Lecture Notes in Computer Science 5502

Commenced Publication in 1973
Founding and Former Series Editors:
Gerhard Goos, Juris Hartmanis, and Jan van Leeuwen

Giuseppe Castagna (Ed.)

Programming Languages and Systems

18th European Symposium on Programming, ESOP 2009
Held as Part of the Joint European Conferences
on Theory and Practice of Software, ETAPS 2009
York, UK, March 22-29, 2009
Proceedings

 Springer

Volume Editor

Giuseppe Castagna
PPS Laboratory, CNRS
Université Denis Diderot - Paris 7, France
E-mail: giuseppe.castagna@pps.jussieu.fr

Library of Congress Control Number: Applied for

CR Subject Classification (1998): D.3, D.2.2, F.3.2, D.2.4, D.2.5, D.3.3

LNCS Sublibrary: SL 1 – Theoretical Computer Science and General Issues

ISSN   0302-9743
ISBN-10   3-642-00589-6 Springer Berlin Heidelberg New York
ISBN-13   978-3-642-00589-3 Springer Berlin Heidelberg New York

springer.com

© Springer-Verlag Berlin Heidelberg 2009
Printed in Germany

Typesetting: Camera-ready by author, data conversion by Scientific Publishing Services, Chennai, India
Printed on acid-free paper   SPIN: 12632244   06/3180   5 4 3 2 1 0

Foreword

ETAPS 2009 was the 12th instance of the European Joint Conferences on Theory and Practice of Software. ETAPS is an annual federated conference that was established in 1998 by combining a number of existing and new conferences. This year it comprised five conferences (CC, ESOP, FASE, FOSSACS, TACAS), 22 satellite workshops (ACCAT, ARSPA-WITS, Bytecode, COCV, COMPASS, FESCA, FInCo, FORMED, GaLoP, GT-VMT, HFL, LDTA, MBT, MLQA, OpenCert, PLACES, QAPL, RC, SafeCert, TAASN, TERMGRAPH, and WING), four tutorials, and seven invited lectures (excluding those that were specific to the satellite events). The five main conferences received 532 submissions (including 30 tool demonstration papers), 141 of which were accepted (10 tool demos), giving an overall acceptance rate of about 26%, with most of the conferences at around 25%. Congratulations therefore to all the authors who made it to the final programme! I hope that most of the other authors will still have found a way of participating in this exciting event, and that you will all continue submitting to ETAPS and contributing towards making it the best conference on software science and engineering.

The events that comprise ETAPS address various aspects of the system development process, including specification, design, implementation, analysis and improvement. The languages, methodologies and tools which support these activities are all well within its scope. Different blends of theory and practice are represented, with an inclination towards theory with a practical motivation on the one hand and soundly based practice on the other. Many of the issues involved in software design apply to systems in general, including hardware systems, and the emphasis on software is not intended to be exclusive.

ETAPS is a confederation in which each event retains its own identity, with a separate Programme Committee and proceedings. Its format is open-ended, allowing it to grow and evolve as time goes by. Contributed talks and system demonstrations are in synchronised parallel sessions, with invited lectures in plenary sessions. Two of the invited lectures are reserved for 'unifying' talks on topics of interest to the whole range of ETAPS attendees. The aim of cramming all this activity into a single one-week meeting is to create a strong magnet for academic and industrial researchers working on topics within its scope, giving them the opportunity to learn about research in related areas, and thereby to foster new and existing links between work in areas that were formerly addressed in separate meetings.

ETAPS 2009 was organised by the University of York in cooperation with

▷ European Association for Theoretical Computer Science (EATCS)
▷ European Association for Programming Languages and Systems (EAPLS)
▷ European Association of Software Science and Technology (EASST)

and with support from ERCIM, Microsoft Research, Rolls-Royce, Transitive, and Yorkshire Forward.

The organising team comprised:

Chair	Gerald Luettgen
Secretariat	Ginny Wilson and Bob French
Finances	Alan Wood
Satellite Events	Jeremy Jacob and Simon O'Keefe
Publicity	Colin Runciman and Richard Paige
Website	Fiona Polack and Malihe Tabatabaie.

Overall planning for ETAPS conferences is the responsibility of its Steering Committee, whose current membership is:

Vladimiro Sassone (Southampton, Chair), Luca de Alfaro (Santa Cruz), Roberto Amadio (Paris), Giuseppe Castagna (Paris), Marsha Chechik (Toronto), Sophia Drossopoulou (London), Hartmut Ehrig (Berlin), Javier Esparza (Munich), Jose Fiadeiro (Leicester), Andrew Gordon (MSR Cambridge), Rajiv Gupta (Arizona), Chris Hankin (London), Laurie Hendren (McGill), Mike Hinchey (NASA Goddard), Paola Inverardi (L'Aquila), Joost-Pieter Katoen (Aachen), Paul Klint (Amsterdam), Stefan Kowalewski (Aachen), Shriram Krishnamurthi (Brown), Kim Larsen (Aalborg), Gerald Luettgen (York), Rupak Majumdar (Los Angeles), Tiziana Margaria (Göttingen), Ugo Montanari (Pisa), Oege de Moor (Oxford), Luke Ong (Oxford), Catuscia Palamidessi (Paris), George Papadopoulos (Cyprus), Anna Philippou (Cyprus), David Rosenblum (London), Don Sannella (Edinburgh), João Saraiva (Minho), Michael Schwartzbach (Aarhus), Perdita Stevens (Edinburgh), Gabriel Taentzer (Marburg), Dániel Varró (Budapest), and Martin Wirsing (Munich).

I would like to express my sincere gratitude to all of these people and organisations, the Programme Committee Chairs and PC members of the ETAPS conferences, the organisers of the satellite events, the speakers themselves, the many reviewers, and Springer for agreeing to publish the ETAPS proceedings. Finally, I would like to thank the Organising Chair of ETAPS 2009, Gerald Luettgen, for arranging for us to hold ETAPS in the most beautiful city of York.

January 2009   Vladimiro Sassone, Chair
                                                   ETAPS Steering Committee

Preface

This volume contains 26 regular papers and two abstracts of invited talks presented at the 18th European Symposium on Programming held during March 25–27, 2009 in York (UK).

We received 130 abstracts and 98 full paper submissions. Some abstracts were never followed by a full paper because of the 15-page limit for submissions imposed by ETAPS to all member conferences. Many, myself included, believe that this limit strongly penalizes ESOP with respect to most programming language conferences (such as POPL, PLDI, PPoPP, PPDP, ICFP, OOPSLA, ECOOP). By a rough calculation, submissions to ECOOP and to 10-page ACM conferences have two-thirds more space than ESOP papers. The gap is much wider with 12-page ACM conference (ICFP, POPL, PPDP) or even 18-page ACM conferences such as OOPSLA. I personally know authors who did not submit to ESOP because of the page limit and then had their paper accepted in one of the other conferences mentioned above. The 15-page limit is inadequate for ESOP, not only relatively to other major conferences, but also in the absolute sense. This was felt by authors, reviewers, and Program Committee (PC) members. The most common, printable, adjective used to described this limit in the PC discussions was "absurd": reviewers complained that some papers were butchered to fit in the allotted page count, and that they had to download full versions and read appendixes in order to be able to judge the work (as this was not uniformly the case, with some reviewers judging only the submitted version, it added a further degree of randomness to the decision process). The inadequacy was further confirmed by two questionnaires submitted to authors and PC members (and, rather surprisingly, dissatisfaction with the page limit was higher among the PC members). The consensus is that ESOP will not reach its full potential as long as such a limit is maintained, which is why several persons wrote to invite me to argue at the ETAPS Steering Committee meeting to relax this limit and/or to stop imposing the same limit to all ETAPS conferences.

Now for more mundane matters. This year competition was tough. We loosely applied the *Identify the Champion* selection strategy[1] and 30 of the 98 submissions had at least one strong proponent, that is, one review with the highest possible score. Two papers were immediately rejected because of simultaneous submission to other conferences. In one case the authors explained that the double submission was due to reviews obtained during a rebuttal phase, which were so negative that they assumed it meant the paper was rejected. However, since they did not formally withdraw their submission from the first conference, it was considered as a double submission and the paper was rejected. In the second case

---

[1] See http://www.iam.unibe.ch/ oscar/Champion/.

the authors justified their double submission by the fact they did not carefully read submission policies. For the remaining papers the discussion was organized in four phases: we first selected the clear accepts and clear rejects; then divided the remaining papers in thematic groups and performed a further selection on a per group basis; the remaining papers of different topics were then further classified according to individual PC members' rankings, independently from their topics; finally, five last submissions were accepted in a final ballot requiring at least one-third of the PC members votes.

A novelty of this year's ESOP was the introduction of a rebuttal phase. Authors were given a 60-hour period and 500 words to point out factual errors and answer direct questions from reviewers. Rebuttals went smoothly (apart from a single PC member who, despite several repeated reminders, uploaded all his reports eight hours *after* the start of the rebuttal phase) and, according to the questionnaires, they were unanimously appreciated by both authors and PC members. I admit that before this experience I believed that the only benefit of a rebuttal phase was to "put the pressure" on external reviewers so as to obtain more detailed reviews. However, and somewhat to my surprise, rebuttals turned out to be quite useful for decision making. In most cases in which rebuttals influenced the decision, they did so in a negative way, since they somehow confirmed or strengthened reviewers' doubts. But in a few cases, they made reviewers change their assessments and the paper switched from rejection to acceptance.

I was truly impressed by the work done by the PC members and the 145 external reviewers: they prepared 313 reports and produced over 1100 comments in the subsequent discussion. The discussion took place electronically and was managed by *EasyChair*, a wonderful conference management system developed by Andrei Voronkov, which made this PC Chair's life much easier. I am particularly grateful to the many external reviewers who, during the discussion phase and on short notice, accepted to prepare reports in a few days, thus giving a decisive help in deciding controversial papers. But above all I am grateful to the many authors that submitted a paper to ESOP, especially those that were not gratified by seeing their paper accepted: for them I do hope that the feedback they received from our reviews turned out to be useful to improve their work.

January 2009   Giuseppe Castagna

Organization

Program Chair

Giuseppe Castagna   CNRS, Université Denis Diderot - Paris 7
                     (France)

Program Committee

Martín Abadi   UCSC and Microsoft Research (USA)
Torben Amtoft   Kansas State University (USA)
John Boyland   University of Wisconsin-Milwaukee (USA)
Michele Bugliesi   Università "Ca' Fóscari" di Venezia (Italy)
Silvano Dal Zilio   CNRS-LAAS (France)
Vincent Danos   University of Edinburgh (UK)
Mariangiola Dezani   Università di Torino (Italy)
Maribel Fernández   King's College London (UK)
Tim Harris   Microsoft Research, Cambridge (UK)
Martin Hofmann   Ludwig-Maximilians-Universität München
                       (Germany)
Joxan Jaffar   National University of Singapore (Singapore)
Xavier Leroy   INRIA Paris-Rocquencourt (France)
Eugenio Moggi   Università di Genova (Italy)
Greg Morrisett   Harvard University (USA)
George Necula   Rinera Networks and University of California
                       Berkeley (USA)
James Noble   Victoria University of Wellington
                       (New Zealand)
Kostis Sagonas   National Technical University of Athens
                       (Greece)
Peter Sestoft   IT University of Copenhagen (Denmark)
Peter Sewell   University of Cambridge (UK)
Jean-Pierre Talpin   INRIA Rennes-Bretagne-Atlantique (France)
Peter Thiemann   Unversität Freiburg (Germany)
Jan Vitek   Purdue University (USA)
Kwangkeun Yi   Seoul National University (Korea)
Gianluigi Zavattaro Università degli Studi di Bologna (Italy)

External Reviewers

Abel, Andreas
Acciai, Lucia
Ahmed, Amal
Andrei, Oana
Ariola, Zena
Axelsson, Roland
Balakrishnan, Gogul
Bergel, Alexandre
Beringer, Lennart
Berthomieu, Bernard
Bieniusa, Annette
Bloom, Bard
Bonfante, Guillaume
Bonilla, Lidia
Borgstrom, Johannes
Bravetti, Mario
Calcagno, Cristiano
Cameron, Nicholas
Chang, Bor-Yuh Evan
Chaudhuri, Swarat
Chevalier, Yannick
Chitil, Olaf
Chlipala, Adam
Conchon, Sylvain
Coppo, Mario
Dagnat, Fabien
Dalla Preda, Mila
de' Liguoro, Ugo
Degen, Markus
Delzanno, Giorgio
Dryer, Derek
Dubois, Catherine
Ducasse, Stéphane
ElBendary, Mohamed
Feret, Jérôme
Field, John
Findler, Robby
Flatt, Matthew
Fluet, Matthew
Foster, J. Nathan
Gabbrielli, Maurizio
Gaboardi, Marco
Garoche, Pierre-Loïc
Garrigue, Jacques

Gerakios, Prodromos
Giannini, Paola
Gordon, Andrew D.
Gorla, Daniele
Gotsman, Alexey
Grossman, Dan
Gulwani, Sumit
Guts, Nataliya
Hamlen, Kevin
Heidegger, Phillip
Hildebrandt, Thomas
Hirschfeld, Robert
Hobor, Aquinas
Hoffmann, Jan
Hyvernat, Pierre
Igarashi, Atsushi
Jeannet, Bertrand
Jouvelot, Pierre
Kim, Ik-Soon
Knowles, Kenn
Lagorio, Giovanni
Laird, James
Lakin, Matthew R.
Lanese, Ivan
Lange, Martin
Le Botlan, Didier
Lee, Oukseh
Ligatti, Jay
Liu, Yang
Loidl, Hans-Wolfgang
Loreti, Michele
Macedonio, Damiano
Maffei, Matteo
Mainland, Geoffrey
Marché, Claude
McBride, Conor
Mezzina, Leonardo Gaetano
Might, Matthew
Milazzo, Paolo
Miné, Antoine
Momigliano, Alberto
Mostrous, Dimitris
Müller, Peter
Myreen, Magnus O.

Nanevski, Aleks
Navas, Jorge
Oh, Hakjoo
Ostlund, Johan
Owens, Scott
Pantel, Marc
Park, Sungwoo
Passerone, Roberto
Pearce, David
Piazza, Carla
Pierce, Benjamin
Pittarello, Fabio
Pontelli, Enrico
Potanin, Alex
Potop Butucaru, Dumitru
Potter, John
Pottier, François
Pous, Damien
Pouzet, Marc
Pratikakis, Polyvios
Rajamani, Sriram
Rathke, Julian
Retert, William
Ridge, Tom
Rodriguez, Dulma
Roychoudhury, Abhik
Salibra, Antonino
Santosa, Andrew

Sarkar, Susmit
Sauciuc, Raluca
Schmitt, Alan
Schoepp, Uli
Sezgin, Ali
Shkaravska, Olha
Siafakas, Nikolaos
Simmons, Robert
Søndergaard, Harald
Spoto, Fausto
Sridharan, Manu
Staton, Sam
Strecker, Martin
Sun, Jun
Teller, David
Tuch, Harvey
Valencia, Frank
Vecchie, Eric
Versari, Cristian
Vieira, Hugo
Voicu, Razvan
Vouillon, Jérôme
Wehr, Stefan
Wrigstad, Tobias
Zappa Nardelli, Francesco
Zdancewic, Steve
Zhao, Tian
Zucca, Elena

Table of Contents

ESOP Invited Talk

Security

Concurrency

Service-Oriented Computing

Parallel and Concurrent Programming

Well-Typed Programs Can't Be Blamed

Philip Wadler[1] and Robert Bruce Findler[2]

[1] University of Edinburgh
[2] University of Chicago

Abstract. We introduce the *blame calculus*, which adds the notion of blame from Findler and Felleisen's *contracts* to a system similar to Siek and Taha's *gradual types* and Flanagan's *hybrid types*. We characterise where positive and negative blame can arise by decomposing the usual notion of subtype into positive and negative subtypes, and show that these recombine to yield naive subtypes. Naive subtypes previously appeared in type systems that are unsound, but we believe this is the first time naive subtypes play a role in establishing type soundness.

1 Introduction

Much recent work has focused on integrating dynamic and static typing using *contracts* [4] to ensure that dynamically-typed code meets statically-typed invariants. Examples include *gradual types* [15], *hybrid types* [5, 8], *dynamic dependent types* [13], and *multi-language programming* [10]. Both Meijer [11] and Bracha [2] argue in favor of mixing dynamic and static typing. Static and dynamic typing are both supported in Visual Basic, and similar integration is planned for Perl 6 and ECMAScript 4.

Here we unify some of this work, by introducing a notion of blame (from contracts) into a type system with casts (similar to intermediate languages for gradual and hybrid types), yielding a system we dub the *blame calculus*. In this calculus, programmers may add casts to evolve dynamically typed code into statically typed, (as with gradual types) or to evolve statically typed code to use subset types (as with hybrid types).

The technical content of this paper is to introduce notions of positive and negative subtypes, and prove a theorem that characterises when positive and negative blame can occur. A corollary is that when a program integrating less-typed and more-typed components goes wrong the blame must lie with the less-typed component. Though obvious, this result has either been ignored in previous work or required a complex proof; here we give a simple proof.

Our work involves both ordinary subtypes (which, for functions, is contravariant in the domain and covariant in the range) and naive subtypes (which is covariant in both the domain and the range). Ordinary subtypes characterize a cast that cannot fail, while naive subtypes characterize which side of a cast is less typed (and hence will be blamed if the cast fails). We show that ordinary subtypes decompose into positive and negative subtypes, and that these recombine in a different way to yield naive subtypes. A striking analogy is a tangram, where a square decomposes into parts that recombine into a different shape (see Figure 1). Naive subtypes previously appeared in type systems that are unsound, notably that of Eiffel [12], but we believe this is the first time naive subtypes play a role in establishing type soundness.

G. Castagna (Ed.): ESOP 2009, LNCS 5502, pp. 1–16, 2009.

Gradual types [15], hybrid types [5, 8], and dynamic dependent types [13] use source languages where most or all casts are omitted, but inferred by a type-directed translation; all three use similar translations which target similar intermediate languages. The blame calculus resembles these intermediate languages. Our point is that the intermediate language is in itself suitable as a source language, with the advantage that it becomes crystal clear where static guarantees hold and where dynamic checks are enforced.

Fig. 1. Tangram as metaphor: Ordinary subtyping decomposes and recombines to yield naive subtyping

The blame calculus uses subset types as found in hybrid types and dynamic dependent types, but it lacks the dependent function types found in these systems (an important area for future work). Hybrid types and dynamic dependent types are parameterized by a theorem prover, which returns true, false, or maybe when supplied with a logical implication required by a subtyping relationship; the blame calculus corresponds to the extreme case where the theorem prover always returns maybe.

We make the following contributions.

- We introduce the blame calculus, showing that a language with explicit casts is suited to many of the same purposes as gradual types and hybrid types (Section 2).
- We give a framework similar to that of hybrid types and dynamic dependent types, but with a decidable type system for the source language (Section 3).
- We factor ordinary subtypes positive and negative subtypes, which recombine into naive subtypes. We prove that a cast from a positive subtype cannot give rise to positive blame, and that a cast from a negative subtype cannot give rise to negative blame (Section 4).

An earlier version of this paper appeared in a workshop [19]. The current version is completely rewritten and some technicalities differ. A rule merging positive blame and negative blame from distinct casts has been eliminated, and as a consequence we use a simpler notation with one label rather than two. A rule making every ground type a subtype of type Dyn has been added, making the subtyping relations less conservative. Detailed proofs may be found in the accompanying technical report [20].

2   The Blame Calculus

2.1   From Untyped to Typed

Figure 2 presents a series of example programs, which we consider in turn.

Program (a) is untyped. By default, our programming language is typed, so we indicate untyped code by surrounding it with ceiling brackets. Untyped code is really uni-typed (a slogan due to Robert Harper); it is a special case of typed code where every term has type Dyn. Here the term evaluates to $\lceil 4 \rceil$: Dyn.

(a) $\lceil$let $x = 2$ (b) let $x = 2$
    let $f = \lambda y.\, y + 1$ let $f = \langle$Int $\to$ Int $\Leftarrow$ Dyn$\rangle^p$ $\lceil\lambda y.\, y + 1\rceil$
    let $h = \lambda g.\, g\,(g\,x)$ let $h = \lambda g : $ Int $\to$ Int. $g\,(g\,x)$
    in $h\,f\rceil$ in $h\,f$

(c) let $x = \langle$Nat $\Leftarrow$ Int$\rangle^p$ 2
    let $f = \langle$Nat $\to$ Nat $\Leftarrow$ Int $\to$ Int$\rangle^q$ $(\lambda y : $ Int. $y + 1)$
    let $h = \lambda g : $ Nat $\to$ Nat. $g\,(g\,x)$
    in $h\,f$

(d) let $x = \lceil$true$\rceil$
    let $f = \lambda y : $ Int. $y + 1$
    let $h = \langle($Int $\to$ Int$) \to$ Int $\Leftarrow$ Dyn$\rangle^p$ $\lceil\lambda g.\, g\,(g\,x)\rceil$
    in $h\,f$

(e) let $x = \lceil$true$\rceil$
    let $f = \langle$Dyn $\Leftarrow$ Int $\to$ Int$\rangle^p$ $(\lambda y : $ Int. $y + 1)$
    let $h = \lceil\lambda g.\, g\,(g\,x)\rceil$
    in $\lceil h\,f\rceil$

(f) let $x = \langle$Nat $\Leftarrow$ Int$\rangle^p$ 3
    let $f = \langle$Nat $\to$ Nat $\Leftarrow$ Int $\to$ Int$\rangle^q$ $(\lambda y : $ Int. $y - 2)$
    let $h = \lceil\lambda g.\, g\,(g\,x)\rceil$
    in $\lceil h\,f\rceil$

Fig. 2. Example programs

As a matter of software engineering, when we add types to our code we may not wish to do so all at once. Progam (b) contains typed and untyped parts, fit together by casting the untyped code to a suitable type. and the term evaluates to 4 : Int. Gradual evolution is overkill for such a short piece of code, but in real systems it plays an important role [17, 18]. Here $\lceil\lambda y.\, y + 1\rceil$ has type Dyn, and the cast converts it to type Int $\to$ Int.

In general, a cast from source type S to target type T is written $\langle T \Leftarrow S\rangle^p\, s$, where subterm s has type S and the whole term has type T, and p is a *blame label*. We assume an involutive operation of negation on blame labels: if p is a blame label then $\bar{p}$ is its negation, and $\bar{\bar{p}}$ is the same as p. Consider a cast with blame label p: blame is allocated to p when the *term contained* in the cast fails to satisfy the contract associated with the cast, while blame is allocated to $\bar{p}$ when the *context containing* the cast fails to satisfy the contract.

Our notation is chosen for clarity rather than compactness. Writing the source type is redundant, but convenient for a core calculus. Our notation is based on that of Gronski and Flanagan [7].

2.2 Contracts and Subset Types

Findler and Felleisen [4] introduced higher-order contracts, and Flanagan [5] and Ou *et al.* [13] observed that contracts can be incorporated into a type system as a form of *subset* (or *refinement*) type. An example is $\{x : \text{Int} \mid x \geq 0\}$, the type of all integers greater than zero, which we will write Nat. A cast from Int to Nat performs a dynamic test, checking that the integer is indeed greater than or equal to zero. Just as we can start with an untyped program and add types, we can start with a typed program and add subset types. Program (c) is a version of the previous program with subset types added.

Unlike hybrid or dependent types, the blame calculus does not require subsumption. As a technical nicety, this allows us to design a type system which (like gradual types) satisfies *unicity*: every well-typed term has exactly one type. In order to achieve unicity, we must add new value forms corresponding to the result of casting to a subset type. Thus, the value of Program (c) is not $4 : \text{Int}$ but $4_{\text{Nat}} : \text{Nat}$.

2.3   The Blame Game

The above examples execute with no errors, but in general we may not be so lucky. Casts perform dynamic tests at run-time that fail if a value cannot be coerced to the given type. A cast to a subset type reduces to a dynamic test of the condition on the type. Recall that Nat denotes $\{x : \text{Int} \mid x \geq 0\}$. Here is a successful test:

$$\langle\text{Nat} \Leftarrow \text{Int}\rangle^p\, 4 \quad\longrightarrow\quad 4 \geq 0 \,\triangleright^p\, 4_{\text{Nat}} \quad\longrightarrow\quad \text{true} \,\triangleright^p\, 4_{\text{Nat}} \quad\longrightarrow\quad 4_{\text{Nat}}$$

And here is a failed test:

$$\langle\text{Nat} \Leftarrow \text{Int}\rangle^p\, {-4} \quad\longrightarrow\quad -4 \geq 0 \,\triangleright^p\, {-4_{\text{Nat}}} \quad\longrightarrow\quad \text{false} \,\triangleright^p\, {-4_{\text{Nat}}} \longrightarrow \Uparrow p$$

The middle steps show a new term form that performs a dynamic test, of the form $s \triangleright^p v_{\{x:B\mid t\}}$. If s evaluates to true, the value of subset type is returned; if s evaluates to false, blame is allocated to p, written $\Uparrow p$.

Given an arbitrary term that takes integers to integers, it is not decidable whether it also takes naturals to naturals. Therefore, when casting a function type the test is deferred until the function is applied. This is the essence of higher-order contracts.

Here is an example of casting a function and applying the result.

$$
\begin{aligned}
&(\langle\text{Nat} \to \text{Nat} \Leftarrow \text{Int} \to \text{Int}\rangle^p\, (\lambda y : \text{Int}.\, y + 1))\, 2_{\text{Nat}} \longrightarrow \\
&\langle\text{Nat} \Leftarrow \text{Int}\rangle^p((\lambda y : \text{Int}.\, y + 1)\, (\langle\text{Int} \Leftarrow \text{Nat}\rangle^{\bar{p}}\, 2_{\text{Nat}}) \longrightarrow \\
&\langle\text{Nat} \Leftarrow \text{Int}\rangle^p\, ((\lambda y : \text{Int}.\, y + 1)\, 2) \longrightarrow \\
&\langle\text{Nat} \Leftarrow \text{Int}\rangle^p\, 3 \longrightarrow 3_{\text{Nat}}
\end{aligned}
$$

The cast on the function breaks into two casts, each in opposite directions: the cast on the result takes the range of the *source* to the range of the *target*, while the cast on the argument takes the domain of the *target* to the domain of the *source*. Preserving order for the range while reversing order for the domain is analogous to the standard rule for function subtyping, which is covariant in the range and contravariant in the domain.

Observe that the blame label on the reversed cast has been negated, because if that cast fails it is the fault of the context, which supplies the argument to the function. Conversely, the blame label is not negated on the result cast, because if that cast fails it is the fault of the function itself.

The above cast took a function with range and domain $\texttt{Int}$ to a function with more precise range and domain $\texttt{Nat}$. Now consider a cast to a function with less precise range and domain $\texttt{Dyn}$.

$$(\langle \texttt{Dyn} \to \texttt{Dyn} \Leftarrow \texttt{Int} \to \texttt{Int} \rangle^p \,(\lambda y : \texttt{Int}.\, y + 1)) \lceil 2 \rceil \longrightarrow$$
$$\langle \texttt{Dyn} \Leftarrow \texttt{Int} \rangle^p((\lambda y : \texttt{Int}.\, y + 1)\,(\langle \texttt{Int} \Leftarrow \texttt{Dyn} \rangle^{\bar{p}} \lceil 2 \rceil)) \longrightarrow$$
$$\langle \texttt{Dyn} \Leftarrow \texttt{Int} \rangle^p((\lambda y : \texttt{Int}.\, y + 1)\, 2) \longrightarrow \langle \texttt{Dyn} \Leftarrow \texttt{Int} \rangle^p \, 3 \longrightarrow \lceil 3 \rceil$$

Again, a cast on the function breaks into two casts, each in opposite directions.

If we consider a well-typed term of the form

$$(\langle \texttt{Nat} \to \texttt{Nat} \Leftarrow \texttt{Int} \to \texttt{Int} \rangle^p \, f)\, x$$

we can see that negative blame *never* adheres to this cast, because the type checker guarantees that x has type $\texttt{Nat}$, and the cast from $\texttt{Nat}$ to $\texttt{Int}$ always succeeds. However positive blame may adhere, for instance if f is $\lambda y : \texttt{Int}.\, y - 2$ and x is 1.

Conversely, if we consider a well-typed term of the form

$$(\langle \texttt{Dyn} \to \texttt{Dyn} \Leftarrow \texttt{Int} \to \texttt{Int} \rangle^p \, f)\, x$$

we can see that positive blame *never* adheres to this cast, because the types guarantee that f returns an $\texttt{Int}$, and the cast from $\texttt{Int}$ to $\texttt{Dyn}$ always succeeds. However negative blame may adhere, for instance if f is $\lambda y : \texttt{Int}.\, y + 1$ and x is $\lceil \texttt{true} \rceil$.

The key result of this paper is to show that casting from a more precise type to a less precise type cannot give rise to positive blame (but may give rise to negative); and that casting for a less precise type to a more precise type cannot give rise to negative blame (but may give rise to positive). Here are the two examples considered above, with the more precise type on the left, and the less precise type on the right.

$$\texttt{Nat} \to \texttt{Nat} <:_n \texttt{Int} \to \texttt{Int} \qquad \texttt{Int} \to \texttt{Int} <:_n \texttt{Dyn} \to \texttt{Dyn}$$

We call this *naive* subtyping (hence the subscript n) because it is covariant in both the domain and the range of function types, in contrast to traditional subtyping, which is contravariant in the domain and covariant in the range. We formally define both subtyping and naive subtyping in Section 3.3.

2.4 Well-Typed Programs Can't Be Blamed

Consider a program that mixes typed and untyped code; it will contain two sorts of casts. One sort gives types to untyped code. Such casts make types more precise, and so cannot give rise to negative blame. For instance, Program (d) in Figure 2 fails blaming p. Because the blame is positive, the fault lies with the untyped code inside the cast.

The other sort takes typed code and makes it untyped. Such a cast makes types less precise, and so cannot give rise to positive blame. For instance, Program (e) fails blaming $\bar{p}$. Because the blame is negative, the fault lies with the code outside the cast.

Both times the fault lies with the untyped code! This is of course what we would expect, since typed code should contain no type errors. Understanding positive and negative blame, and knowing when each can arise, is the key to giving a simple proof of this expected fact.

Syntax	variables	x, y	blame labels	p, q

$$\text{base types} \quad B \quad ::= \text{Bool} \mid \text{Int} \mid \cdots$$

$$\text{constants} \quad c \quad ::= \text{true} \mid \text{false} \mid 0 \mid 1 \mid \cdots \mid + \mid - \mid \geq \cdots$$

$$\text{types} \quad S, T \quad ::= \text{Dyn} \mid B \mid S \to T \mid \{x : B \mid t\}$$

$$\text{terms} \quad s, t, u ::= x \mid c \mid \lambda x : S. \, t \mid t \, s \mid \langle T \Leftarrow S \rangle^p \, s$$

Compile-time typing

$$\frac{x : T \in \Gamma}{\Gamma \vdash x : T} \qquad \frac{T = \text{ty}(c)}{\Gamma \vdash c : T} \qquad \boxed{\Gamma \vdash t : T}$$

$$\frac{\Gamma, x : S \vdash t : T}{\Gamma \vdash \lambda x : S. \, t : S \to T} \qquad \frac{\Gamma \vdash t : S \to T \quad \Gamma \vdash s : S}{\Gamma \vdash t \, s : T} \qquad \frac{\Gamma \vdash s : S \quad S \sim T}{\Gamma \vdash \langle T \Leftarrow S \rangle^p \, s : T}$$

Compatibility

$$B \sim B \qquad \text{Dyn} \sim T \qquad S \sim \text{Dyn} \qquad \boxed{S \sim T}$$

$$\frac{S \sim S' \quad T \sim T'}{S \to T \sim S' \to T'} \qquad \frac{B \sim T}{\{x : B \mid s\} \sim T} \qquad \frac{S \sim B}{S \sim \{y : B \mid t\}}$$

Fig. 3. Compile-time types

The same analysis generalizes to code containing subset types. For instance, Program (f) fails blaming q. In this case, both casts make the types more precise, so cannot give rise to negative blame. Because the blame is positive, the fault lies with the less refined code inside the cast.

3 Types, Reduction, Subtyping

Compile-time type rules of our system are presented in Figure 3, run-time type rules and reduction rules in Figure 4, and rules for subtyping in Figure 5. We discuss each of these in turn in the following three subsections.

3.1 Types and Terms

Figure 3 presents the syntax of types and terms and the compile-time type rules. The language is explicitly and statically typed. (See Section 3.4 for embedding untyped terms.)

We let S, T range over types, and s, t range over terms. A type is either a base type B, the dynamic type Dyn, a function type $S \to T$, or a subset type $\{x : B \mid t\}$. A term is either a variable x, a constant c, a lambda expression $\lambda x : S. \, t$, an application $s \, t$, or a cast expression $\langle T \Leftarrow S \rangle^p \, s$. We write let $x = s$ in t as an abbreviation for $(\lambda x : S. \, t) \, s$ where s has type S.

We assume a denumerable set of constants. Every constant c is assigned a unique type ty(c). We assume Bool is a base type with true and false as constants of type Bool; and that Int is a base type with 0, 1, and so on, as constants of type Int, and $+$ and $-$ as constants of type Int $\to$ Int $\to$ Int, and $\geq$ as a contant of type Int $\to$ Int $\to$ Bool, and possibly other constants. Constants must have base type or function type; this guarantees that every value of type Dyn has the form $\text{Dyn}_G(v)$ and that every value of subset type has the form $v_{\{x:B|t\}}$. Constants of function type must not raise blame when evaluated; this guarantees that only casts can raise blame.

Syntax

ground types G $::= B \mid \texttt{Dyn} \to \texttt{Dyn}$

terms $s,t,u ::= \cdots \mid \texttt{Dyn}_G(v) \mid v_{\{x:B\mid t\}} \mid s \triangleright^p v_{\{x:B\mid t\}}$

values $v,w ::= x \mid c \mid \lambda x : S.\, t \mid \langle S' \to T' \Leftarrow S \to T\rangle^p\, v \mid \texttt{Dyn}_G(v) \mid v_{\{x:B\mid t\}}$

results $r   ::= t \mid \Uparrow p$

eval contexts $E   ::= [\,] \mid E\, s \mid v\, E \mid \langle T \Leftarrow S\rangle^p\, E \mid E \triangleright^p v_{\{x:B\mid t\}}$

Run-time typing

$$\dfrac{\Gamma \vdash s : \texttt{Bool} \qquad \Gamma \vdash v : B \qquad t[x := v] \longrightarrow^* s}{\Gamma \vdash s \triangleright^p v_{\{x:B\mid t\}} : \{x : B \mid t\}} \qquad \boxed{\Gamma \vdash t : T}$$

$$\dfrac{\Gamma \vdash v : G}{\Gamma \vdash \texttt{Dyn}_G(v) : \texttt{Dyn}} \qquad \dfrac{\Gamma \vdash v : B \qquad t[x := v] \longrightarrow^* \texttt{true}}{\Gamma \vdash v_{\{x:B\mid t\}} : \{x : B \mid t\}}$$

Reductions

$\boxed{s \longrightarrow r}$

$$E[c\, v] \longrightarrow E[[\![c]\!](v)] \tag{1}$$

$$E[(\lambda x : S.\, t)\, v] \longrightarrow E[t[x := v]] \tag{2}$$

$$E[\langle B \Leftarrow B\rangle^p\, v] \longrightarrow E[v] \tag{3}$$

$$E[(\langle S' \to T' \Leftarrow S \to T\rangle^p\, v)\, w] \longrightarrow E[\langle T' \Leftarrow T\rangle^p\, (v\, (\langle S \Leftarrow S'\rangle^{\bar p}\, w))] \tag{4}$$

$$E[\langle \texttt{Dyn} \Leftarrow \texttt{Dyn}\rangle^p\, v] \longrightarrow E[v] \tag{5}$$

$$E[\langle \texttt{Dyn} \Leftarrow B\rangle^p\, v] \longrightarrow E[\texttt{Dyn}_B(v)] \tag{6}$$

$$E[\langle \texttt{Dyn} \Leftarrow S \to T\rangle^p\, v] \longrightarrow E[\texttt{Dyn}_{\texttt{Dyn}\to\texttt{Dyn}}(\langle \texttt{Dyn} \to \texttt{Dyn} \Leftarrow S \to T\rangle^p\, v)] \tag{7}$$

$$E[\langle T \Leftarrow \texttt{Dyn}\rangle^p\, \texttt{Dyn}_G(v)] \longrightarrow E[\langle T \Leftarrow G\rangle^p\, v], \quad \text{if } G \sim T \tag{8}$$

$$E[\langle T \Leftarrow \texttt{Dyn}\rangle^p\, \texttt{Dyn}_G(v)] \longrightarrow \Uparrow p, \quad \text{if } G \nsim T \tag{9}$$

$$E[\langle\{x : B \mid t\} \Leftarrow S\rangle^p\, v] \longrightarrow E[\texttt{let } x = \langle B \Leftarrow S\rangle^p\, v \texttt{ in } t \triangleright^p x_{\{x:B\mid t\}}] \tag{10}$$

$$E[\texttt{true} \triangleright^p v_{\{x:B\mid t\}}] \longrightarrow E[v_{\{x:B\mid t\}}] \tag{11}$$

$$E[\texttt{false} \triangleright^p v_{\{x:B\mid t\}}] \longrightarrow \Uparrow p \tag{12}$$

$$E[\langle T \Leftarrow \{x : B \mid s\}\rangle^p\, v_{\{x:B\mid s\}}] \longrightarrow E[\langle T \Leftarrow B\rangle^p\, v] \tag{13}$$

Fig. 4. Run-time types and reduction

The type system is explained in terms of three judgements, which are presented in Figure 3. We write $\Gamma \vdash t : T$ if term t has type T in environment Γ, and we write $S \sim T$ if type S is compatible with type T. We let Γ range over type environments, which are a list of variable-type pairs $x : T$.

A type is well-formed if for every subset type $\{x : B \mid t\}$ we have that t has type Bool on the assumption that x has type B (no other free variables may appear in t). In what follows, we assume all types are well-formed. We call B the *domain* of the subset type $\{x : B \mid t\}$.

The type rules for variables, constants, lambda abstraction, and application are standard. The type rule for casts is straightforward: if term s has type S and type S is compatible with type T (defined below), then the term $\langle T \Leftarrow S\rangle^p\, s$ has type T.

We write $S \sim T$ for the *compatibility* relation, which holds if it may be sensible to cast type S to type T. A base type is compatible with itself, type Dyn is compatible with any type, two function types are compatible if their domains and ranges are compatible, and a subset type is compatible with every type that is compatible with its domain.

Compatibility is reflexive and symmetric but not transitive. For example, $S \sim$ Dyn and Dyn $\sim T$ hold for any types S and T, but $S \sim T$ does not hold if one of S or T is a function type and the other is a base type. Requiring compatibility ensures that there are no obviously foolish casts, but does not rule out the possibility of two successive casts, one from S to Dyn and the next from Dyn to T.

Our cast rule is inspired by the similar rules found for gradual types and hybrid types. Gradual types introduce compatibility, but do not have subset types. Hybrid types include subset types, but do not bother with compatibility. Neither system uses both positive and negative blame labels, as we do here.

Hybrid types also have a subsumption rule: if s has type S, and S is a subtype of T, then s also has type T. This greatly increases the power of the type system. For instance, in hybrid types each constant is assigned the singleton type $c : \{x : B \mid c = x\}$; and by subtyping and subsumption it follows that each constant belongs to every subset type $\{x : B \mid t\}$ for which $t[x := c] \longrightarrow^*$ true. However, the price paid for this is that type checking for hybrid types is undecidable, because the subtype relation is undecidable.

A pleasant consequence of omitting subsumption from the blame calculus is that each term has a unique type, and an even more pleasant consequence is that the type system for the source language is decidable.

Proposition 1. *(Unicity) If $\Gamma \vdash s : S$ and $\Gamma \vdash s : T$ then $S = T$.*

Proposition 2. *(Decidability) Given Γ and t, it is decidable whether there is a T such that $\Gamma \vdash t : T$ (using the compile-time type rules of Figure 3).*

Both propositions are easy inductions.

However, there are some less pleasant consequences. (The tiger is caged, not tamed!) Reduction may introduce terms that are not permitted in the source language, and we need additional semidecidable run-time rules to check the types of these terms. We explain the details of how this works below.

3.2   Reductions

Figure 4 defines additional term forms, values, evaluation contexts, additional run-time type rules, and reduction.

We let v, w range over values. A value is either a variable, a constant, a lambda term, a cast to a function type from another function type, an injection into dynamic from a ground type, or an injection into a subset type from its domain type. The first three of these are standard, and we explain the other three below.

We take a cast to a function type from another function type as a value for technical convenience. Other work [15, 5] makes the opposite choice, and reduce a cast to a function type from another function type to a lambda expression.

Values of dynamic type take the form $\mathrm{Dyn}_G(v)$, where G is ground type, which is either a base type B or the function type Dyn $\to$ Dyn, and v is a value of type G. For example, the cast $\langle \text{Dyn} \Leftarrow \text{Int} \to \text{Int} \rangle^p (\lambda x : \text{Int. } x + 1)$ reduces to the value $\text{Dyn}_{\text{Dyn} \to \text{Dyn}}(\langle \text{Dyn} \to \text{Dyn} \Leftarrow \text{Int} \to \text{Int} \rangle^p (\lambda x : \text{Int. } x + 1))$. Note that the inner cast is a value, since it is to a function type from another function type.

Values of subset type take the form $v_{\{x:B|t\}}$ where v is a value of type B and $t[x := v] \longrightarrow^*$ true. We also need an intermediate term to test the predicate associated with a cast to a subset type. This term has the form $s \vartriangleright^p v_{\{x:B|t\}}$, where v is a value of type T, and s is a boolean term such that $t[x := v] \longrightarrow^* s$. If s reduces to true the term reduces to $v_{\{x:B|t\}}$, and if s reduces to false the term allocates blame to p.

(In contrast, Flanagan [5] has essentially the following rule.

$$\frac{t[x := v] \longrightarrow^* \text{true}}{\langle \{x : B \mid t\} \Leftarrow B \rangle^p v \longrightarrow v_{\{x:B|t\}}}$$

This formulation is unusual, in that a single reduction step in the conclusion depends on multiple steps in the hypothesis. The rule makes it awkward to formulate a traditional progress theorem, because if reduction of $t[x := v]$ proceeds forever, then evaluation gets stuck.)

We let E range over evaluation contexts, which are standard. The cast operation is strict, and reduces the term being cast to a value before the cast is performed, and the subset test is strict in its predicate.

We write $s \longrightarrow r$ to indicate that a single reduction step takes term s to result r, which is either a term t or the form $\Uparrow p$, which indicates allocation of blame to label p. We write $s \longrightarrow^* r$ for the reflexive and transitive closure of reduction.

There are three additional type rules for the three additional term forms. These are straightforward, save that the two rules for subset types involve reduction, and hence are semi-decidable. Hence, Proposition 2 (Decidability) holds only for the compile-time syntax type rules of Figure 3, and fails when these are extended with the run-time type rules of Figure 4. However, it is easy to check that Proposition 1 (Unicity), holds even when the compile-time type rules are extended with the run-time type rules.

The good news is that semi-decidability is not a show stopper. We introduce the semi-decidable type rules precisely in order to prove preservation and progress. Typing of the source language is decidable, and reduction is decidable. We never need to check whether a term satisfies the semi-decidable rules, since this is guaranteed by preservation and progress!

We now go through each of the reductions in turn. (1) Constants of function type are interpreted by a semantic function consistent with their type: if $\text{ty}(c) = S \to T$ and value v has type S, then $[\![c]\!](v)$ is a term of type T. For example, $\text{ty}(+) = \text{Int} \to \text{Int} \to \text{Int}$, with $[\![+]\!](3) = +_3$, where $\text{ty}(+_3) = \text{Int} \to \text{Int}$ and $[\![+_3]\!](4) = 7$. (2) The rule for applying a lambda expression is standard. (3) A cast to a base type from itself is the identity. (4) A cast to a function type from another function type decomposes into separate casts on the argument and result. Note the reversal in the argument cast, and the corresponding negating of the blame label.

The next three rules concern casts to the dynamic type. (5) A cast to Dyn from itself is the identity. (6) A cast to Dyn from a base type is a value. (7) A cast to Dyn from a function type $S \to T$ decomposes into a cast to Dyn from the ground type $\text{Dyn} \to \text{Dyn}$, and a cast to $\text{Dyn} \to \text{Dyn}$ from $S \to T$.

Entailment

$$\boxed{x : T \Leftarrow S \models t}$$

$$\frac{S \sim T \qquad \text{for all } v \text{ and } w, \text{ if } \vdash v : S \text{ and } \langle T \Leftarrow S \rangle^p\, v \longrightarrow^* w \text{ then } t[x := w] \longrightarrow^* \text{true}}{x : T \Leftarrow S \models t}$$

Subtype

$$B <: B \qquad \text{Dyn} <: \text{Dyn} \qquad \boxed{S <: T}$$

$$\frac{S' <: S \qquad T <: T'}{S \to T <: S' \to T'} \qquad \frac{B <: T}{\{x : B \mid s\} <: T} \qquad \frac{S <: B \quad x : B \Leftarrow S \models t}{S <: \{x : B \mid t\}} \qquad \frac{S <: G}{S <: \text{Dyn}}$$

Positive subtype

$$B <:^+ B \qquad S <:^+ \text{Dyn} \qquad \boxed{S <:^+ T}$$

$$\frac{S' <:^- S \qquad T <:^+ T'}{S \to T <:^+ S' \to T'} \qquad \frac{B <:^+ T}{\{x : B \mid s\} <:^+ T} \qquad \frac{S <:^+ B \quad x : B \Leftarrow S \models t}{S <:^+ \{x : B \mid t\}}$$

Negative subtype

$$B <:^- B \qquad \text{Dyn} <:^- T \qquad \boxed{S <:^- T}$$

$$\frac{S' <:^+ S \qquad T <:^- T'}{S \to T <:^- S' \to T'} \qquad \frac{B <:^- T}{\{x : B \mid s\} <:^- T} \qquad \frac{S <:^- B}{S <:^- \{x : B \mid t\}} \qquad \frac{S <:^- G}{S <:^- T}$$

Naive subtype

$$B <:_n B \qquad S <:_n \text{Dyn} \qquad \boxed{S <:_n T}$$

$$\frac{S <:_n S' \qquad T <:_n T'}{S \to T <:_n S' \to T'} \qquad \frac{B <:_n T}{\{x : B \mid s\} <:_n T} \qquad \frac{S <:_n B \quad x : B \Leftarrow S \models t}{S <:_n \{x : B \mid t\}}$$

Fig. 5. Subtypes

The next two rules concern casts from the dynamic type. (8) A cast to type T from the value $\text{Dyn}_G(v)$ of dynamic type collapses to a cast to type T directly from type G if the types T and G are compatible. (9) Otherwise, such a cast fails.

The next three rules concern casts to subset type. (10) A cast to subset type with domain B from type S decomposes into a cast to B from S, followed by a test that the value satisfies the predicate. (11) If the predicate evaluates to true the test reduces to the subset type. (12) Otherwise the test fails.

The last rule concerns casts from a subset type. (13) Consider a cast to type T from a subset type. Recall that values of subset type have the form $v_{\{x:B|s\}}$, where v has type B. The cast collapses to a cast directly to T from B. Note that B and T must be compatible, since a subset type is only compatible with a type that is compatible with its domain.

3.3   Subtyping

We do not need subtyping to assign types to terms, but we will use subtyping to characterise when a cast cannot give rise to blame. Figure 5 presents entailment and four subtyping judgements—ordinary, positive, negative, and naive.

Entailment is written

$$x : T \Leftarrow S \models t$$

and holds if for all values v of type S and w of type T such that $\langle T \Leftarrow S \rangle^p \, v \longrightarrow^* w$ we have that $t[x := w] \longrightarrow^*$ true.

We write $S <: T$ if S is a subtype of T. Function subtyping is contravariant in the domain and covariant in the range. A subset type is a subtype of its domain, and a type is a subtype of a subset type if membership in the type entails satisfaction of the subset type's predicate. Every subtype of a ground type is a subtype of Dyn, since casts from subtypes of a ground type to Dyn cannot allocate blame.

For example, say that we define Pos $= \{x : \text{Int} \mid x > 0\}$ and Nat $= \{x : \text{Int} \mid x \geq 0\}$. Then $x : \text{Int} \Leftarrow \text{Pos} \models x \geq 0$, and so Pos $<:$ Nat by the sixth rule. For another example, Int $<:$ Int by the first rule, so Pos $<:$ Int by the fifth rule, so Pos $<:$ Dyn by the third rule.

Entailment, and hence subtyping, are undecidable. This is not a hindrance, since our type system does not depend on subtyping. Rather it is an advantage, since it means we can show more types are in the subtype relation, making our results more powerful.

Our rules for subtyping are similar to those found in earlier work [5, 8, 13]. However, they take every type to be a subtype of Dyn. In contrast, we only take S to be a subtype of T if a cast from S to T can never receive any blame, and therefore the only subtypes of Dyn are Dyn itself and subtypes of ground types. It is not appropriate to take function types (other that Dyn $\rightarrow$ Dyn) as subtypes of Dyn, because a cast to Dyn from a function type may receive negative blame. The issues are similar to the treatment of the contract Any [3].

In order to characterize when positive and negative blame cannot occur, we factor subtyping into two subsidiary relations, positive subtyping, written $S <:^+ T$ and negative subtyping, written $S <:^- T$. The two judgements are defined in terms of each other, and track the swapping of positive and negative blame labels that occurs with function types, with the contravariant position in the function typing rule reversing the roles. We have $S <:^+$ Dyn and Dyn $<:^- T$ for every type S and T, since casting to Dyn can never give rise to positive blame, and casting from Dyn can never give rise to negative blame. We only check entailment between subtypes for positive subtyping, since failure of a subset predicate gives rise to positive blame. Finally, on the negative side, if $S <:^- G$, then $S <:^- T$, since no cast from a subtype of a ground type to any other type can allocate negative blame.

Proposition 3. *(Subtyping is transitive and reflexive) If $S <: S'$ and $S' <: S''$ then $S <: S''$, for all S, S', S'', and $S <: S$, for all S. Similarly for $<:^+$, $<:^-$, and $<:_n$.*

Proposition 4. *(Subtyping and compatibility) If $S <: T$ then $S \sim T$. Similarly for $<:^+$ and $<:_n$, but not $<:^-$.*

The main results concerning positive and negative subtyping are given in Section 4. We show that $S <: T$ if and only if $S <:^+ T$ and $S <:^- T$. We also show that if $S <:^+ T$ then a cast from S to T cannot receive positive blame, and that if $S <:^- T$ then a cast from S to T cannot receive negative blame.

We also define a naive subtyping judgement, $S <:_n T$, which corresponds to our informal notion of type S being more precise than type T, and is covariant for both

Syntax   untyped terms $M, N ::= x \mid k \mid \lambda x.\ N \mid M\ N \mid \lfloor t \rfloor$

Well-formed terms $\boxed{\Gamma \vdash M\ \text{wf}}$

$$\frac{(x : \text{Dyn}) \in \Gamma}{\Gamma \vdash x\ \text{wf}} \qquad \frac{\Gamma, x : \text{Dyn} \vdash N\ \text{wf}}{\Gamma \vdash (\lambda x.\ N)\ \text{wf}} \qquad \frac{\Gamma \vdash M\ \text{wf} \quad \Gamma \vdash N\ \text{wf}}{\Gamma \vdash (M\ N)\ \text{wf}} \qquad \frac{\Gamma \vdash t : \text{Dyn}}{\Gamma \vdash \lfloor t \rfloor\ \text{wf}}$$

Embedding $\boxed{\lceil M \rceil}$

$$
\begin{aligned}
\lceil x \rceil &= x \\
\lceil c \rceil &= \langle \text{Dyn} \Leftarrow \text{ty}(c) \rangle\ c \\
\lceil \lambda x.\ N \rceil &= \langle \text{Dyn} \Leftarrow \text{Dyn} \to \text{Dyn} \rangle\ (\lambda x : \text{Dyn}.\ \lceil N \rceil) \\
\lceil M\ N \rceil &= (\langle \text{Dyn} \to \text{Dyn} \Leftarrow \text{Dyn} \rangle\ \lceil M \rceil)\ \lceil N \rceil \\
\lceil \lfloor t \rfloor \rceil &= t
\end{aligned}
$$

Fig. 6. Untyped lambda calculus

---

the domain and range of functions. In Section 4, we show that $S <:_n T$ if and only if $S <:^+ T$ and $T <:^- S$. (Note the reversal! In the similar statement for ordinary subtyping, we wrote $S <:^- T$, where here we write $T <:^- S$.)

Here are some examples:

```
Int → Nat <:  Nat → Int        Nat → Nat <:ₙ Int → Int
Int → Nat <:⁺ Nat → Int        Nat → Nat <:⁺ Int → Int
Int → Nat <:⁻ Nat → Int        Int → Int <:⁻ Nat → Nat
```

The left-hand side line shows that ordinary subtyping is contravariant in the domain and covariant in the range, while the right-hand side shows that naive subtyping is covariant in both. In both cases, the first line is equivalent to the second and third.

3.4 Typed and Untyped Lambda Calculus

We introduce a separate grammar for untyped terms, and show how to embed untyped terms into typed terms (and vice versa). The relevant definitions are in Figure 6.

Let M, N range over untyped terms. The term form $\lfloor t \rfloor$ lets us embed typed terms into untyped terms; it is well-formed only if the typed term t has type Dyn. Below we define a mapping $\lceil M \rceil$, that lets us embed untyped terms into typed terms.

An untyped term is well-formed if every variable appearing free in it has type Dyn, and if every typed subterm has type Dyn. We write $\Gamma \vdash M$ wf to indicate that M is well-formed.

A simple mapping takes untyped terms into typed terms. An untyped term M is well-formed if and only if the corresponding typed term $\lceil M \rceil$ is well-typed with type Dyn.

Lemma 1. *We have* $\Gamma \vdash M$ wf *if and only if* $\Gamma \vdash \lceil M \rceil : \text{Dyn}$.

It is straightforward to define reduction for untyped terms, and show that the embedding preserves and reflects reductions.

$$\frac{S <:^+ T \quad s \text{ safe for } p}{\langle T \Leftarrow S \rangle^p s \text{ safe for } p} \qquad \frac{S <:^- T \quad s \text{ safe for } p}{\langle T \Leftarrow S \rangle^{\bar p} s \text{ safe for } p} \qquad \frac{p \neq q \quad \bar p \neq q \quad s \text{ safe for } p}{\langle T \Leftarrow S \rangle^q s \text{ safe for } p}$$

$$\frac{v \text{ safe for } p}{\mathtt{Dyn}_G(v) \text{ safe for } p} \qquad \frac{s \longrightarrow^* \mathtt{true}}{s \rhd^p v_{\{x:B|t\}} \text{ safe for } p} \qquad \frac{q \neq p \quad s \text{ safe for } p}{s \rhd^q v_{\{x:B|t\}} \text{ safe for } p}$$

$$\overline{x \text{ safe for } p} \qquad \overline{c \text{ safe for } p} \qquad \frac{t \text{ safe for } p}{\lambda x : S. \ t \text{ safe for } p} \qquad \frac{t \text{ safe for } p \quad s \text{ safe for } p}{t \ s \text{ safe for } p}$$

Fig. 7. Safe terms

3.5   Type Safety

We have usual substitution and canonical forms lemmas, and preservation and progress results.

Lemma 2. *(Substitution) If $\Gamma \vdash v : S$ and $\Gamma, x : S \vdash t : T$, then $\Gamma \vdash t[x := v] : T$.*

Lemma 3. *(Canonical forms) Let v be a value that is well-typed in the empty context. One of three cases applies.*

- *If $\vdash v : S \to T$ then either*
  - *$v = \lambda x : S. \ t$, with $x : S \vdash t : T$, or*
  - *$v = c$, with $\mathtt{ty}(c) = S \to T$, or*
  - *$v = \langle S \to T \Leftarrow S' \to T' \rangle^p v'$ with $\vdash v' : S' \to T'$.*
- *If $\vdash v : \{x : B \mid t\}$ then $v = v'_{\{x:B|t\}}$ with $\vdash v' : B$ and $t[x := v'] \longrightarrow^* \mathtt{true}$.*
- *If $\vdash v : \mathtt{Dyn}$ then $v = \mathtt{Dyn}_G(v')$ with $\vdash v' : G$.*

Proposition 5. *(Preservation) If $\Gamma \vdash s : T$ and $s \longrightarrow t$ then $\Gamma \vdash t : T$.*

Proposition 6. *(Progress) If $\vdash s : T$ then either*

- *s is a value, or*
- *$s \longrightarrow t$ for some result t, or*
- *$s \longrightarrow \Uparrow p$ for some blame label p.*

In this case, preservation and progress do not guarantee a great deal, since they do not rule out blame as a result. However, Section 4 gives results that let us identify circumstances where certain kinds of blame cannot arise.

4   The Blame Theorem

Subtyping factors into positive and negative subtyping, and naive subtyping also factors into positive and negative subtyping, this time with the direction of negative subtyping reversed.

Proposition 7. *(Factoring subtyping) We have $S <: T$ if and only if $S <:^+ T$ and $S <:^- T$.*

Proposition 8. *(Factoring naive subtyping) We have* $S <:_n T$ *if and only if* $S <:^+ T$ *and* $T <:^- S$.

The following is the central result of this paper and depends on the definition of the safe for relation. A term t is safe for a blame label p if all of the casts that have the label p are positive subtypes, all of the casts that have the label $\neg p$, are negative subtypes, and all of the predicate tests with the label p succeed. The precise definition is given in Figure 7.

Proposition 9. *(Preservation of safe terms) For any well-typed term t and blame label p, if t safe for p and $t \longrightarrow t'$ then t' safe for p.*

Proposition 10. *(Progress of safe terms) For any well-typed term t and blame label p, if t safe for p then $t \not\longrightarrow \Uparrow p$.*

Corollary 1. *(Well-typed programs can't be blamed) Let t be a well-typed term with a subterm $\langle T \Leftarrow S \rangle^p s$ containing the only occurrences of p in t.*

- *If $S <:^+ T$ then $t \not\longrightarrow^* \Uparrow p$.*
- *If $S <:^- T$ then $t \not\longrightarrow^* \Uparrow \bar{p}$.*
- *If $S <: T$ then $t \not\longrightarrow^* \Uparrow p$ and $t \not\longrightarrow^* \Uparrow \bar{p}$*

In particular, since $S <:^+ \mathtt{Dyn}$, any failure of a cast from a well-typed term to a dynamically-typed context must be blamed on the dynamically-typed context. And since $\mathtt{Dyn} <:^- T$, any failure of a cast from a dynamically-typed term to a well-typed context must be blamed on the dynamically-typed term.

Further, consider a cast from a more precise type to a less precise type, which we can capture using naive subtyping. Since $S <:_n T$ implies $S <:^+ T$, any failure of a cast from a more-precisely-typed term to a less-precisely-typed context must be blamed on the less-precisely-typed context. And since $T <:_n S$ implies $S <:^- T$, any failure of a cast from a less-precisely-typed term to a more-precisely-typed context must be blamed on the less-precisely-typed term.

5   Related Work

Integrating static and dynamic typing is not new, and previous work includes type Dynamic [1], soft types [21], and partial types [16]. Contracts for dynamic testing of specifications were popularized by the language Eiffel [12]. Findler and Felleisen [4] introduced the use of higher-order contracts with blame in functional programming.

Henglein [9] lays much of the theoretical ground work for combining typed and untyped program fragments in a single program. Our work's principal technical debt concerns canonical coercions and the results surrounding them which justify our writing of casts as just a pair of types, instead of a pair of types combined with an explicit coercion (as Henglein does). Due to a coincidence of terminology, it is natural to compare Henglein's positive and negative coercions with our positive and negative subtyping relations, but they are essentially unrelated. Henglein's positive and negative coercions simply characterize naive subtyping [9, Proposition 23].

Siek and Taha [15] introduced gradual types, inspired by Gray et al [6]. Our results augment theirs, since we show how the blame for a failed cast always lies with the less-typed portion of the code. Siek, Garcia, and Taha [14] compare various approaches to subtyping for gradual types, including the one considered in this paper.

Flanagan et al [5, 8] introduced hybrid types and a new programming language, Sage. Ou et al [13] present a closely-related language with dynamically-checked dependent types. These support dependent function types, while our work here is restricted to ordinary function types.

Acknowledgements. This paper benefited enormously from conversations with John Hughes. Thanks to Samuel Bronson, Matthias Felleisen, Cormac Flanagan, Oleg Kiselyov, Jeremy Siek, and anonymous referees of earlier drafts for their comments on the paper. A special thanks to Michael Greenberg, Nate Foster, and Benjamin Pierce for discovering a technical flaw in an earlier version.

References

[1] Abadi, M., Cardelli, L., Pierce, B., Plotkin, G.: Dynamic typing in a statically typed language. ACM Trans. Prog. Lang. Syst. 13(2), 237–268 (1991)

[2] Bracha, G.: Pluggable type systems. In: OOPSLA 2004 Workshop on Revival of Dynamic Languages (October 2004)

[3] Findler, R., Blume, M.: Contracts as pairs of projections. In: Hagiya, M., Wadler, P. (eds.) FLOPS 2006. LNCS, vol. 3945, pp. 226–241. Springer, Heidelberg (2006)

[4] Findler, R.B., Felleisen, M.: Contracts for higher-order functions. In: ACM International Conference on Functional Programming (ICFP) (October 2002)

[5] Flanagan, C.: Hybrid type checking. In: ACM Symposium on Principles of Programming Languages (POPL) (Janurary 2006)

[6] Gray, K.E., Findler, R.B., Flatt, M.: Fine-grained interoperability through contracts and mirrors. In: ACM Conference on Object-Oriented Programming: Systems, Languages, and Applications (OOPSLA), pp. 231–246 (2005)

[7] Gronski, J., Flanagan, C.: Unifying hybrid types and contracts. In: Trends in Functional Programming (TFP) (April 2007)

[8] Gronski, J., Knowles, K., Tomb, A., Freund, S.N., Flanagan, C.: Sage: Hybrid checking for flexible specifications. In: Workshop on Scheme and Functional Programming (September 2006)

[9] Henglein, F.: Dynamic typing: Syntax and proof theory. Sci. Comput. Programming 22(3), 197–230 (1994)

[10] Matthews, J., Findler, R.B.: Operational semantics for multi-language programs. In: ACM Symposium on Principles of Programming Languages (POPL) (Janurary 2007)

[11] Meijer, E.: Static typing where possible, dynamic typing where needed. In: OOPSLA 2004 Workshop on Revival of Dynamic Languages (October 2004)

[12] Meyer, B.: Object-Oriented Software Construction. Prentice Hall, Englewood Cliffs (1988)

[13] Ou, X., Tan, G., Mandelbaum, Y., Walker, D.: Dynamic typing with dependent types. In: IFIP International Conference on Theoretical Computer Science (August 2004)

[14] Siek, J., Garcia, R., Taha, W.: Exploring the design space of higher-order casts. In: Castagna, G. (ed.) ESOP 2009. LNCS, vol. 5502, pp. 17–31. Springer, Heidelberg (2009)

[15] Siek, J.G., Taha, W.: Gradual typing for functional languages. In: Workshop on Scheme and Functional Programming (September 2006)

[16] Thatte, S.: Type inference with partial types. In: Lepistö, T., Salomaa, A. (eds.) ICALP 1988. LNCS, vol. 317. Springer, Heidelberg (1988)

[17] Tobin-Hochstadt, S., Felleisen, M.: Interlanguage migration: From scripts to programs. In: Dynamic Languages Symposium (DLS) (2006)

[18] Tobin-Hochstadt, S., Felleisen, M.: The design and implementation of typed scheme. In: ACM Symposium on Principles of Programming Languages (POPL) (2008)

[19] Wadler, P., Findler, R.B.: Well-typed programs can't be blamed. In: Workshop on Scheme and Functional Programming (September 2007)

[20] Wadler, P., Findler, R.B.: Well-typed programs can't be blamed. Technical Report TR-2009-01, University of Chicago (2009)

[21] Wright, A.K., Cartwright, R.: A practical soft typing system for Scheme. ACM Trans. Prog. Lang. Syst. 19(1) (1997)

Exploring the Design Space of Higher-Order Casts

Jeremy Siek[1,*], Ronald Garcia[2], and Walid Taha[2,**]

[1] University of Colorado, Boulder, CO 80309, USA
[2] Rice University, Houston, TX 77005, USA
jeremy.siek@colorado.edu, ronald.garcia@rice.edu, taha@rice.edu

Abstract. This paper explores the surprisingly rich design space for the simply typed lambda calculus with casts and a dynamic type. Such a calculus is the target intermediate language of the gradually typed lambda calculus but it is also interesting in its own right. In light of diverse requirements for casts, we develop a modular semantic framework, based on Henglein's Coercion Calculus, that instantiates a number of space-efficient, blame-tracking calculi, varying in what errors they detect and how they assign blame. Several of the resulting calculi extend work from the literature with either blame tracking or space efficiency, and in doing so reveal previously unknown connections. Furthermore, we introduce a new strategy for assigning blame under which casts that respect traditional subtyping are statically guaranteed to never fail. One particularly appealing outcome of this work is a novel cast calculus that is well-suited to gradual typing.

1 Introduction

This paper explores the design space for $\lambda_{\rightarrow}^{\langle \cdot \rangle}$, the simply typed lambda calculus with a dynamic type and cast expressions. Variants of this calculus have been used to express the semantics of languages that combine dynamic and static typing [2, 3, 5, 6, 8–11].

The syntax of $\lambda_{\rightarrow}^{\langle \cdot \rangle}$ is given in Fig. 1. The dynamic type Dyn is assigned to values that are tagged with their run-time type. The cast expression, $\langle T \Leftarrow S \rangle^l e$, coerces a run-time value from type S to T or halts with a cast error if it cannot perform the coercion. More precisely, the calculus evaluates e to a value v, checks whether the run-time type of v is consistent with T, and if so, returns the coercion of v to T. Otherwise execution halts and signals that the cast at location l of the source program caused an error.

The semantics of first-order casts (casts on base types) is straightforward. For example, casting an integer to Dyn and then back to Int behaves like the identity function.

$$\langle \text{Int} \Leftarrow \text{Dyn} \rangle^{l_2} \langle \text{Dyn} \Leftarrow \text{Int} \rangle^{l_1} 4 \longmapsto^* 4$$

On the other hand, casting an integer to Dyn and then to Bool raises an error and reports the source location of the cast that failed.

$$\langle \text{Bool} \Leftarrow \text{Dyn} \rangle^{l_2} \langle \text{Dyn} \Leftarrow \text{Int} \rangle^{l_1} 4 \longmapsto^* \text{blame } l_2$$

We say that the cast at location l_2 is *blamed* for the cast error.

---

* Supported by NSF grant CCF-0702362.
** Supported by NSF grants CCF-0747431 and CCF-0439017.

G. Castagna (Ed.): ESOP 2009, LNCS 5502, pp. 17–31, 2009.

Base Types	B	$\supset \{\texttt{Int}, \texttt{Bool}\}$
Types	S, T	$::= B \mid \texttt{Dyn} \mid S \to T$
Blame labels	l	$\in \mathbb{L}$ Integers $n \in \mathbb{Z}$
Constants	k	$\in \mathbb{K} \supset \{n, \texttt{True}, \texttt{False}\}$
Variables	x	$\in \mathbb{V}$
Expressions	e	$::= x \mid k \mid \lambda x : T.\ e \mid e\ e \mid \langle T \Leftarrow S \rangle^l e$

Fig. 1. Syntax for the lambda calculus with casts ($\lambda_{\to}^{\langle \cdot \rangle}$)

Extending casts from first-order to higher-order (function) types raises several issues. For starters, higher-order casts cannot always be checked immediately. In other words, it is not generally possible to decide at the point where a higher-order cast is applied to a value whether that value will always behave according to the type ascribed by the cast. For example, when the following function is cast to $\texttt{Int} \to \texttt{Int}$, there is no way to immediately tell if the function will return an integer every time it is called.

$$\langle \texttt{Int} \to \texttt{Int} \Leftarrow \texttt{Int} \to \texttt{Dyn} \rangle (\lambda x : \texttt{Int}.\ \text{if}\ 0 < x\ \text{then}\ \langle \texttt{Dyn} \Leftarrow \texttt{Bool} \rangle \texttt{True}\ \text{else}\ \langle \texttt{Dyn} \Leftarrow \texttt{Int} \rangle 2)$$

So long as the function is only called with positive numbers, its behavior respects the cast. If it is ever called with a negative number, however, its return value will violate the invariant imposed by the cast.

The standard solution, adopted from work on higher-order contracts [1], defers checking the cast until the function is applied to an argument and then checks the cast against the particular argument and return value. This can be accomplished by using the cast as a wrapper and splitting it when the wrapped function is applied to an argument:

(AppCst) $$((\langle T_1 \to T_2 \Leftarrow S_1 \to S_2 \rangle v_1)\ v_2 \longrightarrow \langle T_2 \Leftarrow S_2 \rangle (v_1\ \langle S_1 \Leftarrow T_1 \rangle v_2))$$

Because a higher-order cast is not checked immediately, it might fail in a context far removed from where it was originally applied. To help diagnose such failures, dynamic semantics are enhanced with *blame tracking*, a facility that traces failures back to their origin in the source program [1, 4, 10].

Several dynamic semantics for casts have been proposed in the literature and their differences, though subtle, produce surprisingly different results for some programs. We use the following abbreviations: **ST** for Siek and Taha [8], **HTF-L** for Herman et al. [7] (lazy variant), **HTF-E** for Herman et al. [7] (eager variant), **WF-1** for Wadler and Findler [10], and **WF-2** for [11]. Consider how these five semantics for $\lambda_{\to}^{\langle \cdot \rangle}$ produce different results for a few small examples.

The following program casts a function of type $\texttt{Int} \to \texttt{Int}$ to $\texttt{Dyn}$ and then to $\texttt{Bool} \to \texttt{Int}$. It produces a run-time cast error in **ST**, **WF-1**, and **HTF-E** but not in **WF-2** and **HTF-L**.

(1) $$\langle \texttt{Bool} \to \texttt{Int} \Leftarrow \texttt{Dyn} \rangle \langle \texttt{Dyn} \Leftarrow \texttt{Int} \to \texttt{Int} \rangle (\lambda x : \texttt{Int}.\ x)$$

With a small change, the program runs without error for four of the semantics but fails in **HTF-E**:

(2) $$\langle \texttt{Bool} \to \texttt{Int} \Leftarrow \texttt{Dyn} \to \texttt{Dyn} \rangle \langle \texttt{Dyn} \to \texttt{Dyn} \Leftarrow \texttt{Int} \to \texttt{Int} \rangle (\lambda x : \texttt{Int}.\ x)$$

It seems surprising that any of the semantics allows a function of type Int → Int to be cast to Bool → Int!

Next consider the semantics of blame assignment. The following program results in a cast error, but which of the three casts should be blamed?

(3) $(\langle \text{Dyn} \rightarrow \text{Int} \Leftarrow \text{Dyn}\rangle^{l_3} \langle \text{Dyn} \Leftarrow \text{Bool} \rightarrow \text{Bool}\rangle^{l_2} \lambda x : \text{Bool}. \ x)\langle \text{Dyn} \Leftarrow \text{Int}\rangle^{l_1} 1$

The semantics **ST**, **HTF-E**, and **HTF-L** do not perform blame tracking. Both **WF-1** and **WF-2** blame l_2. This is surprising because, intuitively, casting a value up to Dyn always seems safe. On the other hand, casting a dynamic value down to a concrete type is an opportunity for type mismatch.

In this paper we map out the design space for $\lambda^{\langle \cdot \rangle}_{\rightarrow}$ using two key insights. First, the semantics of higher-order casts can be categorized as detecting cast errors using an eager, partially eager, or lazy strategy (Section 2). Second, different blame tracking strategies yield different notions of a statically safe cast (a cast that will never be blamed for a run-time cast error) which are characterized by different "subtyping" relations, i.e., partial orders over types (Section 3).

In Section 5 we develop a framework based on Henglein's Coercion Calculus in which we formalize these two axes of the design space and instantiate four variants of the Coercion Calculus, each of which supports blame tracking. Two of the variants extend **HTF-E** and **HTF-L**, respectively, with blame tracking in a natural way. The lazy variant has the same blame assignment behavior as **WF-2**, thereby establishing a previously unknown connection. The other two variants use a new blame tracking strategy in which casts that respect traditional subtyping are guaranteed to never fail. Of these two, the one with eager error detection provides a compelling semantics for gradual typing, as explained in Sections 2 and 3.

In Section 6 we show how the approach of Herman et al. [7] can be applied to obtain a space-efficient reduction strategy for each of these calculi. In doing so, we provide the first space-efficient calculi that also perform blame tracking. We conclude in Section 7.

2   From Lazy to Eager Detection of Higher-Order Cast Errors

The $\lambda^{\langle \cdot \rangle}_{\rightarrow}$ cast can be seen as performing two actions: run-time type checking and coercing. Under the *lazy error detection strategy*, no run-time type checking is performed when a higher-order cast is applied to a value. Thus, higher-order casts never fail immediately; they coerce their argument to the target type and defer checking until the argument is applied. Both **HTF-L** and **WF-2** use lazy error detection, which is why neither detects cast errors in programs (1) and (2).

Under the *partially-eager error detection strategy*, a higher-order cast is checked immediately only when its source type is Dyn, otherwise checking is deferred according to the lazy strategy. Both **ST** and **WF-1** use the partially eager error detection strategy. Under this strategy program (1) produces a cast error whereas program (2) does not.

Examples like program (2) inspire the *eager error detection strategy*. Under this strategy, a higher-order cast always performs some checking immediately. Furthermore, the run-time checking is "deep" in that it not only checks that the target type is consistent with the outermost wrapper, but it also checks for consistency at every layer of wrapping including the underlying value type. Thus, when the cast $\langle$Bool $\rightarrow$ Int$\rangle$ in program (2) is evaluated, it checks that Bool $\rightarrow$ Int is consistent with the prior cast $\langle$Dyn $\rightarrow$ Dyn$\rangle$ (which it is) and with the type of the underlying function Int $\rightarrow$ Int (which it is not). The **HTF-E** semantics is eager in this sense.

For the authors, the main use of $\lambda_{\rightarrow}^{\langle \cdot \rangle}$ is as a target language for the gradually typed lambda calculus, so we seek the most appropriate error detection strategy for gradual typing. With gradual typing, programmers add type annotations to their programs to increase static checking and to express *invariants that they believe to be true about their program*. Thus, when a programmer annotates a parameter with the type Bool $\rightarrow$ Int, she is expressing the invariant that all the run-time values bound to this parameter will behave according to the type Bool $\rightarrow$ Int. With this in mind, it makes sense that the programmer is notified as soon as possible if the invariant does not hold. The eager error detection strategy does this.

3   Blame Assignment and Subtyping

When programming in a language based on $\lambda_{\rightarrow}^{\langle \cdot \rangle}$, it helps to statically know which parts of the program might cause cast errors and which parts never will. A graphical development environment, for instance, could use colors to distinguish safe casts, unsafe casts which might fail, and inadmissible casts which the system rejects because they always fail. The inadmissible casts are statically detected using the consistency relation $\sim$ of Siek and Taha [8], defined in Fig. 2. A cast $\langle T \Leftarrow S \rangle e$ is rejected if $S \nsim T$. Safe casts are statically captured by subtyping relations: if the cast *respects subtyping*, meaning $S <: T$, then it is safe. For unsafe casts, $S \sim T$ but $S \not<: T$[1].

$$\frac{}{T \sim \text{Dyn}} \qquad \frac{}{\text{Dyn} \sim T} \qquad \frac{}{B \sim B} \qquad \frac{S_1 \sim T_1 \quad S_2 \sim T_2}{S_1 \rightarrow S_2 \sim T_1 \rightarrow T_2}$$

Fig. 2. The consistency relation

Formally establishing that a particular subtype relation is sound with respect to the semantics requires a theorem of the form:

If there is a cast at location l of the source program that respects subtyping, then no execution of the program will result in a cast error that blames l.

Wadler and Findler [10], [11] prove this property for their two semantics and their definitions of subtyping, respectively. Fig. 3 shows their two subtyping relations as well as the traditional subtype relation with Dyn as its top element.

We consider the choice of subtype relation to be a critical design decision because it directly affects the programmer, i.e., it determines which casts are statically safe and

---

[1] Subtyping is a conservative approximation, so some of the unsafe casts are "false positives" and will never cause cast errors.

Traditional subtyping:

$$\frac{}{T <: \mathtt{Dyn}} \qquad \frac{}{B <: B} \qquad \frac{T_1 <: S_1 \quad S_2 <: T_2}{S_1 \to S_2 <: T_1 \to T_2}$$

Subtyping of **WF-1**:

$$\frac{}{B <: B} \qquad \frac{}{\mathtt{Dyn} <: \mathtt{Dyn}} \qquad \frac{T_1 <: S_1 \quad S_2 <: T_2}{S_1 \to S_2 <: T_1 \to T_2}$$

Subtyping of **WF-2**:

$$\frac{}{B <: B} \qquad \frac{}{\mathtt{Dyn} <: \mathtt{Dyn}} \qquad \frac{S <: G}{S <: \mathtt{Dyn}} \qquad \frac{T_1 <: S_1 \quad S_2 <: T_2}{S_1 \to S_2 <: T_1 \to T_2}$$

$$\text{where } G ::= B \mid \mathtt{Dyn} \to \mathtt{Dyn}$$

Fig. 3. Three subtyping relations

unsafe. The traditional subtype relation is familiar to programmers, relatively easy to explain, and matches our intuitions about which casts are safe. This raises the question: is there a blame tracking strategy for which the traditional subtype relation is sound?

First, it is instructive to see why traditional subtyping is not sound with respect to the blame tracking in **WF-2** (**WF-1** is similar in this respect). Consider program (3).

$$(\langle \mathtt{Dyn} \to \mathtt{Int} \Leftarrow \mathtt{Dyn} \rangle^{l_3} \langle \mathtt{Dyn} \Leftarrow \mathtt{Bool} \to \mathtt{Bool} \rangle^{l_2} \lambda x : \mathtt{Bool}.\ x) \langle \mathtt{Dyn} \Leftarrow \mathtt{Int} \rangle^{l_1} 1$$

The cast at location l_2 respects the traditional subtyping relation: $\mathtt{Bool} \to \mathtt{Bool} <: \mathtt{Dyn}$. The following reduction sequence uses the blame tracking strategy of **WF-2**. The expression $\mathtt{Dyn}_G(v)$ represents values that have been injected into the dynamic type. The subscript G records the type of v and is restricted to base types, the dynamic type, and the function type $\mathtt{Dyn} \to \mathtt{Dyn}$. Their interpretation of a cast is closer to that of an obligation expression [1], so each blame label has a *polarity*, marked by the presence or absence of an overline, which directs blame toward the interior or exterior of the cast.

$$(\langle \mathtt{Dyn} \to \mathtt{Int} \Leftarrow \mathtt{Dyn} \rangle^{l_3} \langle \mathtt{Dyn} \Leftarrow \mathtt{Bool} \to \mathtt{Bool} \rangle^{l_2} \lambda x : \mathtt{Bool}.\ x) \langle \mathtt{Dyn} \Leftarrow \mathtt{Int} \rangle^{l_1} 1$$
$$\longrightarrow (\langle \mathtt{Dyn} \to \mathtt{Int} \Leftarrow \mathtt{Dyn} \rangle^{l_3} \mathtt{Dyn}_{\mathtt{Dyn} \to \mathtt{Dyn}}(\langle\ \mathtt{Dyn}\ \to \mathtt{Dyn} \Leftarrow\ \mathtt{Bool}\ \to \mathtt{Bool} \rangle^{l_2} \lambda x : \mathtt{Bool}.\ x)) \langle \mathtt{Dyn} \Leftarrow \mathtt{Int} \rangle^{l_1} 1$$
$$\longrightarrow (\langle \mathtt{Dyn} \to \mathtt{Int} \Leftarrow \mathtt{Dyn} \to \mathtt{Dyn} \rangle^{l_3} \langle\ \mathtt{Dyn}\ \to \mathtt{Dyn} \Leftarrow\ \mathtt{Bool}\ \to \mathtt{Bool} \rangle^{l_2} \lambda x : \mathtt{Bool}.\ x) \langle \mathtt{Dyn} \Leftarrow \mathtt{Int} \rangle^{l_1} 1$$
$$\longrightarrow \langle \mathtt{Int} \Leftarrow \mathtt{Dyn} \rangle^{l_3} (\langle\ \mathtt{Dyn}\ \to \mathtt{Dyn} \Leftarrow\ \mathtt{Bool}\ \to \mathtt{Bool} \rangle^{l_2} \lambda x : \mathtt{Bool}.\ x) \langle \mathtt{Dyn} \Leftarrow \mathtt{Dyn} \rangle^{\overline{l_3}} \langle \mathtt{Dyn} \Leftarrow \mathtt{Int} \rangle^{l_1} 1$$
$$\longrightarrow \langle \mathtt{Int} \Leftarrow \mathtt{Dyn} \rangle^{l_3} (\langle\ \mathtt{Dyn}\ \to \mathtt{Dyn} \Leftarrow\ \mathtt{Bool}\ \to \mathtt{Bool} \rangle^{l_2} \lambda x : \mathtt{Bool}.\ x) \langle \mathtt{Dyn} \Leftarrow \mathtt{Int} \rangle^{l_1} 1$$
$$\longrightarrow \langle \mathtt{Int} \Leftarrow \mathtt{Dyn} \rangle^{l_3} \langle \mathtt{Dyn} \Leftarrow \mathtt{Bool} \rangle^{l_2} ((\lambda x : \mathtt{Bool}.\ x)\ \langle \mathtt{Bool} \Leftarrow \mathtt{Dyn} \rangle^{\overline{l_2}} \langle \mathtt{Dyn} \Leftarrow \mathtt{Int} \rangle^{l_1} 1)$$
$$\longrightarrow \mathbf{blame}\ \overline{l_2}$$

The example shows that under this blame tracking strategy, a cast like l_2 can respect traditional subtyping yet still be blamed. We trace back to the source of the cast error by highlighting the relevant portions of the casts in gray. The source of the cast error is the transition that replaces the cast $\langle \mathtt{Dyn} \Leftarrow \mathtt{Bool} \to \mathtt{Bool} \rangle^{l_2}$ with $\langle \mathtt{Dyn} \to \mathtt{Dyn} \Leftarrow \mathtt{Bool} \to \mathtt{Bool} \rangle^{l_2}$. This reduction rule follows from restrictions on the structure of $\mathrm{Dyn}_G(v)$: the only function type allowed for G is $\mathrm{Dyn} \to \mathrm{Dyn}$. This choice forces casts from function types to Dyn to always go through $\mathrm{Dyn} \to \mathrm{Dyn}$. However, adding the intermediate step does not preserve traditional subtyping: $S \to T <: \mathrm{Dyn}$ is always true, but because of the contravariance of subtyping in the argument position, it is not always the case that $S \to T <: \mathrm{Dyn} \to \mathrm{Dyn}$. For instance, if $S = \mathrm{Bool}$, then it is not the case that $\mathrm{Dyn} <: \mathrm{Bool}$.

It seems reasonable, however, to inject higher-order types directly into Dyn. Consider the following alternative injection and and projection rules for Dyn:

$$\langle \mathrm{Dyn} \Leftarrow S \rangle^l v \longrightarrow_s \mathrm{Dyn}_S(v)$$

$$\langle T \Leftarrow \mathrm{Dyn} \rangle^l \mathrm{Dyn}_S(v) \longrightarrow_s \langle T \Leftarrow S \rangle^l v \qquad \text{if } S \sim T$$

$$\langle T \Leftarrow \mathrm{Dyn} \rangle^l \mathrm{Dyn}_S(v) \longrightarrow_s \mathbf{blame}\ l \qquad \text{if } S \nsim T$$

We define the *simple blame tracking semantics*, written $\longrightarrow_s$, to include the above rules together with APPCST and the standard β and δ reduction rules. The following is the corresponding reduction sequence for program (3).

$$(\langle \mathrm{Dyn} \to \mathrm{Int} \Leftarrow \mathrm{Dyn} \rangle^{l_3} \langle \mathrm{Dyn} \Leftarrow \mathrm{Bool} \to \mathrm{Bool} \rangle^{l_2} \lambda x : \mathrm{Bool}.\ x)\ \langle \mathrm{Dyn} \Leftarrow \mathrm{Int} \rangle^{l_1} 1$$

$\longrightarrow_s (\langle \mathrm{Dyn} \to \mathrm{Int} \Leftarrow \mathrm{Dyn} \rangle^{l_3} \mathrm{Dyn}_{\mathrm{Bool} \to \mathrm{Bool}}(\lambda x : \mathrm{Bool}.\ x))\ \langle \mathrm{Dyn} \Leftarrow \mathrm{Int} \rangle^{l_1} 1$

$\longrightarrow_s (\langle \mathrm{Dyn} \to \mathrm{Int} \Leftarrow \mathrm{Bool} \to \mathrm{Bool} \rangle^{l_3} (\lambda x : \mathrm{Bool}.\ x))\ \langle \mathrm{Dyn} \Leftarrow \mathrm{Int} \rangle^{l_1} 1$

$\longrightarrow_s (\langle \mathrm{Dyn} \to \mathrm{Int} \Leftarrow \mathrm{Bool} \to \mathrm{Bool} \rangle^{l_3} (\lambda x : \mathrm{Bool}.\ x))\ \mathrm{Dyn}_{\mathrm{Int}}(1)$

$\longrightarrow_s \langle \mathrm{Int} \Leftarrow \mathrm{Bool} \rangle^{l_3} ((\lambda x : \mathrm{Bool}.\ x)\ \langle \mathrm{Bool} \Leftarrow \mathrm{Dyn} \rangle^{l_3} \mathrm{Dyn}_{\mathrm{Int}}(1))$

$\longrightarrow_s \mathbf{blame}\ l_3$

Under this blame tracking strategy, the downcast from Dyn to $\mathrm{Dyn} \to \mathrm{Int}$ at location l_3 is blamed instead of the upcast at location l_2. This particular result better matches our intuitions about what went wrong, and in general the simple blame strategy never blames a cast that respects the traditional subtype relation.

Theorem 1 (Soundness of subtyping wrt. the simple semantics)
If there is a cast labeled l in program e that respects subtyping, then $e \nrightarrow_s^* \mathbf{blame}\ l$.

Proof. The proof is a straightforward induction on $\longrightarrow_s^*$ once the statement is generalized to say "all casts labeled l". This is necessary because the APPCST rule turns one cast into two casts with the same label.

While the simple blame tracking semantics assigns blame in a way that respects traditional subtyping, it does not perform eager error detection; it is partially eager. We conjecture that the simple semantics could be augmented with deep checks to achieve eager error detection. However, there also remains the issue of space efficiency. In the next section we discuss the problems regarding space efficiency and how these problems can be solved by moving to a framework based on the semantics of Herman et al. [7] which in turn uses the Coercion Calculus of Henglein [6]. We then show how the variations in blame tracking and eager checking can be realized in that framework.

4   Space Efficiency

Herman et al. [7] observe two circumstances where the wrappers used for higher-order casts can lead to unbounded space consumption. First, some programs repeatedly apply casts to the same function, resulting in a build-up of wrappers. In the following example, each time the function bound to k is passed between even and odd a wrapper is added, causing a space leak proportional to n.

```
let rec even(n : Int, k : Dyn→Bool) : Bool =
    if (n = 0) then k(⟨Dyn ⇐ Bool⟩True)
    else odd(n - 1, ⟨Bool → Bool ⇐ Dyn → Bool⟩k)
and odd(n : Int, k : Bool→Bool) : Bool =
    if (n = 0) then k(False)
    else even(n - 1, ⟨Dyn → Bool ⇐ Bool → Bool⟩k)
```

Second, some casts break proper tail recursion. Consider the following example in which the return type of even is Dyn and odd is Bool.

```
let rec even(n : Int) : Dyn =
    if (n = 0) then True else ⟨Dyn ⇐ Bool⟩odd(n - 1)
and odd(n : Int) : Bool =
    if (n = 0) then False else ⟨Bool ⇐ Dyn⟩even(n - 1)
```

Assuming tail call optimization, cast-free versions of the even and odd functions require only constant space, but because the call to even is no longer a tail call, the run-time stack grows with each call and space consumption is proportional to n. The following reduction sequence for a call to even shows the unbounded growth.

$$\text{even}(n) \longmapsto \langle \text{Dyn} \Leftarrow \text{Bool}\rangle \text{odd}(n-1)$$
$$\longmapsto \langle \text{Dyn} \Leftarrow \text{Bool}\rangle\langle \text{Bool} \Leftarrow \text{Dyn}\rangle \text{even}(n-2)$$
$$\longmapsto \langle \text{Dyn} \Leftarrow \text{Bool}\rangle\langle \text{Bool} \Leftarrow \text{Dyn}\rangle\langle \text{Dyn} \Leftarrow \text{Bool}\rangle \text{odd}(n-3)$$
$$\longmapsto \cdots$$

Herman et al. [7] show that space efficiency can be recovered by 1) merging sequences of casts into a single cast, 2) ensuring that the size of a merged cast is bounded by a constant, and 3) checking for sequences of casts in tail-position and merging them before making function calls.

5   Variations on the Coercion Calculus

The semantics of $\lambda_{\rightarrow}^{\langle\cdot\rangle}$ in Henglein [6] and subsequently in Herman et al. [7] use a special sub-language called the Coercion Calculus to express casts. Instead of casts of the form $\langle T \Leftarrow S\rangle e$ they have casts of the form $\langle c\rangle e$ where c is a coercion expression. The Coercion Calculus can be viewed as a fine-grained operational specification of casts. It is not intended to be directly used by programmers, but instead casts of the form $\langle T \Leftarrow S\rangle e$ are compiled into casts of the form $\langle c\rangle e$. In this section we define a translation function $\langle\!\langle T \Leftarrow S\rangle\!\rangle$ that maps the source and target of a cast to a coercion. We define $\langle\!\langle e\rangle\!\rangle$ to be the natural extension of this translation to expressions. The syntax and type system of the Coercion Calculus is shown in Fig. 4. We add blame labels to the syntax to introduce blame tracking to the Coercion Calculus.

The coercion $T!$ injects a value into Dyn whereas the coercion $T?$ projects a value out of Dyn. For example, the coercion Int! takes an integer and injects it into the type Dyn, and conversely, the coercion $\text{Int}?^l$ takes a value of type Dyn and projects it to

Syntax: Coercions $c, d ::= \iota \mid T! \mid T?^l \mid c \to d \mid d \circ c \mid \mathtt{Fail}^l$
               Coercion contexts $C ::= \square \mid C \to c \mid c \to C \mid c \circ C \mid C \circ c$

Type system:

$$\frac{}{\vdash \iota : T \Leftarrow T} \qquad \frac{}{\vdash T! : \mathtt{Dyn} \Leftarrow T} \qquad \frac{}{\vdash T?^l : T \Leftarrow \mathtt{Dyn}} \qquad \frac{}{\vdash \mathtt{Fail}^l : T \Leftarrow S}$$

$$\frac{\vdash c : S_1 \Leftarrow T_1 \qquad \vdash d : T_2 \Leftarrow S_2}{\vdash c \to d : (T_1 \to T_2) \Leftarrow (S_1 \to S_2)} \qquad \frac{\vdash d : T_3 \Leftarrow T_2 \qquad \vdash c : T_2 \Leftarrow T_1}{\vdash d \circ c : T_3 \Leftarrow T_1}$$

Fig. 4. Syntax and type system for the Coercion Calculus

type Int, checking to make sure the value is an integer, blaming location l otherwise. Our presentation of injections and projections differs from that of Henglein [6] in that the grammar in Fig. 4 allows arbitrary types in $T!$ and $T?^l$. When modeling Henglein's semantics, we restrict T to base types and function types of the form $\mathtt{Dyn} \to \mathtt{Dyn}$. Thus, $(\mathtt{Dyn} \to \mathtt{Dyn})!$ is equivalent to Henglein's Func! and $(\mathtt{Dyn} \to \mathtt{Dyn})?^l$ is equivalent to Func?. The calculus also has operators for aggregating coercions. The function coercion $c \to d$ applies coercion c to a function's argument and d to its return value. Coercion composition $d \circ c$ applies coercion c then coercion d.[2] In addition to Henglein's coercions, we adopt the $\mathtt{Fail}^l$ coercion of Herman et al. [7], which compactly represents coercions that are destined to fail but have not yet been applied to a value.

In this section we add blame tracking to the Coercion Calculus using two different blame assignment strategies, one that shares the blame between higher-order upcasts and downcasts, thereby modeling **WF-1** and **WF-2**, and a new strategy that places responsibility on downcasts only. To clearly express not only these two blame assignment strategies but also the existing strategies for eager and lazy error detection (**HTF-E** and **HTF-L**), we organize the reduction rules into four sets that can be combined to create variations on the Coercion Calculus.

L The core set of reduction rules that is used by all variations. This set of rules, when combined with either **UD** or **D**, performs *lazy* error detection.

E The additional rules needed to perform *eager* error detection.

UD The rules for blame assignment that share responsibility between higher-order *upcasts* and *downcasts*.

D The rules for blame assignment that place all the responsibility on *downcasts*.

Fig 5 shows how the sets of reduction rules can be combined to create four distinct coercion calculi.

All of the reduction strategies share the following parameterized rule for single-step evaluation, where X stands for a set of reduction rules.

$$\frac{c \cong C[c_1] \qquad c_1 \longrightarrow_X c_2 \qquad C[c_2] \cong c'}{c \longmapsto_X c'}$$

---

[2] We use the notation $d \circ c$ instead of the notation $c; d$ of Henglein to be consistent with the right to left orientation of our type-based cast expressions.

	Lazy error detection	Eager error detection
Blame upcasts and downcasts	$L \cup UD$	$L \cup UD \cup E$
Blame downcasts	$L \cup D$	$L \cup D \cup E$

Fig. 5. Summary of the Coercion Calculi

The above rule relies on a congruence relation, written $\cong$, to account for the associativity of coercion composition: $(c_3 \circ c_2) \circ c_1 \cong c_3 \circ (c_2 \circ c_1)$. The reduction rules simplify pairs of adjacent coercions into a single coercion. The congruence relation is used during evaluation to reassociate a sequence of coercions so that a pair of adjacent coercions can be reduced. A coercion c is *normalized* if $\nexists c'. \ c \longmapsto_X c'$ and we indicate that a coercion is normalized with an overline, as in $\bar{c}$.

$$B?^l \circ B! \longrightarrow \iota \qquad\qquad B'?^l \circ B! \longrightarrow \mathtt{Fail}^l$$
$$\iota \to \iota \longrightarrow \iota \qquad\qquad B?^l \circ (S_1 \to S_2)! \longrightarrow \mathtt{Fail}^l$$
$$c \circ \iota \longrightarrow c \qquad\qquad (T_1 \to T_2)?^l \circ B! \longrightarrow \mathtt{Fail}^l$$
$$\iota \circ c \longrightarrow c \qquad\qquad d \circ \mathtt{Fail}^l \longrightarrow \mathtt{Fail}^l$$
$$\mathtt{Fail}^l \circ T! \longrightarrow \mathtt{Fail}^l \quad \text{(FAILIN)}$$
$$(d_1 \to d_2) \circ (c_1 \to c_2) \longrightarrow (c_1 \circ d_1) \to (d_2 \circ c_2)$$

Fig. 6. The core reduction rules (**L**)

The set **L** of core reduction rules is given in Fig. 6. These rules differ from those of Herman et al. [7] in several ways. First, the rules propagate blame labels. Second, we factor the rule for handling injection-projection pairs over functions types into **UD** and **D**. Third, we omit a rule of the form

(FAILL) $\mathtt{Fail}^l \circ c \longrightarrow \mathtt{Fail}^l$

This change is motivated by the addition of blame tracking which makes it possible to distinguish between failures with different causes. If we use FAILL, then the optimizations for space efficiency change how blame is assigned. Suppose there is a context waiting on the stack of the form $\langle \mathtt{Fail}^{l_2} \circ \mathtt{Int}?^{l_1} \rangle \square$ and the value returned to this context is $\langle \mathtt{Bool}! \rangle \mathtt{True}$. Then in the un-optimized semantics we have

$$\langle \mathtt{Fail}^{l_2} \circ \mathtt{Int}?^{l_1} \rangle \square \longmapsto \langle \mathtt{Fail}^{l_2} \circ \mathtt{Int}?^{l_1} \rangle \langle \mathtt{Bool}! \rangle \mathtt{True} \longmapsto \langle \mathtt{Fail}^{l_2} \circ \mathtt{Int}?^{l_1} \circ \mathtt{Bool}! \rangle \mathtt{True}$$
$$\longmapsto \langle \mathtt{Fail}^{l_2} \circ \mathtt{Fail}^{l_1} \rangle \mathtt{True} \longmapsto \langle \mathtt{Fail}^{l_1} \rangle \mathtt{True} \longmapsto \mathtt{blame}\ l_1$$

whereas in the optimized semantics we have

$$\langle \mathtt{Fail}^{l_2} \circ \mathtt{Int}?^{l_1} \rangle \square \longmapsto \langle \mathtt{Fail}^{l_2} \rangle \square \longmapsto \langle \mathtt{Fail}^{l_2} \rangle \langle \mathtt{Bool}! \rangle \mathtt{True} \longmapsto \langle \mathtt{Fail}^{l_2} \circ \mathtt{Bool}! \rangle \mathtt{True}$$
$$\longmapsto \langle \mathtt{Fail}^{l_2} \rangle \mathtt{True} \longmapsto \mathtt{blame}\ l_2$$

On the other hand, the rule FAILIN is harmless because an injection can never fail. When we embed a coercion calculus in $\lambda_{\to}^{\langle \cdot \rangle}$, we do not want an expression such as

Syntax:

Expressions	$e ::= x \mid k \mid \lambda x : T.\, e \mid e\, e \mid \langle c \rangle e$
Simple Values	$s ::= k \mid \lambda x : T.\, e$
Regular Coercions	$\hat{c} ::= \bar{c}$ where $\bar{c} \neq \iota$ and $\bar{c} \neq \mathtt{Fail}^l$
Values	$v ::= s \mid \langle \hat{c} \rangle s$
Evaluation contexts	$E ::= \square \mid E\, e \mid v\, E \mid \langle c \rangle E$

Type system:

$$\frac{}{\Gamma \vdash x : \Gamma(x)} \qquad \frac{}{\Gamma \vdash k : \mathit{typeof}(k)} \qquad \frac{\Gamma[x \mapsto S] \vdash e : T}{\Gamma \vdash \lambda x : S.\, e : S \to T}$$

$$\frac{\Gamma \vdash e_1 : S \to T \quad \Gamma \vdash e_2 : S}{\Gamma \vdash e_1\, e_2 : T} \qquad \frac{\vdash c : T \Leftarrow S \quad \Gamma \vdash e : S}{\Gamma \vdash \langle c \rangle e : T}$$

Reduction rules:

$$
\begin{array}{lll}
(\beta) & (\lambda x : T.e)\, v \longrightarrow e[x \mapsto v] & \\
(\delta) & k\, v \longrightarrow \delta(k, v) & \\
(\textsc{StepCst}) & \langle c \rangle s \longrightarrow \langle c' \rangle s & \text{if } c \longmapsto_X c' \\
(\textsc{IdCst}) & \langle \iota \rangle s \longrightarrow s & \\
(\textsc{CmpCst}) & \langle d \rangle \langle \hat{c} \rangle s \longrightarrow \langle d \circ \hat{c} \rangle s & \\
(\textsc{AppCst}) & \langle \bar{c} \to \bar{d} \rangle s\, v \longrightarrow \langle d \rangle (s\, \langle c \rangle v) & \\
(\textsc{FailCst}) & \langle \mathtt{Fail}^l \rangle s \longrightarrow \textbf{blame } l & \\
(\textsc{FailFC}) & \langle \mathtt{Fail}^l \circ (\bar{c} \to \bar{d}) \rangle s \longrightarrow \textbf{blame } l & \\
\end{array}
$$

Single-step evaluation:

$$\frac{e \longrightarrow e}{E[e] \longmapsto E[e']} \qquad \frac{e \longrightarrow \textbf{blame } l}{E[e] \longmapsto \textbf{blame } l}$$

Fig. 7. A semantics for $\lambda^{\langle \cdot \rangle}_{\rightarrow}$ based on coercion calculi

$\langle \mathtt{Fail}^l \circ (\iota \to \mathtt{Int!}) \rangle (\lambda x : \mathtt{Int}.\ x)$ to be a value. It should instead reduce to **blame** l. Instead of trying to solve this in the coercion calculi, we add a reduction rule (FAILFC) to $\lambda^{\langle \cdot \rangle}_{\rightarrow}$ to handle this situation.

Fig. 7 shows a semantics for $\lambda^{\langle \cdot \rangle}_{\rightarrow}$ based on coercion calculi (it is parameterized on the set of coercion reduction rules X). We write $\lambda^{\langle \cdot \rangle}_{\rightarrow}(X)$ to refer to an instantiation of the semantics with the coercion calculus X. The semantics includes the usual rules for the lambda calculus and several rules that govern the behavior of casts. The rule STEPCST simplifies a cast expression by taking one step of evaluation inside the coercion. The rule IDCST discards an identity cast and CMPCST turns a pair of casts into a single cast with composed coercions. The APPCST rule applies a function wrapped in a cast. The cast is split into a cast on the argument and a cast on the return value. The rule FAILCST signals a cast error when the coercion is $\mathtt{Fail}^l$.

5.1 Blame Assignment Strategies

In this section we present two blame assignment strategies: the strategy shared by **WF-1** and **WF-2**, where upcasts and downcasts share responsibility for blame, and a new strategy where only downcasts are responsible for blame. The first strategy will be modeled by the set of reduction rules **UD** (for upcast-downcast) and the second by the set of reduction rules **D** (for downcast).

The UD Blame Assignment Strategy. As discussed in Section 3, the blame assignment strategy that shares responsibility for blame between upcasts and downcasts is based on the notion that a cast between an arbitrary function type and Dyn must always go through Dyn $\rightarrow$ Dyn. As a result, at the level of the coercion calculus, the only higher-order injections and projections are (Dyn $\rightarrow$ Dyn)! and (Dyn $\rightarrow$ Dyn)$?^l$. The compilation of type-based casts to coercion-based casts is responsible for introducing the indirection through Dyn $\rightarrow$ Dyn. Fig. 8 shows the compilation function. The last two lines of the definition handle higher-order upcasts and downcasts and produce coercions that go through Dyn $\rightarrow$ Dyn. Consider the coercion produced from the higher-order cast that injects Bool $\rightarrow$ Bool into Dyn.

$$\langle\!\langle \text{Dyn} \Leftarrow \text{Bool} \rightarrow \text{Bool} \rangle\!\rangle^l = (\text{Dyn} \rightarrow \text{Dyn})! \circ (\text{Bool}?^l \rightarrow \text{Bool}!)$$

The projection Bool$?^l$ in the resulting coercion can cause a run-time cast error, which shows how, with this blame assignment strategy, higher-order upcasts such as Dyn $\Leftarrow$ Bool $\rightarrow$ Bool share the responsibility for cast errors.

The set of reduction rules for **UD** is given in Fig. 8. With **UD**, the only higher-order coercions are to and from Dyn $\rightarrow$ Dyn, so the only injection-projection case missing from the **L** rules is the case handled by the INOUTDD rule in Fig. 8.

The combination **L** $\cup$ **UD** simulates the semantics of **WF-2**.

Theorem 2. *If $e \longrightarrow^* e'$ in WF-2 and e' is a value or blame l, then there is an e'' such that $\langle\!\langle e \rangle\!\rangle \longmapsto^*_{\text{L}\cup\text{UD}} e''$ and $\langle\!\langle e' \rangle\!\rangle = e''$.*

Proof. The proof is a straightforward induction on $\longrightarrow^*$.

The combination **L** $\cup$ **UD** can also be viewed as the natural way to add blame tracking to **HTF-L**, revealing an interesting and new connection between **HTF-L** and **WF-2**.

The D Blame Assignment Strategy. To obtain a blame assignment strategy that coincides with traditional subtyping, we lift the restriction on injections and projections to allow direct coercions between arbitrary function types and Dyn, analogous to what we did in Section 3. With this change the compilation from type-based casts to coercions no longer needs to go through the intermediate Dyn $\rightarrow$ Dyn. Fig. 9 shows the new compilation function. Consequently the reduction rules for **D** need to be more general to handle arbitrary higher-order projections and injections. The rule INOUTFF in Fig. 9 does just that. The blame label l used to create the coercion on the right-hand side is from the projection. This places all of the responsibility for a potential error on the projection.

We now prove that the **D** strategy fulfills its design goal: traditional subtyping should capture the notion of a safe cast, i.e., a cast that is guaranteed not to be blamed for any run-time cast errors. It turns out that this is rather straightforward to prove because a cast from S to T, where $S <: T$, compiles to a coercion with no projection or failure coercions. In fact, the coercion will not contain any blame labels.

Compilation from type-based casts to coercions:

$$\langle\!\langle B \Leftarrow B \rangle\!\rangle^l = \iota$$

$$\langle\!\langle B' \Leftarrow B \rangle\!\rangle^l = \text{Fail}^l \quad \text{if } B \neq B'$$

$$\langle\!\langle \text{Dyn} \Leftarrow \text{Dyn} \rangle\!\rangle^l = \iota$$

$$\langle\!\langle \text{Dyn} \Leftarrow B \rangle\!\rangle^l = B!$$

$$\langle\!\langle B \Leftarrow \text{Dyn} \rangle\!\rangle^l = B?^l$$

$$\langle\!\langle B \Leftarrow S_1 \rightarrow S_2 \rangle\!\rangle^l = \text{Fail}^l$$

$$\langle\!\langle T_1 \rightarrow T_2 \Leftarrow B \rangle\!\rangle^l = \text{Fail}^l$$

$$\langle\!\langle T_1 \rightarrow T_2 \Leftarrow S_1 \rightarrow S_2 \rangle\!\rangle^l = \begin{cases} \iota & \text{if } c = \iota \text{ and } d = \iota \\ \text{Fail}^l & \text{if } c = \text{Fail}^l \text{ or } d = \text{Fail}^l \\ c \rightarrow d & \text{otherwise} \end{cases}$$

$$\text{where } c = \langle\!\langle S_1 \Leftarrow T_1 \rangle\!\rangle^l, d = \langle\!\langle T_2 \Leftarrow S_2 \rangle\!\rangle^l$$

$$\langle\!\langle \text{Dyn} \Leftarrow S_1 \rightarrow S_2 \rangle\!\rangle^l = (\text{Dyn} \rightarrow \text{Dyn})! \circ \langle\!\langle \text{Dyn} \rightarrow \text{Dyn} \Leftarrow S_1 \rightarrow S_2 \rangle\!\rangle^l$$

$$\langle\!\langle T_1 \rightarrow T_2 \Leftarrow \text{Dyn} \rangle\!\rangle^l = \langle\!\langle T_1 \rightarrow T_2 \Leftarrow \text{Dyn} \rightarrow \text{Dyn} \rangle\!\rangle^l \circ (\text{Dyn} \rightarrow \text{Dyn})?^l$$

Reduction rules:

$$(\text{INOUTDD}) \; (\text{Dyn} \rightarrow \text{Dyn})?^l \circ (\text{Dyn} \rightarrow \text{Dyn})! \longrightarrow \iota$$

Fig. 8. The **UD** blame assignment strategy

Lemma 1 (Subtype coercions do not contain blame labels)

If $S <: T$ then $labels(\langle\!\langle T \Leftarrow S \rangle\!\rangle^l) = \emptyset$, where $labels(c)$ is the labels that occur in c.

Proof. The proof is by strong induction on the sum of the height of the two types followed by case analysis on the types. Each case is straightforward.

Next we show that coercion evaluation does not introduce blame labels.

Lemma 2 (Coercion evaluation monotonically decreases labels)

If $c \longmapsto_{\text{L}\cup\text{D}} c'$ then $labels(c') \subseteq labels(c)$.

Proof. The proof is a straightforward case analysis on $\longmapsto_{\text{L}\cup\text{D}}$ and $\longrightarrow_{\text{L}\cup\text{D}}$.

The same can be said of $\lambda^{\langle\cdot\rangle}_{\rightarrow}(\text{L} \cup \text{D})$ evaluation.

Lemma 3 ($\lambda^{\langle\cdot\rangle}_{\rightarrow}(\text{L} \cup \text{D})$ evaluation monotonically decreases labels)

If $e \longmapsto e'$ then $labels(e') \subseteq labels(e)$, where $labels(e)$ is the labels that occur in e.

Proof. The proof is a straightforward case analysis on $\longmapsto$ and $\longrightarrow$.

Thus, when a cast failure occurs, the label must have come from a coercion in the original program, but it could not have been from a cast that respects subtyping because such casts produce coercions that do not contain any blame labels.

Theorem 3 (Soundness of subtyping wrt. $\lambda^{\langle\cdot\rangle}_{\rightarrow}(\text{L} \cup \text{D})$)

*If every cast labeled l in program e respects subtyping, then $e \not\longmapsto^*$ **blame** l.*

Proof. The proof is a straightforward induction on $\longmapsto^*$.

Compilation from type-based casts to coercions:

$$\vdots \text{ (same as in Fig. 8)}$$
$$\langle\!\langle \text{Dyn} \Leftarrow S_1 \rightarrow S_2 \rangle\!\rangle^l = (S_1 \rightarrow S_2)!$$
$$\langle\!\langle T_1 \rightarrow T_2 \Leftarrow \text{Dyn} \rangle\!\rangle^l = (T_1 \rightarrow T_2)?^l$$

Reduction rules:

$$(\textsc{InOutFF}) \; (T_1 \rightarrow T_2)?^l \circ (S_1 \rightarrow S_2)! \longrightarrow \langle\!\langle T_1 \rightarrow T_2 \Leftarrow S_1 \rightarrow S_2 \rangle\!\rangle^l$$

Fig. 9. The **D** blame assignment strategy

5.2 An Eager Error Detection Strategy for the Coercion Calculus

To explain the eager error detection strategy in **HTF-E**, we first review why the reduction rules in **L** detect higher-order cast errors in a lazy fashion. Consider the reduction sequence for program (2) under **L ∪ D**:

$$\langle\!\langle\!\langle \text{Bool} \rightarrow \text{Int} \Leftarrow \text{Dyn} \rightarrow \text{Dyn} \rangle^{l_2} \langle \text{Dyn} \rightarrow \text{Dyn} \Leftarrow \text{Int} \rightarrow \text{Int} \rangle^{l_1} (\lambda x : \text{Int. } x) \rangle\!\rangle$$
$$= \langle \text{Bool!} \rightarrow \text{Int}?^{l_2} \rangle \langle \text{Int}?^{l_1} \rightarrow \text{Int!} \rangle (\lambda x : \text{Int. } x)$$
$$\longmapsto \langle (\text{Bool!} \rightarrow \text{Int}?^{l_2}) \circ (\text{Int}?^{l_1} \rightarrow \text{Int!}) \rangle (\lambda x : \text{Int. } x)$$
$$\longmapsto \langle (\text{Int}?^{l_1} \circ \text{Bool!}) \rightarrow (\text{Int}?^{l_2} \circ \text{Int!}) \rangle (\lambda x : \text{Int. } x)$$
$$\longmapsto \langle \text{Fail}^{l_1} \rightarrow \iota \rangle (\lambda x : \text{Int. } x)$$

The cast $\langle \text{Fail}^{l_1} \rightarrow \iota \rangle$ is in normal form and, because the Fail^{l_1} does not propagate to the top of the cast, the lazy reduction strategy does not signal a failure in this case.

The eager error detection strategy therefore adds reduction rules that propagate failures up through function coercions. Fig 10 shows the two reduction rules for the **E** strategy. Note that in FAILFR we require the coercion in argument position to be normalized but not be a failure. This restriction is needed for confluence.

Using the eager reduction rules, program (2) produces a cast error.

$$\cdots \longmapsto \langle \text{Fail}^{l_1} \rightarrow \iota \rangle (\lambda x : \text{Int. } x) \longmapsto \langle \text{Fail}^{l_1} \rangle (\lambda x : \text{Int. } x) \longmapsto \text{blame } l_1$$

The combination **L ∪ UD ∪ E** can be viewed as adding blame tracking to **HTF-E**. The combination **L∪D∪E** is entirely new and particularly appealing as an intermediate language for gradual typing because it provides thorough error detection and intuitive blame assignment. The combination **L ∪ D** is well-suited to modeling languages that combine dynamic and static typing in a manner that admits as many correctly-behaving programs as possible because it avoids reporting cast errors until they are immediately relevant and provides intuitive guidance when failure occurs.

$$(\textsc{FailFL}) \; (\text{Fail}^l \rightarrow d) \longrightarrow \text{Fail}^l$$
$$(\textsc{FailFR}) \; (\bar{c} \rightarrow \text{Fail}^l) \longrightarrow \text{Fail}^l \quad \text{where } \bar{c} \neq \text{Fail}^{l'}$$

Fig. 10. The eager detections reduction rules (**E**)

6   A Space-Efficient Semantics for $\lambda_{\rightarrow}^{\langle \cdot \rangle}(X)$

The semantics of $\lambda_{\rightarrow}^{\langle \cdot \rangle}(X)$ given in Fig. 7 is only partially space-efficient. Rule CMPCST merges adjacent casts and the normalization of coercions sufficiently compresses them, but casts can still accumulate in the tail position of recursive calls. It is straightforward to parameterize the space-efficient semantics and proofs of Herman et al. [7] with respect to coercion calculi, thereby obtaining a space-efficient semantics for $\lambda_{\rightarrow}^{\langle \cdot \rangle}(X)$.

The proof of space-efficiency requires several properties that depend on the choice of X. First, the size of a coercion (number of AST nodes) in normal form must be bounded by its height.

Lemma 4 (Coercion size bounded by height)
For each coercion calculus X in this paper, if $\vdash c : T \Leftarrow S$ and c is in normal form for X, then $size(c) \leq 5(2^{height(c)} - 1)$.

Proof. The proofs are by structural induction on c. In the worst-case, c has the form $(\text{Dyn} \rightarrow \text{Dyn})! \circ (c_1 \rightarrow c_2) \circ (\text{Dyn} \rightarrow \text{Dyn})?$. Thus, $size(c) = 5 + size(c_1) + size(c_2)$. Applying the induction hypothesis to $size(c_1)$ and $size(c_2)$, we have $size(c) \leq 5 + 2 \cdot 5(2^{height(c)-1} - 1) = 5(2^{height(c)} - 1)$.

Second, the height of the coercions produced by compilation from type-based casts is bounded by the the sum of the source and target type.

Lemma 5. *If $c = \langle\!\langle T \Leftarrow S \rangle\!\rangle^l$ then $height(c) \leq max(height(S), height(T))$.*

Third, coercion evaluation must never increase the height of a coercion.

Lemma 6 (Coercion height never increases)
For each coercion calculi X in this paper, if $c \longmapsto_X c'$ then $height(c') \leq height(c)$.

7   Conclusion and Future Work

In this paper we explore the design space of higher-order casts along two axes: blame assignment strategies and eager versus lazy error detection. This paper introduces a framework based on Henglein's Coercion Calculus and instantiates four variants, each of which supports blame tracking and guarantees space efficiency. Of the four variants, one extends the semantics of Herman et al. [7] with blame tracking in a natural way. This variant has the same blame tracking behavior as [11], thereby establishing a previously unknown connection between these works. One of the variants combines eager error detection with a blame tracking strategy in which casts that respect traditional subtyping are guaranteed to never fail. This variant provides a compelling dynamic semantics for gradual typing.

Our account of the design space for cast calculi introduces new open problems. The **UD** blame strategy has a constant-factor speed advantage over the **D** strategy because **D** must generate coercions dynamically. We would like an implementation model for **D** that does not need to generate coercions. We are also interested in characterizations of statically safe casts that achieve greater precision than subtyping.

Bibliography

[1] Findler, R.B., Felleisen, M.: Contracts for higher-order functions. In: ACM International Conference on Functional Programming (October 2002)

[2] Flanagan, C.: Hybrid type checking. In: POPL 2006: The 33rd ACM SIGPLAN-SIGACT Symposium on Principles of Programming Languages, Charleston, South Carolina, pp. 245–256 (January 2006)

[3] Flanagan, C., Freund, S.N., Tomb, A.: Hybrid types, invariants, and refinements for imperative objects. In: FOOL/WOOD2006: International Workshop on Foundations and Developments of Object-Oriented Languages (2006)

[4] Gronski, J., Flanagan, C.: Unifying hybrid types and contracts. In: Trends in Functional Prog. (TFP) (2007)

[5] Henglein, F.: Dynamic typing. In: Krieg-Brückner, B. (ed.) ESOP 1992. LNCS, vol. 582, pp. 233–253. Springer, Heidelberg (1992)

[6] Henglein, F.: Dynamic typing: syntax and proof theory. Science of Computer Programming 22(3), 197–230 (1994)

[7] Herman, D., Tomb, A., Flanagan, C.: Space-efficient gradual typing. In: Trends in Functional Prog. (TFP), p. XXVIII (April 2007)

[8] Siek, J.G., Taha, W.: Gradual typing for functional languages. In: Scheme and Functional Programming Workshop, pp. 81–92 (September 2006)

[9] Siek, J.G., Taha, W.: Gradual typing for objects. In: Ernst, E. (ed.) ECOOP 2007. LNCS, vol. 4609, pp. 2–27. Springer, Heidelberg (2007)

[10] Wadler, P., Findler, R.B.: Well-typed programs can't be blamed. In: Workshop on Scheme and Functional Programming, pp. 15–26 (2007)

[11] Wadler, P., Findler, R.B.: Well-typed programs can't be blamed. In: Castagna, G. (ed.) ESOP 2009. LNCS, vol. 5502, pp. 1–16. Springer, Heidelberg (2009)

Practical Variable-Arity Polymorphism

T. Stephen Strickland, Sam Tobin-Hochstadt, and Matthias Felleisen

PLT @ Northeastern University

Abstract. Just as some functions have uniform behavior over distinct types, other functions have uniform behavior over distinct arities. These variable-arity functions are widely used in scripting languages such as Scheme and Python. Statically typed languages also accommodate modest forms of variable-arity functions, but even ML and Haskell, languages with highly expressive type systems, cannot type check the wide variety of variable-arity functions found in untyped functional languages. Consequently, their standard libraries contain numerous copies of the same function definition with slightly different names.

As part of the Typed Scheme project—an on-going effort to create an explicitly typed sister language for PLT Scheme—we have designed and implemented an expressive type system for variable-arity functions. Our practical validation in the context of our extensive code base confirms the usefulness of the enriched type system.

1 Types for Variable-Arity Functions

For the past two years, Tobin-Hochstadt and Felleisen [1,2] have been developing Typed Scheme, an explicitly and statically typed sister language of PLT Scheme [3]. In many cases, Typed Scheme accommodates existing Scheme programming idioms as much as possible. One remaining obstacle concerns functions of variable arity. Such functions have a long history in programming languages, especially in LISP and Scheme systems where they are widely used for a variety of purposes, ranging from arithmetic operations to list processing. In response, we have augmented Typed Scheme so that its type system can cope with variable-arity functions of many kinds.

Some variadic functions in Scheme are quite simple. For example, the function + takes any number of numeric values and produces their sum. This function, and others like it, could be typed in a system that maps a variable number of arguments into a homogeneous data structure.[1] Other variable-arity functions, however, demand a more sophisticated approach than collecting the extra arguments in such a fashion.

Consider Scheme's *map* function, which takes a function as input as well as an arbitrary number of lists. It then applies the function to the elements of the lists in a pointwise fashion. The function must therefore take precisely as many arguments as the number of lists provided. For example, if the *make-student*

---

[1] Languages like C, C++, Java, and C# support such variable-arity functions.

G. Castagna (Ed.): ESOP 2009, LNCS 5502, pp. 32–46, 2009.

function consumes two arguments, a name as a string and a number for a grade, then the expression

$$(map \ make\text{-}student \ (list \ \texttt{"Al"} \ \texttt{"Bob"} \ \texttt{"Carol"}) \ (list \ 87 \ 98 \ 64))$$

produces a list. We refer to variable-arity functions such as + and *map* as having *uniform* and *non-uniform* polymorphic types, respectively.

For Typed Scheme to be useful to working programmers, its type system must handle this form of polymorphism. Further, although *map* and + are part of the standard library, language implementers cannot arrogate the ability to abstract over the arities of functions. Scheme programmers routinely define such functions, and if they wish to refactor their Scheme programs into Typed Scheme, our language must allow such function definitions.

Of course, our concerns are relevant beyond the confines of Scheme. Variable-arity functions are also useful in statically typed languages, but are barely supported because of a lack of pragmatic approaches. Even the standard libraries of highly expressive typed functional languages contain functions that would benefit from non-uniform variable-arity, but instead are defined via copying of code. For example, the SML Basis Library [4] includes the ARRAY and ARRAY2 signatures, which include functions that differ only in arity. The GHC standard library [5] also features close to a dozen families of functions (such as zip and zipWith) defined at a variety of arities. We conjecture that if their type systems provided variable-arity polymorphism, Haskell and ML programmers would routinely define such functions, too.

In this paper, we present the first pragmatic and comprehensive approach to variable-arity polymorphism: its design, implementation, and evaluation. Our new version of Typed Scheme can assign types to hundreds of programmer-introduced function definitions with variable arities, something that was simply impossible before. Furthermore, we can now type check library functions such as *map* and *fold-left* without resorting to special tricks or duplication.

In the next two sections, we describe Typed Scheme in general terms and then present the type system for variable-arity functions. In section 4, we introduce a formal model of our variable-arity type system. In section 5 we present preliminary results of our evaluation effort with respect to the PLT Scheme code base and the limitations of our system. In section 6 we discuss related work.

2   Typed Scheme ...

The goal of our Typed Scheme [2] project is to design a typed sister language for an untyped scripting language in which programmers can transfer programs to the typed world one module at a time. Like PLT Scheme, Typed Scheme is a modular programming language; unlike plain Scheme programs, Typed Scheme programs have explicit type annotations for function and structure definitions that are statically checked. Typed Scheme also supports integration with untyped Scheme code, allowing a typed program to link in untyped modules and vice versa. The mechanism exploits functional contracts [6] to guarantee a generalized type soundness theorem [1].

Typed Scheme supports this gradual refactoring with a type system that accommodates standard Scheme programming idioms with minimal code modification. In principle, Scheme programmers need only annotate structure and function headers with types to move a module to the Typed Scheme world; on occasion, they may also wish to define a type alias to keep type expressions concise. The type system combines true union types, recursive types, first-class polymorphic functions, and the novel discipline of occurrence typing. Additionally, Typed Scheme infers types for instantiations of polymorphic functions, based on locally-available type information.

2.1   Basic Typed Scheme

Scheme programmers typically describe the structure of their data in comments, rather than in executable code. For example, a shape data type might be represented as:

   ;; A *shape* is either a rectangle or a circle
   (**define-struct** *rectangle* (*l w*))   (**define-struct** *circle* (*r*))

To accommodate this style in Typed Scheme, programmers can specify true, untagged unions of types:

   (**define-type-alias** *shape* (⋃ *rectangle circle*))
   (**define-struct:** *rectangle* ([*l* : **Integer**] [*w* : **Integer**]))
   (**define-struct:** *circle*   ([*r* : **Integer**]))

Typed Scheme also supports explicit recursive types, which, for example, are necessary for typing uses of *cons* pairs in Scheme programs. This allows the specification of both fixed-length heterogeneous lists and arbitrary-length homogeneous lists, or even combinations of the two.

Finally, Typed Scheme introduces *occurrence typing*, which allows the types of variable occurrences to depend on their position in the control flow graph. For example, the program fragment

   (*display* "Enter a number to double: ")
   (**let** ([*val* (*read*)]) ;; an arbitrary S-expression
     (**if** (*number? val*) (*display* (∗ 2 *val*))
           (*display* "That wasn't a number!")))

type-checks correctly because the use of ∗ is guarded by the *number?* check.

2.2   Polymorphic Functions and Local Type Inference

Typed Scheme supports first-class polymorphic functions. For example, *list-ref* has the type ($∀$ ($α$) ((**Listof** $α$) **Integer** → $α$)). It can be defined in Typed Scheme as follows:

   (: *list-ref* ($∀$ ($α$) ((**Listof** $α$) **Integer** → $α$)))
   (**define** (*list-ref l i*)
     (**cond** [(*not* (*pair? l*)) (*error* "empty list")]
            [(= 0 *i*) (*car l*)]
            [**else** (*list-ref* (*cdr l*) (− *i* 1))]))

The example shows two important aspects of polymorphism in Typed Scheme. First, the abstraction over types is explicit in the polymorphic type of *list-ref* but implicit in the function definition. Second, typical uses of polymorphic functions, e.g., *car* and *list-ref*, do not require explicit type instantiation. Instead, the required type instantiations are synthesized from the types of the arguments.

Argument type synthesis uses the local type inference algorithm of Pierce and Turner [7]. It greatly facilitates the use of polymorphic functions and makes conversions from Scheme to Typed Scheme convenient, while dealing with the subtyping present in the rest of the type system in an elegant manner. Furthermore, it ensures that type inference errors are always locally confined, rendering them reasonably comprehensible to programmers.

3 ... with Variable-Arity Functions

A Scheme programmer defines functions with **lambda** or **define**. Both syntactic forms support fixed and variable-arity parameter specifications:

1. (**lambda** $(x\ y)$ $(+\ x\ (*\ y\ 3)))$ creates a function of two arguments and (**define** $(f\ x\ y)$ $(+\ x\ (*\ y\ 3)))$ creates the same function and names it f;
2. the function (**lambda** $(x\ y\ .\ z)$ $(+\ x\ (apply\ max\ y\ z)))$ consumes at least two arguments and otherwise as many as needed;
3. (**define** $(g\ x\ y\ .\ z)$ $(+\ x\ (apply\ max\ y\ z)))$ names this function g;
4. (**lambda** z $(apply\ +\ z))$ creates a function of arbitrary arity; and
5. (**define** $(h\ .\ z)$ $(apply\ +\ z))$ is the analogue to this **lambda** expression.

The parameter z in the last four cases is called the *rest parameter*.

The application of a variable-arity function combines any arguments in excess of the number of required parameters into a list. Thus, $(g\ 1\ 2\ 3\ 4)$ binds x to 1 and y to 2, while z becomes $(list\ 3\ 4)$ for the evaluation of g's function body. In contrast, $(h\ 1\ 2\ 3\ 4)$ sets z to $(list\ 1\ 2\ 3\ 4)$.

The *apply* function, used in the examples above, takes a function f, a sequence of fixed arguments $v_1 \ldots v_n$, and a list of additional arguments r. If the list r is the value $(list\ w_1\ \ldots\ w_n)$, then $(apply\ f\ v_1\ \ldots\ v_n\ r)$ is the same as $(f\ v_1\ \ldots\ v_n\ w_1\ \ldots\ w_n)$. The *apply* function plays a critical role in conjunction with rest arguments.

This section sketches how the revised version of Typed Scheme accommodates variable-arity functions. Our revision focuses on the uses of such functions that accept arbitrarily many arguments. Scheme programmers sometimes use variable-arity functions to simulate optional or keyword arguments. In PLT Scheme, such programs typically employ **case-lambda** [8] or equivalent **define** forms instead.

3.1 Uniform Variable-Arity Functions

Uniform variable-arity functions are those that expect their rest parameter to be a homogeneous list. Consider the following three examples of type signatures:

(: + (**Integer*** → **Integer**))
(: *string-append* (**String*** → **String**))
(: *list* (∀ (α) (α^* → (**Listof** α))))

The syntax *Type** for the type of rest parameters alludes to the Kleene star for regular expressions. It signals that in addition to the other arguments, the function takes an arbitrary number of arguments of the given base type. The form *Type** is dubbed a *starred pre-type*, because it is not a full-fledged type and may appear only as the last element of a function's domain.

Here is a definition of variable-arity + in Scheme:

;; assumes *binary-+*, a binary addition operator
(**define** (+ . *xs*) (**if** (*null?* *xs*) 0 (*binary-+* (*car* *xs*) (*apply* + (*cdr* *xs*)))))

Typing this definition is straightforward. The type assigned to the rest parameter of starred pre-type τ^* in the body of the function is (**Listof** τ), a pre-existing type in Typed Scheme.

3.2   Beyond Uniform Variable-Arity Functions

Not all variable-arity functions assume that their rest parameter is a homogeneous list of values. We can allow heterogeneous rest parameters by finding other constraints. For example, the length of the list assigned to the rest parameter may be connected to the types of other parameters or the returned value.

For example, Scheme's *map* function is not restricted to mapping unary functions over single lists, unlike its counter-parts in ML or Haskell. When *map* receives a function f and n lists, it expects f to accept n arguments. Also, the type of the kth function parameter must match the element type of the kth list.

Scheme's *apply* function provides its own challenges. It is straightforward to type the use of *apply* with a uniform variable-arity function, as in the hypothetical definition of + from section 3.1. If the type of f involves the starred pre-type τ^*, then the list r must have type (**Listof** τ).

However, take the following example taken from the PLT Scheme code base:

;; implements a wrapper that prints f's arguments
(**define** (*verbose* f)
    (**if** *quiet?* f (**lambda** a (*printf* "xform-cpp: ~a\n" a) (*apply* f a))))

The intent of the programmer is clear—the result of applying *verbose* to a function f should have the same type as f for *any* function type. With uniform variable-arity functions, we can type the internal **lambda**'s argument a only as a homogeneous list of arbitrary length. Thus, if f has some fixed arity n, then there is no way to statically guarantee that the list of arguments a has n elements, and thus applying the function f to the list a via *apply* may go wrong. Our type system should protect the programmer from arity mismatches, whether through function application or uses of *apply*, while allowing functions like *verbose*.

3.3 Non-uniform Variable-Arity Functions

As of the latest release, Typed Scheme can represent the types of *non-uniform* variable-arity functions. Below are the types for some example functions:

```
;; map is the standard Scheme map
(: map
   (∀ (γ α β ...)
      ((α β ...β → γ) (Listof α) (Listof β) ...β → (Listof γ))))

;; map-with-funcs takes any number of functions,
;; and then an appropriate set of arguments, and then produces
;; the results of applying all the functions to the arguments
(: map-with-funcs
   (∀ (β α ...) ((α ...α → β)* → (α ...α → (Listof β)))))
```

Our first key innovation is the possibility to attach ... to the last type variable in the binding position of a ∀ type constructor. Such type variables are dubbed *dotted type variables*. Dotted type variables signal that this polymorphic type can be instantiated with an arbitrary number of types.

Next, the body of ∀ types with dotted type variables may contain expressions of the form $\tau \ldots_\alpha$ for some type τ and a dotted type variable α. These are *dotted pre-types*; they classify non-uniform rest parameters just like starred pre-types classify uniform rest parameters. A dotted pre-type has two parts: the base τ and the bound α. Only dotted type variables can be used as the bound of a dotted pre-type. Since ∀-types are nestable and thus multiple dotted type variables may be in scope, dotted pre-types must specify the bound.

When a dotted polymorphic type is instantiated, any dotted pre-types are expanded by copying the base an appropriate number of times and by replacing free instances of the bound in each copy with the corresponding type argument. For example, instantiating *map-with-funcs* as follows:

(**inst** *map-with-funcs* **Number Integer Boolean String**)

results in a value with the type:

((**Integer Boolean String → Number**)* →
(**Integer Boolean String → (Listof Number**)))

Typed Scheme also provides local inference of the appropriate type arguments for dotted polymorphic functions, so explicit type instantiation is rarely needed [9]. Thus, the following uses of *map* are successfully inferred at the appropriate types:

```
(map not (list #t #f #t))
;; map is instantiated (via local type inference) at:
;; ((Boolean → Boolean) (Listof Boolean) → (Listof Boolean))

(map make-book (list "Flatland") (list "A. Square") (list 1884))
;; ((String String Integer → book)
;;  (Listof String) (Listof String) (Listof Integer) → (Listof book))
```

Typed Scheme can also type-check the definitions of non-uniform variable-arity functions:

```
(: fold-left
  (∀ (γ α β ...) ((γ α β ...β → γ) γ (Listof α) (Listof β) ...β → γ)))
(define (fold-left f c as . bss)
  (if (or (null? as) (ormap null? bss)) c
      (apply fold-left (apply f c (car as) (map car bss)) (cdr as)
             (map cdr bss))))
```

The example introduces a definition of *fold-left*. Its type shows that it accepts at least three arguments: a function f; an initial element c; and at least one list *as*. Optionally, *fold-left* consumes another sequence *bss* of lists. For this combination to work out, f must consume as many arguments as there are lists plus one; in addition, the types of these lists must match the types of f's parameters because each list item becomes an argument.

Beyond this, the example illustrates that the rest parameter is treated as if it were a place-holder for a plain list parameter. In this particular case, *bss* is thrice subjected to *map*-style processing. In general, variable-arity functions should be free to process their rest parameters with existing list-processing functions.

The challenge is to assign types to such expressions. On the one hand, list-processing functions expect lists, but the rest parameter has a dotted pre-type. On the other hand, the result of list-processing a rest parameter may flow again into a rest-argument position. While the first obstacle is simple to overcome with a conversion from dotted pre-types to list types, the second one is onerous. Since list-processing functions do not return dotted pre-types but list types, we cannot possibly expect that such list types come with enough information for an automatic conversion.

Thus we use special type rules for the list processing of rest parameters with *map*, *andmap*, and *ormap*. Consider *map*, which returns a list of the same length as the given one and whose component types are in a predictable order. If xs is classified by the dotted pre-type $\tau \ldots_\alpha$, and f has type $(\tau \to \sigma)$, we classify $(map$ f $xs)$ with the dotted pre-type $\sigma \ldots_\alpha$. Thus, in the definition of *fold-left* $(map$ car $bss)$ is classified as the dotted pre-type $\beta \ldots_\beta$ because car is instantiated at $((\textbf{Listof } \beta) \to \beta)$ and bss is classified as the dotted pre-type $(\textbf{Listof } \beta) \ldots_\beta$.

One way to use such processed rest parameters is in conjunction with *apply*. Specifically, if *apply* is passed a variable-arity function f, then its final argument l, which must be a list, must match up with the rest parameter of f. If the function is a uniform variable-arity procedure and the final argument is a list, typing the use of *apply* is straightforward. If it is a *non-uniform* variable-arity function, the number and types of parameters must match the elements and types of l.

Here is an illustrative example from the definition of *fold-left*:

```
(apply f c (car as) (map car bss))
```

By the type of *fold-left*, f has type $(\gamma \ \alpha \ \beta \ldots_\beta \to \gamma)$. The types of c and $(car$ $as)$ match the types of the initial parameters to f. Since the *map* application

$$p ::= \texttt{=} \mid \texttt{plus} \mid \texttt{minus} \mid \texttt{mult} \mid \texttt{car} \mid \texttt{cdr} \mid \texttt{null?}$$
$$v ::= n \mid b \mid p \mid \texttt{null}_\tau \mid (\texttt{cons}_\tau\ v\ v) \mid (\lambda\ (\overrightarrow{[x:\tau]})\ e) \mid (\Lambda\ (\overrightarrow{\alpha})\ e)$$
$$\mid (\Lambda\ (\overrightarrow{\alpha}\ \alpha\ ...)\ e) \mid (\lambda\ (\overrightarrow{[x:\tau]}\ .\ [x:\tau^*])\ e) \mid (\lambda\ (\overrightarrow{[x:\tau]}\ .\ [x:\tau\ ..._\alpha])\ e)$$
$$e ::= v \mid x \mid (e\ \overrightarrow{e}) \mid (\texttt{if}\ e\ e\ e) \mid (\texttt{cons}_\tau\ e\ e) \mid \texttt{error}_L$$
$$\mid (@\ e\ \overrightarrow{\tau}) \mid (@\ e\ \overrightarrow{\tau}\ \tau\ ..._\alpha) \mid (\texttt{apply}\ e\ \overrightarrow{e}\ e)$$
$$\mid (\texttt{map}\ e\ e) \mid (\texttt{ormap}\ e\ e) \mid (\texttt{andmap}\ e\ e)$$
$$\tau ::= \textbf{Integer} \mid \textbf{Boolean} \mid \alpha \mid (\textbf{Listof}\ \tau) \mid (\overrightarrow{\tau} \to \tau)$$
$$\mid (\overrightarrow{\tau}\ \tau^* \to \tau) \mid (\overrightarrow{\tau}\ \tau\ ..._\alpha \to \tau) \mid (\forall\ (\overrightarrow{\alpha})\ \tau) \mid (\forall\ (\overrightarrow{\alpha}\ \alpha\ ...)\ \tau)$$

Fig. 1. Syntax

has dotted pre-type (**Listof** β) $..._\beta$ and since the rest parameter position of f is bounded by β, we are guaranteed that the length of the list produced by (*map car bss*) matches f's expectations about its rest argument. In short, we use the type system to show that we cannot have an arity mismatch, even in the case of *apply*.

4   A Variable-Arity Type System

The development of our formal model starts from the syntax of a multi-arity version of System F [10], enriched with variable-arity functions. An accompanying technical report [9] contains the full set of type rules as well as a semantics and soundness theorem for this model.

4.1   Syntax

We extend System F with multiple-arity functions at both the type and term level, lists, and uniform rest-argument functions. The use of multiple-arity functions establishes the proper problem context. Lists and uniform rest-argument functions suffice to explain how both kinds of variable-arity functions interact.

The grammar in figure 1 specifies the abstract syntax. We use a syntax close to that of Typed Scheme, including the use of @ to denote type application. The use of the vector notation $\overrightarrow{e}$ denotes a (possibly empty) sequence of forms (in this case, expressions). In the form $\overrightarrow{e_k}^n$, n indicates the length of the sequence, and the term e_{k_i} is the ith element. The subforms of two sequences of the same length have the same subscript, so $\overrightarrow{e_k}^n$ and $\overrightarrow{\tau_k}^n$ are identically-sized sequences of expressions and types, respectively, whereas $\overrightarrow{e_j}^m$ is unrelated. If all vectors are the same size the sizes are dropped, but the subscripts remain. Otherwise the addition of starred pre-types, dotted type variables, dotted pre-types, and special forms is needed to operate on non-uniform rest arguments.

A *starred pre-type*, which has the form τ^*, is used in the types of uniform variable-arity functions whose rest parameter contains values of type τ. It only appears as the last element in the domain of a function type or as the type of a uniform rest argument.

A *dotted type variable*, which has the form α ..., serves as a placeholder in a type abstraction. Its presence signals that the type abstraction can be applied to an arbitrary number of types. A dotted type variable can only appear as the last element in the list of parameters to a type abstraction. We call type abstractions that include dotted type variables *dotted type abstractions*.

A *dotted pre-type*, which has the form τ ...$_\alpha$, is a type that is parameterized over a dotted type variable. When a type instantiation associates the dotted type variable α ... with a sequence $\overrightarrow{\tau_k}^n$ of types, the dotted pre-type τ ...$_\alpha$ is replaced by n copies of τ, where α in the ith copy of τ is replaced with τ_{k_i}. In the syntax, dotted pre-types can appear only in the rightmost position of a function type, as the type of a non-uniform rest argument, or as the last argument to @.

In this model the special forms `ormap`, `andmap`, and `map` are restricted to applications involving non-uniform rest arguments, and `apply` is restricted to applications involving rest arguments. In Typed Scheme, they also work for applications involving lists.

4.2 Type System

The type system is an extension of the type system of System F to handle the new linguistic constructs. We start with the changes to the environments and judgments, plus the major changes to the type validity relation. Next we present relations used for dotted types and expressions that have dotted pre-types instead of types. Then we discuss the changes to the standard typing relation, and finally we discuss the metafunctions used to define the new typing judgments.

The environments and judgments used in our type system are similar to those used for System F except as follows:

- The type variable environment (Δ) includes both dotted and non-dotted type variables.
- There is a new class of environments (Σ), which map non-uniform rest parameters to dotted pre-types.
- There is also an additional validity relation $\Delta \rhd \tau$ ...$_\alpha$ for dotted pre-types.
- The use of Σ makes typing relation $\Gamma, \Delta, \Sigma \vdash e : \tau$ a five-place relation.
- There is an additional typing relation $\Gamma, \Delta, \Sigma \vdash e \rhd \tau$ ...$_\alpha$ for assigning dotted pre-types to expressions.

The type validity relation checks the validity of two forms—types and dotted type variables. The additional rules for establishing type validity of non-uniform variable-arity types are provided below, along with an additional relation which checks the validity of dotted pre-types.

$$
\begin{array}{cccc}
& \text{TE-DF\scriptsize UN} & & \text{TDE-P\scriptsize RETYPE} \\
\text{TE-DV\scriptsize AR} & \dfrac{\Delta \rhd \tau_r \,...\,_\alpha}{} & \text{TE-DA\scriptsize LL} & \dfrac{\Delta \vdash \alpha \,...}{} \\
\dfrac{\alpha \,...\, \in \Delta}{\Delta \vdash \alpha \,...} & \dfrac{\overrightarrow{\Delta \vdash \tau_j} \quad \Delta \vdash \tau}{\Delta \vdash (\overrightarrow{\tau_j}\ \tau_r \,...\,_\alpha \to \tau)} & \dfrac{\Delta \cup \{\overrightarrow{\alpha_j}, \beta \,...\} \vdash \tau}{\Delta \vdash (\forall\ (\overrightarrow{\alpha_j}\ \beta \,...)\ \tau)} & \dfrac{\Delta \cup \{\alpha\} \vdash \tau}{\Delta \rhd \tau \,...\,_\alpha}
\end{array}
$$

When validating a dotted pre-type $\tau \ldots_\alpha$, the bound α is checked to make sure that it is indeed a valid dotted type variable. Then τ is checked in an environment where the bound is allowed to appear free. It is possible for a dotted pre-type to be nested somewhere within a dotted pre-type over the same bound, e.g.

$$(\forall\, (\alpha \ldots)\, ((\alpha \ldots_\alpha \rightarrow \alpha) \ldots_\alpha \rightarrow (\alpha \ldots_\alpha \rightarrow (\textbf{Listof Integer}))))$$

To illustrate how such a type might be used, we instantiate this sample type with the sequence of types **Integer Boolean**:

((**Integer Boolean** → **Integer**) (**Integer Boolean** → **Boolean**)
→ (**Integer Boolean** → (**Listof Integer**)))

There are two functions in the domain of the type, each of which corresponds to an element in our sequence. All functions have the same domain—the sequence of types; the ith function returns the ith type in the sequence.

TD-VAR
$$\frac{\Sigma(x) = \tau \ldots_\alpha}{\Gamma, \Delta, \Sigma \vdash x \triangleright \tau \ldots_\alpha}$$

TD-MAP
$$\frac{\Gamma, \Delta, \Sigma \vdash e_r \triangleright \tau_r \ldots_\alpha \qquad \Gamma, \Delta \cup \{\alpha\}, \Sigma \vdash e_f : (\tau_r \rightarrow \tau)}{\Gamma, \Delta, \Sigma \vdash (\texttt{map } e_f\ e_r) \triangleright \tau \ldots_\alpha}$$

The preceding rules are the typing rules for the two forms of expressions that have dotted pre-types. The TD-VAR rule just checks for the variable in Σ. The TD-MAP rule assigns a type to a function position. Since the function needs to operate on each element of the sequence represented by e_r, not on the sequence as a whole, the domain of the function's type is the base τ_r instead of the dotted type $\tau_r \ldots_\alpha$. This type may include free references to the bound α, however. Therefore, we must check the function in an environment extended with α as a regular type variable.

As expected, most of the typing rules are simple additions of multiple-arity type and term abstractions and lists to System F. For uniform variable-arity functions, the introduction rule treats the rest parameter as a variable whose type is a list of the appropriate type. There is only one elimination rule, which deals with the special form `apply`; other eliminations such as direct application to arguments are handled via the coercion rules.

The type rules in figure 2 concern non-uniform variable-arity functions. These functions also have one introduction and one elimination rule. The rule T-ORMAP and its absent counterpart T-ANDMAP are similar to that of TD-MAP in that the dotted pre-type bound of the second argument is allowed free in the type of the first argument. In contrast to uniform variable-arity functions, non-uniform ones cannot be applied directly to arguments in this calculus.

While T-DTABS, the introduction rule for dotted type abstractions, follows from the rule for normal type abstractions, the elimination rules are quite different. There are two elimination rules: T-DTAPP and T-DTAPPDOTS. The former handles type application of a dotted type abstraction where the dotted type variable corresponds to a sequence of types, and the latter deals with the case when the dotted type variable corresponds to a dotted pre-type.

T-DABS

$$\frac{\Delta \vdash \overrightarrow{\tau_k} \qquad \Delta \rhd \tau_r \ ...\alpha \qquad \Gamma[\overrightarrow{x_k \mapsto \tau_k}], \Delta, \Sigma[x_r \mapsto \tau_r \ ...\alpha] \vdash e : \tau}{\Gamma, \Delta, \Sigma \vdash (\lambda \ ([\overrightarrow{x_k : \tau_k}] . [x_r : \tau_r \ ...\alpha]) \ e) : (\overrightarrow{\tau_k} \ \tau_r \ ...\alpha \to \tau)}$$

T-DAPPLY

$$\frac{\Gamma, \Delta, \Sigma \vdash e_f : (\overrightarrow{\tau_k} \ \tau_r \ ...\alpha \to \tau)}{\Gamma, \Delta, \Sigma \vdash e_k : \overrightarrow{\tau_k} \qquad \Gamma, \Delta, \Sigma \vdash e_r \rhd \tau_r \ ...\alpha}{\Gamma, \Delta, \Sigma \vdash (\mathtt{apply} \ e_f \ \overrightarrow{e_k} \ e_r) : \tau}$$

T-ORMAP

$$\frac{\Gamma, \Delta, \Sigma \vdash e_r \rhd \tau_r \ ...\alpha}{\Gamma, \Delta \cup \{\alpha\}, \Sigma \vdash e_f : (\tau_r \to \mathbf{Boolean})}{\Gamma, \Delta, \Sigma \vdash (\mathtt{ormap} \ e_f \ e_r) : \mathbf{Boolean}}$$

T-DTABS

$$\frac{\Gamma, \Delta \cup \{\overrightarrow{\alpha_k}, \beta \ ...\}, \Sigma \vdash e : \tau}{\Gamma, \Delta, \Sigma \vdash (\Lambda \ (\overrightarrow{\alpha_k} \ \beta \ ...) \ e) : (\forall \ (\overrightarrow{\alpha_k} \ \beta \ ...) \ \tau)}$$

T-DTAPP

$$\frac{\Delta \vdash \overrightarrow{\tau_j}^n \qquad \Delta \vdash \overrightarrow{\tau_k}^m \qquad \overrightarrow{\beta_k}^m \ \text{fresh} \qquad \Gamma, \Delta, \Sigma \vdash e : (\forall \ (\overrightarrow{\alpha_j}^n \ \beta \ ...) \ \tau)}{\Gamma, \Delta, \Sigma \vdash (@ \ e \ \overrightarrow{\tau_j}^n \ \overrightarrow{\tau_k}^m) : td_\tau(\tau[\overrightarrow{\alpha_j \mapsto \tau_j}^n], \beta, \overrightarrow{\beta_k}^m)[\overrightarrow{\beta_k \mapsto \tau_k}^m]}$$

T-DTAPPDOTS

$$\frac{\Delta \vdash \overrightarrow{\tau_k} \qquad \Delta \rhd \tau_r \ ...\beta \qquad \Gamma, \Delta, \Sigma \vdash e : (\forall \ (\overrightarrow{\alpha_k} \ \alpha_r \ ...) \ \tau)}{\Gamma, \Delta, \Sigma \vdash (@ \ e \ \overrightarrow{\tau_k} \ \tau_r \ ...\beta) : sd(\tau[\overrightarrow{\alpha_k \mapsto \tau_k}], \alpha_r, \tau_r, \beta)}$$

Fig. 2. Selected Type Rules

$$sd(\alpha_r, \alpha_r, \tau_r, \beta) \qquad\qquad\quad = \tau_r$$
$$sd(\alpha, \alpha_r, \tau_r, \beta) \qquad\qquad\quad = \alpha \qquad \text{where } \alpha \ne \alpha_r$$
$$sd((\overrightarrow{\tau_j} \ \tau_r' \ ...\alpha_r \to \tau), \alpha_r, \tau_r, \beta) =$$
$$\qquad (\overrightarrow{sd(\tau_j, \alpha_r, \tau_r, \beta)} \ sd(\tau_r', \alpha_r, \tau_r, \beta) \ ...\beta \to sd(\tau, \alpha_r, \tau_r, \beta))$$
$$sd((\overrightarrow{\tau_j} \ \tau_r' \ ...\alpha \to \tau), \alpha_r, \tau_r, \beta) =$$
$$\qquad (\overrightarrow{sd(\tau_j, \alpha_r, \tau_r, \beta)} \ sd(\tau_r', \alpha_r, \tau_r, \beta) \ ...\alpha \to sd(\tau, \alpha_r, \tau_r, \beta)) \qquad \text{where } \alpha \ne \alpha_r$$
$$sd((\forall \ (\overrightarrow{\alpha_j} \ \alpha \ ...) \ \tau), \alpha_r, \tau_r, \beta) \quad = (\forall \ (\overrightarrow{\alpha_j} \ \alpha \ ...) \ sd(\tau, \alpha_r, \tau_r, \beta))$$

$$td_\tau((\overrightarrow{\tau_j}^n \ \tau_r \ ...\beta \to \tau), \beta, \overrightarrow{\beta_k}^m) =$$
$$\qquad (\overrightarrow{td_\tau(\tau_j, \beta, \overrightarrow{\beta_k}^m)}^n \ \overrightarrow{td_\tau(\tau_r, \beta, \overrightarrow{\beta_k}^m)[\beta \mapsto \beta_k]}^m \to td_\tau(\tau, \beta, \overrightarrow{\beta_k}^m))$$
$$td_\tau((\overrightarrow{\tau_j}^n \ \tau_r \ ...\alpha \to \tau), \beta, \overrightarrow{\beta_k}^m) =$$
$$\qquad (\overrightarrow{td_\tau(\tau_j, \beta, \overrightarrow{\beta_k}^m)}^n \ td_\tau(\tau_r, \beta, \overrightarrow{\beta_k}^m) \ ...\alpha \to td_\tau(\tau, \beta, \overrightarrow{\beta_k}^m)) \qquad \text{where } \alpha \ne \beta$$

Fig. 3. Subst-dots and trans-dots

The T-DTAPPDOTS rule is more straightforward, as it is just a substitution
rule. Replacing a dotted type variable with a dotted pre-type is more involved
than normal type substitution, however, because we need to replace the dotted
type variable where it appears as a dotted pre-type bound. The metafunction
sd performs this substitution. Selected cases of the definition of *sd* appear in
figure 3; the remaining clauses perform structural traversals.

The T-DTApp rule must first expand out dotted pre-types that use the dotted type variable before performing the appropriate substitutions. To do this it uses the metafunction td_τ on a sequence of fresh type variables of the appropriate length to expand dotted pre-types that appear in the body of the abstraction's type into a sequence of copies of their base types. These copies are first expanded with td_τ and then in each copy the free occurrences of the bound are replaced with the corresponding fresh type variable. Normal substitution is performed on the result of td_τ, mapping each fresh type variable to its corresponding type argument. The interesting cases of the definition of td_τ also appear in figure 3.

5   Evaluation

Mining the extensive PLT Scheme code base provides significant evidence that variable-arity functions are frequently defined and used; examining a fair number of examples shows that our type system is able to cope with a good portion of these definitions and uses.

5.1   Measurements of Existing Code

A simple pattern-based search of the code base for definitions of variable-arity functions and uses of certain built-in core functions produces the following:

- There are at least 1761 definitions of variable-arity functions.
- There are 488 uses of *map*, *for-each*, *foldl*, *foldr*, *andmap*, and *ormap* with more than the minimum number of arguments.

These numbers demonstrate the need for a type system that deals with variable-arity functions. Programmers use those from the core library at multiple arities. Furthermore, programmers define such functions regularly.

It is this kind of inspection of our code base that inspires a careful investigation of the issue of variable-arity functions. We cannot reasonably ask our programmers to duplicate their code or to duplicate type cases just because our type system does not accommodate their utilization of the expressive power of plain Scheme.

5.2   Evaluation of Examples

Simply counting definitions and uses of variable-arity functions is insufficient. Each definition and use demands a separate inspection in order to validate that our type system can cope with it. This is particularly necessary for function definitions, because our pattern-based search does not indicate whether a definition introduces a uniform or non-uniform variable-arity function.

Uses The sample set for uses of variable-arity functions from the core library covers 30 cases, i.e., 10 randomly-chosen example function applications using each of *map*, *for-each*, and *andmap* with at least two list arguments. For *map*, we are able to type 9 of 10, for *for-each* we are able to type 10 of 10, for *andmap* we are able to type 10 of 10.

In short, our technique is extremely successful for the list-processing functions, checking 29 of the 30 examples. The one failure is due to the use of a list to represent a piece of information that comprises four pieces. In this case, our type system simply does not preserve the length information for the list from the input to *map*.

Definitions. The sample set for definitions of variable-arity functions covers some 120 cases (or some 7%) from the code base. Our findings naturally sort these samples into three categories:

– A majority of the functions can be typed with uniform rest arguments or use variable arity to simulate optional arguments. For the latter, we recommend that programmers rewrite such functions using **case-lambda**.
– Twelve of the 120 inspected definitions are non-uniform and require variable-arity polymorphism. Our type checker can assign types to all of them. Returning to our example in section 3.2, *verbose* can be given the type

$$(\forall \, (\beta \, \alpha \, \dots) \, ((\alpha \dots_\alpha \to \beta) \to (\alpha \dots_\alpha \to \beta))).$$

– The small remainder cannot be typed using our system.

These inspections demonstrate two important points. First, all of the various ways in which Typed Scheme handles varying numbers of arguments are important for type-checking existing Scheme code. Second, our design choices for variable-arity polymorphism mostly capture the programming style used in practice by working PLT Scheme programmers. In conclusion, we conjecture that our type system can validate more than 95% of the uses of heterogeneous library functions such as *map*, that it can check 70% of the close to 1800 definitions, 10% of which require the heterogeneous version of variable-arity polymorphism.

6   Related Work

Variable-arity functions are nearly ubiquitous in the world of programming languages, but no typed language supports them in a systematic and principled manner. Here we survey existing systems as well as several theoretical efforts.

ANSI C provides "varargs," but the functions that implement this functionality serve as a thin wrapper around direct access to the stack frame. Java [11] and C# are two statically typed languages that have only uniform variable-arity functions, since access occurs via a homogeneous array.

Dzeng and Haynes [12] come close to our goal of providing a practical type system for variable-arity functions. As part of the Infer system for type-checking Scheme [13], they use an encoding of "infinitary tuples" as row types for an ML-like type inference system that handles optional arguments and uniform and non-uniform variable-arity functions.

By comparison to our work, Dzeng and Haynes' system has several limitations. Most importantly, since their system does not support first-class polymorphic functions, they are unable to type many of the definitions of variable-arity functions, such as *map* or *fold*. Additionally, their system requires full type inference to avoid exposing users to the underlying details of row types, and it is also designed around a Hindley-Milner style algorithm. This renders it incompatible with the remainder of the design of Typed Scheme, which is based on a system with subtyping.

Gregor and Järvi [14] propose an extension for variadic templates to C++ for the upcoming C++0x standard. This proposal has been accepted by the C++ standardization committee. Variadic templates provide a basis for implementing non-uniform variable-arity functions in templates. Since the approach is grounded in templates, it is difficult to translate their approach to other languages without template systems. The template approach addresses a simpler problem, since template expansion is a pre-processing step and types are only checked after template expansion. It also significantly complicates the language, since arbitrary computation can be performed during template expansion. Further, the template approach prevents checking of variadic functions at the definition site, meaning that errors in the definition are only caught when the function is used.

Tullsen [15] attempts to bring non-uniform variable-arity functions to Haskell via the Zip Calculus, a type system with restricted dependent types and special kinds that serve as tuple dimensions. This work is theoretical and comes without practical evaluation. The presented limitations of the Zip Calculus imply that it cannot assign a variable-arity type to the definition of `zipWith` (Haskell's name for Scheme's *map*) without further extension, whereas Typed Scheme can do so.

Similarly, McBride [16] and Moggi [17] present restricted forms of dependent typing in which the number of arguments is passed as a parameter to variadic functions. Our system, while not allowing the expression of every dependently-typable program, is simpler than dependent typing, suffices for most examples we have encountered, and does not require an extra function parameter.

7   Conclusion

In this paper, we have presented a design for polymorphic functions with variable arity. Our system accommodates both uniform and non-uniform variadic functions. We also validated our design against existing Scheme and Typed Scheme code. Typed Scheme with variable-arity polymorphism is part of the latest release of PLT Scheme (4.1), available from http://plt-scheme.org/.

In closing, we leave the reader with a final observation on the nature of variable-arity polymorphism. Many existing languages allow functions that accept a variable number of arguments, all of a uniform type. Such functions have types of the form $\tau^* \to \tau$. To accommodate variable-arity polymorphism, however, we must lift this abstraction one level up. For example, given the type $(\forall\ (\alpha \ldots)\ (\alpha \ldots_\alpha \to \textbf{Boolean}))$, the *kind* of this type is simply $\star^* \to \star$. So we see that *non-uniform* variable arity at the type level is reflected in *uniform* variable arity at the kind level.

References

1. Tobin-Hochstadt, S., Felleisen, M.: Interlanguage Migration: From Scripts to Programs. In: DLS 2006, Companion to OOPSLA, pp. 964–974 (2006)
2. Tobin-Hochstadt, S., Felleisen, M.: The Design and Implementation of Typed Scheme. In: POPL, pp. 395–406 (2008)
3. Flatt, M.: PLT MzScheme: Language Manual. Technical Report PLT-TR2008-1-v4.0.2, PLT Scheme Inc. (2008), http://www.plt-scheme.org/techreports/
4. Gansner, E.R., Reppy, J.H.: The Standard ML Basis Library. Cambridge University Press, New York (2002)
5. The GHC Team: The Glasgow Haskell Compiler User's Guide (2008)
6. Findler, R.B., Felleisen, M.: Contracts for Higher-Order Functions. In: ACM SIGPLAN International Conference on Functional Programming, pp. 48–59 (2002)
7. Pierce, B.C., Turner, D.N.: Local Type Inference. ACM Trans. Program. Lang. Syst. 22(1), 1–44 (2000)
8. Dybvig, R.K., Hieb, R.: A new approach to procedures with variable arity. Lisp and Symbolic Computation: An International Journal 3(3) (1990)
9. Strickland, T.S., Tobin-Hochstadt, S., Felleisen, M.: Variable-Arity Polymorphism. Technical Report NU-CCIS-08-03, Northeastern University (2008)
10. Girard, J.Y.: Une extension de l'interprétation de Gödel à l'analyse, et son application à l'élimination de coupures dans l'analyse et la théorie des types. In: Fenstad, J.E. (ed.) Proceedings of the Second Scandinavian Logic Symposium, pp. 63–92. North-Holland Publishing Co., Amsterdam (1971)
11. Gosling, J., Joy, B.: The Java Language Specification, 3rd edn. Addison-Wesley, Reading (2005)
12. Dzeng, H., Haynes, C.T.: Type Reconstruction for Variable-Arity Procedures. In: LFP 1994, pp. 239–249. ACM Press, New York (1994)
13. Haynes, C.T.: Infer: A Statically-typed Dialect of Scheme. Technical Report 367, Indiana University (1995)
14. Gregor, D., Järvi, J.: Variadic templates for C++. In: SAC 2007, pp. 1101–1108. ACM Press, New York (2007)
15. Tullsen, M.: The Zip Calculus. In: Backhouse, R., Oliveira, J.N. (eds.) MPC 2000. LNCS, vol. 1837, pp. 28–44. Springer, Heidelberg (2000)
16. McBride, C.: Faking it: Simulating Dependent Types in Haskell. J. Funct. Program. 12(5), 375–392 (2002)
17. Moggi, E.: Arity polymorphism and dependent types. In: APPSEM Workshop on Subtyping and Dependent Types in Programming (July 7, 2000) (invited talk)

Resolving Inductive Definitions with Binders in Higher-Order Typed Functional Programming*

Matthew R. Lakin and Andrew M. Pitts

University of Cambridge Computer Laboratory, Cambridge CB3 0FD, UK
{Matthew.Lakin,Andrew.Pitts}@cl.cam.ac.uk

Abstract. This paper studies inductive definitions involving binders, in which aliasing between free and bound names is permitted. Such aliasing occurs in informal specifications of operational semantics, but is excluded by the common representation of binding as meta-level λ-abstraction. Drawing upon ideas from functional logic programming, we represent such definitions with aliasing as recursively defined functions in a higher-order typed functional programming language that extends core ML with types for name-binding, a type of "semi-decidable propositions" and existential quantification for types with decidable equality. We show that the representation is sound and complete with respect to the language's operational semantics, which combines the use of evaluation contexts with constraint programming. We also give a new and simple proof that the associated constraint problem is NP-complete.

1 Introduction

Perhaps the single most important technique in the study of programming language semantics is the use of inductive definitions. This is especially the case for operational semantics, which in broad terms consists of one or more inductively defined relations between data structures involving programming language syntax. The inductive definition commonly takes the form of finitely many "schematic" rules containing parameters that can be instantiated, usually in infinitely many different ways, to get concrete rules for inductively generating instances of the relations. Schematic rules are necessarily written in some meta-language whose definition is often left implicit in published research. Having to be completely precise about the meta-language of rule schemes is an inescapable part of the current trend toward mechanization of semantics, whether it be machine-assisted proof construction/checking, or executable semantic specifications. In this paper we are concerned with the latter, but in either case it is clear that the ubiquitous presence of binding constructs in the "object-language" (that is, the programming language whose semantics is being formalized) creates difficulties for mechanized meta-languages (see the *POPLmark Challenge* wiki, for example). Ideally one would like the executable meta-language for rule schemes to provide a fully automatic treatment of α-conversion of bound names

---

* Research supported by UK EPSRC grant EP/D000459/1.

in object-languages. Here we investigate a way of doing that within the context of higher-order typed functional programming. In doing so we take a "nominal" approach to object-level binders for the following reasons to do with *name aliasing*.

One way of dealing with issues of α-conversion is to make the representation of object-level binders completely anonymous. This can be achieved through a case-by-case use of de Bruijn indices [8], or more systematically by use of Higher-Order Abstract Syntax (HOAS) [21] to enforce that object-level bound names are only represented by meta-level bound names. In either case the conceptually simple operation of instantiating parameters in a rule scheme, which may involve capture of a free name by a binder of the same name, has to be replaced by something more complicated—simply because "binder of the same name" makes no sense if binders have been anonymized. But there is a more serious problem with anonymous representations of object-level binding: they rule out the common practice of *name-aliasing* involving binders, be it the use of the same name at two different binding occurrences, or the use of the same name for both a free and a binding occurrence. For example, in an inductive definition of β-reduction of λ-terms it is natural to use the rule scheme

$$\frac{t \to t'}{\lambda x.\, t \to \lambda x.\, t'}$$

where the two different binding occurrences within the conclusion are both named x. In this case the name-aliasing does not cause a problem for a formalization using HOAS, which might render the above rule as

$$\frac{f(x) \to f'(x)}{\lambda(f) \to \lambda(f')}$$

where f and f' are meta-variables of function type. The top half of Fig. 1 contains another example. (The bottom half of the figure will be explained in Sect. 2.) In this case the conclusion of the third rule contains both free (the first x) and binding (the x within L(<x>t)) occurrences with the same name. We leave the reader to ponder how to convert these rules into an extensionally equivalent HOAS formalization (probably by ignoring the third rule completely). In fact we do not know any definitive results comparing the class of relations (on tuples of α-equivalence classes of λ-terms, say) defined by HOAS rule schemes with the class defined by first-order rule schemes with conventional, named binders. In any case, the phenomenon of name-aliasing seems too convenient to give up unless we really have to.

So we advocate the study of executable meta-languages for rule schemes that allow object-level binders to be named. More specifically we study such an executable meta-language which is a higher-order, typed functional programming language, drawing upon the ideas of *functional logic programming* [14]. Our motivation for favouring this paradigm over the relational paradigm of first-order logic programming has to do with the expressiveness and modularity afforded by

$\mathtt{nfv}(x, t)$: "$x : \mathtt{vr}$ is not a free variable of the λ-term $t : \mathtt{tm}$"

$$\frac{x \,\#\, x'}{\mathtt{nfv}(x, \mathtt{V}\,x')} \qquad \frac{\mathtt{nfv}(x, t) \,\&\, \mathtt{nfv}(x, t')}{\mathtt{nfv}(x, \mathtt{A}(t, t'))} \qquad \frac{}{\mathtt{nfv}(x, \mathtt{L}(\langle x \rangle t))} \qquad \frac{\mathtt{nfv}(x, t) \,\&\, x \,\#\, x'}{\mathtt{nfv}(x, \mathtt{L}(\langle x' \rangle t))}$$

Equivalent standard form $\dfrac{\varphi}{\mathtt{nfv}\, y}$ has

$\varphi \triangleq \exists x, x'(y = (x, \mathtt{V}\,x') \,\&\, x \,\#\, x') \,\vee\, \exists x, t, t'(y = (x, \mathtt{A}(t, t')) \,\&\, \mathtt{nfv}(x, t) \,\&\, \mathtt{nfv}(x, t'))$
$\quad \vee\, \exists x, t(y = \mathtt{nfv}(x, \mathtt{L}(\langle x \rangle t))) \,\vee\, \exists x, x', t(y = \mathtt{nfv}(x, \mathtt{L}(\langle x' \rangle t)) \,\&\, \mathtt{nfv}(x, t) \,\&\, x \,\#\, x')$

Fig. 1. Example α-inductive definition

higher-order functions. For example, having higher-order functions allows one to encode definitions that are parameterised by other definitions (such as the various operations on relations that occur in the relational approach to contextual equivalence of programs [12, 17, 25]).

Contributions of this paper. We begin by fixing a simple, yet expressive class of inductive definitions permitting name-aliasing in binders, where binding is handled generically through the existing notion of a "nominal signature". These α-*inductive definitions* (Sect. 2) may involve side-conditions asserting constraints in terms of α-equivalence and the "not-a-free-variable-of" relation. In Sect. 3 we make the apparently new observation that such constraints can express membership in finite sets; consequently the associated constraint satisfaction problem is NP-complete (Theorem 3.3). Section 4 introduces the main contribution of the paper, a typed higher-order functional programming language that extends core ML with name-binding types, a type of "semi-decidable propositions" and existential quantification for types in a class of equality types coinciding with the arities of a user-declared nominal signature. This language, which we call αML, draws upon the ideas of αProlog [7], extending them to higher-order functional programming. αML is a simplification of both our first attempt to do this [16] and of αProlog itself, in that *it avoids the use of concrete names and name-permutations in programs* (see Remark 2.2 and Sect. 6 for the significance of this). αML has a remarkably simple operational semantics that combines the use of Felleisen-style evaluation contexts with constraint programming; we show that it restricts to the usual operational semantics on the purely functional part of αML (Theorem 4.1). By design, αML represents α-inductive definitions as certain recursively defined functions; we prove that this representation is sound and complete (Corollary 5.3). Finally, Sect. 6 discusses related and future work.

2 α-Inductive Definitions

In this section we give a simple, yet expressive class of *inductively defined relations between α-equivalence classes of expressions*, or *α-inductive definitions* for short. Alpha-equivalence arises from the presence of binding constructs in the expressions and we will deal with this in a generic way by using *nominal signatures* [28], Σ. These generalize the usual notion of many-sorted algebraic signature to encompass constructors that bind names of various sorts. Such a Σ is given by a finite set of *name sorts* N, a disjoint finite set of *data sorts* S, and a finite set of *constructors* $K : A \rightarrow S$, each with a specified result sort S and argument arity A—where the *nominal arities* of the signature are given by:

$$
\begin{aligned}
A ::= \ & S && \text{(data sort)} \\
& A * \cdots * A && \text{(tuples)} \\
& N && \text{(name sort)} \\
& [N]\,A && \text{(name-abstractions).}
\end{aligned} \tag{1}
$$

For example, the nominal signature for untyped λ-calculus has a name sort vr for variables, a data sort tm for λ-terms and constructors V : vr -> tm, A : tm*tm -> tm and L : [vr] tm -> tm. For other examples, see [24, Sect. 2]. As in that paper, we associate with each arity A of a nominal signature Σ a set $\alpha\text{-}Tree_\Sigma(A)$ of *α-equivalence classes of abstract syntax trees*, or *α-trees* for short. The elements of each $\alpha\text{-}Tree_\Sigma(A)$ are equivalence classes $[g]_\alpha$ of syntax trees $g \in Tree_\Sigma(A)$ built up from countably many *names* $n \in Name(N)$ (for each name sort N of Σ) by repeatedly applying the following three operations.

Constructor application: $K\,g \in Tree_\Sigma(S)$, if $g \in Tree_\Sigma(A)$ and $K : A \rightarrow S$.
Tupling: $(g_1, \ldots, g_n) \in Tree_\Sigma(A_1 * \cdots * A_n)$, if $g_i \in Tree_\Sigma(A_i)$ for $i = 1..n$.
Name-abstraction: $\langle n \rangle g \in Tree_\Sigma([N]\,A)$, if $n \in Name(N)$ and $g \in Tree_\Sigma(A)$.

(These trees are the *ground* nominal terms from [28], that is, the ones not involving variables.) The third operation, name-abstraction, is the generic binding form provided by nominal signatures: renaming $\langle n \rangle (-)$-bound names in trees gives an equivalence relation $=_\alpha$ [24, Fig. 1] and $\alpha\text{-}Tree_\Sigma(A)$ is the quotient $Tree_\Sigma(A)/=_\alpha$. To specify inductively defined relations between α-trees we make use of a simple meta-language of patterns.

Definition 2.1 (patterns and valuations). The *patterns* $p \in Pat_\Sigma(A)$ for describing α-trees of each arity A of Σ are built up from countably many *variables* $x \in Var(A)$ (for each A) by repeatedly applying the three tree-forming operations mentioned above:
Constructor application: $K\,p \in Pat_\Sigma(S)$, if $p \in Pat_\Sigma(A)$ and $K : A \rightarrow S$.
Tupling: $(p_1, \ldots, p_n) \in Pat_\Sigma(A_1 * \cdots * A_n)$, if $p_i \in Pat_\Sigma(A_i)$ for $i = 1..n$.
Name-abstraction: <x>p $\in Pat_\Sigma([N]\,A)$, if $x \in Var(N)$ and $p \in Pat_\Sigma(A)$.

A *valuation* V is a finite function mapping variables to α-trees (of the same arity). If the variables occurring in a pattern $p \in Pat_\Sigma(A)$ are in $dom(V)$ (the domain of definition of V), then $[\![p]\!]_V \in \alpha\text{-}Tree_\Sigma(A)$ denotes the α-tree resulting from p by replacing each $x \in dom(V)$ with $V(x)$.

Remark 2.2. The following points about patterns should be noted.

(a) *Variables stand for unknown α-trees, not unknown trees, and (hence) a pattern $p \in Pat_\Sigma(A)$ describes an α-tree rather than a tree* (just which one depends upon how its variables are instantiated by a valuation). This reflects the common practice of leaving α-equivalence implicit and referring to a class via a representative, signalled by a phrase like "we identify expressions up to α-equivalence". (Our own Figs. 2 and 3 in Sect. 4 provide examples of this!)

(b) *No concrete names $n \in Name(N)$ occur in patterns.* In particular, although the meta-language allows us to name object-level binding occurrences, $<x>p$, we use variables x of name sort rather than names themselves to do so. Again, this reflects common practice. For example, in Barendregt's classic text [1], Definition 2.1.1 says that λ-terms are words over an alphabet containing, among other things, "variables $v_0, v_1, \ldots$"; then Notation 2.1.2 says that "$x, y, z \ldots$ denote arbitrary variables"; the concrete variables $v_0, v_1, \ldots$ are never mentioned again and only the meta-variables $x, y, z \ldots$ are used throughout the rest of the book.

(c) *There are no meta-level variable-binding constructs in patterns—all variables in a pattern are free.* In particular x occurs free in the name-abstraction pattern $<x>p$. This allows patterns to support the phenomenon of name-aliasing discussed in the Introduction.

(d) *Valuation of patterns is a form of "possibly-capturing" substitution.* Once again, this reflects common practice when instantiating the meta-variables of schematic rules in operational semantics. Note that, in addition to the previous point, this is another reason why it makes no sense to try to identify patterns up to renaming $<x>(-)$-scoped variables, since valuations do not respect such a notion of α-equivalence. For example, we cannot regard $<x>z$ and $<y>z$ as equivalent (where x, y and z are distinct), since the valuation $V = \{x \mapsto [n]_\alpha, y \mapsto [n']_\alpha, z \mapsto [n]_\alpha\}$ (with $n \neq n'$) has $[\![<x>z]\!]_V = [\langle n \rangle n]_\alpha \neq [\langle n' \rangle n]_\alpha = [\![<y>z]\!]_V$.

Fix a finite set of *relation symbols* $r <: A$, each with a specified arity A. Such an r is intended to denote a subset of $\alpha\text{-}Tree_\Sigma(A)$. Schematic rules for inductively defining such subsets take the form

$$\frac{r_1(p_1) \And \cdots \And r_m(p_m) \And c_1 \And \cdots \And c_n}{r(p)} \tag{2}$$

(see Fig. 1 for an example). The conclusion of (2) is an *atomic formula* $r(p)$ with $r <: A$ and $p \in Pat_\Sigma(A)$ for some arity A; the hypothesis is a finite (possibly empty) conjunction of such atomic formulas and "side-conditions" c_i, that is, constraints on how the rule may be instantiated by a valuation. What form of constraints should we use? At the very least we need *name-inequality* constraints $x \neq x'$, where $x, x' \in Var(N)$ with N a name sort. Experience with nominal logic [23, 11] and nominal logic programming [7] shows that it is useful to generalize name-inequality to *name freshness* constraints, $x \# p$ where $x \in Var(N)$ and $p \in Pat_\Sigma(A)$, even though these can be inductively defined in terms of name-inequality (cf. Fig. 1). The intended meaning of $x \# p$ on α-trees is as follows.

Definition 2.3 (free names and freshness). If $t \in \alpha\text{-}Tree_\Sigma(A)$ we write $FN\,t$ for the finite set of names that occur freely in some (indeed, any) tree g with $[g]_\alpha = t$; in other words, $n \in FN[g]_\alpha$ iff n occurs in g, but not within the scope of any name-abstraction $\langle n \rangle(-)$. Note that each α-tree $t \in \alpha\text{-}Tree_\Sigma(N)$ of name sort N is of the form $t = [n]_\alpha = \{n\}$ for some $n \in Name(N)$ (because the constructors of a nominal signature only produce results of data sort, rather than of more general arities, and these are disjoint from the name sorts). Given $t \in \alpha\text{-}Tree_\Sigma(N)$ and $t' \in \alpha\text{-}Tree_\Sigma(A)$, we write $t \mathrel{\#} t'$ and say t *is fresh for* t' if $t = [n]_\alpha$ and $n \notin FN\, t'$.

Note that the case of several mutually inductively defined relation symbols $r_1 <: A_1, \ldots, r_k <: A_k$ reduces to the case of a single one at the expense of extending the signature: we add a new data sort S and new constructors $I_i : A_i \to S$ for $i \in \{1..k\}$ and use the fact that subsets $R \subseteq \alpha\text{-}Tree_\Sigma(S)$ are in bijection with n-tuples of subsets, $R_1 \subseteq \alpha\text{-}Tree_\Sigma(A_1), \ldots, R_n \subseteq \alpha\text{-}Tree_\Sigma(A_n)$. So from now on *we will fix on a single arity A_r of a nominal signature Σ and a single relation symbol $r <: A_r$.*

Definition 2.4 (formulas and satisfaction). Let $Form_\Sigma$ be the set of first-order formulas built up from atomic formulas $r(p)$ (where $p \in Pat_\Sigma(A_r)$), equalities $p = p'$ $(p, p' \in Pat_\Sigma(A)$, some $A)$ and freshnesses $x \mathrel{\#} p$ $(x \in Var(N)$, $p \in Pat_\Sigma(A)$, some $N, A)$ just using finite conjunctions &, finite disjunctions ∨ and existential quantification $\exists x(-)$ $(x \in Var(A)$, some $A)$. Given an interpretation $R \subseteq \alpha\text{-}Tree_\Sigma(A_r)$ for the relation symbol r and a valuation V (Definition 2.1) for the free variables of $\varphi \in Form_\Sigma$ (i.e. those not within the scope of an $\exists x$), let $(R, V) \models \varphi$ denote the associated *satisfaction relation*. Thus $(R, V) \models r(p)$ holds if $[\![p]\!]_V \in R$; $(R, V) \models p = p'$ holds if $[\![p]\!]_V = [\![p']\!]_V$; $(R, V) \models x \# p$ holds if $V(x) \# [\![p]\!]_V$ (Definition 2.3); and satisfaction is extended to compound formulas in the usual way.

Generalizing (2), we will allow the hypothesis of a schematic rule to be a formula in $Form_\Sigma$. Allowing equality, disjunction and existential quantification in addition to freshness and conjunction does not increase the expressive power of inductive definitions; but it does allow us to write inductive definitions in a "standard form", illustrated in Fig. 1.

Definition 2.5 (standard α-inductive definitions). An α-*inductive definition* $\mathcal{D}$ *in standard form* of a set of α-trees of arity A_r is given by

$$\frac{\varphi}{r(x)} \tag{3}$$

where $x \in Var(A_r)$ and $\varphi \in Form_\Sigma$ is a formula with at most x free. The *meaning* $[\![\mathcal{D}]\!] \subseteq \alpha\text{-}Tree_\Sigma(A_r)$ of $\mathcal{D}$ is by definition the least fixed point of the monotone function $\Phi_\mathcal{D}$ on subsets of α-trees that maps each $R \subseteq \alpha\text{-}Tree_\Sigma(A_r)$ to

$$\Phi_\mathcal{D}(R) \triangleq \{t \in \alpha\text{-}Tree_\Sigma(A_r) \mid (R, \{x \mapsto t\}) \models \varphi\}. \tag{4}$$

The definition of $[\![\mathcal{D}]\!]$ via (4) is a fancy way of stating the usual meaning of a rule-based inductive definition: the rule (3) is schematic in the sense that it has the variable x as parameter; we instantiate x to get many concrete rules (this is the effect of the valuations $\{x \mapsto t\}$ in the definition of $\Phi_{\mathcal{D}}$) and take the least set of α-trees closed under these rules, in other words, the least R such that $\Phi_{\mathcal{D}}(R) \subseteq R$. The existence of $[\![\mathcal{D}]\!]$ is an application of the usual Tarski fixed point theorem ($\Phi_{\mathcal{D}}$ is monotone because the relation symbol r only occurs positively in φ). Indeed $\Phi_{\mathcal{D}}$ is finitary and we can construct $[\![\mathcal{D}]\!]$ as the union of the countable chain of subsets $\emptyset \subseteq \Phi_{\mathcal{D}}(\emptyset) \subseteq \Phi_{\mathcal{D}}(\Phi_{\mathcal{D}}(\emptyset)) \subseteq \cdots$ of $\alpha\text{-}Tree_\Sigma(A_r)$.

3 α-Tree Constraint Problems

The hypothesis φ of an α-inductive definition (3) contains non-inductive equality and freshness constraints. When instantiated by a particular valuation, the validity of such constraints amounts to α-equivalence of trees $g \in Tree_\Sigma(A)$ and to non-membership of the set of free names of such trees. These are properties that can be decided in linear time; see [3] for example. However, the problem of checking whether or not there is some valuation that validates a collection of equality and freshness constraints is surprisingly more complicated, mainly because of the presence of variables x in binding position in name-abstraction patterns $<x>p$ (see points (c) and (d) in Remark 2.2).

Definition 3.1 (constraints and their satisfaction). A formula $\varphi \in Form_\Sigma$ is an α-tree *constraint* if it is of the form $\exists x_1 \cdots \exists x_m \, (c_1 \, \& \cdots \& \, c_n)$ with each c_i either an equality $(p = p')$ or a freshness $(x \# p)$. Since such formulas do not involve the relation symbol $r <: A_r$, the satisfaction relation of Definition 2.4 restricts to a relation $V \models \varphi$ between valuations and constraints. A *constraint problem* is a closed constraint formula and it is *satisfiable* if $\emptyset \models \varphi$ holds, where $\emptyset$ denotes the valuation with empty domain.

That satisfaction of α-tree constraint problems is decidable and in NP can be deduced from results about nominal unification [28]: see [5, Theorem 7.1.2]. One can show that it is also NP-hard via the following simple observation, which seems to be new.[1] In stating it we use the abbreviation $<x_1, \ldots, x_n>(-)$ to stand for iterated name-abstraction $<x_1>(\cdots <x_n>(-) \cdots)$.

Lemma 3.2 (set membership as an α-tree constraint). *Given distinct variables* $x, x_1, \ldots, x_k, x', x_1', \ldots, x_k' \in Var(N)$ *(for some name sort N), define* $mem(x, x_1, \ldots, x_k) \triangleq \exists x' \exists x_1' \cdots \exists x_k' \, (x \# x' \, \& \, <x_1, \ldots, x_k>x = <x_1', \ldots, x_k'>x')$. *Then a valuation V on $\{x, x_1, \ldots, x_k\}$ satisfies $mem(x, x_1, \ldots, x_k)$ iff $V(x)$ is a member of the finite set $\{V(x_i) \mid i = 1..k\}$.*   □

We can use this lemma to show NP-hardness by reduction of GRAPH 3-COLOUR-ABILITY. Given a finite graph with vertices $v_1, \ldots, v_n$ (which we can take to be variables of some name sort), edges $e_1, \ldots, e_m$ and source/target functions $s, t : \{e_1, \ldots, e_m\} \rightrightarrows \{v_1, \ldots, v_n\}$, then the formula

---

[1] Cheney's proof of NP-hardness [4] for his constraint problems is not applicable here, because it relies upon the use of concrete names and name-permutations.

$\exists r, g, b, v_1, \ldots, v_n \left(r \# g \& g \# b \& b \# r \& \&_{i=1}^{n} mem(v_i, r, g, b) \& \&_{j=1}^{m} s(e_j) \# t(e_j) \right)$

is logically equivalent to an α-tree constraint problem which is satisfiable iff the graph's vertices can be coloured with one of three colours (r, g, b) so that no edge connects vertices of the same colour. So altogether we have:

Theorem 3.3. *Satisfiability of α-tree constraint problems is NP-complete.* □

4 αML

We are going to make the α-inductive definitions of Sect. 2 executable by embedding the simple meta-language language of patterns and formulas in which they are expressed within an ML-like functional programming language, called αML. The embedding has two attractive features:

(a) *nominal signatures Σ are subsumed within recursive data type declarations;*

(b) *α-inductive definitions $\mathcal{D}$ become instances of recursively defined functions.*

To achieve point (a) we mimic FreshML [26] and extend ML's type system with types of name N and name-abstraction types $[N]T$. However, unlike FreshML and for the reasons given below, we will restrict the use of $[N]T$ to the case when T is an *equality type* in the sense of Standard ML [20, Sect. 4.4]. To achieve point (b) we note that the meaning $[\![\mathcal{D}]\!]$ of $\mathcal{D}$ is the fixed point of a higher-order function (4). We represent subsets of α-$Tree_\Sigma(A)$ by αML functions of type $A \rightarrow$ prop, where prop is a new type of "semi-decidable propositions"; and then $\Phi_\mathcal{D}$ is represented by a function of type $(A \rightarrow \text{prop}) \rightarrow (A \rightarrow \text{prop})$. In order to be able to write this function, αML extends the pure functional core of ML with name-binding patterns, with equality and freshness constraints, and with existential quantification over values of equality types. The syntax of αML types and expressions is given in Fig. 2. For simplicity's sake αML has a monomorphic type system with a single, top-level data type declaration of some name sorts (N), of some data sorts $(S$, including a distinguished one bool with constructors T () and F ()) whose recursive definitions may only involve equality types (E), and of some general data types (D) whose recursive definitions may involve function types and prop. Note that in accord with point (a) above, such a declaration subsumes the notion of nominal signature [28] that we used in Sect. 2; in particular, the signature's nominal arities (1) coincide with equality types.

Turning to αML's operational semantics, the behaviour of the pure functional constructs is completely straightforward and could be formalized in any of the standard ways. We use Felleisen-style evaluation contexts [9], formalized using *frame stacks* [22], because this makes the combination with αML's impure features smoother. These impure features are α-tree equality and freshness constraints, and existentially quantified variables of equality type. We describe their behaviour by combining the use of frame stacks with the techniques of *constraint logic programming* (CLP) [15] applied to the α-tree constraint problems of the previous section. A constraint-based approach gives a clean, abstract presentation that avoids the use of unifying substitutions; this is especially useful here

		Expressions $e, v ::=$	
		x, f	(variables)
		`let` $x = e$ `in` e	(sequencing)
Equality types $E ::=$		$K\,v$	(constructor application)
S	(data sort)		
$E * \cdots * E$	(tuples, including nullary case, `unit`)	`case` v `of` $K\,x \Rightarrow e$	
N	(name sort)	$\mid \cdots$	(case analysis)
$[N]\,E$	(name-abstraction)	$\mid K\,x \Rightarrow e$	
		$(v, \ldots, v)$	(tuple)
Types $T ::=$		$e.i$	(projections, $i \in \mathbb{N}$)
E	(equality type)	`fun` $f\,x = e$	(recursive function)
D	(data type)	$v\,v$	(function application) *pure*
$T * \cdots * T$	(tuples)		
$T \rightarrow T$	(functions)		
`prop`	(semi-decidable propositions)	$\langle v \rangle v$	(name-abstraction) *impure*
		$\top$	(empty constraint)
		c	(atomic constraint)
Data type declaration:		$\exists x\,e$	(existential)
`names` $N \cdots$		*Atomic constraints* $c ::=$	
`data`		$v = v$	(equality)
`bool` $= \top$ `of unit` $\mid F$ `of unit`		$v \# v$	(freshness)
$S = K_1$ `of` $E_1 \mid \cdots \mid K_n$ `of` E_n		*Frame stacks* $s ::=$	
$\vdots$		id	(empty)
$D = K'_1$ `of` $T_1 \mid \cdots \mid K'_{n'}$ `of` $T_{n'}$		$s \circ (x.\,e)$	(non-empty)
$\vdots$			

Expressions and frame stacks in *A-normal form* are obtained by restricting v to range over

Values $v ::=$

$x, f \mid K\,v \mid (v, \ldots, v) \mid$ `fun` $f\,x = e \mid \langle v \rangle v \mid \top$

- *We only consider well-typed expressions and frame stacks.* We use explicitly typed variables $x \in Var(T)$ as T ranges over types. The typing of the pure functional part of αML is entirely standard; the types of αML's impure features are:

Name-abstraction	$\langle e \rangle e' : [N]\,E$ if $e : N$ and $e' : E$
Empty constraint	$\top : $ `prop`
Equality constraint	$e = e' : $ `prop` if $e : E$ and $e' : E$
Freshness constraint	$e \# e' : $ `prop` if $e : N$ and $e' : E$
Existential	$\exists x\,e : T$ if $x \in Var(E)$ and $e : T$.

- *We identify αML expressions up to renaming bound variables.* Despite the fact that αML is a meta-language for object-level languages with binding, there is no reason not to adopt the usual conventions (see Remark 2.2(a)) for αML's own variable-binding constructs. In the pure part, variable-binding occurs in the usual way, in `let`, `case` and `fun` expressions and in frame stacks $s \circ (x.\,-)$; and in the impure part, $\exists x(-)$ is a binder. We write $FV(e)$ for the finite set of free variables of an expression e and say e is *closed* if this set is empty. We write $e[e'/x]$ for the capture-avoiding substitution of e' for all free occurrences of x in e (well-defined up to renaming bound variables).

Fig. 2. αML syntax

	Pure transitions $s, e \to s', e'$
(P1)	$s \circ (x.e), v \to s, e[v/x]$
(P2)	$s, (\mathtt{let}\, x = e\, \mathtt{in}\, e') \to s \circ (x.e'), e$
(P3)	$s, (v_1, \ldots, v_n).i \to s, v_i$ if $i \in \{1..n\}$
(P4)	$s, (\mathtt{case}\, K_i\, v\, \mathtt{of}\, K_1\, x_1 \Rightarrow e_1 \mid \cdots \mid K_n\, x_n \Rightarrow e_n) \to s, e_i[v/x_i]$ if $i \in \{1..n\}$
(P5)	$s, v\, v' \to s, e[v/f, v'/x]$ if v is $\mathtt{fun}\, f\, x = e$
	Impure transitions $\exists \vec{x}(\bar{c}; s; e) \to \exists \vec{x}'(\bar{c}'; s'; e')$
(I1)	$\exists \vec{x}(\bar{c}; s; e) \to \exists \vec{x}(\bar{c}; s'; e')$ if $s, e \to s', e'$
(I2)	$\exists \vec{x}(\bar{c}; s; x.i) \to \exists \vec{x}, x_1, \ldots, x_n(\bar{c}\, \&\, x{=}(x_1, \ldots, x_n); s; x_i)$
(I3)	$\exists \vec{x}(\bar{c}; s; \mathtt{case}\, x\, \mathtt{of}\, K_1\, x_1 \Rightarrow e_1 \mid \cdots \mid K_n\, x_n \Rightarrow e_n) \to \exists \vec{x}, x_i(\bar{c}\, \&\, x{=}K_i x_i; s; e_i)$
	if $i \in \{1..n\}$ and $\emptyset \models \exists \vec{x}, x_i(\bar{c}\, \&\, x{=}K_i x_i)$
(I4)	$\exists \vec{x}(\bar{c}; s; c) \to \exists \vec{x}(\bar{c}\, \&\, c; s; \mathsf{T})$ if $\emptyset \models \exists \vec{x}(\bar{c}\, \&\, c)$
(I5)	$\exists \vec{x}(\bar{c}; s; \exists x\, e) \to \exists \vec{x}, x(\bar{c}; s; e)$ if $\emptyset \models \exists x(\mathsf{T})$

- $e, s, e', s', e_i, \ldots$ range over expressions and frame stacks in A-normal form (Fig. 2).
- Impure transitions are between *configurations* $\exists \vec{x}(\bar{c}; s; e)$ where $\bar{c}$ is a finite conjunction of atomic constraints and $\vec{x}$ is a finite list of distinct variables of equality type containing the free variables of $\bar{c}$, s and e. As for expressions, *we identify configurations up to renaming of* $\exists$-*bound variables*. The initial configuration is $\exists \emptyset(\mathsf{T}; id; e)$.
- In (I2) $x \in Var(E_1 * \cdots * E_n)$ and $x_i \in Var(E_i) - \vec{x}$ for $i = 1..n$.
- In (I3) $x \in Var(S)$, $S = K_1\, \mathtt{of}\, E_1 \mid \cdots \mid K_n\, \mathtt{of}\, E_n$ and $x_i \in Var(E_i) - \vec{x}$ for $i = 1..n$.
- In (I5) $x \notin \vec{x}$. If $x \in Var(E)$ say, then constraint $\exists x(\mathsf{T})$ is satisfiable iff E is nonempty, in the sense that there is an α-tree of arity E. We allow empty data sorts, e.g. that given by the declaration $\mathsf{es} = K\, \mathtt{of}\, \mathsf{es}$.

Fig. 3. αML operational semantics

because the "possibly-capturing" nature of substitution (cf. Remark 2.2(d)) complicates unification—see for example the use of terms involving explicit name-permutations in nominal [28] and equivariant [6] unification algorithms. αML's operational semantics is specified in Fig. 3. To simplify the presentation we have restricted to the *A-normal forms* [10] from Fig. 2; transitions for general expressions can be derived by reducing them to A-normal form. The αML transition relation is non-deterministic, because of the "narrowing" that occurs when evaluating a `case`-expression whose subject is an existentially quantified variable (transition (I3) in Fig. 3). There is a considerable literature about this specific source of non-determinism, centred around the semantics of the functional logic programming language Curry; see [14] for a survey. Since αML features non-trivial computational effects and we do not wish to impose a monadic programming style, we prefer a strict evaluation strategy, rather than the call-by-need strategy that is more common in the functional logic programming literature; and for simplicity's sake we wish to avoid residuation and concurrent execution [14, Sect. 2.4]. So we use a simple-minded design where the "rigid/flexible" behaviour of `case`-analysis is part of the dynamics (pure transition (P4) versus impure transition (I3)), rather than user-specified.

The following theorem shows that we do achieve the design goal of embedding within αML the usual operational behaviour of pure functional programming with recursive data types and call-by-value higher-order functions. It depends on a notion of configurations being well-typed, $\exists \vec{x}(\vec{c}; s; e) : T$, whose straightforward definition we omit here.

Theorem 4.1 (embedded pure functional language). *An αML expression or frame stack is* pure *if it does not contain sub-expressions of the form* $\langle e \rangle e'$, T, $e = e'$, $e \# e'$, *or $\exists x\, e$. Suppose s and e are pure and that $\exists \emptyset(\mathsf{T}; s; e) : T$ holds for some type T. Then $\exists \emptyset(\mathsf{T}; s; e) \rightarrow \exists \vec{x}(\vec{c}; s'; e')$ holds iff $\vec{x} = \emptyset$, $\vec{c} = \mathsf{T}$, s' and e' are pure, and there is a pure transition $(s; e) \rightarrow (s'; e')$.* □

αML restricts the name-abstraction type-former $[N](-)$ to apply only to equality types E (that is, to nominal arities) rather than to general types T, for which equality constraints are in general uncomputable. This allows expressions of name-abstraction type to be deconstructed by unification with name-abstraction patterns $\langle x \rangle p$ in the presence of freshness constraints on x, rather than using the "generative name unbinding" [25] mechanism of FreshML, which is based on a supply of dynamically allocated fresh names ("gensym"). Here is an example.

Example 4.2. If the nominal signature for λ-terms mentioned in Sect. 2 is part of the data type declaration, then the λ-term substitution operation $(t, t', x') \mapsto t[t'/x']$ can be encoded in αML by the following function of type `tm*tm*vr -> tm`

$$
\begin{aligned}
&\mathbf{fun}\ subst\,(t, t', x') = \mathbf{case}\,t\ \mathbf{of} \\
&\quad \mathsf{V}\,x \Rightarrow \mathbf{if}\,x = x'\ \mathbf{then}\,t'\ \mathbf{else}\,t \\
&\ |\ \mathsf{A}\,x \Rightarrow \mathsf{A}(subst(x.1, t', x'), subst(x.2, t', x')) \\
&\ |\ \mathsf{L}\,x \Rightarrow \exists x_1\,\exists t_1\ \underline{x_1 \# (t', x')}\ \&\ \langle x_1 \rangle t_1 = x\ \&\ \mathsf{L}(\langle x_1 \rangle subst(t_1, t', x'))
\end{aligned}
\tag{5}
$$

where we have used some syntactic sugar for tuple-pattern matching, together with the following abbreviations:

$$
e_1 \,\&\, e_2 \triangleq \mathbf{let}\ x = e_1\ \mathbf{in}\ e_2 \tag{6}
$$

$$
\mathbf{if}\ e\ \mathbf{then}\ e_1\ \mathbf{else}\ e_2 \triangleq \mathbf{case}\ e\ \mathbf{of}\ \mathsf{T}\,x_1 \Rightarrow e_1\ |\ \mathsf{F}\,x_2 \Rightarrow e_2 \tag{7}
$$

(where $x \notin FV(e_2)$ in (6) and $x_i \notin FV(e_i)$ in (7)). The underlined freshness constraint in (5) enforces the usual "capture-avoiding" property when substituting under a λ-binder (cf. [7, Example 2.3]).

Remark 4.3 (dynamically allocated names). We can add dynamically allocated names to αML without breaking the "names as meta-variables" aspect of its design (Remark 2.2(b)): extend its syntax with expressions $\mathbf{fresh}_N$ of type N (for each name sort N) and its operational semantics with the impure transition:

$$
\text{(I6)} \qquad \exists \vec{x}(\vec{c}; s; \mathbf{fresh}_N) \rightarrow \exists \vec{x}, x(\vec{c}\,\&\, x \# \vec{x}; s; x)
$$

where $x \in Var(N)$ is not in $\vec{x}$ and $x \# \vec{x}$ is the constraint $x \# x_1\,\&\,\cdots\,\&\,x \# x_n$ when $\vec{x} = x_1, \ldots, x_n$. Using this we can define a uniform operation of *generative name-unbinding*

$$
\mathbf{unbind}\,e\ \mathbf{as}\ \langle x \rangle x'\ \mathbf{in}\ e' \triangleq \mathbf{let}\ x = \mathbf{fresh}_N\ \mathbf{in}\ \exists x'\,\langle x \rangle x' = e\,\&\,e' \tag{8}
$$

where $e : [N]E$ and $x \in Var(N), x' \in Var(E)$ are distinct variables not occurring in e. Then, for example, we can replace the last branch of the case expression in (5) with $L\,x \Rightarrow \mathtt{unbind}\,x$ as $<x_1>t_1$ in $L(<x_1>subst\,(t_1, t', x'))$. Rule (I6) and definition (8) together give a version of generative unbinding that is like the one used by MLSOS [16]. It is operationally different from FreshML's version [26], which pushes a swap of x with a fresh name into the body e'. Are these two forms of generative unbinding behaviourally equivalent? To determine this requires developing the properties of *contextual equivalence* for αML, which we defer to a future paper. Is $\mathtt{fresh}_N$ definable up to contextual equivalence in terms of the language presented in Figs 2 and 3? It seems unlikely, but we do not have a proof.

5 α-Inductive Definitions as αML Recursive Functions

We remarked in the previous section that nominal arities are the same thing as αML equality types. Regarding the relation symbol $r <: A_r$ of nominal arity A_r as a variable of type $A_r \to \mathtt{prop}$, we identify α-inductive definitions in standard form $\mathcal{D}$ (Definition 2.5) with certain αML recursive function values $v_{\mathcal{D}}$ of type $A_r \to \mathtt{prop}$:

$$v_{\mathcal{D}} \triangleq (\mathtt{fun}\,r\,x = \varphi) \quad \text{where } \mathcal{D} \text{ is } \frac{\varphi}{r(x)}. \tag{9}$$

For this to make sense we have to embed formulas $\varphi \in Form_\Sigma$ over a nominal signature Σ (Definition 2.4) as αML expressions of type $\mathtt{prop}$. Clearly the patterns p of each arity A (Definition 2.1) coincide with values v (Fig. 2) of equality type A. So αML syntax has all the necessary constituents for expressing formulas except possibly for conjunction and disjunction. We define conjunction as in (6) and express disjunction using a flexible case-expression (cf. [27, Sect. 3.1]):

$$e_1 \vee e_2 \triangleq \exists x\,(\mathtt{case}\,x\,\mathtt{of}\,\mathsf{T}\,x_1 \Rightarrow e_1 \mid \mathsf{F}\,x_2 \Rightarrow e_2) \tag{10}$$
$$(\text{where } x, x_1, x_2 \notin FV(e_1, e_2)).$$

So given an α-inductive definition $\mathcal{D}$ in standard form with associated αML function $v_{\mathcal{D}} : A_r \to \mathtt{prop}$ as in (9), for each formula $\varphi' \in Form_\Sigma$ we get an αML expression $\varphi'[v_{\mathcal{D}}/r]$ of type $\mathtt{prop}$. The following theorem characterizes satisfaction of φ' in terms of the operational behaviour of this expression. It uses the *solution set* of φ' (with respect to a set of variables $\vec{x}$ containing those free in φ'): this is defined to be the set $solns(\varphi')$ of constraints $\exists \vec{x}'(\vec{c})$ such that $\exists \vec{x}(\mathsf{T}; id; \varphi'[v_{\mathcal{D}}/r]) \to \cdots \to \exists \vec{x}, \vec{x}'(\vec{c}; id; \mathsf{T})$ and $\emptyset \models \exists \vec{x}, \vec{x}'(\vec{c})$.

Theorem 5.1. *For any formula φ' and valuation V we have:*

Soundness: *if $\exists \vec{x}'(\vec{c}) \in solns(\varphi')$ and $V \models \exists \vec{x}'(\vec{c})$ then $([\![\mathcal{D}]\!], V) \models \varphi'$.*
Completeness: *if $([\![\mathcal{D}]\!], V) \models \varphi'$ then there is $\exists \vec{x}'(\vec{c}) \in solns(\varphi')$ with $V \models \exists \vec{x}'(\vec{c})$.*

Proof. The theorem can be deduced using standard techniques from constraint logic programming (CLP) [15, Sect. 4.4 and 4.5]. This is because one can prove that αML's operational semantics agrees with the semantics of CLP goal states $\langle \varphi, \varphi_1, \ldots, \varphi_n \mid \bar{c} \rangle$ if the latter are encoded as αML configurations of the form $\exists \vec{x}(\bar{c}; s_{\varphi_n, \ldots, \varphi_1}; \varphi)$, where the frame stack $s_{\varphi_n, \ldots, \varphi_1}$ is defined by: $s_\emptyset \triangleq id$ and $s_{\vec{\varphi}, \varphi} \triangleq s_{\vec{\varphi}} \circ (x. \varphi)$ (where $x \notin FV(\varphi)$). $\qquad\square$

Definition 5.2 (success). We say that a configuration $\exists \vec{x}(\bar{c}; s; e) : \mathtt{prop}$ *may succeed* and write $\exists \vec{x}(\bar{c}; s; e)\downarrow$ if there is a finite sequence of transitions from $\exists \vec{x}(\bar{c}; s; e)$ to a configuration of the form $\exists \vec{x}, \vec{x}'(\bar{c}'; id; \mathsf{T})$, for some $\vec{x}'$ and $\bar{c}'$ with $\emptyset \models \exists \vec{x}, \vec{x}'(\bar{c}')$.

We can use Theorem 5.1 to deduce that the operational semantics of $v_{\mathcal{D}} : A_r \to \mathtt{prop}$ in αML detects, through the above notion of success, all and only the α-trees $t \in \alpha\text{-}Tree(A_r)$ lying in the inductively defined subset $[\![\mathcal{D}]\!]$ (Definition 2.5). To do so, we first have to discuss how αML represents α-trees, since they involve concrete names $n \in Name(N)$ whereas αML follows the common practice (Remark 2.2(b)) of only using variables of name sort, $x \in Var(N)$. What matters about names when they are used to describe binding structure is not their particular identity, but rather the *distinctions* between them—and those can be expressed using constraints asserting that all the variables in a list $\vec{x} = x_1, \ldots, x_k$ are distinct:

$$\#_{\vec{x}} \triangleq \underset{1 \le i < j \le k}{\&} x_i \# x_j.$$

A valuation V with domain $\vec{x}$ satisfies $\#_{\vec{x}}$ iff $V(x_1), \ldots, V(x_k)$ are (α-equivalence classes of) mutually distinct names. We can represent a particular α-tree in αML by a pattern in the presence of such a constraint: if $t \in \alpha\text{-}Tree(A_r)$ is the α-equivalence class of a tree involving k distinct names (bound or free), we can find a pattern $p : A_r$ with k variables $\vec{x}$ of name sort and a valuation V with $t = [\![p]\!]_V$ and $V \models \#_{\vec{x}}$. Then taking φ' to be $\#_{\vec{x}} \& r(p)$ in Theorem 5.1 we get:

Corollary 5.3. *Let $\mathcal{D}$ be an α-inductive definition in standard form with associated αML function $v_{\mathcal{D}} : A_r \to \mathtt{prop}$. If $t \in \alpha\text{-}Tree(A_r)$ is represented as above by a pattern $p : A_r$ and a valuation V (with $dom(V) = \vec{x}$, the variables of p), then $t \in [\![\mathcal{D}]\!]$ iff $\exists \vec{x}(\#_{\vec{x}}; id; v_{\mathcal{D}}\, p)\downarrow$.* $\qquad\square$

6 Related and Future Work

A popular approach to executable operational semantics is to use *higher-order logic programming*, where binders in inductive definitions are represented via higher-order abstract syntax (HOAS): see Miller [19] for an overview. We think it is both useful and interesting to study executable operational semantics also using *functional logic programming* [14]. It has proved harder to integrate HOAS representations with functional programming: see [18] for a recent view on this. In any case, in the Introduction we advocated leaving the HOAS mainstream and pursuing a nominal approach, for reasons to do with name-aliasing. As far as we know the first such approach was Cheney and Urban's first-order logic programming language αProlog [7]. Our first attempt to combine αProlog's computational mechanism (resolution based on nominal unification [28]) with higher-order typed functional programming was influenced by the work on FreshML [26] and produced MLSOS [16]. Byrd and Friedman's αKanren [2] combines it with the untyped functional language Scheme. αProlog, MLSOS and αKanren allow the use of constants to name object-level bound entities. We argued in Remark 2.2(b) that such concrete names are never used in practice when specifying inductively defined relations. Moreover their use naturally leads to "equivariance" (that is, invariance under permutations of concrete names) becoming an explicit part of the meta-language's operational semantics [6], rather than just a useful meta-theoretic property of the semantics. By contrast, αML only uses *meta-variables* rather than constants to name object-level bound entities, plus freshness constraints on meta-variables when distinctions between names are needed. As well as being closer to informal practice, this approach leads both to a pleasingly simple design for αML's operational semantics (Fig. 3) and a correctness result (Corollary 5.3) that was lacking for MLSOS. Our design also avoids the use of explicit name-swapping; although this is a characteristic feature of nominal logic [23], nominal unification and αProlog, it is not needed from the point of view of a user specifying operational semantics in an executable meta-language.

The presence of unifiable meta-variables in binding position in αML patterns does mean that, as for Cheney's equivariant unification [4], our constraint satisfaction problem is NP-complete (Theorem 3.3). There are at least two different approaches to obtaining a practically useful implementation of αML that should be investigated. One approach is to identify restrictions on α-inductive definitions that do not limit their applicability for specifying operational semantics too much, but for which the associated α-tree constraint problems are in P rather than NP; cf. Cheney and Urban [7, Sect. 5.3]. Since degrees of "applicability for specifying operational semantics" are hard to pin down, perhaps a more attractive alternative is to stick with the general and conceptually simple form of α-inductive definitions used in this paper, but investigate transformations on α-tree constraint problems that allow the highly developed technology of SAT-solvers to be applied.

References

[1] Barendregt, H.P.: The Lambda Calculus: Its Syntax and Semantics. North-Holland, Amsterdam (1984) (revised edition)
[2] Byrd, W.E., Friedman, D.P.: alphaKanren: A fresh name in nominal logic programming. In: Proc. 2007 Workshop on Scheme and Functional Programming, number DIUL-RT-0701 in Université Laval Technical Reports, pp. 79–90 (2007)
[3] Calvès, C., Fernández, M.: Nominal matching and alpha-equivalence. In: Hodges, W., de Queiroz, R. (eds.) Logic, Language, Information and Computation. LNCS, vol. 5110, pp. 111–122. Springer, Heidelberg (2008)
[4] Cheney, J.: The complexity of equivariant unification. In: Díaz, J., Karhumäki, J., Lepistö, A., Sannella, D. (eds.) ICALP 2004. LNCS, vol. 3142, pp. 332–344. Springer, Heidelberg (2004)
[5] Cheney, J.: Nominal Logic Programming. PhD thesis, Cornell Univ. (2004)

[6] Cheney, J.: Equivariant unification. In: Giesl, J. (ed.) RTA 2005. LNCS, vol. 3467, pp. 74–89. Springer, Heidelberg (2005)

[7] Cheney, J., Urban, C.: Nominal logic programming. Trans. Prog. Lang. and Systems 30(5), 1–47 (2008)

[8] de Bruijn, N.G.: Lambda calculus notation with nameless dummies, a tool for automatic formula manipulation, with application to the Church-Rosser theorem. Indag. Math. 34, 381–392 (1972)

[9] Felleisen, M., Hieb, R.: The revised report on the syntactic theories of sequential control and state. Theoret. Comput. Science 103, 235–271 (1992)

[10] Flanagan, C., Sabry, A., Duba, B.F., Felleisen, M.: The essence of compiling with continuations. SIGPLAN Not. 28, 237–247 (1993)

[11] Gabbay, M.J.: Fresh logic: Proof-theory and semantics for FM and nominal techniques. J. Appl. Logic 5, 356–387 (2007)

[12] Gordon, A.D.: Operational equivalences for untyped and polymorphic object calculi. In: Gordon and Pitts [13], pp. 9–54

[13] Gordon, A.D., Pitts, A.M. (eds.): Higher Order Operational Techniques in Semantics. Cambridge University Press, Cambridge (1998)

[14] Hanus, M.: Multi-paradigm declarative languages. In: Dahl, V., Niemelä, I. (eds.) ICLP 2007. LNCS, vol. 4670, pp. 45–75. Springer, Heidelberg (2007)

[15] Jaffar, J., Maher, M., Marriott, K., Stuckey, P.: Semantics of constraint logic programming. J. Logic Programming 37, 1–46 (1998)

[16] Lakin, M.R., Pitts, A.M.: A metalanguage for structural operational semantics. In: Trends in Functional Programming, vol. 8, pp. 19–35. Intellect (2008)

[17] Lassen, S.B.: Relational reasoning about contexts. In: Gordon and Pitts [13], pp. 91–135

[18] Licata, D.R., Zeilberger, N., Harper, R.: Focusing on binding and computation. In: LICS 2008 Proceedings, pp. 241–252. IEEE Computer Society, Los Alamitos (2008)

[19] Miller, D.A.: Abstract syntax for variable binders: An overview. In: Palamidessi, C., Moniz Pereira, L., Lloyd, J.W., Dahl, V., Furbach, U., Kerber, M., Lau, K.-K., Sagiv, Y., Stuckey, P.J. (eds.) CL 2000. LNCS, vol. 1861, pp. 239–253. Springer, Heidelberg (2000)

[20] Milner, R., Tofte, M., Harper, R., MacQueen, D.: The Definition of Standard ML (Revised). MIT Press, Cambridge (1997)

[21] Pfenning, F., Elliott, C.: Higher-order abstract syntax. In: PLDI 1988 Proceedings, pp. 199–208. ACM Press, New York (1988)

[22] Pitts, A.M.: Operational semantics and program equivalence. In: Barthe, G., Dybjer, P., Pinto, L., Saraiva, J. (eds.) APPSEM 2000. LNCS, vol. 2395, pp. 378–412. Springer, Heidelberg (2002)

[23] Pitts, A.M.: Nominal logic, a first order theory of names and binding. Inf. and Comput. 186, 165–193 (2003)

[24] Pitts, A.M.: Alpha-structural recursion and induction. J. ACM 53, 459–506 (2006)

[25] Pitts, A.M., Shinwell, M.R.: Generative unbinding of names. Logical Methods in Comput. Science 4, 1–33 (2008)

[26] Shinwell, M.R., Pitts, A.M., Gabbay, M.J.: FreshML: Programming with binders made simple. In: ICFP 2003 Proceedings, pp. 263–274. ACM Press, New York (2003)

[27] Tolmach, A., Antoy, S.: A monadic semantics for core Curry. In: WFLP 2003 Proceedings. Electr. Notes in Theoret. Comp. Science, vol. 86(3), pp. 16–34. Elsevier, Amsterdam (2003)

[28] Urban, C., Pitts, A.M., Gabbay, M.J.: Nominal unification. Theoret. Comp. Science 323, 473–497 (2004)

Using Category Theory to Design Programming Languages

John C. Reynolds*

Computer Science Department, Carnegie Mellon University,
Pittsburgh, U.S.A.
john.reynolds@cs.cmu.edu

In a 1980 paper entitled "Using Category Theory to Design Conversions and Generic Operators", the author showed how the concepts of category theory can guide the design of a programming language to avoid anomalies in the interaction of implicit conversions and generic operators. He wrote:

> ... Our intention is not to use any deep theorems of category theory, but merely to employ the basic concepts of this field as organizing principles. This might appear as a desire to be concise at the expense of being esoteric. But in designing a programming language, the central problem is to organize a variety of concepts in a way which exhibits uniformity and generality. Substantial leverage can be gained in attacking this problem if these concepts can be defined concisely within a framework which has already proven its ability to impose uniformity and generality upon a wide variety of mathematics.

In this talk, we will revisit these ideas and generalize them to other aspects of language design. We intend to demonstrate that language design is an unusual form of applied mathematics, where one uses, rather than theorems, the underlying structural principles of a field such as category theory.

- We will review the treatment of implicit conversions and generic operators, in which the conversions are specified by a functor on the preorder of subtypes, and the operators are natural transformations.
- We will describe the treatment of side-effects as monads, where each side-effect-free type is mapped into the corresponding type with effects by a monadic functor.
- We will present the description of block structure by functor categories, which insures that the values of local variables do not escape from the block in which the variables are declared.

---

* Research supported in part by National Science Foundation Grant CCF-0541021.

G. Castagna (Ed.): ESOP 2009, LNCS 5502, pp. 62–63, 2009.

- If time permits, we will describe the treatment of type variables and polymorphism by PL-categories, where type expressions are described by a base category, and ordinary expressions by a functor from the base category to a category of (cartesian closed) categories.

In each case, we will show how desirable properties of a programming language can be enforced by using an appropriate categorial definition.

No prior knowledge of category theory will be assumed.

Modular Monad Transformers

Mauro Jaskelioff

Functional Programming Laboratory—University of Nottingham

Abstract. During the last two decades, monads have become an indispensable tool for structuring functional programs with computational effects. In this setting, the mathematical notion of a monad is extended with operations that allow programmers to manipulate these effects. When several effects are involved, monad transformers can be used to build up the required monad one effect at a time. Although this seems to be modularity nirvana, there is a catch: in addition to the construction of a monad, the effect-manipulating operations need to be lifted to the resulting monad. The traditional approach for lifting operations is non-modular and ad-hoc. We solve this problem with a principled technique for lifting operations that makes monad transformers truly modular.

1 Introduction

Since monads were introduced by Moggi [13,14] to model computational effects, they have proven to be extremely useful to structure functional programs [20,19,9]. Monads are usually accompanied with operations that manipulate the effects they model. For example, an exception monad may come with operations for throwing an exception and for handling it, and a state monad may come with operations for reading and updating the state. Consequently, the structure one is really working with is a monad and a set of operations associated to it.

In order to combine computational effects, one must combine monads. There are many ways of combining monads: distributive laws [2], coproduct of monads [11], and monad transformers [10,15,3]. However, these technologies fall short in combining monads with operations, as they only provide means to combine monads. Liang et al. [10] identified this problem more than a decade ago and proposed a workaround, which is not modular. In fact, they have to *lift* operations associated to a monad through a monad transformer in an ad-hoc manner, and therefore the number of liftings of operation grows like the product of the number of monad transformers and operations involved (see Section 3.)

More recently, Plotkin et al. [17,7] have proposed to look at monads induced by algebraic theories, and to address the problem of combining monads (and associated operations) as a problem of combining algebraic theories. Their approach works very smoothly, but can only deal with monads induced by algebraic theories (and lifting is limited to algebraic operations).

Of all the techniques for combining monads, monad transformers are the most popular among functional programmers, as they are easy to implement and capture all the desired combinations for standard effects[1]. We show that for

---

[1] We take as standard the monads and operations described in [10].

G. Castagna (Ed.): ESOP 2009, LNCS 5502, pp. 64–79, 2009.

monad transformers with a *functorial behaviour* there is a uniform definition of lifting for a class of operations, which includes (after some minor repackaging) all the operations described in [10]. The main contributions of this article are:

- Identifying a class of operations associated to a monad, called *algebraic $\hat{\Sigma}$-operations*, that are easy to lift along any *monad morphism* (Section 4).
- Showing that all $\hat{\Sigma}$-operations for a monad can be lifted (through any *functorial monad transformer*) by interpreting them as algebraic $\hat{\Sigma}$-operations for a related monad (Section 5).
- Comparing our uniform lifting to more ad-hoc liftings found in the literature or in Haskell's libraries. This has revealed a mismatch with one definition in Haskell's monad transformer library (as discussed in Section 4).

Our approach extends both the traditional monad transformer approach [10] with the addition of uniform liftings, and the algebraic approach [7], since algebraic operations are a special case of algebraic $\hat{\Sigma}$-operations.

Remark 1. This article is aimed at researchers and programmers interested in using monads to structure functional programs with computational effects. Formally we work with system $F\omega$. In examples and remarks we may freely use extensions of $F\omega$ or idioms that are customary in functional languages.

Much of the terminology we introduce is borrowed from Category Theory. Usually, there is not an exact correspondence between category-theoretic notions and their formalization in a calculus. For instance, monads expressible in the simple typed lambda calculus correspond to strong monads in a CCC [14]. In what follows, when we say *monad* we mean *expressible monad* in $F\omega$ (and similarly for other category-theoretic notions).

2   Preliminaries

We work with system $F\omega$ and its equational theory induced by $\beta\eta$-equivalence (for details, see [1,5]). One may replace $F\omega$ with a weaker system, like HML [6] (which distinguishes types from type schemas), or a stronger system, like CC [4]. To fix the notation, we recall the syntax of $F\omega$

$$
\begin{array}{ll}
\text{kinds} & k ::= * \mid k \to k \\
\text{type constuctors} & U ::= X \mid U \to U \mid \forall X : k.\, U \mid \Lambda X : k.\, U \mid U\, U \\
\text{terms} & e ::= x \mid \lambda x : X.\, e \mid \Lambda X : k.\, e \mid e\, U
\end{array}
$$

We write e_U for $e\,U$ (polymorphic instantiation) and we often write definitions $g_X(x : A) \stackrel{\wedge}{=} t$ when we mean $g \stackrel{\wedge}{=} \forall X : *.\, \lambda x : A.\, t$. We often write term application using a tuple, that is, we write $t\,(z_1, \ldots, z_n)$ for $t\, z_1\, \ldots\, z_n$.

Following [18] we express in the setting of $F\omega$ several category-theoretic notions, such as functors, natural transformations, monads, monad transformers. Familiarity with these notions is not needed to understand the rest of the paper, but interested readers may want to look at [16,3].

Definition 2 (Functor [18]). *The set* **Functor** *of functors consists of pairs* $\hat{F} = (F, \mathsf{map}^F)$, *where* $F : * \to *$ *is a type constructor and*

$$\mathsf{map}^F : \mathsf{Map}(F) \triangleq \forall X, Y : *. \ (X \to Y) \to FX \to FY$$

is a term such that for all $f : A \to B$ *and* $g : B \to C$

$$\mathsf{map}^F_{A,A} \ \mathsf{id}_A = \mathsf{id}_{FA} \tag{1}$$

$$\mathsf{map}^F_{A,C} \ (g \cdot f) = \mathsf{map}^F_{B,C} \ g \cdot \mathsf{map}^F_{A,B} \ f \tag{2}$$

where, $\mathsf{id} \triangleq \Lambda X : *. \ \lambda x : X. \ x$ *and* $g \cdot f$ *is function composition* $\lambda x : A.g(f \ x)$.
The composite functor $\hat{F} \circ \hat{G}$ *is the pair* $(F \cdot G, \mathsf{map})$ *where*

$$\mathsf{map}_{A,B} \ (f : A \to B) \triangleq \mathsf{map}^F_{GA,GB}(\mathsf{map}^G_{A,B}f).$$

Definition 3 (Natural Transformation). *Given two functors* $\hat{F}$ *and* $\hat{G}$, *the set* **Nat**$(\hat{F}, \hat{G})$ *of natural transformations from* $\hat{F}$ *to* $\hat{G}$ *consists of terms* $\tau : F \overset{\bullet}{\to} G \triangleq \forall X : *. \ FX \to GX$, *such that for all* $f : A \to B$

$$\mathsf{map}^G_{A,B} \ f \cdot \tau_A \ = \ \tau_B \cdot \mathsf{map}^F_{A,B} \ f \tag{3}$$

The term $\iota \triangleq \Lambda(M : * \to *)(X : *). \ \lambda m : MX. \ m$ *is the identity natural transformation,* $\sigma \circ \tau \triangleq \Lambda X : *. \ \sigma_X \cdot \tau_X$ *is composition of natural transformations, and* $\hat{\Sigma}(\tau : F \overset{\bullet}{\to} G) : \Sigma \cdot F \overset{\bullet}{\to} \Sigma \cdot G \triangleq \Lambda X : *. \ \mathsf{map}^\Sigma_{FX,GX}(\tau_X)$ *is the application of a functor* $\hat{\Sigma}$ *to a natural transformation* τ *from* $\hat{F}$ *to* $\hat{G}$.

Definition 4 (Monad). *The set* **Monad** *of monads consists of triples* $\hat{M} = (M, \mathsf{ret}^M, \mathsf{bind}^M)$, *where* $M : * \to *$ *is a type constructor and*

$$\mathsf{ret}^M : \mathsf{Ret}(M) = \forall X : *. \ X \to MX$$

$$\mathsf{bind}^M : \mathsf{Bind}(M) = \forall X, Y : *. \ MX \to (X \to MY) \to MY$$

are terms such that for every $a : A$, $f : A \to MB$, $m : MA$ *and* $g : B \to MC$:

$$\mathsf{bind}^M_{A,B}(\mathsf{ret}^M_A \ a, f) \ = \ f \ a \tag{4}$$

$$\mathsf{bind}^M_{A,A}(m, \mathsf{ret}^M_A) \ = \ m \tag{5}$$

$$\mathsf{bind}^M_{A,C}(m, \lambda a : A. \ \mathsf{bind}^M_{B,C}(f \ a, g)) \ = \ \mathsf{bind}^M_{B,C}(\mathsf{bind}^M_{A,B}(m, f), g) \tag{6}$$

Every monad $\hat{M} = (M, \mathsf{ret}^M, \mathsf{bind}^M)$ *has an underlying functor* (M, map^M), *denoted by* $\check{M}$, *where* $\mathsf{map}^M_{A,B} \ (f : A \to B) \ (m : MA) \triangleq \mathsf{bind}^M_{A,B}(m, \mathsf{ret}^M_B \cdot f)$.

Example 5 (State Monad). The monad for modelling side-effects on a state of type S is $\hat{S} = (S, \mathsf{ret}^S, \mathsf{bind}^S)$, where $S \ (X : *) \triangleq S \to X \times S$ and

$$\mathsf{ret}^S_X(x : X) : S \ X \triangleq \lambda s : S. \ (x, s)$$
$$\mathsf{bind}^S_{X,Y}(m : S \ X, f : X \to S \ Y) : S \ Y \triangleq \lambda s : S. \ \mathsf{let} \ (a, s') = m \ s \ \mathsf{in} \ f \ a \ s'$$

Intuitively, a computation SX takes an initial state and produces a value of type X and a final state, ret^S does not change the state, and bind^S threads the state. A simple calculation shows that equations 4–6 hold. $\qquad\square$

Example 6 (Continuation Monad). The monad for modelling continuations of result type R is $\hat{\mathsf{C}} = (\mathsf{C}, \mathsf{ret}^{\mathsf{C}}, \mathsf{bind}^{\mathsf{C}})$, where $\mathsf{C}(X : *) \triangleq (X \to R) \to R$ and

$$\mathsf{ret}^{\mathsf{C}}_X (x : X) : \mathsf{C}X \triangleq \lambda k : X \to R.\ k\,x$$

$$\mathsf{bind}^{\mathsf{C}}_{X,Y}(m : \mathsf{C}X, f : X \to \mathsf{C}Y) : \mathsf{C}Y \triangleq \lambda k : Y \to R.\ m\,(\lambda x : X.\ f\,x\,k)$$

Intuitively, $\mathsf{C}X$ is a computation that given a continuation $X \to R$ returns a result in R, $\mathsf{ret}^{\mathsf{C}}$ simply runs a continuation, and $\mathsf{bind}^{\mathsf{C}}(m, f)$ runs m with a continuation constructed by running f in the current continuation. □

Definition 7 (Monad Morphism). *Given two monads $\hat{M}$ and $\hat{N}$, the set* $\mathbf{MM}(\hat{M}, \hat{N})$ *of* monad morphisms *from $\hat{M}$ to $\hat{N}$ consists of terms $\xi : M \overset{\cdot}{\to} N$, such that for every $a : A$, $m : MA$ and $f : A \to MB$*

$$\mathsf{ret}^N_A\,a\ =\ \xi_A(\mathsf{ret}^M_A\,a) \tag{7}$$

$$\xi_B(\mathsf{bind}^M_{A,B}(m, f))\ =\ \mathsf{bind}^N_{A,B}(\xi_A\,m, \xi_B \cdot f) \tag{8}$$

Remark 8. A simple consequence of equations 7–8 is that a monad morphism is also a natural transformation between the underlying functors.

In order to combine effects, instead of writing a monad from scratch, one can add more effects to a pre-existing monad using monad transformers.

Definition 9 (Monad Transformer). *The set* $\mathbf{MT}$ *of* monad transformers *consists of tuples $\hat{T} = (T, \mathsf{ret}^T, \mathsf{bind}^T, \mathsf{lift}^T)$, where $T : (* \to *) \to (* \to *)$ and*

$$\mathsf{ret}^T : \forall M : * \to *.\ \mathsf{Ret}(M) \to \mathsf{Bind}(M) \to \mathsf{Ret}(TM)$$

$$\mathsf{bind}^T : \forall M : * \to *.\ \mathsf{Ret}(M) \to \mathsf{Bind}(M) \to \mathsf{Bind}(TM)$$

$$\mathsf{lift}^T : \forall M : * \to *.\ \mathsf{Ret}(M) \to \mathsf{Bind}(M) \to \forall X : *.\ MX \to TMX$$

are terms such that for every monad $\hat{M}$, the tuple $\hat{T}\hat{M} \triangleq (TM, \mathsf{ret}^T_{\hat{M}}, \mathsf{bind}^T_{\hat{M}})$ is a monad and $\mathsf{lift}^T_{\hat{M}}$ is a monad morphism from $\hat{M}$ to $\hat{T}\hat{M}$, where

$$\mathsf{ret}^T_{\hat{M}} \triangleq \mathsf{ret}^T_M(\mathsf{ret}^M, \mathsf{bind}^M),\ \ \mathsf{bind}^T_{\hat{M}} \triangleq \mathsf{bind}^T_M(\mathsf{ret}^M, \mathsf{bind}^M),$$

$$\mathsf{lift}^T_{\hat{M}} \triangleq \mathsf{lift}^T_M(\mathsf{ret}^M, \mathsf{bind}^M).$$

From now on we will drop type information of kind $*$ from examples, in order to make them more readable.

Example 10. The state monad transformer $\hat{\mathcal{S}} = (\mathcal{S}, \mathsf{ret}^{\mathcal{S}}, \mathsf{bind}^{\mathcal{S}}, \mathsf{lift}^{\mathcal{S}})$ adds side-effects to an existing monad, where $\mathcal{S}(M : * \to *)(X : *) \triangleq S \to M(X \times S)$, and

$$\mathsf{ret}^{\mathcal{S}}_{\hat{M}}(x : X) : \mathcal{S}MX \triangleq \lambda s.\ \mathsf{ret}^M(x, s)$$

$$\mathsf{bind}^{\mathcal{S}}_{\hat{M}}(t : \mathcal{S}MX, f : X \to \mathcal{S}MY) : \mathcal{S}MY \triangleq \lambda s.\ \mathsf{bind}^M(t\,s, \lambda(x, s').\ f\,x\,s')$$

$$\mathsf{lift}^{\mathcal{S}}_{\hat{M}}(m : MX) : \mathcal{S}MX \triangleq \lambda s.\ \mathsf{bind}^M(m, \lambda x.\ \mathsf{ret}^M(x, s))$$

A simple calculation shows that equations 4–6 hold for $\hat{\mathcal{S}}\hat{M}$ and equations 7–8 hold for $\mathsf{lift}^{\mathcal{S}}_{\hat{M}}$, whenever equations 4–6 hold for $\hat{M}$. □

Example 11. The exception monad transformer $\hat{\mathcal{X}} = (\mathcal{X}, \mathsf{ret}^{\mathcal{X}}, \mathsf{bind}^{\mathcal{X}}, \mathsf{lift}^{\mathcal{X}})$ adds exceptions to an existing monad, where $\mathcal{X}(M : * \to *)(X : *) \,\hat{=}\, M(Z + X)$ (here Z is the type of exceptions), and

$$\mathsf{ret}^{\mathcal{X}}_{\hat{M}}(x : X) : \mathcal{X}MX \,\hat{=}\, \mathsf{ret}^{M}(\mathsf{inr}\, x)$$

$$\mathsf{bind}^{\mathcal{X}}_{\hat{M}}(t : \mathcal{X}MX, f : X \to \mathcal{X}MY) : \mathcal{X}MY \,\hat{=}\,$$
$$\mathsf{bind}^{M}(t, \lambda c.\, \mathsf{case}\ c\ \mathsf{of}\ \mid \mathsf{inl}\, z \Rightarrow \mathsf{ret}^{M}(\mathsf{inl}\, z)$$
$$\mid \mathsf{inr}\, x \Rightarrow f\, x)$$

$$\mathsf{lift}^{\mathcal{X}}_{\hat{M}}(m : MX) : \mathcal{X}MX \,\hat{=}\, \mathsf{bind}^{M}(m, \mathsf{ret}^{\mathcal{X}}_{\hat{M}}\, x)$$

A simple calculation shows that equations 4–6 hold for $\hat{\mathcal{X}}\hat{M}$ and equations 7–8 hold for $\mathsf{lift}^{\mathcal{X}}_{\hat{M}}$ whenever equations 4–6 hold for $\hat{M}$.   □

3   Operations and Lifting

We seek a general technique for lifting operations associated to a monad $\hat{M}$ to another monad $\hat{N}$. In this section we make precise what kind of operations our technique will be able to handle, and what lifting means.

Definition 12 ($\hat{\Sigma}$-operation). *If $\hat{\Sigma}$ is a functor and $\hat{M}$ is a monad, then a $\hat{\Sigma}$-operation for $\hat{M}$ is a natural transformation* op *in* $\mathbf{Nat}(\hat{\Sigma} \circ \hat{M}, \hat{M})$.

Example 13. The standard operations for the state monad are

$$\mathsf{get}\,(k : S \to SX) : SX \,\hat{=}\, \lambda s.\, k\, s\, s$$
$$\mathsf{set}\,(s : S, m : SX) : SX \,\hat{=}\, \lambda\_.\, m\, s.$$

The operation get applies the current state to its argument, and set sets runs a stateful computation in the provided state. They are $\hat{\Sigma}$-operations for the following functors

$$\Sigma^{\mathsf{get}}X \,\hat{=}\, S \to X \qquad \mathsf{map}^{\Sigma^{\mathsf{get}}}(f : X \to Y, t : \Sigma^{\mathsf{get}}X) : \Sigma^{\mathsf{get}}Y \,\hat{=}\, \lambda s.\, f\,(t\, s)$$
$$\Sigma^{\mathsf{set}}X \,\hat{=}\, S \times X \qquad \mathsf{map}^{\Sigma^{\mathsf{set}}}(f : X \to Y, (s, x) : \Sigma^{\mathsf{set}}X) : \Sigma^{\mathsf{set}}Y \,\hat{=}\, (s, f\, x).$$

In Fig. 1, we show some $\hat{\Sigma}$-operations (all the monads and $\hat{\Sigma}$-operations are presented along the paper, except for the list monad and its operations for which the reader may consult [19]). Interestingly, all the operations considered in [10] for these monads are *definable* in terms of $\hat{\Sigma}$-operations. For example, we can use the $\hat{\Sigma}$-operations in Example 13 to define the more usual operations

$$\underline{\mathsf{get}} : \mathsf{S}\, S \,\hat{=}\, \mathsf{get}_S(\mathsf{ret}^{\mathsf{S}}_S) = \lambda s.\, (s, s)$$
$$\underline{\mathsf{set}} : S \to \mathsf{S}\, \mathbf{1} \,\hat{=}\, \lambda s.\, \mathsf{set}_1(s, \mathsf{ret}^{\mathsf{S}}_1(\bullet)) = \lambda s\ s'.\, (\bullet, s)$$

where $\bullet$ is the sole inhabitant of the unit type $\mathbf{1}$. In the same manner, we can define

$$\underline{\mathsf{ask}} : \mathsf{R}\, E \,\hat{=}\, \mathsf{ask}_E(\mathsf{ret}^{\mathsf{R}}_E) = \lambda e.\, e$$

for the environment monad, and

Monad	Signature	$\hat{\Sigma}$-operations
List $LX \triangleq [X]$	$\Sigma^{\mathrm{empty}} X \triangleq 1$ $\Sigma^{\mathrm{append}} X \triangleq X \times X$	$\mathrm{empty}_X : 1 \to LX$ $\mathrm{append}_X : LX \times LX \to LX$
Output $OX \triangleq X \times [A]$	$\Sigma^{\mathrm{output}} X \triangleq [A] \times X$ $\Sigma^{\mathrm{flush}} X \triangleq X$	$\mathrm{output}_X : [A] \times OX \to OX$ $\mathrm{flush}_X : OX \to OX$
State $SX \triangleq S \to X \times S$	$\Sigma^{\mathrm{get}} X \triangleq S \to X$ $\Sigma^{\mathrm{set}} X \triangleq S \times X$	$\mathrm{get}_X : (S \to SX) \to SX$ $\mathrm{set}_X : S \times SX \to SX$
Environment $RX \triangleq E \to X$	$\Sigma^{\mathrm{ask}} X \triangleq E \to X$ $\Sigma^{\mathrm{local}} X \triangleq (E \to E) \times X$	$\mathrm{ask}_X : (E \to RX) \to RX$ $\mathrm{local}_X : (E \to E) \times RX \to RX$
Exception $XX \triangleq Z + X$	$\Sigma^{\mathrm{throw}} X \triangleq 1$ $\Sigma^{\mathrm{handle}} X \triangleq X \times (Z \to X)$	$\mathrm{throw}_X : 1 \to XX$ $\mathrm{handle}_X : XX \times (Z \to XX) \to XX$
Continuation $CX \triangleq (X \to R) \to R$	$\Sigma^{\mathrm{abort}} X \triangleq R$ $\Sigma^{\mathrm{callcc}} X \triangleq (X \to R) \to X$	$\mathrm{abort}_X : R \to CX$ $\mathrm{callcc}_X : ((CX \to R) \to CX) \to CX$

Fig. 1. $\hat{\Sigma}$-operations for the standard monads

$$\underline{\mathrm{output}} : [A] \to O1 \triangleq \lambda w.\, \mathrm{output}_1(w, \mathrm{ret}_1^O(\bullet)) = \lambda w.\, (\bullet, w)$$

for the output monad. The usual call-with-current-continuation $\underline{\mathrm{callcc}}$ and the $\hat{\Sigma}$-operation callcc are defined as:

$$\underline{\mathrm{callcc}}\,(f : (X \to CY) \to CX) : CX \triangleq \lambda k.\, f\,(\lambda x \_.\, k\,x)\,k$$
$$\mathrm{callcc}\,(f : (CX \to R) \to CX) : CX \triangleq \lambda k.\, f\,(\lambda m.\, m\,k)\,k$$

The operation $\underline{\mathrm{callcc}}$ can be defined from callcc as:

$$\underline{\mathrm{callcc}}\, f \triangleq \mathrm{callcc}\,(\lambda k.\, f\,(\lambda x \_.\, k\,(\mathrm{ret}^C x))) \tag{9}$$

Definition 14 (Lifting). *Let* op *be a* $\hat{\Sigma}$-operation *for* $\hat{M}$ *and* ξ *be a monad morphism from* $\hat{M}$ *to* $\hat{N}$. *A lifting of* op *to* $\hat{N}$ *along* ξ *is a* $\hat{\Sigma}$-operation op^N *for* $\hat{N}$ *such that for all* $X : *$,

$$\xi_X \cdot \mathrm{op}_X = \mathrm{op}_X^N \cdot (\mathrm{map}_{MX,NX}^{\Sigma}\, \xi_X) \tag{10}$$

or equivalently, such that the following diagram commutes:

$$
\begin{array}{ccc}
\Sigma(NX) & \xrightarrow{\mathrm{op}_X^N} & NX \\
\big\uparrow{\scriptstyle \mathrm{map}^{\Sigma}\xi_X} & & \big\uparrow{\scriptstyle \xi_X} \\
\Sigma(MX) & \xrightarrow{\mathrm{op}_X} & MX
\end{array}
$$

This definition can be specialised to the case of a monad transformer $\hat{T}$ by taking $\hat{N} \triangleq \hat{T}\hat{M}$ and $\xi \triangleq \mathrm{lift}_{\hat{M}}^T$. In this case we call op^N a lifting of op through $\hat{T}$.

In the absence of a general technique, the only way to lift an operation is to do it in an ad-hoc manner, for each monad transformer [10]. Although this works, the approach has significant shortcomings:

- The number of liftings grows like the product of the number of operations and monad transformers. This is clearly non-modular: adding a new monad transformer with some operations involves showing how to lift every existing operation through the new monad transformer, and showing how to lift the new operations through every existing monad transformer.
- Without a uniform definition of lifting, one could have different ad-hoc liftings of the same operation through a monad transformer, and no clear criteria to choose among them.
- There is no division of concerns: defining a lifting involves understanding the intended semantics of both the transformer and the operation.

We show that for well-behaved $\hat{\Sigma}$-operations, called algebraic, there is a unique way to lift them among a monad morphism. Moreover, for all $\hat{\Sigma}$-operations (not necessarily algebraic) there is a uniform way to lift them through a wide class of monad transformers, called functorial monad transformers.

4   Unique Lifting of Algebraic Operations

We characterize operations that interact well with bind.

Definition 15 (Algebraic $\hat{\Sigma}$-operation). *A $\hat{\Sigma}$-operation* op *for $\hat{M}$ is algebraic provided that for every* $f : A \to MB$ *and* $t : \Sigma(MA)$

$$\mathsf{bind}^M_{A,B}(\mathsf{op}_A\, t, f) \;=\; \mathsf{op}_B(\mathsf{map}^\Sigma_{MA,MB}(\lambda m : MA.\ \mathsf{bind}^M_{A,B}(m, f))\, t) \quad (11)$$

or equivalently, that the following diagram commutes:

$$
\begin{array}{ccc}
\Sigma(MA) & \xrightarrow{\;\mathsf{op}_A\;} & MA \\
{\scriptstyle \mathsf{map}^\Sigma \mathsf{bind}^M(-,f)}\big\downarrow & & \big\downarrow {\scriptstyle \mathsf{bind}^M(-,f)} \\
\Sigma(MB) & \xrightarrow[\;\mathsf{op}_B\;]{} & MB
\end{array}
$$

Remark 16. The notion of algebraic operation given in [17] corresponds to algebraic $\hat{\Sigma}$-operations for functors $\hat{\Sigma}$ of the form $\Sigma X = A \times (B \to X)$.

As examples of algebraic $\hat{\Sigma}$-operations we have all the operations in Fig.1, except for flush, local and handle, for which equation 11 does not hold. Remarkably, callcc is an algebraic $\hat{\Sigma}$-operation despite not being algebraic in the sense of [17] and hence, not tractable in that approach. With our generalization, callcc is not only tractable, but also well-behaved.

The following proposition presents a bijection between algebraic operations and natural transformations of a particular type. It provides an alternative way of verifying that an operation is algebraic and it will play a crucial role in showing how to lift algebraic operations.

Proposition 17. *There is a bijection between algebraic $\hat{\Sigma}$-operations for $\hat{M}$ and natural transformations from Σ to $\hat{M}$ given by:*

$$\phi(\text{op}\colon \Sigma \cdot M \overset{\bullet}{\to} M)\colon (\Sigma \overset{\bullet}{\to} M) \doteq \Lambda X\colon *.\ \text{op}_X \cdot (\text{map}^{\Sigma}_{X,MX}\text{ret}^M_X)$$

$$\psi(\text{op}'\colon \Sigma \overset{\bullet}{\to} M)\colon \Sigma \cdot M \overset{\bullet}{\to} M \doteq \Lambda X\colon *.\ \text{join}^M_X \cdot \text{op}'_{MX}$$

where $\text{join}^M_X \doteq \lambda m\colon M(MX).\ \text{bind}^M_{MX,X}(m, \text{id}_{MX})\colon M(MX) \to MX$ *is the multiplication of $\hat{M}$. We call* op' *the natural transformation corresponding to the algebraic $\hat{\Sigma}$-operation* op.

Remark 18. When $\Sigma X = A \times (B \to X)$ there is a further bijection between algebraic $\hat{\Sigma}$-operations op for $\hat{M}$ and maps $\text{op}''\colon A \to MB$, namely

$$\text{op}''(a\colon A) \doteq \text{op}_B(a, \text{ret}^M_B).$$

Theorem 19 (Algebraic Lifting). *Given an algebraic $\hat{\Sigma}$-operation* op *for $\hat{M}$ and a monad morphism ξ from $\hat{M}$ to $\hat{N}$, define the term* $\text{op}^N\colon \Sigma \cdot N \overset{\bullet}{\to} N$ *as*

$$\text{op}^N_X \doteq \text{join}^N_X \cdot \xi_{NX} \cdot \text{op}_{NX} \cdot (\text{map}^{\Sigma}_{NX,M(NX)}\text{ret}^M_{NX})$$

op^N *is an algebraic $\hat{\Sigma}$-operation for $\hat{N}$ and a lifting of* op *along ξ. Moreover,* op^N *is the unique lifting of* op *which is algebraic.*

Proof. The operation op^N is a lifting since the following diagram commutes:

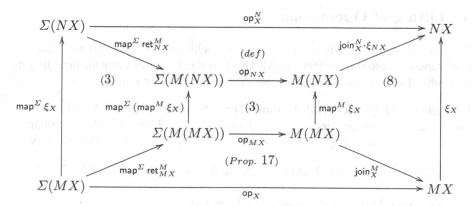

By Prop. 17, op^N is algebraic and, by the same proposition, it must be the unique lifting of op which is algebraic. $\square$

For example, when $\hat{N} = \hat{\mathcal{X}}\hat{S}$ and $\xi = \text{lift}^{\mathcal{X}}_{\hat{S}}$, thus $NX = S \to ((Z + X) \times S)$, then the algebraic lifting of the algebraic $\hat{\Sigma}$-operation get yields the operation

$$\text{get}^{\mathcal{X}}_X(k\colon S \to \mathcal{X}\text{S}X)\colon \mathcal{X}\text{S}X \doteq \lambda s.\, k\, s\, s.$$

Since callcc is an algebraic $\hat{\Sigma}$-operation, we can apply the algebraic lifting and obtain for every monad morphism ξ from C to $\hat{N}$ a lifted algebraic operation callcc^N: $\forall X : *.\ ((NX \to R) \to NX) \to NX$. For example, for $\hat{N} = \hat{S}\hat{C}$ and $\xi = \text{lift}^S_{\hat{C}}$, thus $NX = S \to ((X \times S) \to R) \to R$, then the operation simplifies to:

$$\text{callcc}^S\ (f : (SCX \to R) \to SCX):\ SCX = \lambda s\ k.\ f\ (\lambda m.\ m\ (s, k))\ s\ k.$$

We can define a lifted version of <u>callcc</u> in terms of callcc^S in the same manner as equation 9 and obtain:

$$\underline{\text{callcc}}^S\ (f : (X \to SCY) \to SCX):\ SCX = \lambda s\ k.\ f\ (\lambda x\ s'\ \_.\ k\ (x, s))\ s\ k.$$

The author has used the uniform lifting of callcc to verify the ad-hoc liftings of callcc in Haskell's monad transformer library (mtl). This verification revealed that the uniform lifting above coincided with all of the library's liftings, except for one: the library's lifting of callcc through the state monad transformer is not consistent with the rest of the liftings.[2] The ad-hoc lifting of callcc in mtl is:

$$\underline{\text{callcc}-\text{mtl}}^S\ (f : (X \to SCY) \to SCX):\ SCX = \lambda s\ k.\ f\ (\lambda x\ s'\ \_.\ k\ (x, s'))\ s\ k.$$

The difference is that the ad-hoc lifted operation preserves changes in the state produced during the construction of the new continuation even when the current continuation is used. However, all the other liftings of <u>callcc</u> in the library do not preserve produced effects when using the current continuation.

5   Lifting of Operations

We now show how to lift $\hat{\Sigma}$-operations. To achieve this, we need to refine the definition of monad transformer. All the standard monad transformers fit into this refined definition, except the monad transformer for continuations.

Definition 20 (Functorial Monad Transformer). *The set* **FMT** *of functorial monad transformers consists of tuples* $\hat{T} = (T, \text{ret}^T, \text{bind}^T, \text{lift}^T, \text{hmap}^T)$, *where the first four components give a monad transformer (see Def. 9), and*

$$\text{hmap}^T : \forall M, N : * \to *.\ \text{Map}(M) \to \text{Map}(N) \to (M \overset{\bullet}{\to} N) \to (TM \overset{\bullet}{\to} TN)$$

is a term such that for all monads $\hat{M}$, $\hat{N}$ *and* $\hat{P}$,

- hmap^T *preserves natural transformations and monad morphisms, i.e.*
  - $\tau : \mathbf{Nat}(\hat{M}, \hat{N})$ *implies* $\text{hmap}^T_{\hat{M}, \hat{N}}\ \tau : \mathbf{Nat}(\hat{T}\hat{M}, \hat{T}\hat{N})$
  - $\xi : \mathbf{MM}(\hat{M}, \hat{N})$ *implies* $\text{hmap}^T_{\hat{M}, \hat{N}}\ \xi : \mathbf{MM}(\hat{T}\hat{M}, \hat{T}\hat{N})$
- hmap^T *respects identities and composition of natural transformations, i.e.*
  - $\text{hmap}^T_{\hat{M}, \hat{M}}\ \iota_M = \iota_{TM}$

---

[2] In another monad transformer library by Iavor S. Diatchki, called MonadLib, all the liftings correspond to the uniform lifting obtained above.

- $\tau : \mathbf{Nat}(\hat{M}, \hat{N})$ and $\sigma : \mathbf{Nat}(\hat{N}, \hat{P})$ imply

$$(\mathsf{hmap}^T_{\hat{N},\hat{P}}\sigma) \circ (\mathsf{hmap}^T_{\hat{M},\hat{N}}\tau) = \mathsf{hmap}^T_{\hat{M},\hat{P}}(\sigma \circ \tau)$$

- lift^T is natural, i.e.

$$\tau : \mathbf{Nat}(\hat{M}, \hat{N}) \text{ implies } (\mathsf{hmap}^T_{\hat{M},\hat{N}}\tau)_X \cdot \mathsf{lift}^T_{\hat{M},X} = \mathsf{lift}^T_{\hat{N},X} \cdot \tau_X \qquad (12)$$

where $\mathsf{hmap}^T_{\hat{M},\hat{N}} \triangleq \mathsf{hmap}^T_{M,N}(\mathsf{map}^M, \mathsf{map}^N)$.

Example 21. The monad transformer $\hat{S}$ becomes functorial with hmap^S given by

$$\mathsf{hmap}^S_{\hat{F},\hat{G}}(\tau : F \overset{\bullet}{\to} G)(X:*)(t:SFX): SGX \triangleq \lambda s:S.\ \tau(t\,s)$$

Some tedious calculations show that it satisfies all the required properties.   □

Example 22. The monad transformer $\hat{\mathcal{X}}$ becomes functorial with $\mathsf{hmap}^{\mathcal{X}}$ given by

$$\mathsf{hmap}^{\mathcal{X}}_{\hat{F},\hat{G}}(\tau : F \overset{\bullet}{\to} G)(X:*)(t:\mathcal{X}FX): \mathcal{X}GX \triangleq \tau(t)$$

□

In order to lift $\hat{\Sigma}$-operations we will exploit impredicative polymorphism of system $F\omega$ to define a monad transformer $\mathcal{K}$ (which is not functorial) such that every $\hat{\Sigma}$-operation op for $\hat{M}$ induces an algebraic $\hat{\Sigma}$-operation $\mathsf{op}^{\mathcal{K}}$ for $\hat{\mathcal{K}M}$, and op can be recovered from $\mathsf{op}^{\mathcal{K}}$ by pre- and post-composition of $\mathsf{op}^{\mathcal{K}}$ with two natural transformations. The unique algebraic lifting allows to lift $\mathsf{op}^{\mathcal{K}}$ through any monad transformer $\hat{T}$, and obtain an algebraic $\hat{\Sigma}$-operation $\mathsf{op}^{\mathcal{K},T}$ for $\hat{T}(\hat{\mathcal{K}M})$. Finally, when $\hat{T}$ is functorial, one recovers from $\mathsf{op}^{\mathcal{K},T}$ a lifting of op through $\hat{T}$, in the same way as one recovers op from $\mathsf{op}^{\mathcal{K}}$.

Definition 23 (Codensity). $\hat{\mathcal{K}}$ is the monad transformer $(\mathcal{K}, \mathsf{ret}^{\mathcal{K}}, \mathsf{bind}^{\mathcal{K}}, \mathsf{lift}^{\mathcal{K}})$ such that for every monad $\hat{M}$

$$\mathcal{K}MX \triangleq \forall Y : *.\ (X \to MY) \to MY$$

$$\mathsf{ret}^{\mathcal{K}}_{\hat{M},X}(x:X): \mathcal{K}MX \triangleq \Lambda Y : *.\lambda k : X \to MY.\ k\,x$$

$$\mathsf{bind}^{\mathcal{K}}_{\hat{M},X,Y}(c:\mathcal{K}MX, f:X \to \mathcal{K}MY): \mathcal{K}MY \triangleq$$

$$\Lambda Z : *.\ \lambda k : Y \to MZ.\ c\,(\lambda x : X.\ (f\,x)_Z\,k)$$

$$\mathsf{lift}^{\mathcal{K}}_{\hat{M},X}(m:MX): \mathcal{K}MX \triangleq \Lambda Y : *.\lambda k : X \to MY.\mathsf{bind}^M_{X,Y}(m,k)$$

Remark 24. The monad transformer $\hat{\mathcal{K}}$ is related to the construction of the condensity monad for an endofunctor (see [12]). In what follows, we use only some properties of $\hat{\mathcal{K}}$, which are provable by simple calculations in system $F\omega$. Thus, we do not exploit in full the universal property of the codensity monad.

Definition 25. *Let $\hat{M}$ be a monad. Then, we define the terms*

$$\kappa(\tau \colon \Sigma \cdot M \overset{\bullet}{\to} M) \colon \Sigma \overset{\bullet}{\to} \mathcal{K}M \mathrel{\hat{=}} \Lambda X \colon *. \ \lambda s \colon \Sigma X.$$

$$\Lambda Y \colon *. \ \lambda k \colon X \to MY. \ \tau_Y(\mathrm{map}^{\Sigma} k\, s)$$

$$\mathrm{from}_{\hat{M}} \colon \mathcal{K}M \overset{\bullet}{\to} M \mathrel{\hat{=}} \Lambda X \colon *. \ \lambda c \colon \mathcal{K}MX. \ c_X\,(\mathrm{ret}^{M}_{X})$$

and for every $\hat{\Sigma}$-operation op *for $\hat{M}$ we define*

$$\mathrm{op}^{\mathcal{K}} \colon \Sigma \cdot \mathcal{K}M \overset{\bullet}{\to} \mathcal{K}M \mathrel{\hat{=}} \psi(\kappa\ \mathrm{op})$$

where ψ is defined in Prop. 17.

Proposition 26. *Given a monad $\hat{M}$ and a $\hat{\Sigma}$-operation* op *for $\hat{M}$, then*

a) $\mathrm{from}_{\hat{M}}$ *is a natural transformation from $\hat{\mathcal{K}}\hat{M}$ to $\hat{M}$ such that*

$$\iota_M = \mathrm{from}_{\hat{M}} \circ \mathrm{lift}^{\mathcal{K}}_{\hat{M}}$$

b) $\mathrm{op}^{\mathcal{K}}$ *is an algebraic $\hat{\Sigma}$-operation for $\hat{\mathcal{K}}\hat{M}$ such that*

$$\mathrm{op} = \mathrm{from}_{\hat{M}} \circ \mathrm{op}^{\mathcal{K}} \circ (\hat{\Sigma}\ \mathrm{lift}^{\mathcal{K}}_{\hat{M}}) \tag{13}$$

where ι and $\circ$ are the identity and composition of natural transformations, and $\hat{\Sigma}$ is the application of a functor to a natural transformation (see Definition 3).

Theorem 27 (Lifting). *Given a $\hat{\Sigma}$-operation* op *for a monad $\hat{M}$ and a functorial monad transformer $\hat{T}$, let* $\mathrm{op}^{T} \colon \Sigma \cdot (TM) \overset{\bullet}{\to} TM$ *be the term*

$$\mathrm{op}^{T} = (\mathrm{hmap}^{T}_{\hat{\mathcal{K}}\hat{M},\hat{M}}\mathrm{from}_{\hat{M}}) \circ \mathrm{op}^{\mathcal{K},T} \circ (\hat{\Sigma}(\mathrm{hmap}^{T}_{\hat{M},\hat{\mathcal{K}}\hat{M}}\mathrm{lift}^{\mathcal{K}}_{\hat{M}})) \tag{14}$$

where $\mathrm{op}^{\mathcal{K},T}$ *is the algebraic lifting of* $\mathrm{op}^{\mathcal{K}}$ *through $\hat{T}$, then* op^{T} *is a lifting of* op *through $\hat{T}$.*

Proof. The following diagram commutes:

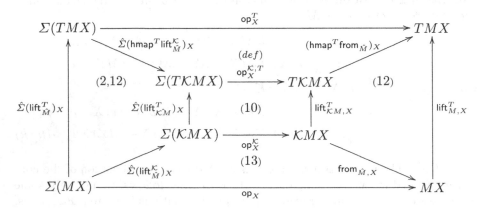

$\square$

When op is an algebraic $\hat{\Sigma}$-operation for $\hat{M}$, there is a simpler way to lift op through $\hat{T}$. The following result says that when both liftings are defined, they yield the same result.

Proposition 28. *If* op *is an algebraic $\hat{\Sigma}$-operation for $\hat{M}$ and $\hat{T}$ a functorial monad transformer, then the algebraic lifting of* op *along* lift^T_M *given by Theorem 19 coincides with the lifting of* op^T *given by Theorem 27.*

Example 29. We specialize the lifting in Theorem 27 to several concrete functorial monad transformers and an arbitrary $\hat{\Sigma}$-operation op for a monad $\hat{M}$.

- When $\hat{T} = \hat{S}$, thus $\mathcal{S}MX = S \to M(X \times S)$, the lifting simplifies to:

$$\mathsf{op}^{\mathcal{S}}_X (t : \Sigma(\mathcal{S}MX)) : \mathcal{S}MX = \lambda s.\, \mathsf{op}_{X \times S}(\mathsf{map}^{\Sigma} \tau^s\, t)$$

  where $\tau^s(f : S \to M(X \times S)) = f\, s$.
- When $\hat{T} = \hat{\mathcal{X}}$, thus $\mathcal{X}MX = M(Z + X)$, the lifting simplifies to:

$$\mathsf{op}^{\mathcal{X}}_X(t : \Sigma(\mathcal{X}MX)) : \mathcal{X}MX = \mathsf{op}_{Z+X}\, t.$$

- When $\hat{T}$ is $\hat{\mathcal{R}}$, the functorial monad transformer for environments of type E [10], thus $\mathcal{R}MX = E \to MX$, the lifting simplifies to:

$$\mathsf{op}^{\mathcal{R}}_X (t : \Sigma(\mathcal{R}MX)) : \mathcal{R}MX = \lambda e.\, \mathsf{op}_X(\mathsf{map}^{\Sigma} \tau^e\, t)$$

  where $\tau^e(f : E \to MX) = f\, e$.
- When $\hat{T}$ is $\hat{\mathcal{O}}$, the functorial monad transformer for output of type $[A]$ [10], thus $\mathcal{O}MX = M(X \times [A])$, and the lifting simplifies to:

$$\mathsf{op}^{\mathcal{O}}_X(t : \Sigma(\mathcal{O}MX)) : \mathcal{O}MX = \mathsf{op}_{X \times [A]}\, t.$$

$\square$

The example above shows that Theorem 27 subsumes the incremental approach in [15,3]. In the following, we apply the lifting theorem to the remaining non-algebraic operations local, handle, and flush. Because of Proposition 28, for algebraic operations it makes more sense to use the simpler algebraic lifting.

Example 30. The monad for environments of type E and its operations for reading the environment and performing a computation in a modified environment are shown below.

$$\mathsf{R}(X : *) \mathrel{\hat{=}} E \to X$$

$$\mathsf{ret}^{\mathsf{R}} (x : X) : \mathsf{R}X \mathrel{\hat{=}} \lambda_\_ .\, x$$

$$\mathsf{bind}^{\mathsf{R}}(m : \mathsf{R}X, f : X \to \mathsf{R}Y) : \mathsf{R}Y \mathrel{\hat{=}} \lambda e.\, f\,(m\,e)\,e$$

$$\mathsf{ask}\,(f : E \to \mathsf{R}X) : \mathsf{R}X \mathrel{\hat{=}} \lambda e.\, f\,e\,e$$

$$\mathsf{local}\,(f : E \to E, m : \mathsf{R}X) : \mathsf{R}X \mathrel{\hat{=}} \lambda e.\, m\,(f\,e)$$

Applying Theorem 27 to the non-algebraic, $\hat{\Sigma}$-operation local we obtain the following lifted operation for any functorial monad transformer $\hat{T}$:

$$\text{local}^T\,(f: E \to E, t: TRX): TRX \,\hat{=}\, \text{hmap}^T_{\mathcal{K}\hat{R},\hat{R}}\,\text{from}_{\hat{R}}\,(\text{local}^{\mathcal{K},T}(f,t'))$$

$$\text{where} \qquad t': T\mathcal{K}RX \,\hat{=}\, \text{hmap}^T_{\hat{R},\mathcal{K}\hat{R}}\,\text{lift}^{\mathcal{K}}_{\hat{R}}\,t$$

$$\text{local}^{\mathcal{K},T}\,(f: E \to E, t: T\mathcal{K}RX): T\mathcal{K}RX \,\hat{=}\, \text{join}^T_{\mathcal{K}\hat{R}}\,(\text{lift}^T_{\mathcal{K}\hat{R}}\,(\Lambda Y.\,\lambda k.\,\text{local}\,(f,k\,t)))$$

– When $\hat{T} = \hat{\mathcal{S}}$, thus $\mathcal{S}RX = S \to E \to (X \times S)$, the lifting simplifies to:

$$\text{local}^{\mathcal{S}}\,(f: E \to E, t: \mathcal{S}RX): \mathcal{S}RX = \lambda s\,e.\,t\,s\,(f\,e).$$

– When $\hat{T} = \hat{\mathcal{X}}$, thus $\mathcal{X}RX = E \to (Z + X)$, the lifting simplifies to:

$$\text{local}^{\mathcal{X}}\,(f: E \to E, t: \mathcal{X}RX): \mathcal{X}RX = \lambda e.\,t\,(f\,e).$$

– When $\hat{T} = \hat{\mathcal{R}}$, thus $\mathcal{R}RX = E \to E \to X$, the lifting simplifies to:

$$\text{local}^{\mathcal{R}}\,(f: E \to E, t: \mathcal{R}RX): \mathcal{R}RX = \lambda e\,e'.\,t\,e\,(f\,e')$$

– When $\hat{T} = \hat{\mathcal{O}}$, thus $\mathcal{O}MX = E \to (X \times [A])$, the lifting simplifies to:

$$\text{local}^{\mathcal{O}}\,(f: E \to E, t: \mathcal{O}RX): \mathcal{O}RX = \lambda e.\,t\,(f\,e)$$

$\square$

Note that we can arrive at the concrete liftings above—where both $\hat{T}$ and op are fixed—by either Example 29 (where we first fix $\hat{T}$) or the definition of local^T above (where we first fix op), but only by fixing the monad transformer we get a significant simplification of the lifting.

Example 31. The monad for exceptions of type Z and its operations for throwing and handling exceptions are shown below.

$$X(X:*) \,\hat{=}\, Z + X$$
$$\text{ret}^X(x: X): X\,X \,\hat{=}\, \text{inr}\,x$$
$$\text{bind}^X(m: X\,X, f: X \to X\,Y): X\,Y \,\hat{=}\, \text{case}\,m\,\text{of}\,|\,\text{inl}\,z \Rightarrow \text{inl}\,z\,|\,\text{inr}\,x \Rightarrow f\,x$$
$$\text{throw}\,(z: Z): X\,X \,\hat{=}\, \text{inl}\,z$$
$$\text{handle}\,(m: X\,X, h: Z \to X\,X): X\,X \,\hat{=}\, \text{case}\,m\,\text{of}\,|\,\text{inl}\,z \Rightarrow h\,z\,|\,\text{inr}\,x \Rightarrow \text{inr}\,x$$

We obtain the following liftings for the non-algebraic $\hat{\Sigma}$-operation handle.

– When $\hat{T} = \hat{\mathcal{S}}$, thus $\mathcal{S}XX = S \to Z + (X \times S)$, the lifting is:

$$\text{handle}^{\mathcal{S}}\,(t: \mathcal{S}XX, h: Z \to \mathcal{S}XX): \mathcal{S}XX = \lambda s.\,\text{case}\,t\,s\,\text{of}\,|\,\text{inl}\,z \Rightarrow h\,z\,s$$
$$|\,\text{inr}\,x \Rightarrow \text{inr}\,x$$

- When $\hat{T} = \hat{\mathcal{X}}$, thus $\mathcal{X}XX = Z + (Z + X)$, the lifting is:

$$\mathsf{handle}^{\mathcal{X}}(t\colon \mathcal{X}XX, h\colon Z \to \mathcal{X}XX)\colon \mathcal{X}XX = \mathsf{case}\ t\ \mathsf{of}\ |\ \mathsf{inl}\ z \Rightarrow h\ z$$
$$|\ \mathsf{inr}\ x \Rightarrow \mathsf{inr}\ x.$$

- When $\hat{T} = \hat{\mathcal{R}}$, thus $\mathcal{R}XX = E \to (Z + X)$, the lifting is:

$$\mathsf{handle}^{\mathcal{R}}(t\colon \mathcal{R}XX, h\colon Z \to \mathcal{R}XX)\colon \mathcal{R}XX = \lambda e.\ \mathsf{case}\ t\ e\ \mathsf{of}\ |\ \mathsf{inl}\ z \Rightarrow h\ z\ e$$
$$|\ \mathsf{inr}\ x \Rightarrow \mathsf{inr}\ x$$

- When $\hat{T} = \hat{\mathcal{O}}$, thus $\mathcal{O}XX = Z + (X \times [A])$, the lifting is:

$$\mathsf{handle}^{\mathcal{O}}(t\colon \mathcal{O}XX, h\colon Z \to \mathcal{O}XX)\colon \mathcal{O}XX = \mathsf{case}\ t\ \mathsf{of}\ |\ \mathsf{inl}\ z \Rightarrow h\ z$$
$$|\ \mathsf{inr}\ x \Rightarrow \mathsf{inr}\ x.$$

$\square$

Example 32. The monad for output of a type $[A]$ and its operations for outputting a list, and flushing the output are shown below.

$$\mathsf{O}\,(X\colon *) \triangleq X \times [A]$$
$$\mathsf{ret}^{\mathsf{O}}\,(x\colon X)\colon \mathsf{O}X \triangleq (x, \mathsf{empty}(\bullet))$$
$$\mathsf{bind}^{\mathsf{O}}(m\colon \mathsf{O}X, f\colon X \to \mathsf{O}Y)\colon \mathsf{O}X \triangleq \mathsf{let}\ (x, w) = m\ \mathsf{in}$$
$$\mathsf{let}\ (x', w') = f\ x\ \mathsf{in}\ (x', \mathsf{append}(w, w'))$$
$$\mathsf{output}\,(\,(w, m) : W \times \mathsf{O}X)\colon \mathsf{O}X \triangleq \mathsf{let}\ (x, w') = m\ \mathsf{in}\ (x, \mathsf{append}(w', w))$$
$$\mathsf{flush}\,(m\colon \mathsf{O}X)\colon \mathsf{O}X \triangleq \mathsf{let}\ (x, \_) = m\ \mathsf{in}\ (x, \mathsf{empty}(\bullet))$$

where $\mathsf{empty}(\bullet)$ is the empty list, and append appends two lists. We obtain the following liftings for the non-algebraic $\hat{\Sigma}$-operation flush.

- When $\hat{T} = \hat{\mathcal{S}}$, thus $\mathcal{S}OX = S \to ((X \times S) \times [A])$, the lifting is:

$$\mathsf{flush}^{\mathcal{S}}\,(t\colon \mathcal{S}OX)\colon \mathcal{S}OX = \lambda s.\ \mathsf{let}\ (x, \_) = t\ s\ \mathsf{in}\ (x, \mathsf{empty}(\bullet))$$

- When $\hat{T} = \hat{\mathcal{X}}$, thus $\mathcal{X}OX = (Z + X) \times [A]$, the lifting is:

$$\mathsf{flush}^{\mathcal{X}}\,((c, w)\colon \mathcal{X}OX, h\colon Z \to \mathcal{X}OX)\colon \mathcal{X}OX = (c, \mathsf{empty}(\bullet))$$

- When $\hat{T} = \hat{\mathcal{R}}$, thus $\mathcal{R}OX = E \to (X \times [A])$, the lifting is:

$$\mathsf{flush}^{\mathcal{R}}\,(t\colon \mathcal{R}OX)\colon \mathcal{R}OX = \lambda e.\ \mathsf{let}\ (x, \_) = t\ e\ \mathsf{in}\ (x, \mathsf{empty}(\bullet))$$

- When $\hat{T} = \hat{\mathcal{O}}$, thus $\mathcal{O}OX = (X \times [A]) \times [A]$, the lifting is:

$$\mathsf{flush}^{\mathcal{O}}\,((p, w)\colon \mathcal{O}OX, h\colon Z \to \mathcal{O}OX)\colon \mathcal{O}OX = (p, \mathsf{empty}(\bullet))$$

$\square$

6   Conclusion

Monad transformers allow programmers to modularly construct a monad, but for their potential to be fully realized, the lifting of operations should also be modular. We have defined a uniform lifting through any monad transformer with a *functorial behaviour*. This lifting is applicable to a wide class of operations which includes all operations considered in [10] and all the operations in Haskell's mtl, except for listen. Through several examples, we have given evidence that our uniform lifting subsumes the more or less ad-hoc definitions of lifting that could be found in the literature.

Our initial focus on algebraic operations is inspired by Plotkin et al. [7], where a monad is constructed from an algebraic theory presented by algebraic operations and equations, and combined monads are obtained by combination of theories. This approach is appealing, but it can cope only with monads corresponding to algebraic theories and with algebraic operations.

The current design of monad transformer libraries is based on the traditional approach to operation lifting which has other problems besides non-modularity. The experimental library Monatron [8] implements a new design which not only lifts operations uniformly, but also avoids many of these problems.

There are several possible directions for further research:

- The lifting of $\hat{\Sigma}$-operations assumes functorial monad transformers. In order to accomodate the continuation monad transformer, we plan to extend the results in the article to mixed-variant functorial monad transformers.
- Instead of assuming an operation $\Sigma \cdot M \overset{\bullet}{\to} M$, we can consider operations $HM \overset{\bullet}{\to} M$, where H is a functor in an endofunctor category. This allows us to model the mtl operation listen and obtain a lifting for it. However, in general, obtaining a lifting seems to depend on the operation inducing an algebraic $\hat{\Sigma}$-operation for another monad. General techniques for finding such a lifting need to be investigated.
- Given a $\hat{\Sigma}$-operation for $\hat{M}$, we can obtain its lifting through any functorial monad transformer. However, its general formulation is rather involved, and we would like to obtain a simpler lifting (perhaps under certain extra assumptions, as in Proposition 28).

Since the traditional non-modular solution for lifting operations through monad transformers was introduced, there has been little progress in this area. We hope that the new approach developed in this article leads to new and exciting ways of designing structured effectful functional programs.

Acknowledgments. I would like to thank Nils Anders Danielsson, Neil Ghani, Graham Hutton, Peter Morris, Wouter Swierstra, and the anonoymous referees for their detailed and insightful comments. Finally, I would like to specially thank Eugenio Moggi for his generous assistance in significantly improving this article.

References

1. Barendregt, H.: Lambda calculi with types. In: Abramsky, S., Gabbay, D.M., Maibaum, T.S.E. (eds.) Handbook of Logic in Computer Science, pp. 117–309. Oxford University Press, Oxford (1992)
2. Barr, M., Wells, C.: Toposes, Triples and Theories. Grundlehren der mathematischen Wissenschaften, vol. 278. Springer, New York (1985)
3. Benton, N., Hughes, J., Moggi, E.: Monads and effects. In: Barthe, G., Dybjer, P., Pinto, L., Saraiva, J. (eds.) APPSEM 2000. LNCS, vol. 2395, pp. 42–122. Springer, Heidelberg (2002)
4. Coquand, T., Huet, G.P.: The calculus of constructions. Inf. Comput. 76(2/3), 95–120 (1988)
5. Ghani, N.: Eta-expansions in F-omega. In: van Dalen, D., Bezem, M. (eds.) CSL 1996. LNCS, vol. 1258, pp. 182–197. Springer, Heidelberg (1997)
6. Harper, R., Mitchell, J.C., Moggi, E.: Higher-order modules and the phase distinction. In: POPL, pp. 341–354 (1990)
7. Hyland, M., Plotkin, G.D., Power, J.: Combining effects: Sum and tensor. Theor. Comput. Sci. 357(1-3), 70–99 (2006)
8. Jaskelioff, M.: Monatron: an extensible monad transformer library (submitted for publication) (2008), http://www.cs.nott.ac.uk/~mjj/pubs/monatron.pdf
9. Peyton Jones, S.L., Wadler, P.: Imperative functional programming. In: POPL, pp. 71–84 (1993)
10. Liang, S., Hudak, P., Jones, M.: Monad transformers and modular interpreters. In: POPL, pp. 333–343 (1995)
11. Lüth, C., Ghani, N.: Composing monads using coproducts. In: ICFP, pp. 133–144 (2002)
12. Mac Lane, S.: Categories for the Working Mathematician. Graduate Texts in Mathematics, vol. 5. Springer, Heidelberg (1971)
13. Moggi, E.: Computational lambda-calculus and monads. In: LICS, pp. 14–23. IEEE Computer Society, Los Alamitos (1989)
14. Moggi, E.: Notions of computation and monads. Information and Computation 93(1), 55–92 (1991)
15. Moggi, E.: Metalanguages and applications. In: Semantics and Logics of Computation. Publications of the Newton Institute. CUP (1997)
16. Pierce, B.C.: Basic Category Theory for Computer Scientists (Foundations of Computing). MIT Press, Cambridge (1991)
17. Plotkin, G.D., Power, J.: Semantics for algebraic operations. In: ENTCS, vol. 45 (2001)
18. Reynolds, J.C., Plotkin, G.D.: On functors expressible in the polymorphic typed lambda calculus. Inf. Comput. 105(1), 1–29 (1993)
19. Wadler, P.: Comprehending monads. MSCS 2(4), 461–493 (1992)
20. Wadler, P.: The essence of functional programming. In: POPL, pp. 1–14 (1992)

Handlers of Algebraic Effects

Gordon Plotkin* and Matija Pretnar**

Laboratory for Foundations of Computer Science,
School of Informatics, University of Edinburgh, Scotland

Abstract. We present an algebraic treatment of exception handlers and, more generally, introduce handlers for other computational effects representable by an algebraic theory. These include nondeterminism, interactive input/output, concurrency, state, time, and their combinations; in all cases the computation monad is the free-model monad of the theory. Each such handler corresponds to a model of the theory for the effects at hand. The handling construct, which applies a handler to a computation, is based on the one introduced by Benton and Kennedy, and is interpreted using the homomorphism induced by the universal property of the free model. This general construct can be used to describe previously unrelated concepts from both theory and practice.

1 Introduction

In seminal work, Moggi proposed a uniform representation of computational effects by monads [14,15,1]. The computations that return values from a set X are modelled by elements of TX, for a suitable monad T. Examples include exceptions, nondeterminism, interactive input/output, concurrency, state, time, continuations, and combinations thereof. Plotkin and Power later proposed to focus on *algebraic* effects, that is, effects that allow a representation by operations and equations [18,20,21]; the operations give rise to the effects at hand. All of the effects mentioned above are algebraic, with the notable exception of continuations [6], which have to be treated differently: see [9] for initial ideas.

In the algebraic approach, an operation gives rise to an occurrence of an effect and its arguments are the possible computations after that occurrence. For example, using a binary choice operation or : 2, a nondeterministically chosen boolean is given by the term or(return true, return false) : Fbool, where $F\sigma$ stands for the type of computations that return values of type σ (we are working in Levy's call-by-push-value (CBPV) framework [11]). The equations of the theory, for example the ones stating that or is a semi-lattice operation, generate the free-model functor, which is used to interpret the type $F\sigma$.

Modulo the forgetful functor, the free model functor is exactly the monad proposed by Moggi to model the corresponding effect [19]. When operations are viewed as a family of functions parametric in X, e.g., $\mathrm{or}_X : TX^2 \to TX$, one

---

* Supported by EPSRC grant GR/586371/01 and a Royal Society-Wolfson Award Fellowship.

** Supported by EPSRC grant GR/586371/01.

G. Castagna (Ed.): ESOP 2009, LNCS 5502, pp. 80–94, 2009.

obtains the so-called *algebraic operations*; such families are characterised by a certain naturality condition [20].

Although the algebraic approach has given ways of constructing, combining [10], and reasoning [22] about effects, it has not yet accounted for their handling. The difficulty is that exception handlers, a well-known programming concept, fail to be algebraic operations [20]. Conceptually, algebraic operations and effect handlers are dual: the former could be called *effect constructors* as they give rise to the effects; the latter could be called *effect deconstructors* as they depend on the effects already created. Filinski's reflection and reification operations provide general effect constructors and deconstructors in the context of layered monads [5].

This paper presents an account of deconstructors for arbitrary algebraic effects, and introduces a handling construct for them. The central new semantic idea is that deconstructing a computation amounts to applying to it a unique homomorphism guaranteed by universality. The domain of this homomorphism is a free model of the algebraic theory of the effects at hand; its range is a programmer-defined model of the algebraic theory; and it extends a programmer-defined map on values. Our new handling construct generalises the exception-handling construct of Benton and Kennedy [2]. It also includes many other, previously unrelated, examples, such as: stream redirection of shell processes, renaming and hiding in CCS [8], timeout, and rollback.

In Section 2, we illustrate the use of homomorphisms via an informal discussion of exception handlers. Then in Sections 3, 4, and 5, we develop a formal calculus in the call-by-push-value framework. This framework includes both call-by-value and call-by-name and proved convenient for the logic of effects in [22]. Section 3 describes the algebraic theory of effects over a given base signature and interpretation. A natural need for two languages arises: one describing handlers, given in Section 4, and one using them to handle computations, given in Section 5. The second parts of these sections give the relevant denotational semantics; readers may wish to omit them at first reading. We give examples in Section 6, where CBPV enables us to define handlers using non-free algebras.

We outline a version of a logic for algebraic effects [22] with handlers in Section 7. In Section 8, we sketch the inclusion of recursion: until then we work only with sets and functions, but everything adapts straightforwardly to ω-cpos (partial orders with sups of increasing sequences) and continuous functions (monotone functions preserving sups of increasing sequences). We conclude in Section 9 with a discussion of some open questions and possible future work.

2   Exception Handlers

We start our study with exception handlers, both because they are an established concept [2,12] and also because exceptions provide the simplest example of algebraic effects. To focus on the exposition of ideas, we write this section in a rather informal style, mixing syntax and semantics.

Taking a set of exceptions E, the computations that return values from a set X are modelled by elements γ of the monad $TX =_{\mathrm{def}} X + E$ with unit

$\eta_X = \text{inl}_X: X \to X + E$. Algebraically, one may take a nullary operation, i.e., a constant, $\text{raise}_e: 0$ for each $e \in E$ and no equations, and then FX has carrier TX with raise_e interpreted as $\text{inr}(e)$.

Fixing X, an exception handler $\gamma \, \text{handle} \, \{e \mapsto \gamma_e\}_{e \in E}$ takes a computation $\gamma \in X + E$ and intercepts raised exceptions $e \in E$, carrying out predefined computations $\gamma_e \in X + E$ instead (if one chooses not to handle a particular exception e one takes $\gamma_e = \text{raise}_e$). So we have the two equations:

$$\eta_X(x) \, \text{handle} \, \{e \mapsto \gamma_e\}_{e \in E} = \text{inl}_X(x) \, ,$$
$$\text{raise}_e \, \text{handle} \, \{e \mapsto \gamma_e\}_{e \in E} = \gamma_e \, .$$

From an algebraic point of view, the γ_e provide a model $\overline{X + E}$ for the theory of exceptions. This model has carrier $X + E$ and, for each e, raise_e is interpreted by γ_e. We then see from the above two equations that

$$\theta(\gamma) =_{\text{def}} \gamma \, \text{handle} \, \{e \mapsto \gamma_e\}_{e \in E}$$

is the unique homomorphism $\theta: X + E \to \overline{X + E}$ extending $\text{inl}_X: X \to X + E$ along η_X (we confuse the free model on X with its carrier).

Benton and Kennedy [2] generalised the handling construct to one of the form

$$\text{try} \, x \Leftarrow \gamma \, \text{in} \, g(x) \, \text{unless} \, \{e \mapsto \gamma_e\}_{e \in E} \, ,$$

where exceptions e may be handled by computations γ_e of any given type M (here a model of the theory) and returned values are "handled" with a map $g: X \to M$. (This construct is actually a bit more general than in [2] as E may be infinite and as we are in a call-by-push-value framework rather than a call-by-value one.) We now have:

$$\text{try} \, x \Leftarrow \eta_X(x) \, \text{in} \, g(x) \, \text{unless} \, \{e \mapsto \gamma_e\}_{e \in E} = g(x) \, ,$$
$$\text{try} \, x \Leftarrow \text{raise}_e \, \text{in} \, g(x) \, \text{unless} \, \{e \mapsto \gamma_e\}_{e \in E} = \gamma_e \, .$$

As remarked in [2], this handling construct allows a more concise programming style, program optimisations, and a stack-free small-step operational semantics.

Algebraically we now have a model $\overline{M}$ on (the carrier of) M, interpreting raise_e by γ_e, and the handling construct corresponds to the homomorphism θ induced by g, that is the unique homomorphism $\theta: X + E \to \overline{M}$ extending g along η_X. Note that *all* the homomorphisms from the free model are obtained in this way, and so (this version of) Benton and Kennedy's handling construct is the most general one possible from the algebraic point of view.

We can now see how to give handlers of other algebraic effects. To give a model of a finitary algebraic theory on a set X is to give a map $f_{\text{op}}: X^n \to X$ for each operation $\text{op}: n$, on condition that those maps satisfy the equations of the theory. As before, computations are interpreted in the free model and handling constructs are interpreted by the induced homomorphisms. Intuitively, while exceptions are replaced by handling computations, operations are recursively replaced by handling functions on computations.

3 Effects

We start with a *base signature* Σ_{base}, consisting of: a set of *base types* β; a subset of the base types, called the *arity types* α; a collection of *function symbols* $f : (\boldsymbol{\beta}) \to \beta$; and a collection of *relation symbols* $R : (\boldsymbol{\beta})$. We use vector notation $\boldsymbol{a}$ to abbreviate lists $a_1, \ldots, a_n$.

Base terms v are built from variables x and function symbols, while *base formulas* ψ are built from equations between base terms, relation symbols applied to base terms, logical connectives, and quantifiers over base types; we may omit empty parentheses in terms and formulas, and in similar constructs introduced below. In a context Γ of variables bound to base types, we type base terms as $\Gamma \vdash v : \beta$ and base formulas as $\Gamma \vdash \psi : \textbf{form}$.

An *interpretation of the base signature* is given by: a set $[\![\beta]\!]$ for each base type β, countable if β is an arity type; a map $[\![f]\!] : [\![\boldsymbol{\beta}]\!] \to [\![\beta]\!]$ for each function symbol $f : (\boldsymbol{\beta}) \to \beta$; and a subset $[\![R]\!] \subseteq [\![\boldsymbol{\beta}]\!]$ for each relation symbol $R : (\boldsymbol{\beta})$, where $[\![\boldsymbol{\beta}]\!] = [\![\beta_1]\!] \times \ldots [\![\beta_n]\!]$. Terms $\Gamma \vdash v : \beta$ and formulas $\Gamma \vdash \psi : \textbf{form}$ are interpreted by maps $[\![v]\!] : [\![\Gamma]\!] \to [\![\beta]\!]$ and subsets $[\![\psi]\!] \subseteq [\![\Gamma]\!]$ as usual [4].

3.1 Effect Theories

Standard equational logic does not give a finitary notation for describing effects given by an infinite family of operations, having an infinite number of outcomes, or described by an infinite number of equations [20]. We present a more general notation to do this, at least in some cases.

To avoid infinite families of operation symbols, we allow operations to have parameters of base types. For example, instead of having a family of operation symbols $\textsf{update}_{l,d} : 1$ for each location l and datum d, we employ a single operation symbol $\textsf{update} : \textbf{loc}, \textbf{dat}; 1$ that takes parameters $l : \textbf{loc}$ and $d : \textbf{dat}$, giving a memory location to be updated and a datum to be stored there.

To avoid operation symbols of infinite arity, their arguments are allowed to depend on an element of an arity type. For example, $\textsf{lookup} : \textbf{loc}; \textbf{dat}$ has parameter $l : \textbf{loc}$ and a single argument, dependent on a $d : \textbf{dat}$. The parameter gives a memory location to be looked-up and the argument gives the computation to be then carried out, dependent on the datum stored in that location.

Thus, given a base signature Σ_{base}, an *effect signature* Σ_{eff} consists of *operation symbols* $\textsf{op} : \boldsymbol{\beta}; \boldsymbol{\alpha}_1, \ldots, \boldsymbol{\alpha}_n$, where $\boldsymbol{\beta}$ is a list of *parameter* base types, and $\boldsymbol{\alpha}_1, \ldots, \boldsymbol{\alpha}_n$ are lists of *argument* arity types. We omit the semicolon when $\boldsymbol{\beta}$ is empty, and write n instead of $\boldsymbol{\alpha}_1, \ldots, \boldsymbol{\alpha}_n$ when every $\boldsymbol{\alpha}_i$ is empty. *Effect terms* T are given by the following grammar:

$$T ::= z(\boldsymbol{v}) \mid \textsf{op}_{\boldsymbol{v}}(\boldsymbol{x}_i : \boldsymbol{\alpha}_i.T_i)_i \,,$$

where z ranges over *effect variables*, and $\textsf{op}_{\boldsymbol{v}}(\boldsymbol{x}_i : \boldsymbol{\alpha}_i.T_i)_i$ is an abbreviation for $\textsf{op}_{\boldsymbol{v}}(\boldsymbol{x}_1 : \boldsymbol{\alpha}_1.T_1, \ldots, \boldsymbol{x}_n : \boldsymbol{\alpha}_n.T_n)$. We may omit empty binders here and in similar constructs below.

We type effect terms as $Z; \Gamma \vdash T$, where Z consists of effect variables $z : (\alpha)$, according to the following rules:

$$\frac{\Gamma \vdash v : \alpha}{Z; \Gamma \vdash z(v)} \quad (z : (\alpha) \in Z)$$

$$\frac{\Gamma \vdash v : \beta \qquad Z; \Gamma, x_i : \alpha_i \vdash T_i \quad (i = 1, \ldots, n)}{Z; \Gamma \vdash \mathsf{op}_v(x_i : \alpha_i . T_i)_i} \quad (\mathsf{op} : \beta; \alpha_1, \ldots, \alpha_n \in \Sigma_{\mathrm{eff}}) \, .$$

Next, *conditional equations* have the form $Z; \Gamma \vdash T_1 = T_2 \, (\psi)$, assuming that $Z; \Gamma \vdash T_1$, $Z; \Gamma \vdash T_2$, and $\Gamma \vdash \psi : \mathbf{form}$. Finally, a *conditional effect theory* $\mathfrak{T}_{\mathrm{eff}}$ *(over base and effect signatures Σ_{base} and Σ_{eff})* is a collection of such equations. It would be interesting to develop an equational logic for such theories [17].

Example 1. To describe a set E of exceptions, the base signature consists of a base type **exc** and a constant function symbol $e : () \to \mathbf{exc}$ for each $e \in E$. We interpret **exc** by E and function symbols by their corresponding elements. The effect signature consists of an operation symbol raise : **exc**; 0, while the effect theory is empty. Then, omitting empty parentheses, raise_e is the computation that raises the exception e.

Example 2. For nondeterminism, we take the empty base signature, the empty interpretation, the effect signature with a single nondeterministic choice operation symbol or : 2, and the effect theory for a semi-lattice, which states that or is idempotent, commutative, and associative.

Example 3. For state, the base signature contains a base type **loc** of memory locations, an arity type **dat** of data, and appropriate function and relation symbols for the locations and data. We interpret **loc** by a finite set L and **dat** by a countable set D. The effect signature consists of operation symbols lookup : **loc**; **dat** and update : **loc**, **dat**; 1, while the effect theory consists of seven conditional equations [19,17]. As an example, $\mathsf{lookup}_l(d : \mathbf{dat}.\mathsf{update}_{l',d}(z))$ is the computation that copies d from l to l' and then proceeds as z.

Each effect theory $\mathfrak{T}_{\mathrm{eff}}$ and interpretation of the base signature induces a standard, possibly infinitary, equational theory [7]. For each $\mathsf{op} : \beta; \alpha_1, \ldots, \alpha_n$ and $b \in [\![\beta]\!]$, we take an operation symbol op_b of countable arity $\sum_i |[\![\alpha_i]\!]|$. Then each effect term $Z; \Gamma \vdash T$ and $c \in [\![\Gamma]\!]$ gives rise to a, possibly infinitary, term T_c, with variables of the form z_a $(z : (\alpha) \in Z, a \in [\![\alpha]\!])$. The equations of the theory are $T_c = T'_c$ for each $Z; \Gamma \vdash T = T' \, (\psi)$ in $\mathfrak{T}_{\mathrm{eff}}$ and $c \in [\![\psi]\!]$ $(\subseteq [\![\Gamma]\!])$.

An *interpretation* of Σ_{eff} has a set M, its *carrier*, together with a map

$$\mathsf{op}_M : [\![\beta]\!] \times \prod_i M^{[\![\alpha_i]\!]} \to M$$

for each $\mathsf{op} : \beta; \alpha_1, \ldots, \alpha_n \in \Sigma_{\mathrm{eff}}$; it is a *model of the effect theory* $\mathfrak{T}_{\mathrm{eff}}$ if the corresponding maps $\mathsf{op}_M(b, -)$, where $b \in [\![\beta]\!]$, satisfy the equations of the induced equational theory. A *homomorphism* between models M and N is a map $\theta \colon M \to N$ such that $\mathsf{op}_N \circ (\mathbf{id}_{[\![\beta]\!]} \times \prod_i \theta^{[\![\alpha_i]\!]}) = \theta \circ \mathsf{op}_M$ holds for all $\mathsf{op} \colon \beta; \alpha_1, \ldots, \alpha_n \in \Sigma_{\text{eff}}$.

Models and homomorphisms form a category $\mathrm{Mod}_{\mathcal{T}_{\text{eff}}}$, equipped with the forgetful functor $U \colon \mathrm{Mod}_{\mathcal{T}_{\text{eff}}} \to \mathbf{Set}$, which maps a model to its carrier and a homomorphism to its underlying map. This functor has a left adjoint F, which constructs the free model FX on a set of generators X. The set UFX represents the set of computations that return values in X, and the monad UF agrees [19] with the monad proposed by Moggi to model the corresponding effect [15] (assuming the effect theory appropriately chosen).

The monad induced by the theory for exceptions in Example 1 maps a set X to $X + E$, the one for non-determinism in Example 2 maps it to the set $\mathcal{F}^+(X)$ of finite non-empty subsets of X, while the one for state in Example 3 maps it to $(S \times X)^S$, where $S = D^L$. One can give an equivalent treatment using countable Lawvere theories [23].

4 Handlers

Exception handlers are usually described and used within the same language: for each exception, we give a replacement computation term, which can contain further exception handlers. Repeating the same procedure for other algebraic effects is less straightforward: in order to interpret the handling construct, the handlers have to be correct in the sense that the redefinition of the operations they provide yields a model of the effect theory.

Equipping a single calculus with a mechanism to verify that handlers are correct would result in a complex interdependence between well-formedness and correctness. We avoid this by providing two calculi: one, given in this section, enables the language designer to specify handlers; another, given in the next section, enables the programmer to use them. In this way the selection of correct handlers is delegated to the meta-level.

Handler types χ, *handler terms* w, and *handlers* h are given by the following grammar:

$$\chi ::= X \mid F\sigma \mid \mathbf{1} \mid \chi_1 \times \chi_2 \mid \sigma \to \chi$$
$$w ::= \varphi(v) \mid \mathsf{op}_v(x_i \colon \alpha_i . w_i)_i \mid \text{if } \psi \text{ then } w_1 \text{ else } w_2 \mid \text{return } v \mid$$
$$\quad \text{let } x \colon \sigma \text{ be } w \text{ in } w' \mid \star \mid \langle w_1, w_2 \rangle \mid \mathsf{fst}\, w \mid \mathsf{snd}\, w \mid \lambda x \colon \sigma . w \mid wv$$
$$h ::= (\varphi_p \colon \chi; x_p \colon \sigma).\{\mathsf{op}_x(\varphi) \mapsto w_{\mathsf{op}}\}_{\mathsf{op} \in \Sigma_{\text{eff}}},$$

where X ranges over *type variables*, σ ranges over *value types* (here the same as the base types), φ ranges over *handler variables*, and ψ ranges over quantifier-free formulas. A handler is given by a handling term for each operation, dependent on parameters x_p and φ_p. We may omit the semicolon in handlers when either σ or χ is empty, and also in similar constructs introduced below. When $\mathsf{op}_x(\varphi) \mapsto w_{\mathsf{op}}$ is omitted, we assume that $w_{\mathsf{op}} = \mathsf{op}_x(x_i \colon \alpha_i . \varphi_i(x_i))_i$, so that op is not handled.

We type handler terms as $\Phi; \Gamma \vdash w : \chi$ where Φ is a context of handler variables $\varphi : (\alpha) \rightarrow \chi$, according to the following rules:

$$\frac{\Gamma \vdash v : \alpha}{\Phi; \Gamma \vdash \varphi(v) : \chi} \quad (\varphi : (\alpha) \rightarrow \chi \in$$

$$\Phi) \frac{\Gamma \vdash v : \beta \qquad \Phi; \Gamma, x_i : \alpha_i \vdash w_i : \chi \quad (i = 1, \ldots, n)}{\Phi; \Gamma \vdash \mathsf{op}_v(x_i : \alpha_i. w_i)_i : \chi} \quad (\mathsf{op} : \beta; \alpha_1, \ldots, \alpha_n \in \Sigma_{\mathrm{eff}})$$

$$\frac{\Gamma \vdash v : \sigma}{\Phi; \Gamma \vdash \mathsf{return}\, v : F\sigma} \qquad \frac{\Phi; \Gamma \vdash w : F\sigma \qquad \Phi; \Gamma, x : \sigma \vdash w' : \chi}{\Phi; \Gamma \vdash \mathsf{let}\, x : \sigma\, \mathsf{be}\, w\, \mathsf{in}\, w' : \chi},$$

and the standard rules for conditionals, products, and functions.

Handlers are typed as $\vdash h : (\chi; \sigma) \rightarrow \chi$ **handler** by the following rule:

$$\frac{\varphi_p : \chi, (\varphi_i : (\alpha_i) \rightarrow \chi)_{i=1}^{n}; x_p : \sigma, x : \beta \vdash w_{\mathsf{op}} : \chi \quad (\mathsf{op} : \beta; \alpha_1, \ldots, \alpha_n \in \Sigma_{\mathrm{eff}})}{\vdash (\varphi_p : \chi; x_p : \sigma).\{\mathsf{op}_x(\varphi) \mapsto w_{\mathsf{op}}\}_{\mathsf{op} \in \Sigma_{\mathrm{eff}}} : (\chi; \sigma) \rightarrow \chi\ \mathbf{handler}}.$$

Note that a handler may be polymorphic, as type variables may occur in χ or χ. We say that a handler $\vdash h : (\chi; \sigma) \rightarrow \chi$ **handler** is *uniform* if $\chi = X$, and *parametrically uniform* if $\chi = \sigma \rightarrow X$.

4.1 Semantics

For each assignment ρ of models to type variables, handler types χ are interpreted by models $[\![\chi]\!]_\rho$, given by

$$[\![X]\!]_\rho = \rho(X) \qquad\qquad [\![F\sigma]\!]_\rho = F[\![\sigma]\!] \qquad [\![1]\!]_\rho = 1$$

$$[\![\chi_1 \times \chi_2]\!]_\rho = [\![\chi_1]\!]_\rho \times [\![\chi_2]\!]_\rho \qquad [\![\sigma \rightarrow \chi]\!]_\rho = [\![\chi]\!]_\rho^{[\![\sigma]\!]},$$

where the model is given component-wise on $M_1 \times M_2$ and point-wise on M^A.

Then, we interpret contexts $\Phi = \varphi_1 : (\alpha_1) \rightarrow \chi_1, \ldots, \varphi_n : (\alpha_n) \rightarrow \chi_n$ by $[\![\Phi]\!]_\rho = U[\![\chi_1]\!]_\rho^{[\![\alpha_1]\!]} \times \cdots \times U[\![\chi_n]\!]_\rho^{[\![\alpha_n]\!]}$ and handler terms $\Phi; \Gamma \vdash w : \chi$ by maps $[\![w]\!]_\rho : [\![\Phi]\!]_\rho \times [\![\Gamma]\!] \rightarrow U[\![\chi]\!]_\rho$, defined inductively on valid typing judgements by

$$[\![\Phi; \Gamma \vdash \varphi_i(v) : \chi_i]\!]_\rho = \mathbf{ev}_{[\![\alpha_i]\!], U[\![\chi_i]\!]_\rho} \circ \langle \mathbf{pr}_i \circ \mathbf{pr}_1, \langle [\![v]\!] \rangle \circ \mathbf{pr}_2 \rangle$$

$$[\![\Phi; \Gamma \vdash \mathsf{op}_v(x_i : \alpha_i. w_i)_i : \chi]\!]_\rho = \mathsf{op}_{[\![\chi]\!]_\rho} \circ \langle \langle [\![v]\!] \rangle \circ \mathbf{pr}_2, \widehat{[\![w_1]\!]}_\rho, \ldots, \widehat{[\![w_n]\!]}_\rho \rangle$$

$$[\![\Phi; \Gamma \vdash \mathsf{return}\, v : F\sigma]\!]_\rho = \eta_{[\![\sigma]\!]} \circ [\![v]\!] \circ \mathbf{pr}_2$$

$$[\![\Phi; \Gamma \vdash \mathsf{let}\, x : \sigma\, \mathsf{be}\, w\, \mathsf{in}\, w' : \chi]\!]_\rho = [\![w']\!]_\rho^{\dagger} \circ \langle \mathbf{id}_{[\![\Phi]\!]_\rho \times [\![\Gamma]\!]}, [\![w]\!]_\rho \rangle,$$

where judgements are abbreviated to terms on the right. The maps $\mathbf{ev}$ and $\mathbf{pr}$ are evaluation and projection functions; $\widehat{}$ is the transpose operation (associativity isomorphisms are omitted here, and below); and η is the unit of UF. The map $f^{\dagger} =_{\mathrm{def}} U(\varepsilon_M \circ Ff) \circ \mathsf{st}_{A,B} : A \times UFB \rightarrow UM$ is the *parameterised lifting* of $f : A \times B \rightarrow UM$, where ε is the counit of FU, and st is the strength of UF. Conditionals, products, and functions are interpreted as usual [11].

A handler $h : (\chi; \sigma) \to \chi$ **handler** is interpreted by a parameterised family $[\![h]\!]_\rho(m_p, a_p)$ of Σ_{eff}-interpretations, where $m_p \in U[\![\chi]\!]_\rho$ and $a_p \in [\![\sigma]\!]$; each such interpretation has carrier $U[\![\chi]\!]_\rho$, and, for each $\text{op}:\beta; \alpha_1, \ldots, \alpha_n$, the map

$$\text{op}_{U[\![\chi]\!]_\rho} =_{\text{def}} (m, a) \mapsto [\![w_{\text{op}}]\!]((m_p, m), (a_p, a))$$

(identifying models M with their trivial powers M^1).

We say that h is *correct (with respect to $\mathfrak{T}_{\text{eff}}$)* if for all assignments ρ, and for all $m_p \in U[\![\chi]\!]_\rho$ and $a_p \in [\![\sigma]\!]$, the Σ_{eff}-interpretation $[\![h]\!]_\rho(m_p, a_p)$ defines a model of the effect theory $\mathfrak{T}_{\text{eff}}$ on $U[\![\chi]\!]_\rho$. If the effect theory is empty, then any handler is correct, but, in general, correctness is undecidable. In particular, the following problem is Π_1-complete: given a multi-sorted finitary equational theory with finite signature and finitely many axioms, decide whether, in the initial model, a given interpretation of the theory in itself satisfies the axioms.

5   Computations

We assume a *handler signature* Σ_{hand} of *handler symbols*

$$H:(\chi; \sigma) \to \chi \textbf{ handler}.$$

Then, *computation types* $\underline{\tau}$ and *terms* t are given by the following grammar:

$$\underline{\tau} ::= F\sigma \mid 1 \mid \underline{\tau}_1 \times \underline{\tau}_2 \mid \sigma \to \underline{\tau},$$
$$t ::= \text{op}_v(x_i:\alpha_i.t_i)_i \mid \text{if } \psi \text{ then } t_1 \text{ else } t_2 \mid \text{return } v \mid \text{let } x:\sigma \text{ be } t \text{ in } t' \mid$$
$$\text{try } t \text{ with } H(t; v) \text{ as } x:\sigma \text{ in } t' \mid \star \mid \langle t_1, t_2 \rangle \mid \text{fst } t \mid \text{snd } t \mid \lambda x:\sigma.t \mid tv,$$

where ψ ranges over quantifier-free formulas, as before.

One can see that computation types and terms mirror their handler counterparts, with the omission of type and handler variables, and with the addition of the handling construct. When the full handling construct is not necessary, we write $\text{handle } t$ with $H(t; v)$ instead of $\text{try } t$ with $H(t; v)$ as $x:\sigma$ in $\text{return } x$, and when the handler signature consists of a single handler symbol H, we omit it, writing $\text{try } t$ with $v; t$ as $x:\sigma$ in t' or $\text{handle } t$ with $t; v$ instead.

We can extend both handlers and computations with other call-by-push-value types and terms [11,22]. A problem arises if we introduce thunks: handler terms then contain value terms, which contain thunked computation terms, which contain the handling construct. To resolve the issue, one further splits the handler types and terms into value and computation ones.

Computation terms are typed as $\Gamma \vdash t : \underline{\tau}$ according to rules similar to the ones for handling terms, except that the handling construct for a handler symbol $H:(\chi; \sigma) \to \chi \textbf{ handler} \in \Sigma_{\text{hand}}$ is typed by

$$\frac{\Gamma \vdash t:F\sigma \quad \Gamma \vdash t:\chi[\underline{\tau}/X] \quad \Gamma \vdash v:\sigma \quad \Gamma, x:\sigma \vdash t':\chi[\underline{\tau}/X]}{\Gamma \vdash \text{try } t \text{ with } H(t; v) \text{ as } x:\sigma \text{ in } t':\chi[\underline{\tau}/X]},$$

where $\chi[\underline{\tau}/X]$ is the computation type obtained by replacing all the type variables X in χ by the computation types $\underline{\tau}$.

5.1 Semantics

To interpret computation terms, we assume given a *handler definition* Δ, mapping each handler symbol $H : (\chi; \sigma) \to \chi$ **handler** $\in \Sigma_{\text{hand}}$ to a correct handler $\vdash \Delta(H) : (\chi; \sigma) \to \chi$ **handler**. Then, computation types and terms are interpreted in the same way as their handler counterparts, except that the handling construct $\Gamma \vdash$ try t with $H(t; v)$ as $x : \sigma$ in $t' : \chi[\underline{\tau}/X]$ is interpreted along the lines discussed in Section 2, as we now see.

Take $c \in \llbracket \Gamma \rrbracket$ and let ρ be an assignment that maps X_i to $\llbracket \underline{\tau}_i \rrbracket$. Since each handler $\Delta(H)$ is correct, the Σ_{eff} interpretation $\llbracket \Delta(H) \rrbracket_\rho (\langle \llbracket t \rrbracket \rangle (c), \langle \llbracket v \rrbracket \rangle (c))$ is a model $\overline{U \llbracket \chi \rrbracket}_\rho$ of the effect theory $\mathfrak{T}_{\text{eff}}$ with carrier $U \llbracket \chi \rrbracket_\rho$. By the universality of the free model $F \llbracket \sigma \rrbracket$, there is a unique homomorphism $\theta_c : F \llbracket \sigma \rrbracket \to \overline{U \llbracket \chi \rrbracket}_\rho$ extending $\llbracket t' \rrbracket (c, -)$ in the sense that the following diagram commutes:

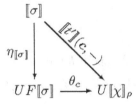

The handling construct $\Gamma \vdash$ try t with $H(t; v)$ as $x : \sigma$ in $t' : \chi[\underline{\tau}/X]$ is then interpreted by the map

$$c \mapsto \theta_c(\llbracket t \rrbracket(c)) : \llbracket \Gamma \rrbracket \to U \llbracket \chi[\underline{\tau}/X] \rrbracket$$

(note that $\llbracket \chi \rrbracket_\rho$ is equal to $\llbracket \chi[\underline{\tau}/X] \rrbracket$ by the definition of ρ).

6 Examples

We give a number of examples to demonstrate the versatility of our handling construct.

6.1 Exceptions

The standard uniform exception handler is given by

$$(\varphi : \text{exc} \to X).\{\text{raise}_e \mapsto \varphi e\} : (\text{exc} \to X) \to X \text{ handler} .$$

Benton and Kennedy's construct try $x \Leftarrow t$ in t' unless $\{e_1 \Rightarrow t_1 \mid \cdots \mid e_n \Rightarrow t_n\}$ can then be written as try t with t_{exc} as $x : \sigma$ in t' for a suitable σ and $t_{\text{exc}} : \text{exc} \to \underline{\tau}$.

Benton and Kennedy noted a few issues about the syntax of their construct when used for programming [2]. It is not obvious that t is handled whereas t' is not, especially when t' is large and the handler is obscured. An alternative they propose is try $x \Leftarrow t$ unless $\{e_1 \Rightarrow t_1 \mid \ldots \mid e_n \Rightarrow t_n\}_i$ in t', but then it is not obvious that x is bound in t', but not in the handler. The syntax of our construct try t with $H(t; v)$ as $x : \sigma$ in t' addresses those issues and clarifies the order of evaluation: after t is handled with H, its results are bound to x and used in t'.

6.2   Stream Redirection

Shell processes in UNIX-like operating systems communicate with the user using input and output streams, usually connected to a keyboard and a terminal window. However, such streams can be rerouted to other processes so simple commands can be combined into more powerful ones.

One case is the redirection `proc > outfile` of the output stream of a process `proc` to a file `outfile`, usually used to store the output for a future analysis. An alternative is the redirection `proc > /dev/null` to the null device, which effectively discards the standard output stream.

Another case is the pipe `proc1 | proc2`, where the output of `proc1` is fed to the input of `proc2`. For example, to get a way (not necessarily the best one) of routinely confirming a series of actions, for example deleting a large number of files, we write `yes | proc`, where the command `yes` outputs an infinite stream made of a predetermined character (the default one being y).

We represent interactive input/output by: a base signature, consisting of a base type **char** of characters and constants $a, b, \dots$ of type **char**, together with the obvious interpretation; an effect signature, consisting of operation symbols out : **char**; 1 and in : **char**, with the empty effect theory. Then, if t is a computation, we can express `yes | t > /dev/null` by handle t with H_{red}, where $H_{\mathrm{red}} : () \to X$ **handler** is defined to be $\{\mathrm{out}_c(\varphi) \mapsto \varphi, \mathrm{in}(\varphi) \mapsto \varphi(\mathrm{y})\}$.

6.3   CCS Renaming and Hiding

In functional programming, processes are regarded as programs of empty type **0**. The subset of CCS processes [13], given by action prefix and sum, can be represented by: a base signature, consisting of a base type **act** of actions and appropriate constants for actions, interpreted in the evident way; an effect signature, consisting of operation symbols $0:0$, do:**act**; 1, and $+:2$, with the obvious effect theory [22]. Then, process renaming $t[b/a]$ can be written as handle t with $H_{\mathrm{ren}}(a, b)$, where, writing $a.\varphi$ for $\mathrm{do}_a(\varphi)$, $H_{\mathrm{ren}} : (\mathbf{act}, \mathbf{act}) \to F\mathbf{0}$ **handler** is defined by:

$$H_{\mathrm{ren}} = (a:\mathbf{act}, b:\mathbf{act}).\{a'.\varphi \mapsto \text{if } a' = a \text{ then } b.\varphi \text{ else } a'.\varphi\} .$$

Note that 0 and + are handled by themselves, following the convention given above regarding operation symbols omitted from handlers.

Hiding can be implemented in a similar way, but whether parallel can be is an open question. The difficulty is that the natural definition of parallel is by a simultaneous recursion on the structure of *both* its arguments, whereas the handler mechanism provides only recursion on one argument. We should mention that some attempts at finding a binary variant of handlers were unsuccessful.

6.4   Explicit Nondeterminism

The evaluation of a nondeterministic computation usually takes only one of all the possible paths. But in logic programming [3], we do an exhaustive search for all solutions that satisfy given constraints in the order given by the solver implementation. Such nondeterminism is represented slightly differently from the one in Example 2. We take: the empty base signature; an effect signature, consisting of operation symbols $\mathsf{fail}:0$ and $\mathsf{pick}:2$, with the effect theory consisting of the following equations stating that the operations form a monoid:

$$z \vdash \mathsf{pick}(z, \mathsf{fail}) = \mathsf{pick}(\mathsf{fail}, z) = z \ ,$$
$$z_1, z_2, z_3 \vdash \mathsf{pick}(z_1, \mathsf{pick}(z_2, z_3)) = \mathsf{pick}(\mathsf{pick}(z_1, z_2), z_3) \ .$$

The free-model monad maps a set to the set of all finite sequences of its elements, which is Haskell's nondeterminism monad [16].

A user is usually presented with a way of browsing through those solutions, for example extracting all the solutions into a list. Since our calculus has no polymorphic lists (although it can easily be extended with them), we take base types α and list_α, function symbols $\mathsf{nil}:() \to \mathsf{list}_\alpha$, $\mathsf{cons}:(\alpha, \mathsf{list}_\alpha) \to \mathsf{list}_\alpha$, $\mathsf{head}:(\mathsf{list}_\alpha) \to \alpha$, $\mathsf{tail}:(\mathsf{list}_\alpha) \to \mathsf{list}_\alpha$, and $\mathsf{append}:(\mathsf{list}_\alpha, \mathsf{list}_\alpha) \to \mathsf{list}_\alpha$. Then, all the results of a computation of type $F\alpha$ can be extracted into a returned value of type $F\mathsf{list}_\alpha$ using the handler

$\{\mathsf{fail} \mapsto \mathsf{return\ nil}\ ,$

$\quad \mathsf{pick}(\varphi_1, \varphi_2) \mapsto \mathsf{let}\ x_1 : \mathsf{list}_\alpha\ \mathsf{be}\ \varphi_1\ \mathsf{in\ let}\ x_2 : \mathsf{list}_\alpha\ \mathsf{be}\ \varphi_2\ \mathsf{in\ return\ append}(x_1, x_2)\}\ .$

We can similarly devise a handler that returns the first solution, or one that prints out a solution and asks the user whether to continue the search or not.

6.5   Handlers with Parameter Passing

Sometimes, we wish to handle different instances of the same operation differently, for example suppressing output after a certain number of characters. Although we handle operations in a fixed way, we can use handlers on a function type $\sigma \to \chi$ to simulate handlers on χ that pass around a parameter of type σ.

Instead of

$$(\varphi_p : \chi; x_p : \sigma).\{\mathsf{op}_x(\varphi) \mapsto \lambda x : \sigma.w_{\mathsf{op}}\}_{\mathsf{op} \in \Sigma_{\mathsf{eff}}} : (\chi; \sigma) \to (\sigma \to \chi)\ \mathbf{handler}\ .$$

where all the occurrences of $\varphi_i(v)$ are applied to some $v : \sigma$, the changed parameter, we write

$$(\varphi_p : \chi; x_p : \sigma).\{\mathsf{op}_x(\varphi) @ x : \sigma \mapsto w'_{\mathsf{op}}\}_{\mathsf{op} \in \Sigma_{\mathsf{eff}}} : (\chi; \sigma) \to \chi @ \sigma\ \mathbf{handler}\ ,$$

where w'_{op} results from substituting $\varphi_i(v) @ v$ for $\varphi_i(v)v$ in w_{op}. We also write

$$\mathsf{try}\ t\ \mathsf{with}\ H(t; v) @ v\ \mathsf{as}\ y : \sigma' @ x : \sigma\ \mathsf{in}\ t'$$

instead of

$$(\mathsf{try}\ t\ \mathsf{with}\ H(t; v)\ \mathsf{as}\ y : \sigma'\ \mathsf{in}\ \lambda x : \sigma.t')v\ .$$

We could similarly simulate mutually defined handlers by handlers on product types, but we know no interesting examples of their use.

6.6   Timeout

When the evaluation of a computation takes too long, we may want to abort it and provide a predefined result instead, a behaviour called *timeout*.

We represent time by: a base signature with a base type **int** of integers, appropriate function symbols and a relation symbol $>:(\mathbf{int},\mathbf{int})$, with the evident interpretation; an effect signature consisting of delay:1, to represent the passage of some fixed amount of time, with the empty effect theory. Then timeout can be described by a handler which passes around a parameter $T:\mathbf{int}$ representing how long we are willing to wait before we abort the evaluation and return φ_p.

$$(\varphi_p:X).\{\mathsf{delay}(\varphi)\,@\,T:\mathbf{int}\mapsto \mathsf{delay}(\text{if }T>0\text{ then }\varphi@(T-1)\text{ else }\varphi_p)\}$$

Note that the handling term is wrapped in delay in order to preserve the time spent during the evaluation of the handled computation.

6.7   Input Redirection

With parameter passing, we can implement the redirection proc < infile, which feeds the contents of infile to the standard input of proc. We take the base signature, etc., of Section 6.2, extended by the base type $\mathsf{list}_{\mathsf{char}}$, etc., of Section 6.4. Then a handler $H_{\mathrm{in}}:()\rightarrow X@\mathsf{list}_{\mathsf{char}}$ handler to pass a string to a process is defined by

$$\{\mathsf{in}(\varphi)\,@\,\ell:\mathsf{list}_{\mathsf{char}}\mapsto \text{if }\ell=\mathsf{nil}\text{ then }\mathsf{in}(a.\varphi(a)@\mathsf{nil})\text{ else }\varphi(\mathsf{head}(\ell))@\mathsf{tail}(\ell)\}\;.$$

Unfortunately we do not see how to implement the pipe $t_1\,|\,t_2$: the difficulty is very much like that with the CCS parallel combinator.

6.8   Rollback

When a computation raises an exception while modifying the memory, for example, when a connection drops half-way through a database transaction, we want to revert all the modifications made. This behaviour is termed *rollback*.

We take the base and the effect signatures for exceptions as in Example 1 and state as in Example 3, and the effect theory for state, together with the equation $\mathsf{update}_{l,d}(\mathsf{raise}_e)=\mathsf{raise}_e$ for each exception e [10]. The standard exception handler, extended to state, is no longer correct. Instead, working in an extended language as described above, we use a parametrically uniform handler $H_{\mathrm{rollback}}:()\rightarrow X@U(\mathbf{exc}\rightarrow X)$ handler with parameter a thunked function to revert modified locations. It is defined, omitting some type declarations, by

$$\{\mathsf{update}_{l,d}(\varphi)\,@\,f:U(\mathbf{exc}\rightarrow X)\mapsto$$

$\quad\mathsf{lookup}_l(d'.\mathsf{update}_{l,d}(\varphi@\mathsf{thunk}(\lambda e.\,\mathsf{let}\,x\,\mathsf{be}\,(\mathsf{force}\,f)e\,\mathsf{in}\,\mathsf{update}_{l,d'}(\mathsf{return}\,x))))\;,$

$\quad\mathsf{lookup}_l(\varphi)\,@\,f:U(\mathbf{exc}\rightarrow X)\mapsto \mathsf{lookup}_l(d.\varphi(d)@f)\;,$

$\quad\mathsf{raise}_e\,@\,f:U(\mathbf{exc}\rightarrow X)\mapsto (\mathsf{force}\,f)e\}\;,$

and is used on $t:F\sigma$ by handle t with $H_{\mathrm{rollback}}@t_0$ for some $t_0:\mathbf{exc}\rightarrow F\sigma$.

We can also give a variant of rollback that passes around a list of changes to the memory, committed only after the computation has returned a value.

7 Logic

We sketch an adaptation of the logic for algebraic effects of [22] to account for handlers. This is relatively straightforward as the notions needed to interpret the handling construct are embodied in the computation induction (CI) and free algebra principles of [22]: the latter allows the ad-hoc construction of models and guarantees the existence of the required unique homomorphism.

We add handler types and terms to the language of the logic and state that handling is a homomorphic extension by:

$$\Gamma \vdash \mathsf{try\ return}\ v\ \mathsf{with}\ H(\boldsymbol{t}_p; \boldsymbol{v}_p)\ \mathsf{as}\ x : \sigma\ \mathsf{in}\ t = t[v/x]\ ,$$

$$\Gamma \vdash \mathsf{try\ op}_{\boldsymbol{v}}(\boldsymbol{x}_i.t_i)_i\ \mathsf{with}\ H(\boldsymbol{t}_p; \boldsymbol{v}_p)\ \mathsf{as}\ x : \sigma\ \mathsf{in}\ t = w'_{\mathsf{op}}\ ,$$

where, if $\Delta(H) = (\varphi_p : \chi\ ;\ \boldsymbol{x}_p : \boldsymbol{\sigma}).\{\mathsf{op}_{\boldsymbol{x}}(\varphi) \mapsto w_{\mathsf{op}}\}_{\mathsf{op} \in \Sigma_{\mathrm{eff}}}$, then w'_{op} is obtained by substituting $\boldsymbol{t}_p$ for $\varphi_p()$ and try $t_i[\boldsymbol{v}_i/\boldsymbol{x}_i]$ with $H(\boldsymbol{t}_p; \boldsymbol{v}_p)$ as $x : \sigma$ in t for $\varphi_i(\boldsymbol{v}_i)$ in $w_{\mathsf{op}}[\boldsymbol{v}_p/\boldsymbol{x}_p, v/\boldsymbol{x}]$; CI yields uniqueness. These two equations generalise the first two 'handle-sequencing' equations of [12].

The fourth 'associativity' equation has no valid generalisation of the form

$$\mathsf{try}\ (\mathsf{try}\ t_1\ \mathsf{with}\ m_2\ \mathsf{as}\ x_1 : \sigma_1\ \mathsf{in}\ t_2)\ \mathsf{with}\ m_3\ \mathsf{as}\ x_2 : \sigma_2\ \mathsf{in}\ t_3$$

$$= \mathsf{try}\ t_1\ \mathsf{with}\ m'_3\ \mathsf{as}\ x_1 : \sigma_1\ \mathsf{in}\ (\mathsf{try}\ t_2\ \mathsf{with}\ m_3\ \mathsf{as}\ x_2 : \sigma_2\ \mathsf{in}\ t_3)\ ,$$

for some m'_3, given the t_i and the m_j (m ranges over *model expressions* $H(\boldsymbol{t}; \boldsymbol{v})$): such an m'_3 may not exist, and there may even be no possible model for it to denote. There are generalisations of the third and fourth equations provable by CI, subject to conditions involving the model expressions.

Still, the associativity of exception handlers is expressible, and provable by CI. We then have $m_1 = H_{\mathrm{exc}}(t)$ for some $t : \mathbf{exc} \to F\sigma_2$, and we set

$$m_3 =_{\mathrm{def}} H_{\mathrm{exc}}(\lambda e : \mathbf{exc}.\ \mathsf{try}\ t e\ \mathsf{with}\ m_2\ \mathsf{as}\ x_2 : \sigma_2\ \mathsf{in}\ t_3)\ .$$

(Note that, although handlers cannot contain handler constructs, it is possible to achieve something of that effect through the use of parameters, as we do here.) It may be, more generally, that unconditional associativity is provable for limited classes of handlers, such as the uniform ones. Further equations for exception-handling (also provable by CI) are given in [2]; it remains to consider their possible general forms.

8 Recursion

We sketch how to adapt the above ideas to deal with recursion. Base signatures are as before; for their interpretations we use ω-cpos and continuous functions, still, however, interpreting arity types by countable sets, equipped with the trivial order (with some additional effort this can be generalised to ω-cpos countable in the categorical sense). Effect syntax is as before, except that we allow conditional *inequations* $Z; \Gamma \vdash T_1 \leq T_2\ (\psi)$ and assume there is always a constant Ω and the inequation $\vdash \Omega \leq z$. We again obtain a category of models, now using

ω-cpos (necessarily with a least element) as carriers and continuous functions (necessarily strict) as homomorphisms; free models exist as before.

The handler and computation syntax is also as before except that we add recursion terms $\mu\varphi\!:\!\chi.w$ and $\mu y\!:\!\underline{\tau}.t$ (and so also computation variables y) with the usual least fixed-point interpretation. Correct handlers cannot redefine Ω because of the inequation $\Omega \leq z$. The adaptation of the logic of effects to allow recursion in [22] further adapts to handlers, analogously to the above; in this regard one notes that inequations are admissible and therefore one may still use computation induction to prove associativity and so on.

9 Conclusions

Some immediate questions stem from the current work. The most important is how to simultaneously handle two computations to describe parallel operators, e.g., that of CCS or the UNIX pipe combinator; that would bring parallelism within the ambit of the algebraic theory of effects. More routinely, perhaps, the logic should be worked out more fully, the work done on combinations of effects in [10] should be extended to combinations of handlers, and there should be a general operational semantics [18] including that of Benton and Kennedy in [2].

The separation between the languages for handlers and computations is essential in the development of this paper. A possible alternative is to give a single language and a mechanism limiting well-typed handlers to correct ones. This might be done by means of a suitable type-theory.

It is interesting to compare our approach to that taken in Haskell [16], where a monad is given by a type with unit and binding maps. The type-checker only checks the signature of the maps, but not the monadic laws they should satisfy. Still, the only way to use effects in Haskell is through the use of the built-in monads, and their laws were checked by their designers. Building on this similarity, one can imagine extending Haskell in two ways: enriching the built-in effects with operations and handlers; and giving programmers a means to write their own handlers which could be used to program in an extension of the monadic style.

A given handler may or may not be computationally feasible for a given effect and so there is a question as to which are. We may expect uniform, or parametrically uniform, handlers to be feasible, as they cannot use the properties of a specific data-type and so, one may imagine, cannot be as contrived. In this connection, note too that a single monad or algebraic theory may model distinct effects. For example, the complexity monad $\mathbb{N}\times-$ may be used to model either space or time.

Lastly, one advantage of Benton and Kennedy's handling construct is the elegant programming style it introduces. We gave various examples of our more general construct above; some used parameter-passing, but none, unfortunately, used mutually defined handlers. We hope our new programming construct proves useful, and we look forward to feedback from the programming community.

Acknowledgments. The authors thank Andrej Bauer, Andrzej Filinski, Paul Levy, John Power, Mojca Pretnar, and Alex Simpson for their insightful comments and support.

References

1. Benton, N., Hughes, J., Moggi, E.: Monads and effects. In: Barthe, G., Dybjer, P., Pinto, L., Saraiva, J. (eds.) APPSEM 2000. LNCS, vol. 2395, pp. 42–122. Springer, Heidelberg (2002)
2. Benton, N., Kennedy, A.: Exceptional syntax. Journal of Functional Programming 11(4), 395–410 (2001)
3. Clocksin, W.F., Mellish, C.: Programming in Prolog, 3rd edn. Springer, Heidelberg (1987)
4. Enderton, H.B.: A Mathematical Introduction to Logic, 2nd edn. Academic Press, London (2000)
5. Filinski, A.: Representing layered monads. In: 26th Symposium on Principles of Programming Languages, pp. 175–188 (1999)
6. Flanagan, C., Sabry, A., Duba, B.F., Felleisen, M.: The essence of compiling with continuations. In: PLDI, pp. 237–247 (1993)
7. Grätzer, G.A.: Universal Algebra, 2nd edn. Springer, Heidelberg (1979)
8. Hennessy, M., Milner, R.: Algebraic laws for nondeterminism and concurrency. Journal of the ACM 32(1), 137–161 (1985)
9. Hyland, M., Levy, P.B., Plotkin, G.D., Power, A.J.: Combining algebraic effects with continuations. Theoretical Computer Science 375(1-3), 20–40 (2007)
10. Hyland, M., Plotkin, G.D., Power, A.J.: Combining effects: Sum and tensor. Theoretical Computer Science 357(1-3), 70–99 (2006)
11. Levy, P.B.: Call-by-push-value: Decomposing call-by-value and call-by-name. Higher-Order and Symbolic Computation 19(4), 377–414 (2006)
12. Levy, P.B.: Monads and adjunctions for global exceptions. Electronic Notes in Theoretical Computer Science 158, 261–287 (2006)
13. Milner, R.: A Calculus of Communicating Systems. Springer, Heidelberg (1980)
14. Moggi, E.: Computational lambda-calculus and monads. In: 4th Symposium on Logic in Computer Science, pp. 14–23 (1989)
15. Moggi, E.: Notions of computation and monads. Information And Computation 93(1), 55–92 (1991)
16. Peyton Jones, S.L.: Haskell 98. Journal of Functional Programming 13(1), 255 (2003)
17. Plotkin, G.D.: Some varieties of equational logic. In: Futatsugi, K., Jouannaud, J.-P., Meseguer, J. (eds.) Algebra, Meaning, and Computation. LNCS, vol. 4060, pp. 150–156. Springer, Heidelberg (2006)
18. Plotkin, G.D., Power, A.J.: Adequacy for algebraic effects. In: Honsell, F., Miculan, M. (eds.) FOSSACS 2001. LNCS, vol. 2030, pp. 1–24. Springer, Heidelberg (2001)
19. Plotkin, G.D., Power, A.J.: Notions of computation determine monads. In: Nielsen, M., Engberg, U. (eds.) FOSSACS 2002. LNCS, vol. 2303, pp. 342–356. Springer, Heidelberg (2002)
20. Plotkin, G.D., Power, A.J.: Algebraic operations and generic effects. Applied Categorical Structures 11(1), 69–94 (2003)
21. Plotkin, G.D., Power, A.J.: Computational effects and operations: An overview. Electronic Notes in Theoretical Computer Science 73, 149–163 (2004)
22. Plotkin, G.D., Pretnar, M.: A logic for algebraic effects. In: 23rd Symposium on Logic in Computer Science, pp. 118–129 (2008)
23. Power, A.J.: Countable Lawvere theories and computational effects. Electronic Notes in Theoretical Computer Science 161, 59–71 (2006)

Is Structural Subtyping Useful?
An Empirical Study

Donna Malayeri and Jonathan Aldrich

Carnegie Mellon University, Pittsburgh, PA 15213, USA
{donna,aldrich}@cs.cmu.edu

Abstract. Structural subtyping is popular in research languages, but all mainstream object-oriented languages use nominal subtyping. Since languages with structural subtyping are not in widespread use, the empirical questions of whether and how structural subtyping is useful have thus far remained unanswered. This study aims to provide answers to these questions. We identified several criteria that are indicators that nominally typed programs could benefit from structural subtyping, and performed automated and manual analyses of open-source Java programs based on these criteria. Our results suggest that these programs could indeed be improved with the addition of structural subtyping. We hope this study will provide guidance for language designers who are considering use of this subtyping discipline.

1 Introduction

Structural subtyping is popular in the research community and is used in languages such as O'Caml [15], PolyToil [6], Moby [11], Strongtalk [5], and a number of type systems and calculi (e.g., [7, 1]). In the research community, many believe that structural subtyping is beneficial and is superior to nominal subtyping. But, structural subtyping is not used in any mainstream object-oriented programming language—perhaps due to lack of evidence of its utility. Accordingly, we ask: what empirical evidence could show that structural subtyping can be beneficial?

Let us consider the characteristics that a nominally-typed program might exhibit that would indicate that it could benefit from structural subtyping. First, the program might systematically make use of a subset of methods of a type, with no nominal type corresponding to this method set. A particular such implicit type might be used repeatedly throughout the program. Structural subtyping would allow these types to be easily expressed, without requiring that the type hierarchy of the program change.

Second, there might be methods in two different classes that share the same name and perform the same operation, but that are not contained in a common nominal supertype. This could happen due to oversight, or perhaps the need did not yet exist to call that method in a generic manner for both classes. Alternatively, perhaps such a need did exist, but programmers resorted to code duplication rather than refactoring the type hierarchy. With structural subtyping, the two classes would automatically share a common supertype.

Or, programs might use the Java reflection method Class.getMethod to call a method with a particular signature in a generic manner. Structural subtyping provides

G. Castagna (Ed.): ESOP 2009, LNCS 5502, pp. 95–111, 2009.
© Springer-Verlag Berlin Heidelberg 2009

exactly this capability, with no need for reflection. Finally, what might a class do if it can only support a subset of its declared interface, but no such super-interface can be defined (due to library use)? One implementation strategy is to have some of its methods always throw an UnsupportedOperationException. In contrast, with structural subtyping, the intended structural super-interface could simply be used.

With these characteristics in mind, we examined up to 29 open-source Java programs, using both manual and automated analyses (in the case of manual analyses, a subset of the subject programs were considered). Each aimed to answer one question: are nominally-typed programs using implicit structural types? We found that indeed they were; representing these types explicitly could therefore be advantageous.

In our empirical evaluation, we sought to answer the following questions:

1. Does the body of a method use only a subset of the methods of its parameters? If so, structural types could ease the task of making the method more general. (Sect. 3)
2. If structural types are inferred for method parameters, do there exist types that are used repeatedly, suggesting that they represent a meaningful abstraction? (Sect. 3.3)
3. How many methods always throw "unsupported operation" exceptions? In such cases, classes support a structural supertype of the class type. (Sect. 4)
4. Do there exist *common methods*—methods with the same name and signature, but that are not contained in a common supertype of the enclosing classes? (Sect 5.1)
5. How many common methods represent an accidental name clash? (Sect 5.2)
6. Can structural subtyping reduce code duplication? (Sect. 5.3)
7. Is there synergy between structural subtyping and other proposed language features, such as multimethods? (Sect. 6)
8. Do programs use reflection where structural types would be preferable? (Sect. 7)

Thus, we considered a variety of facets of existing programs. While none of these aspects is conclusive on its own, taken together, the answers to the above questions provide evidence that even programs written with a nominal subtyping discipline could benefit from structural subtyping. This study provides initial answers to the above questions; further study is needed to fully examine all aspects of some questions, particularly questions 6 and 7. Additionally, this study considers only the potential benefits of structural subtyping, while there are situations where nominal types are more appropriate [23, 17].

To our knowledge, this is the first systematic corpus analysis to determine the benefits of structural subtyping. This paper makes the following contributions: (1) identification of a number of characteristics in a program that suggest the use of implicit structural types; and (2) results from automated and manual analyses that measure the identified characteristics.

2   Corpus and Methodology

For this study, we analyzed the source code of up to 29 open-source Java applications (details, including version numbers, are provided in [18]). The full set of subject programs were used for the automated analyses; due to practical considerations, for manual analysis we chose a subset thereof (ranging from 2 to 8 in size). The applications were chosen from the following sources: popular applications on SourceForge, Apache Foundation applications, and the DaCapo benchmark suite. The full set of programs range from

12 kLOC to 161 kLOC, and for both kinds of analysis we selected programs based on size, type (library vs. standalone program) and domain (selecting for variety). For some of the manual analyses, we favored applications with which we were familiar, as this aided analysis. All of the manual analyses, including the subjective analyses, were performed by the first author. The methodology for each analysis is described in the corresponding section; further details are available in the companion technical report [18].

For space considerations, in this paper we have omitted data from the 10 smallest applications that were not already the subject of a manual analysis (in order that the manual analysis subject programs be a subset of the included automated analysis programs). (There is one exception: Azureus was used in one manual analysis (Sect. 5.3), but was too large for our whole-program automated analyses.) We refer the reader to the companion technical report for full results [18].

3 Inferring Structural Types for Method Parameters

It is considered good programming practice to make parameters as general as the program allows. Bloch, for example, recommends favoring interfaces over classes in general—particularly so in the case of parameter types [3]. An analogous situation arises in the generic programming community, where it is recommended that generic algorithms and types place as few requirements as possible on their type parameters (e.g., what methods they should support) [22].

Bloch acknowledges that sometimes an appropriate interface does not exist (e.g., class java.util.Random does not implement any non-marker interfaces). In such a case the programmer is forced to use classes for parameter types—even though it is possible that multiple implementations of the same functionality could exist [3]. This is a situation where structural subtyping could be beneficial, as it allows programmers to create supertypes after-the-fact.

As it is impossible to retroactively implement interfaces in Java, we hypothesized that method parameter types are often overly specific, and sought to determine both (1) the degree and (2) the character of over-specificity. To answer question (1), we performed an automated whole-program analysis to infer structural types for method parameters. Methodology and quantitative results are described in Sect. 3.1. To properly interpret this data, however, we must consider question (2). Accordingly, we manually examined the inferred structural types from the previous analysis and considered the qualitative question of whether changing a method to have the most general structural type could potentially improve the method's interface (Sect. 3.2). Across all applications, we also counted occurrences of inferred structural types that were supertypes of classes and interfaces of the Java Collections Library. Of these, in Sect. 3.3 we present those structural types that a client might plausibly wish to implement while *not* simultaneously implementing a more specific nominal type (e.g., Collection, Map, etc.).

3.1 Quantitative Results

Our analysis infers structural types for method parameters, based on the methods that were actually called on the parameters. (For example, a method may take a List as an argument, but may only use the add and iterator methods.) The analysis, a simple inter-procedural dataflow analysis, re-computes structural types for each parameter of a method until a fixpoint is reached. Details of the algorithm are described in the companion technical report [18]. Structural types were not inferred in the following cases: calls to library methods, assignments to fields and local variables, uses of primitive types, uses of types such as String and Object, and cases where the inferred structural type would have a non-public member.

The analysis is conservative; in the case where a parameter is not used (or only methods of class Object are used), no structural type is inferred for it. (A parameter may be unused because (a) it is expected that overriding methods will use the parameter, or (b) because the method may make use of the parameter when the program evolves, or (c) because it is no longer needed, due to changes in the program.) In the case of method overriding, the analysis ensures that the same structural types are inferred for corresponding parameters in the method family.

Our results suggest that a refactoring that infers structural types is of limited utility unless structural types are used in libraries. On average, only 15% of parameters could have a structural type inferred. The remaining parameters fell into the following three categories: an average of 14% were either a primitive type or were unused; an average of 25% were uses of Object, String or StringBuffer; an average of 49% were parameters on which a library method was transitively called, or were stored to fields/local variables, or which called non-public instance methods. Thus, our results do not paint a complete picture, though the fact that several of the subjects were libraries does increase confidence in our findings. In our future work, we plan to analyze some of the libraries used by the subject applications, in order to increase the percentage of inferrable parameters.

Analysis results for 19 programs are displayed in Table 1. For example, in Ant, 16.5% of parameters could have a structural type inferred. Of these, 98.6% of the parameters were declared with an *overly specific* nominal type (i.e., the nominal type contained more methods than were actually needed). For only 2.4% of the inferred parameters did a corresponding nominal type exist that would make the parameter type as *general* as possible (i.e., a nominal type that contained only those methods transitively called on the object). There were an average of 2.0 methods in the inferred structural types, while there were 33.3 methods in the corresponding nominal types. Finally, there was a median of 1 structural type inferred for each nominal type in the program, and a maximum of 27 structural types.

Several conclusions can be drawn from the data. First, most parameter types for which a structural type can be inferred (15% on average) are overly specific (94% on average). Moreover, for most inferred parameters (91% on average), no nominal type existed in the program that was as general as possible.

Second, inferred structural types do not have many methods (3.5 on average), while the corresponding nominal types have quite a few methods (37.8 on average). This shows that there is quite a large *degree* of over specificity—more than a full order of magnitude—in addition to the large percentage of overly specific parameters. This is likely due to the overhead of naming and defining nominal types, as well as the lack of retroactive interface implementation. We also found that when nominal types were

Table 1. Results of running structural type inference. *Percent inferrable* is the percentage of parameters that could have a structural type inferred for them (i.e., where neither library methods were transitively called, nor was the parameter unused, etc.), *percent overly specific* is the percentage of the inferrable parameters that have an overly specific nominal type, *percent structural needed* is the percentage of the inferrable parameters for which a most general nominal type does *not* exist, *average methods per structural type* is the average number of methods in the inferred structural types, *average methods per nominal type* is the average number of methods in nominal types that appear as parameter types (including inherited methods), and *median/maximum structural types per nominal* are the median and maximum, respectively, of the number of inferred structural types corresponding to each nominal type.

	LOC	% inferrable	% overly specific	% structural needed	Avg methods/ structural type	Avg methods/ nominal type	Struct types/nominal median	max
Ant	62k	16.5%	98.6%	97.6%	2.0	33.3	1	27
Apache collect.	26k	10.9%	90.1%	83.6%	1.9	9.9	1	11
Areca	35k	15.0%	99.1%	97.0%	2.6	35.1	1	35
Cayenne	95k	21.1%	96.8%	93.0%	2.4	27.6	2	27
Columba	70k	12.0%	99.6%	98.7%	2.0	55.3	1	19
Crystal	12k	15.9%	97.7%	92.5%	3.5	13.7	1	19
hsqldb	62k	7.8%	99.4%	99.4%	1.9	50.8	2	34
jEdit	71k	6.7%	95.1%	95.1%	2.2	105.2	1	20
JFreeChart	93k	17.2%	97.4%	94.4%	3.2	53.4	1	35
JHotDraw	52k	17.5%	100.0%	99.6%	2.7	55.2	2	19
JRuby	86k	24.6%	97.4%	96.7%	4.4	66.1	1	85
LimeWire	97k	16.7%	98.4%	94.8%	2.1	35.2	1	21
Log4j	13k	17.1%	96.7%	95.0%	1.9	54.9	1	6
Lucene	24k	9.2%	80.5%	77.4%	1.6	9.9	1.5	8
OpenFire	90k	20.6%	99.3%	99.2%	2.5	34.3	1	45
PLT collections	19k	10.3%	49.7%	51.0%	1.6	15.2	1	25
Smack	40k	13.7%	100.0%	90.8%	4.6	25.2	1	13
Tomcat	126k	13.4%	96.7%	96.3%	4.5	34.4	2	32
Xalan	161k	12.4%	95.5%	95.1%	3.1	55.7	1	16
Average		**15.0%**	**93.5%**	**91.3%**	**3.5**	**37.8**	**1.2**	**23.4**

as general as possible, they had very few members—one or two on average. This is in accordance with previous work which found that interfaces are generally smaller than classes [25].

Next, for a given nominal type, there were not many corresponding structural types (2.5 on average, a median of 1.2). The data followed a power law distribution, with an average maximum of 24; that is, small values were heavily represented, but there were also a few large values. The low median suggests that the overhead of naming structural types is not necessarily high; it is plausible that programmers would be able to name and use structural types for around half of the nominal parameter types.

Finally, if we were to define new interfaces everywhere possible, the average increase in the number of interfaces is 313%, the median is 287%, and the maximum is 1000%. This illustrates the infeasibility of defining new nominal types for the inferred structural types. Note that we considered only those interfaces for which the `implements` clause of a class could be modified (i.e., those classes in the program's source); in general, the situation is even worse, as programmers may wish to define new supertypes for types contained in libraries.

3.2 Qualitative Results

Though our results show that many parameters are overly specific, we do not necessarily recommend that every parameter be made as general as possible. This is because a method might be currently only using a particular set of methods, but later code modifications may make it necessary to use a larger set; a more general type could hinder program evolution. On the other hand, more general types make methods more reusable, which aids program evolution. For this reason, a refactoring to structural types (or even structural type inference) cannot be a fully automated process—programmers must consider each type carefully, keeping in view the kinds of program modifications that are likely to occur. Additionally, for some structural types, there may ever be only one corresponding nominal type, in which case using a structural type is of limited utility.

Accordingly, we considered the empirical question of whether changing a given method to have the most general structural types for its parameters would make the method more general in a way that could improve the program. To determine this, we inspected each method and asked two questions. First, does the inferred parameter type S generalize the abstract operation performed by the method, as determined by the method name? Second, does it seem likely that there would be multiple subtypes of S?

We studied two applications: Apache Collections (a collections library) and Crystal (a static analysis framework). Of methods for which a structural type was inferred on one or more parameters, we found that 58% and 66%, respectively, would be generalized in a potentially useful manner if the inferred types were used.

For example, in Apache Collections, in the class `OnePredicate` (a predicate class that returns true only if one of its enclosing predicates returns true), the factory method `getInstance(Collection)` had the structural type `{iterator(); size();}` inferred for its parameter. This would make the method applicable to any collection that supported only iteration and retrieving the collection size, even if it didn't support collection addition and removal methods. There were 25 other methods in the library that used this structural type. Another example is the method `ListUtils.intersection` which takes two `List` objects. However, the first `List` need only have a `contains` method, and the second `List` need only have an `iterator` method (for this latter parameter, the interface `Iterable` could be used). There were also 8 methods that took an `Iterator` as a parameter, but never called the `remove` method. With a structural type for the method, the type would clearly specify that a read-only iterator can be passed as an argument.

In Crystal, two methods took a `Map` parameter that used only the `get` and `put` methods. Converting the method to use this structural type would make it applicable to a map that did not support iteration (such a type exists in Apache Collections, for example). Also, there were 11 methods that use only the methods `getModifiers()` and `getName()` on an `IBinding` object (an interface in the Eclipse JDT). Replacing the nominal type with a structural type would allow the program to substitute a different "bindings" class that supported only those two methods.

Of course, for some of these structural types, there may not be a large number of classes that implement its methods but not all of the methods of a more specific nominal type, e.g., `Collection`. However, we believe that all of the aforementioned types represent meaningful abstractions. Furthermore, since it is conceivable that a programmer may define a class implementing that abstraction, using these more general types would increase the applications' reusability.

Translation to Whiteoak. Using the inference algorithm, we also developed an automated translation of programs from Java to Whiteoak [14], a research language that extends Java with support for structural subtyping. We performed this translation on two programs: Apache Collections and Lucene, validating the results of the analysis and demonstrating its practical use.

3.3   Uses of Java Collections Library

We examined the inferred structural types that were generalizations of types in the Java Collections Library. Over all applications, there were 67 distinct types in total, though not all appeared to express an important abstraction. We made a conservative subjective finding that at least 10 of these types *were* potentially useful; these are displayed in Table 2, along with a description of possible implementations. The relatively high number of occurrences of each of these structural types further suggests their utility, even though the types contain few methods. It further shows that programs routinely make use of types that the library designers either did not anticipate or chose not to support.

Table 2. Uses of Java Collections classes across 19 programs, as inferred using the parameter structural type inference. (Erasures are used in lieu of generic types.).

Methods in type	Uses	Description
`get(Object); containsKey(Object);`	168	Read-only non-iterable map; for instance, a read-only hashtable
`iterator(); isEmpty(); size();`	114	Read-only iterable collection that knows its size; for instance, a read-only list
`add(Object); addAll(Collection);`	101	Write-only collection; for instance, a log
`put(Object, Object);`	55	Write-only map
`hasNext(); next();`	28	Read-only iterator
`contains(Object);`	21	Read-only collection that does not support iteration; for instance, a read-only hashset
`get(Object); put(Object, Object);`	15	Non-iterable map; for instance, a hashtable
`contains(Object); iterator(); size();`	11	Read-only iterable collection that knows its size and can be polled for the existence of an element; for instance, an iterable hashset
`add(Object); contains(Object); iterator(); size();`	10	Same as above, but that also supports adding elements
`iterator(); size(); toArray(Object[]);`	8	Read-only collection that can be converted to an array; for instance, a read-only array

In summary, the data shows that programs make repeated use of many implicit structural types. A language that would allow defining these types explicitly could be beneficial, as it can help programmers make their methods more generally applicable.

3.4   Related Work

Forster [12] and Steimann [24] have described experience using the *Infer Type* refactoring, which generates new interfaces for inferred types and replaces uses of overly

Table 3. A selection of the structural interfaces "implemented" by classes in the subject programs once methods unconditionally throwing an `UnsupportedOperationException` are removed. (Actual method sets are omitted to conserve space.).

	Number of classes
Read-only `Iterator`	50
Read-only `Collection`	19
Read-only `Map`	9
Read-only `Map.Entry`	6
Read-only `ListIterator`	6
`Collection` supporting everything but removal	5
`Map` supporting everything but removal	4
`Collection` supporting only read and removal methods	1
`Collection` supporting iteration, addition, and size only	1
`ListIterator` supporting read, add, and remove (but not `set()`)	1
`ListIterator` supporting only read and `set()` operation	1
`Map` supporting read, put, and size only	1
`Map` supporting read and put, but not size or removal	1
`Map` supporting everything but `entrySet()`, `values()` and `containsValue()`	1

specific types with these interfaces. This analysis is more general than ours, because it considers all type references, not just parameter types. However, the refactoring is limited by the fact that classes in libraries cannot retroactively implement new interfaces. Steimann found that when applying this refactoring, the number of total interfaces almost quadrupled—an increase of 369%.[1]

4   Throwing "Unsupported Operation" Exceptions

In the Java Collections Library, there are a number of "optional" methods whose documentation permits them to always throw an exception. This decision was due to the practical consideration of avoiding an "explosion" of interfaces; the library designers mentioned that at least 25 new interfaces would be otherwise required [19].

To determine if such super-interfaces would be useful in practice, we totalled the methods in the subject programs that unconditionally throw an `UnsupportedOperationException`. The program that had the most such methods was Apache Collections: there were 148 methods that unconditionally throw the exception (out of 3669 total methods, corresponding to 4%). Next, we considered those methods that were overriding a method in the Java Collections Library. To encode these optional methods directly would require 18 additional interfaces. There are only 27 interfaces defined in the library, so this represents a 67% increase. Note that this is a conservative estimate, as we did not consider interactions between classes (e.g., an `Iterable` returning a read-only `Iterator`). A selection of these structural super-interfaces are summarized in Table 3. For instance, there were 50 iterator classes that did not support the `remove()` operation, and 19 subclasses of `Collection` that supported a read-only interface.

---

[1] This differs slightly from our average of 313%, though this difference is likely due to the fact that Steimann considered only two applications.

Note that, with the exception of the read-only iterator, the sets of interfaces in Tables 3 and 2 are distinct from one another (though some are subtypes). This is likely due to the fact that different applications use different subsets of the methods of a class.

Structural subtyping could be helpful for statically ensuring that "unsupported operation" exceptions cannot occur, as it would allow programmers to express these super-interfaces directly.

5   Common Methods

In our experience, there are situations where two types share an implicit common supertype, but this relationship is not encoded in the type hierarchy. For example, suppose two classes both have a `getName` method with the same signature, but there does not exist a supertype of both classes containing this method. We call `getName`, and methods like it, *common methods*. Common methods can occur when programmers do not anticipate the utility of a shared supertype or when two methods have the same name, but perform different operations; e.g., `Cowboy.draw()` and `Circle.draw()` [16].

Accordingly, this section aims to answer three questions: (1) how often do common methods occur, (2) how many common methods represent an accidental name clash, and (3) do common methods result in code clones.

5.1   Frequency

We performed a simple whole-program analysis to count the number of common methods in each application. Only public instance methods were considered (resulting in slightly different data than that previously presented [17]). Results are in Table 4. Overall, common methods comprise an average of 19% of all public instance methods. That is, for 19% of methods, there existed another method with the same name and signature and the method was not contained in a common supertype of the enclosing types.

We also computed the number of types that share at least two common methods with another type; there were an average of 9% of such types. These are the cases in which a structural supertype is most likely to be useful. This high percentage indicates that there are a number of implicit structural types in most applications.

For example, in Apache Collections, `UnmodifiableSortedMap` and `OrderedMap` share the methods `firstKey()` and `lastKey()`. And, `AbstractLinkedList` and `SequencedHashMap` share the methods `getFirst()` and `getLast()`. Finally, `BoundedMap` and `BoundedCollection` have the common methods `isFull()` and `maxSize()`.

In Lucene, a document indexing and search library, `RAMOutputStream` and `RAMInputStream` both support the `seek()`, `close()`, and `getFilePointer()` methods, which might be useful to move to a supertype. Also, the classes `PhraseQuery` and `MultiPhraseQuery` both support the methods `add(Term)`, `getPositions()`, `getSlop()`, and `setSlop(int)`.

5.2   Accidental Name Clashes

Of course, to interpret this data, we must consider cases where the common methods have the same *meaning*, and where callers are likely to call the methods with the same

Table 4. Common methods for each application. *Number of types* indicates the total number of types in the application, *types with greater than one common method* is the number of types that share more than one common method, *percentage* is the percentage of this compared to the total number of types, *percent common methods* is the percentage of public instance methods that is a common method, and *average number of classes per common signature* is the average number of classes for each common method signature.

	LOC	Number of types	Types with >1 common method	Percentage	% common methods	Avg # classes/ common signature
Ant	62k	945	65	6.9%	31.3%	3.7
Apache Collections	26k	550	19	3.5%	7.3%	2.7
Areca	35k	362	30	8.3%	15.4%	2.7
Cayenne	95k	1415	104	7.3%	18.1%	2.8
Columba	70k	1232	48	3.9%	17.3%	3.1
Crystal	12k	211	4	1.9%	5.1%	2.9
hsqldb	62k	355	31	8.7%	19.5%	2.6
jEdit	71k	880	40	4.5%	11.7%	2.5
JFreeChart	93k	789	301	38.1%	39.5%	3.9
JHotDraw	52k	616	59	9.6%	19.0%	2.8
JRuby	86k	997	83	8.3%	15.6%	3.1
LimeWire	97k	1689	88	5.2%	17.7%	3.1
log4j	13k	201	4	2.0%	13.6%	2.4
Lucene	24k	398	21	5.3%	13.4%	2.6
OpenFire	90k	1039	110	10.6%	19.0%	3
plt collections	19k	812	60	7.4%	7.5%	2.8
Smack	40k	847	115	13.6%	23.5%	3.3
Tomcat	126k	1727	234	13.5%	32.6%	3.6
xalan	161k	1223	94	7.7%	16.1%	2.9
Average				**9.3%**	**19.0%**	**2.9**

purpose in mind. If two methods have the same meaning, it might be useful to define a structural type consisting of that method. Two methods are defined as "having the same meaning" if they perform the same abstract operation, taking into account (a) the semantics of the method, and (b) the semantics of the enclosing types. This determination was made by examining the source code, using javadoc where available.

We studied two applications: Apache Collections and Lucene. In Collections, under condition (a), there were no methods that had the same signature but performed different abstract operations. However, there were 2 cases (1% of all common methods) where the methods had the same meaning, but the enclosing classes did not appear to be semantic subtypes of some common supertype containing that method; i.e., condition (b) was not satisfied. For example, the classes ChainedClosure and SwitchClosure both had a getClosures() method, but ChainedClosure calls each of these closures in turn, while SwitchClosure calls that closure whose predicate returns true.

In Lucene, there were 42 instances of methods that had the same signature, but did not have the same meaning (19% of all common methods). In 32 of these cases, the methods were actually performing a different abstract operation. For example, HitIterator.length() returned the number of hits for a particular query, while Payload.length() returned the length of the payload data. An additional 10 cases did not satisfy condition (b) above. For example, in a high-level class IndexModifier, there were several cases where a method m performed some operation, then called

```
// repeated exactly in 19 classes
if (property == EXPRESSION_PROPERTY) {
  if (get) {
    return getExpression();
  } else {
    setExpression((Expression) child);
    return null;
  }
}
```

(a)

```
private InlineMethodRefactoring(ICompilationUnit unit,
    MethodInvocation node, int offset, int length)
{
  this(unit, (ASTNode)node, offset, length);
  fTargetProvider= TargetProvider.create(unit, node);
  fInitialMode= fCurrentMode= Mode.INLINE_SINGLE;
  fDeleteSource= false;
}

private InlineMethodRefactoring(ICompilationUnit unit,
    SuperMethodInvocation node, int offset, int length)
{
  ... // same method body as above
}
```

(b)

Fig. 1. Examples of code duplication in the Eclipse JDT. Structural subtyping could eliminate this duplication.

IndexWriter.m, the latter performing a lower-level operation. So, the semantics of the methods were similar, but the semantics of each class was different.

Overall, the data is very promising, as it indicates that most common methods have the same meaning and would benefit from being contained in a structural supertype—90% on average, across both applications. Structural subtyping would allow these methods to be called in a generic manner, without the need to create additional interfaces.

5.3   Code Clones

We hypothesized that common methods can lead to code clones, as there is a common structure that is not expressed in the type system. To determine this, we examined two applications: Eclipse JDT and Azureus.

In the Eclipse Java Development Tools (JDT), many AST classes have methods getExpression and setExpression, but these methods are not contained in a supertype. As a result, there is repeated code in each of these classes, e.g., related to reading and storing these attributes in a generic internal AST map. The code for this is shown in Fig. 1a. This could be re-written using structural subtyping by writing a helper method taking a parameter of structural type { getExpression; setExpression; }. The repeated code would then be replaced with something similar to getSetExpr(this, get, child). A similar situation occurs with the methods typeArguments() and getBody().

Similarly, the classes FieldAccess and SuperFieldAccess have no superclass other than Expression. The same problem occurs with MethodInvocation and SuperMethodInvocation, and ConstructorInvocation and SuperConstructorInvocation. We found 44 code clones involving these types (though some were only a few lines long). An example of a code clone involving MethodInvocation and SuperMethodInvocation appears in Fig. 1b.

In the Eclipse SWT (Simple Windowing Toolkit), there are 13 classes (such as Button, Label, and Link) with the methods getText and setText that get and set the main text for the control. But, there is no common IText interface. Azureus, a

```
if (widget instanceof Label)                    if (widget instanceof CoolBar) {
   ((Label) widget).setText(message);              CoolItem[] items = ((CoolBar)widget).getItems();
else if (widget instanceof CLabel)                 for(int i = 0; i < items.length; i++) {
   ((CLabel) widget).setText(message);                Control control = items[i].getControl();
else if (widget instanceof Group)                     updateLanguageForControl(control);
   ((Group) widget).setText(message);               }
... // 5 more items                              } else if (widget instanceof TabFolder) {
                                                    ... // same code
                                                 } else if (widget instanceof CTabFolder) {
                                                    ... // same code
                                                 ... // 5 more items
              (a)                                              (b)
```

Fig. 2. Code excerpts from Azureus, illustrating an awkward coding style and duplication

BitTorrent client, is an application that requires the ability to call these methods in a generic fashion. Azureus is localized for a number of languages, which can be changed at runtime. Accordingly, there are several instances of code similar to that of Fig. 2.

Note that some of this code duplication might be avoided if the class hierarchy were refactored. Obviously, this is not always possible—e.g., Azureus cannot modify SWT.

In summary, common methods can lead to undesirable code duplication. Structural subtyping can help eliminate this problem, without refactoring the class hierarchy.

6 Cascading "Instanceof" Tests

We considered the question of whether structural subtyping could provide benefits if used in conjunction with other language features—external methods in particular. *External methods* (also known as open classes) are similar to ordinary methods and provide the the usual dispatch semantics, but can be implemented outside of a class's definition, providing more flexibility. Multimethods are a generalized form of external method, defined outside all classes and allowing dispatch on any subset of a method's arguments [9, 4, 10, 17].

Since Java does not support any form of external dispatch, programmers often compensate by using cascading instanceof tests. This programming pattern is problematic because it is tedious, error-prone, and lacks extensibility [10]. Many instances of this pattern could be re-written to use external methods, but a problem arises if an instanceof test is performed on an expression of type Object.

To illustrate this, let us consider how instanceof tests would be translated to external methods. Suppose we have a cascaded instanceof, with each case of the form "[else] if expr instanceof C_i { $block_i$ }." This would be translated to an external method f defined on expr's class, and overridden for each C_i by defining $C_i.f$ { $block_i$ }. The top part of Fig. 3b shows the external methods translated from the instanceof tests in Fig. 3a (but without an external method defined on Object, the type of query, which we will come to in a moment).

A problem arises when the target expression in the instanceof test is of type Object, as an external method must be defined on Object, then overridden for each

<table>
<tr><td>

```
List qlist = ...
Object query = qlist.get(i);
Query q = null;
if (query instanceof String)
  q = parser.parse((String) query);
else if (query instanceof Query)
  q = (Query) query;
else
  System.err.println(
    "Unsupported query type");
```

(a)
</td><td>

```
// external methods
Query String.toQuery(QueryParser parser) {
  return parser.parse(this);
}
Query Query.toQuery(QueryParser parser) {
  return this;
}
  ...
// structural type
struct QueryConvert { Query toQuery(QueryParser) };
List<QueryConvert> qlist = ...
Query q = qlist.get(i).toQuery(parser);
```

(b)
</td></tr>
</table>

Fig. 3. Rewriting `instanceof` using structural subtyping and external dispatch. Listing (a) is the original code; listing (b) is the translated code, which defines the structural type `QueryConvert` and external methods on `Query` and `String`. Note that the translated code eliminates the need for the error condition.

Table 5. Total `instanceof` tests, the number present in cascading `if` statements that perform the test on an expression of type `Object`, and that number expressed as a percentage. Code written using this pattern can be translated to a language with structural subtyping and external dispatch.

	`instanceof`	Expression of type `Object`	Percentage
Apache collections	225	75	33%
Areca	77	10	13%
JHotDraw	229	50	22%
log4j	54	8	15%
Lucene	56	10	18%
PLT collections	119	64	54%
Smack	56	20	36%
Tomcat	959	158	16%
Average			**26%**

type tested via an `instanceof`. The problem with this solution is that it pollutes the interface of `Object`. In many cases, the implementation of this method performs a generic fallback operation that does not make sense for an object of arbitrary type—but this method becomes part of every class's interface and implementation. (While it is also possible to pollute the interface of an arbitrary class *C*, this is generally less severe, and detecting such a situation requires application-specific knowledge.)

To determine the prevalence of this pattern, we manually searched for `instanceof` tests in 8 applications, and found that 13% to 54% (with an average of 26%) were performing a cascading `instanceof` test on an expression of type `Object` (see Table 5).

Structural subtyping provides one solution to this problem. We have previously defined a language with both structural subtyping and external dispatch [17]. The type of the expression on which the `instanceof` is performed would be changed from `Object` to the structural type consisting of the newly defined external method *f*. That is, instead of making the target operation applicable to an arbitrary object, it would be applicable to only those objects that contain method f. Figure 3b defines an external method toQuery on String and Query, then uses the structural type { toQuery(...) } as the type for the List elements. The advantage of using structural subtyping is that the main code can call this method uniformly. [2]

Thus, for many applications, there is a potential benefit to using structural subtyping in a language that supports external dispatch; an average of 26% of instanceof tests could be eliminated.

Note that since we refined the element type of the List object, this obviates the need for the error condition—an additional advantage. However, it is not always possible to refine types to a structural type; an expression may simply have type Object, due to the loss of type information. In such a case, it would be possible to re-write the code using a structural downcast. Though the use of casts would not be eliminated, there are still several advantages to this implementation style. First, the external methods could be changed without having to also modify the method that uses them. Also, if subclasses are added, a new internal or external method could be defined for them. Finally, since the proposed cast would use a structural type, it would be more general, applying to any type for which the method were defined.

7   Java Reflection Analysis

We aimed to answer the following question: do Java programs use reflection where structural types would be more appropriate? We hypothesized that uses of reflection fall into two categories: cases where dynamic class instantiation and classloading are used, and cases where the type system is not sufficiently powerful to express the programming pattern used. It is difficult to eliminate reflection in the first category, as these uses represent an inherently dynamic operation. However, some of the uses in the second category could potentially be rewritten using structural downcasts. Reducing the uses of reflection is beneficial as it decreases the number of runtime errors and can improve performance.

We examined 28 applications, and found that an average of 32% of uses of the reflection method Class.getMethod could be re-written using a structural downcast (see Table 6). A structural downcast is preferable to reflection because type information is retained when later calling methods, as opposed to Method.invoke, which is passed an Object array and must typecheck the arguments at runtime. Additionally, it is easier to combine sets of methods in a downcast; when using reflection, each method must be selected individually. There is also the potential to make method calls more efficient, which is difficult with reflection, due to the low-level nature of the available operations. (For example, the language Whiteoak [14] supports efficient structural downcasts.)

In summary, the high percentage of reflection uses that can be translated to structural downcasts suggests that programmers may sometimes use reflection as a workaround for lack of structural types.

---

[2] Note that it would not be possible to make use of a nominal interface containing the method f to call the method in a generic manner. For external methods to be modular, once a method is defined as an internal method, it cannot be implemented with an external method; see [20, 10].

Table 6. Uses of the reflection method `Class.getMethod`, and the number and percentage that could be re-written using a structural downcast. Programs that did not call this method are omitted. The percentage entry in the last row is calculated by dividing the total "*could be rewritten*" by the total "*uses of getMethod.*"

	Uses of `getMethod`	Could be rewritten	Percentage
Ant	36	9	25%
Apache Collections	4	3	75%
Areca	1	0	0%
Azureus	27	6	22%
Cayenne	28	4	14%
Columba	10	8	80%
hsqldb	2	0	0%
jEdit	10	7	70%
JFreeChart	1	1	100%
JHotDraw	26	1	4%
JRuby	17	6	35%
log4j	4	1	25%
OpenFire	2	0	0%
Tomcat	37	10	27%
Xalan	28	11	39%
Totals	**233**	**67**	**29%**

8 Related Work

A number of research languages support structural subtyping, such as O'Caml [15], PolyToil [6], Moby [11], and Strongtalk [5]. We have also previously defined a language supporting both external dispatch and structural subtyping [17]. An evaluation of the benefits of each of nominal and structural subtyping is available in [23, 17].

As mentioned in Sect. 3, researchers have studied the problem of refactoring programs to use most general nominal types where possible [12, 24]. Structural subtyping would make such refactorings more feasible (since new types would not have to be defined) and applicable to more type references in the program (since structural supertypes for library types could be created, while new interfaces cannot).

Muschevici et al. measured the number of cascading `instanceof` tests in a number of Java programs, to determine how often multiple dispatch might be applicable [21]. They found that cascading `instanceof` tests were quite common, and that many cases could be rewritten to use multimethods; this is consistent with our results.

Corpus analysis is commonly used in empirical software engineering research. For example, it has been used to examine non-nullness [8], aspects [2], micro patterns [13], and inheritance [25].

9 Summary and Conclusions

In summary, we found that a number of different aspects of Java programs suggest the potential utility of structural subtyping. While some of the results are not as strong as others, taken together the data suggests that programs could benefit from the addition of structural subtyping, even if they were written in a nominally-typed language.

We hope that the results of this study will be used to inform designers of future programming languages, as well as serve as a starting point for further empirical studies in this area. Ultimately, one must study the way structural subtyping is eventually used by mainstream programmers; this work serves as a step in that direction.

Acknowledgements. We would like to thank Ewan Tempero for helpful discussions and feedback, and Nels Beckman and the reviewers for comments on an earlier version of this paper. This research was supported in part by the U.S. Department of Defense, Army Research Office grant number DAAD19-02-1-0389 entitled "Perpetually Available and Secure Information Systems," and NSF CAREER award CCF-0546550.

References

[1] Amadio, R., Cardelli, L.: Subtyping recursive types. ACM TOPLAS 15(4) (1993)

[2] Baldi, P., Lopes, C., Linstead, E., Bajracharya, S.: A theory of aspects as latent topics. In: OOPSLA (2008)

[3] Bloch, J.: Effective Java, 2nd edn. Addison-Wesley, Reading (2008)

[4] Boyland, J., Castagna, G.: Parasitic methods: an implementation of multi-methods for Java. In: OOPSLA 1997, pp. 66–76 (1997)

[5] Bracha, G., Griswold, D.: Strongtalk: typechecking Smalltalk in a production environment. In: OOPSLA 1993, pp. 215–230 (1993)

[6] Bruce, K., Schuett, A., van Gent, R., Fiech, A.: PolyTOIL: A type-safe polymorphic object-oriented language. ACM Trans. Program. Lang. Syst. 25(2), 225–290 (2003)

[7] Cardelli, L.: Structural subtyping and the notion of power type. In: POPL 1988 (1988)

[8] Chalin, P., James, P.: Non-null references by default in Java: Alleviating the nullity annotation burden. In: Ernst, E. (ed.) ECOOP 2007. LNCS, vol. 4609, pp. 227–247. Springer, Heidelberg (2007)

[9] Chambers, C.: Object-oriented multi-methods in Cecil. In: Lehrmann Madsen, O. (ed.) ECOOP 1992. LNCS, vol. 615, pp. 33–56. Springer, Heidelberg (1992)

[10] Clifton, C., Millstein, T., Leavens, G., Chambers, C.: MultiJava: Design rationale, compiler implementation, and applications. ACM TOPLAS 28(3), 517–575 (2006)

[11] Fisher, K., Reppy, J.: The design of a class mechanism for Moby. In: PLDI (1999)

[12] Forster, F.: Cost and benefit of rigorous decoupling with context-specific interfaces. In: PPPJ 2006, pp. 23–30 (2006)

[13] Gil, J., Maman, I.: Micro patterns in Java code. In: OOPSLA 2005, pp. 97–116 (2005)

[14] Gil, J., Maman, I.: Whiteoak: Introducing structural typing into Java. In: OOPSLA (2008)

[15] Leroy, X., Doligez, D., Garrigue, J., Rémy, D., Vouillon, J.: The Objective Caml system, release 3.10 (2007), http://caml.inria.fr/pub/docs/manual-ocaml

[16] Magnusson, B.: Code reuse considered harmful. Journal of Object-Oriented Programming 4(3) (November 1991)

[17] Malayeri, D., Aldrich, J.: Integrating nominal and structural subtyping. In: Vitek, J. (ed.) ECOOP 2008. LNCS, vol. 5142, pp. 260–284. Springer, Heidelberg (2008)

[18] Malayeri, D., Aldrich, J.: Is structural subtyping useful? An empirical study. Technical Report CMU-CS-09-100, School of Computer Science, Carnegie Mellon University (January 2009)

[19] Sun Microsystems. Java collections API design FAQ (2003), http://java.sun.com/j2se/1.4.2/docs/guide/collections/designfaq.html

[20] Millstein, T., Chambers, C.: Modular statically typed multimethods. Inf. Comput. 175(1), 76–118 (2002)

[21] Muschevici, R., Potanin, A., Tempero, E., Noble, J.: Multiple dispatch in practice. In: OOP-SLA 2008 (October 2008)

[22] Musser, D., Stepanov, A.: Generic programming. In: Gianni, P. (ed.) An Optimized Translation Process and Its Application to ALGOL 68. LNCS, vol. 38, pp. 13–25. Springer, Heidelberg (1989)

[23] Pierce, B.: Types and Programming Languages. MIT Press, Cambridge (2002)

[24] Steimann, F.: The infer type refactoring and its use for interface-based programming. Journal of Object Technology 6(2) (2007)

[25] Tempero, E.D., Noble, J., Melton, H.: How do Java programs use inheritance? An empirical study of inheritance in Java software. In: Vitek, J. (ed.) ECOOP 2008. LNCS, vol. 5142, pp. 667–691. Springer, Heidelberg (2008)

An Interval-Based Inference of Variant Parametric Types*

Florin Craciun[1], Wei-Ngan Chin[2], Guanhua He[1], and Shengchao Qin[1]

[1] Department of Computer Science, Durham University, UK
{florin.craciun,guanhua.he,shengchao.qin}@durham.ac.uk
[2] Department of Computer Science, National University of Singapore, Singapore
chinwn@comp.nus.edu.sg

Abstract. Variant parametric types represent the successful integration of subtype and parametric polymorphism to support a more flexible subtyping for Java-like languages. A key feature that helps strengthen this integration is the use-site variance. Depending on how the fields are used, each variance denotes a covariant, a contravariant, an invariant or a bivariant subtyping. By annotating variance properties on each type argument to a parametric class, programmers can choose various desirable variance properties for each use of the parametric class. Although Java library classes have been successfully refactored to use variant parametric types, these mechanisms are often criticized, due to the difficulty of choosing appropriate variance annotations. Several algorithms have been proposed for automatically refactoring legacy Java code to use generic libraries, but none can support the full flexibility of the use-site variance-based subtyping. This paper addresses this difficulty by proposing a novel interval-based approach to inferring both the variance annotations and the type arguments. Each variant parametric type is regarded as an interval type with two type bounds, a lower bound for writing and an upper bound for reading. We propose a constraint-based inference algorithm that works on a per method basis, as a summary-based analysis.

1 Introduction

Recently, several mainstream object-oriented languages, such as Java and C#, have successfully integrated traditional *subtype polymorphism* and *parametric polymorphism* to support better type-safe reusable code with significant reduction of runtime cast operations. Subtype polymorphism is a nominal relation, based on a given class hierarchy. Parametric polymorphism allows a data or a function to be parameterized by types and supports structural subtyping [1]. In handling objects with mutable fields, a crucial feature that helps strengthen the integration of subtype and parametric polymorphism is the adoption of *variance*. Variance annotations predict the flow of values for fields and provide a richer subtyping hierarchy. Depending on how the fields are being accessed, each variance denotes a covariant, a contravariant, an invariant or a bivariant subtyping. Generics types of Java 5 (also called Wildcard Types) [23,24,12] are based on the variant parametric types (or VPTs) [14]. VPTs is based on *use-site variance* whereby each use of a class type is marked with suitable variances that indicate how the fields are to be accessed.

---

* The work is supported in part by the EPSRC project EP/E021948/1.

G. Castagna (Ed.): ESOP 2009, LNCS 5502, pp. 112–127, 2009.

Variant Parametric Types. Consider a variant parametric class `Pair` with two fields which are captured as type parameters:

$$\text{class Pair}\langle A, B \rangle \ \{ \ \text{A fst;} \quad \text{B snd;} \quad \cdots \ \}$$

Assume three methods to retrieve the first field, to set the second field and to swap the two fields for a `Pair` object. In these methods, the parameter `this` is the `Pair` object whose variant parametric type must be provided with suitable variances. The type of the `this` parameter is specified prior to delimiter $'|'$ (as in [4]):

```
Pair⟨⊕A,⊛⟩ | C getFst⟨A,C⟩() where A<:C  { return this.fst; }
Pair⟨⊛,⊖B⟩ | void setSnd⟨B,C⟩(C y) where C<:B  { this.snd=y; }
Pair⟨⊙A,⊙A⟩ | void swap⟨A⟩(){A y=this.fst; this.fst=this.snd; this.snd=y; }
```

As can be seen, four kinds of variance annotations (denoted by α) are possible: (i) $\alpha = \oplus$ captures a *flow-out* from the field to support covariant subtyping; (ii) $\alpha = \ominus$ captures a *flow-in* to the field to support contravariant subtyping; (iii) $\alpha = \odot$ captures both *flow-in* and *flow-out* to support invariant subtyping; and (iv) $\alpha = \circledast$ captures *no access* for the field to support bivariant subtyping. For simplicity, $\circledast t$ can be abbreviated as $\circledast$. More generally, given an object with variant parametric type $c_1\langle \alpha_1 t_1 \rangle$, we may pass it to a location with type $c_2\langle \alpha_2 t_2 \rangle$, in accordance with the following subsumption relations:

$$\frac{c_1 <: c_2 \quad \alpha_1 t_1 <: \alpha_2 t_2}{c_1\langle \alpha_1 t_1 \rangle <: c_2\langle \alpha_2 t_2 \rangle} \qquad \frac{(\alpha_1 <: \odot) \quad t_1 = t_2}{\alpha_1 t_1 <: \odot t_2} \qquad \frac{}{\alpha_1 t_1 <: \circledast t_2}$$

$$\frac{(\alpha_1 <: \oplus \wedge t_1 <: t_2) \vee t_2 = \text{Object}}{\alpha_1 t_1 <: \oplus t_2} \qquad \frac{(\alpha_1 <: \ominus \wedge t_2 <: t_1) \vee t_2 = \bot}{\alpha_1 t_1 <: \ominus t_2}$$

The bottom of the class hierarchy is $\bot$ denoting the type of `null` value, while the top of the class hierarchy is `Object`. For simplicity, the first rule assumes that each class constructor has only a single inheritable type parameter. The above rules use nominal subtyping $c_1 <: c_2$ from traditional class hierarchy and also a reflexive and transitive variance subtyping with a simple hierarchy: $\odot <: \oplus <: \circledast \quad \odot <: \ominus <: \circledast$. The $<:$ operator is overloaded to handle variance subtyping, nominal class subtyping and two VPT subtypings for t and αt, respectively. The above subsumption relations form the basis of the VPT system to provide a richer subtyping system. Two provisos highlighted in the above rules for parametric fields are (i) to allow each such field to be retrievable as an `Object`, and (ii) a null value (of $\bot$ type) to be written into any such field, regardless of its variant annotation. Types $\oplus$`Object` and $\ominus\bot$ are essentially equivalent to $\circledast t$.

Motivation. Although VPT mechanisms have now been validated in the full-scale implementation of Java 5 [12] and Java library classes have been successfully refactored to use variant parametric types, these mechanisms are often criticized, due to the difficulty of choosing appropriate variance annotations. By annotating variance properties on each type argument to a parametric class, programmers can choose various desirable variance properties for each use of the parametric class. For example, the types `Pair⟨⊕A, ⊕B⟩` or `Pair⟨⊙A, ⊙B⟩` are still correct types for the receiver of the above method `getFst`. However the best generic type is `Pair⟨⊕A, ⊛⟩`, since the first field is read and the second field is not accessed. In order to establish the most flexible correct variance annotations (those which do not restrict the code genericity) for a type declaration, the programmer has to analyse all the places where that type declaration is used in the program. Although several algorithms have been proposed for refactoring legacy Java code [9,8,7,11], they are restricted either to parametric types [1] or to variant parametric types with known variance annotations. No one can support the full flexibility of the use-site variance-based subtyping. Moreover these algorithms require global analysis.

Contributions. We propose a novel approach to automatically inferring the variance annotations and the type variables for the variant parametric types of method parameters (including receiver), method result and method body's local variables. In addition, the expected value flow that may arise from the method body is captured as a precondition. The inference is designed as *a summary-based analysis* that works on a per method basis: the variant parametric types of a method are inferred only based on how they are used in the method body, while each call site is a specific instance of the method's type declaration. Our inference is guided by a dependency graph such that all the methods which are called by the current method have been already analyzed. Our inference also assumes that the generic class hierarchy is known. In order to support the full flexibility of the subtyping based on the use-site variance, our inference algorithm starts with unknown variance annotations. Each variant parametric type is represented as an *interval type* [2], namely two type bounds that allow us to distinguish a *read flow* from a *write flow* for each object's field. Based on a flow-based approach for VPTs [4], we reduce the problem of inferring variance annotations and type arguments to the problem of solving specialized *flow constraints*. To the best of our knowledge this is *the first algorithm* that decouples variance inference from the type inference itself. In order to allow more generic types for the method parameters we introduce *dual types* to support *unknown variance flow*. Dual types make a distinction between flow via an object, *object flow* and the flow via the object's fields, *field flow*. We also use *intersection and union types* to capture the *divergent flow* and *convergent flow*, respectively. A safe yet precise approximation is used to avoid disjunctive constraints. We also provide special solutions to handle runtime cast operations and method overriding.

Related Work. The task of introducing generics to an existing Java code [9,8,7,11,16] consists of two distinct problems, parameterization and instantiation. Class parameterization selects the class fields that can be promoted as class type parameters. Since class parameterization decisions may be quite hard to automate due to trade-offs in the possible design outcomes, our solution is to let programmers focus on high-level design decisions for parameterization, while leaving the more tedious annotations on value flows of methods to be automatically inferred. Previous algorithms for instantiation have been restricted to parametric types based on invariant subtyping [9,8,7,11]. Although the most recent Java refactoring paper [16] claims being able to infer wildcard types, it conservatively assumes invariant subtyping even with wildcard types.

At each call site, Java compiler [12] performs a local inference of the method's type parameters. The algorithm follows the local type inference designed for parametric types [17] . Recently, a significant revision of Java local inference has been proposed in [21]. The new proposal has introduced two bounds for a type variable similar to our interval types. However it does not perform variance inference since the variance annotations are known. Our approach is more general and subsuming the local type inference.

Our variant parametric type inference algorithm produces subtyping (flow) constraints. To solve them, we work on a closed constraint graph employing techniques from [25,18,22,10]. It seems also possible to formalize our constraint solver on a pre-transitive graph [13] to have a more scalable implementation. In general the constraint solving techniques assume that the polarities of term constructors are known. However the inference of variant parametric types may generate term constructors with unknown polarities (variances). Therefore our approach uses an interval type (a contravariant lower bound and a covariant upper bound) to represent each unknown polarity of a term constructor. The idea of using interval types for updatable values has already been applied to reference type [20,19] and also in the context of object calculi [2]. An open problem (discussed in [2]) is whether the interval types can be used to infer types with variance information from non-annotated terms. Our variance inference provides a constraint-based solution to this open problem.

Outline. The following section presents our interval-based view of VPTs. Section 3 introduces the key features of our approach. Section 4 formalizes our inference algorithm. Section 5 solves the method overriding problem. A brief conclusion is then given.

2 Variant Parametric Types as Interval Types

The underlying idea behind our solution is to view each variant parametric type αX as an interval (of types) with a low-bound $X.L$ and a high-bound $X.H$ such that $X.L <: X.H$. The low-bound variable captures each value of type t_1 that may *flow into* αX using the constraint $t_1 <: X.L$, while the high-bound variable captures each value of type t_2 that may *flow out* of αX using $X.H <: t_2$. By default, it is always safe for each low-bound $X.L$ to be bounded by $\perp <: X.L$ and each high-bound can be bounded by $X.H <: Object$. For example, given a variant parametric type $c\langle \alpha X \rangle$ (where X is a type variable) denoting a class with a field of type αX, it can always be translated into an interval type as follows:

$$\frac{X = X.H}{c\langle \oplus X \rangle \Longleftrightarrow c\langle [\perp, X.H] \rangle} \quad \frac{X = X.L}{c\langle \ominus X \rangle \Longleftrightarrow c\langle [X.L, Object] \rangle} \quad \frac{}{c\langle \odot X \rangle \Longleftrightarrow c\langle [X, X] \rangle}$$

$$\frac{}{c\langle \circledast \rangle \Longleftrightarrow c\langle [\perp, Object] \rangle} \quad \frac{X.L = \texttt{fresh}() \quad X.H = \texttt{fresh}()}{c\langle \alpha X \rangle \Longrightarrow c\langle [X.L, X.H] \rangle}$$

Translation rules are bidirectional where the variance is known. The last rule is a key rule for variance inference, as it splits a type variable with an unknown variance into two type variables. Thus, field selection (reading) uses the type $X.H$, while field updating (writing) is based on type $X.L$.

The *interval type subtyping* subsumes VPT subtyping and is defined as a contravariant subtyping on low-bounds and a covariant subtyping on high-bounds, as follows:

$$\frac{c_1 <: c_2 \quad t_2.L <: t_1.L \quad t_1.H <: t_2.H}{c_1 \langle [t_1.L, t_1.H] \rangle <: c_2 \langle [t_2.L, t_2.H] \rangle}$$

The annotations .L and .H make a flow-based distinction among the types, such that:

- $X.L$ denotes a type that expects a *write flow* (flow in),
- $X.H$ denotes a type that expects a *read flow* (flow out),
- X (without annotation) denotes a type that expects both *read* and *write* flows.

Using the flow expectations, we identified a special group of flow constraints that we called *closed flow constraints*. They denote a matching of a flow-out with a flow-in, namely a consumption of a read flow by a write flow.

Definition 1 (Closed Flow Constraint). *A closed flow constraint is a flow constraint that has one of the following forms:* $X_1.H{<:}X_2.L$, $X_1.H{<:}X_2$, $X_1{<:}X_2.L$, *and* $X_1{<:}X_2$, *where* X_1, X_2, *are different from Object and* $\bot$.

Proposition 1 (Variance Inference Rule-1). *If a low-bound type variable* X.L *does not occur in any closed flow constraint, it is resolved to be* $\bot$. *If a high-bound type variable* X.H *does not occur in any closed flow constraint, it is resolved to be Object.*

3   Inference of Variant Parametric Types

3.1   Main Algorithm

This section illustrates the main steps of our inference algorithm using the following method of a non-generic `Pair` class:

```
Pair | Object move(Pair a) { Object y=a.getFst(); this.setSnd(y); return y; }
```

Our goal is to infer its generic version that corresponds to the variant parametric class $Pair\langle A, B\rangle$. Internally, our algorithm works with interval types to generate and solve the flow constraints. Therefore, we use the following interval type based specifications of the methods `getFst` and `setSnd` of the variant parametric class $Pair\langle A, B\rangle$:

$$Pair\langle[\bot, A.H], [\bot, Object]\rangle \mid C\ getFst\langle A.H, C\rangle()\ \text{where}\ A.H{<:}C\ \{..\}$$
$$Pair\langle[\bot, Object], [B.L, Object]\rangle \mid void\ setSnd\langle B.L, C\rangle(C\ y)\ \text{where}\ C{<:}B.L\ \{..\}$$

Step 0. Decoration with Fresh Interval Types. This is a pre-processing step. It consists of the annotation with fresh type variables of the non-generic types and non-generic methods. We use the following naming conventions: the letters V_i for the global type variables (visible outside the method), the letter Y for the method result, the letters N_i for the arguments of new expressions, and the letters T_i for other annotations:

$$Pair\langle[V_1.L, V_1.H], [V_2.L, V_2.H]\rangle \mid Y\ move(Pair\langle[V_3.L, V_3.H], [V_4.L, V_4.H]\rangle\ a)$$
$$\{T_0\ y=a.getFst\langle T_1.H, T_2\rangle();\ this.setSnd\langle T_3.L, T_4\rangle(y);\ return\ y; \}$$

Step 1. Collect Flow Constraints. This step gathers the constraints from the method body using the type inference rules given in Section 4.1, as follows:

$$Pair\langle[V_3.L, V_3.H], [V_4.L, V_4.H]\rangle{<:}Pair\langle[\bot, T_1.H], [\bot, Object]\rangle \wedge T_1.H{<:}T_2 \wedge T_2{<:}T_0 \wedge T_0{<:}T_4 \wedge$$
$$T_4{<:}T_3.L \wedge Pair\langle[V_1.L, V_1.H], [V_2.L, V_2.H]\rangle{<:}Pair\langle[\bot, Object], [T_3.L, Object]\rangle \wedge T_0{<:}Y$$

Step 2. Simplify Flow Constraints. This is a closure algorithm that iteratively decomposes the constraints into their elementary components. It primarily applies the interval subtyping rules with transitivity. The closure algorithm is invoked each time a new constraint is added to the set. For brevity, in the following examples, we omit the transitivity and the default constraints like $\bot{<:}X$, $X{<:}Object$, and $X.L{<:}X.H$. The result of this step is the following:

$$V_3.H{<:}T_1.H \wedge T_1.H{<:}T_2 \wedge T_2{<:}T_0 \wedge T_0{<:}T_4 \wedge T_4{<:}T_3.L \wedge T_3.L{<:}V_2.L \wedge T_0{<:}Y$$

Step 3. Variance Inference. This step generates a set of closed flow constraints and then applies the variance inference rule from Section 2. Since $V_1.L, V_1.H, V_4.L, V_4.H, V_2.H, V_3.L$ do not occur in any closed flow constraint, they are accordingly solved as follows:

$$V_1.L{=}\bot \wedge V_1.H{=}Object \wedge V_4.L{=}\bot \wedge V_4.H{=}Object \wedge V_2.H{=}Object \wedge V_3.L{=}\bot$$

Step 4. Type Variables Inference. This step solves the type variables T_i, N_i, and Y in term of the global type variables V_i and ground types (which are types without type variables). It consists of three substeps:

1. Cycle elimination: This causes all type variables of a cycle to be equal. Note that there isn't a cycle in the current example.
2. Ordering: The type variables are ordered based on the number of constraints in which they appear as an upper bound.
3. Unification: Following the order defined before, the type variables are solved by equating to their low bounds. Type variables occuring in fewer constraints have a higher priority.

For our example, the result of the unification is summarized by the last column of the following table. The first column contains the constraints in which the type variables from the second column occur as upper bounds. Multiple type variables in the second column denotes type variables having the same priority.

Constraints	TVars	Result
$V_3.H<:T_1.H$	$\{T_1.H\}$	$T_1.H=V_3.H$
$V_3.H<:T_2 \wedge T_1.H<:T_2$	$\{T_2\}$	$T_2=V_3.H$
$V_3.H<:T_0 \wedge T_1.H<:T_0 \wedge T_2<:T_0$	$\{T_0\}$	$T_0=V_3.H$
$V_3.H<:T_4 \wedge V_3.H<:Y \wedge T_1.H<:T_4 \wedge T_1.H<:Y \wedge T_2<:T_4 \wedge T_2<:Y \wedge T_0<:T_4 \wedge T_0<:Y$	$\{T_4, Y\}$	$Y=T_4=V_3.H$
$V_3.H<:T_1.H<:T_2<:T_0<:T_4<:T_3.L$	$\{T_3.L\}$	$T_3.L=V_3.H$

Step 5. Result Refining. This step simplifies the inferred types of the method. The goal is to reduce the number of the global type variables using the residual flow constraint (namely the remaining flow constraints among the global type variables). The residual flow constraint of the current example is: $V_3.H<:V_2.L$. These type variables can be unified to a fresh type variable V, such that $V=V_3.H=V_2.L$. Since V stands for both low-bound and high-bound, it is not marked with either. The result of our inference (including the above refinements) is the following:

$$\text{Pair}\langle[\bot, Object], [V, Object]\rangle \mid V \text{ move}\langle V\rangle(\text{Pair}\langle[\bot, V], [\bot, Object]\rangle \text{ a})$$
$$\{V \text{ y=a.getFst}\langle V, V\rangle(); \text{ this.setSnd}\langle V, V\rangle(y); \text{ return y; }\}$$

Step 6. VPT Result. This step translates the inferred interval types into VPTs:

$$\text{Pair}\langle\circledast, \ominus V\rangle \mid V \text{ move}\langle V\rangle(\text{Pair}\langle\oplus V, \circledast\rangle \text{ a})$$
$$\{V \text{ y=a.getFst}\langle V, V\rangle(); \text{ this.setSnd}\langle V, V\rangle(y); \text{ return y; }\}$$

3.2 Interval Types Versus Variant Parametric Types

The interval types are more expressive than variant parametric types, since they can support two different non-default bounds. A variant parametric type can only support two equal non-default bounds in the case of invariant subtyping $\odot$. Note that the default low-bound is $\bot$, while the default high-bound is *Object*. Considering the following code fragment, we like to infer the interval type of obj:

```
class Cell⟨A⟩ { A fst; ···          class Integer extends Number{..}
    Cell⟨⊕A⟩ | A get⟨A⟩(){..}        class MyInt extends Integer{..}
    Cell⟨⊖A⟩ | void set⟨A⟩(A y){..}..}
    ...
Cell⟨[T.L, T.H]⟩ obj = new Cell⟨Integer⟩(new Integer(1)); // T.L<:Integer<:T.H
Number n = obj.get⟨T₁⟩();                                  // T.H<:T₁<:Number
MyInt m = new MyInt(2); obj.set⟨T₂⟩(m);                     // MyInt<:T₂<:T.L
```

Our algorithm can infer the interval type $Cell\langle[MyInt, Number]\rangle$ for obj. However this interval type cannot be translated into a variant parametric type, since it consists of two different bounds. In order to keep the equivalence between interval types and variant parametric types, we add one more rule to the variance inference:

Proposition 2 (Variance Inference Rule-2). *If both bounds* X.L *and* X.H *of an interval type occur in the closed flow constraints, then the default constraint of an interval type* X.L<:X.H *is strengthened to the equality* X.L=X.H.

In our example, adding T.L=T.H to the above set of constraints will generate a cycle such that T.L<:Integer<:T.H ∧ T.L=T.H. Cycle elimination generates T.L=Integer=T.H. Thus new inference result is the interval type $Cell\langle[Integer, Integer]\rangle$, that can be directly translated into the variant parametric type $Cell\langle\odot Integer\rangle$.

3.3 Main Flow and Conditional Flow

Cast operations give rise to *conditional flow constraints* (or dynamic subtype constraints in [9]). These constraints are conditional in the sense that they are only required to hold if the corresponding dynamic downcasts succeed at runtime. Our analysis separates the *main flow* gathered from the method body without the cast operations and the *conditional flow* corresponding to the cast operations. Conditional constraints use a different subtyping notation ($<:_c$). One benefit of our analysis is that it can guarantee that some of the cast operations are redundant, and therefore they can be safely eliminated at compile time. The number of the eliminated casts is used as an accuracy measure of generic type systems [8,11,4,16]. The following example illustrates how our inference algorithm handles the cast operations:

Original code   Inference Result
Cell | void fill(Cell a)   Cell⟨⊕V⟩| void fill(Cell⟨⊕Cell⟨⊖V⟩⟩ a)
{Cell b = (Cell)a.fst; b.fst = this.fst; } {Cell⟨⊖V⟩ b = a.fst; b.fst = this.fst; }
Code annotated with Fresh Interval Types
Cell⟨[V₁.L, V₁.H]⟩ | void fill(Cell⟨[V₂.L, V₂.H]⟩ a)
    { Cell⟨[T₁.L, T₁.H]⟩ b = (Cell⟨[T₂.L, T₂.H]⟩)a.fst; b.fst = this.fst; }

1. *Collect* *Constraints*	Cell⟨[T₂.L, T₂.H]⟩<:Cell⟨[T₁.L, T₁.H]⟩∧V₁.H<:T₁.L V₂.H<:_cCell⟨[T₂.L, T₂.H]⟩
2. Simplify	V₁.H<:T₁.L<:T₂.L<:T₂.H<:T₁.H V₂.H<:_cCell⟨[T₂.L, T₂.H]⟩
3. *Infer* *Variance*	V₁.L=V₂.L=⊥∧T₁.H=T₂.H=*Object*∧V₁.H<:T₁.L<:T₂.L V₂.H<:_cCell⟨[T₂.L, *Object*]⟩
4. Infer Type Vars	{T₁.L} T₁.L=V₁.H {T₂.L} T₂.L=V₁.H
5. *Solve Conditional*	V₂.H<:_cCell⟨[V₁.H, *Object*]⟩ ⇒ V₂.H<:Cell⟨[V₁.H, *Object*]⟩
6. Refine Results	V=fresh() V₁.H=V ∧ V₂.H=Cell⟨[V, *Object*]⟩

Though the conditional flow is kept separately, it is still used by the variance inference in Step 3. If Step 3 ignores the conditional flow, it infers the incorrect result $V_2.H{=}Object$. A new step (Step 5) is added to the main algorithm. This step combines together the conditional flow and the (already solved) main flow in order to find a common solution. In our example, adding the conditional constraint to the main flow does not generate any contradiction as the type variables $V_2.H$ and $V_1.H$ are unconstrained in the main flow. However it is not always possible to find a common solution for the main and conditional flow, as illustrated by the following example:

```
V₃ foo2(Cell⟨[V₄.L, V₄.H]⟩ obj) {
    if(...) {... return (Integer)obj.fst; } else{... return (Float)obj.fst; }}
    //Integer<:V₃∧Float<:V₃  V₄.H<:꜀Integer∧V₄.H<:꜀Float
```

In this example the conditional constraints can be added to the method precondition to be checked at each call site where the casts could be selectively eliminated (with the help of a polyvariant program specializer):

```
Number foo2(Cell⟨[⊥, V₄.H]⟩ obj) where V₄.H<:꜀Integer∧V₄.H<:꜀Float
```

3.4 Convergent Flow and Divergent Flow

Multiple low bounds denote a *convergent flow*, while multiple high bounds denote a *divergent flow*. Our analysis uses union types for multiple low bounds and intersection types for multiple high bounds. An union type $t_1|t_2$ represents the least upper bound of t_1 and t_2, while an intersection type $t_1\&t_2$ is the greatest lower bound of t_1 and t_2. Some of their subtyping rules may generate disjunctions. In order to keep our analysis simple, we propose a safe yet precise approximation that avoids those disjunctions:

AND rules	OR rules	Our OR rules
$t_1\|t_2{<}{:}t$	$t{<}{:}t_1\|t_2$	$t{<}{:}t_1\|t_2 \quad T_1{=}\text{fresh}()$
$t_1{<}{:}t \land t_2{<}{:}t$	$t{<}{:}t_1 \lor t{<}{:}t_2$	$t{<}{:}T_1 \land t_1{<}{:}T_1 \land t_2{<}{:}T_1$
$t{<}{:}t_1\&t_2$	$t_1\&t_2{<}{:}t$	$t_1\&t_2{<}{:}t \quad T_2{=}\text{fresh}()$
$t{<}{:}t_1 \land t{<}{:}t_2$	$t_1{<}{:}t \lor t_2{<}{:}t$	$T_2{<}{:}t_1 \land T_2{<}{:}t_2 \land T_2{<}{:}t$

where T_1 and T_2 are fresh type variables. Another solution to avoid disjunctions is the tautology $t_1\&t_2{<}{:}t_1|t_2$, but sometimes this approximation may lead to no solutions. One benefit of using union and intersection types is that they are more expressive so that more casts can be directly eliminated as the following example (from [8,4]) can illustrate:

class B1 extends A implements I {..};	class B2 extends A implements I {..};
Original code	Code annotated with Fresh Interval Types
void foo(Boolean b){	void foo(Boolean b){
Cell c1 = new Cell(new B1());	Cell⟨[T₁.L, T₁.H]⟩ c1 = new Cell⟨N₁⟩(new B1());
Cell c2 = new Cell(new B2());	Cell⟨[T₂.L, T₂.H]⟩ c2 = new Cell⟨N₂⟩(new B2());
Cell c = b?c1 : c2;	Cell⟨[T₃.L, T₃.H]⟩ c = b?c1 : c2;
A a = (A) c.get();	A a = (A) c.get⟨T₄⟩();
I i = (I) c.get();	I i = (I) c.get⟨T₅⟩();
B1 b1 = (B1) c1.get();	B1 b1 = (B1) c1.get⟨T₆⟩();
B2 b2 = (B2) c2.get(); }	B2 b2 = (B2) c2.get⟨T₇⟩(); }

The following table contains the inference steps for the above code with interval types. At the step 4.4, $T_3.H$ is resolved as to the union type B1|B2 due to two distinct flows converging to it, $B1<:T_3.H \land B2<:T_3.H$. The solutions of the main flow can prove that all conditional constraints succeed, and therefore all casts can be eliminated.

1. Collect Constraints	$B1<:N_1 \land Cell\langle[N_1,N_1]\rangle <:Cell\langle[T_1.L,T_1.H]\rangle \land$
	$B2<:N_2 \land Cell\langle[N_2,N_2]\rangle <:Cell\langle[T_2.L,T_2.H]\rangle \land$
	$Cell\langle[T_1.L,T_1.H]\rangle <:Cell\langle[T_3.L,T_3.H]\rangle \land Cell\langle[T_2.L,T_2.H]\rangle <:Cell\langle[T_3.L,T_3.H]\rangle$
	$\land T_3.H<:T_4 \land T_3.H<:T_5 \land T_1.H<:T_6 \land T_2.H<:T_7$
	$T_4<:_c A \land T_5<:_c I \land T_6<:_c B1 \land T_7<:_c B2$
2. Simplify	$B1<:N_1 \land T_1.L<:N_1<:T_1.H \land B2<:N_2 \land T_2.L<:N_2<:T_2.H \land T_3.L<:T_1.L \land T_1.H<:T_3.H$
	$\land T_3.L<:T_2.L \land T_2.H<:T_3.H \land T_3.H<:T_4 \land T_3.H<:T_5 \land T_1.H<:T_6 \land T_2.H<:T_7$
	$T_4<:_c A \land T_5<:_c I \land T_6<:_c B1 \land T_7<:_c B2$
3. Infer Variance	$T_1.L=T_2.L=T_3.L=\bot \land B1<:N_1<:T_1.H \land B2<:N_2<:T_2.H \land$
	$T_1.H<:T_3.H \land T_2.H<:T_3.H \land T_3.H<:T_4 \land T_3.H<:T_5 \land T_1.H<:T_6 \land T_2.H<:T_7$
	$T_4<:_c A \land T_5<:_c I \land T_6<:_c B1 \land T_7<:_c B2$
4. Infer Type Vars	$\{N_1,N_2\}$ $N_1=B1 \land N_2=B2$
	$\{T_1.H,T_2.H\}$ $T_1.H=B1 \land T_2.H=B2$
	$\{T_6,T_7\}$ $T_6=B1 \land T_7=B2$
	$\{T_3.H\}$ $T_3.H=B1|B2$
	$\{T_4,T_5\}$ $T_5=T_4=B1|B2$
5. Solve Conditional	$B_1|B_2<:_c A$ $B_1|B_2<:_c I$
	$B1<:_c B1$ $B2<:_c B2$

3.5   Field Flow and Object Flow

A key feature of our approach is the distinction between the flow via an object, called *object flow* and the flow via the fields of that object, called *field flow*. We introduce a special type notation, that we called *dual type* to support these two views: (1) object as a black box, and (2) object as a glass box. For example, a dual type for a Pair is of the form $X \doteq Pair\langle[V_1.L,V_1.H],[V_2.L,V_2.H]\rangle$, where the type variable X (called *object part*) is used for the flow of the entire object, while $Pair\langle[V_1.L,V_1.H],[V_2.L,V_2.H]\rangle$ (called *field part*) caters to the flow via its fields. This dualism can improve the genericity of our inference results. Specifically, given the following method dup (from [4,14]):

```
Pair dup(Pair a) { Pair p = new Pair(a, a); return p; }
```

Without using the dual types, our inference can get the following types:

```
Pair⟨⊛,⊛⟩ dup(Pair⟨⊛,⊛⟩ a){
        Pair⟨⊛,⊛⟩ p=new Pair⟨Pair⟨⊛,⊛⟩,Pair⟨⊛,⊛⟩⟩(a, a); return p; }
```

The type of the method result is too imprecise, but still correct as fields are not accessed (bivariant ⊛) in the method body. Using dual types our approach can get more precise types by inferring an intersection type for the method parameter a, namely:

```
Pair⟨⊙X₁,⊙X₁⟩ dup⟨X₁⟩(X₁&Pair⟨⊛,⊛⟩ a) {
        Pair⟨⊙X₁,⊙X₁⟩ p = new Pair⟨X₁,X₁⟩(a, a); return p; }
```

The type variable X_1 plays an important role, it allows the unknown variance to flow unchanged, such that the variance annotations of the parameter a fields are preserved in the type of the method result. As can be seen below, the type variable X_1 comes from the object part of the dual type:

Y dup($X_1 \doteq$Pair$\langle[V_1.L, V_1.H], [V_2.L, V_2.H]\rangle$ a) {
    $X_2 \doteq$Pair$\langle[T_1.L, T_1.H], [T_2.L, T_2.H]\rangle$ p $=$ new Pair$\langle N_1, N_2\rangle$(a, a); return p; }

1. Collect Constraints	$X_1 \doteq$Pair$\langle[V_1.L,V_1.H],[V_2.L,V_2.H]\rangle <: N_1 \wedge X_1 \doteq$Pair$\langle[V_1.L,V_1.H],[V_2.L,V_2.H]\rangle <: N_2$ $\wedge$Pair$\langle[N_1,N_1],[N_2,N_2]\rangle <: X_2 \doteq$Pair$\langle[T_1.L,T_1.H],[T_2.L,T_2.H]\rangle$ $\wedge X_2 \doteq$Pair$\langle[T_1.L, T_1.H], [T_2.L, T_2.H]\rangle <: Y$
2. Simplify Dual Types	$X_1 <: N_1 \wedge X_1 <: N_2 \wedge$Pair$\langle[N_1, N_1], [N_2, N_2]\rangle <: X_2$ $\wedge$Pair$\langle[N_1,N_1],[N_2,N_2]\rangle <:$Pair$\langle[T_1.L, T_1.H], [T_2.L, T_2.H]\rangle \wedge X_2 <: Y$
3. Simplify	$X_1 <: N_1 \wedge X_1 <: N_2 \wedge$Pair$\langle[N_1, N_1], [N_2, N_2]\rangle <: X_2 <: Y$ $\wedge T_1.L <: N_1 <: T_1.H \wedge T_2.L <: N_2 <: T_2.H$
4. Infer Variance	$V_1.L = V_2.L = T_1.L = T_2.L = \perp \wedge V_1.H = V_2.H = T_1.H = T_2.H = Object$ $X_1 <: N_1 \wedge X_1 <: N_2 \wedge$Pair$\langle[N_1, N_1], [N_2, N_2]\rangle <: X_2 <: Y$
5. Infer Type Vars	$\{N_1, N_2\}\ N_1 = X_1 \wedge N_2 = X_1$ $\{X_2\}\ X_2 =$Pair$\langle[X_1, X_1], [X_1, X_1]\rangle$ $\{Y\}\ Y =$Pair$\langle[X_1, X_1], [X_1, X_1]\rangle$
6. Refine Results	$X_1 \doteq$Pair$\langle[\perp, Object], [\perp, Object]\rangle \Rightarrow X_1$&Pair$\langle[\perp, Object], [\perp, Object]\rangle$ Pair$\langle[X_1,X_1],[X_1,X_1]\rangle \doteq$Pair$\langle[\perp,Object],[\perp,Object]\rangle \Rightarrow$Pair$\langle[X_1,X_1],[X_1,X_1]\rangle$

A new step (Step 2) is added to the main algorithm in order to simplify the dual types. The simplification rules always prefer the object flow over the field flow (e.g. first constraint of Step 1 is reduced to $X_1 <: N_1$). However, when the type variables of the field part are used by the other constraints, both flows are generated (e.g. the third constraint of Step 1 is decomposed into two constraints). The last step is adapted to refine the dual types. A dual type can be refined to an intersection type (e.g. first line of Step 6). Since an intersection type is the greatest lower bound of its parts, it could be further simplified (e.g. the second line of Step 6).

4   Inference Algorithm

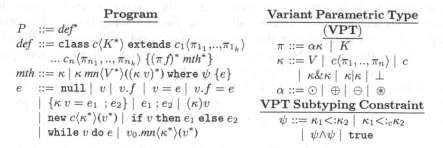

Program	Variant Parametric Type (VPT)

Fig. 1. SYNTAX OF VARIANT CORE-JAVA

We design our inference algorithm as a *summary-based analysis*, on a per method basis guided by a global method call graph. Our approach is flow-insensitive within each method, but context-sensitive across the methods. The algorithm takes as input a well-typed non-generic program and the VPT class hierarchy, before it outputs a program that uses VPTs.

We use two assumptions to avoid recursive constraints: (1) no F-bounded quantification over the VPT class hierarchy, and (2) no polymorphic recursion for the classes and the methods. Techniques for avoiding recursive constraints are presented in [4,5]. Nevertheless, our algorithm can cope with F-bounds, as long as we use constraint solving techniques that support recursive constraints and inductive simplification (from [25,18]). Our current approach can infer generic types for mutually-recursive methods under the monomorphic recursion assumption.

We formalize the algorithm on Variant Core-Java (Fig. 1), a core calculus for Java-like languages. Both input and output programs are encoded in Core-Java since VPTs can subsume non-generic types. For ease of presentation, the features related to static methods, exception handling, inner classes and overloading are omitted. Multiple interface inheritance is supported as in Java [12], each class may extend from a single superclass but may implement multiple interfaces. VPT's syntax is also shown in Fig. 1. There are two kinds of type variables: κ denoting a variance and a type together, and ν denoting only a type. For simplicity, primitive types (e.g. bool, void) are represented by their corresponding classes (such as Bool, Void). Specifically, for each method our analysis can be divided into two main steps: (1) gathering the flow constraints based on the type inference rules (Section 4.1), and (2) solving the flow constraints (Section 4.2).

4.1   Type Inference Rules

The inference process is driven by the following main rule for each method:

$$\frac{G \vdash c_i \Rightarrow_{dcr} t_i \qquad G; \{(v_i{:}t_i)_{i=2}^n, \texttt{this}{:}t_1\} \vdash e \Rightarrow_e e'{:}t, \varphi_0 \\ Y = \texttt{fresh}() \qquad Q_1 = \bigcup_{i=1}^n \texttt{fv}(t_i) \qquad G \vdash \varphi_0 \wedge t <: Y; Q_1 \Rightarrow_{solver} \varphi; Q; \sigma \\ \sigma t_1 | \sigma Y \ mn\langle Q \rangle ((\sigma t_i \ v_i)_{i=2}^n) \ \texttt{where} \ \varphi \ \{\sigma e'\} \Rightarrow_{vpt} \kappa_1 | \kappa \ mn\langle Q' \rangle ((\kappa_i \ v_i)_{i=2}^n) \ \texttt{where} \ \psi \ \{e''\}}{G \vdash c_1 | c_0 \ mn((c_i \ v_i)_{i=2}^n) \ \{e\} \ \Rightarrow \ \kappa_1 | \kappa \ mn\langle Q' \rangle ((\kappa_i \ v_i)_{i=2}^n)) \ \texttt{where} \ \psi \ \{e''\}}$$

that takes a non-generic method and the VPT class hierarchy G, decorates the method parameters ($\Rightarrow_{dcr}$) with fresh interval types, collects the flow constraints ($\Rightarrow_e$) from the method body, and then passes the constraints to the constraint solver ($\Rightarrow_{solver}$). The solver (Section 4.2) returns the list of method type parameters Q and a substitution σ. The substitution maps the type variables (introduced by the decoration) either to ground types or to the type variables from Q. Interval types (and dual types), their flow constraints and the substitutions σ are detailed in Fig. 2. The final step $\Rightarrow_{vpt}$ translates the interval types inferred for the method into VPTs. We summarize below the main judgments employed by this phase of our analysis (a complete description is in [5]):

- $G \vdash c \Rightarrow_{dcr} t$ denotes the decoration with fresh type variables of a non-generic class c with respect to its parameterized version from VPT class hierarchy G. The result t is either a dual type, or the class c (when c is not parameterized), or a type variable.
- $\rho \vdash \kappa \Rightarrow_{\kappa t} t$ and $\rho \vdash \pi \Rightarrow_{\pi \tau} \tau$ denote the translation of a VPT into an interval type with respect to a substitution ρ. A substitution ρ maps a type variable κ (denoting a type and a variance) into two bounds $[\tau_L, \tau_H]$.
- $G \vdash t, \texttt{fn} \Rightarrow_{fld} [\tau_L, \tau_H]$ returns the low-bound and high-bound $[\tau_L, \tau_H]$ of a field fn with respect to an interval type t and the VPT class hierarchy G.
- $G \vdash t, \texttt{mn} \Rightarrow_{mth} \texttt{mth}$ returns the interface mth (with fresh interval types) of a method mn with respect to a receiver t and the VPT class hierarchy G.

Interval Type	Flow Constraint

$$\tau ::= t \mid t.L \mid t.H$$

$$\varphi ::= \tau_1 <:\tau_2 \mid \tau_1 <:_c \tau_2 \mid \varphi \wedge \varphi \mid \text{true}$$

$$t ::= X \mid d \mid c\langle[\tau_{1L}, \tau_{1H}], .., [\tau_{nL}, \tau_{nH}]\rangle$$

Substitution

$$\sigma ::= X{=}\tau \mid X.L{=}\tau \mid X.H{=}\tau \mid d{=}t$$

$$c \mid t_1 \& t_2 \mid t_1 | t_2 \mid \bot \mid Object$$

$$X ::= V \mid T \mid N \mid Y$$

Closed Flow Constraint

Dual Type

$$\phi ::= t_1.H{<}:t_2.L \mid t_1{<}:t_2.L \mid t_1.H{<}:t_2$$

$$d ::= X \doteq c\langle[\tau_{1L}, \tau_{1H}], ..., [\tau_{nL}, \tau_{nH}]\rangle$$

$$\mid t_1.H{<}:_c t_2.L \mid t_1{<}:_c t_2.L \mid t_1.H{<}:_c t_2$$

Fig. 2. INFERENCE TYPES AND FLOW CONSTRAINTS

- $G; \Gamma \vdash e \Rightarrow_e e':t, \varphi$ denotes the type inference for the expression e with respect to the type environment Γ and the VPT class hierarchy G. The inference result consists of the expression e' annotated with interval types, its interval type t and the derived flow constraint φ. The type environment Γ consists of the interval types generated by $\Rightarrow_{dcr}$.

4.2 Constraint Solver

The constraint solver takes as input a flow constraint φ_0, a set of visible type variables Q_0, a VPT class hierarchy G and performs the following sequence of steps:

$$\frac{\vdash \varphi_0 \Rightarrow_{set} C_0 \quad \vdash C_0 \Rightarrow_{tr} C_1 \quad G \vdash C_1 \Rightarrow_{simplify} C_2 \quad \vdash C_2 \Rightarrow_{dual} C_3; D \quad G \vdash C_3 \Rightarrow_{simplify} C_4}{G \vdash C_4; Q_0 \Rightarrow_{variance} C_5; Q_1; \sigma_1 \quad \vdash C_5; Q_1 \Rightarrow_{typvar} C_6; Q_2; \sigma_2 \quad G \vdash C_6 \Rightarrow_{cond} C_7}$$

$$\frac{G \vdash C_7; D; Q_2; \sigma_2 \circ \sigma_1 \Rightarrow_{refine} C_8; Q; \sigma \quad \vdash C_8 \Rightarrow_{cnj} \varphi}{G \vdash \varphi_0; Q_0 \Rightarrow_{solver} \varphi; Q; \sigma}$$

The goal is first to simplify the constraints φ_0 to atomic constraints among type variables and ground types and then to solve the type variables in term of the ground type and the visible type variables Q. The result consists of a residual constraint φ among the visible type variables, a reduced set of type variables Q and the solution itself given as a substitution σ. Since our solver internally works with a set of constraints C instead of a conjunction φ, the judgments $\Rightarrow_{set}$ and $\Rightarrow_{cnj}$ make the corresponding translations. We summarize below the main steps of our solver (a complete description is in [5]).

Transitive Closure ($\Rightarrow_{tr}$). The constraint set is always closed by transitivity such that this step is performed each time a new constraint is added. The transitivity takes into account the conditional constraints, it generates a conditional constraint from a conditional constraint and non-conditional constraint. VPT subtyping (and also interval type subtyping) is transitive since the VPT class declarations are well-formed as in [15].

Simplification ($\Rightarrow_{simplify}$). It consists of a constraint decomposition $\Rightarrow_s$ followed by a transitive closure:

$$\frac{G \vdash C_0 \Rightarrow_s C' \quad \vdash C' \Rightarrow_{tr} C}{G \vdash C_0 \Rightarrow_{simplify} C}$$

Constraint decomposition $\Rightarrow_s$ is performed with respect to the class subtyping given by the VPT class hierarchy G, the interval subtyping rule and the subtyping rules for intersection and union types. Using the mechanism presented before the intersection and union types constraints always decompose into conjunctions. A conditional constraint is decomposed into new conditional constraints. The step is performed until the constraint set remains unchanged. In the solver, the first call of $\Rightarrow_{simplify}$ step decomposes the outermost intersection and union types to reduce the complexity of the step $\Rightarrow_{dual}$.

Dual Types Simplification($\Rightarrow_{dual}$). It decomposes all the dual types from the input constraint set C_0. The result consists of a new constraint set C and the list of the decomposed dual types D:

$$\frac{\vdash C_0 \Rightarrow_d D; C_1 \quad \vdash C_1 \Rightarrow_{tr} C_1' \quad D \vdash C_1' \Rightarrow_{cd} C_2 \quad \vdash C_2 \Rightarrow_{tr} C}{\vdash C_0 \Rightarrow_{dual} C; D}$$

The process is performed in two stages. In the first stage ($\Rightarrow_d$), all the flow constraints with dual types are decomposed. When it needs to choose, $\Rightarrow_d$ prefers the flow through the object part of a dual type rather than that through the field part. In the second stage ($\Rightarrow_{cd}$), the flow through the field part is selectively added to the constraint set when it is required by the other constraints.

Variance Inference ($\Rightarrow_{variance}$). It computes the high-bound type variables and the low-bound type variables that do not occur in the closed flow constraints, and resolves them to their default values by the substitutions σ_H and σ_L respectively.

$$L_H = \{V.H \mid V.H <: V_1.L \in C_0 \vee V.H <: V_2 \in C_0 \vee V.H <:_c V_3.L \in C_0 \vee V.H <:_c V_4 \in C\}$$
$$L_L = \{V.L \mid V_1.H <: V.L \in C_0 \vee V_2 <: V.L \in C_0 \vee V_3.H <:_c V.L \in C_0 \vee V_4 <:_c V.L \in C_0\}$$
$$\sigma_H = [[V.H \mapsto Object] \mid V.H \in \mathbf{fv}(C_0) \wedge V.H \notin L_H]$$
$$\sigma_L = [[V.L \mapsto \bot] \mid V.L \in \mathbf{fv}(C_0) \wedge V.L \notin L_L]$$
$$\sigma_{HL} = [[V.L \mapsto V, V.H \mapsto V] \mid V.H \in L_H \wedge V.L \in L_L]$$
$$\frac{Q = Q_0 \cup \mathrm{ran}(\sigma_{HL}) \setminus (\mathrm{dom}(\sigma_L) \cup \mathrm{dom}(\sigma_H) \cup \mathrm{dom}(\sigma_{HL})) \quad C = \sigma_H \circ \sigma_L \circ \sigma_{HL} C_0}{\vdash C_0; Q_0 \Rightarrow_{variance} C; Q; \sigma_H \circ \sigma_L \circ \sigma_{HL}}$$

The substitution σ_{HL} implements the second variance inference rule, making equal the bounds of an interval when both of them occur in the closed flow constraints. The initial list of the visible type variables Q can be affected by the variance inference. This step works on all constraints, either from conditional flow or from main flow.

Type Variables Inference ($\Rightarrow_{typvar}$). This step solves the non-visible type variables in terms of the visible type variables Q_0:

$$\frac{\vdash C_0; Q_0 \Rightarrow_{cycle} C_1; Q_1; \sigma_1 \quad \vdash C_1; Q_1 \Rightarrow_{order} L \quad \vdash L; C_1 \Rightarrow_{unify} C; \sigma_2 \quad Q = Q_1 \cup \mathbf{fv}(C)}{\vdash C_0; Q_0 \Rightarrow_{typvar} C; Q; \sigma_2 \circ \sigma_1}$$

First substep ($\Rightarrow_{cycle}$) makes equal all the type variables of a cycle. This process may also affect the visible type variables, resulting in a new set Q_1. We use techniques from [10] to eliminate the cycles. The non-visible type variables are then solved ($\Rightarrow_{unify}$) in an order given by the number of their low bounds ($\Rightarrow_{order}$). The substep $\Rightarrow_{order}$ iteratively computes the order taking into account the situations when the low bounds are class type parameterized with type variables. The substep $\Rightarrow_{unify}$ unifies the type variables with their low-bounds producing a substitution σ_2. Multiple low-bounds are combined together as an union type. Non-visible type variables of final constraint set C are promoted as visible in Q. Though this step works only on the main flow constraints, its computed substitutions are also applied on the constraints of the conditional flow.

Solving conditional constraints ($\Rightarrow_{cond}$). This step translates the conditional constraints into non-conditional constraints if the non-conditional constraints hold. Since it is always safe to add more constraints on the method interface type variables and the constraint set is transitively closed, this step only checks ($\vdash_?$) the conditional constraints with the ground types with respect to the class hierarchy G. First check is for ground constraints, while the last two are to verify if an intersection and an union type can exist in G. If the checks do not hold, the conditional constraints are not translated.

$$B=\{c_1<:_cc_2 \mid c_1<:_cc_2 \in C_0\} \quad G\vdash_?B$$
$$\forall V \in \mathtt{fv}(C_0).G\vdash_?\{c \mid V<:_cc \in C_0\}\&\{c \mid V<:c \in C_0\}$$
$$\forall V \in \mathtt{fv}(C_0).G\vdash_?\{c \mid c<:_cV \in C_0\}\mid\{c \mid c<:V \in C_0\}$$
$$C'=\{\tau_1<:\tau_2 \mid \tau_1<:_c\tau_2 \in C_0\} \quad C_0'=C_0\setminus\{\tau_1<:_c\tau_2 \mid \tau_1<:_c\tau_2 \in C_0\}$$
$$\overline{G\vdash C_0\Rightarrow_{cond}C'\cup C_0'}$$

Refining the results ($\Rightarrow_{refine}$). The goal of this step is to reduce the number of visible type variables of a method interface. The first three substitutions are based on the closed flow constraints which are in C_0. The last two substitutions are for the high bound (low bound) type variables occurring on low bound (high bound) positions. Dual types are also translated into intersection types by the substitution σ_d.

$$\sigma_1=[V_1.H\mapsto V, V_2.L\mapsto V \mid V_1.H<:V_2.L \in C_0 \wedge V=\mathtt{fresh}()] \quad \sigma_2=[V.H\mapsto t \mid V.H<:t \in \sigma_1C_0]$$
$$\sigma_3=[V.L\mapsto t \mid t<:V.L \in \sigma_2\circ\sigma_1C_0] \quad \sigma_4=[V\mapsto t \mid t<:V \in \sigma_3\circ\sigma_2\circ\sigma_1C_0 \vee V<:t \in \sigma_3\circ\sigma_2\circ\sigma_1C_0]$$
$$\sigma'=\sigma_3\circ\sigma_2\circ\sigma_1\circ\sigma_t \quad G\vdash\sigma'D\Rightarrow_{refineduel}\sigma_d$$
$$\sigma_1'=[V.H\mapsto V \mid V_1.L\mapsto V.H \in \sigma' \wedge V=\mathtt{fresh}()] \quad \sigma_2'=[V.L\mapsto V \mid V_1.H\mapsto V.L \in \sigma' \wedge V=\mathtt{fresh}()]$$
$$\sigma=\sigma_2'\circ\sigma_1'\circ\sigma_d\circ\sigma'$$
$$\overline{G\vdash C_0;D;Q_0;\sigma_0\Rightarrow_{refine}\sigma C_0;\sigma Q_0;\sigma}$$

5 Method Overriding

Consider the following method overriding example, where the method boo of the class Cell is overridden by the subclass Pair (note that class Pair extends Cell{..}):

Cell | Object boo(Cell a) {this.fst = a.fst; return a.fst; }
Pair | Object boo(Cell a) {a.fst = this.fst; this.snd = a.fst; return a.fst; }

Applying our inference to each method, we obtain the following results:

Cell$\langle\ominus P\rangle$ | P boo(Cell$\langle\oplus P\rangle$ a){..}   Pair$\langle\oplus P_1,\ominus P_1\rangle$ | P_1 boo(Cell$\langle\odot P_1\rangle$ a){..}

The method overriding is sound only if the overriding method is a subtype of the overridden method and the overriding method's receiver is a subtype of the overridden method's receiver [3]. As can be seen, this property does not hold for the above inferred methods:

Pair$\langle\oplus P_1,\ominus P_1\rangle<:$Cell$\langle\ominus P\rangle$ Cell$\langle\oplus P\rangle<:$Cell$\langle\odot P_1\rangle$ $P_1<:$P

To ensure this property, we augment our inference algorithm with the following considerations: (i) we can strengthen the receiver type and the result type of the overriding method; (ii) we can strengthen the parameters types and the precondition of the overridden method. Thus the method overriding problem is solved as follows:

1. Infer the overridden method as: $\text{Cell}\langle[\text{P},\textit{Object}]\rangle \mid \text{P boo}(\text{Cell}\langle[\bot,\text{P}]\rangle \text{ a})$
2. Undo the variance of the overridden method parameters by using fresh interval type variables ($P_1.H$ and $P_1.L$) that keep the relation with the other type variables of the receiver and the result: $\text{Cell}\langle[\text{P},\textit{Object}]\rangle \mid \text{P boo}(\text{Cell}\langle[P_1.L,P_1.H]\rangle \text{ a})$ where $P_1.H<:P$
3. Do inference for the overriding method: The process starts with the sound overriding assumptions (Step 1):

$$\text{Pair}\langle[V_1.L,V_1.H],[V_2.L,V_2.H]\rangle \mid \text{Y boo}(\text{Cell}\langle[V_3.L,V_3.H]\rangle \text{ a})$$
$$\{\text{a.fst=this.fst;this.snd=a.fst;return a.fst;}\}$$

1.Overriding Assumptions	$\text{Pair}\langle[V_1.L,V_1.H],[V_2.L,V_2.H]\rangle<:\text{Cell}\langle[\text{P},\textit{Object}]\rangle \wedge Y<:P \wedge$ $\text{Cell}\langle[P_1.L,P_1.H]\rangle<:\text{Cell}\langle[V_3.L,V_3.H]\rangle \wedge P_1.H<:P$
2.Collect Constraints	$V_1.H<:V_3.L \wedge V_3.H<:V_2.L \wedge V_3.H<:Y$
3.Simplify	$P<:V_1.L \wedge Y<:P \wedge V_3.L<:P_1.L \wedge P_1.H<:V_3.H \wedge P_1.H<:P$
	$V_1.H<:V_3.L \wedge V_3.H<:V_2.L \wedge V_3.H<:Y$
4.Infer Variance	$V_2.H=\textit{Object} \wedge V_1.L=V_1.H \wedge V_3.L=V_3.H \wedge P_1.L=P_1.H$
5.Infer Type Vars	$P=P_1.H=P_1.L=V_1.H=V_1.L=V_2.L=V_3.H=V_3.L$

4. The result of the previous step is applied on both overridden and overriding methods and we obtain the following sound result:

$$\text{Cell}\langle\ominus P\rangle \mid \text{P boo}(\text{Cell}\langle\odot P\rangle \text{ a}) \qquad \text{Pair}\langle\odot P,\ominus P\rangle \mid \text{P boo}(\text{Cell}\langle\odot P\rangle \text{ a})$$

6   Conclusion

We have formalized a novel constraint-based algorithm to infer variant parametric types for non-generic Java code. In contrast to the previous refactoring algorithms [9,8,7,11,16] which mainly support invariant subtyping and are designed as whole program analyses, our approach offers full support for use-site variance based subtyping and it is designed as a summary-based analysis that works on a per method basis. The main technical novelty of our approach is a systematic variance inference based on interval types. With the full support for use-site variance based subtyping, our approach can generate better generic types than those derived by existing systems. For instance, none of the previous algorithms can automatically infer the examples from Section 3.4 and Section 3.5.

Although our inference algorithm internally works with sophisticated mechanisms, its output is expressed in terms of variant parametric types extended with restricted forms of intersection/union types as used in [4]. We have proven the soundness of our inference algorithm with respect to our variant parametric type system in [4]. However the completeness requirement is a difficult problem since the decidability of nominal subtyping with use-site variance is still an open problem as was discussed in [15].

We have built an inference prototype which works for a core subset of Java. Our previous VPT checker from [4] is used to validate the inferred results. In our initial experiments we have tested the quality of our inference system results on a small set of non-generic programs by comparing the inferred generic types with the best generic types that one can manually provide. In all the cases, our system was able to infer the same types as those manually provided. The inference time was less than one second for each test program. Currently we are working to extend our experiments to larger programs by using our translator of Java to a core subset [6].

References

1. Bracha, G., Oderski, M., Stoutamire, D., Wadler, P.: Making the future safe for the past: Adding genericity to the Java programming language. In: ACM OOPSLA (1998)
2. Bugliesi, M., Geertsen, S.M.P.: Type inference for variant object types. Information and Computation 177(1) (2002)
3. Castagna, G.: Covariance and contravariance: Conflict without a cause. ACM TOPLAS 17(3) (1995)
4. Chin, W.N., Craciun, F., Khoo, S.C., Popeea, C.: A flow-based approach for variant parametric types. In: ACM OOPSLA (2006)
5. Craciun, F., Chin, W.N., He, G., Qin, S.: An Interval-based Inference of Variant Parametric Types. Technical report, Department of Computer Science, Durham University, UK (December 2008), http://www.durham.ac.uk/shengchao.qin/papers/VPTinfer.pdf
6. Craciun, F., Goh, H.Y., Chin, W.N.: A framework for object-oriented program analyses via Core-Java. In: IEEE Internationl Conference on Intelligent Computer Communication and Processing (2006)
7. Dincklage, D., Diwan, A.: Converting Java Classes to use Generics. In: ACM OOPSLA (2004)
8. Donovan, A., Kiezun, A., Tschantz, M.S., Ernst, M.D.: Converting Java Programs to Use Generic Libraries. In: ACM OOPSLA (2004)
9. Duggan, D.: Modular Type-based Reverse Engineering of Parameterized Types in Java Code. In: ACM OOPSLA (1999)
10. Fähndrich, M., Foster, J.S., Su, Z., Aiken, A.: Partial online cycle elimination in inclusion constraint graphs. In: ACM PLDI (1998)
11. Fuhrer, R., Tip, F., Kiezun, A., Dolby, J., Keller, M.: Efficiently Refactoring Java Applications to Use Generic Libraries. In: Black, A.P. (ed.) ECOOP 2005. LNCS, vol. 3586, pp. 71–96. Springer, Heidelberg (2005)
12. Gosling, J., Joy, B., Steele, G., Bracha, G.: The Java Language Specification. Addison-Wesley, Reading (2005)
13. Heintze, N., Tardieu, O.: Ultra-fast aliasing analysis using cla: A million lines of c code in a second. In: ACM PLDI (2001)
14. Igarashi, A., Viroli, M.: Variant parametric types: A flexible subtyping scheme for generics. ACM TOPLAS 28(5) (2006)
15. Kennedy, A., Pierce, B.: On Decidability of Nominal Subtyping with Variance. In: FOOL/WOOD (2007)
16. Kieżun, A., Ernst, M.D., Tip, F., Fuhrer, R.M.: Refactoring for parameterizing Java classes. In: ICSE (2007)
17. Odersky, M.: Inferred Type Instantiation for GJ, Notes (January 2002)
18. Pottier, F.: Simplifying Subtyping Constraints. In: ACM ICFP (1996)
19. Pottier, F.: Type inference in the presence of subtyping: from theory to practice. PhD thesis, Universite Paris 7 (1998)
20. Reynolds, J.C.: Preliminary design of the programming language Forsythe. Technical report, CMU-CS-88-159, Carnegie Mellon (1988)
21. Smith, D., Cartwright, R.: Java type inference is broken: Can we fix it? In: ACM OOPSLA (2008)
22. Su, Z., Fahndrich, M., Aiken, A.: Projection merging: Reducing redundancies in inclusion constraint graphs. In: ACM POPL (2000)
23. Torgersen, M., Ernst, E., Hansen, C.P., von der Ahe, P., Bracha, G., Gafter, N.: Adding Wildcards to the Java Programming Language. JOT 3(11) (2004)
24. Torgersen, M., Ernst, E., Hansen, C.P.: WildFJ. In: FOOL (2005)
25. Trifonov, V., Smith, S.: Subtyping Constrained Types. In: SAS (1996)

Existential Quantification for Variant Ownership

Nicholas Cameron* and Sophia Drossopoulou

Imperial College London
{ncameron,scd}@doc.ic.ac.uk

Abstract. Ownership types characterize the topology of objects in the heap, through a characterization of the context to which an object belongs. They have been used to support reasoning, memory management, concurrency, *etc.* Subtyping is traditionally invariant w.r.t. contexts, which has often proven inflexible in some situations. Recent work has introduced restricted forms of subtype variance and unknown context, but in a rather ad-hoc and restricted way.

We develop Jo∃, a calculus which supports parameterisation of types, as well as contexts, and allows variant subtyping of contexts based on existential quantification. Jo∃ is more expressive, general, and uniform than previous works which add variance to ownership languages. Our explicit use of existential types makes the connection to type-theoretic foundations from existential types more transparent. We prove type soundness for Jo∃ and extend it to Jo∃$_{deep}$ which enforces the owners-as-dominators property.

1 Introduction

Ownership types [9,10,11] support a characterization of the topology of objects in the heap. They have been successfully applied in many areas. Boyapati [3] et al. annotated several Java library classes and multithreaded server programs, effectively preventing data races. Vitek et al. used ownership types to support memory management in real time systems, with applications such as flying unmanned aircraft [2], while Aldrich et al. used ownership to enforce software architectures in large, real-world software [1].

Usually ownership types are expressed by classes parameterised by formal *context parameters*, *e.g.,* class C<o1,o2,o3> {...}, and types parameterised by actuals, *e.g.,* C<this,o2,o2>. Context parameters represent objects. The first context parameter denotes the *owner* of the corresponding object. We say that an object is *inside* its owner, and all transitive owners of the latter. This implicitly defines a tree structure of owners in the heap.

Deep ownership systems enforce the *owners-as-dominators* property [11,9], which requires that the path to any object o from the root object passes through the owner of o. That is, objects are *dominated* by their owners. Such encapsulated objects are protected from direct and indirect access.

---

* Author's current address is Victoria University of Wellington, New Zealand.

G. Castagna (Ed.): ESOP 2009, LNCS 5502, pp. 128–142, 2009.

In many variations of ownership types [9,10,22,23], actual context parameters must be *known* and invariant: they must not vary with execution or subtyping; *i.e.,* C<o1> is not a subtype of C<o2> even if o1 is inside o2. This follows generic types: List<Dog> is not a subtype of List<Animal>.

Recent work on ownership types has introduced the concept of *unknown*, flexible contexts: universe types [13] support the annotation any, MOJO [6] uses the context parameter ?, and effective ownership [19] uses an any context. These unknown owners introduce *variant subtyping*, whereby, *e.g.,* C<o> is a subtype of C<?>. Variant ownership types [18] support variance annotations to more precisely describe variance properties of ownership types.

All these systems are somewhat ad hoc in formalisation — there is no direct link to the underlying theory of existential types. In particular, they do not support:

1 two or more context parameters are unknown, but known to be the same, *e.g.,* in the type ∃o.C<o,o>;
2 context polymorphic methods [9,23] in the presence of variant contexts;
3 upper *and* lower bounds on variant contexts;
4 scoping of unknown contexts, *e.g.,* to distinguish a list of students which may have different owners, from a list of student which share the same unknown owners, *i.e.,* List<this, ∃o.Student<o>>, and ∃o.List<this, Student<o>>.

To bridge this gap, we develop Jo∃, which has its foundations in existential types and supports all these features. Jo∃ is a purely descriptive system, in that it only describes the heap topology, and guarantees that the topology is preserved, but does not restrict the topology in any way. We then develop a flavour of Jo∃, called Jo∃*deep*, which also supports deep ownership. We have distinguished deep ownership from the existential aspects, because descriptive ownership systems are useful in their own right (*e.g.,* to support reasoning with effects).

Jo∃ is a foundational, rather than usable, system. We expect it to be useful to reason about variance in ownership systems and to compare the various implementations of ownership variance. Whilst it is expressive and powerful, Jo∃ is verbose. Practical adoption of Jo∃ would require heavy syntactic sugaring.

Recent work with Java wildcards and similar systems [7,5,16,20] has used existential types to implement and formalise subtype variance in object-oriented languages. In these systems existential types are often implicit [20,16], a more programmer-friendly syntax obscures the underlying existential types. Packing and unpacking are usually implicit, even where quantification is explicit [5].

We use existential quantification of contexts to implement variant ownership. This solution is uniform and clearly related to its theoretical underpinnings; typing and the underlying mechanisms are refelcted in the syntax. Furthermore, in combination with type parameterisation, it is extremely expressive.

Outline. In Sect. 2 we give an example explaining and motivating Jo∃. We present Jo∃ in Sect. 3 and Jo∃*deep* in Sect. 4. We discuss these languages in Sect. 5 and their relation to related work in Sect. 6. We conclude in Sect. 7

2 Example

In this example we use a sugared syntax[1], rather than the verbose $\exists$ syntax, with implicit packing and unpacking of existential types. Such implicit packing and unpacking appears, for example, in Java wildcards; mapping from the sugared version to $\exists$ is simple [4]. We use o→[a b] to denote that the formal context parameter o has the lower bound a and upper bound b, that is, any instantiation of o must be inside b and outside[2] a in the ownership hierarchy.

```
class Worker<manager, company outside manager> {
    List<this, Worker<manager, company>> colleagues;
    ∃o→[⊥ company].List<this, Worker<o, company>> workGroup;
    ∃o→[manager company].Worker<o, company> mentor;

    void mixGroups() {
        workGroup = colleagues;
        //colleagues = workGroup;                      ERROR
        //colleagues.add(workGroup.get(0));            ERROR
        //workGroup.add(colleagues.get(0));            ERROR
    }
}

class Company extends Object<◯> {
    Worker<this, this> director;
    Worker<director, this> headOfMarketing;
    ∃o→[⊥ director].Worker<o, this> employeeOfTheMonth;
    List<this, ∃o→[⊥ this].Worker<o, this>> payroll;

    <m> void processColleagues(Worker<m, this> w) {
        for (Worker<m, this> c : w.colleagues) { ... }
    }

    void mentorEmpMonth() {
        employeeOfTheMonth.mentor = director;
        //employeeOfTheMonth.mentor =
        //   new Worker<headOfMarketing, this>;       ERROR
    }
}
```

Our example is part of a human resources system for a large company. Each worker in the company is owned by its manager; the employees form a hierarchy with the director at its root. In the Worker class, each worker keeps a list of his

---

[1] We also use fields as context parameters. This is not implemented in $\exists$, but is a relatively easy extension. It is present in, for example, MOJO [6].

[2] We say o outside o′ to mean o′ inside o.

colleagues. Each colleague is a `Worker` with the same `manager` as `this`. In the `Company` class, we store references to the `director` and the head of marketing, whose immediate `manager` is the `director`.

So far, we have only used features present in classical ownership types systems. We use existential types where the precise owner of objects is unknown and highlight the features listed in the previous section, *e.g.*, **1**. In the `Worker` class, `mentor` is some worker who either works with or indirectly manages that worker, but whose exact position in the management hierarchy is not specified (**3**). A worker may work with some other team of workers in the company (a team is assumed to have a single manager). For example, an engineer may have contact with the management team. This group (`workGroup`) may have any manager in the company, and this is represented by the existential type. Since we assume all members of the group have the same owner, the existential quantification is outside the `List` (**4**).

In the `Company` class, the `employeeOfTheMonth` may be any `Worker` in the company, her manager is not important. The `payroll` keeps track of every worker in the company. Each worker on the `payroll` may have a different manager.

The method `processColleagues` takes a worker (`w`) as a parameter and performs some action on each of his colleagues. Since the method is polymorphic in the manager (`m`) of `w`, we can name `m` as the owner of `w`'s colleagues, `c` (**2**).

In `mixGroups` we can set `workGroup` to `colleagues` because `manager` (the manager of `colleagues`) is within the bounds specified in the type of `workGroup`. We cannot set `colleagues` to `workGroup`, nor add an element of `colleagues` to `workGroup`, because `workGroup` may have any manager, not necessarily `this`. Even though we can set `workGroup` to `colleagues`, we cannot add an element of `colleagues` to `workGroup` because although the owner of the `workGroup` may be any owner, it is a specific owner and not necessarily `manager`[3].

Owners-as-dominators. Even in a deep ownership system it can be safe and desirable to support subtype variance. A `Worker` instance and his `mentor` (though not his `workGroup`) satisfy owners-as-dominators in $Jo\exists_{deep}$. `mentorEmpMonth` sets the `mentor` of the `employeeOfTheMonth` to the `director`. This preserves owners-as-dominators since the `director` must transitively manage (own) the `employeeOfTheMonth`, no matter who that is. Setting the `employeeOfTheMonth`'s `mentor` to a new worker owned by the `headOfMarketing` would violate owners-as-dominators and is not allowed. This is because the `employeeOfTheMonth` may not be transitively owned by this new worker.

3   Jo∃

In this section we present the most interesting parts of Jo∃, a minimal object-oriented language in the style of FGJ [15], with parametrisation of methods and classes by context and type parameters, and existential quantification of contexts. In order to demonstrate ownership properties, we include field assignment

---

[3] Here, the owner is `manager` due to the earlier assignment, but in general it will be unknown.

and a mutable heap. Jo∃ is fully described in the first author's PhD thesis [4] along with much extra detail that could not be included here for space reasons.

Subtype variance in Jo∃ is implemented by existential quantification. Existential types are explicit and are introduced and eliminated (packed and unpacked) using `close` and `open` expressions. Thus, we follow the more traditional model of existential types [7], rather than the Java 5.0 approach of using implicit packing and unpacking.

Neither the ownership or existential quantification features of Jo∃ interact with subclassing. Furthermore, the benefits of existential quantification in Jo∃ do not depend on subclassing, nor the absence of subclassing. For these reasons, and because the standard solution to subclassing in ownership types systems is long known [10], we elide subclassing and inheritance. This simplifies the presentation of Jo∃ and its proofs. Jo∃ could be extended to include subclassing by extending the subtyping and method and field lookup rules following FGJ [15]. Subclassing must preserve the formal owner of an object [10]. There are no changes to any of the rules involving quantification.

We are primarily interested in type parameterisation to increase expressiveness of ownership types, rather than to investigate features of generic types. We therefore treat type parameterisation simply and do not support bounds on formal type parameters, nor existential quantification of type variables.

e	::=	null | x | γ.f | γ.f = e | γ.<$\overline{a}$, $\overline{T}$>m($\overline{e}$) | new C<$\overline{a}$, $\overline{T}$> | open e as x,$\overline{o}$ in e | close e with $\overline{o \to [b\ b]}$ hiding $\overline{a}$ | ι | err	*expressions*

Q	::=	class C<Δ, $\overline{X}$> {$\overline{Tf}$; $\overline{W}$}	*class declarations*
W	::=	<Δ, $\overline{X}$> T m($\overline{Tx}$) {return e;}	*method declarations*

v	::=	close v with $\overline{o \to [b\ b]}$ hiding $\overline{r}$ | ι | null | err	*values*

N	::=	C<$\overline{a}$, $\overline{T}$>	*class types*	a	::=	o | x | $\bigcirc$ | ι	*contexts*
R	::=	C<$\overline{r}$, $\overline{T}$>	*runtime types*	r	::=	$\bigcirc$ | ι	*runtime contexts*
M	::=	N | X	*non-existential types*	b	::=	a | $\perp$	*bounds*
T	::=	M | $\exists\Delta$.N	*types*				

Ψ	::=	$\overline{X \to [b_l\ b_u]}$	*type environments*	x, y	*variables*
Δ	::=	$\overline{o \to [b_l\ b_u]}$	*context environments*	X, Y	*type variables*
γ	::=	x | ι | null	*vars and addresses*	o	*formal owners*
Γ	::=	$\overline{\gamma:T}$	*var environments*	C	*classes*
$\mathcal{H}$	::=	$\overline{\iota \to (R, \overline{f \to v})}$	*heaps*	ι	*addresses*

Fig. 1. Syntax of Jo∃

Syntax. The syntax of Jo∃ is given in Fig. 1. Entities only used at runtime are in grey . Jo∃ includes expressions for accessing variables (x, which includes this) and addresses (ι), object creation, null (for field initialisation), field access and assignment, method invocation, and packing and unpacking of existential types.

Class and method declarations (Q and W) are parameterised by context (o) and type (X) parameters. The former have upper and lower bounds (bounds are actual context parameters — not subtype bounds — and limit the bounded formal context to some part of the ownership hierarchy), and so methods and classes are considered to be parameterised by *context environments* (Δ). These are mappings from formal context parameters to their bounds (o→[b$_l$ b$_u$]).

Contexts (a) consist of context variables (o), variables (x) and the *world context* (the root object), $\bigcirc$. At runtime we may also use addresses. Runtime contexts (r) are restricted to addresses and $\bigcirc$.

Variable environments, Γ, map variables to their types. Type environments, Ψ, map type variables to bounds on a context. Type variables do not have bounds on the types they may take. The bounds contained in Ψ define upper and lower bounds on the owner of actual types. If the lower and upper bounds on the owner of X are b$_l$ and b$_u$, then for C<o> to instantiate X, o must be outside b$_l$ and inside b$_u$. The bounds in Ψ are manufactured by the type system (in T-CLASS in Fig. 4 and T-METHOD [4]) and cannot be defined by the programmer. In Jo∃ and Jo∃$_{deep}$, upper bounds in Ψ are always $\bigcirc$ and, in effect, are never used; however, we keep upper bounds to allow for easy extension. We only use the lower bound to support deep ownership in Jo∃$_{deep}$ (Sect. 4).

To model execution we use a heap, $\mathcal{H}$, which maps addresses (ι) to records representing objects. Each record contains the type of the object and a mapping from field names to values. Values (v) are addresses or close expressions that pack addresses.

Types in Jo∃. The syntax of types in Jo∃ is given in Fig. 1. Class types (N) are class names parameterised by actual type and context parameters. The first context parameter is the owner of objects with that type. Class types may be existentially quantified by a context environment to give existential types. For example, ∃o.List<o, Animal> denotes a list owned by *some* owner. For conciseness in examples, we omit bounds and empty parameter lists where convenient.

By combining existential quantification with type parameterisation we can express many interesting and useful types: ∃o.List<o, Animal<this>> denotes a list owned by some unknown owner where each element is an Animal owned by this, while ∃o1,o2.List<o1, Animal<o2>> denotes a list owned by some owner where all elements are owned by the same owner which may be different from the owner of the list, and ∃o1.List<o1, ∃o2.Animal<o2>> denotes a list where each element is owned by some owner and the owner of each element may be different, finally, ∃o.List<o, Animal<o>> denotes a list where each element in the list and the list itself are owned by the same, unknown, owner.

Subtyping and the Inside Relation. The inside relation relates contexts and is defined by the rules given in Fig. 2. We say that o$_1$ is inside o$_2$ ($\Delta; \Gamma \vdash$ o$_1 \preceq$ o$_2$), if o$_1$ is transitively owned by o$_2$. The inside relation is reflexive, transitive, and

$$\frac{}{\Delta; \Gamma \vdash M <: M} \qquad \frac{\Delta; \Gamma \vdash \overline{b_u \preceq b_u'} \qquad \Delta; \Gamma \vdash \overline{b_l' \preceq b_l}}{\Delta; \Gamma \vdash \exists o \to [\overline{b_l \ b_u}].N <: \exists o \to [\overline{b_l' \ b_u'}].N}$$

$$\text{(S-Reflex)} \qquad\qquad\qquad\qquad \text{(S-Full)}$$

$$\frac{}{\Delta; \Gamma \vdash b \preceq b} \qquad \frac{\Delta; \Gamma \vdash b \preceq b'' \qquad \Delta; \Gamma \vdash b'' \preceq b'}{\Delta; \Gamma \vdash b \preceq b'} \qquad \frac{\Delta; \Gamma \vdash b \ \text{OK}}{\Delta; \Gamma \vdash b \preceq \bigcirc}$$

$$\text{(I-Reflex)} \qquad\qquad \text{(I-Trans)} \qquad\qquad\qquad \text{(I-World)}$$

$$\frac{\Delta; \Gamma \vdash b \ \text{OK}}{\Delta; \Gamma \vdash \bot \preceq b} \qquad \frac{\Gamma(\gamma) = C<\overline{a}, \ \overline{T}>}{\Delta; \Gamma \vdash \gamma \preceq a_0} \qquad \frac{\Delta(o) = [\overline{b_l \ b_u}]}{\Delta; \Gamma \vdash o \preceq b_u} \\ \qquad\qquad\qquad\qquad\qquad\qquad\qquad \Delta; \Gamma \vdash b_l \preceq o$$

$$\text{(I-Bottom)} \qquad\qquad \text{(I-Owner)} \qquad\qquad\qquad \text{(I-Bound)}$$

Fig. 2. Jo∃ subtyping, and the inside relation for owners and environments

has top and bottom elements — the world and bottom contexts, respectively. I-Owner asserts that every variable and address is inside the declared owner of its type (if its type is a class type). For example, if `this` has type C<o>, then `this` is inside o. I-Bound gives that a formal context is within its bounds.

Subtyping is also given in Fig. 2. Since there is no subclassing in Jo∃, subtyping of non-existential types is given only by reflexivity. Subtyping between existential types follows the full variant of existential subtyping [14,7]. Existential types are subtypes where the bounds of quantified contexts in the subtype are more strict than in the supertype.

$$\frac{o \in dom(\Delta)}{\Delta; \Gamma \vdash o \ \text{OK}} \qquad \frac{}{\Delta; \Gamma \vdash \bigcirc \ \text{OK}} \qquad \frac{}{\Delta; \Gamma \vdash \bot \ \text{OK}} \qquad \frac{\Gamma(\gamma) = N}{\Delta; \Gamma \vdash \gamma \ \text{OK}}$$

$$\text{(F-Owner)} \qquad\quad \text{(F-World)} \qquad\quad \text{(F-Bottom)} \qquad\quad \text{(F-Var)}$$

$$\text{class } C<o \to [\overline{b_l \ b_u}], \ \overline{X}>... \qquad \Delta; \Gamma \vdash \overline{a} \ \text{OK}$$
$$\frac{\Delta; \Gamma, \text{this}:C<\overline{a}, \ \overline{X}> \vdash \overline{[a/o]b_l} \preceq a \qquad \Delta; \Gamma, \text{this}:C<\overline{a}, \ \overline{X}> \vdash a \preceq \overline{[a/o]b_u}}{\Psi; \Delta; \Gamma \vdash \overline{T} \ \text{OK} \qquad |\overline{T}| = |\overline{X}|}$$
$$\frac{}{\Psi; \Delta; \Gamma \vdash C<\overline{a}, \ \overline{T}> \ \text{OK}}$$

$$\text{(F-Class)}$$

$$\frac{X \in dom(\Psi)}{\Psi; \Delta; \Gamma \vdash X \ \text{OK}} \qquad \frac{\Delta; \Gamma \vdash \overline{o \to [b_l \ b_u]} \ \text{OK}}{\Psi; \Delta, \overline{o \to [b_l \ b_u]}; \Gamma \vdash N \ \text{OK}}{\Psi; \Delta; \Gamma \vdash \exists o \to [\overline{b_l \ b_u}].N \ \text{OK}}$$

$$\text{(F-Type-Var)} \qquad\qquad\qquad \text{(F-Exist)}$$

Fig. 3. Jo∃ well-formed contexts and types

Well-formedness. Well-formed contexts and types are given in Fig. 3. An owner variable is well-formed if it has class type; this guarantees precise information about all unquantified contexts, and that the set of contexts is closed under substitution. This restriction abides by the philosophy of existential types, that abstract packages must be unpacked to be used.

Well-formed class types (F-CLASS) require the class name to have been declared, actual context parameters to be within the bounds of formal context parameters, the number of actual type parameters to match the number of formal type parameters, and actual context and type parameters to be well-formed. Well-formed environments (used in F-EXISTS) are elided, the only interesting aspect is that we require the lower bound of each context variable to be inside its corresponding upper bound.

To check that actual context parameters are within their corresponding bounds, the judging environments are extended with this mapped to C<$\bar{a}$, $\bar{X}$>, i.e., the class type with actual context parameters and formal type parameters. This is necessary because $\overline{b_l}$ and $\overline{b_u}$ may involve this. We cannot substitute for this, because there may not be a variable or address that contains the object to be substituted. We use a mixture of actual context parameters ($\bar{a}$) and formal type parameters ($\bar{X}$) because of the order of application of substitution lemmas in the proofs. Using $\bar{X}$ is safe, even though $\bar{X}$ are not in scope, because the type parameters of types are never used in the rules defining the inside relation.

$$\frac{\Psi;\Delta;\Gamma \vdash \gamma : \mathbb{N} \quad fType(\mathtt{f},\gamma,\mathbb{N}) = \mathtt{T}}{\Psi;\Delta;\Gamma \vdash \gamma.\mathtt{f} : \mathtt{T}}$$

(T-FIELD)

$$\frac{\begin{array}{c}\Psi;\Delta;\Gamma \vdash \gamma : \mathbb{N} \\ fType(\mathtt{f},\gamma,\mathbb{N}) = \mathtt{T} \\ \Psi;\Delta;\Gamma \vdash \mathtt{e} : \mathtt{T}\end{array}}{\Psi;\Delta;\Gamma \vdash \gamma.\mathtt{f} = \mathtt{e} : \mathtt{T}}$$

(T-ASSIGN)

$$\frac{\Psi;\Delta;\Gamma \vdash \mathtt{C}\mathtt{<}\bar{\mathtt{a}},\ \bar{\mathtt{U}}\mathtt{>}\ \text{OK}}{\Psi;\Delta;\Gamma \vdash \mathtt{new}\ \mathtt{C}\mathtt{<}\bar{\mathtt{a}},\ \bar{\mathtt{U}}\mathtt{>} : \mathtt{C}\mathtt{<}\bar{\mathtt{a}},\ \bar{\mathtt{U}}\mathtt{>}}$$

(T-NEW)

$$\frac{\begin{array}{c}\Psi;\Delta;\Gamma \vdash \gamma : \mathbb{N} \quad \Psi;\Delta;\Gamma \vdash \overline{\mathtt{e}} : \overline{\mathtt{T}} \\ \Delta;\Gamma \vdash \bar{\mathtt{a}}\ \text{OK} \quad \Psi;\Delta;\Gamma \vdash \bar{\mathtt{U}}\ \text{OK} \\ mType_{\Delta;\Gamma}(\mathtt{m}\mathtt{<}\bar{\mathtt{a}},\ \gamma,\ \bar{\mathtt{U}}\mathtt{>},\mathbb{N}) = \overline{\mathtt{T}}{\to}\mathtt{T}\end{array}}{\Psi;\Delta;\Gamma \vdash \gamma.\mathtt{<}\bar{\mathtt{a}},\ \bar{\mathtt{U}}\mathtt{>}\mathtt{m}(\overline{\mathtt{e}}) : \mathtt{T}}$$

(T-INVK)

$$\frac{\begin{array}{c}\Psi;\Delta;\Gamma \vdash \mathtt{e} : \exists\mathtt{o}{\to}[\mathtt{b}_l\ \mathtt{b}_u].\mathbb{N} \\ \Psi;\Delta,\mathtt{o}{\to}[\mathtt{b}_l\ \mathtt{b}_u];\Gamma,\mathtt{x}{:}\mathbb{N} \vdash \mathtt{e}' : \mathtt{T} \\ \Psi;\Delta;\Gamma \vdash \mathtt{T}\ \text{OK}\end{array}}{\Psi;\Delta;\Gamma \vdash \mathtt{open}\ \mathtt{e}\ \mathtt{as}\ \mathtt{x},\bar{\mathtt{o}}\ \mathtt{in}\ \mathtt{e}' : \mathtt{T}}$$

(T-OPEN)

$$\frac{\begin{array}{c}\Delta;\Gamma \vdash \overline{[\mathtt{a}/\mathtt{o}]\mathtt{b}_l} \preceq \mathtt{a} \quad \Delta;\Gamma \vdash \overline{\mathtt{a} \preceq [\mathtt{a}/\mathtt{o}]\mathtt{b}_u} \quad \Delta;\Gamma \vdash \bar{\mathtt{a}}\ \text{OK} \\ \Psi;\Delta;\Gamma \vdash \mathtt{e} : [\mathtt{a}/\mathtt{o}]\mathbb{N} \quad \Psi;\Delta;\Gamma \vdash \exists\mathtt{o}{\to}[\mathtt{b}_l\ \mathtt{b}_u].\mathbb{N}\ \text{OK}\end{array}}{\Psi;\Delta;\Gamma \vdash \mathtt{close}\ \mathtt{e}\ \mathtt{with}\ \mathtt{o}{\to}[\mathtt{b}_l\ \mathtt{b}_u]\ \mathtt{hiding}\ \bar{\mathtt{a}} : \exists\mathtt{o}{\to}[\mathtt{b}_l\ \mathtt{b}_u].\mathbb{N}}$$

(T-CLOSE)

$$\frac{\begin{array}{c}\Psi = \overline{\mathtt{X}{\to}[\bot\bigcirc]} \\ \emptyset;\mathtt{this}{:}\mathtt{C}\mathtt{<}\bar{\mathtt{o}},\ \bar{\mathtt{X}}\mathtt{>} \vdash \overline{\mathtt{o}{\to}[\mathtt{b}_l\ \mathtt{b}_u]}\ \text{OK} \quad \Psi;\overline{\mathtt{o}{\to}[\mathtt{b}_l\ \mathtt{b}_u]};\mathtt{this}{:}\mathtt{C}\mathtt{<}\bar{\mathtt{o}},\ \bar{\mathtt{X}}\mathtt{>} \vdash \bar{\mathtt{W}},\ \bar{\mathtt{T}}\ \text{OK}\end{array}}{\vdash\ \mathtt{class}\ \mathtt{C}\mathtt{<}\mathtt{o}{\to}[\mathtt{b}_l\ \mathtt{b}_u],\ \bar{\mathtt{X}}\mathtt{>}\ \{\overline{\mathtt{T}\,\mathtt{f}};\ \bar{\mathtt{W}}\}\ \text{OK}}$$

(T-CLASS)

Fig. 4. Jo∃ expression and class typing rules

Typing. Type rules are given in Fig. 4. Field and variable access (T-FIELD and T-VAR) are close to those of FGJ [15]. Field assignment (T-ASSIGN) is a straightforward extension of field access. We adopt the standard subsumption rule (T-SUB). In object creation (T-NEW), we create uninitialised objects, we do not support constructors. T-NULL allows `null` to take any well-formed type. Method invocation is also close to FGJ, with the addition that actual context parameters must be well-formed and within their corresponding formal bounds.

In T-FIELD, T-ASSIGN, and T-INVK, the receiver is restricted to γ. This allows us to substitute γ for `this` in field and method types without requiring dependent typing. Expressivity is not lost since the programmer can use an `open` expression with empty $\bar{o}$ to act as a let expression.

To type check `open` and `close` expressions we follow Fun [8] and other classical existential types systems. The type of expression e is unpacked to an owner environment, $\overline{o \rightarrow [b_l\ b_u]}$, and unquantified type, N. We then judge the body of open (e′) by extending Δ with $\overline{o \rightarrow [b_l\ b_u]}$ and adding a fresh variable, x, with type N to Γ; x stands for the unpacked value of e. We ensure no variables escape the scope of the `open` expression by checking that the result type, T, is well-formed without $\bar{o}$ or x.

The `close` expression packs an expression e by hiding some of the context parameters present in e's type. For example, if e has type C<this>, then the expression `close e with o hiding this` has the existential type $\exists$o.C<o>.

Example. The assignment `employeeOfTheMonth.mentor = director` from the example in Sect. 2 is represented with explicit packing and unpacking as:

```
open employeeOfTheMonth as e,m in
    e.mentor = close director with o→[m this] hiding this;
```

Under an environment where e has type Worker<m, this>, the close and assignment expressions have type $\exists$o→[m this].Worker<o, this> by T-CLOSE, and by T-ASSIGN and S-REFLEX, respectively. By T-SUBS, S-FULL, and I-BTTM, the assignment has the m-free type $\exists$o→[⊥ this].Worker<o, this>. employeeOfTheMonth (of type $\exists$m→[⊥ director].Worker<m, this>) can be unpacked as e (of type Worker<m, this>), used in type checking the assignment, and therefore T-OPEN can be applied, giving the entire expression the type $\exists$o→[⊥ this].Worker<o, this>.

Dynamic Semantics. We elide most of the operational semantics of Jo$\exists$, they are mostly standard[4]. Reduction of open and close expressions is given by the following rule, taken from the classical formulations of existential types [21]:

$$\text{open (close } v \text{ with } \overline{o \rightarrow [b_l\ b_u]} \text{ hiding } \bar{r}) \text{ as } x,\bar{o} \text{ in } e; \mathcal{H} \rightsquigarrow [r/o,\ v/x]e; \mathcal{H}$$

The `open` and `close` sub-expressions are eliminated, leaving the body of open (e) with formal variables replaced by the packed value and hidden contexts. For example, `open (close 3 with o hiding 2) as x,o in (this.<o>m(x))`, where 2 and 3 are addresses, reduces to `this.<2>m(3)` (we replace x by 3 and o by 2).

---

[4] Object creation, performed in R-NEW, creates a new object with all its fields set to `null`; i.e., we do not support constructors.

$$\frac{\begin{array}{c} \forall \iota \to \{\text{C<}\overline{\text{r}},\ \overline{\text{T}}\text{>};\overline{\text{f}\to\text{v}}\} \in \mathcal{H}: \\ \emptyset; \varDelta; \mathcal{H} \vdash \text{C<}\overline{\text{r}},\ \overline{\text{T}}\text{> OK} \\ fType(\text{f}, \iota, \text{C<}\overline{\text{r}},\ \overline{\text{T}}\text{>}) = \text{T}' \qquad \emptyset; \varDelta; \mathcal{H} \vdash \text{v} : \text{T}' \\ \forall \text{v} \in \overline{\text{v}} : add(\text{v})\ defined \Rightarrow add(\text{v}) \in dom(\mathcal{H}) \end{array}}{\varDelta \vdash \mathcal{H}\ \text{OK}} \qquad \frac{\begin{array}{c} \varDelta \vdash \mathcal{H}\ \text{OK} \\ \forall \iota \in fv(\text{e}) : \iota \in dom(\mathcal{H}) \end{array}}{\varDelta; \mathcal{H} \vdash \text{e OK}}$$

$$\text{(F-Heap)} \qquad\qquad\qquad\qquad \text{(F-Config)}$$

Fig. 5. Jo∃ well-formed heaps and configurations

In Fig. 5 we give the definitions of well-formed heaps and configurations. Most premises are standard. We insist that the address of all referenced values are in the domain of the heap. The address of a value is given by the partial function add, defined as:

$$add(\text{v}) = \begin{cases} \iota, & \text{if } \text{v} = \iota \\ add(\text{v}'), & \text{if } \text{v} = \text{close } \text{v}' \ldots \\ undefined, & \text{otherwise} \end{cases}$$

which recursively unwraps abstract packages, returning the address within. Thus, $add(v)$ is defined if v is neither null nor null wrapped in a close expression.

Type Soundness. Type soundness in Jo∃ guarantees that the types of variables accurately reflect their contents, including ownership information. Furthermore, the ownership hierarchy defined statically in a program describes the heap when that program is executed. Although these properties do not constitute an encapsulation property, they are necessary when using ownership information to reason about programs, for example using effects [10]. We show type soundness for Jo∃ by proving progress and preservation (subject reduction):

Theorem (progress). *For any* $\mathcal{H}, \text{e}, \text{T},$ *if* $\emptyset; \emptyset; \mathcal{H} \vdash \text{e} : \text{T}$ *and* $\emptyset \vdash \mathcal{H}$ OK *then either there exists* $\mathcal{H}', \text{e}'$ *such that* $\text{e}; \mathcal{H} \rightsquigarrow \text{e}'; \mathcal{H}'$ *or there exists* v *such that* $\text{e} = \text{v}.$

Theorem (subject reduction). *For any* $\varDelta, \mathcal{H}, \mathcal{H}', \text{e}, \text{e}', \text{T},$ *if* $\emptyset; \varDelta; \mathcal{H} \vdash \text{e} : \text{T}$ *and* $\text{e}; \mathcal{H} \rightsquigarrow \text{e}'; \mathcal{H}'$ *and* $\varDelta; \mathcal{H} \vdash \text{e}$ OK *and* $\emptyset; \mathcal{H} \vdash \varDelta$ OK *and* $\text{e}' \neq \text{err}$ *then* $\emptyset; \varDelta; \mathcal{H}' \vdash \text{e}' : \text{T}$ *and* $\varDelta; \mathcal{H}' \vdash \text{e}'$ OK.

Proofs are given in [4] and can be downloaded from:

http://www.doc.ic.ac.uk/~ncameron/papers/cameron_esop09_proofs.pdf

4   Jo∃$_{deep}$

Jo∃$_{deep}$ enforces the owners-as-dominators property. It differs from Jo∃ only in its definition of well-formed types, heaps, and classes. We define auxiliary functions to find the owner of an object in the heap ($own_{\mathcal{H}}(\text{v})$) and the owner of objects with type T ($own_{\Psi}(\text{T})$) in Fig. 6.

The owner of objects of type X is the lower bound on the owner of X, recorded in Ψ. To find the owner of objects with existential type ($\exists \varDelta.\text{C<}\overline{\text{a}},\ \overline{\text{T}}\text{>}$), we must

$$\frac{}{own_\Psi(\text{C}<\overline{\text{a}},\ \overline{\text{T}}>) = \text{a}_0} \qquad \frac{\Psi(\text{X}) = [\text{b}_l\ \text{b}_u]}{own_\Psi(\text{X}) = \text{b}_l} \qquad \frac{}{own_\Psi(\exists\Delta.\text{C}<\overline{\text{a}},\ \overline{\text{T}}>) = glb_\Delta(\text{a}_0)}$$

$$\frac{\text{b} \notin dom(\Delta)}{glb_\Delta(\text{b}) = \text{b}} \qquad \frac{\Delta(o) = [\text{b}_l\ \text{b}_u]}{glb_\Delta(o) = glb_\Delta(\text{b}_l)}$$

$$\frac{\mathcal{H}(\iota) = \{\text{C}<\overline{\text{r}},\ \overline{\text{T}}>\ \ldots\}}{own_\mathcal{H}(\iota) = \text{r}_0} \qquad \frac{}{own_\mathcal{H}(\text{close v with } \overline{o \rightarrow [\text{b}_l\ \text{b}_u]} \text{ hiding } \overline{\text{r}}) = own_\mathcal{H}(\text{v})}$$

Fig. 6. Owner lookup functions for Jo$\exists_{deep}$

find a context that is not quantified and that is inside the declared owner of the type (a_0). This is accomplished by the glb function; $glb_\Delta(\text{b})$ finds the outermost object that is inside b and not in the domain of Δ.

The owners-as-dominators property manifests itself as an extra constraint on well-formed heaps; thus, we extend F-HEAP (Fig. 5) as follows:

$$\cdots$$
$$\frac{\forall \iota \in \mathcal{H} \qquad \forall \text{v} \in \mathcal{H}(\iota) \qquad \Delta; \mathcal{H} \vdash \iota \preceq own_\mathcal{H}(\text{v})}{\Delta \vdash \mathcal{H} \text{ OK}}$$

(F-HEAP)

Similarly, Jo$\exists_{deep}$ requires some modifications to the well-formedness rules for class types and classes of Jo$\exists$:

$$\cdots \qquad\qquad\qquad\qquad \cdots$$
$$\frac{\begin{array}{c}\forall \text{a}_i \in \overline{\text{a}} : \Delta; \Gamma \vdash \text{a}_0 \preceq \text{a}_i \\ \forall \text{T}_i \in \overline{\text{T}} : \Delta; \Gamma \vdash \text{a}_0 \preceq own_\Psi(\text{T}_i)\end{array}}{\Psi; \Delta; \Gamma \vdash \text{C}<\overline{\text{a}},\ \overline{\text{T}}> \text{ OK}} \qquad \frac{\begin{array}{c}\Psi = \overline{\text{X} \rightarrow [\text{o}_0\ \bigcirc]} \\ \bot \notin \overline{\text{T}}, o \rightarrow [\text{b}_l\ \text{b}_u]\end{array}}{\vdash \text{class } \text{C}<o \rightarrow [\text{b}_l\ \text{b}_u],\ \overline{\text{X}>} \{\overline{\text{T f}};\ \overline{\text{W}}\} \text{ OK}}$$

(F-CLASS)   (T-CLASS)

The extra premises in F-CLASS (together with the well-formedness rules for contexts) ensure that only contexts that are outside an object can be formed by substitution of actual for formal parameters in its class. The owner of an object (a_0) is, by definition, outside that object. The first extra premise ensures that the actual context parameters are outside a_0. The second premise ensures that the owners of any actual type parameters are outside a_0. Therefore, all types formed by substitution of contexts or types will have an owner outside this.

In T-CLASS we change the way Ψ is created; the lower bounds in Ψ are the formal owner of the class rather than $\bot$. This is required because of the changes we made to F-CLASS. The class declaration class C<o, X> { C<o, X> f; } would not type check without this change: otherwise C<o, X> would not be well-formed because $own_\Psi(\text{X})$ could not be derived to be outside o.

The second extra premise in T-CLASS requires that $\bot$ cannot appear as a bound in the formal context parameters of the class, nor in any existential types given to fields in the class. The intention is to ensure that the owner of all objects referenced by objects of the class (including the hidden owner of objects with existential type) is outside the referring object. Therefore, in the example in Sect. 2, the declaration of workGroup would be illegal in $\text{Jo}\exists_{deep}$.

We state the owners-as-dominators property in $\text{Jo}\exists_{deep}$ as:

Theorem (Owners-as-dominators). *For any* $\mathcal{H}$, *if* $\Delta \vdash \mathcal{H}$ OK *then* $\forall \iota \to \{\text{R}; \{\overline{\text{f} \to \text{v}}\}\} \in \mathcal{H}, \forall v_i \in \overline{\text{v}} : \Delta; \mathcal{H} \vdash \iota \preceq own_{\mathcal{H}}(v_i)$

This is given by the added premise to F-HEAP; we prove that this is maintained under execution as part of the proof of subject-reduction [4].

5   Discussion

The expressivity of types in $\text{Jo}\exists$ comes from the combination of existential quantification of contexts and type parameterisation. The formalisation of $\text{Jo}\exists$ follows from these starting points and the decision to use explicit packing and unpacking, which simplifies the type rules and proofs for $\text{Jo}\exists$. The natural and uniform emergence of the calculus is reassuring.

Allowing packed values to be be values (and thus stored in the heap) follows earlier work [8,21,14] on existential types and is a natural consequence of explicit packing. However, the owners-as-dominators property is usually phrased assuming that all values are objects (addresses in $\text{Jo}\exists$). We must therefore consider how to describe owners-as-dominators in the presence of packed values. We do this by not distinguishing between packed values and the objects that they abstract. This ensures that existential quantification cannot hide violations of owners-as-dominators.

In the type system of $\text{Jo}\exists_{deep}$, we had to extend the usual restrictions found in ownership systems to enforce owners-as-dominators. Requiring context parameters to be outside an object's owner is standard, we needed to extend this to deal with quantified context variables and type parameters. The crucial observation is that, in enforcing owners-as-dominators, we always wish to show that a value is outside the object that refers to it. It is therefore conservative to use a lower bound on a value's owner rather than the value's owner itself. The additional premises in F-CLASS of $\text{Jo}\exists_{deep}$ can thus deal with lower bounds on parameters. In the case of quantified context parameters this means that we can use their greatest lower bound. For type parameters we use the lower bound stored in Ψ; this motivates using Ψ in $\text{Jo}\exists$ rather than just a set of type variables.

6   Related Work

Generics and Ownership Types. Type and ownership information in ownership types systems is usually kept separate [9,12,25], as in $\text{Jo}\exists$. Surprisingly, in OGJ [22], these two kinds of parameters can be expressed using only type parameters. This leads to a small and uniform extension of generic Java that implements deep ownership. The fact that context parameterisation can be encoded using type extension highlights the similarity of the two systems. It will be interesting future work to add $\text{Jo}\exists$'s existential types to OGJ and, it is hoped, reap the benefits of $\text{Jo}\exists$ in a more realistic language.

Existential Types. Existential quantification of ownership domains in *System* F_{own} [17] allows domains to be passed around even if they cannot be named. System F_{own} supports existential quantification of types, absent in Jo∃, but does not support subtyping and so existential quantification does not lead to variance.

Infinitary ownership types [9] use existential types to abstract contexts which cannot be named. Because of dynamically created contexts, this is necessary to avoid dependent typing. Existential types in Jo∃ can be used in the same way. However, since contexts cannot be dynamically created, abstraction is not necessary to avoid dependent typing.

Existential owners can be used in dynamic casts [24]. Casts are not supported in Jo∃, but they should be straightforward to add. Existential downcasting could then be encoded in Jo∃ by casting using an existential type.

Variance. *Variant ownership types* [18] are a programmer friendly way to support use-site subtype variance, and have very similar behaviour to existential types. Jo∃ types are more expressive as they allow lower and upper bounds on contexts (as opposed to upper *or* lower bounds), type parameters, and explicit quantification (to express types such as ∃o.C<o, o>).

MOJO [6] uses ? to denote an unknown context parameter. This corresponds to an existentially quantified context bounded by ⊥ and ◯ in Jo∃. In MOJO, ? may be used as an actual context parameter.

In the case of field access, substitution of ? (not found in other systems such as Wild FJ [20]) produces a similar behaviour to existential types in Jo∃. To prevent field assignment and method call where ? would appear as a type parameter by substitution (but not where ? is written in the type), *strict* method and field lookup are used. Likewise in Jo∃, field assignment or method call where the receiver has existential type is type incorrect. Variant types in MOJO are, therefore, treated in the same way as unbounded existential types in Jo∃.

Universes [13] support limited subtype variance through the **any** notation. Universe types can be given corresponding types in Jo∃: **any** C corresponds to ∃o→[⊥◯].C<o>, **peer** C corresponds to C<o> (where o is the owner of the class declaration in which the type appears), and **rep** C corresponds to C<this>. The viewpoint adaptation[5] rules of universes correspond to substitution of owners and unpacking and packing in Jo∃. Generic universes [12] can be described using this correspondence and Jo∃'s type parameterisation.

An **any** context is used to facilitate variance in *effective ownership* [19]. During field and method type lookup, all substitutions of **any** for x are replaced with substitutions of **unknown** for x. This mechanism is similar to the abstract contexts of variant ownership types [18] and ? in MOJO. Similarly to these systems, it should be possible to encode the ownership structure of effective ownership in Jo∃. Effective owners (per-method owners) are currently beyond the scope of Jo∃. An effective owner cannot be **any**, and so there is no variance aspect to these owners.

---

[5] Viewpoint adaptation is the change in universe annotations when considering a type in a different context from the one in which it was declared.

In most related work [6,13,18], the treatment of unknown contexts is specific to the underlying system; our approach is founded in the theory of existential types and makes clear the relationship between variant types and their behaviour. We discuss in more detail how Jo∃ can be used to encode and compare the systems described in this section in [4].

7   Conclusion and Future Work

Jo∃ supports context variance in a uniform and transparent fashion using existential types. Expressivity is improved by combining existential quantification of contexts with type parameterisation. We have extended Jo∃ to support owners-as-dominators and proved both versions sound.

Jo∃ can be used to compare and encode ownership systems with different kinds of variance or existential types. Existing mechanisms for supporting context variance have the same behaviour as existential types in Jo∃ and can be easily encoded (even if other language features cannot). Explicit existential types can give us a clearer picture of the underlying mechanisms used in type checking. Jo∃ can also be used to encode existing kinds of existential types in ownership systems with similar benefits.

We would like to use type parameterisation and context quantification to improve the expressivity of multiple ownership and ownership domains systems, and to investigate how existentially quantified contexts can be used in an effects system. It might be useful to extend Jo∃ with subclassing, bounds on type variables, and existential quantification of type variables.

Acknowledgement. We would like to thank Werner Dietl and the anonymous reviewers for their detailed and useful feedback, and James Noble for ideas and inspiration from discussions on the MOJO project.

References

1. Abi-Antoun, M., Aldrich, J.: Ownership Domains in the Real World. In: International Workshop on Aliasing, Confinement and Ownership in object-oriented programming (IWACO) (2008)
2. Armbruster, A., Baker, J., Cunei, A., Flack, C., Holmes, D., Pizlo, F., Pla, E., Prochazka, M., Vitek, J.: A Real-Time Java Virtual Machine with Applications in Avionics. Transactions on Embedded Computing Systems 7(1), 1–49 (2007)
3. Boyapati, C., Rinard, M.: A Parameterized Type System for Race-free Java Programs. In: Object-Oriented Programming, Systems, Languages, and Applications (OOPSLA) (2001)
4. Cameron, N.: Existential Types for Variance — Java Wildcards and Ownership Types. PhD thesis, Imperial College London (2009)
5. Cameron, N., Drossopoulou, S., Ernst, E.: A Model for Java with Wildcards. In: Vitek, J. (ed.) ECOOP 2008. LNCS, vol. 5142, pp. 2–26. Springer, Heidelberg (2008)

6. Cameron, N., Drossopoulou, S., Noble, J., Smith, M.: Multiple Ownership. In: Object-Oriented Programming, Systems, Languages, and Applications (OOPSLA) (2007)
7. Cameron, N., Ernst, E., Drossopoulou, S.: Towards an Existential Types Model for Java Wildcards. In: Formal Techniques for Java-like Programs (FTfJP) (2007)
8. Cardelli, L., Wegner, P.: On Understanding Types, Data Abstraction, and Polymorphism. ACM Computing Surveys 17(4), 471–522 (1985)
9. Clarke, D.: Object Ownership and Containment. PhD thesis, School of Computer Science and Engineering, The University of New South Wales, Sydney, Australia (2001)
10. Clarke, D.G., Drossopoulou, S.: Ownership, Encapsulation and the Disjointness of Type and Effect. In: Object-Oriented Programming, Systems, Languages, and Applications (OOPSLA) (2002)
11. Clarke, D.G., Potter, J.M., Noble, J.: Ownership Types for Flexible Alias Protection. In: Object-Oriented Programming, Systems, Languages, and Applications (OOPSLA) (1998)
12. Dietl, W., Drossopoulou, S., Müller, P.: Generic Universe Types. In: European Conference on Object Oriented Programming (ECOOP) (2007)
13. Dietl, W., Müller, P.: Universes: Lightweight Ownership for JML. Journal of Object Technology 4(8), 5–32 (2005)
14. Ghelli, G., Pierce, B.: Bounded existentials and minimal typing. Theoretical Computer Science 193(1-2), 75–96 (1998)
15. Igarashi, A., Pierce, B.C., Wadler, P.: Featherweight Java: a Minimal Core Calculus For Java and GJ. ACM Trans. Program. Lang. Syst. 23(3), 396–450 (2001); an earlier version of this work appeared at OOPSLA 1999 (1999)
16. Igarashi, A., Viroli, M.: Variant Parametric Types: A Flexible Subtyping Scheme for Generics. Transactions on Programming Languages and Systems 28(5), 795–847 (2006)
17. Krishnaswami, N., Aldrich, J.: Permission-Based Ownership: Encapsulating State in Higher-Order Typed Languages. In: Programming Language Design and Implementation (PLDI) (2005)
18. Lu, Y., Potter, J.: On Ownership and Accessibility. In: Thomas, D. (ed.) ECOOP 2006. LNCS, vol. 4067, pp. 99–123. Springer, Heidelberg (2006)
19. Lu, Y., Potter, J.: Protecting Representation with Effect Encapsulation. In: Principles of Programming Languages (POPL) (2006)
20. Torgersen, M., Ernst, E., Hansen, C.P.: Wild FJ. In: Foundations of Object-Oriented Languages (FOOL) (2005)
21. Mitchell, J.C., Plotkin, G.D.: Abstract Types have Existential Type. Transactions on Programming Languages and Systems 10(3), 470–502 (1988)
22. Potanin, A., Noble, J., Clarke, D., Biddle, R.: Generic Ownership for Generic Java. In: Object-Oriented Programming, Systems, Languages, and Applications (OOPSLA) (2006)
23. Wrigstad, T.: Ownership-Based Alias Managemant. PhD thesis, KTH, Sweden (2006)
24. Wrigstad, T., Clarke, D.: Existential Owners for Ownership Types. Journal of Object Technology 6(4) (2007)
25. Zhao, T., Palsberg, J., Vitek, J.: Type-based Confinement. J. Funct. Program 16(1), 83–128 (2006)

Formalising and Verifying Reference Attribute Grammars in Coq

Max Schäfer, Torbjörn Ekman, and Oege de Moor

Programming Tools Group, University of Oxford, UK
{max.schaefer,torbjorn.ekman,oege.de.moor}@comlab.ox.ac.uk

Abstract. Reference attribute grammars are a powerful formalism for concisely specifying and implementing static analyses. While they have proven their merit in practical applications, no attempt has so far been made to rigorously verify correctness properties of the resulting systems. We present a general method for formalising reference attribute grammars in the theorem prover Coq. The formalisation is supported by tools for generating standard definitions from an abstract description and custom proof tactics to help automate verification. As a small but typical application, we show how closure analysis for the untyped lambda calculus can easily be implemented and proved correct with respect to an operational semantics. To evaluate the feasibility of our approach on larger systems, we implement name lookup for a naming core calculus of Java and give a formal correctness proof of the centrepiece of a rename refactoring for this language.

1 Introduction

Verifying program analyses and transformations is hard, even with the assistance of modern proof tools. Previous work [17,18] has followed standard practice in the compilers community by focussing on simple intermediate languages, where issues like complex scoping have been transformed away. For verifying optimisations in a batch compiler this approach is successful and adequate.

However, many modern development tools such as refactoring editors and code checkers operate at source level, and not on an intermediate language. This requires the implementation of analyses and transformations that align with the 'middle' phases of a compiler that deal with name binding, type checking and complex control flow structures, which are often the most intricate and error prone [10,6].

This paper presents a framework for verifying analyses and transformations on source, consisting of a specification formalism for source-level analyses and transformations, namely Circular Reference Attribute Grammars, and an embedding of that formalism in Coq. Our embedding is supported by tools that reduce the tedium of working with a complex language definition and allow proofs to be conducted at a high level of abstraction.

The particular variant of attribute grammars we have chosen is the basis of the JastAdd system [7]. It enhances standard attribute grammars [16] with a notion of node identity (reference attributes), and the ability to express least fixed point computations (circular attributes). Both these extensions are well-known: most industrial attribute

G. Castagna (Ed.): ESOP 2009, LNCS 5502, pp. 143–159, 2009.

grammar systems support reference attributes [1,23], and the idea of circular attributes goes at least back to Farrow [8].

The success of JastAdd [28] amply demonstrates the power of circular reference attribute grammars and their practical usability. Particularly relevant are its use in the implementation of JastAddJ, a full, highly compliant Java compiler [7], and in the construction of a refactoring framework for Java [24].

While it is well-known that pure attribute grammars can be regarded as non-strict functional programs [15], reference attributes and circular attributes require a more sophisticated translation. We demonstrate that these complications can be handled gracefully by generating boilerplate definitions and judicious use of proof strategies.

The result is a completely general framework for conducting proofs of analyses and transformations that deal with the full complexity of modern source languages. We illustrate its use on two examples: verification of a closure analysis, and the core of the refactoring framework of [24]. The complete formalisation including mechanised proofs is available for download [25]. Major contributions of this paper are:

- The first generic framework for mechanised proofs of the correctness of program analyses and transformations specified at source level.
- Tool support for conducting such proofs in Coq, at a high level of abstraction.
- A substantial case study that illustrates how our framework copes with the complex scoping issues in modern object-oriented languages, an issue that has hitherto not been considered in a formal setting.
- Evidence that proofs in our framework are scalable: non-trivial extensions to the object language require only modest additions to the proofs themselves.

The paper is structured as follows. First we introduce the notion of circular reference attribute grammars in Sec. 2. Next we show in Sec. 3 how this variant of attribute grammars is formalised in Coq. Sections 2 and 3 use a simple closure analysis as a running example. As a more substantial case study, we describe a formalisation of name analysis in an object-oriented language in Sec. 4, and show how it can be used to give a correctness proof of the central component of the Rename refactoring. Section 5 evaluates the development effort for both examples, and investigates scalability issues. Related work is discussed in Sec. 6, and we conclude in Sec. 7.

2   Reference Attribute Grammars

Attribute grammars [16] are a high-level formalism for declaratively specifying and implementing programs working on trees, in particular programming language processors such as compilers. Nodes of the underlying trees are endowed with attributes defined in terms of other attributes on the same node, or attributes on the surrounding nodes.

As originally proposed, attribute grammars make no special provisions for non-local dependencies, i.e. attributes that are defined in terms of other attributes on nodes far away in the tree. This situation commonly occurs in the static analysis of programming languages: For example, to typecheck the use of a variable, information about its type is needed, which has to be obtained from its declaration arbitrarily far away in the tree.

Solutions such as the explicit construction of symbol tables tend to become quite complicated, compromising the conceptual clarity of the underlying approach. Many extensions have been proposed to remedy this and similar problems, a particularly simple one being Reference Attribute Grammars, or RAGs [11], which are closely related to Remote Attribute Grammars [3]. The idea here is to allow attributes to evaluate to node references, on which other attributes can be evaluated in turn, thus superimposing a graph structure on the abstract syntax tree. This alleviates the need for secondary structures such as symbol tables and enables the use of the abstract syntax tree as the only data structure. RAGs become especially useful when combined with circular attributes, i.e. attributes defined by recursive equations; the combined formalism of Circular Reference Attribute Grammars, or CRAGs [20], will be our focus in this paper.

To introduce the key features of attribute grammars in general and reference attribute grammars in particular, we show how to implement closure analysis for the untyped lambda calculus. Closure analysis is a static analysis that predicts the reduction behaviour of terms. Take, for example, the term $(\lambda f.(f\,I)\,(f\,K))\,(\lambda x.x)$ where $I = \lambda a.a$ and $K = \lambda b.\lambda c.b$. Closure analysis will be able to predict that during reduction x can only be bound to the terms I and K; we say that the set of closures of (the single occurence of) x is $\{I, K\}$. For a discussion of the uses of closure analysis we refer to the literature [26,22], we concentrate on how to compute the set of closures using an attribute grammar.

2.1 Abstract Syntax Trees

Our object language is the simply typed lambda calculus with its reduction relation $t \Downarrow v$, indicating that term t evaluates to value v. The definitions of syntax and reduction relation are standard and we elide them for brevity.

Lambda terms are represented as abstract syntax trees (ASTs): Every node in an AST corresponds to a nonterminal of the grammar (here always `term`). Its children may either be terminals or other nodes, corresponding to a particular production in the grammar. In our example, a `term` node is either a variable node with a single identifier as its only child; or an abstraction node with an identifier (the bound variable) and a `term` node as its children; or an application node with two `term` nodes as its children. A node represents a subterm *at a certain position*, hence in the example the two occurrences of variable f will be represented by different nodes, albeit with the same content (namely the term f).

We want to implement an attribute `closures` that, for each node in the abstract syntax tree of a lambda term, returns the set of possible closures it could evaluate to. We want to prove a coherence result to show that our closure analysis agrees with the reduction relation and correctly predicts reduction outcomes:

Lemma 1 (Coherence). *For any lambda term t and closure v, if $t \Downarrow v$ then there is some node $nd \in$* `closures`(t) *such that v is the content of nd.*

2.2 The Attributes

To start with, we need to define a parameterised `lookup` attribute which looks up a name from a position within the term. Proceeding outwards, it returns a reference to the innermost enclosing lambda abstraction binding that name, if there is any. Thus, the result of looking up a name y at a node nd depends on the context of the node:

- if nd is the body of a lambda abstraction binding a variable x, we compare y and x; if they are the same, nd's parent node (the lambda abstraction) is returned as result; otherwise, we proceed with the lookup of y from the parent node
- if nd is the left child of an application node, lookup proceeds outwards
- if nd is the right child of an application node, lookup proceeds outwards

These three cases correspond to the clauses of the definition of name lookup as an *inherited attribute*, which is given in Fig. 1 using pseudocode. In these equations, **this** refers to the node lookup is invoked on, whereas **parent** is that node's parent node. The equations are defined by pattern matching on the position of **this** relative to **parent**, which is here symbolically indicated as a term with a bullet showing the position of **this**.

$$\textbf{inh lookup} \quad :: \textbf{id} \times \textbf{node} \rightarrow \textbf{node}$$
$$\texttt{lookup}(y, \lambda x.\bullet) = \begin{cases} \textbf{parent} & \text{if } y \equiv x \\ \texttt{lookup}(y, \textbf{parent}) & \text{otherwise} \end{cases}$$
$$\texttt{lookup}(y, \bullet\, t_2) = \texttt{lookup}(y, \textbf{parent})$$
$$\texttt{lookup}(y, t_1\, \bullet) = \texttt{lookup}(y, \textbf{parent})$$

Fig. 1. Informal specification of name lookup

The closure analysis itself is specified as a *synthesised attribute* closures, which computes an overapproximation of the closures a term could evaluate to, and a *collection attribute* args, which computes an overapproximation of the closures a closure could be applied to. These two attributes are mutually defined as shown in Fig. 2.

$$\textbf{syn closures} \quad :: \textbf{node} \rightarrow \textbf{set node}$$
$$\texttt{closures}(x) \quad = \texttt{args}(\texttt{lookup}(x, \textbf{this}))$$
$$\texttt{closures}(\lambda x.t) = \{\textbf{this}\}$$
$$\texttt{closures}(t_1\, t_2) = \bigcup \{\texttt{closures}(\texttt{body}(c)) \mid c \in \texttt{closures}(t_1)\}$$

$$\textbf{coll args} \quad :: \textbf{node} \rightarrow \textbf{set node}$$
$$\texttt{args}(c, t_1\, t_2) \quad \supseteq \texttt{closures}(t_2) \quad \text{if } c \in \texttt{closures}(t_1)$$
$$\texttt{args}(c, \_) \quad \supseteq \emptyset \quad \text{otherwise}$$

Fig. 2. Informal specification of closure analysis

The attribute closures is defined by case analysis over the *content* of its argument node, not its position as with attribute lookup above: this is the crucial difference between synthesised and inherited attributes. The equations are quite straightforward:

- a name can be bound to any value its binding abstraction is applied to
- a lambda abstraction's only possible value is itself
- an application's possible values are those of the body of its first child

Note the use of reference attributes in the third equation: The attribute `closures` returns a set of node references, on which other attributes may in turn be evaluated.

The attribute `args` is a globally defined collection attribute: Every node in the tree contributes a value, and all these contributions are combined using set theoretic union to yield the attribute's final value. The attribute has type node $\rightarrow$ set node; for a closure c, $\text{args}(c)$ is the set of all possible arguments c could be applied to. The contribution clauses (written using $\supseteq$) have type node $\times$ node $\rightarrow$ set node; for a closure c and a node n, they specify what the node n contributes to the value of $\text{args}(c)$. In particular, an application $t_1\ t_2$ with c as a possible value of t_1 contributes all possible values of t_2.

The attributes `closures` and `args` circularly depend on each other, thus it is not immediately clear that this definition is sensible. The classical solution [5] is to take least fixed points, which can here be constructed by iteration: the definitions are monotonic (as we will prove) and have values over a complete partial order of finite height.

Since the inception of attribute grammars, much research has been done on how to statically detect circularities. It turns out, however, that even the very simple extension of allowing attributes to take additional parameters (like `lookup`) defeats all checks:

Theorem 1 (Undecidability of Circularity). *It is undecidable whether a parameterised attribute is circularly defined.*

Proof. See the technical report for details [25].

3 Formalisation of Reference Attribute Grammars

We now show how to implement reference attribute grammars, such as the example presented in the previous section, in Coq. We choose to use a shallow embedding of reference attribute grammars into Coq: Abstract syntax trees are represented as terms, with attributes as functions on them. This means that attribute equations can use the full power of the Coq language, in particular they can exploit its powerful type system.

3.1 Formalising Abstract Syntax

For the formalisation of the object language's abstract syntax, we make use of Ott [27], a tool for specifying the syntax and semantics of programming languages and calculi. Given an abstract grammar, Ott generates one Coq datatype per nonterminal, with one constructor per production. In our case this yields

```
Inductive term : Set := Var : string → term
                      | Abs : string → term → term
                      | App : term → term → term.
```

This representation, however, is not sufficient to model reference attributes. The attribute `lookup`, for example, should return a reference to a lambda abstraction, which is not only characterised by its content (given by term of type `term`), but also its position in the syntax tree to distinguish it from other abstractions that might happen to have the same body. This leads to our first implementation challenge:

Challenge 1 (Node Identity) *We need a datatype representing nodes with an identity such that they can be distinguished from other nodes, even if they have identical content.*

To achieve this, we use Huet's zipper [12]. The basic idea of the zipper is to describe a node's position as a "path" from the node to the root of the tree. Let n be the node under consideration. If it is the root node, its path is empty. Otherwise, n must be the ith child of some node p and has left siblings $n_1, \ldots, n_{i-1}$ and right siblings $n_{i+1}, \ldots, n_m$, where m is the total number of children of p. Then the path of n consists of a first "step" containing all the siblings $n_1, \ldots, n_{i-1}, n_{i+1}, n_m$ (represented by their subtrees), and a path for p.

The possible steps are prescribed by the grammar: since every abstract syntax tree must be derivable from the start symbol, a step can only go from the occurrence of a nonterminal t′ on the right hand side of some production p to the nonterminal t on its left hand side. In our grammar, there are only three possible steps and only one nonterminal, hence the definition of the step datatype is very simple:

```
Inductive step : Set := Term1InApp : term → step
                      | Term2InApp : term → step
                      | TermInAbs  : string → step.
```

The three constructors correspond exactly to the position patterns used in our informal specification of the lookup attribute in the previous section: A step Term1InApp t2 describes (the position of) a node which is the first child of a node representing an application, and whose right sibling is t2 − in the pseudocode, this was written as ($\bullet\, t_2$). Likewise, Term2InApp tt1 corresponds to ($t_1\, \bullet$) and TermInAbs x is ($\lambda x.\bullet$).

In order to fully describe a node's position, we need to give the complete sequence of steps all the way to the root of the syntax tree. Thus the datatype of positions is

```
Inductive pos : Set := Root : pos
                     | Step : step → pos → pos.
```

Finally, nodes are nothing but pairs of positions and content (i.e., terms), with convenience functions node_pos and node_content to access these two parts.

The example term from Sec. 2 is represented in Coq as

```
App (Abs "f" (App (App (Var "f") I) (App (Var "f") K)))
    (Abs "x" (Var "x"))
```

where I and K are Coq representations of the terms I and K, respectively. The position of the only occurrence of x is

```
 Step (TermInAbs "x")
(Step (Term2InApp (Abs "f" (App (App (Var "f") I)
                                (App (Var "f") K)))) Root)
```

If we "plug" the content of the node into the first step on its path, we obtain the tree representation of the parent node's content. If we continue plugging all the way up to the root node, we get back the representation of the whole tree. These operations can be implemented systematically for every nonterminal as two functions plug_step and root which can be understood as tree navigation primitives for going "upwards".

The definitions of the zipper datatypes `step`, `pos`, `node`, and the helper functions `plug_step` and `root` can clearly be automatically derived from the abstract grammar. Indeed, we have extended Ott to provide this facility, but since the general case of grammars with multiple nonterminals requires somewhat more involved definitions than the ones given above, we defer discussion of this feature until Sec. 4.

3.2 Formalising Attributes

A pleasant side effect of using a zipper-based representation of nodes is that it yields a nice characterisation of the difference between synthesised and inherited attributes: A synthesised attribute works on the first component of a node (its children), whereas an inherited attribute works on its second component (its siblings and ancestors).

We start out by rephrasing our informal specification of `lookup` from Sec. 2 in Coq. First, we need to remedy a loophole of that specification: if we try to lookup an unbound variable, the inherited attribute described in Fig. 1 will reach the root of the syntax tree without having found any binding abstraction, and the specification does not say what is supposed to happen in this case. Our implementation of the attribute as a Coq function will have an option type as its return type, with a designated value `None` indicating that no binder was found.

If a binder *was* found, what should the function return? In the specification, it returns the binder's node. However, given our current node implementation, all nodes have type `node`, so we cannot by its type distinguish a node representing an abstraction from a node representing, say, an application. Hence we introduce a type that contains the same information as a node containing an abstraction, but in more explicit form[1]:

Definition closure := pos * string * term.

The type of the `lookup` attribute is now `string → node → option closure`. When evaluated to lookup an unbound variable, it will return `None`, otherwise `Some c` where c is the closure representing the binding abstraction:

```
Definition lookup (y:string) :=
  inh (fun _ ⇒ option closure) (fun _ ⇒ None)
      (fun s p t up ⇒
        match s with
        | TermInAbs x ⇒
            if string_eq x y then Some (p, x, t) else up
        | _ ⇒ up
        end).
```

The implementation makes use of the `inh` combinator which takes three arguments:

1. The result type of the attribute. .
2. The default value of the inherited attribute at the root node.
3. A function to compute the attribute value on a non-root node. The four parameters of this function are

---

[1] A perhaps more elegant alternative would be to have a grammar with a separate nonterminal for abstractions; our syntax tree would then be more strongly typed, and we could directly return a node from lookup. This is the path followed in Sec. 4.

(a) the first step of the node's position
(b) the parent node's position
(c) the contents of the node
(d) the attribute value at the parent node.

The definition of the combinator is automatically derived from the specification of the grammar by our framework. Its use greatly improves the legibility of inherited attributes; the implementation of `lookup` closely resembles the informal specification.

Next, we implement the synthesised attribute `closures`. According to its specification, it should return a set of nodes representing closures; instead of sets, our implementation uses lists (without duplicate elements). The implementation of the attribute is shown in Fig. 3, where the underlined code should be ignored for the moment. It makes use of some user-defined syntactic sugar for handling sets to improve legibility.

The collection attribute `args` from Sec. 2 is implemented in two parts: One is the contribution function `args`, which, for every node in the tree, specifies what it contributes to the value of the attribute. Its implementation is given in Fig. 3, again with some additional underlined code to be discussed shortly. The attribute `closures` uses the combinator `coll` to perform a traversal of the syntax tree, collecting contributions from all the nodes, and combining them by set `union`, with `[]` (the empty set) as neutral element. The combinator's definition is automatically derived from the grammar.

3.3 Circularity

The functions `closures` and `args` are defined by mutual recursion. However, Coq does not allow general recursion, requiring recursive functions to use well-founded recursion instead to ensure termination, which leads to our second main formalisation challenge:

Challenge 2 (Circularity) *Many attributes are most easily given (mutually) circular definitions. We need a way to formalise such definitions in Coq.*

In line with classical work on circular attribute grammars [5,8], we require all possibly circular attributes to be monotonic functions whose range is partially ordered; the actual attribute value is then computed as the least fixed point.

In our example, the attributes take values in the poset of (finite) lists of closures[2]. The iterative fixed point computation is formalised by giving all circularly defined attributes an extra "time to live" (TTL) parameter `ttl`, which is a natural number that is decreased on every unsafe recursive invocation. If it ever reaches 0, the recursion stops and `[]` (the bottom element of the poset) is returned. To achieve this, we need to introduce extra code (underlined in Fig. 3), which makes use of a convenience function to effect the "cut-off" once the counter drops to zero:

Definition TTLcut f ttl := **match** ttl **with** 0 ⇒ []
                                              | S ttl' ⇒ f ttl' **end**.

This solution is quite lightweight and requires pleasantly little extra machinery.

---

[2] This partial order is a priori infinite (and of infinite height), but for any given term t the attribute `closures` will only return closures from t, which form a finite set.

```
Fixpoint closures (nd:node) ttl := TTLcut (fun ttl ⇒
  match node_content nd with
  | Var x ⇒ match lookup x nd with
            | Some c ⇒ coll union [] (args c ttl)
            | None ⇒ []
            end
  | Abs x t ⇒ [nd]
  | App t1 t2 ⇒
      let f := Node (Step (Term1InApp t2) (node_pos nd)) t1 in
      ⋃ {{ closures (closure_body c) ttl | c ← closures f ttl }}
  end) ttl
with args c ttl (nd:node) := TTLcut (fun ttl ⇒
  let p := node_pos nd in
  match node_content nd with
  | App t1 t2 ⇒
      let n1 := Node (Step (Term1InApp t2) p) t1 in
      let n2 := Node (Step (Term2InApp t1) p) t2 in
      if contains (closures n1 ttl) c then closures n2 ttl
      else []
  | _ ⇒ []
  end) ttl.
```

Fig. 3. Definition of `closures` and `args`; circularity handling code underlined

Our first and most urgent task is to prove monotonicity of the definitions to ensure that we can sensibly speak about their least fixed points. Since the two attributes are mutually defined, the Coq proof simultaneously establishes their monotonicity by induction on `ttl`.

We can now proceed to the formalisation of the coherence lemma. The reduction relation on terms can be abstractly specified in Ott and is extracted to Coq as a binary predicate `reduce`. Lemma 1 then reads like this:

```
Lemma closures_sound : ∀ t v, reduce t v →
  ∃ ttl, In v (closures (Node Root t) ttl).
```

In words, this asserts that for any term t and any value v such that $t \Downarrow v$ there is a sufficiently large TTL value such that the analysis predicts a closure c containing v. The proof proceeds by induction on the reduction of t to v.

To summarise, we have shown how the implementation of closure analysis as a CRAG from Sec. 2 can be translated to Coq. The two features of reference attributes and circular attributes pose the two challenges of how to represent nodes with identity and how to accommodate non-wellfounded mutual recursion. These challenges are overcome via automatically generated datatype definitions and combinators that make it easy to translate the informal attribute specifications into Coq code, on which we can then prove the desired coherence property.

4   Case Study: Name Analysis

The example in the previous section is quite simple and could easily have been written without using CRAGs. As a case study in using our framework to formalise a more substantial attribute grammar, we will now briefly discuss the formalisation of name analysis for a subset of Java. Although this is a much more complicated object language than the untyped lambda calculus, the same techniques are applicable; in fact, name analysis can be implemented using only inherited and synthesised attributes, there is no need for collection attributes. Tool support for automatic generation of definitions for the abstract syntax and the zipper datatypes is much more important now, as are carefully chosen tactics to simplify proofs. These two facilities ensure easy extensibility of the language: adding a non-naming related feature to the language usually can be done by changing only the high-level specification.

4.1   The Grammar

We define NameJava, a subset of Java that concentrates on the language's naming features for fields and classes, to the exclusion of almost all "operational" aspects.In particular it supports compilation units and packages, nested classes, initialisers with nested blocks, member fields and local variables, qualified names for variables and classes, and the keywords **this** and **super**.

The name lookup rules for NameJava are the same as for Java [9]; an example program that highlights some of the salient points appears in Fig. 4. The five local variables a1 to a5 are assigned as follows: a1 is bound to the local variable a, a2 to the field a of class D, a3 to the field a of class B, a4 to the field a of class B (since the local variable A obscures the class of the same name), and a5 to the field a of class A.

```
package p;           class B {
                        A a;
class A {
  A a;                  class D extends A {
  class C { }            C c; // 1
}                        A a;
                        { A a = a; B A = A; A a1 = a; A a2 = this.a;
                          A a3 = B.this.a; A a4 = A.a; A a5 = p.A.a; }
                        }
                      }
```

Fig. 4. Example NameJava program

The grammar of NameJava is, as for the untyped lambda calculus, specified in Ott, so datatype definitions for the abstract syntax and the zipper are automatically generated. For example, the inductive datatype for programs is

Inductive program : **Set** := CProgram : list compunit → program.

expressing that a program is a list of compilation units.

For the zipper datatypes, our automatic extraction actually generates a more strongly typed version than the one shown in Section 2: there is not a single datatype node of nodes, but rather a family of datatypes indexed by the nonterminal they represent. The index type is an enumeration type with one constructor per nonterminal of the grammar:

```
Inductive nt : Set := Program | Compunit | Classdecl | Extclause
  | Bodydecl | Block | Stmt | Vardecl | Expr | Access | ...
```

The datatype of steps is doubly indexed over nt. A step t' t describes the position of a subtree derived from nonterminal t' within its parent, which is derived from nonterminal t, i.e. it is a "step from t' to t". We cannot give the definition of step for NameJava in full due to space constraints, but a fairly typical constructor is

```
BodydeclInClassdecl : string → extclause →
  list bodydecl → list bodydecl → step Bodydecl Classdecl
```

describing the position of a body declaration within a class declaration: To reconstruct the complete class declaration given one of its body declarations b, we need to know the class name (a string), the **extends** clause, the body declarations to the left of b, and the body declarations to the right of b—exactly the data stored in the step constructor.

As before, the pos datatype is a sequence of steps. It is, however, likewise indexed over a nonterminal (thus pos t describes the type of positions of subtrees derived from t), and it ensures that the steps it is composed of "fit together":

```
Inductive pos : nt → Type :=
  Root : pos Program
| Step : ∀ t t', step t t' → pos t' → pos t.
```

Finally, to define the type of nodes, we need to ensure that the content of a node t actually is of the right type, i.e., a term of the inductive datatype corresponding to the index t. To this end we make use of an (automatically generated) function content, that maps indices to datatypes—for example, content Program is program:

```
Inductive node : nodetype → Type :=
  Node : ∀ t, pos t → content t → node t.
```

The upshot of using this more complicated, indexed representation of zippers is that it rules out many positions and nodes that could never occur in a well-formed program. For example, with the given NameJava grammar we can prove (in Coq) that the parent of a node Stmt will always be a node Block. This is crucial for the definition of plug_step and root, which both map nodes to trees; if the nodes were improperly nested, no corresponding trees could be constructed.

4.2 Attributes for Name Analysis

Name lookup in NameJava proceeds basically in an "outwards" movement, searching through enclosing lexical scopes until a matching declaration is found. Member classes and fields, however, can also be inherited from an ancestor class, hence an "upwards" movement (up the inheritance chain) is superimposed on the underlying outwards movement. Qualified names, finally, contribute a third type of movement: first, the declaration of the qualifier (resp. its type if it is a variable) is looked up, then the qualified name is looked up as a member within this declaration (again possibly following the inheritance chain upwards, but never going outwards through enclosing scopes).

Name lookup for classes is implemented using five attributes, modelled after the implementation in the JastAddJ Java compiler [7]:

- `toplevel_class` looks up a toplevel class within a compilation unit
- `canonical_class` looks up a class by name and package
- `local_class` looks up a local member class within a class
- `member_class` looks up a member class in a class or one of its ancestors
- `lookup_class` looks up a class, starting from an arbitrary node and searching through enclosing scopes

The first three of these just iterate over a list of declarations, looking for the first one with the right name. The behaviour of `lookup_class` and `member_class` and their interaction, is more interesting, since they circularly depend on each other: Suppose that `lookup_class` is used to lookup the type name `"C"` from the line marked with "1" in Fig. 4. First, class D is searched for a `member_class` named C. Member classes include both locally defined classes and inherited member classes. Since no `local_class` C exists, we need to invoke `member_class` on D's super class.

To resolve the super class, we need to lookup the name `"A"` by `lookup_class`, causing `member_class` to depend on `lookup_class`. That lookup will search for a `member_class` named `"A"` in the enclosing class B, causing `lookup_class` to depend on `member_class` in turn. Since A is not a member class of B, it will be found as a `toplevel_class`. Once we have a reference to A, class C is successfully looked up as a `member_class` of A.

Observe that this last step makes crucial use of reference attributes: The node of class A is retrieved as the value of attribute `lookup_class`, and then attribute `member_class` is in turn evaluated on it. The example also shows that the two attributes recursively invoke each other, and thus are circularly defined.

4.3   Circularity in Name Analysis

Nevertheless, this circularity is quite different from the one encountered when implementing closure analysis: Whereas the specification of closure analysis is genuinely circular and the actual result of the analysis is the least fixed point of the given equations, the circularity of the definitions of `lookup_class` and `member_class` is somewhat accidental. We would, in fact, hope that the mutual recursive invocations of these two attributes are well-founded so that the attribute evaluation eventually terminates.

However, the language described so far allows classes that extend themselves, i.e. definitions like **class** A **extends** A { }. Looking up a member in A will lead the two attributes to repeatedly invoking each other on the same arguments, and thus to nontermination. The Java Language Specification [9] forbids programs like the above: Well-formed Java programs must not contain classes that are their own descendants.

It is clear that lookup on classes with acyclic inheritance hierarchy always terminates: When `member_class` recursively invokes itself on the superclass (as determined by `lookup_class`), we have moved up one level of inheritance, so eventually we will arrive at a class that extends no other class, and the member lookup will terminate. So in order to implement a version of lookup_class that is guaranteed to terminate, we need to require that the node it is invoked on belongs to a program with acyclic inheritance hierarchy. However, in order to define the concept of an acyclic inheritance hierarchy we need a definition of inheritance, and for this we need lookup_class!

There does not seem to be an easy solution to this chicken-and-egg problem, so we accept the presence of a possible circularity, and treat it in the same way as for closure analysis: The circularly defined attributes take an additional TTL parameter and produce values over the flat poset of optional values, defined by the Coq type option, with None standing for nontermination.

Once we have implemented class lookup as a partial function, we can define what it means for a class to have an acyclic inheritance hierarchy, and we can give a (constructive) proof that when looking up a member class of such a class, there is a sufficiently large number n for which lookup will always return a value when invoked with n as its TTL counter. In other words, we can now prove that member lookup on classes with acyclic inheritance hierarchy always terminates.

Note that the need for circularly defined class lookup arises from the presence of nested classes. In a language without nested classes, all classes are toplevel classes within compilation units, so class lookup could be implemented by the two attributes toplevel_class and canonical_class alone, without any circularity.

4.4 Towards the Verification of Rename Refactorings

We cannot prove the correctness of our lookup implementation, since there is no formal specification to validate it against, so we apply our framework to a different problem: In [24], we describe how the well-known *Rename* refactoring, i.e. changing the name of a declaration and all its uses, can be implemented using right inverses to the lookup functions. We start from the observation that a reasonable correctness criterion for a renaming would be that the "binding structure" of the program does not change, i.e. all names in the program still refer to the same declarations as before.

We therefore define an *access computation* function that is a right inverse to lookup: Whereas lookup computes the declaration d a name n binds to at a program location p, access computes a name n that a declaration d can be accessed under from a location p, where n might be qualified to avoid capture. The inversion property means that if access gives a name n to access d from p, looking up n from p will yield d.

Given an implementation of access computation with this property, it is, in principle, easy to implement a rename refactoring: Given an input program, we first determine which declaration every individual name refers to. Then we perform the requested name change. Now we go over the program again. For every name, we know the declaration it ought to refer to, and if it does not do so anymore we can use access computation to determine an alternative name that does, and replace the old name with it.

In our current case study we concentrate on proving the inversion property. Given the implementation of the attributes for class and variable lookup, we can write corresponding access computation attributes. For member_class, which looks up a member class, we have an attribute access_member, which constructs an access to a member class; for lookup_class we have access_class, and so on. The inversion of an attribute definition is quite systematic, and it is easily verified that all the access computation attributes are indeed right inverse to their corresponding lookup attributes.

Many of the proofs proceed by induction on either trees or positions, and hence have to handle (at least) one case per language construct to establish the induction step. Only a limited number of cases is actually interesting for every given proof, however: When proving properties of name lookup, for example, only constructs corresponding to naming scopes need special attention, in all the other cases the induction hypothesis can be applied directly. This situation can be handled gracefully by the Coq tactic language: When doing an induction, we specify a default tactic to be tried on all new subgoals; usually, Coq's `auto` tactic is sufficient to discharge all the trivial cases, if its hint database has been populated with enough domain specific lemmas.

5 Evaluation

5.1 Statistics

Figure 5 gives some statistics about the size of the complete Coq development for both our examples: the implementation of closure analysis in Sec. 3 and the name analysis for NameJava in Sec. 4. For both we give the line count for the Ott specification and for the Coq code automatically extracted from that specification, written as a sum: The first summand represents the size of the code extracted by Ott, and the second the size of the code extracted by our extension. Furthermore, we give the line count for the handwritten Coq specification, and for the proof scripts, as well as the total line count.

	Closure Analysis	NameJava
Ott specification (LOC)	80	322
extracted Coq code (LOC)	118+163	403+443
Coq specification (LOC)	301	2219
proof scripts (LOC)	233	1694
total LOC	**614**	**4235**

Fig. 5. Size of development

As expected, the name analysis is far bigger than the closure analysis, at almost seven times the size. In both cases, we have profited clearly from writing a high-level specification in Ott and automatically extracting the definitions of tree and zipper datatypes: the Ott specification is only about a third of the size of the extracted code. It is worth noting, however, that we use Ott merely as a convenient language for describing the object language syntax. All the proofs are carried out inside Coq, on the generated abstract syntax, and are fully certified by the Coq kernel.

It is interesting to see that the proof scripts are smaller than the specification they verify, only comprising about 40% of the total line count on both projects. This number is similar to other formalisation projects, such as Leroy's CompCert [19].

5.2   Extensibility

Although NameJava has all the major naming related features of full Java, it is a much smaller language. We have shown how the same implementation techniques can be used to specify closure analysis on the lambda calculus and to prove the inversion property of access computation and lookup in NameJava. But what about extending to a larger subset of Java, or even the full language? Will all the proofs have to be redone?

Fortunately, the answer is no. Adding a non-naming related feature to the language is possible without breaking any of the proofs: Introducing an `if` statement to the language only needs five additional lines of Ott. Neither lookup nor access computation have to be changed, and all the proofs still go through unchanged. For language features such as the `for` loop, which do influence the lookup without introducing any new naming related concepts, the effort is still moderate (40 lines of specification, 50 lines of proof). Adding, e.g., interfaces would certainly require more effort, but the experience of JastAddJ shows that CRAGs are powerful enough to handle the full Java language.

6   Related Work

Proofs of analyses and transformations. Cachera et al. [4] derive a dataflow analysis in Coq by abstract interpretation, independent of an implementation language. On the other end of the spectrum, Lerner et al. [18] introduce a domain specific language to encode analyses, which are then automatically proved correct. Our work is positioned in the middle: Using CRAGs offers a convenient implementation language, which is nevertheless fully integrated with Coq; the price we pay is less automation.

Formalising attribute grammars. Traditionally, attribute grammars have been encoded in lazy functional languages as families of functions, one per nonterminal, that take inherited attributes as parameters and return synthesised attributes as results [15]. Our method represents different attributes by different functions, thus staying closer to the original attribute grammar. It is not clear if the traditional encoding could accommodate reference attributes. The zipper has been used before to implement inherited attributes [29,2], but without making the connection to reference attributes.

Formalisations of Java. There has been much interest in the formalisation of (subsets of) the Java language [14,21], but most formalisations focus on the semantics of the language and mostly ignore more syntactic aspects like lookup rules. Only FJI [13] makes an effort to model nested classes, but the formalisation is geared towards minimality and does not give a satisfying solution to the name lookup circularity problem.

7   Conclusions

We have presented a novel framework for formalisation and verification of analyses and transformations that are expressed at source level, rather than on a simplified intermediate language. The key to this framework are circular reference attribute grammars, which have proven their practical worth in compiler generation tools [1,23,8,7].

We have presented a general method for formalising them in Coq, enabling the expression of specifications and proofs at a high level of abstraction. We provide tools that automatically generate datatype definitions and utility functions from a high-level description of the object language, which are complemented by domain-specific tactics to simplify proofs. We have validated these tools and tactics with a non-trivial case study, namely renaming in the presence of the complex binding rules of modern object-oriented languages. The verification effort is manageable, and the proofs are scalable, so that they do not have to be redone from scratch when the object language changes.

As future work, we would like to explore the implementation of a domain specific language for attribute grammars on top of Coq. This would give additional possibilities for automation, and it might be possible to support automatic proofs of common lemmas such as the monotonicity of circularly defined attributes. Still, we feel that it is essential to provide close integration of the attribute implementations with the Coq language in general, so as not to lock the user into the DSL, since the more complex proofs can likely not be fully automated and certainly benefit from the power of the full system.

We hope this paper has enthused others to venture into the formalisation and verification of source level analyses . Modern development tools need to stay at the source level to interact with the user, but bugs are common even in production quality environments. Our work shows that rigorous verification of the underlying analyses is feasible, which can help in improving tools used by developers on a daily basis.

References

1. Augusteijn, L.: Definition of the programming language Elegant, 2000. Release 7.1, Philips Research Laboratories, Eindhoven, the Netherlands (February 2000)
2. Badouel, É., Fotsing, B., Tchougong, R.: Yet Another Implementation of Attribute Evaluation. Technical Report 6315, INRIA Rennes (2007)
3. Boyland, J.T.: Remote attribute grammars. J. ACM 52(4), 627–687 (2005)
4. Cachera, D., Jensen, T., Pichardie, D., Rusu, V.: Extracting a data flow analyser in constructive logic. Theor. Comput. Sci. 342(1), 56–78 (2005)
5. Chirica, L.M., Martin, D.F.: An Order-Algebraic Definition of Knuthian Semantics. Mathematical Systems Theory 13, 1–27 (1979)
6. Ekman, T., Ettinger, R., Schäfer, M., Verbaere, M.: Refactoring bugs (2008), http://progtools.comlab.ox.ac.uk/refactoring/bugreports
7. Ekman, T., Hedin, G.: The JastAdd Extensible Java Compiler. In: OOPSLA (2007)
8. Farrow, R.: Automatic generation of fixed-point-finding evaluators for circular, but well-defined, attribute grammars. In: CC, pp. 85–98 (1986)
9. Gosling, J., Joy, B., Steele, G., Bracha, G.: The Java Language Specification (2005)
10. Hanson, D., Proebsting, T.: A research C# compiler. SPE 34(13) (2004)
11. Hedin, G.: Reference Attributed Grammars. Informatica (24), 301–317 (2000)
12. Huet, G.P.: The Zipper. J. Funct. Program. 7(5), 549–554 (1997)
13. Igarashi, A., Pierce, B.C.: On inner classes. Inf. and Comp. 177(1), 56–89 (2002)
14. Igarashi, A., Pierce, B.C., Wadler, P.: Featherweight Java: A Minimal Core Calculus for Java and GJ. In: OOPSLA, pp. 132–146 (1999)
15. Johnsson, T.: Attribute grammars as a functional programming paradigm. In: Kahn, G. (ed.) FPCA 1987. LNCS, vol. 274, pp. 154–173. Springer, Heidelberg (1987)
16. Knuth, D.E.: Semantics of context-free languages. Mathematical Systems Theory 2, 127–146 (1968); correction: Mathematical Systems Theory 5, 95–96 (1971)
17. Lacey, D., Jones, N.D., Van Wyk, E., Frederiksen, C.C.: Proving Correctness of Compiler Optimizations by Temporal Logic. In: POPL, pp. 283–294. ACM Press, New York (2002)

18. Lerner, S., Millstein, T., Rice, E., Chambers, C.: Automated soundness proofs for dataflow analyses and transformations via local rules. SIGPLAN Not. 40(1), 364–377 (2005)
19. Leroy, X.: Formal certification of a compiler back-end. In: POPL, pp. 42–54 (2006)
20. Magnusson, E., Hedin, G.: Circular Reference Attributed Grammars. Sci. Comput. Program. 68(1), 21–37 (2007)
21. von Oheimb, D., Nipkow, T.: Machine-checking the java specification: Proving type-safety. In: Alves-Foss, J. (ed.) Formal Syntax and Semantics of Java. LNCS, vol. 1523, p. 119. Springer, Heidelberg (1999)
22. Palsberg, J.: Closure Analysis in Constraint Form. TOPLAS 17(1), 47–62 (1995)
23. Reps, T.W., Teitelbaum, T.: The Synthesizer Generator: A system for constructing language-based editors. In: Texts and Monographs in Computer Science. Springer, Heidelberg (1989)
24. Schäfer, M., Ekman, T., de Moor, O.: Sound and Extensible Renaming for Java. In: Kiczales, G. (ed.) OOPSLA. ACM Press, New York (2008)
25. Schäfer, M., Ekman, T., de Moor, O.: Formalising and Verifying Reference Attribute Grammars in Coq (Technical Report and Implementation) (2009), http://progtools. comlab.ox.ac.uk/projects/refactoring/formalising-rags
26. Sestoft, P.: Analysis and Efficient Implementation of Funct. Prog. Ph.D. thesis (1991)
27. Sewell, P., Nardelli, F.Z., Owens, S., Peskine, G., Ridge, T., Sarkar, S., Strnisa, R.: Ott: effective tool support for the working semanticist. In: ICFP, pp. 1–12 (2007)
28. Ekman, T.: JastAdd (2008), http://www.jastadd.org
29. Uustalu, T., Vene, V.: Comonadic functional attribute evaluation. In: TFP (2005)

Verified, Executable Parsing

Aditi Barthwal[1] and Michael Norrish[2]

[1] Australian National University
Aditi.Barthwal@anu.edu.au
[2] Canberra Research Lab., NICTA
Michael.Norrish@nicta.com.au

Abstract. We describe the mechanisation of an SLR parser produced by a parser generator, covering background properties of context-free languages and grammars, as well as the construction of an SLR automaton. Among the various properties proved about the parser we show, in particular, *soundness*: if the parser results in a parse tree on a given input, then the parse tree is valid with respect to the grammar, and the leaves of the parse tree match the input; *completeness*: if the input is in the language of the grammar then the parser constructs the correct parse tree for the input with respect to the grammar; and *non-ambiguity*: grammars successfully converted to SLR automata are unambiguous.

We also develop versions of the algorithms that are executable by automatic translation from HOL to SML. These alternative versions of the algorithms require some interesting termination proofs.

1 Introduction

The (context-free) parsing problem is one of determining whether or not a string of terminal symbols belongs to a language that has been specified by means of a context-free grammar. In addition, we imagine that the input is to be processed by some later form of analysis, *e.g.*, a compiler. Therefore, we wish to generate the parse tree that demonstrates this membership when the string is in the language, rather than just a yes/no verdict.

The parsing problem can be solved in a general way for large classes of grammars through the construction of deterministic push-down automata. Given any grammar in the acceptable class, the application of one function produces an automaton embodying the grammar. This automaton then analyses its input, producing an appropriate parse tree. The particular function we have chosen to formally characterise and verify produces what is known as an SLR automaton.

Thus, at a high level, our task is to specify and verify two functions

```
slrmac : grammar -> automaton option
parse : automaton -> token list -> ptree option
```

The `slrmac` function returns SOME m if the grammar is in the SLR class, and NONE otherwise. The `parse` function uses the machine m to consume the input and produce a parse tree for the input string, returning NONE in case of a failure. A parser generator

G. Castagna (Ed.): ESOP 2009, LNCS 5502, pp. 160–174, 2009.

is used to produce such a `parse` function for any context-free grammar. In this paper we will concentrate on implementation and verification of the `parse` function.

In the rest of the paper, we will describe the types and functions that appear above. In Section 1.1, we describe grammars and their properties. In Section 1.2, we describe the type of SLR automata, and the type of the results. In Section 1.3, we describe the construction of automata from input grammars. We are then in a position to verify important properties about these functions. Our theorems are described in Section 2. Finally, we also wish to be able to turn our verified HOL functions into functions that can be executed in SML. To do this, a number of definitions that have rather abstract or "semantic" characterisations need to be shown to have executable equivalents. The derivation of executable forms is described in Section 3.

Literature and Technology. Being one of our field's earliest examples of theory leading to successful practice, parsing and language theory has a large literature. On the other hand, we are not aware of any existing work on a mechanised theory of parsing. Our mechanisation has been performed in the HOL4 system [2,5], and has been inspired principally by Hopcroft and Ullman's standard text [3].

Parsers as External Proof Oracles. If an external, potentially untrusted, tool were to generate the parse tree for a given string, it would be easy to verify that this parse tree was indeed valid for the given grammar. The parse tree would be serving as a proof that the input string was indeed in the grammar's language, and the trusted infrastructure need only check that proof. It is natural then to ask what additional value a verified parser-generator might provide. Apart from the intellectual appeal in mechanising interesting mathematics, we believe there is at least one pragmatic benefit: if the (verified) construction of an SLR automaton succeeds, one has a proof that the grammar in question is unambiguous. When a parse is produced by the automaton, one knows that no other parse is possible.

1.1   Context-Free Grammars

A context-free grammar (CFG) is represented in HOL using the following type definitions:

```
symbol = TS of string | NTS of string

rule = rule of string => symbol list

grammar = G of rule list => string
```

(The `=>` arrow indicates curried arguments to an algebraic type's constructor. Thus, the `rule` constructor is a term of type `string -> symbol list -> rule`. We use lists rather than sets for the grammar's rules for ease of later translation to SML, and to avoid frequent finite-ness side conditions.)

A rule is a mapping from a string to a symbol list, where the string is interpreted as a non-terminal. Similarly, a grammar consists of a list of rules and a string giving the start

symbol. Traditional presentations of grammars often include separate sets corresponding to the grammar's terminals and non-terminals. We extract these sets with functions
`terminals` and `nonTerminals` respectively.

Definition 1. *A* list of symbols *(or* sentential form*) s derives t in a single step if s is of
the form* $\alpha A \gamma$, *t is of the form* $\alpha \beta \gamma$, *and if* $A \rightarrow \beta$ *is one of the rules in the grammar.
In HOL:*

```
derives g sf1 sf2 =
  ∃s1 s2 rhs N.
    (sf1 = s1 ++ [NTS N] ++ s2) ∧
    (sf2 = s1 ++ rhs ++ s2) ∧
    MEM (rule N rhs) (rules g)
```

(The infix ++ *denotes list concatenation. The* MEM *relation denotes list membership.)*

We can form the reflexive and transitive closure of a binary relation like `derives g`
with the `^*` operator, written as a suffix. Thus, `(derives g)^* sf1 sf2` indicates
that `sf2` is derived from `sf1` in zero or more steps, also denoted as `sf1` $\Rightarrow^*$ `sf2` w.r.t
a grammar.
    Later we will also use the rightmost derivation relation, `rderives`, and its closure.

Definition 2. *The* language *of a grammar consists of all the words that can be derived
from the start symbol.*

```
language g =
  { tsl | (derives g)^* [NTS (startSym g)] tsl ∧
          EVERY isTmnlSym tsl }
```

(Predicate `isTmnlSym` *is true of a symbol if it is of the form* TS s *for some string s.
EVERY checks that every element of a list satisfies the given predicate.)*

We also define the concept of nullability and relations for finding first sets and follow
sets for a symbol as stated below. These notions are central when the actions for the
SLR automaton are calculated (see Section 1.2).

Definition 3. *A* list of symbols α is nullable *iff* $\alpha \Rightarrow^* \epsilon$:

```
nullable g sl = (derives g)^* sl []
```

Definition 4. *The* first set *of a symbol is the set of terminals that can appear first in the
sentential forms derivable from it:*

```
firstSet g sym =
  { (TS fst) | ∃rst.(derives g)^* [sym] (TS fst::rst) }
```

(:: *represents the list 'cons' operator.)*

Definition 5. *The* follow set *of a symbol N is the set of terminals that can occur after
N in a sentential form derivable from any of the right-hand sides belonging to a rule in
the grammar.*

```
followSet g N =
  { TS ts | ∃M rhs p s.
              MEM (rule M rhs) (rules g) ∧
              (derives g)^* rhs (p ++ [N;TS ts] ++ s) }
```

(This definition might be simplified by only considering derivations from the start symbol of the grammar. However, we choose to present it in the above way so it is compatible with our executable definition, which ignores reachability of non-terminals.)

Executable versions of these functions (which do not need to scan all possible derivations) are described in Section 3.1.

1.2 SLR Automata

An SLR machine is a push-down automaton where each state in the automaton corresponds to a list of *items*. An item $N \rightarrow \alpha \cdot \beta$, is a grammar rule that has been split in two by the dot ($\cdot$) marking the progress that has been made in recognising the given right-hand side ($\alpha\beta$). In HOL:

```
item = item of string => symbol list # symbol list
state = item list
```

In the mechanisation, an automaton state is a list of items, and the empty list represents an error state. The state of an execution is the current input, coupled with a stack of pairs of automaton states and parse trees. The root of each parse tree corresponds to a terminal symbol that has been shifted from the input, or to a non-terminal that has been produced through a reduction step.

Based on the next symbol in the input (we are implementing SLR with one symbol lookahead), and the state the parser is in, the parser will perform one of the following actions:

- REDUCE: the parser recognizes a valid handle on the stack and reduces it to the left-hand side of the rule
- GOTO: the parser shifts an input symbol on to the stack and goes to the indicated state
- NA: the parser throws an error

In our framework, the automaton is presented by two functions, goto and reduce. The goto function takes a symbol and a state as arguments and returns a new state. We have thus merged two tables in the traditional presentation: the shift table encoding information for terminals, and the goto table for non-terminals.

The reduce function takes a symbol and a state and returns a list of possible rules that can be reduced in the given state. When the machine has been constructed from an SLR grammar the list will always be empty or just one element long. If a reduction is to be performed for rule $N \rightarrow \alpha$, the symbols α are popped off the stack, revealing a state s_0. The non-terminal N is pushed onto the stack, and the machine shifts to the state given by goto applied to N and s_0.

Given a state and input symbol, the next action is a shift if the `goto` function returns a non-error state. The next action is a reduction if the `reduce` function returns a list containing one rule. The SLR construction ensures that both conditions can't be true simultaneously. If neither is true, the machine throws an error.

These functions are combined using a while combinator of type

```
('a -> bool) -> ('a -> 'a option) -> 'a ->
'a option option
```

The type `'a` is the type of the execution state. The first argument is a boolean condition on states specifying when the loop should continue. The second argument encodes the loop body, allowing for the possibility that the loop execution terminates abnormally (*e.g.* the parser detects a string not in the grammar's language). The third argument is the initial state. The result encodes normal termination, abnormal termination (`SOME NONE`) and failure to terminate (`NONE`).

1.3   Constructing the Parser

The architecture of the parser-construction process is shown in Figure 1. The first step in creating the SLR machine is to augment the grammar. The augmentation adds an extra rule that introduces a new start symbol and a marker (a terminal symbol) that appears at the end of all the words in the language of the grammar. The parser uses this rule for reduction exactly when it has accepted the input word. This ensures that the parser always 'spots' the end of input. The augmentor `auggr` is a function of type

```
grammar -> string -> string -> grammar option
```

We use `SOME g'` to return the augmented grammar g' when the symbols being introduced are 'fresh' (not part of the old grammar). Otherwise failure is indicated by returning `NONE`.

The `slrmac` function creates the `goto` and `reduce` functions which represent the three transition tables of the traditional presentation of an LR automaton. It checks that

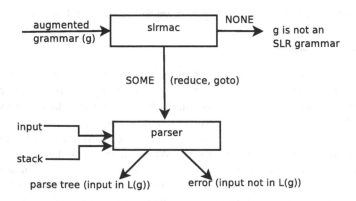

Fig. 1. Architecture of the Parser Construction Process

the functions don't produce any shift-reduce or reduce-reduce conflicts. If the functions pass this test, they can be passed onto the `parser` function which implements the machine (as described above in Section 1.2).

Building the Parsing Tables. The construction of the `goto` function is conceptually simple: let the result of applying `goto` to a state σ and the symbol s (terminal or non-terminal) be the list of items $N \rightarrow \alpha s \cdot \beta$, where $N \rightarrow \alpha \cdot s\beta$ is an element of σ. This behaviour is captured in the HOL function `moveDot`. Unfortunately, it is not sufficient.

When an item's dot is before a non-terminal, say $A \rightarrow \alpha \cdot B\beta$, this indicates that the parser expects to parse the non-terminal (B) next. To ensure the item set contains all possible rules the parser may be in the midst of parsing, it must additionally include all items describing how B itself will be parsed. If there are rules for B that themselves have non-terminals as the first element of a RHS, then those non-terminals' items must also be included. Thus we must take a closure: repeatedly including all referenced non-terminals until we reach a fix-point.

The final `goto` function is calculated by `nextState` (which gets access to the input grammar). The new state is computed by moving the dot over all the items in the current state that have the input symbol after the dot, and then taking the closure.

```
nextState g itl sym = closure g (moveDot itl sym)
```

The other table we must compute is `reduce`. This really is simple: for every complete item (of the form $N \rightarrow \alpha\cdot$) in a state, return the rule $N \rightarrow \alpha$ if the input symbol is in the follow set of N. Because we use the entire follow set of N, we are computing an SLR machine. If we didn't use a follow set at all, and always reduced on complete items, we would be implementing an LR(0) parser. If we computed follow sets for states that depended on where a non-terminal had been used, we would be implementing an LALR parser.

Checking for Conflicts. When `slrmac` has constructed the functions `goto` and `reduce`, it then checks them for possible shift-reduce or reduce-reduce conflicts. Checking for such an error in a given state on a given symbol is done by the `noError` function:

```
noError (go,rd) sym st =
  case rd st sym of
      []    -> T
   || [r] -> (go st sym = [])
   || otherwise -> F
```

The `slrmac` function then tests `noError` on all reachable states in the automaton, and for all possible terminal symbols. This is easy to express logically:

```
okSlr g initState =
  ∀syms state tok.
      trans g (initState, syms) = SOME state ⟹
      noError (goto g, reduce g) tok state
```

where `trans` `g` iterates `goto` `g` over a sequence of symbols to find the resulting state (if any). Hopcroft and Ullman call this function δ.

Expressing this check executably is discussed in Section 3.

Putting it all Together. The `parser` function is as given in Figure 1.

```
parser (initState, eof, oldS) m sl  =
    let out = mwhile (¬ ∘ exitCond eof oldS)
                        (λs.parse m s) (init initState sl)
    in
        case out of
            NONE -> NONE
        || SOME (SOME (sl',[(state,ptree)],csl')) ->
            SOME (SOME ptree)
        || SOME NONE -> SOME NONE
        || SOME _ -> SOME NONE
```

The `parse` function implements a single step of the SLR machine (Section 1.2). `init` provides the initial execution state to get this process started. The `exitCond` function is true of an execution state if the stack consists of just the non-augmented grammar's start symbol, and if the input consists of just the `eof` token. The while combinator `mwhile` (Section 1.2) repeatedly performs the `parse` step until `exitCond` is true.

2 Proofs

We now have a parser generator formally specified in HOL. To verify that our specification is indeed correct, we would like to demonstrate that the language accepted by the automaton is the same as the language defined by the grammar. This goal is naturally split into two inclusion results: that everything accepted by the machine is in the language ("soundness"), and that everything in the language is accepted by the machine ("completeness").

Before we delve into the proofs, we describe what it means to be a valid parse tree with respect to a grammar:

```
(validptree g (Node n ptl) =
   MEM (rule n (getSymbols ptl)) (rules g) ∧
   (∀e. MEM e ptl ∧ isNode e ⟹ validptree g e)) ∧
(validptree g (Leaf tm) = F)
```

Here, `getSymbols` gives the list of symbols at the roots of a list of trees. Thus, a tree is valid with respect to a grammar if there is a rule in the grammar that corresponds to the root node deriving the roots of its sub-trees, and if (recursively) all the sub-trees are also valid.

The proofs to come also depend on a number of simple invariants on the state of a parse execution:

- **parser_inv** states implementation-specific properties about the stack. These properties ensure the items in each of the state on the stack correspond to some grammar rule (validStates) and that the initial start state is never popped off from the stack.

```
parser_inv g csl = validStates g csl ∧ ¬NULL csl
```

- The SLR automaton works by computing valid items for each viable prefix. Predicate **validItem_inv** asserts that each of the states contains only those items that are valid for the viable prefix γ, which is the string of symbols that has been pushed on to the stack to reach that state (stk).

```
validItem_inv g initState stk =
  ∀stk'.
    IS_PREFIX stk stk' ∧ ¬NULL stk'
    ⟹
      trans g (initState, stackSyms stk') =
      SOME (topState stk')
```

2.1 Validity of the Parse Tree Generated

If the parser results in a parse tree, the tree is valid with respect to the grammar for which the parser was generated. Alternatively, the parse tree was built using rules present in the given grammar.

Below we abbreviate validptree_inv for conditions which state that for all the non-terminals on the stack, the associated parse trees are valid with respect to the given grammar. We prove that this property is preserved by the parse function, which takes a single step of the execution. By induction over the while-loop, if the parser is able to reduce the stack symbols to the start symbol, then the corresponding parse tree must be valid as well.

Theorem 1
```
∀g sl stl.
    auggr g s eof = SOME ag ∧ slrmac ag = SOME m ∧
    parser_inv ag csl ∧ validptree_inv g stl ∧
    parser (initState, eof, oldS) (SOME m) sl =
      SOME (SOME tree)
⟹
    validptree ag tree
```

2.2 Equivalence of the Output Parse Tree and the Input String Parsed

The main predicate of interest here is the leaves_eq_inv. Below it abbreviates conditions which assert that at each state the leaves of the tree are equal to the parsed string. This ensures that the grammar rules being applied to form the parse tree, correspond to the input string being parsed and the leaves of the resulting parse tree are equal to the original input string.

Theorem 2

```
∀m g s eof sl csl.
   auggr g s eof = SOME ag ∧ slrmac ag = SOME m ∧
   parser_inv ag csl ∧ leaves_eq_inv sl sl [] ∧
   parser (initState, eof, startSym g) (SOME m) sl =
      SOME (SOME tree))
⟹
   (sl=leaves tree)
```

2.3 Soundness of the Parser

To prove soundness, we have to show that the input string for which a valid parse tree can be constructed, is in the language of the grammar.

Theorem 3

```
∀m g s eof sl csl.
   auggr g s eof = SOME ag ∧ slrmac ag = SOME m ∧
   parser_inv ag (stl, csl) ∧
   validptree_inv ag (stl, csl) ∧
   leaves_eq_inv sl sl [] ∧
   parser (initState, eof, startSym g) (SOME m) sl =
      SOME (SOME tree))
⟹
   sl ∈ language ag
```

In turn, this result depends on a simple result stating the equivalence of being able to derive a sentential form and having a valid parse tree with that form as its leaves.

2.4 Completeness of the Parser

To show completeness, we have to prove that if a string is in the language of a grammar then the parser will terminate with a parse tree. Soundness (Theorem 3) already ensures the validity of the output tree. We assume that the grammar does not have useless non-terminals, *i.e.* all the non-terminal symbols generate some terminal string ('generates a word', gaw). We earlier proved that removing useless symbols does not affect the language of a grammar, so we might extend slrmac to do this for us, or just have it report an error if given a grammar containing useless non-terminals.

Theorem 4

```
   auggr g st eof = SOME ag ∧ sl ∈ language ag ∧
   slrmac ag = SOME m ∧
   (∀nt. nt ∈ nonTerminals ag ⟹ gaw ag nt)
⟹
   ∃tree.
   parser (initState, eof, startSym g) (SOME m) sl =
      SOME (SOME tree)
```

This result has by far the most complicated proof in the mechanisation, and took a considerable proportion of the total time spent. Much of the time was spent casting about for a detailed version of the argument for LR(0) grammars in Hopcroft and Ullman [3, §10.7]. That argument specifies the construction of the automaton and continues:

> We claim that when M starts with w in $L(G)$ on its input and only s_0 on the stack, it will construct a rightmost derivation for w in reverse order. The only point still requiring proof...

Our eventual proof recasts this somewhat. We already have an (arbitrary) rightmost derivation for w by virtue of the fact that it is in $L(G)$. (We proved the lemma stating that any derivation of a word has a rightmost equivalent.) We then argue that the machine will take a sequence of steps that mirror this derivation.

We make the actual derivation concrete (it is a list of sentential forms), and write $R \vdash d \lhd sf_0 \rightarrow sf_1$ if d is a derivation of sf_1, starting at sf_0, and respecting derivation relation R (*i.e.*, R holds between each successive pair of elements in the list d).

Each sentential form is derived from its predecessor by the expansion of a nonterminal. When moving backwards through the derivation, this corresponds to a reduction step.

The crucial lemma supporting our proof states that if we have `rderives` $g \vdash d \lhd$ $sf_0 \rightarrow w$, then there is a sequence of n `parse`-steps bringing the SLR automaton to a state where it is just about to perform the first reduction of the derivation d. This is by induction on d. This result in turn relies on knowing that when the current *handle*, or RHS of the next reduction, is still partly or completely in the input, the machine will perform a sequence of shift moves in order to bring the handle onto the stack.

All of these results depend on the invariants already described, and the fact that the automaton is SLR. For example, in the last lemma: if we know that a shift is possible, then we also know that a reduction is not.

2.5   SLR Grammars Are Unambiguous

A grammar is unambiguous if for each string $w \in$ L(G), w has a unique rightmost derivation.

Definition 6. *A word w in the language of grammar g is represented by a derivation list starting from the start symbol of g and ending in w. A derivation for w is unique iff all possible derivation lists are identical.*

```
isUnambiguous g =
  ∀sl dl dl'.
    sl ∈ language g ∧
    rderives g ⊢ dl ⊲ [NTS (startSym g)] → sl ∧
    rderives g ⊢ dl' ⊲ [NTS (startSym g)] → sl ∧
    ⟹
    dl=dl'
```

Theorem 5
```
auggr g st eof = SOME ag ∧ slr ag = SOME m
  ⟹
isUnambiguous ag
```

A corollary of completeness and the fact that the SLR machine is deterministic.

3   An Executable Parser

For the most part, the HOL definitions turn out to be executable. However, for the sake of simplicity and clarity, many of our definitions were written in a style that favoured mathematical ease of expression. The use of existential quantifiers, and the reflexive and transitive closure in such definitions make them non-executable. Here we describe how the defined functions can be re-expressed in a way that makes them acceptable to HOL4's emitML technology. Our general approach was to take an existing function f, and define a new fML constant. After proving termination for the typically complicated recursion equations defining fML, we then had to show that fML's behaviour was equivalent to f's.

Would it save work to just use executable functions from the outset? Sadly no; the important thing about these executable functions is that they should compute some mathematical property. Proving that this is the case is the same problem as showing the equivalences we describe here.

In this section we describe our executable implementations of the non-executable, or "mathematical" HOL definitions. Even though the HOL versions were more tractable for proving properties such as our language inclusion results, there have been places where it was decided to value executability over succinctness of presentation.

3.1   Executable Calculation of Nullable Non-terminals

The executable counterpart of the nullable function is given below.

```
nullableML g sn [] = T ∧
nullableML g sn (TS ts::rest) = F ∧
nullableML g sn (NTS A::rest) =
  if (MEM (NTS A) sn) then F
  else
    EXISTS (nullableML g (NTS A::sn))
           (getRhs A (rules g)) ∧
    nullableML g sn rest
```

The nullableML function determines whether or not a list of symbols (a sentential form) can derive the empty string. When the string includes a terminal symbol, the result is false. When a non-terminal is encountered, we recursively determine if any of that non-terminal's RHSes might derive the empty string.

In order to ensure that this recursion terminates, we introduce a "seen" list and update this with the non-terminal that is being visited when we expand it. To then convince HOL that this function terminates, we must find a wellfounded relation on the arguments of `nullableML`. Because a singleton list containing a non-terminal may expand into a list of symbols of arbitrary length, we cannot simply use the length of the sentential form as a measure. Instead we use the lexicographic combination:

```
measure (λ(g,sn). |nonTerminals g \ set sn|)
   LEX
measure LENGTH
```

We assert that either the number of symbols except the ones in the seen list decreases, or that the length of the sentential form decreases. The former corresponds to the first conjunct in the third clause in the definition while the latter takes care of the second conjunct.

The next step is to show the equivalence between the new HOL constants and the originals. Proving the equivalence requires showing the following two implications.

$$\forall g \; sn \; sf. \; \texttt{nullableML} \; g \; sn \; sf \implies \texttt{nullable} \; g \; sf$$

$$\forall g \; sf. \; \texttt{nullable} \; g \; sf \implies sn = [] \implies \texttt{nullableML} \; g \; sn \; sf$$

As previously outlined, for a sentential form to be nullable, it cannot have a terminal symbol. We look at the non-trivial case, *i.e.* when the sentential form itself is not empty. A sentential form $N_1 N_2 ... N_n$ is nullable iff the individual derivations for the Ns itself are nullable.

$$N_1 \Rightarrow^* \epsilon$$
$$N_2 \Rightarrow^* \epsilon$$
.
.
.
$$N_n \Rightarrow^* \epsilon$$

`nullable` asserts the existence of *some* derivation from sf to ϵ. On the other hand, `nullableML` looks at a concrete derivation with a specific property, *i.e.* in each individual derivation, the symbols cannot be repeated. This property gives us termination but it also makes the equivalence proof harder.

The first implication turns out to be easy to prove since we are showing the existence of a particular form of derivation from a more generic one.

To prove the latter implication, we need to show that each derivation without any constraints on its form, can be recast into a derivation where the individual derivations of ϵ do not have repeated symbols. We do this by a complete induction on the length of the derivation and show that any derivation of the form $N \Rightarrow^* \epsilon$ can be recasted into a new derivation (possibly smaller), that gets accepted by *nullableML*.

This 'obvious' property of nullable derivations is usually 'assumed' in textbook proofs, but plays a centre role when proving the equivalence between a mathematical definition and an executable one.

With this equivalence we now know that execution of SML code will provide a behaviour corresponding to that of the formal HOL entity.

The executable `firstSet` and `followSet` definitions were defined in a similar way (by introducing a "seen" list in the computation). The termination and equivalence proof follow similar lines of reasoning.

An Executable `slrmac`. Another interesting termination case is encountered when we try to make `slrmac` definition executable. `slrmac` checks whether the resulting table for the grammar has any conflict or not. It is not strictly a necessary component of the parser generator but does assist in stating some of the proofs. For example, with this function we can assert that if we can build a parse table for a grammar and the input belongs in the language of the grammar, then the parser will output a parse tree.

Building the parse table involves traversing the state space to find the next state for each of the symbols in the grammar, starting from the initial state. `neighbours` takes a state and returns a state list. The state list contains states that can be reached by following each of the symbols in the input (*i.e.*, transitions one-level deep). It uses `symNeighbour` to shift the dot past the current symbol and get the state corresponding to it. The resulting state contains no duplicates (`rmDupes`). The condition `DISTINCT` ensures that we don't loop forever by considering states where the same items might be repeated. Another check, `validItl` makes sure that the items in the state do correspond to some rule in the grammar.

```
symNeighbour g itl sym =
        rmDupes (closure g (moveDot itl sym))

neighbours g itl [] = [] ∧
neighbours g itl (x::xs) =
  symNeighbour g itl x::neighbours g itl xs

visit g sn itl =
  if ¬(DISTINCT itl) ∨ ¬(validItl g itl) then []
  else let s = neighbours g itl set (allSyms g) in
    let rem = diff s sn in
            rem++(FLAT (MAP (visit g (sn++rem)) rem))
```

The parse table builder here is the `visit` function. Starting in the initial state it follows the transitions for each of the symbols in the grammar until it can reach no more new states. The important thing here is to make sure states are not repeated otherwise we end up following the same path over and over again. Here, the number of states seen increases at each recursive call. We also know that the number of possible states (even though it might be large) is finite (`allGrammarItls`). This is because we have a finite number of symbols in our grammar and a finite number of rules as well. From this we can deduce that the number of states that have not been encountered decreases at each call. This forms our termination argument.

```
measure (λ(g,sn,itl). |allGrammarItls g \ set sn|)
```

With this on hand, we can implement an executable `slrmac` that checks the entire table for shift-reduce and reduce-reduce conflicts.

```
slrML4Sym g [] sym = SOME (goto g, reduce g) ∧
slrML4Sym g (i::itl) sym =
    let s = goto g i sym in
        let r = reduce g i (sym2Str sym) in
            case (s,r) of ([],[]) -> slrML4Sym g itl sym
            || ([],[v12]) -> slrML4Sym g itl sym
            || ([],h::h'::t) -> NONE
            || (h::t,[]) -> slrML4Sym g itl sym
            || (h::t,h'::t') -> NONE

slrML g itl [] = SOME (goto g, reduce g) ∧
slrML g itl (sym::rst) =
    if (slrML4Sym g itl sym = NONE) then NONE
        else slrML g itl rst
```

4 Future Work

One piece of future work we would like to pursue is to demonstrate that SLR parsers terminate on all inputs, not just on strings in the language. This would then demonstrate the decidability of language membership. (Our mechanisation currently admits the possibility that parser goes into an infinite loop.)

We would also like to improve the efficiency of the parser. Currently, the DFA states are computed on the fly. This gives us simpler proof goals, assisting in reasoning about the program's properties. Changing this to be computed statically would enhance the performance of the parser when emitted as executable SML code.

For the sake of simplicity, we have dealt with SLR parsers. In practice however, compiler-compilers such as yacc and GNU bison generate LALR parsers. Instead of follow sets, LALR parsers uses lookahead sets, which are more specific as they take more of the parsing context into account, allowing finer distinctions. It will be interesting to see to what extent the existing work on SLR will assist us in verifying other parsing algorithms such as LR(1), LALR or GLR parser generator. We anticipate that most of the proof framework will not change excepting the work related to calculating lookahead sets.

5 Related Work

To realise the ambition of fully verified translation from source to machine code, all phases in the compilation process should either be verified or subject to verification after the fact. These two strategies are implemented in what have been termed *verified* or *verifying* compilers respectively. As we have already commented, one might imagine that the appropriate strategy for parsing would be to verify the output of an external tool. This then would be what one might call *verifying parsing*. For example, a verifying parser would mesh with Blazy, Dargaye and Leroy's work on the formal verification of a compiler front-end for a subset of the C language [1], which otherwise ignores parsing as an issue.

In the field of language theory, Nipkow [4] provided a verified and executable lexical analyzer generator. This is the closest in nature to the verification we have done. As with our work, Nipkow faced issues in making his definitions executable, principally because of the inductively defined transitive closure.

6 Conclusions

We have presented work on formal verification of an SLR parser generator. Most of the functions are directly executable. For those that we thought were better expressed more "mathematically", we have presented executable definitions of behaviourally equivalent alternatives. This conversion also illustrated the gap between simple textbook definitions and a verifiable executable implementation in a theorem prover. Issues like termination which can be ignored when dealing with semantic definitions, become necessary when executability comes into play. This also highlights how eminently suitable HOL is for developments of this kind, especially with its facility of emitting verified HOL definitions as SML code.

HOL sources for the work are available at http://users.rsise.anu.edu.au/~aditi/. The definitions and proofs are 21000 LOC. It took 7 months to complete the work which includes over 700 lemmas/theorems. This includes the definitions, major proofs related to SLR grammars and also lemmas about existing HOL types (*e.g.*, sets,lists) that were not already present in the system.

References

1. Blazy, S., Dargaye, Z., Leroy, X.: Formal verification of a C compiler front-end. In: Misra, J., Nipkow, T., Sekerinski, E. (eds.) FM 2006. LNCS, vol. 4085, pp. 460–475. Springer, Heidelberg (2006)
2. Gordon, M.J.C., Melham, T. (eds.): Introduction to HOL: a theorem proving environment for higher order logic. Cambridge University Press, Cambridge (1993)
3. Hopcroft, J.E., Ullman, J.D.: Introduction to Automata Theory, Languages and Computation. Addison-Wesley, Reading (1979)
4. Nipkow, T.: Verified lexical analysis. In: Grundy, J., Newey, M. (eds.) TPHOLs 1998. LNCS, vol. 1479, pp. 1–15. Springer, Heidelberg (1998)
5. Slind, K., Norrish, M.: A brief overview of HOL4. In: Mohamed, O.A., Muñoz, C., Tahar, S. (eds.) TPHOLs 2008. LNCS, vol. 5170, pp. 28–32. Springer, Heidelberg (2008), http://hol.sourceforge.net

An Efficient Algorithm for Solving the Dyck-CFL Reachability Problem on Trees

Hao Yuan and Patrick Eugster

Department of Computer Science, Purdue University
{yuan3,peugster}@cs.purdue.edu

Abstract. The context-free language (CFL) reachability problem is well known and studied in computer science, as a fundamental problem underlying many important static analyses such as points-to-analysis. Solving the CFL reachability problem in the general case is very hard. Popular solutions resorting to a graph traversal exhibit a time complexity of $O(k^3 n^3)$ for a grammar of size k. For Dyck CFLs, a particular class of CFLs, this complexity can be reduced to $O(kn^3)$. Only recently the first subcubic algorithm was proposed by Chaudhuri, dividing the complexity of predating solutions by a factor of $\log n$.

In this paper we propose an effective algorithm for solving the CFL reachability problem for Dyck languages when the considered graph is a bidirected tree with specific constraints. Our solution pre-processes the graph in $O(n \log n \log k)$ time in a space of $O(n \log n)$, after which any Dyck-CFL reachability query can be answered in $O(1)$ time, while a naïve online algorithm will require $O(n)$ time to answer a query or require $O(n^2)$ to store the pre-computed results for all pairs of nodes.

1 Introduction

In this paper, we study a well-known problem called the *context-free language reachability* (CFL reachability) problem [1]. This problem is of particular interest in the context of static analyses, such as type-based flow analysis [2] or points-to analysis [3,4]. Consider a directed graph $G = (V, E)$ with n vertices and a context-free grammar, each directed edge $(u, v) \in E$ is labeled by a terminal symbol $\mathcal{L}(u, v)$ from Σ. For any path $p = v_0 v_1 v_2 \ldots v_m$ (which can have loops), we say that this path realizes a string $R(p)$ which is the concatenation of the symbols on the path, i.e., $R(p) = \mathcal{L}(v_0, v_1)\mathcal{L}(v_1, v_2)\mathcal{L}(v_2, v_3) \ldots \mathcal{L}(v_{m-1}, v_m)$.

The CFL reachability problem has several facets:

- *Source and destination specified.* Given a source node and a destination node, is there a path p connecting them, whose corresponding string $R(p)$ can be generated by the context-free grammar?
- *Single source.* Given a source node u, answer the questions: for each node v, is there a path p connecting u and v, whose corresponding string $R(p)$ can be generated by the context-free grammar?

G. Castagna (Ed.): ESOP 2009, LNCS 5502, pp. 175–189, 2009.
© Springer-Verlag Berlin Heidelberg 2009

- *Single destination.* Given a destination node v, answer the questions: for each node u, is there a path p connecting u and v, whose corresponding string $R(p)$ can be generated by the context-free grammar?
- *All pair queries.* Answer for every pair of nodes u and v: is there a path p connecting u and v, whose corresponding string $R(p)$ can be generated by the context-free grammar?

A context-free language is called *Dyck* language if it is used to generate matched parentheses. Basically, it has the following form: a size k (i.e., k kinds of parentheses) Dyck language can be defined by

$$ S \longrightarrow \epsilon \mid S\,S \mid (_1 S)_1 \mid (_2 S)_2 \mid \cdots \mid (_k S)_k $$

where S is the start symbol, and ϵ is the empty string.

When the context-free language is a Dyck language, the CFL reachability problem on that language is referred to as the *Dyck-CFL reachability* problem. In this paper we give an efficient algorithm for solving this problem when the given digraph is in a *specific bidirected tree structure*, as detailed in Sections 3 and 4. A bidirected tree corresponds to some situation in which an object flow (sub-)graph only involves objects of non-recursive types.

In short, our algorithm pre-processes the specific tree graph in $O(n \log n \log k)$ time within $O(n \log n)$ space, which allows for a Dyck-CFL reachability query for any pair of nodes to be performed in $O(1)$ time. Note that a naïve online algorithm will in contrast take $O(n)$ time to answer a query online, or need $O(n^2)$ space to store the pre-computed results for all pairs of nodes.

The speedups in the pre-processing, which are central to the efficiency of our algorithm, are made possible by the following two key ideas:

1. We build linear data structures for a *pivot node* x to answer queries on paths leading through x. To that end, we construct *tries* [5] of size n representing strings of unmatched parentheses for the path from any node to x in a single tree walk using $O(n \log k)$ time.
2. To handle the case where a given path does not lead through x, we apply the above scheme recursively for the subtrees obtained by removing x; x is chosen to be a *centroid node* of the tree [6,7].

Roadmap. This paper is organized as follows. Section 2 covers the related work on the CFL reachability problem. The motivation of studying the Dyck-CFL reachability problem on trees is given in Section 3, which focuses on the application to points-to analysis. Our algorithm to solve the problem efficiently is described in Section 5, after preliminary definitions and lemmas have been provided in Section 4. Finally, Section 6 concludes with final remarks.

2   Background and Related Work

The CFL reachability problem was first formulated by Yannakakis [8] in his work to solve the datalog chain query evaluation problem in the context of database theory. Since then, it is widely used in the area of program analysis: many program analysis problems can be reduced to it, e.g., interprocedural data flow analysis [9], shape analysis [10], points-to analysis [3,4], alias analysis [11] and type-based flow analysis [2]. For more applications, see the survey paper of [1].

In the work of Yanakakis [8], an $O(k^3n^3)$ algorithm was given to solve the CFL reachability problem, with k the size of the grammar (usually considered to be constant) and n the number of nodes (typically objects in an object graph). Later, Reps gave a very popular iterative algorithm [10], which is still in $O(k^3n^3)$. Since many program analysis problem can be reduced to the CFL reachability problem, it is important to see if we can break the cubic bottleneck.

Recently, Chaudhuri gave the first subcubic time algorithm for the CFL reachability problem [12]. His algorithm runs in $O(k^3n^3/\log n)$ time by using the well-known Four Russians' Trick [13] to speed up set operations under the Random Access Machine model. Similar techniques were used in Rytter's work [14,15]. A closely related problem, the reachability problem on *recursive state machines*, was also studied in [12]. It can be shown that the reachability problem on recursive state machines can be reduced to the CFL reachability problem, and vice versa [16].

It is possible to improve the running time of the CFL reachability algorithm for special cases [1]. One direction is to design algorithm for specific grammars. For example, if the context-free language under consideration is the *Dyck* language, then the general $O(k^3n^3)$ time bound can be reduced to $O(kn^3)$ by a refined analysis [17]; in the type-based flow analysis work of Fähndrich [2], an $O(n^3)$ algorithm is designed to handle the special grammar used in his reduction. The Dyck language captures the nature of the call/return structures of a program execution path, and hence constitutes an important context-free language that is studied within the context of the CFL reachability problem [4,1,12]. In the work of [3], a Dyck language was used to model the PutField and GetField operations in the field-sensitive flow-insensitive points-to analysis for Java. Dyck languages are also studied in the context of visibly pushdown languages [18] and streaming XML [19].

The other direction is to design algorithms for special graph classes. When the directed graph is a chain, the CFL reachability problem can be viewed as the CFL-*recognition* problem, which has an algorithm running in $O(BM(n))$ time given by Valiant [20], where $BM(n)$ is the upper bound to solve the matrix multiplication problem for $n \times n$ boolean matrices. The best such upper bound known is $O(n^{2.376})$. Yannakakis [8] noted that Valiant's algorithm can also be applied to the case when the graph is a directed acyclic graph. In this work, we will consider the special case when the graph is in the form of a bidirected tree.

3   Motivation: Points-to Analysis

In this section, we present the motivation for the Dyck-CFL reachability problem on trees; it is based on the application of the CFL reachability problem to *field-sensitive flow-insensitive points-to analysis* [3].

3.1   Points-to Analysis via Dyck-CFL Reachability

In points-to analysis, we want to compute for each pointer x, the points-to function

$$pt(x) = \{\text{objects allocated in the heap that are possibly pointed by } x\}.$$

Throughout this paper, we will use the other notation $ft(o)$, the flow-to function, to represent the set of pointers that will possibly point to the object o, i.e.

$$ft(o) = \{x \mid o \in pt(x)\}.$$

The underlying model discussed is field-sensitive and flow-insensitive. Field-sensitive means that we take the fields of the classes into consideration. Flow-insensitivity entails that we do not consider the execution order of the codes. Figure 1 gives an example illustrating the basic concepts of flow analysis.

The scenario depicted in the figure is as follows. For the statement x=new Object(); we allocate a new object o_1 in the heap, and then assign it to the pointer x by a directed edge labeled with **new**. Similarly, for the second statement, we make a **new** edge from o_2 to pointer z. For the assignment statement w=x;, we add an **assign** edge to the graph. One can see that object o_1 may flow to pointer w through the execution of the first and third statements, this is reflected on the graph by a path from o_1 to w. The last two statements demonstrate the field-sensitive analysis, i.e., we add two edges GetField[f] and PutField[f] accordingly. Object o_1 is only considered possibly flowing to the field f of v rather than flowing to v even if v is reachable from o_1 in the graph. The reason is that, the path connecting o_1 and v is not closed: there should be a PutField[f] before GetField[f] to make the object flow to v through the field f. It is not difficult to see that o_2 indeed can flow to v through a path

$$o_2 \xrightarrow{\text{new}} z \xrightarrow{\text{PutField[f]}} w \xrightarrow{\text{GetField[f]}} v$$

If we consider a pair of PutField[f] and GetField[f] operations as a kind of parenthesis indexed by the field f, and consider **assign** and **new** as ϵ, then the points-to analysis can be formulated by the reachability problem under the following Dyck Language:

$$\begin{aligned}
S \longrightarrow \epsilon \mid & \, S\,S \mid \text{PutField[f]}\, S\, \text{GetField[f]} \\
& \mid \text{PutField[g]}\, S\, \text{GetField[g]} \\
& \mid \text{PutField[h]}\, S\, \text{GetField[h]} \\
& \mid \cdots
\end{aligned}$$

where f, g and h are the available fields. An object o can flow to a pointer x if and only if there is a path p connecting o to x such that the corresponding $R(p)$ can be generated by the above grammar. In this points-to definition, we do not consider the "may alias" cases (see [3] for more details).

```
x = new Obj(); // o₁
z = new Obj(); // o₂
w = x;
w.f = z;
v = w.f;
```

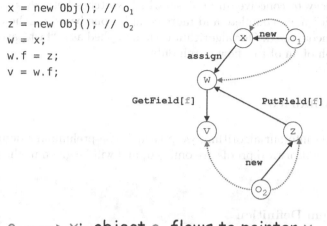

o_1 ┈┈┈▶ x: object o_1 flows to pointer x
⇔ pointer x points to object o_1

Fig. 1. An example of field-sensitive points-to analysis (modified from the talk slides of [3]). The black edges are generated based on the statements. The dotted blue edges are used to illustrate the flows-to/points-to relationship.

3.2 Special Tree Structure Case

If the corresponding directed graph for a set of program statements forms a tree[1] structure, then we can take advantage of the tree structure to provide a better algorithm for solving the Dyck-CFL reachability problem.

For any two neighbor nodes u and v on the tree, we may have both directed edge (u, v) and (v, u) (i.e., the tree digraph can actually have loops!). In such a case, we restrict the labels on them to satisfy the following constraint: if there are both (u, v) and (v, u) on the tree, then either they are both labeled by ϵ, or they are labeled by a pair of parentheses (or PutField/GetField) of the same index. For example, if (u, v) is labeled by PutField[g], then (v, u) must be labeled by GetField[g]. This constraint will enable us to have a fast algorithm to solve the Dyck-CFL reachability problem on a tree.

The constraint corresponds to a special case of instances of non-recursive types. In the a special scenario, if one has a statement x=y.f, then the only other interaction between x and y about the field f must be y.f=x. This constraint ensures that for any path connecting two nodes, there is no reason to go through any loop, because the string labeled by the loop must be well matched. Note that in this case, a special constraint is made: the interaction between x and y must go trough a single field.

Such a constraint and the tree-structure requirement do not imply that our algorithm is restricted to non-tree graphs and languages which *prohibit* recursive

---

[1] Throughout this paper, we use the term "tree" to represent the special bidirected tree graph.

types; it is easy to conceive an analysis which switches between our algorithm and a "classic" more complete and more complex one based on the objects and flow graph encountered. Our algorithm is then applied as a "fast path", possibly to a subgraph of an object flow graph only.

4   Preliminaries

Before delving into our algorithm, we present some preliminary definitions and lemmas. Straightforward proofs are omitted, and will be given in the full version of this paper.

4.1   Problem Definition

Given a bidirected tree $T = (V, E)$, for every neighboring node pair u and v, at least one of the edges $\{(u, v), (v, u)\}$ exists. Each directed edge $(u, v) \in E$ is assigned a label $\mathcal{L}(u, v)$, which is a symbol in either $A = \{a_1, a_2, \cdots, a_k\}$ or $\bar{A} = \{\bar{a}_1, \bar{a}_2, \cdots, \bar{a}_k\}$. Here, A represents the set of opening parentheses, and $\bar{A}$ represents the set of closing parentheses. For any $1 \leq i \leq k$, we call the two symbols a_i and $\bar{a}_i$ a pair of *matched* parentheses.

Let $\mathscr{A}$ be $A \cup \bar{A}$. For any $x \in \mathscr{A}$, we define

$$flip(x) = \begin{cases} \bar{a}_i & \text{if } x = a_i \text{ for some } i, \\ a_i & \text{if } x = \bar{a}_i \text{ for some } i. \end{cases}$$

Note that we will also use $\bar{x}$ to denote $flip(x)$. For any directed edge $(u, v) \in E$, we assume that $\mathcal{L}(v, u) = flip(\mathcal{L}(u, v))$ if (v, u) exists.

A Dyck language $L(G)$ of size k is defined by the following context free grammar G:

- The only non-terminal symbol is S, which is also served as the start symbol.
- The set of terminal symbols is $\mathscr{A} = A \cup \bar{A}$.
- The production rules are

$$S \longrightarrow \epsilon \mid S\,S \mid a_1\,S\,\bar{a}_1 \mid a_2\,S\,\bar{a}_2 \mid \cdots \mid a_k\,S\,\bar{a}_k,$$

where ϵ represents the empty string.

For any path $p = v_0 v_1 v_2 \ldots v_m$ (which can have loops) in the tree, we use $R(p)$ to denote the string that is realized by p. More specifically, we define $R(p)$ to be $R(p) = \mathcal{L}(v_0, v_1)\mathcal{L}(v_1, v_2)\mathcal{L}(v_2, v_3)\mathcal{L}(v_3, v_4)\ldots\mathcal{L}(v_{m-1}, v_m)$, i.e., the concatenation string of the symbols along the path.

The Dyck-CFL reachability problem asks the following query $Q(u, v)$: for any two nodes u and v, is there a path p connecting u and v, such that $R(p)$ can be produced from the grammar G?

4.2   Basic Definitions

For any string s, we call it an S-string if it can be produced from the grammar G by starting from the non-terminal S. Similarly, for any path p, if its realized string $R(p)$ is an S-string, then we call the path p an S-path. Since S is by default the starting non-terminal symbol in grammar G, therefore, the Dyck-CFL reachability problem can be formulated as: for any two nodes u and v, is there an S-path connecting u and v?

Definition 1. *We define a function $R'(s)$ for a string s to be the string generated by repeatedly eliminating matched parentheses from s. Formally, $R'(s)$ is generated based on the following elimination process: for any substring of s, if it is an S-string, then we remove the substring from s and repeat the process on the resulting string.*

For example, if $s = \bar{a}_3 a_1 a_2 a_1 \bar{a}_1 \bar{a}_2 a_3 a_4 \bar{a}_4 a_2$, then we have $R'(s) = \bar{a}_3 a_1 a_3 a_2$, because $a_2 a_1 \bar{a}_1 \bar{a}_2$ and $a_4 \bar{a}_4$ are the two removed S-substrings. Given a string s, the computation of $R'(s)$ can be done in $O(|s|)$ time using a stack. The definition of $R'(s)$ directly gives the following facts:

Lemma 1. *A string s is an S-string if and only if $R'(s) = \epsilon$, where ε represents the empty string.*

Lemma 2. *For any two strings s_1 and s_2, we have $R'(s_1 s_2) = R'(R'(s_1)R'(s_2))$.*

The following definitions and lemmas are used to test if the concatenation of two strings is an S-string.

Definition 2. *For any string s_1, we call it a valid S-prefix if there exists a string s_2 such that $s_1 s_2$ is an S-string. Similarly, for any string s_2, we call it a valid S-suffix if there exists a string s_1 such that $s_1 s_2$ is an S-string.*

Note that testing whether a string is an S-prefix or S-suffix can be done using a stack in linear time.

Definition 3. *For any two strings s_1 and s_2, we say that s_1 matches s_2 if and only if $s_1 s_2$ is an S-string, or equivalently, $R'(s_1 s_2) = \epsilon$.*

Let $reverse(s)$ represent the reversal of a string s, e.g., $reverse(a_1 \bar{a}_4 a_2 a_3) = a_3 a_2 \bar{a}_4 a_1$.

Lemma 3. *For any two strings s_1 and s_2, we have s_1 matches s_2 if and only if $R'(s_1) = flip(reverse(R'(s_2)))$ and s_1 is a valid S-prefix.*

For any two nodes u and v in the tree, we denote the only loopless directed path from u to v by $P(u, v)$ – if such a path exists. We also use $R(u, v)$ and $R'(u, v)$ to denote $R(P(u, v))$ and $R'(P(u, v))$ respectively for short.

5   Dyck-CFL Reachability Algorithm on Trees

In this section, we describe our algorithm for solving the Dyck-CFL reachability problem on bidirected trees, which can be pre-computed using $O(n \log n)$ space and $O(n \log n \log k)$ time to subsequently answer any online query $Q(u, v)$ in $O(1)$ time.

5.1   Loopless Property

In the problem definition, we have assumed that for any directed edge $(u, v) \in E$, $\mathcal{L}(v, u) = flip(\mathcal{L}(u, v))$ if (v, u) exists. This assumption leads to the following lemmas:

Lemma 4. *Any closed directed path $p = v_0 v_1 v_2 \cdots v_m v_0$ in the tree is an S-path.*

Lemma 5. *For any query $Q(u, v)$, it is only required to consider the loopless directed path $P(u, v)$ to see if it is the S-path. If $P(u, v)$ is not an S-path, then we can conclude that no S-path joining u and v exists.*

5.2   Basic Idea

Let x be a *fixed* tree node. We will call this node x a *pivot* node. Now, consider the following set of queries:

$$Q_x = \big\{ Q(u, v) \mid u \text{ and } v \text{ are a query pair such that } P(u, v) \text{ goes through } x \big\}.$$

The goal is to build a linear data structure to answer any query in Q_x efficiently. Later in Section 5.3, we will describe how to handle queries outside Q_x by recursively building the data structures.

For any query $Q(u, v) \in Q_x$, according to Lemma 1 and Definition 3, we know that $P(u, v)$ is an S-path if and only if $R(u, x)$ matches $R(x, v)$. By Lemma 3, this is equivalent to testing whether $R(u, x)$ is a valid S-prefix and $R'(u, x) = flip(reverse(R'(x, v)))$. So we need to build data structures that support the following subqueries

- For any node u, is $R(u, x)$ a valid S-prefix?
- For any nodes u and v, is $R'(u, x) = flip(reverse(R'(x, v)))$?

S-prefix test. If $R'(u, x)$ can be computed efficiently, then we are able to tell whether $R(u, x)$ is a valid S-prefix due to the following Lemma 6.

Lemma 6. *$R(u, x)$ is a valid S-prefix if and only if $R'(u, x)$ does not contain any symbol from $\bar{A}$.*

A naïve algorithm to compute $R'(u, x)$ is to use a stack to cancel matched parentheses in $|R(u, x)|$ time (see the **NaiveStack** procedure in Algorithm 1). If we do that for every u separately, then the total time can be as bad as $\Theta(n^2)$, and the spaces required to store the n realized strings can be as large as $\Theta(n^2)$.

Algorithm 1. Stack-based algorithm to compute $R'(u, x)$ for a single u

Procedure NaiveStack(u)

Input: a tree node u
Output: a string $R'(u, x)$, represented by the stack

1: Initialize an empty stack.
2: $w \leftarrow u$.
3: **while** $w \neq x$ **do**
4:     Let w_p be the parent node of w in the tree.
5:     If the directed edge (w, w_p) does not exist, then we terminate and report that no directed path from u to x exists.
6:     **if** $\mathcal{L}(w, w_p) \in \bar{A}$ **and** the stack is non-empty **and** $\mathcal{L}(w, w_p)$ is the flipped parenthesis of the top of the stack **then**
7:         Pop the top symbol from the stack. // Detected a pair of matched parentheses.
8:     **else**
9:         Push $\mathcal{L}(w, w_p)$ to the stack.
10:    **end if**
11:    $w \leftarrow w_p$. // Move w to the next node on the path to x.
12: **end while**

Constructing a trie. Our idea to speed up the computation is to pre-compute $R'(u, x)$ for all u's in a single tree walk using $O(n \log k)$ time, and represent the realized strings in a trie [7] of size $O(n)$. See Algorithm 2. The trie constructed by **BuildTrie** will have the following properties:

- Denote the trie by TRIE, and its root by r.
- Each edge (z', z) of TRIE will be labeled by a symbol $\mathcal{L}(z', z)$ from $\mathscr{A}$. Here, the edges of the trie are undirected.
- For a trie node z, denote $R(z)$ to be a string that is concatenated by the symbols on the path from z to the root r. Note that this definition is in the bottom-up fashion, in contrast to the traditional top-down reading of the trie. Also, the algorithm processes the path $P(u, x)$ in the order from x to u rather than from u to x (like **NaiveStack**).
- For each tree node $u \in T$, there is a corresponding trie node $z \in$ TRIE such that $R(z) = R'(u, x)$. We store this trie node z in $TriePos(u)$. Note that, if $TriePos(u)$ is not set for some $u \in T$, then it means that there is no directed path from u to x.
- At each node $z \in$ TRIE, we store the set of tree nodes that are associated to z in $TreeNodeSet(z)$, i.e., $TreeNodeSet(z) = \{u \mid TriePos(u) = z\}$.

The correctness of **BuildTrie** is based on the fact that: the trie simulates a stack. Line 5 simulates "stack pop" by moving z to its parent z_p, and line 8 simulates "stack push" by expanding/walking-down the trie. In this way, a trie node z effectively represents a stack, and the contents of the stack is captured by $R(z)$. The space complexity of this tree-walk style pre-processing algorithm is $O(|T|)$, and time complexity is $O(|T| \log k)$. The $\log k$ factor comes from

---

Algorithm 2. Trie-based algorithm to compute $R'(u, x)$ for all u's

---

Make a call to the following recursive procedure by **BuildTrie**(x, r), where r is a pre-allocated root of a trie.

Procedure BuildTrie(u, z)
Input: a tree node u, and a trie node z
 1: $TriePos(u) \leftarrow z$ and add u to the set $TreeNodeSet(z)$.
 2: **for** each child node u' of u such that the directed edge (u', u) exists **do**
 3:   Let z_p be the parent node of z in the trie.
 4:   **if** z_p exists and $\mathcal{L}(u', u) = flip(\mathcal{L}(z, z_p))$ and $\mathcal{L}(u', u) \in A$ **then**
 5:     Call BuildTrie(u', z_p).
 6:   **else**
 7:     Choose a child node z' of z such that $\mathcal{L}(z', z) = \mathcal{L}(u', u)$; if it does not exist, then add a new child node z' to z, and label the edge (z', z) by $\mathcal{L}(u', u)$.
 8:     Call BuildTrie(u', z').
 9:   **end if**
10: **end for**

---

line 7, where a balanced binary tree of size at most $|\mathscr{A}| = 2k$ is used efficiently to search for child nodes in the trie.

Now, we have the trie to compactly represent $R'(u, x)$ for all u's. Getting back to the S-prefix test problem, the validity for $R'(u, x)$ can be easily pre-computed by a top-down tree walk as in Algorithm 3. The correctness is guaranteed from Lemma 6: each time we visit a node z, we have made sure that $R(z)$ contains symbols only from A and the tree walk only passes through edges that are labeled by symbols from A. Therefore, the S-prefix validity test for $R(u, x)$ can be pre-computed in linear time and space, and the subquery can be answered later in $O(1)$ time.

Algorithm 3. Pre-compute the information for S-prefix validity test

---

Make a call to the following procedure by **MarkValidity**(r), where r is the trie root.

Procedure MarkValidity(z)
Input: a trie node z
 1: For each $u \in TreeNodeSet(z)$, we mark down that $R(u, x)$ is a valid S-prefix.
 2: **for** each child node z' of z **do**
 3:   **if** $\mathcal{L}(z', z) \in A$ **then**
 4:     Call MarkValidity(z').
 5:   **end if**
 6: **end for**

Match test. Now, consider the second subquery, i.e., testing whether $R'(u, x) = flip(reverse(R'(x, v)))$. We will first show that $R'(x, v)$ for all v's can also be represented by a trie, and pre-computed efficiently. The previous Algorithm 2 can be modified to construct a trie such that:

- For each trie node z, if we denote $\hat{R}(z)$ to be the string that is concatenated from the symbols along the path from the trie root to z (this time, it is in the top-down fashion), then we have $\hat{R}(z) = R'(x, v)$ for any tree node v that is associated to the trie node z.

The key modifications of Algorithm 2 to compute such a trie are

- Consider downward edges (u, u') instead of upward edges (u', u).
- When testing to "pop" or not (at line 4), change the condition from $\mathcal{L}(u', u) \in A$ to $\mathcal{L}(u, u') \in \bar{A}$. This is important, because when we compute $R'(x, v)$, we should use a symbol from $\bar{A}$ to initiate the cancelation of matched parentheses.

The time and space complexities after the modifications are still $O(n \log k)$ and $O(n)$ respectively.

Assume that we now have two tries TRIE_1 and TRIE_2, where TRIE_1 is constructed to represent $R'(u, x)$, and TRIE_2 is to represent $R'(x, v)$. A naïve way to test whether $R'(u, x) = flip(reverse(R'(x, v)))$ can be done as follows

1. Find out $z_1 = TriePos(u)$ in TRIE_1.
2. Find out $z_2 = TriePos(v)$ in TRIE_2.
3. Let z_1 and z_2 simultaneously walk up the tries towards their corresponding roots. During the walk, test to see if the edge labels are matched (i.e., one label is the flipped version of the other edge label in the other trie).

The correctness is based on the fact that $R(z_2)$ is the reversed string of $\hat{R}(z_2)$, so we are actually testing whether $R(z_1) = R'(u, x)$ is the flipped version of $R(z_2) = reverse(\hat{R}(z_2)) = reverse(R'(x, v))$. This naïve algorithm would use as much as $\Theta(n)$ time if the tries have very large heights.

To speed up the testing, we adapt the following pre-processing algorithm:

1. Flip all the edge labels of TRIE_2.
2. Merge TRIE_1 and TRIE_2 to be a single trie. This can be done in linear time [5]. Denote the new trie by $\mathrm{TRIE}_{\mathrm{merged}}$.
3. For a tree node $u \in T$, let $z_1 \in \mathrm{TRIE}_1$ be the trie node where $R(z_1) = R'(u, x)$, i.e., z_1 is the $TriePos(u)$ in the context of TRIE_1. Then after the merge, we denote $TriePos_1(u)$ to be the new location of z_1 in the merged trie $\mathrm{TRIE}_{\mathrm{merged}}$.
4. For a tree node $v \in T$, let $z_2 \in \mathrm{TRIE}_2$ be the trie node where $\hat{R}(z_2) = R'(x, v)$, i.e., z_2 is the $TriePos(v)$ in the context of TRIE_2. Then after the the merge, we denote $TriePos_2(v)$ to be the new location of z_2 in the merged trie $\mathrm{TRIE}_{\mathrm{merged}}$.

Step 1 and 2 take linear time. The data structures (i.e., $TriePos_1$ and $TriePos_2$) defined in step 3 and 4 can be computed naturally in linear time during the merging.

Using $\mathrm{TRIE}_{\mathrm{merged}}$, we can tell whether $R'(u, x) = flip(reverse(R'(x, v)))$ by simply checking the equality of $TriePos_1(u)$ and $TriePos_2(v)$. More specifically,

$R'(u, x) = flip(reverse(R'(x, v)))$ if and only if $TriePos_1(u) = TriePos_2(v)$ based on the above analysis.

Therefore, the second subquery can be answered in $O(1)$ time, with an $O(n \log k)$-time and $O(n)$-space pre-processing. Combing the results in this subsection, we have the following theorem.

Theorem 1. *There exists a data structure, which can be preprocessed in $O(n \log k)$ time and $O(n)$ space to answer any query pair whose path goes through a pre-defined separator x of the tree.*

5.3   Divide and Conquer

Now the question is how to efficiently handle the cases when the path does not go through the predefined pivot node x. We can solve those cases by recursively building data structures for the subtrees obtained by removing x from the tree. The recursions are expected to be balanced in order to achieve a good time bound, so we choose the *centroid* node of a tree to be such an x.

A node x in a tree T is called a centroid of T if the removal of x will make the size of each remaining connected component no greater than $|T|/2$. A tree may have at most two centroids, and if there are two then one must be a neighbor of the other [6,5]. Throughout this paper, we specify the centroid of a tree to be the one whose numbering is lexicographically smaller (i.e., we number the nodes from 1 to n). There exists a linear time algorithm to compute the centroid of a tree due to the work of Goldman [21]. We use $CT(T)$ to denote the centroid of T computed by the linear time algorithm.

Algorithm 4 is the well-known recursive tree centroid decomposition method (see Figure 2 for an example of the tree centroid decomposition). The time complexity for the recursive tree centroid decomposition algorithm is $O(n \log n)$, since no node will participate in the centroid computations for more than $O(\log n)$ times. The stack space for the recursion is bounded by $O(n + n/2 + n/4 + n/8 + \ldots) = O(n)$.

Algorithm 4. Tree centroid decomposition

Procedure CentroidDecomposition(T)

1: Find the centroid of T. Denote the set of the remaining connected components by Remain $(T) = \{T' \mid T'$ is a connected component after the removal of $CT(T)\}$.

2: Let $c = CT(T)$ be the computed centroid, then for each neighbor x of c in T, we use $T_{c,x}$ to denote the remaining connected component that contains x. Also, we denote the current tree T by T_c.

3: Recursively call CentroidDecomposition(T') for each $T' \in$ Remain (T).

Define *canonical* subtrees to be all the subtrees considered during the recursive call of Algorithm 4 if we start the recursion at T, i.e., the canonical subtrees are $\{T_c \mid c \in V\}$. Please note that, each node $c \in V$ must be a centroid of some

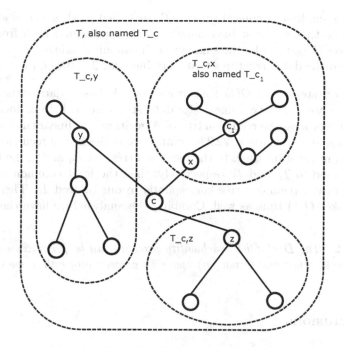

Fig. 2. An example for the tree centroid decomposition. In this example, node c is a centroid of the whole tree, and c_1 is the centroid of the subtree $T_{c,x}$.

canonical subtree; an extreme case is when node c is the centroid of a subtree which only consists of a single node (c itself). Therefore, there are exactly n such canonical subtrees, and one can see that each "remaining connected component" $T_{c,x}$ is just $T_{\mathrm{CT}(T_{c,x})}$. Based on the fact that no node will be in more than $O(\log n)$ canonical subtrees, we have

$$\sum_{c \in V} |T_c| = O(n \log n).$$

For each canonical subtree T_c, we build a trie using the **BuildTrie** algorithm specified in Section 5.2 to preprocess for the following query set

$$Q_c = \{Q(u,v) \mid u \text{ and } v \text{ are a query pair such that } P(u,v) \text{ goes through } c\}.$$

The total time complexity is

$$\sum_{c \in V} |T_c| \log k = O(n \log n \log k).$$

Once the data structures for each canonical subtree are built, we can answer any query $Q(u,v)$ in the following way:

- Locate a smallest canonical subtree T_c such that both u and v are in that tree. Note that we must have node c on the undirected path from u to v, otherwise T_c can not be the smallest such canonical subtree.
- Query on the data structures that were built for T_c since $Q(u, v) \in Q_c$.

The second step takes $O(1)$ time from the trie-based data structures. For the first step, we can have a linear size data structure to help us locate the T_c efficiently: preprocess the recursion tree of Algorithm 4 in linear time so that the least common ancestor query [22,23] for any two nodes in the recursion tree can be answered in constant time. In the recursion tree, let n_u and n_v be two nodes that correspond to T_u and T_v respectively, then the least common ancestor of n_u and n_v in the recursion tree corresponds to our desired T_c. Therefore, the first step takes $O(1)$ time as well. Combing the analysis, we have the following theorem.

Theorem 2. *The Dyck-CFL reachability problem can be preprocessed in* $O(n \log n \log k)$ *time and* $O(n \log n)$ *space to answer any online query in* $O(1)$ *time.*

6   Conclusions

We considered the CFL reachability problem for the case when the underlying graph is a specific bidirected tree of size n, and the grammar is the Dyck language of size k. We have described an efficient algorithm to build a data structure of size $O(n \log n)$ in $O(n \log n \log k)$ time to handle any online query in $O(1)$ time. Possible future work can be considering dynamic graph updates, i.e., graph nodes and edges are added/deleted dynamically and online CFL reachability queries need to be answered efficiently.

References

1. Reps, T.W.: Program analysis via graph reachability. Information & Software Technology 40(11-12), 701–726 (1998)
2. Rehof, J., Fähndrich, M.: Type-based flow analysis: From polymorphic subtyping to CFL-reachability. In: Proceedings of the 28th ACM SIGACT-SIGPLAN Symposium on Principles of Programming Languages (POPL 2001), pp. 54–66 (2001)
3. Sridharan, M., Gopan, D., Shan, L., Bodík, R.: Demand-driven points-to analysis for Java. In: Proceedings of the 20th Annual ACM SIGPLAN Conference on Object-Oriented Programming, Systems, Languages, and Applications (OOPSLA 2005), pp. 59–76 (2005)
4. Sridharan, M., Bodík, R.: Refinement-based context-sensitive points-to analysis for Java. In: Proceedings of the ACM SIGPLAN 2006 Conference on Programming Language Design and Implementation (PLDI 2006), pp. 387–400 (2006)
5. Knuth, D.E.: The art of computer programming, volume III: sorting and searching. Addison-Wesley, Reading (1973)
6. Hakimi, S.: Optimum locations of switching center and the absolute center and medians of a graph. Operations Research 12, 450–459 (1964)

7. Knuth, D.E.: The art of computer programming, volume I: fundamental algorithms. Addison-Wesley, Reading (1973)
8. Yannakakis, M.: Graph-theoretic methods in database theory. In: Proceedings of the 9th ACM SIGACT-SIGMOD-SIGART Symposium on Principles of Database Systems (PODS 1990), pp. 230–242 (1990)
9. Reps, T.W., Horwitz, S., Sagiv, S.: Precise interprocedural dataflow analysis via graph reachability. In: Conference Record of the 22nd ACM SIGPLAN-SIGACT Symposium on Principles of Programming Languages (POPL 1995), pp. 49–61 (1995)
10. Reps, T.W.: Shape analysis as a generalized path problem. In: Proceedings of the ACM SIGPLAN Symposium on Partial Evaluation and Semantics-Based Program Manipulation (PEPM 1995), pp. 1–11 (1995)
11. Zheng, X., Rugina, R.: Demand-driven alias analysis for C. In: Proceedings of the 35th ACM SIGPLAN-SIGACT Symposium on Principles of Programming Languages (POPL 2008), pp. 197–208 (2008)
12. Chaudhuri, S.: Subcubic algorithms for recursive state machines. In: Proceedings of the 35th ACM SIGPLAN-SIGACT Symposium on Principles of Programming Languages (POPL 2008), pp. 159–169 (2008)
13. Arlazarov, V.L., Dinic, E.A., Faradzev, M.A.K.,, I.A.: On economical construction of the transitive closure of an oriented graph. Soviet Mathematics Doklady 11, 1209–1210 (1970)
14. Rytter, W.: Time complexity of loop-free two-way pushdown automata. Inf. Process. Lett. 16(3), 127–129 (1983)
15. Rytter, W.: Fast recognition of pushdown automaton and context-free languages. Inf. Control 67(1-3), 12–22 (1986)
16. Alur, R., Benedikt, M., Etessami, K., Godefroid, P., Reps, T.W., Yannakakis, M.: Analysis of recursive state machines. ACM Transactions on Programming Languags and Systems 27(4), 786–818 (2005)
17. Kodumal, J., Aiken, A.: The set constraint/cfl reachability connection in practice. In: Proceedings of the ACM SIGPLAN Conference on Programming Language Design and Implementation (PLDI 2004), pp. 207–218 (2004)
18. Alur, R., Madhusudan, P.: Visibly pushdown languages. In: STOC 2004: Proceedings of the thirty-sixth annual ACM symposium on Theory of computing, pp. 202–211. ACM, New York (2004)
19. Alur, R.: Marrying words and trees. In: PODS 2007: Proceedings of the twenty-sixth ACM SIGMOD-SIGACT-SIGART symposium on Principles of database systems, pp. 233–242. ACM, New York (2007)
20. Valiant, L.G.: General context-free recognition in less than cubic time. Journal of Computer and System Sciences 10(2), 308–315 (1975)
21. Goldman, A.: Optimal center location in a simple network. Transportation Science 5, 212–221 (1971)
22. Harel, D., Tarjan, R.E.: Fast algorithms for finding nearest common ancestors. SIAM Journal of Computing 13(2), 338–355 (1984)
23. Bender, M.A., Farach-Colton, M.: The lca problem revisited. In: Proceedings of the 4th Latin American Symposium on Theoretical Informatics, pp. 88–94 (2000)

Amortised Memory Analysis Using the Depth of Data Structures

Brian Campbell*

School of Informatics, University of Edinburgh
Brian.Campbell@ed.ac.uk

Abstract. Hofmann and Jost have presented a heap space analysis [1] that finds linear space bounds for many functional programs. It uses an amortised analysis: assigning hypothetical amounts of free space (called potential) to data structures in proportion to their sizes using type annotations. Constraints on these annotations in the type system ensure that the total potential assigned to the input is an upper bound on the total memory required to satisfy all allocations.

We describe a related system for bounding the stack space requirements which uses the depth of data structures, by expressing potential in terms of maxima as well as sums. This is achieved by adding extra structure to typing contexts (inspired by O'Hearn's bunched typing [2]) to describe the form of the bounds. We will also present the extra steps that must be taken to construct a typing during the analysis.

Obtaining bounds on the resource requirements of programs can be crucial for ensuring that they enjoy reliability and security properties, particularly for use in constrained systems such as mobile phones, smartcards and embedded systems. Hofmann and Jost have presented a type-based amortised analysis for finding upper bounds on the heap memory required for programs in a simple functional programming language [1]. The form of these bounds is limited to linear functions with respect to the size of the program's input. Fortunately, this is sufficient for a wide variety of interesting programs. Moreover, the analysis was successfully used to certify such bounds in a Proof Carrying Code system [3].

However, it is also important to bound the stack space requirements, especially for functional programs where it is easy to cause excessive stack usage by accident. The Hofmann-Jost analysis has previously been adapted to measure stack space [4,5], but the form of the bounds was again limited to linear functions in terms of the *total* size of the input.

In this work we present a similar analysis where bounds are given as max-plus expressions on the *depth* of data structures. This is far more precise for programs operating on tree-structured data.

Like Hofmann-Jost, our analysis consists of two parts: a type-system which *certifies* that a given bound really is an upper bound on the stack memory requirements, and an inference procedure based on Linear Programming for that

---

* This work was partially supported by the ReQueST grant (EP/C537068/1) from the Engineering and Physical Sciences Research Council.

G. Castagna (Ed.): ESOP 2009, LNCS 5502, pp. 190–204, 2009.

type system. In our type system we impose extra structure on the typing contexts to represent the form of the bounds (where to take the maximum and where to add), and hence we use extra structural typing rules to manipulate the context. We also add an extra stage to the inference to determine where these structural rules should be used.

We begin by presenting the programming language and its metered operational semantics, then in Section 2 give details of the type system and consider some examples of typings in Section 3. We prove that the type system correctly certifies bounds in Section 4 before presenting the inference procedure in Section 5. In Section 6 we discuss some limitations when analysing programs with nested datatypes. Finally we describe some extensions to the analysis (Section 7) and related work (Section 8).

1 Language and Operational Semantics

We consider a simple first-order call-by-value functional programming language. The syntax of the language is presented in Figure 1, where programs P are given as a sequence of function definitions D with expressions e. For brevity's sake we only consider computations on units ($*$), booleans, pairs, sums and binary trees. The syntax requires programs to be in a 'let-normal' form which makes the evaluation order explicit by requiring variables rather than subexpressions in various places. We will discuss extensions to the language in Section 7.

$$P := \mathsf{let}\ D \mid \mathsf{let}\ D\ P$$
$$D := f(x_1, \ldots, x_p) = e_f$$
$$e := *\ \mid\ \mathsf{true}\ \mid\ \mathsf{false}\ \mid\ x\ \mid\ f(x_1, \ldots, x_p)\ \mid\ \mathsf{let}\ x = e_1\ \mathsf{in}\ e_2\ \mid\ \mathsf{if}\ x\ \mathsf{then}\ e_t\ \mathsf{else}\ e_f$$
$$\mid\ (x_1, x_2)\ \mid\ \mathsf{match}\ x\ \mathsf{with}\ (x_1, x_2) \to e$$
$$\mid\ \mathsf{inl}(x)\ \mid\ \mathsf{inr}(x)\ \mid\ \mathsf{match}\ x\ \mathsf{with}\ \mathsf{inl}(x_l) \to e_l \mathbin{\text{\tiny I}} \mathsf{inr}(x_r) \to e_r$$
$$\mid\ \mathsf{leaf}\ \mid\ \mathsf{node}(x_l, x_r, x_v)\ \mid\ \mathsf{match}\ x\ \mathsf{with}\ \mathsf{leaf} \to e_1 \mathbin{\text{\tiny I}} \mathsf{node}(x_l, x_r, x_v) \to e_2$$

Fig. 1. Syntax

We have a large step operational semantics for the language, which includes metering of the free stack space. Values in the language are units, booleans, pairs, sums and heap locations for trees, with a distinguished location null which represents leaf. A selection of the rules for the operational semantics appear in Figure 2. The judgements have the form

$$m, S, \sigma \vdash e \rightsquigarrow v, \sigma'$$

meaning that with m units of stack space, an environment S mapping variable names to values and a store σ mapping non-null locations to binary tree triplets, the expression e can evaluate to the value v with the new store σ'. We do not

$$\dfrac{\begin{array}{c} S(x_1) = v_1 \ \ldots \ S(x_p) = v_p \qquad m, [y_1 \mapsto v_1, \ldots, y_p \mapsto v_p], \sigma \vdash e_f \leadsto v, \sigma' \\ \text{the } y_i \text{ are the symbolic arguments in the definition of } f \end{array}}{m + \mathsf{stack}(f), S, \sigma \vdash f(x_1, \ldots, x_p) \leadsto v, \sigma'} \ \text{E-Fun}$$

$$\dfrac{m, S, \sigma \vdash e_1 \leadsto v_0, \sigma_0 \qquad m, S[x \mapsto v_0], \sigma_0 \vdash e_2 \leadsto v, \sigma'}{m, S, \sigma \vdash \mathsf{let} \ x = e_1 \ \mathsf{in} \ e_2 \leadsto v, \sigma'} \ \text{E-Let}$$

$$\dfrac{}{m, S, \sigma \vdash \mathsf{leaf} \leadsto \mathsf{null}, \sigma} \ \text{E-Leaf}$$

$$\dfrac{\sigma' = \sigma[l \mapsto \langle S(x_l), S(x_r), S(x_v) \rangle] \qquad l \notin \mathrm{dom}(\sigma)}{m, S, \sigma \vdash \mathsf{node}(x_l, x_r, x_v) \leadsto l, \sigma'} \ \text{E-Node}$$

$$\dfrac{S(x) = \langle v_l, v_r, v_v \rangle \qquad m, S[x_l \mapsto v_l, x_r \mapsto v_r, x_v \mapsto v_v], \sigma \vdash e_2 \leadsto v, \sigma'}{m, S, \sigma \vdash \mathsf{match} \ x \ \mathsf{with} \ \mathsf{leaf} \to e_1 \mid \mathsf{node}(x_l, x_r, x_v) \to e_2 \leadsto v, \sigma'} \ \text{E-MatchNode}$$

Fig. 2. Sample rules from the operational semantics

need to include the amount of stack space afterwards because the stack discipline will ensure that it is m again (this is easily checked in the full set of rules).

Note that we assume that stack space is allocated one frame at a time on function entry, and released on exit. We denote the size of frame required by function f by $\mathsf{stack}(f)$. We expect that our techniques could also be applied to more fine grained stack machines. Indeed, a simpler Hofmann-Jost style stack space analysis has been applied to a stack machine cost model for the Hume language [4].

We will also need to mention an unmetered form of the operational semantics. For this we simply drop the m part of each judgement.

Example 1. The andtrees function computes the point-wise boolean 'and' of two binary trees with boolean values at the nodes:

```
let andtrees(t1,t2) =
    match t1 with leaf → leaf ι node(l1,r1,v1) →
    match t2 with leaf → leaf ι node(l2,r2,v2) →
      let l = andtrees(l1,l2) in
      let r = andtrees(r1,r2) in
      let v = if v1 then v2 else false in
        node(l,r,v)
```

This function requires at most $\mathsf{stack}(\text{andtrees}) \times (\min\{|\text{t1}|_d, |\text{t2}|_d\} + 1)$ units of stack space to run (where depth $|\cdot|_d$ is defined by $|\mathsf{null}|_d = 0$ and $|l|_d = 1 + \max\{|l_1|_d, |l_2|_d\}$ when $\sigma(l) = \langle l_1, l_2, v \rangle$).

2   Type System

We now describe the type system that can be used to provide certified bounds. The key notion in the type system is that the function from input size to the stack space bound is encoded by annotations in the types and the structure of the typing context. This is similar to the 'physicist's view' of amortised analysis described by Tarjan [6]. Following Tarjan, we call this assignment *potential*.

The types and contexts are given by

$$T := 1 \mid \mathsf{bool} \mid T_1 \otimes T_2 \mid (T_1, k_1) + (T_2, k_2) \mid \mathsf{tree}(T, k).$$
$$\Gamma := \cdot \mid x : T \mid k \mid \Gamma_1, \Gamma_2 \mid \Gamma_1; \Gamma_2.$$

where the annotations k are positive rational numbers. For sum types the annotations represent different contributions to the bound depending upon the choice, and for trees the annotations represent a requirement of k times the depth of the tree (not counting the leaves). Fractional amounts are allowed; for instance, a tree with annotation of one half corresponds to one unit of stack space for every second level of the tree.

The typing contexts have two context formers: one for summing the contribution of the subcontexts (,) and one for taking the maximum (;). For example, the context

$$(x : \mathsf{tree}(\mathsf{bool}, 5); y : \mathsf{tree}(\mathsf{bool}, 3)), 6$$

represents the bound

$$\max\{5 \times |x|_d, 3 \times |y|_d\} + 6.$$

Thus our typing contexts take the form of trees. To allow a greater range of bounding functions to be represented we also allow variables to appear several times in the context, so long as the underlying types (but not necessarily the annotations) are the same. We will implicitly take ',' and ';' to be associative throughout.

The formal encoding of this potential in types and typing contexts is given as the Υ_t and Υ_c functions in Figure 3.

Using structured contexts in this way was inspired by O'Hearn's Bunched Typing [2], where a typical application of the structure was to denote heap separation of data structures with one context former, and possible sharing of heap data with the other.

We represent function signatures as a map Σ from function names to a signature $\Gamma \to T, k$ where Γ is a context containing each parameter once, T is the result type and k the fixed amount of potential to add to that from T.

The type system has two groups of rules. The syntax-directed rules feature side conditions which ensure that the potential of the context is a sufficient amount of stack space to evaluate the expression, *and* that there is enough potential in the context to account for all of the potential in the result type (we will make this more formal in Theorem 1, below). The latter requirement is needed to translate bounds for subsequent parts of the program — the typing of these later parts may give a bound in terms of the size of the result of this expression, and we wish to translate it into a bound with respect to the size of the input values *only*. Thanks to this translation we do not need a separate size analysis to give a relationship between the size of the intermediate values and the input.

$$\Upsilon_t(\sigma, *, 1) = \Upsilon_t(\sigma, \mathsf{true}, \mathsf{bool}) = \Upsilon_t(\sigma, \mathsf{false}, \mathsf{bool}) = 0$$
$$\Upsilon_t(\sigma, (v', v''), T' \otimes T'') = \Upsilon_t(\sigma, v', T') + \Upsilon_t(\sigma, v'', T''),$$
$$\Upsilon_t(\sigma, \mathsf{inl}(v), (T', k') + (T'', k'')) = k' + \Upsilon_t(\sigma, v, T'),$$
$$\Upsilon_t(\sigma, \mathsf{inr}(v), (T', k') + (T'', k'')) = k'' + \Upsilon_t(\sigma, v, T''),$$
$$\Upsilon_t(\sigma, \mathsf{null}, \mathsf{tree}(T, k)) = 0$$
$$\Upsilon_t(\sigma, l, \mathsf{tree}(T, k)) = \max\{\Upsilon_t(\sigma, v_l, \mathsf{tree}(T, k)), \Upsilon_t(\sigma, v_r, \mathsf{tree}(T, k)), \Upsilon_t(\sigma, v_v, T)\} + k$$
$$\text{where } \sigma(l) = \langle v_l, v_r, v_v \rangle.$$

$$\Upsilon_c(\sigma, S, \cdot) = 0,$$
$$\Upsilon_c(\sigma, S, x : T) = \Upsilon_t(\sigma, S(x), T),$$
$$\Upsilon_c(\sigma, S, k) = k,$$
$$\Upsilon_c(\sigma, S, (\Gamma, \Delta)) = \Upsilon_c(\sigma, S, \Gamma) + \Upsilon_c(\sigma, S, \Delta),$$
$$\Upsilon_c(\sigma, S, (\Gamma; \Delta)) = \max\{\Upsilon_c(\sigma, S, \Gamma), \Upsilon_c(\sigma, S, \Delta)\}.$$

Fig. 3. Assignment of potential to values and environments according to their types and contexts

However, the syntax-directed rules require the typing context to have a specific structure. To manipulate the context structure to fulfil these requirements we also have a set of *structural* rules.

A representative sample of the syntax-directed rules is given in Figure 4 and all of the structural rules are given in Figure 5. The typing judgements take the form

$$\Gamma \vdash e : T, k'$$

meaning that in the context Γ the expression e can be given type T, and the potential assigned to the result is given by the annotations in T *plus* the fixed amount k'. In some places we use $\Gamma()$ to denote a context with a hole, and $\Gamma(\Delta)$ when that hole is filled by Δ. We write $q \times \Gamma$ to denote the context Γ with every annotation k replaced by qk.

The VAR and LEAF rules are the simplest: evaluation of the expressions requires no stack space and we only need to ensure that the potential of the result, k', is accounted for by a fixed amount in the context, k. Note that the annotation for the leaf's type, k_1, can be anything because we consider the depth of a leaf to be zero. The NODE rule's side condition requires an extra k_1 units because the resulting tree is one level deeper than the larger subtree.

The FUN rule has two side conditions. The first ensures that there is enough potential in the context to account for the allocation of a stack frame for the callee, and the second gives the two possible sources for 'translating' k', either from the potential k used to show that we can allocate the stack frame, or from the amount k'_1 given by the result of the callee (which must ultimately have come from somewhere in Γ).

$$\frac{k \geq k'}{x : T, k \vdash x : T, k'} \ \text{VAR} \qquad\qquad \frac{k \geq k'}{\cdot, k \vdash \text{leaf} : \text{tree}(T, k_1), k'} \ \text{LEAF}$$

$$\frac{k \geq \text{stack}(f) \qquad k + k_1' \geq k' \qquad \Sigma(f) = \Gamma \to T, k_1' \qquad (y_1, \dots, y_p) = \text{names}(\Gamma)}{\Gamma[x_1/y_1, \dots, x_p/y_p], k \vdash f(x_1, \dots, x_p) : T, k'} \ \text{FUN}$$

$$\frac{\Delta \vdash e_1 : T_0, k_0 \qquad \Gamma(x : T_0, k_0) \vdash e_2 : T, k'}{\Gamma(\Delta) \vdash \text{let } x = e_1 \text{ in } e_2 : T, k'} \ \text{LET}$$

$$\frac{k \geq k_1 + k'}{(x_l : \text{tree}(T, k_1); x_r : \text{tree}(T, k_1); x_v : T), k \vdash \text{node}(x_l, x_r, x_v) : \text{tree}(T, k_1), k'} \ \text{NODE}$$

$$\frac{\Gamma(\cdot) \vdash e_1 : T, k' \qquad \Gamma((x_l : \text{tree}(T, k_1); x_r : \text{tree}(T, k_1); x_v : T), k_1) \vdash e_2 : T, k'}{\Gamma(x : \text{tree}(T, k_1)) \vdash \text{match } x \text{ with leaf} \to e_1 \mid \text{node}(x_l, x_r, x_v) \to e_2 : T, k'} \ \text{MATCH}$$

Fig. 4. Sample syntax-directed typing rules

The LET rule is more subtle. Intuitively, we can just take the maximum of the stack space bounds for e_1 and e_2, but we must also consider how to translate the parts of e_2's bound that are expressed in terms of the size of the value of the bound variable x. Hence we locally replace the part of the context used for e_1 with x, which allows for both the stack allocation required for e_1 and the translation of subsequent requirements in e_2 given in terms of the size of x. To be sound this requires that all of the allocations that we consider respect the stack discipline; that is, all allocations in e_1 are deallocated before the evaluation of e_1 is complete. If we consider memory allocations in e_1 that may persist into e_2 (such as heap memory) then we may not have the free memory 'promised' by the annotations in the surrounding context, $\Gamma()$.

The MATCH rule uses a similar local replacement, but this is simply an unfolding of the tree structure into the context and does not require the stack discipline for soundness.

The structural rules allow the manipulation of contexts to fit the requirements of the syntax-directed rules. The two weakening rules remove sections of the context and unnecessary potential. The context equivalence rule $\equiv$ replaces part

$$\frac{\Gamma(\Delta) \vdash e : T, k'}{\Gamma(\Gamma'(\Delta)) \vdash e : T, k'} \ \text{WEAKEN}$$

$$\frac{\Gamma(x : T[k_1/k]) \vdash e : T', k' \qquad k \geq k_1}{\Gamma(x : T) \vdash e : T', k'} \ \text{WEAKEN}A$$

$$\frac{\Gamma(\Delta') \vdash e : T, k' \qquad \Delta \cong \Delta'}{\Gamma(\Delta) \vdash e : T, k'} \ \equiv$$

$$\frac{\Gamma(q \times \Delta, (1 - q) \times \Delta') \vdash e : T, k' \qquad q \in [0, 1]}{\Gamma(\Delta; \Delta') \vdash e : T, k'} \ \text{SPLIT}$$

Fig. 5. Structural typing rules

$$\Gamma, \Delta \cong \Delta, \Gamma \qquad \text{(plus-commute)} \qquad \Gamma; \Delta \cong \Delta; \Gamma \quad \text{(max-commute)}$$

$$\Gamma, (\Delta; \Delta') \cong (\Gamma, \Delta); (\Gamma, \Delta') \qquad \text{(distribute)} \qquad \Gamma \cong \Gamma; \Gamma \quad \text{(max-contract)}$$

$$\Gamma \cong \Gamma, \cdot \qquad \text{(plus-empty)} \qquad \Gamma \cong \Gamma; \cdot \quad \text{(max-empty)}$$

$$\Gamma \cong \Gamma, 0 \qquad \text{(plus-zero)} \qquad \Gamma \cong \Gamma; 0 \quad \text{(max-zero)}$$

$$\Gamma \cong \Delta \quad \text{if} \quad \Delta \cong \Gamma \qquad \text{(symmetry)}$$

$$\Gamma \cong q \times \Gamma, (1 - q) \times \Gamma \quad \text{for } q \in [0, 1] \qquad \text{(plus-contract)}$$

Fig. 6. Equivalent contexts (for the $\equiv$ typing rule)

of the typing context with one whose contents and potential are identical, using any of the equivalences from Figure 6. Note that all of these equivalences are reversible.

The plus-contract case of $\equiv$ illustrates an important difference from the Hofmann-Jost heap analysis. In that system contraction treated the annotations of nested types (such as $\text{tree}(\text{tree}(\text{bool}, 3), 2)$) independently. Here we can only uniformly scale the entire context. This restriction is necessary because we are measuring the depth of the entire data structure weighted by the annotations and treating the annotations independently can change the ratio of the weightings and hence may alter which path through the data structure is the 'deepest'. Uniform scaling maintains the deepest path, ensuring that the potential does not change as a result of applying the typing rule.

SPLIT is the typing rule of last resort — it approximates a bound given as a sum by a bound given as a maximum. For example, when $q = 1/2$ and the potential of Δ and Δ' is given by x and y, SPLIT corresponds to the fact that

$$\forall x, y \in \mathbb{Q}^+, \quad \max\{x, y\} \geq x/2 + y/2,$$

where $\mathbb{Q}^+$ is the set of rationals greater than or equal to zero. The set of inequalities corresponding to SPLIT are the best we can give without requiring extra information about x and y. SPLIT is useful in two places; during inference when conflicting structural requirements force the approximation, and when one of the subcontexts can be ignored for the purposes of giving a bound (for example, because it is a boolean). In the latter case q is 0 or 1 and there is no approximation.

We also give the following two derived rules to manipulate fixed amounts of potential:

$$\frac{\Gamma(k_1, k_2) \vdash e : T, k' \qquad k = k_1 + k_2}{\Gamma(k) \vdash e : T, k'} \text{ CONTRACTA}$$

$$\frac{\Gamma(k) \vdash e : T, k' \qquad k = k_1 + k_2}{\Gamma(k_1, k_2) \vdash e : T, k'} \text{ CONTRACTA}'$$

These two contraction rules replace most of the cases of plus-contract where the factor q is not known. Thus if we fix a value for q in the remaining cases and the uses of SPLIT we will only have linear equalities and inequalities as side conditions, which will allow us to use Linear Programming during the inference.

3 Examples of Typing Derivations

Before proving the soundness of the type system we consider some examples.

Example 1 (Continued). The precise bound given in Section 1 contained a minimum, whereas we only consider max-plus bounds. Hence we hope to show that

$$\text{stack(andtrees)} \times (1 + |t1|_d) \quad \text{and} \quad \text{stack(andtrees)} \times (1 + |t2|_d)$$

are bounds on the stack space required. These correspond to the following two type signatures:

$t1 : \text{tree(bool, stack(andtrees))}, t2 : \text{tree(bool, 0)} \rightarrow \text{tree(bool, stack(andtrees))}, 0$

$t1 : \text{tree(bool, 0)}, t2 : \text{tree(bool, stack(andtrees))} \rightarrow \text{tree(bool, stack(andtrees))}, 0$

Note that these signatures do not include the last stack(andtrees) units of space; this is added by the typing of the function call in the caller. The annotation on the result says that the bound is also at least stack(andtrees) times the depth of the result, too.

We can obtain either of these signatures with a type derivation of the structure shown in Figure 7, where $k_1 = \text{stack(andtrees)}, k_2 = 0$ for the first bound, and vice versa for the second. The only non-trivial side condition in this typing is $k_1 + k_2 = k$ from CONTRACTA′. Note that the uses of LET in the derivation focus in on exactly the subcontext required for the recursive calls and the calculation of v.

Example 2. Using maxima in the potential also allows more precise bounds to be derived than plain Hofmann-Jost is able to. Consider the following function:

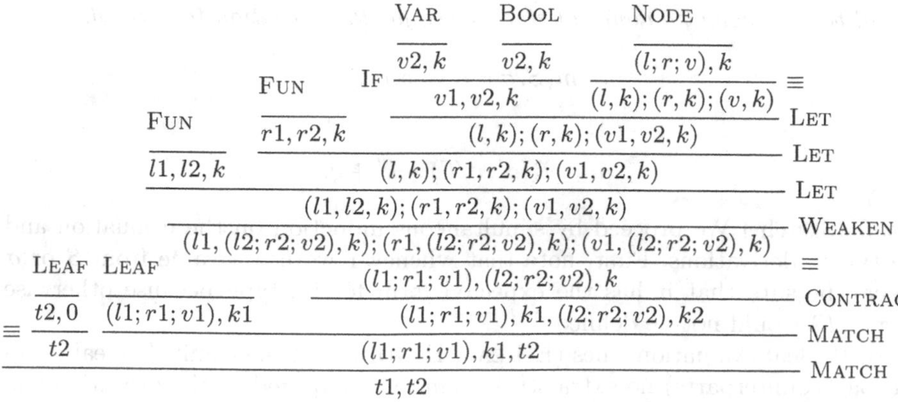

Fig. 7. Typing derivation structure and contexts for andtrees example

```
let maybeleft(t,b) =
    match t with leaf → leaf | node(l,r,v) →
        if b then l else t
```

While the function itself only requires a constant amount of stack space, its typing is used to translate bounds in terms of its result's size into bounds in terms of t. In the present system we can obtain the signature

$$\mathsf{tree}(T, k); \mathsf{bool} \rightarrow \mathsf{tree}(T, k), 0$$

indicating that the size of t is an upper bound on the size of the result. The key part of the typing is that we can use the max-contract form of the $\equiv$ rule to take the maximum of the two branches of the if expression. However, other Hofmann-Jost analyses can only sum the potential for the branches of the if, which doubles the part of the bound expressed in terms of t's size.

4   Soundness

Our main result is that any amount of potential that we can assign to a typing context and still type an expression using it is a sufficient amount of stack space to evaluate that expression. For the induction, we also show that the potential assigned to the result is at most the amount we began with and that any extra space q is preserved.

Theorem 1. *If an expression e in some well-typed program has a typing*

$$\Gamma \vdash e : T, k'$$

and an evaluation $S, \sigma \vdash e \rightsquigarrow v, \sigma'$ and $\Upsilon_c(\sigma, S, \Gamma)$ is defined, then for any $q \in \mathbb{Q}^+$ and $m \in \mathbb{N}$ such that

$$m \geq \Upsilon_c(\sigma, S, \Gamma) + q$$

m will be a sufficient amount of stack space for the execution to succeed,

$$m, S, \sigma \vdash e \rightsquigarrow v, \sigma',$$

and

$$m \geq \Upsilon_t(\sigma', v, T) + k' + q.$$

Proof. (Sketch.) We proceed by simultaneous induction on the evaluation and the typing derivations. First, note that whenever we use a value from S or σ we can be sure that it has the expected form for its type because otherwise $\Upsilon_c(\sigma, S, \Gamma)$ would not be defined.

For the leaf evaluation rules (E-LEAF, E-NODE and their unit, boolean, sum and pair counterparts) no extra stack memory is required so the execution will always succeed. It is then sufficient to check that $\Upsilon_c(\sigma, S, \Gamma)$ plus the given side condition is at least the potential assigned to the result.

The other rules need to use the induction hypothesis. The precondition on m can be satisfied by showing that the original $\Upsilon_c(\sigma, S, \Gamma)$ is larger than or equal to its counterpart for the induction hypothesis. The result of the induction hypothesis is sufficient for most of the rules, where the resulting value and type from the induction hypothesis are also the value and type of the current expression. The FUN rule is a little different due to the stack space used, and LET rule uses the induction hypothesis twice. As these are the most interesting cases, we consider them in a little more detail.

FUN. As the entire program is well-typed there must be a typing of the function body:

$$\Gamma \vdash e_f : T, k_1'.$$

Now we can check that m is sufficient for both the allocation and the induction hypothesis (note that the side condition guarantees that $q + k - \text{stack}(f)$ is positive):

$$m \geq \Upsilon_c(\sigma, S, (\Gamma[x_1/y_1, \ldots, x_p/y_p], k)) + q$$
$$= \Upsilon_c(\sigma, [y_1 \mapsto S(x_1), \ldots, y_p \mapsto S(x_p)], \Gamma) + k + q$$
$$\geq \text{stack}(f) + \Upsilon_c(\sigma, [y_1 \mapsto S(x_1), \ldots, y_p \mapsto S(x_p)], \Gamma) + (q + k - \text{stack}(f)).$$

From the induction hypothesis we also have

$$m \geq \text{stack}(f) + \Upsilon_t(\sigma', v, T) + k_1' + (q + k - \text{stack}(f))$$
$$\geq \Upsilon_t(\sigma', v, T) + k' + q,$$

as required.

LET. It can be easily shown that $\Upsilon_c(\sigma, S, \Gamma(\Delta)) \geq \Upsilon_c(\sigma, S, \Delta)$, which allows us to apply the induction hypothesis to e_1.

We can also use the induction hypothesis to deduce that the potential has not increased. If we set $m_1 = \lceil \Upsilon_c(\sigma, S, \Delta) \rceil$ and $q = m_1 - \Upsilon_c(\sigma, S, \Delta)$ we can see that $m_1 - q = \Upsilon_c(\sigma, S, \Delta)$, and from the induction hypothesis we know that $m_1 - q \geq \Upsilon_t(\sigma_0, v_0, T_0) + k_0$. Thus,

$$\Upsilon_c(\sigma, S, \Delta) \geq \Upsilon_t(\sigma_0, v_0, T_0) + k_0.$$

Thus we can also establish that m is sufficient to apply the induction hypothesis to e_2. $\qquad \square$

5 Checking and Inference

For type checking we assume that we are given the full typing derivation (in the implementation we use an assignment of extra terms to uses of the structural typing rules), including rational values for the annotations. It then remains to check that each arithmetic side condition is satisfied.

Our inference procedure has three main steps:

1. Construct a plain (that is, unannotated) typing;

2. add the context structure and uses of the structural rules to obtain a typing derivation in the system of Section 2, modulo side conditions; then
3. use standard Linear Programming techniques such as the Simplex method to solve the side conditions and minimise the bound.

The first stage can be performed by standard unification methods. The middle stage is new to this analysis; previous Hofmann-Jost systems had relatively little extra structure that might not be present in a plain typing (the exception to this is contraction, which must be explicit in order to sum all the requirements).

To make the inference more tractable we assume that the user provides the *structure* of the function signatures, but they need not give actual values for the annotations. For instance, in the andtrees examples we could supply the structure

$$t1, t2$$

without specifying the types or values for their annotations.

With the typing from the first stage and the structure for function signatures we can derive a 'desired' typing context for each leaf in the typing derivation. For example, the construction of the new node in the andtrees example has a desired context of

$$(l : \mathsf{tree}(\mathsf{bool}, k_1); r : \mathsf{tree}(\mathsf{bool}, k_1); v : \mathsf{bool}), k$$

to match the NODE rule. Note that k_1 and k are just symbolic annotations; the actual values are determined by the Linear Programming solver in the final stage.

We then work outwards in the typing derivation until we have a 'desired' context for the entire function body. For example, if we have an expression if x then e_1 else e_2 and desired contexts Γ_1 and Γ_2 for e_1 and e_2 respectively, then we can take $\Gamma_1; \Gamma_2; x$ (the maximum bound of the branches) as the desired context for the entire expression. Note that we need to add a use of WEAKEN to the typing derivations for e_1 and e_2 to remove the irrelevant subcontexts.

Binding constructs are more challenging. To simplify the problem we note that we can use the $\equiv$ typing rule to expand a context into a maximum of sums form, and also contract an expanded context into its original form. Once we have the contexts for the subexpressions in this form we can factor out the bound variables and use CONTRACTA$'$ to split any fixed amount k between the part of the context changed by the expression's typing rule and the surrounding context (denoted $\Gamma()$ in the typing rules). It is during this factoring that we may need to introduce an approximation using SPLIT. Finally, the expression's typing rule provides us with the desired typing context for the whole expression.

We must also add structural rules to bridge any gap between the desired context inferred for the function body and the given function signature. Fortunately this can be treated as an extreme form of binding construct, where every variable is bound. Should the desired context have any symbolic annotation k without a corresponding source in the function signature the plus-zero or max-zero cases of $\equiv$ can be used to fix k to be zero.

Finally, we gather the side conditions from the resulting typing and use a Linear Programming solver to minimise the overall bound. This step may fail if the resource usage is super-linear, or too subtle for the analysis (for example, because it relies on some unmodelled invariant).

Applying the inference procedure to the examples in Section 3 yields the same bounds as our manual use of the type system. However, the derivations are more verbose, mostly due to the context expansion at every binding construct.

The extra stage in the inference also adds to the amount of work the inference performs. In the worst case the expansion can be exponential with respect to the context size, but in practice the execution times remain similar to earlier Hofmann-Jost analyses [7, Appendix B].

6 Containers

Nested data structures such as trees of trees can present a problem for the analysis. The limitation is that we always take the depth of the *entire* data structure, including all nested contents. In a tree of trees this is the longest path (weighted by the annotations) from the root of the outer tree to a leaf of the inner trees. Hence when we move values around the outer tree (to sort it, for example) we may change the overall depth despite leaving the depth of the outer tree and each inner tree alone.

Ideally we would wish to express the overall 'size' of the data structures differently; namely, as the depth of the outermost structure, plus the maximum depth of the structures in the next layer, and so on for further nested layers: essentially, the sum of the maximum depth of each layer. We conjecture that the present type system could be extended in this direction by allowing constrained movement of 'contents' variables in the context to mimic the corresponding movement of values in their container. However, we leave this to future work.

For containers with simpler contents which carry no potential (units, booleans and pairs thereof in the above language) we can adopt a simpler solution. As these values are assigned no potential, there is no approximation involved in using the SPLIT rule with $q = 0$ to 'lift' these variables to the outermost level of the context. Then the inference procedure described above is able to use them wherever necessary.

We have successfully applied this technique to infer bounds on a functional heap sort, and in particular it can show that the internal routines in the sort use stack space proportional to the heap depth.

7 Extensions

The analysis can be extended in several ways. Algebraic datatypes can be incorporated by assigning structured contexts to constructors in a similar manner to function signatures and generalising the typing rules for trees. These structures can be derived automatically to provide bounds with respect to depth, or left to the user for greater flexibility. For example, two forms of product can be defined using these datatypes: a plus-product that behaves as the product presented above, and a max-product where the maximum of the potential of the two values is taken.

The *resource polymorphism* extension hypothesised in the conclusions to Hofmann and Jost's paper [1] can also be applied to allow different function signatures to be inferred for different uses of a function, reflecting the local resource requirements. Tail call optimisation can also be taken into account, and the soundness proof can be extended to partial evaluations of non-terminating programs.

Details of these extensions, including a full soundness proof and formal details of the inference procedure can be found in the author's thesis [7, Chapters 6 and 7]. The extended type checker and inference procedures have been implemented in Standard ML and are available online[1] along with a small selection of example programs.

8   Related Work

We have already mentioned some of the recent work on Hofmann-Jost, notably the extension to the Hume language in the Embounded project [4,8]. Jost has also worked on extensions for higher-order functions [9] and object oriented programming and mutable references [10], although there is not currently an inference procedure for the latter. These features are largely orthogonal to our work, as they change the language but only infer linear total size bounds. Indeed, one possible avenue of future work is to apply our techniques to these analyses.

Most other analyses are based upon some form of sized-types. An early example is Reistad and Gifford's system for finding execution time estimates to assist parallelisation [11], although they avoid detailed analysis of recursive functions by providing fixed types for a small range of library functions such as `map` and `fold` instead. Hughes and Pareto used their sized-types work to certify heap and stack space bounds in a first-order 'embedded ML' language [12], but do not provide any inference.

A strand of inference work on sized-types systems starts with Chin and Khoo's inference [13]. Like Pareto's checker, the system is based on solving systems of Presburger formulae. Their later work considers properties about the values in containers [14], a language with references [15], space bounds for object-oriented languages [16], and applying similar techniques to assembly programs [17]. Vasconcelos has also studied these inference systems in order to produce a sized types analysis and heap and stack space bounds for Hume [18]. One of the main advantages of a sized-types analysis over our approach is that the size information can be reused for other analyses.

The use of Presburger solvers in these systems raises concerns about efficiency, but it is unclear whether the generated constraints may include arbitrary formulae, or if they are limited to some easily solved subset. The reports cited above suggest that they are reasonable in practice. Similarly, certification using these

---

[1] http://homepages.inf.ed.ac.uk/bcampbe2/depth-analysis/

systems may require the verifier to perform some constraint solving, whereas for our system they need only perform some simple arithmetic after reconstructing the typing using suitable hints.

A different approach which can yield non-linear bounds is to use recurrence solvers to deal with recursive functions, such as Debray and Lin's execution time analysis for logic programs [19], and Vasconcelos and Hammond's analysis [20]. The power of these analyses is dependent on the power of the recurrence solver used. Recent work by Albert et al. has tackled this by producing a specialised recurrence solver for dealing with cost equations [21].

9 Conclusions

We have presented a new stack space analysis similar in concept to the Hofmann-Jost heap space analysis, but with more structure to enable richer, more precise bounds.

Further work on the system could include enhancing the language (perhaps using the existing Hofmann-Jost extensions mentioned above), removing the need for users to provide the structure for type signatures and the containers extension outlined in Section 6. It would also be interesting to apply these techniques to heap space by devising a suitable replacement for the LET rule, especially as we may be able to regain the fine-grained form of plus-contraction when considering total space bounds.

References

1. Hofmann, M., Jost, S.: Static prediction of heap space usage for first-order functional programs. In: POPL 2003: Proceedings of the 30th ACM Symposium on Principles of Programming Languages, New Orleans. ACM Press, New York (2003)
2. O'Hearn, P.: On bunched typing. Journal of Functional Programming 13(4), 747–796 (2003)
3. Aspinall, D., Gilmore, S., Hofmann, M., Sannella, D., Stark, I.: Mobile resource guarantees for smart devices. In: Barthe, G., Burdy, L., Huisman, M., Lanet, J.-L., Muntean, T. (eds.) CASSIS 2004. LNCS, vol. 3362, pp. 1–26. Springer, Heidelberg (2005)
4. Jost, S., Loidl, H.W., Hammond, K.: Report on stack-space analysis (revised). Deliverable D05, The Embounded Project (IST-510255) (2007)
5. Campbell, B.: Prediction of linear memory usage for first-order functional programs. In: Trends in Functional Programming, vol. 9 (2008) (to appear)
6. Tarjan, R.E.: Amortized computational complexity. SIAM Journal on Algebraic and Discrete Methods 6(2), 306–318 (1985)
7. Campbell, B.: Type-based amortized stack memory prediction. PhD thesis, University of Edinburgh (2008)
8. Jost, S., Loidl, H.W., Hammond, K.: Report on heap-space analysis. Deliverable D11, The Embounded Project (IST-510255) (2007)
9. Jost, S.: Amortised Analysis for Functional Programs. PhD thesis, Ludwig-Maximilians-University (forthcoming, provisional title) (2008)

10. Hofmann, M., Jost, S.: Type-based amortised heap-space analysis (for an object-oriented language). In: Sestoft, P. (ed.) ESOP 2006. LNCS, vol. 3924, pp. 22–37. Springer, Heidelberg (2006)

11. Reistad, B., Gifford, D.K.: Static dependent costs for estimating execution time. In: LFP 1994: Proceedings of the 1994 ACM conference on LISP and functional programming, pp. 65–78. ACM Press, New York (1994)

12. Hughes, J., Pareto, L.: Recursion and dynamic data-structures in bounded space: towards embedded ML programming. In: ICFP 1999: Proceedings of the fourth ACM SIGPLAN International Conference on Functional Programming, pp. 70–81. ACM Press, New York (1999)

13. Chin, W.N., Khoo, S.C.: Calculating sized types. Higher Order and Symbolic Computation 14(2-3), 261–300 (2001)

14. Chin, W.N., Khoo, S.C., Xu, D.N.: Extending sized type with collection analysis. In: PEPM 2003: Proceedings of the 2003 ACM SIGPLAN workshop on Partial Evaluation and Semantics-based Program Manipulation, pp. 75–84. ACM Press, New York (2003)

15. Chin, W.N., Khoo, S.C., Qin, S., Popeea, C., Nguyen, H.H.: Verifying safety policies with size properties and alias controls. In: ICSE 2005: Proceedings of the 27th International Conference on Software Engineering, pp. 186–195. ACM Press, New York (2005)

16. Chin, W.N., Nguyen, H.H., Qin, S., Rinard, M.: Memory usage verification for OO programs. In: Hankin, C., Siveroni, I. (eds.) SAS 2005. LNCS, vol. 3672, pp. 70–86. Springer, Heidelberg (2005)

17. Chin, W.N., Nguyen, H.H., Popeea, C., Qin, S.: Analysing memory resource bounds for low-level programs. In: ISMM 2008: Proceedings of the 7th international symposium on Memory management, pp. 151–160. ACM, New York (2008)

18. Vasconcelos, P.: Space Cost Analysis Using Sized Types. PhD thesis, University of St Andrews (2008)

19. Debray, S.K., Lin, N.W.: Cost analysis of logic programs. ACM Transactions on Programming Languages and Systems 15(5), 826–875 (1993)

20. Vasconcelos, P.B., Hammond, K.: Inferring cost equations for recursive, polymorphic and higher-order functional programs. In: Trinder, P., Michaelson, G.J., Peña, R. (eds.) IFL 2003. LNCS, vol. 3145, pp. 86–101. Springer, Heidelberg (2004)

21. Albert, E., Arenas, P., Genaim, S., Puebla, G.: Automatic inference of upper bounds for recurrence relations in cost analysis. In: Alpuente, M., Vidal, G. (eds.) SAS 2008. LNCS, vol. 5079, pp. 221–237. Springer, Heidelberg (2008)

The Financial Crisis, a Lack of Contract Specification Tools: What Can Finance Learn from Programming Language Design?

Jean-Marc Eber

LexiFi, 49 rue de Billancourt, F-92100 Boulogne-Billancourt, France
www.lexifi.com

The magnitude and dramatic consequences of the current "financial crisis" are publicly well documented. Even non professionals may read in, say, newspapers about notions like "derivatives", "over the counter deals", "complexity of contracts", "insufficient regulation" or "impossible to understand portfolios" while reading about bankruptcy or bailouts of big financial institutions.

Even if this crisis has many reasons—a topic of future research for economists, historians, sociologists, politicians and many others—it is often argued that "excessive complexity" or "excessive mathematization" should be considered as one of the original faults. The financial sector—banks, asset managers, hedge funds, insurance companies—is indeed viewed as a highly technical one, driven by rapid innovation and using numerous quantitative analysts ("quants") for achieving precise calculations or risk analyses.

In this informal presentation, we argue on the contrary that the main technical problem faced by the financial industry is not "solving complexity" but "mastering diversity". Similarly to a company that would have to "manage" thousands of informally specified algorithms, a big financial institution "manages" thousands of client tailored financial bilateral contracts (described in "term-sheets" in financial jargon), many of them lasting for years, mentioning important decisions (exercise decisions) to be taken by the institution itself or its counterparty and including transformations to apply to the contract in the future (typically called fixings in finance). The technical difficulty stems not only from the necessity of having a clear understanding of such a portfolio of contracts at a particular date, but also to monitor correctly all "actions" to apply at precise dates. Even if tremendous information technology resources are devoted for implementing software in the finance sector, one should note that contrary to general belief, this activity is typically mainly driven by a mixture of partially adapted "legacy systems", a lot of manual work and a large number of badly integrated spreadsheet macros. This situation is not very publicized for clear reasons but sheds light on why financial institutions have difficulties in knowing their exposures at any time or why they incur significant "operational risk", meaning the risk of not managing correctly a given contract over its lifetime.

At this stage, any serious computer scientist would point to the necessity of a well founded specification formalism with a clearly defined semantics. Designing such a "domain specific language"—the semantics of which should of course be compositional and allow for multiple uses—has been surprisingly difficult,

G. Castagna (Ed.): ESOP 2009, LNCS 5502, pp. 205–206, 2009.

especially when one is considering all implementation tricks necessary to scale efficiently from little toy examples to the most complex real-world cases.

Building on the experience of working more than a decade in a major investment bank followed by the design and implementation since 2001 in our company of such a formalism used by our customers, we present an intuitive, simplified contract with its formal description. We show examples of different semantics uses. Not surprisingly but of tremendous power in everyday use, pricing a contract under certain model hypotheses (a fundamentally important topic) appears to be a denotational semantics—currently implemented as a mapping from the contract description to C source code—while managing a contract over time amounts to implementing and applying operational semantics adequately.

We also comment on our implementation choices—our software is mainly written with an enhanced OCaml system and strongly linked to OCaml's run-time system—and extensions needed to ease industrial acceptance and integration with existing technology or systems. For this reason, we insist on the strategic importance of having the possibility to adapt and enhance our main compiler to our needs. We also show examples of how this machinery integrates into a traditional gui application, hiding all complexity from end-users and giving the look and feel of a traditional application. We finally comment on our attempts to formally prove (some subsets of) our formalism or implementation.

We argue that the relative simplicity of such contract description language, that does not need to be Turing complete as a full-fledged programming language like C or Java, allows for the effective implementation and use of many interesting approaches—let us mention here abstract interpretation, partial application and run-time code generation—which are often very difficult if not impossible to use automatically in a more general setting. The financial sector appears to be a surprisingly good testbed for many of these techniques.

From a technical perspective, financial sector innovation is currently dominated by mathematical models and efficient numerical implementation problems. We are quite convinced that only a combined approach, mixing formal descriptions and manipulations of contracts with efficient numerical approaches can solve some recurrent and fundamental technical problems faced by the financial industry today and in the future.

All Secrets Great and Small

Delphine Demange[1] and David Sands[2]

[1] University of Rennes 1, France
[2] Chalmers University of Technology, Sweden

Abstract. Tools for analysing secure information flow are almost exclusively based on ideas going back to Denning's work from the 70's. This approach embodies an imperfect notion of security which turns a blind eye to information flows which are encoded in the termination behaviour of a program. In exchange for this weakness many more programs are deemed "secure", using conditions which are easy to check. Previously it was thought that such leaks are limited to at most one bit per run. Recent work by Askarov et al (ESORICS'08) offers some bad news and some good news: the bad news is that for programs which perform output, the amount of information leaked by a Denning style analysis is not bounded; the good news is that if secrets are chosen to be sufficiently large and sufficiently random then they cannot be effectively leaked at all. The problem addressed in this paper is that secrets cannot always be made sufficiently large or sufficiently random. Contrast, for example, an encryption key with an "hasHIV"-field of a patient record. In recognition of this we develop a notion of *secret-sensitive noninterference* in which "small" secrets are handled more carefully than "big" ones. We illustrate the idea with a type system which combines a liberal Denning-style analysis with a more restrictive system according to the nature of the secrets at hand.

1 Introduction

Most tools for analysing information flow in programs such as Jif [MZZ+08] and Flow-Caml [Sim03] build upon ideas going back to Denning's work from the 70's [DD77]. These systems enforce an imperfect notion of information flow which has become known as *termination-insensitive noninterference* (TINI). Under this version of noninterference, information leaks are permitted if they are transmitted purely by the program's termination behaviour (i.e., whether it terminates or not). This imperfection is the price to pay for having a security condition which is relatively liberal (e.g. allowing while-loops whose termination may depend on the value of a secret) and easy to check.

How bad is termination-insensitive noninterference? Previously there have been informal arguments that termination-insensitive noninterference leaks at most one bit: either a program terminates or it does not, so at most one bit of information can be encoded in the termination state. However, recent work by Askarov *et al* [AHSS08] shows that for programs which perform output, an arbitrary amount of information can be leaked. The following program outputs an ascending sequence of natural numbers on a public channel until the secret has been output, at which point it goes into a silent loop:

G. Castagna (Ed.): ESOP 2009, LNCS 5502, pp. 207–221, 2009.
© Springer-Verlag Berlin Heidelberg 2009

```
for i = 0 to maxNat (
    output i on public_channel
    if (i = secret) then (while true do skip)
)
```

At the very least we can say that at each output step, the observer is able to narrow down the possible values of the secret. This program (in suitable variants) is accepted as secure by state-of-the-art information flow analysis tools such as Jif [MZZ$^+$08], FlowCaml [Sim03], and the SPARK Examiner [BB03, CH04].

Askarov *et al* formalise the notion of termination-insensitive noninterference and show that although termination-insensitive noninterference can leak an arbitrary amount of information, it cannot do so any more efficiently than the above example. The revised intuition for programs performing public output is that the number of possible "termination states" that can be used to encode information is of the order of the number of public outputs performed by the program – since the program can diverge after 0 outputs, after 1 output, after 2 outputs, etc. This means that to leak n bits of information the program needs to perform 2^n outputs.

For Denning-style analyses this means that if secrets are sufficiently large and sufficiently random then programs are *computationally secure* in the sense that the probability of the attacker guessing the secret after observing a polynomial number of outputs (again, in the size of the secret) gives only a negligible advantage over guessing the secret without running the program.

What does this mean for information flow analysis in practice? Whereas previously the imperfections of a Denning-style analysis were viewed as a reasonable tradeoff between ease of analysis versus degree of security, we believe that in the light of [AHSS08] we need a different perspective. The leak caused by termination-insensitivity is only acceptable for sufficiently large and random secrets. But secrets, in general, are not always parametric: one cannot always freely choose to make a secret larger and more random. For example, an application cannot decide that a credit card CCV number should be made larger. An encryption key, on the other hand, might be something that the application can control, and decide to scale up.

In this paper we consider the information flow problem in an arbitrary multi-level security lattice. We present a way (Section 2) of refining each security level in an information-flow lattice into two levels: *big secrets*, that are sufficiently large and randomized to abide some leakage, and *small secrets*, for which even slow leakage is unacceptable. Then, we define a two-level noninterference (Section 3), following Askarov et al's recent work, which combines the demands of termination-insensitive noninterference (for big secrets) with the stricter requirements of termination-sensitive noninterference (for small secrets). A type system is provided (Section 4) that ensures this notion of noninterference. Additional novelties of the system are a somewhat more liberal treatment of small secrets than found in previous termination-sensitive type systems. Section 5 describes a strengthening of the definition of security to eliminate leakage correlations between big and small secrets.

2   A Refined Multilevel Lattice

In [AHSS08] a definition of termination-insensitive noninterference (**TINI**) was introduced which is suitable for programs with outputs, assuming only two security levels *low* and *high*. They proved that, even if programs verifying this condition can leak more than a bit of information, the attacker cannot reliably (i.e in a single run) learn a secret in polynomial time in the size of the secret. They also proved that, for programs satisfying TINI, if secrets are uniformly distributed, then a particular observation of a computation represents only a negligible hint for the attacker (Theorem 3).

The basic idea in this work is to refine the notion of *high* into two points *bhigh* and *shigh*. These will correspond to "big" secrets and "small" secrets respectively. We will define a notion of secret-sensitive noninterference which allows a low user to learn a little about big secrets, and nothing at all about small secrets (relative to the notion of observation that we model).

How are big and small secrets related? A key point here is that data labelled *bhigh* will depend only on *bhigh* or *low* data sources, whereas data labelled *shigh* might also depend on *shigh* data sources. Thus the label *bhigh* does not mean that the data *is* a large secret – it just means that it does not depend on (contain any information about) a small secret. We can then see that the resulting refined security lattice is as given in Figure 1.

Fig. 1. The refined 2-point lattice

Now we generalise this refinement to the case of an arbitrary multi-level lattice of information levels [Den76]. Denning's lattice model of information considers an arbitrary complete lattice $\langle \mathcal{L}, \sqsubseteq_{\mathcal{L}}, \sqcup_{\mathcal{L}}, \sqcap_{\mathcal{L}}, \perp_{\mathcal{L}} \rangle$ where $\mathcal{L}$ is the set of security *clearance levels* (henceforth just *levels*, ranged over by i, j), and $\sqsubseteq_{\mathcal{L}}$ is the ordering relation which determines when one level is higher than another. The idea is that a principal with a clearance level i is permitted to see data which is classified at level i or below according to the partial ordering. Information from any levels may be combined, in which case the classification for the resulting data is given deterministically by the least-upper-bound operation $\sqcup_{\mathcal{L}}$.

To refine this general case we note that we must split each level $i \in \mathcal{L}$, with the exception of the bottom level $\perp_{\mathcal{L}}$ (which can always be thought of as public data) into two points, corresponding to the big secrets (labelled b) and the small (labelled s). Thus any non-bottom element i will be refined to (i, b) and (i, s). To define the appropriate order between lattice elements we first note that $(i, b) \sqsubseteq (i, s)$ – with the same motivation as given for the refined two-point lattice. Similarly, when comparing secrets of the same kind we have $(i, a) \sqsubseteq (j, a)$ only when $i \sqsubseteq_{\mathcal{L}} j$.

What about the relationship between two points (i, b) and (j, s) – when can information flow between these points? The idea is that information at level b is potentially leaked via a covert channel, so that it may be leaked to *any* level. Because of this we can only permit flow from (i, b) to (j, s), and then only when $i \sqsubseteq_{\mathcal{L}} j$. If we permitted a small secret (i, s) to flow to any (j, b) for $(j \neq i)$ then we would be able to launder small secrets by first allowing them to flow to a big secret and then leaking via the covert channel from there. In summary, we define the refinement of a given security lattice:

Definition 1. *Let S denote the 2-point lattice formed from b and s under the ordering $b \sqsubseteq s$. We define the* refinement *of a security lattice $\mathcal{L}$ as the* partial product *of $\mathcal{L}$ and S, which is the standard product lattice $\mathcal{L} \times S$, quotiented by the equivalence $(\bot_{\mathcal{L}}, b) \equiv (\bot_{\mathcal{L}}, s)$ – and this bottom element will be simply denoted by $\bot_{\mathcal{L}}$.*

Example. Consider the example where $\mathcal{L} = \{secret, financial, medical, public\}$ is the set of the four security levels a program has to deal with, ordered according to the Hasse diagram in Figure 2. Motivating a refinement of the lattice, there could be medical data that is encrypted – or simply very large (e.g. high resolution image data) that could be safely allowed to leak slowly, and other medical data that are to be handled with more care, such as an "hasHIV" boolean flag in a patient record. The partial product of lattices $\mathcal{L}$ and S is presented in Figure 3.

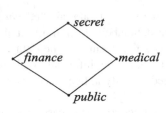

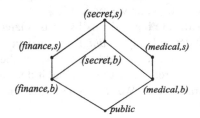

Fig. 2. Example $\mathcal{L}$ Fig. 3. The refinement of $\mathcal{L}$

3   Secret-Sensitive Noninterference

In this section we define the security goal for programs computing over data labelled with a refined lattice. This variant of the notion of noninterference, *secret-sensitive noninterference*, combines the demands of termination-insensitive noninterference for b-data, and the stronger termination-sensitive noninterference for s-data. Further, we develop a bisimulation-style characterisation of *secret-sensitive noninterference* which provides a convenient proof method.

Operational Semantics. We keep our presentation language independent, but we assume some basic structure for an operational semantics. We will consider simple imperative computation modelled by a standard small-step operational semantics defined over configurations of the form $\langle M, C \rangle$ where M is a memory (store) – a finite mapping from variables to values – and C (C', D etc.) is a command. Each variable x is assumed to have a fixed policy denoted $\Gamma(x)$, which we take to be a member of the refinement of some lattice $\mathcal{L}$.

We assume an operational semantics consisting of deterministic labelled transitions between configurations, where a label u is either (i) an observable output $i(v)$, meaning that a value v is output on a channel observable at level $i \in \mathcal{L}$ or above, or (ii) a silent action labelled τ. We write e.g. $\langle M, C \rangle \xrightarrow{i(v)} \langle M', C' \rangle$.

On top of the basic labelled transitions we define a family of transition systems labelled by a particular level:

Definition 2 (*i-observable transitions*). *We can define the transition relations* $\xrightarrow{u}_i$, $i \in \mathcal{L}$ *as:*

$$\frac{\langle M, C \rangle \xrightarrow{j(v)} \langle M', C' \rangle \quad j \sqsubseteq_{\mathcal{L}} i}{\langle M, C \rangle \xrightarrow{v}_i \langle M', C' \rangle}$$

$$\frac{\langle M, C \rangle \xrightarrow{u} \langle M', C' \rangle \quad u = \tau \text{ or } u = j(n) \text{ where } j \not\sqsubseteq_{\mathcal{L}} i}{\langle M, C \rangle \xrightarrow{\tau}_i \langle M', C' \rangle}$$

Thus the i-observable transitions are obtained from the raw transitions by filtering out (replacing by τ) all output actions that are not visible at level i. Note that the non-τ transitions are just the value which is observed and not the channel on which it is observed.

Now we define the "big step" transitions $\langle M, C \rangle \xRightarrow{u}_i \langle M', C' \rangle$ as follows

$$\langle M, C \rangle \xRightarrow{\tau}_i \langle M', C' \rangle \triangleq \langle M, C \rangle \xrightarrow{\tau}^*_i \langle M', C' \rangle$$
$$\langle M, C \rangle \xRightarrow{v}_i \langle M', C' \rangle \triangleq \langle M, C \rangle \xrightarrow{\tau}^*_i \xrightarrow{v}_i \langle M', C' \rangle$$

We also define the multi-step observations $\langle M, C \rangle \xRightarrow{\vec{v}}_i \langle M', C' \rangle$ with $\vec{v} = v_1 v_2 \cdots v_n$ as follows:

$$\langle M, C \rangle \xRightarrow{v_1}_i \langle M_1, C_1 \rangle \xRightarrow{v_2}_i \langle M_2, C_2 \rangle \xRightarrow{v_3}_i \cdots \xRightarrow{v_{n-1}}_i \langle M_{n-1}, C_{n-1} \rangle \xRightarrow{v_n}_i \langle M', C' \rangle$$

for some sequence of intermediate configurations $\langle M_i, C_i \rangle$. We define the multi-step reduction for the empty vector to be synonymous with $\xRightarrow{\tau}_i$.

Attacker's knowledge. Our presentation follows the style of Askarov *et al* [AHSS08] closely. The definition of noninterference developed here builds on the concept of *attacker knowledge* which is what an attacker (an observer of a given clearance level i) can deduce about the initial values of variables based on a particular observation of a program run.

The attacker i knows the initial low part of the memory. The low part of the memory from the perspective of a given level i is all variables with policy (i, s) or lower - and observes some output trace $\vec{v}$ that is not necessarily maximal, knows the program and is able to make perfect deductions about the semantics of the program. For a memory M we let M^i denote the low part of the memory from the perspective of an observer at level i, i.e. the part of the memory that he can see.

Definition 3 (**Observations**). *Given a program C and a low memory M^i, the i-observations is the set of all possible sequences of observable outputs that could arise from a run of C with a memory compatible with M^i. It is defined:*

$$Obs_i(C, M^i) = \{\vec{v} | \langle N, C \rangle \xRightarrow{\vec{v}}_i \langle N', C' \rangle, \quad N^i = M^i\}$$

Definition 4 (**Attacker's knowledge**). *Given a program C, an initial choice M^i of the low part of the memory (for level i) and a trace of i-observable outputs $\vec{v}$, the attacker's knowledge gained from this observation is the set of all possible memories that could have lead to this observation.*

$$k_i(C, M^i, \vec{v}) = \{N | \langle N, C \rangle \xRightarrow{\vec{v}}_i \langle N', C' \rangle, \quad N^i = M^i\}$$

Note that increase in knowledge corresponds to a decrease in the size of the knowledge set. Knowledge increases with outputs: the more outputs the attacker observes, the more precise is his knowledge [AS07]:

$$\forall C, M^i, \vec{v}, v. \quad k_i(C, M^i, \vec{v}v) \subseteq k_i(C, M^i, \vec{v})$$

In order to distinguish between what is learnt about the "big" secrets (variables at levels (i, b)) from what is learnt about the "small secrets" (variables at levels (i, s)) we define the projections of knowledge sets to the b- and s-parts.

Definition 5 (b- **and** s-**restricted memories**). *Given a memory M, and a security size $a \in \mathcal{S}$, we define $M|_a^i$ to be the restriction of M to those variables x such that $\Gamma(x) = (j, a)$, $j \not\sqsubseteq i$ – i.e. the "a-secrets" from i's perspective. We extend the definition pointwise to sets of memories.*

Definition 6 (b- **and** s-**restricted knowledge**). *Given a program C, a security size $a \in \mathcal{S}$ and an initial choice M^i of the low part of the memory and a trace of outputs $\vec{v}$, the a-restricted knowledge of the attacker i, written $k_i^a(C, M^i, \vec{v})$ is defined $(k_i(C, M^i, \vec{v}))|_a^i$.*

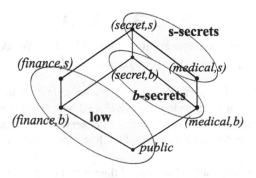

Fig. 4. The *finance*-perspective on the example refined lattice

Informally, the restricted knowledge $k_i^a(C, M^i, \vec{v})$ is i's knowledge about the a-secrets (from i's perspective) after having observed $\vec{v}$ from initial memory M^i.

The idea of "i's secrets" can be illustrated using the lattice presented in Figure 3. For example, the projection $M|_s^{finance}$ restricts M to just those variables with classifications $(medical, s)$ or $(secret, s)$. The *finance*-perspective on the lattice is illustrated in Figure 4, where the b-secrets and s-secrets are marked. The low part of the lattice, from the finance perspective, is also marked.

The s-restricted knowledge for an attacker at level *finance* is thus the knowledge that can be deduced about the s-secret part of the memory.

Noninterference. Several kinds of noninterference can be defined from the notion of knowledge. Here we adapt the definition of termination-(in)sensitive noninterference that was proposed in [AHSS08] and then propose a definition of a two-levelled noninterference.

Definition 7 (Termination-Sensitive Noninterference (TSNI)). *A program C satisfies TSNI if for all i, whenever $\vec{v}v \in Obs_i(C, M^i)$ then*

$$k_i(C, M^i, \vec{v}) = k_i(C, M^i, \vec{v}v).$$

TSNI means that at each step of output, nothing new about the high memory is learnt by the attacker.

Definition 8 (Termination-Insensitive Noninterference (TINI)). *A program C satisfies TINI if for all i, whenever $\vec{v}v \in Obs_i(C, M^i)$ then*

$$k_i(C, M^i, \vec{v}v) = \bigcup_{v'} k_i(C, M^i, \vec{v}v').$$

TINI allows leakage at each low output step, but only through the fact that there is *some* output step. The knowledge leaked by one output is the same as for any other.

In order to deal with our two different kinds of secret (b and s), the idea is here to combine both TSNI and TINI: although we only accept TSNI for s-data which must be handled with more care, we allow TINI for b-data, that abide some leakage since they are randomized and large enough.

Definition 9 (Secret-Sensitive Noninterference (SSNI)). *A program C satisfies SSNI if for all i, whenever $\vec{v}v \in Obs_i(C, M^i)$ then the following two properties hold:*

$$
\begin{aligned}
k_i^s(C, M^i, \vec{v}v) &= k_i^s(C, M^i, \vec{v}) && \text{(s-TSNI)} \\
k_i^b(C, M^i, \vec{v}v) &= \textstyle\bigcup_{v'} k_i^b(C, M^i, \vec{v}v') && \text{(b-TINI)}
\end{aligned}
$$

3.1 Characterising SSNI

The knowledge based definitions are (in our opinion) lucid because they give a clear attacker perspective on the problem. However, for reasoning about secret-sensitive noninterference we find it convenient to work with a more conventional characterisation in terms of bisimulation relations. Here we develop this alternative characterisation, which we will employ in Section 4 in order to prove that the type system there guarantees secret-sensitive noninterference.

The basic idea is to establish the two components of SSNI via two forms of bisimulation relations between configurations.

Definition 10 (Termination-sensitive i-bisimulation (i-TSB)). *A symmetric relation $\mathcal{R}$ on configurations is a termination-sensitive i-bisimulation, if $\langle M, C \rangle \mathcal{R} \langle N, D \rangle$ implies:*

(i) $M^i = N^i$ and $M|_b^i = N|_b^i$, and
(ii) whenever $\langle M, C \rangle \xrightarrow{u}_i \langle M', C' \rangle$ then $\langle N, D \rangle \overset{u}{\Rightarrow}_i \langle N', D' \rangle$ with $\langle M', C' \rangle \mathcal{R} \langle N', D' \rangle$.

Two configurations are said to be i-TSB equivalent (denoted by $\cong_i$) if there exists a i-TSB relating them.

Here, the termination-sensitivity comes from the ability to produce the next output together with the symmetry of the relation.

Definition 11 (Termination-insensitive i-bisimulation (i-TIB)). *We say that a configuration $\langle M, C \rangle$ diverges for i, written $\langle M, C \rangle \Uparrow_i$, if $\langle M, C \rangle$ cannot perform any i-observable output transition $\overset{v}{\to}_i$.*

A symmetric relation $\mathcal{R}$ on configurations is defined to be a termination-insensitive i-bisimulation if whenever $\langle M, C \rangle \mathcal{R} \langle N, D \rangle$ we have

(i) $M^i = N^i$ and
(ii) if $\langle M, C \rangle \overset{u}{\to}_i \langle M', C' \rangle$ then either $\langle N, D \rangle \overset{u}{\Rightarrow}_i \langle N', D' \rangle$ with $\langle M', C' \rangle \mathcal{R} \langle N', D' \rangle$, or $\langle N, D \rangle \Uparrow_i$.

Two configurations are said to be i-TIB equivalent (denoted by $\simeq_i$) if there exists a i-TIB relating them.

Note that the notion of "divergence" used here is purely from the perspective of a remote observer who sees only the outputs on channels. We could make this more conventional if we made program termination an observable event for all levels. We have chosen not to do so, but the technical development in this paper does not depend in a crucial way on this fact.

Before we show how these relations are sufficient to characterise SSNI, we need the following lemmas about i-TSB and i-TIB.

Lemma 1
If $\langle M, C \rangle \cong_i \langle N, D \rangle$ and $\langle M, C \rangle \overset{\vec{v}}{\Rightarrow}_i \langle M', C' \rangle$ then $\langle N, D \rangle \overset{\vec{v}}{\Rightarrow}_i \langle N', D' \rangle$ with $\langle M', C' \rangle \cong_i \langle N', D' \rangle$.

Lemma 2
If $\langle M, C \rangle \simeq_i \langle N, D \rangle$ and $\langle M, C \rangle \overset{\vec{v}}{\Rightarrow}_i \langle M', C' \rangle$ then $\langle N, D \rangle \overset{\vec{v'}}{\Rightarrow}_i \langle N', D' \rangle$ for some $\vec{v'}$ such that either $\vec{v} = \vec{v'}$ and $\langle M', C' \rangle \simeq_i \langle N', D' \rangle$, or $\vec{v'}$ is a prefix of $\vec{v}$ and $\langle N', D' \rangle \Uparrow_i$.

Proof. (Lemmas 1 and 2) By induction on the number of outputs (length of $\vec{v}$), and in the base case by induction on the length of the raw transition sequence.   □

Proposition 1
Suppose that for all levels i and all memories M and N such that $M^i = N^i$ and $M|_b^i = N|_b^i$ we have $\langle M, C \rangle \cong_i \langle N, C \rangle$. Then for all i, whenever $\vec{v}v \in Obs_i(C, M^i)$ then $k_i^s(C, M^i, \vec{v}v) = k_i^s(C, M^i, \vec{v})$.

Proof. See technical report [DS09].   □

A similar proposition can be stated about termination-insensitive noninterference concerning $bhigh$ data.

Proposition 2
Suppose that for all levels i and all M and N, such that $M^i = N^i$ we have that $\langle M, C \rangle \simeq_i \langle N, C \rangle$. Then $\vec{v}v \in Obs_i(C, M_i)$ implies $k_i^b(C, M^i, \vec{v}v) = \bigcup_{v'} k_i^b(C, M^i, \vec{v}v')$.

Proof. See technical report [DS09].   □

Clearly, then, putting the propositions together we get a proof technique for SSNI:

Corollary 1. C *satisfies* $SSNI$ *if, for all levels* i *and all* M *and* N, *we have*

- $M^i = N^i$ *implies* $\langle M, C \rangle \simeq_i \langle N, C \rangle$, *and*
- $M^i = N^i$ *and* $M|_b^i = N|_b^i$ *implies* $\langle M, C \rangle \cong_i \langle N, C \rangle$.

3.2 Computational Security

Definition 9 clearly enforces termination-sensitive noninterference for s-data. Regarding b-data, we can provide the computational security guarantees of [AHSS08] to show that b-secrets, if chosen uniformly, cannot be leaked in polynomial time in their size. To argue this we can first reclassify all secrets as b-data (or equivalently assume that there are no s-secrets). Then we are back in the standard security lattice, and we simply need to generalise the results of [AHSS08] from a two-point lattice to an arbitrary one. This is, as usual, unproblematic since from the perspective of each individual level i there are only two levels of interest: the levels which can be seen (i.e. the levels less than or equal to i) and those which cannot. The main result is that if b-data is randomly chosen, then an observer at level i learns a negligible amount of information (as a function of the size of the b-data) about the data which i cannot see. We will not further develop the details of this argument in the present article. The differences from the development in [AHSS08] would be minor.

4   Secret-Sensitive Noninterference by Typing

In this section, we describe a type system that enforces noninterference Definition 9: well-typed programs are secret-sensitive noninterfering. We study a classical deterministic while programming language defined with expressions and commands.

$$e ::= n \mid x \mid e \; op \; e$$
$$c ::= \textbf{skip} \mid x := e \mid c \, ; \, c \mid \textbf{if } e \textbf{ then } c \textbf{ else } c \mid$$
$$\textbf{while } e \textbf{ do } c \mid \textbf{for } e \textbf{ do } c \mid \textbf{output}_i(e)$$

Here n stands for any integer constant, x for any variable and op for any of the classical binary arithmetical operators. Booleans are represented by integers the classical way (0 is $false$, and everything else is $true$). We also assume that there are no exceptions raised: all binary operators are totally defined.

Note that the language provides two types of loops: **for** loops are always terminating, that is the guard expression is evaluated just once, leading to a constant that is decreased each time the end of the loop body is reached, and **while** loops are potentially non terminating. The distinction will be used in the type system to good effect.

The language includes the **output**$_i$ primitive method that writes the value of its argument to a channel with level i. The operational semantics is standard and is given in the technical report [DS09].

4.1 Type System

This type system is based on the combination of a standard Denning-style analysis (in type system form [VSI96]) for enforcing the termination-insensitive security for b-secrets, and a more restrictive type system for handling the s-secrets. One such termination-sensitive type system is that described in [VS97], but that system is extremely restrictive: loops are only allowed if the guard does not refer to anything except data at the lowest lattice level, and if there is a branch on secret data at any level then no loops are allowed inside the branches. Instead we adapt an idea common to the type systems from [BC01] and [Smi01] for the termination-sensitive part. The idea is here to allow high while loops (i.e. loops with high guards or arbitrary while loops occurring in a high context) so long as no assignment or output to levels below the loop guards follows them.

The form of the typing judgements follows the style of [BC01] in that it handles indirect information flows by recording the write effect of a command (the lowest level to which it writes data). This gives the same power as Denning's popular approach which uses a "program counter" level.

Consider both lattices $\mathcal{L}$ and $\mathcal{S}$, and let $\mathcal{P}$ be their partial product as previously defined. A type is either an expression type denoted $e : \tau$, or a command type written $(\tau, \sigma, \delta)cmd$, where both τ and σ are in $\mathcal{P}$, the set of security levels, and δ, the *termination flag* is a member of the set $\{\downarrow, \uparrow\}$, where we order the elements $\downarrow \leq \uparrow$.

Type judgments are of the form

$$\Gamma \vdash C : (\tau, \sigma, \delta)cmd$$

where Γ is the typing environment i.e. a mapping from variables to variable types. In the following, Γ is kept implicit. The syntactic meaning of such a judgment is that

- τ is a lower bound on the security levels of variables that are assigned to in C.
- σ is the least upper bound on the levels of (for,if,while) guards occurring in C.
- δ is $\downarrow$ if C contains no while loops, and is $\uparrow$ otherwise.

The semantic implication of these typings is that

- τ is a lower bound on the the *write effect* of the command – i.e., the command only modifies variables of level τ or above, and
- σ is the *termination effect*: observing that C produces some output (i.e. "terminates") give us knowledge about data at level at most σ.
- δ is a *termination flag*: if $\delta = \downarrow$ then the command always terminates.

With these intended meanings of τ, σ and δ, there is a natural partial order on types which is contravariant in its first component and covariant in its second and third:

$$(\tau, \sigma, \delta)cmd \leq (\tau', \sigma', \delta')cmd \text{ if } \tau' \sqsubseteq_{\mathcal{P}} \tau \text{ and } \sigma \sqsubseteq_{\mathcal{P}} \sigma' \text{ and } \delta \leq \delta'$$

This relation is not used in the type system, but is used in the statement of e.g. the subject reduction property below.

For elements of $\mathcal{P}$ (the first two components of a command type in particular) we define the first and second projections in the obvious way: $fst(i, a) = i$ and $fst(\bot_{\mathcal{P}}) = \bot_{\mathcal{L}}$; $snd(i, a) = a$ and $snd(\bot_{\mathcal{P}}) = \bot_{\mathcal{S}} = b$.

Rules of the security type system are displayed in Figure 5, where we drop the subscript for the relation $\sqsubseteq_{\mathcal{P}}$.

Explicit flows are handled with rules for expressions, rules T-ASSIG, and T-OUT, while implicit flows are treated in T-IF, T-WHILE and T-FOR which demand that their body is at least as high as their guard level.

Most of the action takes place in the sequential composition rules. The interesting case is T-SEQ2 where the termination effect σ_1 of C_1 is an s-secret, and C_1 is indeed potentially nonterminating. This means that we cannot allow arbitrary assignments in C_2 since these might leak information about the s-secrets which affected the termination of C_1. Thus the write effect of C_2 is constrained so that it does not write below σ_1, the termination effect of C_1. For rule T-SEQ1 we are more liberal, since either the guards do not depend on s-secrets, or C_1 is always terminating.

The same reasoning is applied to while and for loops – their execution may be a sequential composition of the body of the loop and the loop itself.

$$\frac{}{\vdash n : \tau}\text{T-CONST} \qquad \frac{\Gamma(x) = \tau\ var}{\vdash x : \tau}\text{T-VAREXP}$$

$$\frac{\vdash e : \tau' \qquad \tau' \sqsubseteq \tau}{\vdash e : \tau}\text{T-SUBEXP} \qquad \frac{\vdash e_1 : \tau \qquad \vdash e_2 : \tau}{\vdash e_1\ op\ e_2 : \tau}\text{T-BINOP}$$

$$\frac{}{\vdash \mathbf{skip} : (\top_{\mathcal{P}}, \bot_{\mathcal{P}}, \downarrow)cmd}\text{T-SKIP} \qquad \frac{\vdash e : \tau \qquad \Gamma(x) = \tau\ var}{\vdash x := e : (\tau, \bot_{\mathcal{P}}, \downarrow)cmd}\text{T-ASSIG}$$

$$\frac{\vdash e : \tau \qquad fst(\tau) \sqsubseteq_{\mathcal{L}} i}{\vdash \mathbf{output}_i(e) : ((i, s), \bot_{\mathcal{P}}, \downarrow)cmd}\text{T-OUT}$$

$$\frac{\vdash C_i : (\tau_i, \sigma_i, \delta_i)cmd \qquad snd(\sigma_1) = b \quad \text{or} \quad \delta_1 = \downarrow}{\vdash C_1; C_2 : (\tau_1 \sqcap \tau_2, \sigma_1 \sqcup \sigma_2, \delta_1 \sqcup \delta_2)cmd}\text{T-SEQ1}$$

$$\frac{\vdash C_i : (\tau_i, \sigma_i, \delta_i)cmd \qquad \sigma_1 \sqsubseteq \tau_2 \qquad snd(\sigma_1) = s \qquad \delta_1 = \uparrow}{\vdash C_1; C_2 : (\tau_1 \sqcap \tau_2, \sigma_1 \sqcup \sigma_2, \uparrow)cmd}\text{T-SEQ2}$$

$$\frac{\vdash e : \theta \qquad \vdash C_i : (\tau_i, \sigma_i, \delta_i)cmd \qquad \theta \sqsubseteq \tau_i}{\vdash \mathbf{if}\ e\ \mathbf{then}\ C_1\ \mathbf{else}\ C_2 : (\tau_1 \sqcap \tau_2, \sigma_1 \sqcup \sigma_2 \sqcup \theta, \delta_1 \sqcup \delta_2)cmd}\text{T-IF}$$

$$\frac{\vdash e : \theta \qquad \vdash C : (\tau, \sigma, \delta)cmd \qquad \theta \sqsubseteq \tau \qquad snd(\sigma) = s \Rightarrow \sigma \sqsubseteq \tau}{\vdash \mathbf{while}\ e\ \mathbf{do}\ C : (\tau, \sigma \sqcup \theta, \uparrow)cmd}\text{T-WHILE}$$

$$\frac{\vdash e : \theta \qquad \vdash C : (\tau, \sigma, \delta)cmd \qquad \theta \sqsubseteq \tau \qquad snd(\sigma) = s \wedge \delta = \uparrow \Rightarrow \sigma \sqsubseteq \tau}{\vdash \mathbf{for}\ e\ \mathbf{do}\ C : (\tau, \sigma, \delta)cmd}\text{T-FOR}$$

Fig. 5. The security type system

4.2 Type Soundness

In this section we prove some results about well typed programs with regard to the type system in Figure 5. The main proposition establishes that the type system indeed enforces the secret-sensitive noninterference property we defined in Section 3.

Proofs of the following results are only sketched here. A full version of the proofs can be found in the technical report corresponding to the present paper [DS09].

The first property is the standard notion of *subject reduction* which guarantees that execution preserves types.

Theorem 1 (Subject reduction). *If* $\vdash C : (\tau, \sigma, \delta)cmd$ *and* $\langle M, C \rangle \xrightarrow{u} \langle M', C' \rangle$, *then* $\vdash C' : (\tau', \sigma', \delta')cmd$ *with* $(\tau', \sigma', \delta')cmd \leq (\tau, \sigma, \delta)cmd$.

Proof. We proceed by induction on the typing derivation, and then by case analysis on the last rule of the operational semantics. □

We need some preliminary lemmas in order to prove the SSNI enforcement. The following lemmas (using the terminology from [VSI96]) confirm that the informal definitions we gave about both components of a command type in Section 4.1 are enforced by the type system.

Lemma 3 (Simple security). *If* $\vdash e : \tau$ *then every variable occurring in e has type τ' var where $\tau' \sqsubseteq \tau$.*

Lemma 4 (Confinement). *If* $\vdash C : (\tau, \sigma, \delta)cmd$, *then every variable assigned to in program C has type θ var with $\tau \sqsubseteq \theta$.*

Lemma 5 (Guard safety). *If* $\vdash C : (\tau, \sigma, \delta)cmd$, *then every while loop or conditional guard in program C has type θ var with $\theta \sqsubseteq \sigma$.*

Lemma 6 (Termination). *If* $\vdash C : (\tau, \sigma, \downarrow)cmd$, *then C terminates on all memories.*

These four lemmas can be easily proved by induction on the typing derivation.

In the formal development that follows for simplicity's sake we only treat the case of the three point lattice in Figure 1. The following results can be extended to the general case: for a given clearance level i in $\mathcal{L}$, as was depicted in the example of *finance*'s perspective in Figure 4, the refinement of $\mathcal{L}$ can be rethought of as a three point lattice - *low* level, *bhigh* and *shigh* secrets.

Proposition 3 (Noninterference of well typed commands)
If a command C is typable, i.e., $\vdash C : (\tau, \sigma, \delta)cmd$, *then C satisfies SSNI.*

Proof. (Sketch; see technical report [DS09] for details) We use the proof technique provided by Corollary 1. In the construction of the specific bisimulations we adapt the proof from [BC01]. The first step is to show that $\vdash C : (\tau, \sigma, \delta)cmd$ implies $\langle C, M \rangle \cong_i \langle C, N \rangle$ for all levels i, to have the s-TSNI property of Definition 9. The interesting case is $i = low$ since $i = high$ is vacuous (memories and commands are in this case equal).

A command C is said to be *shigh* or *bhigh* if there exists τ and σ such that $\vdash C : (\tau, \sigma, \delta)cmd$ with respectively $\tau = shigh$ or $bhigh \sqsubseteq \tau$. We show that $\vdash C : (\tau, \sigma, \delta)cmd$ implies $\langle C, M \rangle \cong_l \langle C, N \rangle$ for all M and N that are equal on their low and bhigh parts. To do this we define a relation $\mathcal{R}_1 : \langle M, C \rangle \mathcal{R}_1 \langle N, D \rangle$ iff C and D are typable, $M^l = N^l$ and $M|_b^l = N|_b^l$, and one of the following four conditions holds:

(i) C and D are *shigh*;   (ii) $C = D$
(iii) $C = C_1; C_2$, $D = D_1; C_2$ with $\langle M, C_1 \rangle \mathcal{R}_1 \langle N, D_1 \rangle$ and C_2 is *shigh*
(iv) C is *shigh*, $D = D_1; D_2$ with $\langle M, \mathbf{skip} \rangle \mathcal{R}_1 \langle N, D_1 \rangle$ and D_2 is *shigh*

We then show that $\mathcal{R}_1$ is a l-TSB by induction on the definition of $\mathcal{R}_1$, and conclude using Proposition 1. By Clause (ii) and Proposition 1, we have that in well typed programs, there is no flow from $shigh$ data to $bhigh$ and low data.

The next step is to prove that the type system ensures TINI concerning the $bhigh$ data. We proceed in a similar way, providing a l-TIB $\mathcal{R}_2$ over configurations. The relation $\mathcal{R}_2$ is defined: $\langle M, C \rangle \mathcal{R}_2 \langle N, D \rangle$ iff C and D are typable, $M^l = N^l$, and one of the following holds:

(i) C and D are $bhigh$ (ii) $C = D$

(iii) $\langle M, C \rangle \mathcal{R}'_2 \langle N, D \rangle$, where the relation $\mathcal{R}'_2$ is defined inductively as:

$$\frac{C, D \ bhigh}{\langle M, C; C' \rangle \ \mathcal{R}'_2 \ \langle N, D; C' \rangle} \text{R1} \qquad \frac{\langle M, C \rangle \ \mathcal{R}'_2 \ \langle N, D \rangle}{\langle N, C; C' \rangle \ \mathcal{R}'_2 \ \langle N, D; C' \rangle} \text{R2}$$

By Clause (ii) and Proposition 2, we then have the TINI property of well typed programs concerning their $bhigh$ data: there is no flow from $bhigh$ data to low data except via the termination channel. $\qquad \square$

5   Correlation Leaks

In this section we mention a weakness in the definition of secret-sensitive noninterference which allows the attacker to observe *correlations* between big and small secrets. We show how the definition can be strengthened to remove such correlations, and conjecture that the type-system guarantees correlation-freedom without need for modification.

Suppose that b is $bhigh$ and s is $shigh$ (in the lattice in Figure 1). Somewhat surprisingly the program $output_{low}(b == s)$ is secret-sensitive noninterfering (note though that it is not typeable). This is because the low observer can say nothing about the value of e.g. s in isolation. The problem is that although the observer cannot deduce anything about the individual kinds of secret, he can deduce information about their *correlation* (in this example whether they are equal or not).

To eliminate the possibility of learning something about the correlation of big and small secrets we need to demand that the knowledge learnt about big and small secrets together is the same as for the combined knowledge learnt about them independently. To express this precisely we need some additional notation.

In the definitions of secret-sensitive noninterference we have dealt with knowledge as sets of projections of memories. We say that a memory M is *full* if $dom(M)$ is the set of all variables. In order to easily compare and combine knowledge sets we need to work with full memories. Define $M^\star$ to be the set of full memories obtainable by completing M:

$$M^\star = \{N \mid N|_{dom(M)} = M, N \text{ is full}\}.$$

Now lift $\cdot^\star$ to sets of memories K in the natural way by defining

$$K^\star = \bigcup_{M \in K} M^\star$$

Definition 12 (Correlation Freedom). *A program* C *is* Correlation Free *if for all* $\vec{v} \in$ $Obs_i(C, M^i)$, *we have* $k_i^{bs}(C, M^i, \vec{v})^\star = k_i^b(C, M^i, \vec{v})^\star \cap k_i^s(C, M^i, \vec{v})^\star$, *where* $k_i^{bs}(C, M^i, \vec{v}) = \{M|^i \mid M \in k_i(C, M^i, \vec{v})\}$ *and* $M|^i$ *is the complement of* M^i *– i.e., the projection of* M *to the variables* not *visible at level* i.

In the case that C is secret-sensitive noninterfering we can show that this condition is equivalent to $k_i^{bs}(C, M^i, \vec{v})^\star = k_i^b(C, M^i, \vec{v})^\star$, which says that nothing more is learnt about the big and small secrets together than can be deduced from the big secrets alone.

Conjecture 1. Well-typed programs are correlation free.

We leave the proof of this conjecture to further work; the intuition here is that any "correlation information" will always be typed as s-level data, and hence cannot be leaked at all.

6   Conclusions

In this article we provided a way to refine an arbitrary complex security lattice in order to distinguish two levels of secret, the big secrets b and the small ones s. Big secrets can be handled more liberally on the grounds that they can be made sufficiently large and random for slow leakage to be tolerable. We introduced an accompanying notion of secret-sensitive noninterference which combines the relative merits of termination-sensitive and termination-insensitive noninterference. We illustrated the use of the definition in the soundness argument for a simple type system for verifying secret-sensitive noninterference.

Related Work. As mentioned previously, the starting point of this work is [AHSS08]. Our interpretation of the results there is that we need to treat different kinds of secrets in different ways, and to our knowledge this paper is the first to do so in a noninterference setting. It is, however, relatively common to give a special treatment to cryptographic keys as compared to other kinds of secret – e.g. [AHS06] – but usually the goal here is to deal with integrity (a key cannot be modified using a low value) or freshness (a key cannot be used more than once).

Our type system is essentially a fusion of a type-based version of Denning's system [VSI96], and a stricter system based on [BC01]. The latter system is stricter than a Denning-style analysis for quite a different purpose: to deal with multi-threaded programs. Our system, in a sequential setting, improves on [BC01] by additionally tracking whether a program is terminating.

Further Work. A natural and interesting next step would be to combine such a type system with cryptographic primitives (e.g. [Vol00][LV05][AHS06]). The notion of "big" and "small" secrets have a natural interpretation in the cryptographic setting, since "big" secrets correspond to e.g. cryptographic keys. In such a setting it might also be important to handle "size integrity", so that one could know that a variable is not only independent of small secrets, but that it *is* a big secret.

Acknowledgements. Thanks to Andrei Sabelfeld for pointing out the correlation problem discussed in Section 5, and to Niklas Broberg, David Pichardie, Thomas Jensen and the anonymous referees for very helpful comments on an earlier draft. This work was partly supported by grants from the Swedish funding agencies SSF, Vinnova (The Swedish Governmental Agency for Innovation Systems), VR, and by the European IST-2005-015905 MOBIUS project.

References

[AHS06]   Askarov, A., Hedin, D., Sabelfeld, A.: Cryptographically-masked flows. In: Yi, K. (ed.) SAS 2006. LNCS, vol. 4134, pp. 353–369. Springer, Heidelberg (2006)

[AHSS08]   Askarov, A., Hunt, S., Sabelfeld, A., Sands, D.: Termination-insensitive noninterference leaks more than just a bit. In: Jajodia, S., Lopez, J. (eds.) ESORICS 2008. LNCS, vol. 5283. Springer, Heidelberg (2008)

[AS07]   Askarov, A., Sabelfeld, A.: Gradual release: Unifying declassification, encryption and key release policies. In: Proc. IEEE Symp. on Security and Privacy, pp. 207–221 (May 2007)

[BB03]   Barnes, J., Barnes, J.G.: High Integrity Software: The SPARK Approach to Safety and Security. Addison-Wesley Longman Publishing Co., Inc., Amsterdam (2003)

[BC01]   Boudol, G., Castellani, I.: Noninterference for concurrent programs. In: Orejas, F., Spirakis, P.G., van Leeuwen, J. (eds.) ICALP 2001. LNCS, vol. 2076, pp. 382–395. Springer, Heidelberg (2001)

[CH04]   Chapman, R., Hilton, A.: Enforcing security and safety models with an information flow analysis tool. ACM SIGAda Ada Letters 24(4), 39–46 (2004)

[DD77]   Denning, D.E., Denning, P.J.: Certification of programs for secure information flow. CACM 20(7), 504–513 (1977)

[Den76]   Denning, D.E.: A lattice model of secure information flow. Comm. of the ACM 19(5), 236–243 (1976)

[DS09]   Demange, D., Sands, D.: All secrets great and small. Technical report, Chalmers University of Technology, Sweden, Extended Version (2009)

[LV05]   Laud, P., Vene, V.: A type system for computationally secure information flow. In: Liśkiewicz, M., Reischuk, R. (eds.) FCT 2005. LNCS, vol. 3623, pp. 365–377. Springer, Heidelberg (2005)

[MZZ+08]   Myers, A.C., Zheng, L., Zdancewic, S., Chong, S., Nystrom, N.: Jif: Java information flow. Software release (July 2001-2008),
           http://www.cs.cornell.edu/jif

[Sim03]   Simonet, V.: The Flow Caml system. Software release (July 2003),
           http://cristal.inria.fr/~simonet/soft/flowcaml/

[Smi01]   Smith, G.: A new type system for secure information flow. In: Proc. IEEE Computer Security Foundations Workshop, pp. 115–125 (June 2001)

[Vol00]   Volpano, D.: Secure introduction of one-way functions. In: CSFW 2000: Proceedings of the 13th IEEE workshop on Computer Security Foundations, p. 246. IEEE Computer Society, Washington (2000)

[VS97]   Volpano, D., Smith, G.: Eliminating covert flows with minimum typings. In: Proc. IEEE Computer Security Foundations Workshop, pp. 156–168 (June 1997)

[VSI96]   Volpano, D., Smith, G., Irvine, C.: A sound type system for secure flow analysis. J. Computer Security 4(3), 167–187 (1996)

Type-Based Automated Verification of Authenticity in Cryptographic Protocols

Daisuke Kikuchi and Naoki Kobayashi

Graduate School of Information Sciences, Tohoku University
{kikuchi,koba}@kb.ecei.tohoku.ac.jp

Abstract. Gordon and Jeffrey have proposed a type and effect system for checking authenticity in cryptographic protocols. The type system reduces the protocol verification problem to the type checking problem, but protocols must be manually annotated with non-trivial types and effects. To automate the verification of cryptographic protocols, we modify Gordon and Jeffrey's type system and develop a type inference algorithm. Key modifications for enabling automated type inference are introduction of fractional effects and replacement of typing rules with syntax-directed ones. We have implemented and tested a prototype protocol verifier based on our type system.

1 Introduction

Gordon and Jeffrey [1,2,3] developed a series of type systems for verifying authenticity in security protocols. The required authenticity properties are described by using Woo and Lam's correspondence assertions [4], and Gordon and Jeffrey's type systems guarantee that well-typed processes (describing security protocols) satisfy the correspondence assertions. The type systems reduce the problem of verifying authenticity properties in security protocols to the type checking problem. Based on the type systems, Haack and Jeffrey implemented a verifier for cryptographic protocols [5].

One of the main shortcomings of their type systems was that protocols must be explicitly annotated with types. Since the types may contain complex information about how communication channels, cryptographic keys, and nonces should be used in protocols, it seems difficult for non-expert users (especially those who are not familiar with the type systems) to supply such annotations.

In our previous work [6], we have extended Gordon and Jeffrey's type system for checking correspondence assertions [1] in the π-calculus (without cryptographic primitives), the first and simplest one in the series of their type systems, and developed a polynomial-time type inference algorithm for it. The key idea of the extension was to introduce *fractional* effects, which allowed us to reduce the type inference problem to linear programming over rational numbers, rather than integer linear programming.

In this paper, we extend our previous work [6], and show that a similar technique can be used to develop a type inference algorithm for a variant of Gordon

G. Castagna (Ed.): ESOP 2009, LNCS 5502, pp. 222–236, 2009.

and Jeffrey's type system for checking authenticity in cryptographic protocols [2]. The key technique for enabling efficient type inference is to allow fractional effects, as in our previous work [6]. Some new challenges, however, arise in dealing with cryptographic primitives [2]. First, there are two rules for each message/process constructor in their type system: one for trusted data, and the other for untrusted data.[1] Second, there is an explicit cast operation for capturing the role of nonces in cryptographic protocols. These features make even the simple type inference (without effects) non-trivial. We modify Gordon and Jeffrey's type system [2] to remove those problems, so that there is only one rule for each message/process constructor, and no explicit cast operation is required. That modification allows us to develop a type inference algorithm in a manner similar to our previous work [6]. Although the expressive power of our type system is incomparable to that of Gordon and Jeffrey's type system [2] (there are processes typable in their type system but not in our type system, and vice versa), all the examples discussed in [2] are typable in our type system (modulo an extension with labeled variants).

The rest of this paper is structured as follows. Section 2 introduces SpiCA, an extension of the Spi-calculus with correspondence assertions, which is used for describing cryptographic protocols. Section 3 introduces our new type system for checking authenticity of cryptographic protocols. Section 4 describes a type inference algorithm, which serves as an algorithm for automatic verification of authenticity in cryptographic protocols. Section 5 reports preliminary experiments. Section 6 discusses related work and Section 7 concludes. A longer version of this paper is available from http://www.kb.ecei.tohoku.ac.jp/~koba/esop09-long.pdf.

2   SpiCA: Spi-Calculus with Correspondence Assertions

In this section, we introduce the language SpiCA, an extension of the Spi-calculus [8] with correspondence assertions. The language is similar to Gordon and Jeffrey's calculus [2]: our language is obtained from it by removing type annotations and cast operations.

2.1   Syntax

Definition 1 (messages, processes). The sets of *messages* and *processes*, ranged over by M and P respectively, are given by:

$$K, M, N ::= x \mid (M_1, M_2) \mid \mathbf{inl}(M) \mid \mathbf{inr}(M) \mid \{M\}_K$$
$$P, Q ::= \mathbf{0} \mid M!N \mid M?x.P \mid (P_1 \mid P_2) \mid *P \mid (\nu x)P \mid \mathbf{check}\ x\ is\ M.P$$
$$\mid \mathbf{decrypt}\ M\ is\ \{x\}_K.P \mid \mathbf{case}\ M\ is\ \mathbf{inl}(x).P\ is\ \mathbf{inr}(y).Q$$
$$\mid \mathbf{split}\ M\ is\ (x, y).P \mid \mathbf{begin}\ M.P \mid \mathbf{end}\ M.P$$

Here, the meta-variables x and y range over the set $\mathcal{N}$ of variables.

---

[1] In a subsequent paper [7], Gordon and Jeffrey uses subtyping and merges the two rules into one. The subsumption rule still makes type inference difficult.

The variable x is bound in $M?x.P$, $(\nu x)P$ and **decrypt** M is $\{x\}_K.P$. x and y are bound in **case** M is $\mathbf{inl}(x).P$ is $\mathbf{inr}(y).Q$ and **split** M is $(x,y).P$. We write $[M/x]P$ for the process obtained by replacing x in P with M.

(M_1, M_2) is a pair consisting of M_1 and M_2. $\mathbf{inl}(M)$ and $\mathbf{inr}(M)$ are constructors for sums. $\{M\}_K$ is the message obtained by encrypting M with key K. Here, we assume perfect encryption; information about an encrypted message can be obtained only if the key is known.

The process $\mathbf{0}$ is an inaction. The process $M!N$ sends the message N on the channel M. The process $M?x.P$ waits to receive a message on channel M, binds x to it, and then behaves like P. $(P_1 \mid P_2)$ runs P_1 and P_2 in parallel, while $*P$ runs infinitely many copies of P in parallel. The process $(\nu x)P$ creates a fresh name (which may be used as a channel, a nonce, or a symmetric key), binds x to it, and behaves like P. The process **check** x is $M.P$ behaves like P if the values of x and M are the same; otherwise the process is aborted. The process **decrypt** M is $\{x\}_K.P$ decrypts the message M with the symmetric-key K. If the decryption succeeds, the process binds x to the decrypted message, and behaves like P; otherwise, the process is aborted. The process **case** M is $\mathbf{inl}(x).P$ is $\mathbf{inr}(y).Q$ behaves like $[N/x]P$ if M is of the form $\mathbf{inl}(N)$, and behaves like $[N/y]Q$ if M is of the form $\mathbf{inr}(N)$. The process **split** M is $(x,y).P$ splits the pair $M = (M_1, M_2)$, binds x to M_1 and y to M_2, and behaves like P.

The processes **begin** $M.P$ and **end** $M.P$ are special processes for declaring correspondence assertions; **begin** $M.P$ raises a "begin M" event and then behaves like P, while **end** $M.P$ raises an "end M" event and then behaves like P. It is expected (and will be guaranteed by our type system) that whenever an end-event occurs, a corresponding begin-event must have occurred before. Authenticity properties (like "if Alice receives a message m, then Bob must have sent the message") are reduced to such relations between begin- and end-events: See Example 1 below.

Example 1. Consider the following process *System*, taken from [2]:

$$System \stackrel{\triangle}{=} (\nu key)(*Sender(ch, key) \mid *Receiver(ch, key))$$
$$Sender(ch, key) \stackrel{\triangle}{=} ch?n.(\nu msg)\mathbf{begin}\ msg.ch!\{(msg, n)\}_{key}$$
$$Receiver(ch, key) \stackrel{\triangle}{=} (\nu non)(ch!non \mid ch?ctext.\mathbf{decrypt}\ ctext\ is\ \{x\}_{key}.$$
$$\mathbf{split}\ x\ is\ (m, non').\mathbf{check}\ non\ is\ non'.\mathbf{end}\ m)$$

System creates a shared key *key*, and runs infinitely many copies of *Sender*(*ch*, *key*) and *Receiver*(*ch*, *key*) in parallel. Here, *ch* is a public communication channel, on which an attacker may also send/receive messages. The process *Receiver*(*ch*, *key*) creates a fresh name *non* (which is often called a *nonce* in the terminology of security protocols) and sends it on *ch*. The process *Sender*(*ch*, *key*) then receives the nonce and creates a new message. It then raises a "**begin** *msg*"-event and sends the cyphertext $\{(msg, non)\}_{key}$ on *ch*. Here, the event "**begin** *msg*" represents the fact that the process certainly sent the message *msg*. *Receiver*(*ch*, *key*) then receives the cyphertext, decrypts it (as a result, *m* and *non'* are bound to *msg* and *non*), and checks that the second element of the decrypted message matches the nonce it has sent before. The receiver then raises the event **end** *msg*, meaning that it has received the message *msg*. The correspondence between **end** *msg* and **begin** *msg*, (i.e., the property that whenever an "**end** *msg*"-event happens, a "**begin** *msg*"-event must have occurred before) assures that each time *Receiver*(*ch*, *key*) executes **end** *msg*, the message *msg* has certainly been sent by *Sender*(*ch*, *key*).

Note that the nonce check "**check** *non is non'.* · · ·" in the protocol above is essential; if there is no such check, then an attacker can confuse the receiver by duplicating a message $\{(msg, non)\}_{key}$ (by running $ch?x.(ch!x \mid ch!x)$, for instance).   □

2.2   Semantics

The operational semantics is given in Figure 1. (The rules for **split**, **case** and replications are omitted.) Here, a state is represented as a triple $\langle \Psi, E, N \rangle$, where Ψ is a multiset of processes, N is a set of names, and E is a multiset of messages M such that the event **begin** M has been raised but **end** L has not. In other words, E describes capabilities (or, permissions) to raise end-events.

$$\langle \Psi \uplus \{x?y.P, x!M\}, E, N \rangle \longrightarrow \langle \Psi \uplus \{[M/y]P\}, E, N \rangle$$
$$\langle \Psi \uplus \{P \mid Q\}, E, N \rangle \longrightarrow \langle \Psi \uplus \{P, Q\}, E, N \rangle$$
$$\langle \Psi \uplus \{(\nu x)P\}, E, N \rangle \longrightarrow \langle \Psi \uplus \{[y/x]P\}, E, N \cup \{y\} \rangle \ (y \notin N)$$
$$\langle \Psi \uplus \{\mathbf{check} \ x \ is \ x.P\}, E, N \rangle \longrightarrow \langle \Psi \uplus \{P\}, E, N \rangle$$
$$\langle \Psi \uplus \{\mathbf{decrypt} \ \{M\}_K \ is \ \{x\}_K.P\}, E, N \rangle \longrightarrow \langle \Psi \uplus \{[M/x]P\}, E, N \rangle$$
$$\langle \Psi \uplus \{\mathbf{begin} \ L.P\}, E, N \rangle \longrightarrow \langle \Psi \uplus \{P\}, E \uplus \{L\}, N \rangle$$
$$\langle \Psi \uplus \{\mathbf{end} \ L.P\}, E \uplus \{L\}, N \rangle \longrightarrow \langle \Psi \uplus \{P\}, E, N \rangle$$

Fig. 1. Operational Semantics

We write $\langle \Psi, E, N \rangle \longrightarrow$ **Error** if **end** $L.P \in \Psi$ but $L \notin E$. We write $\longrightarrow^*$ for the reflexive and transitive closure of $\longrightarrow$. The required correspondence between begin-events and end-events is stated as follows.

Definition 2 (safety). A process P is *safe* if $\langle \{P\}, \emptyset, N \rangle \not\longrightarrow^*$ **Error**, where N is the set of free names in P.

For security protocols, the safety of the process running protocols alone is not sufficient; the robust safety defined below means that the process is safe in the presence of attackers running in parallel.

Definition 3 (robust safety). A process P is *robustly safe* if $(P \mid O)$ is safe for any process O that contains no begin/end/check-assertions.

Remark 1. In Gordon and Jeffrey's definition [2], attackers may execute check operations. We removed them, as the check operations do not increase the power of attackers. **check** M *is* $N.P$ can be simulated by **decrypt** $\{x\}_M$ *is* $\{y\}_N.P$.

3   Type System

3.1   Types and Effects

Definition 4 (effects). The sets of *types* and *effects*, ranged over by T and e, are given by:

$$
\begin{aligned}
T \text{ (types)} & ::= \mathbf{N}(e) \mid \mathbf{Key}(T) \mid T_1 \times T_2 \mid T_1 + T_2 \\
e \text{ (effects)} & ::= [A_1 \mapsto r_1, \ldots, A_n \mapsto r_n] \\
A \text{ (atomic effects)} & ::= \mathbf{end}\langle M \rangle \mid \mathbf{chk}\langle \alpha \rangle \\
\alpha \text{ (extended names)} & ::= x \mid i \\
i \text{ (indices)} & ::= 0 \mid 1 \mid 2 \mid \cdots
\end{aligned}
$$

Here, $r_1, \ldots, r_n$ ranges over the set of non-negative rational numbers.

The type $\mathbf{N}(e)$ describes names used as channels, nonces, or cyphertexts. When the type describes a nonce, the effect e describes a capability to raise end-events carried by the nonce. For example, *non* passed through *ch* in Example 1 carries a capability to raise one "**end** *msg*"-event, so that its type is $\mathbf{N}([\mathbf{end}\langle msg \rangle \mapsto 1])$. We often write $\mathbf{Un}$ for $\mathbf{N}([\,])$. The type $\mathbf{Key}(T)$ describes keys used for decrypting messages of type T.

The type $T_1 \times T_2$ describes pairs consisting of messages of types T_1 and T_2. Indices are used to express dependencies of the second element on the first element: For example, $\mathbf{Un} \times \mathbf{N}([\mathbf{end}\langle 0 \rangle \mapsto 1])$ describes a pair (a, b), where b's type is $\mathbf{N}([\mathbf{end}\langle a \rangle \mapsto 1])$. The type corresponds to $(x{:}\mathbf{Un}, \mathbf{N}([\mathbf{end}\langle x \rangle \mapsto 1]))$ in Gordon and Jeffrey's notation [2]. The type $\mathbf{Un} \times (\mathbf{Un} \times \mathbf{N}([\mathbf{end}\langle 0 \rangle \mapsto 1, \mathbf{chk}\langle 1 \rangle \mapsto 1]))$ describes a message of the form $(a, (b, c))$ where a and b have type $\mathbf{Un}$, and c has type $\mathbf{N}([\mathbf{end}\langle b \rangle \mapsto 1, \mathbf{chk}\langle a \rangle \mapsto 1])$. We use the nameless representation of dependent types just for technical convenience for formalizing type inference; in terms of the expressiveness of the type system, the nameless dependent types are equivalent to Gordon and Jeffrey's name dependent types [2].

The type $T_1 + T_2$ describes sums of the form $\mathbf{inl}(M)$ (where M is a message of type T_1) or $\mathbf{inr}(M)$ (where M is a message of type T_2).

An effect $[A_1 \mapsto r_1, \ldots, A_n \mapsto r_n]$ denotes the mapping f from the set of atomic events to the set of rational numbers such that $f(A_i) = r_i$ for $i \in \{1, \ldots, n\}$ and $f(M) = 0$ for $M \notin \{A_1, \ldots, A_n\}$. The atomic effect $\mathbf{end}\langle M \rangle$ denotes a capability to execute "**end** M," while the atomic effect $\mathbf{chk}\langle \alpha \rangle$ denotes a capability to execute **check** α *is* $x.P$. The latter kind of effect is used to guarantee that each nonce can be checked at most once. In the rest of this paper, the words "effects" and "capabilities" are used interchangeably.

Example 2. Names in Example 1 have the following types.

$$
ch : \mathbf{Un} \quad x : \mathbf{N}([\,]) \times \mathbf{N}([\mathbf{end}\langle 0 \rangle \mapsto 1]) \quad key : \mathbf{Key}(\mathbf{N}([\,]) \times \mathbf{N}([\mathbf{end}\langle 0 \rangle \mapsto 1]))
$$

A substitution $[x_1/i_1, \ldots, x_k/i_k]$, denoted by meta-variable θ, is a mapping from indices to names. The substitution, summation, and binary relation $\leq$ on effects are defined by:

$$(\theta e)(A) = \Sigma\{e(A') \mid \theta A' = A\} \qquad (e_1 + e_2)(A) = e_1(A) + e_2(A)$$
$$e \leq e' \Leftrightarrow \forall A.e(A) \leq e'(A)$$

The substitution θT on types is defined by:

$$[x/i]\mathbf{N}(e) = \mathbf{N}([x/i]e) \qquad\qquad [x/i]\mathbf{Key}(T) = \mathbf{Key}([x/i]T)$$
$$[x/i](T_1 \times T_2) = [x/i]T_1 \times [x/(i+1)]T_2 \qquad [x/i](T_1 + T_2) = [x/i]T_1 + [x/i]T_2$$

3.2 Typing Rules

We introduce two type judgment forms: $\Gamma; e \vdash M : T$ for messages and $\Gamma; e \vdash P$ for processes. Here, Γ, called a type environment, is a finite sequence of bindings of names to types. $\Gamma; e \vdash M : T$ means that given names described by Γ and capabilities described by e, one can construct a message M of type T. For example, we have

$$x : \mathbf{Un}, y : \mathbf{Un}; [\mathbf{end}\langle x\rangle \mapsto 1] \vdash (x, y) : \mathbf{Un} \times \mathbf{N}([\mathbf{end}\langle 0\rangle \mapsto 1]).$$

In this manner, capabilities (to raise end-events or check nonces) can be attached to a name, and passed to other processes. $\Gamma; e \vdash P$ means that given names described by Γ and capabilities described by e, the process P can be safely executed. For example, $x : \mathbf{Un}, y : \mathbf{Un}; [\mathbf{end}\langle x\rangle \mapsto 1] \vdash \mathbf{end}\ x$ is a valid judgment, but $x : \mathbf{Un}, y : \mathbf{Un}; [\mathbf{end}\langle x\rangle \mapsto 1] \vdash \mathbf{end}\ y$ is invalid since there is no capability to execute $\mathbf{end}\ y$. When we write $\Gamma; e \vdash M : T$ or $\Gamma; e \vdash P$, we implicitly assume that Γ, e, and T are well-formed, in the sense that they do not contain undefined names. For example, when we write "$\Gamma, x{:}T$," only the names bound in Γ may occur in T.

The typing rules for messages are given in Figure 2. In rule MT-VAR, $T + e$ is defined as $\mathbf{N}(e' + e)$ if T is of the form $\mathbf{N}(e')$; otherwise $T + e$ is T. The capabilities e are transferred from the environment to x if x has type $\mathbf{N}(e')$. The role of the rule is similar to that of Gordon and Jeffrey's typing rule for cast-operations [2]. Unlike in Gordon and Jeffrey's type system, however, the transfer of capabilities from the environment to a name is implicitly performed by MT-VAR. The capabilities attached to a name can be extracted at most once by a check operation: see the rule T-CHECK given later.

In rule MT-PAIR, the index 0 in T_2 refers to the first element, so that N must have type $[M/0]T_2$. The other rules are standard.

The typing rules for processes are given in Figure 3. Note that we have only one rule for each process constructor (except T-SUBEF, which can be easily eliminated), while Gordon and Jeffrey's type system [2] had two rules for each process constructor: one for trusted data and the other for untrusted data.

In the figure, $FN(e)$ denotes the set $\bigcup\{FN(A) \mid e(A) > 0\}$, where $FN(A)$ is the set of extended names occurring in A. For example, $FN([\mathbf{end}\langle(x, y)\rangle \mapsto 0.5, \mathbf{end}\langle(y, z)\rangle \mapsto 0]) = \{x, y\}$.

The predicate **pub**(T) used in the figure is defined inductively by:

$$\frac{}{\mathbf{pub}(\mathbf{N}([\,]))} \qquad \frac{\mathbf{pub}(T)}{\mathbf{pub}(\mathbf{Key}(T))}$$

$$\frac{\mathbf{pub}(T_1) \qquad \mathbf{pub}(T_2)}{\mathbf{pub}(T_1 \times T_2)} \qquad \frac{\mathbf{pub}(T_1) \qquad \mathbf{pub}(T_2)}{\mathbf{pub}(T_1 + T_2)}$$

In other words, **pub**(T) holds if T does not carry any effects. The predicate **gen**(T) means that T is of the form $\mathbf{N}([\,])$ or $\mathbf{Key}(T')$.

We explain some of the key typing rules below. A communication channel in our calculus is an untrusted communication device, on which attackers may intercept, duplicate messages, etc. In rules T-OUT and T-IN, therefore, the type of messages sent on a channel must be public, meaning that they must not contain effects. To send a name carrying effects, one must encrypt it; otherwise, an attacker may abuse the effects (or, capabilities) carried by the name. Besides the requirement that it must be public, there is no restriction on the type of messages; thus, well-typed processes may suffer from type mismatch errors at run-time (when executing split and case expressions).

The rule T-PAR splits the capabilities $e_1 + e_2$ into e_1 and e_2 for P_1 and P_2 respectively. In rule T-RES, x is a fresh name, so that a capability to use x as a nonce and check x is added to P.

The rule T-CHECK says that the check-expression extracts the capability e' carried by N, by consuming the capability to check x; the consumption of the capability $\mathbf{chk}\langle x \rangle$ ensures that the capability e' can no longer be extracted. The rules T-BEGIN and T-END say that the begin-expression adds the capability to raise an end-event, while the end-expression consumes the capability to raise an end-event. The rule T-SUBEF allows some capabilities not to be used (so that for a begin-event, there may be no corresponding end-event).

$$\frac{}{\Gamma, x : T \,;\, e \vdash x : T + e} \qquad \text{(MT-VAR)}$$

$$\frac{\Gamma \,;\, e_1 \vdash M : T_1 \qquad \Gamma \,;\, e_2 \vdash N : [M/0]T_2}{\Gamma \,;\, e_1 + e_2 \vdash (M, N) : T_1 \times T_2} \qquad \text{(MT-PAIR)}$$

$$\frac{\Gamma \,;\, e \vdash M : T_1}{\Gamma \,;\, e \vdash \mathbf{inl}(M) : T_1 + T_2} \qquad \text{(MT-INL)}$$

$$\frac{\Gamma \,;\, e \vdash M : T_2}{\Gamma \,;\, e \vdash \mathbf{inr}(M) : T_1 + T_2} \qquad \text{(MT-INR)}$$

$$\frac{\Gamma \,;\, e \vdash M : T \qquad \Gamma \,;\, [\,] \vdash K : \mathbf{Key}(T)}{\Gamma \,;\, e \vdash \{M\}_K : \mathbf{Un}} \qquad \text{(MT-ENCRYPT)}$$

Fig. 2. Typing for Messages

$$\overline{\Gamma\,;\,[\,]\vdash \mathbf{0}} \tag{T-Zero}$$

$$\frac{\Gamma\,;\,[\,]\vdash x:\mathbf{Un}\qquad \Gamma\,;\,e\vdash N:T\qquad \mathbf{pub}(T)}{\Gamma\,;\,e\vdash x!N} \tag{T-Out}$$

$$\frac{\Gamma\,;\,[\,]\vdash x:\mathbf{Un}\qquad \Gamma,y:T\,;\,e\vdash P\qquad \mathbf{pub}(T)\qquad y\notin FN(e)}{\Gamma\,;\,e\vdash x?y.P} \tag{T-In}$$

$$\frac{\Gamma\,;\,e_1\vdash P_1\qquad \Gamma\,;\,e_2\vdash P_2}{\Gamma\,;\,e_1+e_2\vdash P_1\,|\,P_2} \tag{T-Par}$$

$$\frac{\Gamma\,;\,[\,]\vdash P}{\Gamma\,;\,[\,]\vdash *P} \tag{T-Rep}$$

$$\frac{\Gamma,x:T\,;\,e+[\mathbf{chk}\langle x\rangle\mapsto 1]\vdash P\qquad x\notin FN(e)\qquad \mathbf{gen}(T)}{\Gamma\,;\,e\vdash (\nu x)P} \tag{T-Res}$$

$$\frac{\Gamma\,;\,[\,]\vdash x:\mathbf{Un}\qquad \Gamma\,;\,[\,]\vdash N:\mathbf{N}(e')\qquad \Gamma\,;\,e+e'\vdash P}{\Gamma\,;\,e+[\mathbf{chk}\langle x\rangle\mapsto 1]\vdash \mathbf{check}\ x\ is\ N.P} \tag{T-Check}$$

$$\frac{\Gamma\,;\,[\,]\vdash M:\mathbf{Un}\qquad \Gamma\,;\,[\,]\vdash K:\mathbf{Key}(T)\qquad \Gamma,y:T\,;\,e\vdash P\qquad y\notin FN(e)}{\Gamma\,;\,e\vdash \mathbf{decrypt}\ M\ is\ \{y\}_K.P} \tag{T-Decrypt}$$

$$\frac{\Gamma\,;\,[\,]\vdash M:T_1+T_2\qquad \Gamma,y:T_1\,;\,e\vdash P_1\qquad \Gamma,z:T_2\,;\,e\vdash P_2\qquad y,z\notin FN(e)}{\Gamma\,;\,e\vdash \mathbf{case}\ M\ is\ \mathbf{inl}(y).P_1\ is\ \mathbf{inr}(z).P_2} \tag{T-Case}$$

$$\frac{\Gamma\,;\,[\,]\vdash M:T_1\times T_2\qquad \Gamma,y:T_1,z:[y/0]T_2\,;\,e\vdash P\qquad y,z\notin FN(e)}{\Gamma\,;\,e\vdash \mathbf{split}\ M\ is\ (y,z).P} \tag{T-Split}$$

$$\frac{\Gamma\,;\,e+[\mathbf{end}\langle M\rangle\mapsto 1]\vdash P\qquad FN(M)\subseteq \mathbf{dom}(\Gamma)}{\Gamma\,;\,e\vdash \mathbf{begin}\ M.P} \tag{T-Begin}$$

$$\frac{\Gamma\,;\,e\vdash P\qquad FN(M)\subseteq \mathbf{dom}(\Gamma)}{\Gamma\,;\,e+[\mathbf{end}\langle M\rangle\mapsto 1]\vdash \mathbf{end}\ M.P} \tag{T-End}$$

$$\frac{\Gamma\,;\,e'\vdash P\qquad e'\leq e}{\Gamma\,;\,e\vdash P} \tag{T-SubEf}$$

Fig. 3. Typing for Processes

Example 3. Recall Example 1. *Sender*(ch, key) is typed as follows.

$$\cfrac{\cfrac{\cfrac{\cfrac{\cfrac{\Gamma_1 ; [] \vdash key : T_2 \qquad \cfrac{\Gamma_1 ; [] \vdash msg : \mathbf{Un} \quad \Gamma_1 ; e \vdash n : \mathbf{N}(e)}{\Gamma_1 ; e \vdash (msg, n) : T_1}}{\Gamma_1 ; [\mathbf{end}\langle msg \rangle \mapsto 1] \vdash \{(msg, n)\}_{key} : \mathbf{Un}}}{\Gamma_1 ; [\mathbf{end}\langle msg \rangle \mapsto 1] \vdash ch!\{(msg, n)\}_{key}} \qquad \Gamma_1 ; [] \vdash ch : \mathbf{Un}}{\Gamma_1 ; [\mathbf{chk}\langle msg \rangle \mapsto 1, \mathbf{end}\langle msg \rangle \mapsto 1] \vdash ch!\{msg, n\}_{key}}}{\Gamma_1 ; [\mathbf{chk}\langle msg \rangle \mapsto 1] \vdash \mathbf{begin}\ msg. \cdots}}{ch : \mathbf{Un}, key : T, n : \mathbf{Un}; [] \vdash (\nu msg) \cdots}}{ch : \mathbf{Un}, key : T ; [] \vdash Sender(ch, key)}$$

Here, $T_1 = \mathbf{Un} \times \mathbf{N}([\mathbf{end}\langle 0 \rangle \mapsto 1])$, $T_2 = \mathbf{Key}(T_1)$, $e = [\mathbf{end}\langle msg \rangle \mapsto 1]$ and $\Gamma_1 = ch : \mathbf{Un}, key : T, n : \mathbf{Un}, msg : \mathbf{Un}$.

The sub-process $ch?ctext. \cdots$ of *Receiver*(ch, key) is typed as follows.

$$\cfrac{\cfrac{\cfrac{\cfrac{\Gamma_3 ; [] \vdash non : \mathbf{Un} \quad \Gamma_3 ; [] \vdash non' : \mathbf{N}(e') \quad \Gamma_3 ; e' \vdash \mathbf{end}\ m}{\Gamma_3 ; [\mathbf{chk}\langle non \rangle \mapsto 1] \vdash \mathbf{check}\ non\ is\ non'. \cdots}}{\Gamma_2, x : \mathbf{Un} \times \mathbf{N}([\mathbf{end}\langle 0 \rangle \mapsto 1]) ; [\mathbf{chk}\langle non \rangle \mapsto 1] \vdash \mathbf{split}\ x\ is\ (m, non'). \cdots}}{\Gamma_2 ; [\mathbf{chk}\langle non \rangle \mapsto 1] \vdash \mathbf{decrypt}\ ctext\ is\ \{x\}_{key}. \cdots}}{ch : \mathbf{Un}, key : T_2, non : \mathbf{Un}; [\mathbf{chk}\langle non \rangle \mapsto 1] \vdash ch?ctext. \cdots}$$

Here, $e' = [\mathbf{end}\langle m \rangle \mapsto 1]$, $\Gamma_2 = ch : \mathbf{Un}, key : T, non : \mathbf{Un}, ctext : \mathbf{Un}$ and $\Gamma_3 = \Gamma_2, m : \mathbf{Un}, non' : \mathbf{N}([\mathbf{end}\langle m \rangle \mapsto 1])$. From this, we can get $ch : \mathbf{Un}, key : T ; [] \vdash Receiver(ch, key)$.

The entire system *System* is typed as $ch : \mathbf{Un} ; [] \vdash System$. □

3.3   Type Soundness

The soundness of our type system is stated as follows.

Theorem 1 (robust safety). *If* $x_1{:}\mathbf{Un}, \ldots x_n{:}\mathbf{Un}; [] \vdash P$, *then* P *is robustly safe.*

The theorem says that if $x_1{:}\mathbf{Un}, \ldots x_n{:}\mathbf{Un}{:}[] \vdash P$ holds, then the correspondence assertions in P hold even in the presence of attackers.

The rest of this subsection sketches the proof of the above theorem. Gordon and Jeffrey [2] proved the robust safety by showing (i) any well-typed process is safe, and (ii) any attacker (an opponent process) is well-typed. Our proof is similar, but a few modifications are required, because of the following points:

- An attacker process is not necessarily typed in our type system.
- The safety of a well-typed process usually follows from the fact that typing is preserved by reductions. Our type system does not, however, satisfy the type preservation property (recall that the rules T-IN and T-OUT imposes no restriction on the type of messages, except the condition $\mathbf{pub}(T)$).

To remedy the problems above, we first extend the type system. We add the following rules for subtyping and subsumption to the type system presented so far.

$$\frac{\mathbf{pub}(T) \quad \mathbf{pub}(T')}{T \leq T'} \qquad \frac{\Gamma; e \vdash M : T' \quad T' \leq T}{\Gamma; e \vdash M : T}$$

Let us write $\Gamma; e \vdash_{\mathrm{EX}} M : T$ if $\Gamma; e \vdash M : T$ is derivable in the extended type system. Then, we can prove the following lemmas in a manner similar to [2]:

Lemma 1. *If $\Gamma; [\,] \vdash_{\mathrm{EX}} P$, then P is safe.*

Lemma 2. *If O contains no begin/end/check-expressions and $FN(O) \subseteq \{x_1, \ldots, x_n\}$, then $x_1 : \mathbf{Un}, \ldots, x_n : \mathbf{Un}; [\,] \vdash_{\mathrm{EX}} O$ holds.*

We can now prove Theorem 1.

Proof of Theorem 1 Suppose that $x_1 : \mathbf{Un}, \ldots, x_n : \mathbf{Un}; e \vdash P$ holds. Let O be a process such that $FN(O) \subseteq \{x_1, \ldots, x_n\}$ and O contains no begin/end/check-expressions. It suffices to show that $P \,|\, O$ is safe.

By the definition of the extended type system, we have $x_1 : \mathbf{Un}, \ldots, x_n : \mathbf{Un}; [\,] \vdash_{\mathrm{EX}} P$. By Lemma 2, we have $x_1 : \mathbf{Un}, \ldots, x_n : \mathbf{Un}; [\,] \vdash_{\mathrm{EX}} O$. By rule T-PAR, we obtain $x_1 : \mathbf{Un}, \ldots, x_n : \mathbf{Un}; [\,] \vdash_{\mathrm{EX}} P \,|\, O$. By Lemma 1, $P \,|\, O$ is safe. $\qquad\qquad\square$

3.4 On the Expressive Power of the Type System

The expressive power of our type system is incomparable to that of Gordon and Jeffrey's type system [2]. On one hand, the following process, which uses the name x both as a pair and a sum, is typed under $x : \mathbf{Un}$ in Gordon and Jeffrey's type system, but not in our type system (without the extension).

$$\mathbf{split}\ x\ is\ (y, z).\mathbf{case}\ x\ is\ \mathbf{inl}(y).0\ is\ \mathbf{inr}(z).0$$

On the other hand, consider the following process *HalfCap*.

$$(\nu y)(\nu z)(\mathbf{begin}\ x.(c!\{y\}_k \,|\, d!\{z\}_k)$$
$$|\ c?u.d?v.\mathbf{decrypt}\ u\ is\ \{y'\}_k.\mathbf{decrypt}\ v\ is\ \{z'\}_k.$$
$$\mathbf{check}\ y\ is\ y'.\mathbf{check}\ z\ is\ z'.\mathbf{end}\ x.)$$

The first process raises a begin-event, and passes the capability to raise an end-event through the names y and z. The above process *HalfCap* is typed as follows in our type system:

$$x : \mathbf{Un}, c : \mathbf{Un}, d : \mathbf{Un}, k : \mathbf{Key}(\mathbf{N}([\mathbf{end}\langle x \rangle \mapsto 0.5])); [\,] \vdash HalfCap.$$

P is not, however, typable in Gordon and Jeffrey's type system.

Despite the difference of the expressive power, however, we expect that both the type systems are equally effective for realistic protocols. First, with the extension discussed in Section 3.3, our type system is strictly more expressive than Gordon and Jeffrey's type system: If P is well-typed in their type system, then the process obtained from P by removing type annotations and casts is well-typed in our type system. Second, *HalfCap* given above is an artificial example, and we are not aware of realistic protocols that use fractional capabilities.

4   Type Inference Algorithm

A type inference algorithm can be obtained in the same manner as in our previous work [6]. The algorithm consists of the following steps.

- Step 1: Generate constraints on effects based on the typing rules.
- Step 2: Reduce the constraints on effects into linear inequalities on rational numbers.
- Step 3: Check whether the linear inequalities have a solution.

The algorithm is sound and complete: Given a process P, the algorithm always terminates, and it outputs a type-annotated process if and only if $x_1 : \mathbf{Un}, \ldots, x_n : \mathbf{Un}; [\,] \vdash P$.

For the first step, we first eliminate the rule T-SUBEF by combining it with other rules. For example, the rule T-END can be replaced by:

$$\frac{\Gamma; e' \vdash P \qquad FN(M) \subseteq \mathbf{dom}(\Gamma) \qquad e' + [\mathbf{end}\langle M \rangle \mapsto 1] \le e}{\Gamma; e \vdash \mathbf{end}\ M.P} \quad \text{(T-END')}$$

The resulting typing rules are syntax-directed: there is exactly one rule for each message/process constructor. Based on the typing rules, we can easily generate constraints on type and effect variables, and then reduce them to constraints on effect variables of the following forms:

$$e \le e' \qquad FN(e) \subseteq \{\alpha_1, \ldots, \alpha_n\} \qquad \alpha \notin FN(e)$$

Here, e is an expression constructed from effects, effect variables, $+$, and substitutions.

The second step is also straightforward. We first obtain a set of atomic effects $\{A_1, \ldots, A_m\}$ that may occur in effects. We then replace each effect variable ρ with $[A_1 \mapsto \eta_{\rho,1}, \ldots, A_m \mapsto \eta_{\rho,m}]$ by preparing variables $\eta_{\rho,1}, \ldots, \eta_{\rho,m}$ ranging over rational numbers. We can then reduce each effect to linear inequalities. For example, $\rho_1 \le \rho_2$ is reduced to the set of constraints $\{\eta_{\rho_1,1} \le \eta_{\rho_2,1}, \ldots, \eta_{\rho_1,m} \le \eta_{\rho_2,m}\}$. $\alpha \notin FN(e)$ is replaced by: $\{\eta_{\rho,i} = 0 \mid \alpha \text{ occurs in } A_i\}$.

As in [6], the type inference algorithm runs in time polynomial in the size of a process under the following assumptions:

1. The simple type of each message occurring in the process is bound by a constant.
2. The arguments of begin/end-events cannot contain encrypted messages (of the form $\{M\}_K$).

Note that the first assumption ensures that the size of the effect constraints in step 1 is polynomial in the size of the given process. The first and second conditions ensure that the size of the set of relevant atomic effects is also polynomial, hence so is the size of the linear inequalities.

Example 4. Recall Example 1. In step 1, we first prepare the following template of type derivation for $Sender(ch, key)$:

$$\cfrac{\Gamma_2; \rho_4 \vdash ch : \mathbf{Un} \quad \cfrac{\Gamma_2; \rho_6 \vdash key : T \quad \cfrac{\Gamma_2; \rho_8 \vdash msg : \mathbf{N}(\rho_{14}) \quad \Gamma_1; \rho_9 \vdash n : \mathbf{N}(\rho_{13})}{\cfrac{\Gamma_2; \rho_7 \vdash (msg, n) : \mathbf{N}(\rho_{11}) \times \mathbf{N}(\rho_{12})}{\Gamma_2; \rho_5 \vdash \{(msg, n)\}_{key} : \mathbf{N}(\rho_{10})}}}{\cfrac{\Gamma_2; \rho_3 \vdash ch!\{msg, n\}_{key}}{\cfrac{\Gamma_2; \rho_2 \vdash \mathbf{begin}\ msg. \cdots}{\cfrac{\Gamma_1; \rho_1 \vdash (\nu msg) \cdots}{\Gamma_0; \rho_0 \vdash Sender(ch, key)}}}}$$

Here, T, Γ_0, Γ_1, and Γ_2 are given by:

$$T = \mathbf{Key}(\mathbf{N}(\rho_{15}) \times \mathbf{N}(\rho_{16})) \qquad \Gamma_0 = ch : \mathbf{Un}, key : T$$
$$\Gamma_1 = \Gamma_0, n : \mathbf{N}(\rho_n) \qquad \Gamma_2 = \Gamma_1, msg : \mathbf{N}(\rho_{msg})$$

From the derivation tree, we obtain the following constraints:

$$\rho_1 \le \rho_0 \qquad \rho_2 \le \rho_1 + [\mathbf{chk}\langle msg\rangle \mapsto 1] \qquad \rho_3 \le \rho_2 + [\mathbf{end}\langle msg\rangle \mapsto 1]$$
$$\rho_4 = \rho_6 = [] \qquad \rho_7 \le \rho_5 \le \rho_3 \qquad \rho_8 + \rho_9 \le \rho_7$$
$$\mathbf{pub}(\mathbf{N}(\rho_n)) \qquad \mathbf{gen}(\mathbf{N}(\rho_{msg})) \qquad \mathbf{N}(\rho_{15}) \times \mathbf{N}(\rho_{16}) = \mathbf{N}(\rho_{11}) \times \mathbf{N}(\rho_{12})$$
$$\mathbf{N}(\rho_{11}) = \mathbf{N}(\rho_{14}) \qquad \mathbf{N}(\rho_{13}) = [msg/0]\mathbf{N}(\rho_{12}) \qquad \rho_n + \rho_9 = \rho_{13}$$
$$FN(\rho_{15}) \subseteq \{ch\} \qquad FN(\rho_{16}) \subseteq \{ch, 0\} \qquad FN(\rho_n) \subseteq \{ch, key\} \qquad \cdots$$

(The constraints on the last line come from the well-formedness conditions of type judgments.) The constraints on types can be easily reduced to those on effects: for example, $\mathbf{pub}(\mathbf{N}(\rho_n))$ is replaced by $\rho_n = []$.

By analyzing the effect constraints generated from the whole process *System*, we can infer that the relevant atomic effects are $S = \{\mathbf{end}\langle\alpha\rangle, \mathbf{chk}\langle\alpha\rangle \mid \alpha \in \{0, msg, non, non', m\}\}$. Let $\rho_i(A) = \eta_{i,A}$ for $A \in S$. Then, we can generate linear inequalities from the effect constraints. For example, from $\rho_2 \le \rho_1 + [\mathbf{chk}\langle msg\rangle \mapsto 1]$, we obtain the following linear inequalities:

$$\eta_{2,\mathbf{chk}\langle msg\rangle} \le \eta_{1,\mathbf{chk}\langle msg\rangle} + 1 \qquad \forall A \in S \setminus \{\mathbf{chk}\langle msg\rangle\}.\eta_{2,A} \le \eta_{1,A}$$

5   Experiments

We have implemented a prototype protocol verifier SpiCA based on our type system. The implementation is available from `http://www.kb.ecei.tohoku.ac.jp/~koba/spica/`. The system takes a protocol description without type annotations as an input. If the input is well-typed, the system annotates it with types and effects; otherwise, it just reports that the input is ill-typed. The current system uses simplex method routines of the GLPK library [9] (via ocaml-glpk, `http://ocaml-glpk.sourceforge.net/`) to solve linear inequalities; thus, the implementation may suffer from exponential time complexity in the worst-case.

Table 1. Benchmark results

Processes	Typing	#EC	#LC	Time (ms)
nonce-handshake	yes	49	13	20
flawed-handshake	no	45	0	20
HalfCap	yes	60	14	30
woo-lam	yes	273	311	50
flawed-wide-mouth	no	239	1208	90
wide-mouth	yes	349	1328	100
otway-ree	yes	462	2143	180

Table 1 summarizes the results of preliminary experiments. The experiments are conducted on a machine with an Intel(R) Pentium(R) 1.2GHz processor and 500MB memory. The column "Typing" shows whether or not the processes were judged to be well-typed. The columns "#EC" and "#LC" respectively show the number of effect constraints and that of linear inequalities generated in Steps 1 and 2 of the algorithm. The column "Time" shows the running time. The process nonce-handshake is the system in Example 1, while flawed-handshake is a flawed version obtained from nonce-handshake by removing the check operation. The process HalfCap is the one discussed in Section 3.4. The other protocols were taken from Gordon and Jeffrey's paper [2]. The process woo-lam is a corrected version of Woo and Lam's protocol. The processes flawed-wide-mouth and wide-mouth are flawed and corrected versions of Abadi and Gordon's variant of wide mouth frog. The process otway-ree is Abadi and Needham's variant of Otway and Ree's key exchange protocol.

All the processes were correctly verified (or rejected as ill-typed in the case for the flawed protocols), and the inferred types and effects were as expected: for example, $\mathbf{Key}(\mathbf{N}([\mathbf{end}\langle x\rangle \mapsto 0.5]))$ was automatically inferred as the type of k in HalfCap.

In some cases, the number of linear constraints is smaller than that of effect constraints. That is because constraints (such as unification constraints) are simplified before the translation into linear constraints. In particular, for flawed-handshake, inconsistency is detected in the simplification phase for effect constraints.

6   Related Work

This paper combines Gordon and Jeffrey's work [2] on the type system for checking authenticity with our previous work [6] of using fractional effects to enable polynomial-time type inference for π-calculus with correspondence assertions. The combination is non-trivial, however. Since Gordon and Jeffrey's type system has explicit type annotations and cast operations, non-trivial modifications of the type system were necessary to adapt our previous technique.

Gordon and Jeffrey later extended their type system to deal with asymmetric cryptographic protocols [7]. We expect that our approach can also be extended to deal with them.

Gordon, Hüttel, and Hansen [10] have also recently proposed a type inference algorithm for checking correspondence assertions in π-calculus. The algorithm checks one-to-many correspondence (in which there may be more than one end-events for each begin-event), rather than one-to-one correspondence considered in the present paper and our previous work [6]. Their algorithm is quite different from ours, and does not handle cryptographic primitives.

Bugliesi, Focardi, and Maffei [11,12] have proposed type-based static analyses for authentication protocols that are closely related to Gordon and Jeffrey's type systems. They [13] later introduced an algorithm for automatically inferring *tags* (which roughly correspond to Gordon and Jeffrey's types [2,7]). Their inference algorithm is based on exhaustive search of potential taggings by backtracking. Our type inference algorithm is therefore more efficient theoretically. The advantage of our polynomial-time type inference may not be so important in analyzing abstract descriptions of cryptographic protocols, which are usually very short. The advantage may be more significant for analyzing the source code of cryptographic protocols [14].

Blanchet [15] also proposed automated techniques for checking checking correspondence assertions in cryptographic protocols. An advantage of our type-based approach is that the result of type inference gives a better explanation of why the protocol is safe. Blanchet [16] has recently proposed a quite different technique for authenticity verification. His technique can guarantee soundness in the computational model, rather than in the formal model with the assumption of perfect encryption.

The idea of using rational numbers in type systems goes back to the work of Boyland [17], and has been extensively studied by Terauchi [18,19,20].

7   Conclusion

We have modified Gordon and Jeffrey's type system for checking correspondence assertions in cryptographic protocols, and obtained a type inference algorithm, which serves as an algorithm for automated verification of cryptographic protocols. Under certain reasonable assumptions, the algorithm runs in time polynomial in the size of an input process.

Acknowledgment. We would like to thank Koki Nishizawa for comments and discussions on this work, and Kohei Suenaga for his help in using the GLPK library.

References

1. Gordon, A.D., Jeffrey, A.: Typing correspondence assertions for communication protocols. Theor. Comput. Sci. 300, 379–409 (2003)
2. Gordon, A.D., Jeffrey, A.: Authenticity by typing for security protocols. Journal of Computer Security 11(4), 451–520 (2003)
3. Gordon, A.D., Jeffrey, A.: Types and effects for asymmetric cryptographic protocols. In: 15th IEEE Computer Security Foundations Workshop (CSFW-15), pp. 77–91 (2002)

4. Woo, T.Y., Lam, S.S.: A semantic model for authentication protocols. In: RSP: IEEE Computer Society Symposium on Research in Security and Privacy, pp. 178–193 (1993)
5. Haack, C., Jeffrey, A.: Cryptyc (2004), http://www.cryptyc.org/
6. Kikuchi, D., Kobayashi, N.: Type-based verification of correspondence assertions for communication protocols. In: Shao, Z. (ed.) APLAS 2007. LNCS, vol. 4807, pp. 191–205. Springer, Heidelberg (2007)
7. Gordon, A.D., Jeffrey, A.: Types and effects for asymmetric cryptographic protocols. Journal of Computer Security 12(3-4), 435–483 (2004)
8. Abadi, M., Gordon, A.D.: A Calculus for Cryptographic Protocols: The Spi Calculus. Information and Computation 148(1), 1–70 (1999)
9. GNU Linear Programming Kit, http://www.gnu.org/software/glpk
10. Gordon, A.D., Hüttel, H., Hansen, R.R.: Type inference for correspondence types. In: 6th International Workshop on Security Issues in Concurrency (SecCo 2008) (2008)
11. Bugliesi, M., Focardi, R., Maffei, M.: Compositional analysis of authentication protocols. In: Schmidt, D. (ed.) ESOP 2004. LNCS, vol. 2986, pp. 140–154. Springer, Heidelberg (2004)
12. Bugliesi, M., Focardi, R., Maffei, M.: Authenticity by tagging and typing. In: Proceedings of the 2004 ACM Workshop on Formal Methods in Security Engineering (FMSE 2004), pp. 1–12 (2004)
13. Focardi, R., Maffei, M., Placella, F.: Inferring authentication tags. In: Proceedings of the Workshop on Issues in the Theory of Security (WITS 2005), pp. 41–49 (2005)
14. Bengtson, J., Bhargavan, K., Fournet, C., Gordon, A.D., Maffeis, S.: Refinement types for secure implementations. In: Proceedings of the 21st IEEE Computer Security Foundations Symposium (CSF 2008), pp. 17–32 (2008)
15. Blanchet, B.: From Secrecy to Authenticity in Security Protocols. In: Hermenegildo, M.V., Puebla, G. (eds.) SAS 2002. LNCS, vol. 2477, pp. 342–359. Springer, Heidelberg (2002)
16. Blanchet, B.: Computationally sound mechanized proofs of correspondence assertions. In: 20th IEEE Computer Security Foundations Symposium (CSF 2007), pp. 97–111 (2007)
17. Boyland, J.: Checking interference with fractional permissions. In: Cousot, R. (ed.) SAS 2003. LNCS, vol. 2694, pp. 55–72. Springer, Heidelberg (2003)
18. Terauchi, T., Aiken, A.: Witnessing side-effects. In: Proc. of ICFP, pp. 105–115. ACM, New York (2005)
19. Terauchi, T., Aiken, A.: A capability calculus for concurrency and determinism. ACM Trans. Prog. Lang. Syst. 30(5) (2008)
20. Terauchi, T.: Checking race freedom via linear programming. In: Proc. of PLDI, pp. 1–10 (2008)

A Theory of Non-monotone Memory
(Or: Contexts for free)*

Eijiro Sumii

Tohoku University
sumii@ecei.tohoku.ac.jp

Abstract. We develop a general method of proving contextual properties—including (but not limited to) observational equivalence, space improvement, and memory safety *under arbitrary contexts*—for programs
in untyped call-by-value λ-calculus with first-class, higher-order references (**ref**, := and !) and deallocation (**free**). The method significantly
generalizes Sumii et al.'s environmental bisimulation technique, and gives
a sound and complete characterization of each proved property, in the
sense that the "bisimilarity" (the largest set satisfying the bisimulation-
like conditions) equals the set of terms with the property to be proved.
We give examples of contextual properties concerning typical data structures such as linked lists, binary search trees, and directed acyclic graphs
with reference counts, all with deletion operations that release memory.

This shows the scalability of the environmental approach from contextual equivalence to other binary relations (such as space improvement)
and unary predicates (such as memory safety), as well as to languages
with non-monotone store, where Kripke-style logical relations have
difficulties.

1 Introduction

1.1 Background

Memory management is tricky, be it manual or automatic. Manual memory
management is notoriously difficult, leading to memory leaks and segmentation
faults (or, even worse, security holes). Automatic memory management is usually
more convenient. Still, real programs often suffer from performance problems—
in terms of both memory and time—due to automatic memory management,
and require manual tuning. In addition, implementing memory management
routines—such as memory allocators and garbage collectors—is even harder than
writing programs that use them.

To address these problems, various theories for safe memory management
have been developed, including linear types [17], regions [16], and the capability
calculus [6], just to name a few. These approaches typically conduct a sound
and efficient static analysis—often based on types—on programs, and guarantee
their memory safety. However, since static analyses are necessarily incomplete

---

* Extended abstract with appendices online [13].

G. Castagna (Ed.): ESOP 2009, LNCS 5502, pp. 237–251, 2009.
© Springer-Verlag Berlin Heidelberg 2009

$$dag = \nu z := \texttt{null}; \langle addn, deln, gc \rangle$$
$$addn = \lambda x. \lambda p.\, x + 0;\, map(\lambda y.\, y + 0)p;$$
$$\qquad incr_x(!z)p;\, \nu n := \langle x, \texttt{true}, 0, p, !z \rangle;\, z := n$$
$$incr_x = \texttt{fix } f(n).\, \lambda p.\, \texttt{ifnull } n \texttt{ then } \langle \rangle \texttt{ else}$$
$$\qquad \texttt{if } \#_1(!n) \overset{int}{=} x \texttt{ then diverge else}$$
$$\qquad \texttt{if } member(\#_1(!n))p \texttt{ then } \#_3^5(!n) \leftarrow \#_3(!n) + 1;\, f(n)(remove(\#_1(!n))p) \texttt{ else}$$
$$\qquad f(\#_5(!n))p$$
$$deln = \lambda x.\, deln_x(!z)$$
$$deln_x = \texttt{fix } g(n).\, \texttt{ifnull } n \texttt{ then } \langle \rangle \texttt{ else}$$
$$\qquad \texttt{if } \#_1(!n) \overset{int}{=} x \texttt{ then } \#_2^5(!n) \leftarrow \texttt{false else}$$
$$\qquad g(\#_5(!n))$$
$$gc = \lambda x.\, z := decr(!z)[]$$
$$decr = \texttt{fix } h(n).\, \lambda p.\, \texttt{ifnull } n \texttt{ then null else}$$
$$\qquad \texttt{if } member(\#_1(!n))p \texttt{ then } \#_3^5(!n) \leftarrow \#_3(!n) - 1;\, h(n)(remove(\#_1(!n))p) \texttt{ else}$$
$$\qquad \texttt{if } \#_2(!n) \lor \#_3(!n) > 0 \texttt{ then } \#_5^5(!n) \leftarrow h(\#_5(!n))p;\, n \texttt{ else}$$
$$\qquad h(\#_5(!n))(append(\#_4(!n))p) \texttt{ before free}(n)$$

Fig. 1. Directed acyclic graph with garbage collection by reference counting

in the sense that some safe programs are rejected, the programs usually have to be written in a style that is accepted by the analysis.

1.2   Our Contributions

In this paper, we develop a different approach, originating from Sumii et al.'s environmental bisimulations [7, 12, 14, 15]. Unlike most static analyses, our method is not fully automated, but is (sound and) complete in the sense that all (and only) safe programs can potentially be proved safe. Moreover, it guarantees memory safety *under any context*, even if the context—or, in fact, the whole language—is untyped.

For instance, consider the triple *dag* in Figure 1, which implements a directed acyclic graph object with addition, deletion, and garbage collection by reference counting. (Details of this implementation are explained in Section 6. The formal syntax and semantics of our language are given in Section 3.) To verify the memory safety of this implementation, it makes no sense to consider the triple by itself; rather, we must consider all possible uses of it, i.e., put it under arbitrary contexts. Our method gives such a proof in many examples.

Because our method is based on a relational technique (namely, bisimulations), we can also prove binary properties such as observational equivalence, in addition to unary properties such as memory safety. Furthermore, we can prove more general binary properties like "the memory usage (i.e., number of locations) is the same on the left hand side and the right" or "the left hand side uses less memory than the right." Again, such properties between programs are preserved by contexts in the language, like contextual equivalence [10].

1.3   Our Approach

Environmental bisimulations. Suppose that we want to prove the equivalence of two programs e and e'.[1] The basic idea of our approach is to consider the set X of every possible "configuration" of the programs. A configuration takes one of the two forms: $(\mathcal{R}, s \triangleright e, s' \triangleright e')$ and $(\mathcal{R}, s, s')$. The former means that the compared programs e and e' are running under stores s and s', respectively. The latter means that the programs have stopped with stores s and s'. In both forms, $\mathcal{R}$ is a binary relation on values and represents the *knowledge* of a context, called an environment.

For instance, suppose that we have a configuration $(\mathcal{R}, s \triangleright e, s' \triangleright e')$ in X. (Typically, $\mathcal{R}$ is empty at first.) If $s \triangleright e$ reduces to $t \triangleright d$ in one step according to the operational semantics of the language, then it must be that $s' \triangleright e'$ also reduces to some $t' \triangleright d'$ in some number of steps, and the new configuration $(\mathcal{R}, t \triangleright d, t' \triangleright d')$ belongs to X again. Knowledge $\mathcal{R}$ does not change yet, because the context cannot learn anything from these internal transitions.

Now, suppose $(\mathcal{R}, s \triangleright e, s' \triangleright e') \in X$ and e has stopped running, i.e., e is a value v. Then, $s' \triangleright e'$ must also converge to some $t' \triangleright w'$, and the context learns the resulting values v and w'. Thus, $\mathcal{R}$ is extended with the value pair (v, w'), and $(\mathcal{R} \cup \{(v, w')\}, s, t')$ must belong to X.

Once the compared programs have stopped, the context can make use of elements from its knowledge to make more observations. For example, suppose $(\mathcal{R}, s, s') \in X$ and $(\ell, \ell') \in \mathcal{R}$. This means that location ℓ (resp. ℓ') is known to the context on the left (resp. right) hand side. If $s = t \uplus \{\ell \mapsto v\}$ and $s' = t' \uplus \{\ell' \mapsto v'\}$ (where $\_ \uplus \{\_ \mapsto \_\}$ denotes store extension), then the context can read the contents v (resp. v') of ℓ (resp. ℓ') on the left (resp. right) hand side, and add them to its knowledge, requiring $(\mathcal{R} \cup \{(v, v')\}, s, s') \in X$.

Or, the contents can be updated with any values composed from the knowledge of the context. That is, for any $(w, w') \in \mathcal{R}^*$, we require $(\mathcal{R}, t \uplus \{\ell \mapsto w\}, t' \uplus \{\ell' \mapsto w'\}) \in X$. Here, $\mathcal{R}^*$ is the *context closure* of $\mathcal{R}$ and denotes the set of (pairs of) terms that can be composed from values in $\mathcal{R}$. Formally, it is defined as

$$\mathcal{R}^* = \{([v_1, \ldots, v_n / x_1, \ldots, x_n]e, [v'_1, \ldots, v'_n / x_1, \ldots, x_n]e) \mid$$
$$(v_1, v'_1), \ldots, (v_n, v'_n) \in \mathcal{R}, \ fv(e) \subseteq \{x_1, \ldots, x_n\}, \ loc(e) = \emptyset\}$$

where $fv(e)$ is the set of free variables in e and $loc(e)$ is the set of locations that appear in e.

Moreover, the context can also deallocate locations it knows, or allocate fresh ones. For the former case, we require $(\mathcal{R}, t, t') \in X$ for any $(\mathcal{R}, t \uplus \{\ell \mapsto v\}, t' \uplus \{\ell' \mapsto v'\}) \in X$ with $(\ell, \ell') \in \mathcal{R}$. For the latter case, $(\mathcal{R} \cup \{\ell, \ell\}, t \uplus \{\ell \mapsto v\}, t' \uplus \{\ell \mapsto v'\}) \in X$ is required for any $(\mathcal{R}, t, t') \in X$ with fresh ℓ and $(v, v') \in \mathcal{R}^*$.

Of course, there are also conditions on values other than locations. For instance, if $(\mathcal{R}, s, s') \in X$ and $(\lambda x. e, \lambda x. e') \in \mathcal{R}$, then $(\mathcal{R}, s \triangleright (\lambda x. e)v, s' \triangleright$

---

[1] Throughout this paper, we often (though not always) follow the notational convention that meta-variables with $'$ are used for objects on the right hand side of binary relations, and ones without for the left hand side (and unary relations).

$(\lambda x.\, e')v') \in X$ is required for any $(v, v') \in R^\star$, because the context can apply any functions it knows ($\lambda x.\, e$ and $\lambda x.\, e'$) to any arguments it can compose (v and v').

Congruence of environmental bisimilarity. As we shall prove, the largest set X satisfying the above conditions—which exists because all of them are monotone on X—is "contextual" in the following sense:

- If a configuration $(\mathcal{R}, s \triangleright e, s' \triangleright e')$ is in X, then its context-closed version $(\mathcal{R}^{\hat{\star}}, s \triangleright E[e], s' \triangleright E[e'])$ is also in X, for any location-free evaluation context E.
- If a configuration $(\mathcal{R}, s, s')$ is in X, then its context-closed version $(\mathcal{R}^{\hat{\star}}, s \triangleright e, s' \triangleright e')$ is also in X, for any $(e, e') \in \mathcal{R}^\star$.

Here, $\mathcal{R}^{\hat{\star}}$ denotes the restriction of $\mathcal{R}^\star$ to values.

The restriction to location-free evaluation contexts in the first item is *not* a limitation of our approach, as already shown in previous work [7, 15]: If one wants to prove the equivalence of e and e' under non-evaluation contexts, it suffices to prove the equivalence of $\lambda x.\, e$ and $\lambda x.\, e'$ (for fresh x) under evaluation contexts only. In addition, if a context needs access to some locations $\ell_1, \ldots, \ell_n$, just requiring $(\ell_1, \ell_1), \ldots, (\ell_n, \ell_n) \in \mathcal{R}$ is sufficient. Programs with free variables are not a problem, either: instead of open e and e', it suffices to consider $\lambda x_1. \ldots \lambda x_n.\, e$ and $\lambda x_1. \ldots \lambda x_n.\, e'$ for $\{x_1, \ldots x_n\} \supseteq fv(e) \cup fv(e')$.

Generalization to contextual relations. The above approach is not limited to the proof of contextual equivalence, but can be generalized for other binary relations as well. For example, if we add a condition "$|dom(s)| \leq |dom(s')|$ for any $(\mathcal{R}, s \triangleright e, s' \triangleright e') \in X$," then one can conclude that e uses fewer locations than e' under arbitrary (evaluation) contexts. In short, any predicate P on configurations can be added to the conditions of X while keeping it contextual, as long as P itself is contextual (i.e., preserved by contexts). It does not have to be a congruence (or even a pre-congruence), hence the term "contextual" rather than "congruent" (or pre-congruent).

Contextual predicates and memory safety. In fact, there is no reason why the proved contextual relations have to be binary. Rather, they can be of arbitrary arity. In particular, the arity can be 1, meaning unary predicates. To obtain conditions for the unary version of X, we just have to remove everything that belongs to the "right hand side." Again, the resulting X is contextual as long as the predicate P itself is contextual.

A prominent example of such unary properties is memory safety. For proving memory safety under arbitrary contexts, let us first classify all locations into "private" and "public" ones. The intent is that private locations are kept secret to the program under consideration, whereas public locations are under the control of the context. Then, let $P(\mathcal{R}, s \triangleright e)$ be false if and only if e is immediately reading from, writing to, or deallocating a private location that is not in $dom(s)$, and $P(\mathcal{R}, s)$ be true if and only if any $\ell \in \mathcal{R}$ is public. Then, just as in the binary case, we can prove that the largest X satisfying the bisimulation-like conditions is contextual. (Of course, here, we are not considering a congruence or an equivalence relation—or even a binary relation at all!—but the set X is still "bisimulation-like" in the sense that it involves co-induction and is contextual.)

Another example of unary contextual properties is an upper bound on the number of private locations. To be concrete, let $P(\mathcal{R}, s \triangleright e)$ and $P(\mathcal{R}, s)$ be true if and only if the number of private locations in $dom(s)$ is less than a constant c. Then, again, we can use our approach to prove that a term e allocates at most c private locations under arbitrary contexts that do not create private locations.

1.4 Overview of the Paper

The rest of this paper is structured as follows. Section 2 discusses some (not all, because of space constraints) related work. Section 3 defines our target language. Section 4 develops the binary version of our proof technique and Appendix A (available online [13]) gives examples (contextual relations between two multiset implementations). In addition, Appendix B introduces an auxiliary "up-to" technique to simplify the proofs, with examples in Appendix C. Section 5 defines the unary version of our approach and Section 6 gives an example (directed acyclic graphs with garbage collection with reference counting). Appendix D gives another example (bucket sort). Section 7 concludes with future work.

2 Related Work

As stated above, our technique is rooted in Sumii et al.'s previous work on environmental bisimulations [7, 12, 14, 15]. In particular, our language and the binary version of our proof method (for contextual equivalence) is an extension of their environmental bisimulation for untyped call-by-value λ-calculus with references (**ref**, := and !) in [12, Section 4], enriched with deallocation (**free**). It is also similar to the language and bisimulation of [7], except that we adopt small-step reduction semantics while they used big-step evaluation semantics. However, the fact itself that the extension is possible is striking, especially because deallocation is known to be highly non-trivial in other approaches, including type-based analyses and logical relations. In addition, our generalization of their technique—from contextual equivalence to other properties such as memory safety—is entirely new.

Denotational semantics can be used to prove contextual equivalence of programs (see, for example, [9, pp. 77, 344]). In short, two programs are contextually equivalent if their denotations are the same (provided that the semantics is adequate, of course). However, it is known to be hard to develop fully abstract—i.e., equivalence preserving—denotational semantics for languages with local store [8], let alone full references or deallocation.

Logical relations are relations between (semantics of) programs defined by induction on their types, and can be used for proving properties like contextual equivalence and memory safety. Pitts and Stark [11] defined (binary) syntactic logical relations—i.e., relations between the syntax of programs itself rather than their semantics—for a simply-typed call-by-value higher-order language with references to integers, and proved that they characterize contextual equivalence in this language. However, it is known to be hard to extend their result to languages with general references [2, 5] (references to arbitrary values, including functions and references themselves) or deallocation. In particular, the latter seems to break monotonicity (of the domain of a store), which is a crucial assumption of Kripke-style logical relations [9, p. 590] like theirs.

Ahmed [1, Chapter 7] defined (unary) step-indexed logical relations—i.e., relations defined by induction on the number of reduction steps instead of types—for a continuation-passing-style higher-order language with regions and their deallocation (like the capability calculus). In her definition, monotonicity is maintained by marking deallocated regions "dead" instead of removing them, thereby forbidding their reuse *at the type level* (still, region *handles* can be reused at the term level). Completeness is not discussed. Ahmed, Fluet, and Morrisett [3, 4] defined (unary) step-indexed logical relations in languages with linear types and deallocation. Their developments depend on the static guarantee by linear types. None of the work above considers contextual equivalence (or other binary properties).

3   The Language

The syntax of our language is given in Figure 2. It is a standard call-by-value λ-calculus extended with references and deallocation, in addition to first-order primitives (such as Boolean values and integer arithmetic) and tuples, which are added solely for the sake of convenience. The operational semantics is also standard and given in Figure 3 in the Appendices [13]. It is parametrized by the semantics of primitives, given as a partial function $[\![\_]\!]$ to constants from operations on constants.

A location ℓ^π is an atomic symbol that models a reference in ML (though it is untyped and deallocatable in our language) or a pointer in C (although our language omits pointer arithmetic for simplicity, it can easily be added by modeling the store as a finite map from locations to *arrays* of values). It has a "security level" $\top$ or $\bot$ to distinguish private and public locations, as outlined in the introduction. In what follows, we omit security levels when they are unimportant. We assume that there exist a countably infinite number of locations, both private and public. A special location $\texttt{null}^\bot$ is reserved for representing a never allocated location. This treatment is just for the sake of simplicity of examples. We write $loc(e)$ for the set of locations that appear in e (except $\texttt{null}^\bot$), and $fv(e)$ for the set of free variables in e. Note that there is no binder for locations in the syntax of our language.

Allocation $\nu x^\pi := e_1; e_2$ creates a fresh location ℓ^π of the specified security level π, initializes the contents with the value of e_1, binds the location to x, and executes e_2. (It is easy to separate allocation from initialization like $\nu x^\pi. e$, but the present form is more convenient for examples. In addition, we do not like to fix a single, arbitrary initial value of locations.) As outlined in the introduction,

$\pi, \rho ::=$	security level	$u, v, w ::=$	value
$\top$	private	$\lambda x. e$	function
$\bot$	public	c	constant
		$\langle v_1, \ldots, v_n \rangle$	tuple
$d, e, C, D ::=$	term	ℓ^π	location
x	variable		
$\lambda x. e$	function	$E, F ::=$	evaluation context
$e_1 e_2$	application	$[]$	hole
c	constant	$E e$	application (left)
$op(e_1, \ldots, e_n)$	primitive	$v E$	application (right)
if e_1 then e_2 else e_3		$op(v_1, \ldots, v_m, E, e_1, \ldots, e_n)$	primitive
	conditional branch	if E then e_1 else e_2	conditional branch
$\langle e_1, \ldots, e_n \rangle$	tupling	$\langle v_1, \ldots, v_m, E, e_1, \ldots, e_n \rangle$	tupling
$\#_i(e)$	projection	$\#_i(E)$	projection
ℓ^π	location	$\nu x^\pi := E; e$	allocation
$\nu x^\pi := e_1; e_2$	allocation	$\mathbf{free}(E)$	deallocation
$\mathbf{free}(e)$	deallocation	$E := e$	update (left)
$e_1 := e_2$	update	$v := E$	update (right)
$!e$	dereference	$!E$	dereference
$e_1 \overset{ptr}{=} e_2$	pointer equality	$E \overset{ptr}{=} e$	pointer equality (left)
		$v \overset{ptr}{=} E$	pointer equality (right)

Fig. 2. Syntax

our intent is to disallow contexts to allocate private locations. This restriction is a mere matter of a proof technique, and does not limit the computational power of contexts at runtime. In other words, we can always divide locations so that all locations under the control of a context are public.

Deallocation $\mathbf{free}(e)$ releases memory and lets it be reused later. Update $e_1 := e_2$ overwrites the contents of a location.

Pointer equality $e_1 \overset{ptr}{=} e_2$ compares locations themselves (not their contents). We do not use it in our examples (except for comparison with $\mathtt{null}^\bot$), but it is necessary for contexts to have a realistic observational power. If both locations are live, their equality can be tested by writing to one of the locations and reading from the other. However, this is not possible when either (or both) of them is "dead," i.e., already deallocated.

Throughout this paper, we focus on properties of closed terms and values only. (This is not a limitation, as explained in the introduction.) Thus, we can model a (possibly multi-hole) context C just by a term e with free variables $x_1, \ldots, x_n$, and a context application $C[e_1, \ldots, e_n]$ by a variable substitution $[e_1, \ldots, e_n / x_1, \ldots, x_n]e$. For this reason, we use meta-variables C and D for terms that are used for representing contexts. By convention, we implicitly assume that terms denoted by capital letters are location-free (except for $\mathtt{null}^\bot$) and do not include private allocation $\nu x^\top$.

For brevity, we use various syntactic sugar. We write let $x = e_1$ in e_2 for $(\lambda x. e_2)e_1$, and $e_1; e_2$ for let $x = e_1$ in e_2 where x does not appear free in e_2. Recursive function $\mathbf{fix}\ f(x). e$ is defined as (the value of) $Y(\lambda f. \lambda x. e)$ by using some call-by-value fixed-point operator Y as usual. As in Standard ML, e_1 **before** e_2 denotes **let** $x = e_1$ **in** $e_2; x$, again with x not free in e_2. We also write $e_1 \wedge e_2$ for **if** e_1 **then** e_2 **else false** and $e_1 \vee e_2$ for **if** e_1 **then true else** e_2. Note that these conjunction and disjunction operators are not symmetric, as in most programming languages with side effects or divergence. As in Objective Caml, **if** e_1 **then** e_2 abbreviates **if** e_1 **then** e_2 **else** $\langle\rangle$, where $\langle\rangle$ is the nullary tuple. Moreover, **ifnull** e_1 **then** e_2 **else** e_3 abbreviates **if** $e_1 \overset{ptr}{=} \texttt{null}^{\perp}$ **then** e_2 **else** e_3. Finally, $\#^i_j(!e_1) \leftarrow e_2$ stands for **let** $x = e_1$ **in** $x := \langle \#_1(!x),$ $\ldots, \#_{j-1}(!x), e_2, \#_{j+1}(!x), \ldots, \#_i(!x)\rangle$.

We give higher precedence to ; and **before** than λ, **let**, and **if** forms. Thus, for instance, **if** e_1 **then** e_2 **else** $e_3; e_4$ and $\lambda x. e_1; e_2$ mean **if** e_1 **then** e_2 **else** $(e_3; e_4)$ and $\lambda x. (e_1; e_2)$, respectively, rather than (**if** e_1 **then** e_2 **else** e_3); e_4 or $(\lambda x. e_1); e_2$. In addition, we take ; as right-associative, which is more convenient when defining a bisimulation (see Appendix D [13]).

Our operational semantics is a standard small-step reduction semantics with evaluation contexts and stores. Here, a store s is a finite map from locations (except $\texttt{null}^{\perp}$) to values. We write $dom(s)$ for the domain of store s. We also write $s \uplus \{\ell \mapsto v\}$ for the extension of store s with location ℓ mapped to value v, with the assumption that $\ell \notin dom(s)$. It is undefined if $\ell \in dom(s)$. Similarly, $s_1 \uplus s_2$ is defined to be $s_1 \cup s_2$ if $dom(s_1) \cap dom(s_2) = \emptyset$, and undefined otherwise. $s \setminus \tilde{\ell}$ denotes the store obtained from s by removing $\tilde{\ell}$ from its domain. Again, it is undefined if $\tilde{\ell} \notin dom(s)$. We write $\twoheadrightarrow$ for the reflexive and transitive closure of $\rightarrow$.

Note that the reduction is non-deterministic, even up to renaming of locations. For instance, consider $e = \nu x := \langle\rangle; x \overset{ptr}{=} \ell$. Then, we have both $\emptyset \rhd e \rightarrow \{\ell \mapsto \langle\rangle\} \rhd (\ell \overset{ptr}{=} \ell) \rightarrow \{\ell \mapsto \langle\rangle\} \rhd \texttt{true}$ and $\emptyset \rhd e \rightarrow \{m \mapsto \langle\rangle\} \rhd (m \overset{ptr}{=} \ell) \rightarrow \{m \mapsto \langle\rangle\} \rhd \texttt{false}$. This is one of the characteristics of our language, where deallocation makes dangling pointers (like ℓ in the above example), which may or may not get reallocated later.

Throughout the paper, we often abbreviate sequences $A_1, \ldots, A_n$ to $\tilde{A}$, for any kind of meta-variables A_i. We also abbreviate sequences of tuples, like $(A_1, B_1), \ldots, (A_n, B_n)$, as $(\tilde{A}, \tilde{B})$. Thus, for example, $[\tilde{v}/\tilde{x}]e$ denotes $[v_1, \ldots, v_n / x_1, \ldots, x_n]e$.

4   Binary Environmental Relations

In this section, we develop our approach for *binary* relations including contextual equivalence, which is closer to (the small-step version [12] of) the original environmental bisimulations [7, 14, 15].

First, we establish the basic terminology for our developments. Intuitions behind the definitions are given in the introduction.

Definition 1 (state and binary configuration). *The pair $s \rhd e$ of store s and term e is called a* state. *A binary configuration is a quintuple of the form $(\mathcal{R}, s \rhd e, s' \rhd e')$ or a triple of the form $(\mathcal{R}, s, s')$, where $\mathcal{R}$ is a binary relation on values.*

Note that we do not impose well-formedness conditions such as $loc(e) \subseteq dom(s)$ and $loc(e') \subseteq dom(s')$, because deallocation may (rightfully) make dangling pointers.

Definition 2 (context closure). *The* context closure $\mathcal{R}^\star$ *of a binary relation* $\mathcal{R}$ *on values, is defined by* $\mathcal{R}^\star = \{([\tilde{v}/\tilde{x}]C, [\tilde{v}'/\tilde{x}]C) \mid (\tilde{v}, \tilde{v}') \in \mathcal{R}, \; fv(C) \subseteq \{\tilde{x}\}\}$.

We write $R^{\hat{\star}}$ for the restriction of $\mathcal{R}^\star$ to values. Note $\mathcal{R} \subseteq \mathcal{R}^\star = (\mathcal{R}^{\hat{\star}})^\star$.

Then, we give the main definitions in this section. For brevity, we omit some universal and existential quantifications on meta-variables in the conditions below. They should be clear from the context—or, more precisely, from the positions of the first occurrences of the meta-variables. For instance, when we say

For every $(\mathcal{R}, s \triangleright d, s' \triangleright d') \in X$, if $s \triangleright d \to t \triangleright e$, then $s' \triangleright d' \twoheadrightarrow t' \triangleright e'$ and $(\mathcal{R}, t \triangleright e, t' \triangleright e') \in X$

it means

For every $(\mathcal{R}, s \triangleright d, s' \triangleright d') \in X$, and for any t and e, if $s \triangleright d \to t \triangleright e$ then for some t' and e' we have $s' \triangleright d' \twoheadrightarrow t' \triangleright e'$ and $(\mathcal{R}, t \triangleright e, t' \triangleright e') \in X$

because t and e first appear in the assumption, whereas t' and e' first appear in the conclusion.

Definition 3 (reduction closure). *A set* X *of binary configurations is* reduction-closed *if, for every* $(\mathcal{R}, s \triangleright d, s' \triangleright d') \in X$,

i. *If* $s \triangleright d \to t \triangleright e$, *then* $s' \triangleright d' \twoheadrightarrow t' \triangleright e'$ *and* $(\mathcal{R}, t \triangleright e, t' \triangleright e') \in X$.
ii. *If* $s' \triangleright d' \to t' \triangleright e'$, *then* $s \triangleright d \twoheadrightarrow t \triangleright e$ *and* $(\mathcal{R}, t \triangleright e, t' \triangleright e') \in X$.
iii. *If* $d = v$ *and* $d' = v'$, *then* $(\mathcal{R} \cup \{(v, v')\}, s, s') \in X$.

Intuitively, reduction closure means that the property in question is preserved throughout the execution of the programs e and e' (including the returned values v and v', which are then learned by the context). Note that we do not require a condition like "if $d = v$, then $s' \triangleright d' \twoheadrightarrow t' \triangleright v'$" (and vice versa) here. It is a specific property—defined P^{obs} below—of contextual equivalence, while we are interested in other more general properties as well.

In what follows, whenever we say "a predicate P on binary configurations," we silently impose the restriction that if $P(\mathcal{R}, s \triangleright d, s' \triangleright d')$ or $P(\mathcal{R}, s, s')$, and if $(u, u') \in \mathcal{R}$, then the outermost shape of u is the same as that of u'. (This includes equality of constants—that is, $u = c$ if and only if $u' = c$. We assume the existence of equality tests on all constants.) This is for excluding cases where reduction gets stuck on the left hand side and not on the right (or vice versa). For similar reasons, we additionally assume:

– If $(\ell^\pi, \ell'^{\pi'}) \in \mathcal{R}$, then $\pi = \pi' = \bot$ and $\ell^\bot \in dom(s) \iff \ell'^\bot \in dom(s')$.
– If $(\ell_1^\bot, \ell_1'^\bot) \in \mathcal{R}$ and $(\ell_2^\bot, \ell_2'^\bot) \in \mathcal{R}$, then $\ell_1^\bot = \ell_2^\bot \iff \ell_1'^\bot = \ell_2'^\bot$.

Definition 4 (environmental P-simulation). *Let* P *be a predicate on binary configurations. A reduction-closed subset* X *of* P *is called an* environmental P-simulation *if, for every* $(\mathcal{R}, s, s') \in X$ *and* $(u, u') \in \mathcal{R}$,

1. If $u = \lambda x.\, e$ and $u' = \lambda x.\, e'$, then $(\mathcal{R}, s \triangleright uv, t \triangleright u'v') \in X$ for any $(v, v') \in \mathcal{R}^\star$.

2. If $u = \langle v_1, \ldots, v_i, \ldots, v_n \rangle$ and $u' = \langle v'_1, \ldots, v'_i, \ldots, v'_n \rangle$, then $(\mathcal{R} \cup \{(v_i, v'_i)\}, s, s') \in X$.

3. If $u = \ell^\perp$, $u' = \ell'^\perp$, $s = t \uplus \{\ell^\perp \mapsto v\}$ and $s' = t' \uplus \{\ell'^\perp \mapsto v'\}$, then

   (a) $(\mathcal{R}, t, t') \in X$.

   (b) $(\mathcal{R}, t \uplus \{\ell^\perp \mapsto w\}, t' \uplus \{\ell'^\perp \mapsto w'\}) \in X$ for any $(w, w') \in \mathcal{R}^\star$.

   (c) $(\mathcal{R} \cup \{(v, v')\}, s, s') \in X$.

4. For any $\ell^\perp \notin dom(s)$ and $(v, v') \in \mathcal{R}^\star$, we have $(\mathcal{R} \cup \{(\ell^\perp, \ell'^\perp)\}, s \uplus \{\ell^\perp \mapsto v\}, s' \uplus \{\ell'^\perp \mapsto v'\}) \in X$ for some $\ell'^\perp \notin dom(s')$.

An environmental P-simulation X is called an *environmental P-bisimulation* if its inverse

$$X^{-1} = \{(\mathcal{R}^{-1}, s' \triangleright e', s \triangleright e) \mid (\mathcal{R}, s \triangleright e, s' \triangleright e') \in X\}$$
$$\cup \{(\mathcal{R}^{-1}, s', s) \mid (\mathcal{R}, s, s') \in X\}$$

is also an environmental P-simulation (or, if X is an environmental P^{-1}-simulation—this is equivalent because all the other conditions are symmetric). An *environmental bisimulation* X is defined by taking P to be the following P^{obs}.

$$P^{obs}(\mathcal{R}, s \triangleright d, s' \triangleright d') = \text{if } d' = v', \text{ then } s \triangleright d \twoheadrightarrow t \triangleright v$$
$$P^{obs}(\mathcal{R}, s, s') \qquad\qquad = true$$

Since all the conditions of environmental P-simulations are monotone on X, the union of all environmental P-simulations is also an environmental P-simulation, called the *environmental P-similarity*. In what follows, we often omit the adjective "environmental" and just write "a simulation" to mean an environmental simulation. The same holds for all the combinations of P- and bi- simulations and similarity.

As outlined in the introduction, the conditions of P-simulation reflect observations made by contexts. In Definition 3 (reduction closure), Conditions i and ii mean reduction on the left can be simulated by the right hand side and vice versa. Condition iii adds the returned values of programs to the knowledge of a context.

In Definition 4 (P-simulation), Condition 1 corresponds to function application, and Condition 2 to element projection from tuples. Conditions 3a, 3b, 3c, and 4 represent deallocation of, writing to, reading from, and allocation of locations, respectively.

We are now going to prove the main result of this section: let $P_{\star\to}$ be the largest contextual, reduction-closed subset of P (which exists because the union of contextual, reduction-closed sets is again contextual and reduction-closed); then the P-similarity coincides with $P_{\star\to}$, provided that P itself is contextual in the following sense.

Definition 5 (contextuality). *A set P of configurations is* contextual *if its context closure*

$$P^\star = \{(\mathcal{S}, s \triangleright [\tilde{v}/\tilde{x}]E[e], s' \triangleright [\tilde{v}'/\tilde{x}]E[e']) \mid$$
$$(\mathcal{R}, s \triangleright e, s' \triangleright e') \in P, \ \mathcal{S} \subseteq \mathcal{R}^{\hat{\star}}, \ (\tilde{v}, \tilde{v}') \in \mathcal{R}, \ fv(E) \subseteq \{\tilde{x}\}\}$$
$$\cup \{(\mathcal{S}, s \triangleright [\tilde{v}/\tilde{x}]C, s' \triangleright [\tilde{v}'/\tilde{x}]C) \mid$$
$$(\mathcal{R}, s, s') \in P, \ \mathcal{S} \subseteq \mathcal{R}^{\hat{\star}}, \ (\tilde{v}, \tilde{v}') \in \mathcal{R}, \ fv(C) \subseteq \{\tilde{x}\}\}$$
$$\cup \{(\mathcal{S}, s, s') \mid (\mathcal{R}, s, s') \in P, \ \mathcal{S} \subseteq \mathcal{R}^{\hat{\star}}\}$$

is included in P.

Note that $P \subseteq P^\star = (P^\star)^\star$. In short, contextuality means that P is preserved under arbitrary contexts. The inclusion $\mathcal{S} \subseteq \mathcal{R}^{\hat{\star}}$ is necessary for the following technical reason: suppose we have a configuration $(\mathcal{R}, s \triangleright d, s' \triangleright d') \in X$ and put it under an evaluation context E, like $(\mathcal{R}, s \triangleright E[d], s' \triangleright E[d']) \in X$. If d and d' reduce to values v and v', respectively, then the context learns these values and adds them to its knowledge, like $(\mathcal{R} \cup \{(v, v')\}, s \triangleright E[v], s' \triangleright E[v']) \in X$. However, according to the conditions of reduction closure, we need $(\mathcal{R}, s \triangleright E[v], s' \triangleright E[v']) \in X$, where the knowledge $\mathcal{R}$ is *smaller* than $\mathcal{R} \cup \{(v, v')\}$. A similar case occurs when the context by itself allocates a fresh location.

This is not a real problem because smaller knowledge means less observations, i.e., more properties. In fact, instead of taking $\mathcal{S} \subseteq \mathcal{R}^{\hat{\star}}$ here, it is also possible to generalize the definition of simulation to allow the increase of knowledge in the middle of an evaluation. This amounts to an up-to environment technique [12].

Theorem 1 (characterization). *For any P, the $P^\star$-similarity coincides with $(P^\star)_{\star\to}$. In particular, if P is contextual, then the P-similarity coincides with $P_{\star\to}$.*

It is easy to check—by simple induction on the evaluation context E—that the previous P^{obs} for contextual equivalence is indeed contextual. (It does not even refer to $\mathcal{R}$ at all!) Thus:

Corollary 1 (bisimilarity equals contextual equivalence). *The bisimilarity coincides with the contextual equivalence $P^{obs}_{\star\to}$.*

Appendix A [13] gives examples of the use of P-bisimulations, including a proof of contextual equivalence and a property of space usage. Appendix B [13] develops an up-to technique that lightens the burden of bisimulation proof.

5   Unary Environmental Predicates

Suppose that we want to prove the memory safety of the directed acyclic graph implementation *dag*. To do so, we can use the "bisimulation" between *dag* and *dag* itself! This idea formalizes to the following definitions.

Definition 6 (memory safety). *State $s \triangleright e$ is* memory unsafe *if e is either $E[\mathtt{free}(\ell^\top)]$, $E[\ell^\top := v]$, or $E[!\ell^\top]$, with $\ell^\top \notin dom(s)$. It is* memory safe *if not memory unsafe. We often omit "memory" and just say "safe" or "unsafe," and write* safe *for the set of safe $s \triangleright e$.*

Note that the definition above does not imply so-called "type safety," which is a more general property. For instance, *safe* does not preclude stuck states such as $\emptyset \triangleright \ell\ 3$.

Definition 7. *A* unary configuration *is a triple of the form* $(\mathcal{R}, s \triangleright e)$ *or a pair of the form* $(\mathcal{R}, s)$, *where* $\mathcal{R}$ *is a predicate on values.*

Definition 8 (environmental P-predicate). *Let P be a predicate on unary configurations. A set* $X \subseteq P$ *of unary configurations is called an* environmental *P-predicate if its duplication* $X^2 = \{(\mathcal{R}^2, s \triangleright e, s \triangleright e) \mid (\mathcal{R}, s \triangleright e) \in X\} \cup \{(\mathcal{R}^2, s, s) \mid (\mathcal{R}, s) \in X\}$ *is an environmental* P^2*-simulation, where* $\mathcal{R}^2 = \{(v, v) \mid v \in \mathcal{R}\}$. *To spell out all the conditions,*

1. *For every* $(\mathcal{R}, s \triangleright d) \in X$,
   (a) *If* $s \triangleright d \rightarrow t \triangleright e$, *then* $(\mathcal{R}, t \triangleright e) \in X$.
   (b) *If* $d = v$, *then* $(\mathcal{R} \cup \{v\}, s) \in X$.
2. *For every* $(\mathcal{R}, s) \in X$ *and* $u \in \mathcal{R}$,
   (a) *If* $u = \lambda x.\, e$, *then* $(\mathcal{R}, s \triangleright uv) \in X$ *for any* $v \in \mathcal{R}^\star$.
   (b) *If* $u = \langle v_1, \ldots, v_i, \ldots, v_n \rangle$, *then* $(\mathcal{R} \cup \{v_i\}, s) \in X$.
   (c) *If* $u = \ell^\perp$ *and* $s = t \uplus \{\ell^\perp \mapsto v\}$, *then* $(\mathcal{R}, t) \in X$, $(\mathcal{R}, t \uplus \{\ell^\perp \mapsto w\}) \in X$ *for any* $w \in \mathcal{R}^\star$, *and* $(\mathcal{R} \cup \{v\}, s) \in X$.
   (d) $(\mathcal{R} \cup \{\ell^\perp\}, s \uplus \{\ell^\perp \mapsto v\}) \in X$ *for any* $\ell^\perp \notin dom(s)$ *and* $v \in \mathcal{R}^\star$.

where the unary version of context closure is defined as $\mathcal{R}^\star = \{[\tilde{v}/\tilde{x}]C \mid \tilde{v} \in \mathcal{R},\ fv(C) \subseteq \{\tilde{x}\}\}$.

All the results from binary environmental *P*-simulations apply to this unary version, because the latter is just a special case of the former (and because equality satisfies all the restrictions on *P*). This includes soundness and the up-to technique. For pedagogy, we spell out the conditions of environmental *P*-predicate up-to context and allocation.

Definition 9 (allocation closure). *The (unary) allocation closure of* X *is defined as:*

$$X^\nu = \{(\mathcal{R}, s \triangleright e) \mid (\mathcal{R}, s \triangleright e) \in X\}$$
$$\cup \{(\mathcal{S}, s \setminus \tilde{m}^\perp \uplus \{\tilde{\ell}^\perp \mapsto \tilde{w}\}) \mid (\mathcal{R}, s) \in X,\ \tilde{m}^\perp \in \mathcal{R},\ \mathcal{S} = \mathcal{R} \cup \{\tilde{\ell}^\perp\},\ \tilde{w} \in \mathcal{S}^\star\}$$

Definition 10 (environmental P-predicate up-to). *A set* $X \subseteq P$ *of unary configurations is called an* environmental *P-predicate up-to context and allocation (or just a "P-predicate up-to" in short) if:*

1. *For every* $(\mathcal{R}, s \triangleright d) \in X$,
   (a) *If* $s \triangleright d \rightarrow t \triangleright e$, *then* $(\mathcal{S}, t \triangleright e) \in (X^\nu)^\star$.
   (b) *If* $d = v$, *then* $(\mathcal{R} \cup \{v\}, s) \in (X^\nu)^\star$.
2. *For every* $(\mathcal{R}, s) \in X$ *and* $u \in \mathcal{R}$,
   (a) *If* $u = \lambda x.\, e$, *then for any* $(\mathcal{S}, t) \in \{(\mathcal{R}, s)\}^\nu$ *and* $v \in \mathcal{S}^\star$, *we have* $(\mathcal{S}, t \triangleright uv) \in X$.
   (b) *If* $u = \langle v_1, \ldots, v_i, \ldots, v_n \rangle$, *then* $(\mathcal{R} \cup \{v_i\}, s) \in (X^\nu)^\star$.
   (c) *If* $u = \ell^\perp$ *and* $\ell^\perp \in dom(s)$, *then* $(\mathcal{R} \cup \{s(\ell^\perp)\}, s) \in (X^\nu)^\star$.

6 An Example

The code in Figure 1 implements directed acyclic graphs (DAGs), with garbage collection by reference counting. For simplicity, we use *immutable* lists in this example (in addition to a mutable data structure for representing the DAGs themselves), and assume their basic operations such as *member*, *append*, and *remove*.

Here, z is bound to the location of the last added node in the DAG. A node is either null or a quintuple $\langle i, b, n, p, \ell \rangle$, where i is an integer ID of the node, b a Boolean value meaning whether the node is "in the root set" (i.e., cannot be garbage collected), n the reference count of the node, p the (immutable) list of the integer IDs of child nodes, and ℓ the pointer to the second last added node. This pointer is different from child pointers, for which we use the list of integer IDs.

Function *addn* takes integer x and integer list p, and adds a node with ID x and children p. The code $x + 0$ and $map(\lambda y. y + 0)p$ ensures they are indeed an integer and an integer list (assuming that $\_ + 0$ is defined only for integers). An auxiliary function $incr_x$ is used to increment the reference counts of nodes in p, as well as to check if node x already exists (in which case it diverges). Note that the same node may appear more than once in p. Its reference count is increased by the number of appearance.

Function *deln* prepares to delete a node by (un)marking it as non-root. Function *gc* invokes the garbage collector *decr*, which takes a node pointer n and an integer list p. It decreases the reference counts of nodes in p, again according to the number of their appearances. If the reference count becomes 0, and if the root flag is not set, then the node is deleted, and its children are added to p so that their reference counts will be decreased recursively. In the end, *decr* returns the updated node pointer n.

We define the shape predicate for DAGs by induction.

- $DAG_S(\text{null}, \emptyset, \emptyset)$
- $DAG_S(\ell, [(i, b, S_0)] @ L_0, s_0 \uplus \{\ell \mapsto \langle i, b, S(i), S_0, \ell_0 \rangle\})$
  if $\ell \neq \text{null}$, $DAG_{S+S_0}(\ell_0, L_0, s_0)$, and $i \neq i_0$ for any $(i_0, \_, \_) \in L_0$.

Here, the subscript S is a multiset of node IDs, representing the number of references to each node.

We also give a specification of our garbage collector as follows. It is more abstract than the implementation because it looks at only the positiveness of the reference count $S(i)$, not its concrete value (i.e., only whether the node is referred to, not how many times).

$$GC_S([]) \qquad\qquad\qquad = []$$
$$GC_S([(i, b, S_0)] @ L_1) \quad = [(i, b, S_0)] @ GC_{S+S_0}(L_1) \quad \text{if } b = \text{true or } S(i) > 0$$
$$GC_S([(i, \text{false}, S_0)] @ L_1) = GC_S(L_1) \qquad\qquad\qquad\qquad \text{if } S(i) = 0$$

GC_S takes a list of triples (i, b, S_0) that represent nodes, where i is the node ID, b the root flag, and S_0 the multiset of the IDs of the children. Here, the subscript S is the multiset of the IDs of nodes pointed to by "external" nodes, i.e., by nodes that are not in the list.

Now, the following lemma can be proved.

Lemma 1. *Suppose $DAG_S(\ell, L, s)$. Then, for any t and T, we have $s \uplus t \triangleright decr(\ell)T \twoheadrightarrow s_0 \uplus t \triangleright \ell_0$ with $DAG_{S-T}(\ell_0, GC_{S-T}(L), s_0)$. (Here, we are abusing notation and writing T for an integer list representing the integer multiset T.)*

Given the lemma above, it is straightforward to give an environmental predicate for *dag* and prove it to be memory safe under arbitrary (public) contexts. In fact, we can prove more properties, e.g., that the number of private locations matches the number of nodes (and therefore the number of *live* nodes after a call to *gc*) plus one (for z). To be specific, take

$$X = \{(\emptyset, \emptyset \triangleright dag)\}$$
$$\cup \{(F^\omega(\{\tilde{\ell}^\perp\}), t \triangleright e) \mid DAG_\emptyset(\ell^\top, L, s),\ d \in F^\omega(\{\tilde{\ell}^\perp\}),\ v, \tilde{w} \in (F^\omega(\{\tilde{\ell}^\perp\}))^\star,$$
$$s \uplus \{m^\top \mapsto \ell^\top\} \uplus \{\tilde{\ell}^\perp \mapsto \tilde{w}\} \triangleright d(v) \twoheadrightarrow t \triangleright e\}$$
$$\cup \{(F^\omega(\{\tilde{\ell}^\perp\}), s \uplus \{m^\top \mapsto \ell^\top\}) \mid DAG_\emptyset(\ell^\top, L, s)\}$$

where

$$F(\mathcal{R}) = \mathcal{R} \cup \{[m^\top/z]\,addn, [m^\top/z]\,deln, [m^\top/z]\,gc\}$$
$$\cup \{[v/x][m^\top/z](\lambda p.\ x + 0; \ldots) \mid v \in \mathcal{R}^\star\}.$$

Then, X is an environmental P-predicate up-to, where

$$P = \{(\mathcal{R}, s \uplus \{m^\top \mapsto \ell^\top\} \uplus \{\tilde{\ell}^\perp \mapsto \tilde{w}\} \triangleright e) \mid safe(s \uplus \{m^\top \mapsto \ell^\top\} \uplus \{\tilde{\ell}^\perp \mapsto \tilde{w}\} \triangleright e)\}$$
$$\cup \{(\mathcal{R}, s \uplus \{m^\top \mapsto \ell^\top\} \uplus \{\tilde{\ell}^\perp \mapsto \tilde{w}\}) \mid DAG_\emptyset(\ell^\top, L, s)\}.$$

Appendix D gives another example of memory safety proof by environmental P-predicates.

7   Conclusion

As is often the case in programming language theories, our theory may seem trivial in hindsight. In particular, all the proofs are arguably straightforward (though sometimes just lengthy because of case analyses) once organized in the way presented here. However, such an organization and the *definitions* were far from trivial, especially because of the non-monotone stores and non-deterministic reduction.

Future work includes deriving such definitions systematically from the operational semantics of a language (cf. [7]), so that the definitions and proofs do not have to be repeated manually for every language. Another direction is mechanization. Although complete automation is clearly impossible, ideas from model checking and type-based analyses may be useful for sound approximation. Weakening the contextuality to restrict the possible contexts—so that more programs can be proved correct—would also be useful in practice.

References

[1] Ahmed, A.: Semantics of Types for Mutable State. PhD thesis, Princeton University (2004)

[2] Ahmed, A., Dreyer, D., Rossberg, A.: State-dependent representation independence. In: Proceedings of the 36th ACM SIGPLAN-SIGACT Symposium on Principles of Programming Languages (2009) (to appear), http://ttic.uchicago.edu/~amal/papers/sdri.pdf

[3] Ahmed, A., Fluet, M., Morrisett, G.: A step-indexed model of substructural state. In: Proceedings of the Tenth ACM SIGPLAN International Conference on Functional Programming, pp. 78–91 (2005)

[4] Ahmed, A., Fluet, M., Morrisett, G.: L3: A linear language with locations. TLCA 2005 77(4), 397–449 (2007); extended abstract appeared in: Typed Lambda Calculi and Applications. LNCS, vol. 3461, pp. 293–307. Springer (2005)

[5] Bohr, N.: Advances in Reasoning Principles for Contextual Equivalence and Termination. PhD thesis, IT University of Copenhagen (2007)

[6] Crary, K., Walker, D., Morrisett, G.: Typed memory management in a calculus of capabilities. In: Proceedings of the 26th ACM SIGPLAN-SIGACT Symposium on Principles of Programming Languages, pp. 262–275 (1999)

[7] Koutavas, V., Wand, M.: Small bisimulations for reasoning about higher-order imperative programs. In: Proceedings of the 33rd ACM SIGPLAN-SIGACT Symposium on Principles of Programming Languages, pp. 141–152 (2006)

[8] Meyer, A.R., Sieber, K.: Towards fully abstract semantics for local variables: Preliminary report. In: Proceedings of the 15th ACM SIGPLAN-SIGACT Symposium on Principles of Programming Languages, pp. 191–203 (1988)

[9] Mitchell, J.C.: Foundations for Programming Languages. MIT Press, Cambridge (1996)

[10] Morris Jr., J.H.: Lambda-Calculus Models of Programming Languages. PhD thesis, Massachusetts Institute of Technology (1968)

[11] Pitts, A.M., Stark, I.: Operational reasoning for functions with local state. In: Higher Order Operational Techniques in Semantics, pp. 227–273. Cambridge University Press, Cambridge (1998)

[12] Sangiorgi, D., Kobayashi, N., Sumii, E.: Environmental bisimulations for higher-order languages. In: Twenty-Second Annual IEEE Symposium on Logic in Computer Science, pp. 293–302 (2007)

[13] Sumii, E.: A theory of non-monotone memory (or: Contexts for free), http://www.kb.ecei.tohoku.ac.jp/~sumii/pub/non-mono.pdf

[14] Sumii, E., Pierce, B.C.: A bisimulation for dynamic sealing. Theoretical Computer Science 375, 1–3, 169–192 (2007); extended abstract appeared in: Proceedings of the 31st ACM SIGPLAN-SIGACT Symposium on Principles of Programming Languages, pp. 161–172 (2004)

[15] Sumii, E., Pierce, B.C.: A bisimulation for type abstraction and recursion. Journal of the ACM 54, 5–26, 1–43 (2007); extended abstract appeared in: Proceedings of the 32nd ACM SIGPLAN-SIGACT Symposium on Principles of Programming Languages, pp. 63–74 (2005)

[16] Tofte, M., Talpin, J.-P.: Implementation of the typed call-by-value λ-calculus using a stack of regions. In: Proceedings of the 21st ACM SIGPLAN-SIGACT Symposium on Principles of Programming Languages, pp. 188–201 (1994)

[17] Wadler, P.: Linear types can change the world! In: Programming Concepts and Methods. North Holland, Amsterdam (1990)

Abstraction for Concurrent Objects*

Ivana Filipović, Peter O'Hearn, Noam Rinetzky, and Hongseok Yang

Queen Mary University of London, UK

Abstract. Concurrent data structures are usually designed to satisfy correctness conditions such as sequential consistency and linearizability. In this paper, we consider the following fundamental question: what guarantees are provided by these conditions for client programs? We formally show that these conditions can be *characterized* in terms of observational refinement. Our study also provides a new understanding of sequential consistency and linearizability in terms of abstraction of dependency between computation steps of client programs.

1 Introduction

The design and implementation of correct and efficient concurrent programs is a challenging problem. Thus, it is not surprising that programmers prefer to develop concurrent software mainly by utilizing highly-optimized concurrent data structures that have been implemented by experts.

Unfortunately, there is a gap in our theoretical understanding, which can have a serious consequence on the correctness of client programs of those concurrent data structures. Usually, programmers expect that the behavior of their program does not change whether they use experts' data structures or less-optimized but obviously-correct data structures. In the programming language community, this expectation has been formalized as observational refinement [4,8,11]. On the other hand, concurrent data structures are designed with different correctness conditions proposed by the concurrent-algorithm community, such as *sequential consistency* [9] and *linearizability* [6]. Can these correctness conditions meet programmers' expectation? In other words, what are the relationships between these conditions and observational refinement? As far as we know, no systematic studies have been done to answer this question.

The goal of this paper is to close the aforementioned gap. We show that (1) linearizability coincides with observational refinement, and (2) as long as the threads are non-interfering (except through experts' concurrent data structures), sequential consistency is equivalent to observational refinement. Our results pinpoint when it is possible to replace a concurrent data structure by another sequentially consistent or linearizable data structure in (client) programs, while preserving observable properties of the programs. One direction in this connection (that linearizability implies observational refinement) has been folklore amongst concurrent-algorithm researchers, and our results provide the first formal confirmation of this folklore. On the other hand, as far as we are aware the other direction (when observational refinement implies linearizability or sequential consistency) is not prefigured or otherwise suggested in the literature.

---

* We would like to thank anonymous referees, Viktor Vafeiadis and Matthew Parkinson for useful comments. This work was supported by EPSRC.

G. Castagna (Ed.): ESOP 2009, LNCS 5502, pp. 252–266, 2009.

Programs, Object Systems, and Histories. A concurrent data structure provides a set of procedures, which may be invoked by concurrently executing threads of the client program using the data structure. Thus, procedure invocations may overlap. (In our setting, a data structure can neither create threads nor call a procedure of the client.) We refer to a collection of concurrent data structures as an *object system.*

In this paper, we are not interested in the implementation of an object system; we are only interested in the possible interactions between the client program and the object system. Thus, we assume that an object system is represented by a set of *histories.* Every history records a possible interaction between the client application program and the object system. The interaction is given in the form of sequences of procedure invocations made by the client and the responses which it receives. A program can use an object system only by interacting with it according to one of the object system's histories. [1]

Example 1. The history $H_0 = (t_1, call\ q.enq(1)); (t_1, ret()\ q.enq); (t_2, call\ q.deq());$ $(t_2, ret(1)\ q.deq)$ records an interaction in which thread t_1 enqueues 1 into queue q followed by a dequeue by thread t_2. The histories

$$H_1 = (t_1, call\ q.enq(1))(t_1, ret()\ q.enq)(t_2, call\ q.enq(2))(t_2, ret()\ q.enq)$$
$$H_2 = (t_2, call\ q.enq(2))(t_2, ret()\ q.enq)(t_1, call\ q.enq(1))(t_1, ret()\ q.enq)$$
$$H_3 = (t_1, call\ q.enq(1))(t_2, call\ q.enq(2))(t_1, ret()\ q.enq)(t_2, ret()\ q.enq)$$

record interactions in which thread t_1 enqueues 1 into the queue and thread t_2 enqueues 2. In H_1, the invocation made by t_1 happens before that of t_2 (i.e., t_1 gets a response before t_2 invokes its own procedure). In H_2, it is the other way around. In H_3, the two invocations overlap.

Sequential Consistency and Linearizability. Informally, an object system OS_C is *sequentially consistent* wrt. an object system OS_A if for every history H_C in OS_C, there exists a history H_A in OS_A that is just another interleaving of threads' actions in H_C: in both H_C and H_A, the same threads invoke the same sequences of operations (i.e., procedure invocations) and receive the same sequences of responses. We say that such H_C and H_A are *weakly equivalent.* (We use the term *weak* equivalence to emphasis that the only relation between H_C and H_A is that they are different interleavings of the same sequential threads.) OS_C is *linearizable* wrt. OS_A, if for every history H_C in OS_C, there is some H_A in OS_A such that (1) H_C and H_A are weakly equivalent and (2) the global order of non-overlapping invocations of H_C is preserved in H_A. [2] In the context of this paper, the main difference between sequential consistency and linearizability is, intuitively, that the former preserves only the happens-before relation between operations of the *same* thread while the latter preserves this relation between the operations of *all* threads.

---

[1] This is a standard assumption in concurrent algorithms work, which Herlihy and Shavit refer to as *interference freedom* [5]: it is an assumption which would have to be verified by other means when applying the theory to particular programming languages or programs.

[2] It is common to require that OS_A be comprised of sequential histories, i.e., ones in which invocations do not overlap. (In this setting, linearizability intuitively means that every operation appears to happen atomically between its invocation and its response.) However, this requirement is not technically necessary for our results, so we do not impose it.

Example 2. The histories H_1, H_2, and H_3 are weakly equivalent. None of them is weakly equivalent to H_0. The history H_3 is linearizable wrt. H_1 as well as H_2, because H_3 does not have non-overlapping invocations. On the other hand, H_1 is not linearizable with respect to H_2; in H_1, the enqueue of t_1 is completed before that of t_2 even starts, but this global order on these two enqueues is reversed in H_2.

Observational Refinement. Our notion of observational refinement is based on observing the initial and final values of variables of client programs. (One can think of the program as having a final command "print all variables".) We say that an object system OS_C observationally refines an object system OS_A if every program P with OS_A, replacing OS_A by OS_C does not generate new observations: for every initial state s, the execution of P with OS_C at s produces only those output states that can already be obtained by running P with OS_A at s.

The main results of this paper is the following characterization of sequential consistency and linearizability in terms of observational refinement:

1. OS_C observationally refines OS_A iff OS_C is sequential consistent with respect to OS_A, assuming client operations (e.g., assignments to variables) of each thread access thread-local variables (or resources) only.
2. OS_C observationally refines OS_A iff OS_C is linearizable with respect to OS_A, assuming that client operations may use at least one shared global variable.

We start the paper by defining a programming language and giving its semantics together with the formal definition of observational refinement (Sections 2, 3, 4 and 5). Then, we describe a generic technique for proving observational refinement in Section 6, and use this technique to prove the connection between observational refinement and linearizability or sequential consistency in Section 7. The next section revisits the definitions of sequential consistency and linearizability, and provides the analysis of them in terms of the dependency between computation steps. Finally, we conclude the paper in Section 9. For space reasons, some proofs are omitted. They can be found in the full version of the paper [3].

2   Programming Language

We assume that we are given a fixed collection O of objects, with method calls $o.f(n)$. For simplicity, all methods will take one integer argument and return an integer value. We will denote method calls by $x := o.f(e)$.

The syntax of sequential commands C and complete programs P is given below:

$$C ::= \mathtt{c} \mid x := o.f(e) \mid C; C \mid C + C \mid C^\star \qquad P ::= C_1 \parallel \cdots \parallel C_n$$

Here, $\mathtt{c}$ ranges over an unspecified collection PComm of primitive commands, $+$ is nondeterministic choice, ; is sequential composition, and $(\cdot)^\star$ is Kleene-star (iterated ;). We use $+$ and $(\cdot)^\star$ instead of conditionals and while loops for theoretical simplicity: given appropriate primitive actions the conditionals and loops can be encoded. In this paper, we assume that the primitive commands include assume statements $\mathtt{assume}(b)$ and assignments $x := e$ not involving method calls.[3]

---

[3] The $\mathtt{assume}(b)$ statement acts as skip when the input state satisfies b. If b does not hold in the input state, the statement deadlocks and does not produce any output states.

3   Action Trace Model

Following Brookes [2], we will define the semantics of our language in two stages. In the first there will be a trace model, where the traces are built from atomic actions. This model resolves all concurrency by interleaving. In the second stage, which is shown in Section 5, we will define the evaluation of these action traces with initial states.

Definition 1. *An* **atomic action** *(in short, action)* φ *is a client operation or a call or return action:* $\varphi ::= (t, a) \mid (t, call\, o.f(n)) \mid (t, ret(n)\, o.f)$. *Here, t is a thread-id (i.e., a natural number), a in* (t, a) *is an atomic client operation taken from an unspecified set* Cop_t *(parameterized by the thread-id t), and n is an integer. An* **action trace** *(in short, trace)* τ *is a finite sequential composition of actions (i.e.,* $\tau ::= \varphi; \cdots; \varphi$*).*

We identify a special class of traces where calls to object methods run sequentially.

Definition 2. *A trace* τ *is* **sequential** *when all calls in* τ *are immediately followed by matching returns, that is,* τ *belongs to the set*

$$\left(\bigcup_{t,a,o,f,n,m} \{ (t,a), \quad (t, call\, o.f(n)); (t, ret(m)\, o.f) \} \right)^* \left(\bigcup_{t,o,f,n} \{ \epsilon, \quad (t, call\, o.f(n)) \} \right).$$

Intuitively, the sequentiality means that all method calls to objects run atomically. Note that the sequentiality also ensures that method calls and returns are properly matched (possibly except the last call), so that, for instance, no sequential traces start with a return action, such as $(t, ret(3)\, o.f)$.

The execution of a program in this paper generates only well-formed traces.

Definition 3. *A trace* τ *is* **well-formed** *iff for all thread-ids t, the projection of* τ *to the t-thread,* $\tau|_t$*, is sequential.*

The well-formedness formalizes two properties of traces. Firstly, it ensures that all the returns should have corresponding method calls. Secondly, it formalizes the intuition that each thread is a sequential program, if it is considered in isolation. Thus, when the thread calls a method $o.f$, it has to wait until the method returns, before doing anything else. We denote the set of all well-formed traces by *WTraces*.

Our trace model $T(-)$ defines the meaning of sequential commands and programs in terms of traces, and it is shown in Figure 1. In our model, a sequential command C means a set $T(C)t$ of well-formed traces, which is parametrized by the id t of a thread running the command. The semantics of a complete program (a parallel composition) P, on the other hand, is a non-parametrized set $T(P)$ of well-formed traces; instead of taking thread-ids as parameters, $T(P)$ creates thread-ids.

Two cases of our semantics are slightly unusual and need further explanations. The first case is the primitive commands c. In this case, the semantics assumes that we are given an interpretation $[\![c]\!]_t$ of c, where c means finite sequences of atomic client operations (i.e., $[\![c]\!]_t \subseteq Cop_t^+$). By allowing sequences of length 2 or more, this assumed interpretation allows the possibility that c is not atomic, but implemented by a sequence of atomic operations. The second case is method calls. Here the semantics distinguishes calls and returns to objects, to be able to account for concurrency (overlapping operations). Given $x:=o.f(e)$, the semantics non-deterministically chooses two

$$T(\mathbf{c})t = \{ \; (t, a_1); (t, a_2); \ldots; (t, a_k) \;\mid\; a_1; a_2; \ldots; a_k \in [\![\mathbf{c}]\!]_t \; \}$$
$$T(x{:=}o.f(e))t = \{ \; \tau; (t, call\ o.f(n)); (t, ret(n')\ o.f); \tau' \;\mid$$
$$n, n' \in Integers \;\wedge\; \tau \in T(\mathbf{assume}(e{=}n))t \;\wedge\; \tau' \in T(x{:=}n')t \; \}$$
$$T(C_1; C_2)t = \{ \tau_1; \tau_2 \mid \tau_i \in T(C_i)t \} \quad T(C_1{+}C_2)t = T(C_1)t \cup T(C_2)t \quad T(C^*)t = (T(C)t)^*$$
$$T(C_1 \parallel \cdots \parallel C_n) \;=\; \bigcup \{ \; interleave(\tau_1, \ldots, \tau_n) \;\mid\; \tau_i \in T(C_i)i \;\wedge\; 1 \leq i \leq n \; \}$$

Fig. 1. Action Trace Model. Here $\tau \in interleave(\tau_1, \ldots, \tau_n)$ iff every action in τ is done by a thread $1 \leq i \leq n$ and $\tau|_i = \tau_i$ for every such thread i.

integers n, n', and uses them to describe a call with input n and a return with result n'. In order to ensure that the argument e evaluates to n, the semantics inserts the assume statement $\mathbf{assume}(e{=}n)$ before the call action, and to ensure that x gets the return value n', it adds the assignment $x{:=}n'$ after the return action. Note that some of the choices here might not be feasible; for instance, the chosen n may not be the value of the parameter expression e when the call action is invoked, or the concurrent object never returns n' when called with n. The next evaluation stage of our semantics will filter out all these infeasible call/return pairs.

Lemma 1. *For all sequential commands C, programs P and thread-ids t, both $T(C)t$ and $T(P)$ contain only well-formed traces.*

4 Object Systems

The semantics of objects is given using histories, which are sequences of calls and returns to objects. We first define precisely what the individual elements in the histories are.

Definition 4. *An **object action** is a call or return: $\psi ::= (t, call\ o.f(n)) \mid (t, ret(n)$ $o.f)$. A **history** H is a finite sequence of object actions (i.e., $H ::= \psi; \psi; \ldots; \psi$). If a history H is well-formed when viewed as a trace, we say that H is **well-formed**.*

Note that in contrast to traces, histories do not include atomic client operations (t, a). We will use $\mathcal{A}$ for the set of all actions, $\mathcal{A}_o$ for the set of all object actions, and $\mathcal{A}_c$ for $\mathcal{A} - \mathcal{A}_o$, i.e., the set of all client operations.

We follow Herlihy and Wing's approach [6], and define object systems.

Definition 5. *An **object system** OS is a set of well-formed histories.*

Notice that OS is a collective notion, defined for all objects together rather than for them independently. Sometimes, the traces of a system satisfy special properties.

Definition 6. *Let OS be an object system. We say that OS is **sequential** iff it contains only sequential traces; OS is **local** iff for any well-formed history H, $H \in OS \iff (\forall o.\ H|_o \in OS)$.*

A local object system is one in which the set of histories for all the objects together is determined by the set of histories for each object individually. Intuitively, locality means that objects can be specified in isolation. Sequential and local object systems are commonly used as specifications for concurrent objects in the work on concurrent algorithms. (See, e.g., [5]).

5 Semantics of Programs

We move on to the second stage of our semantics, which defines the evaluation of traces. Suppose we are given a trace τ and an initial state s, which is a function from variables $x, y, z, \ldots$ to integers.[4] The second stage is the evaluation of the trace τ with s, and it is formally described by the evaluation function eval below:

$$\text{eval} \quad : \quad \textit{States} \times \textit{WTraces} \to \mathcal{P}(\textit{States})$$
$$\text{eval}(s, (t, \textit{call } o.f(n)); \tau) = \text{eval}(s, \tau) \qquad \text{eval}(s, (t, \textit{ret}(n) \, o.f); \tau) = \text{eval}(s, \tau)$$
$$\text{eval}(s, (t, a); \tau) = \bigcup\nolimits_{(s,s') \in [\![a]\!]} \text{eval}(s', \tau) \qquad \text{eval}(s, \epsilon) = \{s\}$$

The semantic clause for atomic client operations (t, a) assumes that we already have an interpretation $[\![a]\!]$ where a means a binary relation on $\textit{States}$. Note that a state s does not change during method calls and returns. This is because firstly, in the evaluation map, a state describes the values of client variables only, not the internal status of objects and secondly, the assignment of a return value n to a variable x in $x{:=}o.f(e)$ is handled by a separate client operation; see the definition of $T(x{:=}o.f(e))$ in Figure 1.

Now we combine the two stages, and give the semantics of programs P. Given a specific object system OS, the formal semantics $[\![P]\!](OS)$ is defined as follows:

$$[\![P]\!](OS) \quad : \quad \textit{States} \to \mathcal{P}(\textit{States})$$
$$[\![P]\!](OS)(s) \quad = \quad \bigcup\{\, \text{eval}(s, \tau) \mid \tau \in T(P) \wedge \text{getHistory}(\tau) \in OS \,\}$$

Here getHistory(τ) is the projection of τ to object actions. The semantics first calculates all traces $T(P)$ for τ, and then selects only those traces whose interactions with objects can be implemented by OS. Finally, the semantics runs all the selected traces with the initial state s.

Our semantics observes the initial and final values of variables in threads, and ignores the object histories. One can think of the program as having a final command "print all variables", which gives us our observable. We use this notion of observation and compare two different object systems OS_A and OS_C.

Definition 7. *Let OS_A and OS_C be object systems. We say that*

- OS_C **observationally refines** $OS_A \iff \forall P, s.\, [\![P]\!](OS_C)(s) \subseteq [\![P]\!](OS_A)(s)$;
- OS_C *is* **observationally equivalent** *to* $OS_A \iff \forall P.\, [\![P]\!](OS_C) = [\![P]\!](OS_A)$.

Usually, OS_A is a sequential local object system that serves as a specification, and OS_C is a concurrent object system representing the implementation. The observational

---

[4] All the results of the paper except the completeness can be developed without assuming any specific form of s. Here we do not take this general approach, to avoid being too abstract.

refinement means that we can replace OS_A by OS_C in any programs without introducing new behaviors of those programs, and gives a sense that OS_C is a correct implementation of OS_A.

In the remainder of this paper, we will focus on answering the question: how do correctness conditions on concurrent objects, such as linearizability, relate to observational refinement?

6   Simulation Relations on Histories

We start by describing a general method for proving observational refinement. Later, in Section 7, we will show that both linearizability and sequential consistency can be understood as specific instances of this method.

Roughly speaking, our method works as follows. Suppose that we want to prove that OS_C observationally refines OS_A. According to our method, we first need to choose a binary relation $\mathcal{R}$ on histories. This relation has to be a *simulation*, i.e., a relation that satisfies a specific requirement, which we will describe shortly. Next, we should prove that every history H in OS_C is $\mathcal{R}$-related to some history H' in OS_A. Once we finish both steps, the soundness theorem of our method lets us infer that OS_C is an observational refinement of OS_A.

The key part of the method, of course, lies in the requirement that the chosen binary relation $\mathcal{R}$ be a simulation. If we were allowed to use any relation for $\mathcal{R}$, we could pick the relation that relates all pairs of histories, and this would lead to the incorrect conclusion that every OS_C observationally refines OS_A, as long as OS_A is nonempty.

To describe our requirement on $\mathcal{R}$ and its consequence precisely, we need to formalize dependency between actions in a single trace, and define trace equivalence based on this formalization.

Definition 8 (Independent Actions). *An action φ **is independent of** an action φ', denoted $\varphi \# \varphi'$, iff (1)* $\mathsf{getTid}(\varphi) \neq \mathsf{getTid}(\varphi')$ *and (2) for all* $s \in States$, $\mathsf{eval}(s, \varphi\varphi') = \mathsf{eval}(s, \varphi'\varphi)$. *Here,* $\mathsf{getTid}(\varphi)$ *is the thread-id (i.e., the first component) of* φ.

Definition 9 (Dependency Relations). *For each trace τ, we define the **immediate dependency relation** $<_\tau$ to be the following relation on actions in τ:[5]* $\tau_i <_\tau \tau_j \iff i < j \wedge \neg(\tau_i \# \tau_j)$. *The **dependency relation** $<_\tau^+$ on τ is the transitive closure of $<_\tau$.*

Definition 10 (Trace Equivalence). *Traces τ, τ' are **equivalent**, denoted $\tau \sim \tau'$, iff there exists a bijection $\pi : \{1, \ldots, |\tau|\} \to \{1, \ldots, |\tau'|\}$ such that $(\forall i.\ \tau_i = \tau'_{\pi(i)})$ and $(\forall i, j.\ \tau_i <_\tau^+ \tau_j \iff \tau'_{\pi(i)} <_{\tau'}^+ \tau'_{\pi(j)})$.*

Intuitively, $\tau \sim \tau'$ means that τ' can be obtained by swapping independent actions in τ. Since we swap only independent actions, we expect that τ' and τ essentially mean the same computation. The lemma below justifies this expectation, by showing that our semantics cannot observe the difference between equivalent traces.

---

[5] Strictly speaking, $<_\tau$ is a relation on the indices $\{1, \ldots, |\tau|\}$ of τ so that we should have written $i <_\tau j$. In this paper, we use a rather informal notation $\tau_i <_\tau \tau_j$ instead, since we found this notation easier to understand.

Lemma 2. *For all* $\tau, \tau' \in WTraces$, *if* $\tau \sim \tau'$, *then* $(\forall P. \ \tau \in T(P) \iff \tau' \in T(P))$ *and* $(\forall s. \ \text{eval}(s, \tau) = \text{eval}(s, \tau'))$.

We are now ready to give the definition of simulation, which encapsulates our requirement on relations on histories, and to prove the soundness of our proof method based on simulation.

Definition 11 (Simulation). *A binary relation* $\mathcal{R}$ *on histories is a* **simulation** *iff for all well-formed histories* H *and* H' *such that* $(H, H') \in \mathcal{R}$,

$$\forall \tau \in WTraces. \ \text{getHistory}(\tau) = H \implies \exists \tau' \in WTraces. \ \tau \sim \tau' \wedge \text{getHistory}(\tau') = H'.$$

One way to understand this definition is to read a history H as a representation of the trace set $\text{means}(H) = \{\tau \in WTraces \mid \text{getHistory}(\tau) = H\}$. Intuitively, this set consists of the well-formed traces whose interactions with objects are precisely H. According to this reading, the requirement in the definition of simulation simply means that $\text{means}(H)$ is a subset of $\text{means}(H')$ modulo trace equivalence $\sim$. For every relation $\mathcal{R}$ on histories, we define its lifting to a relation $\lhd_{\mathcal{R}}$ on object systems as follows: $OS_C \lhd_{\mathcal{R}} OS_A \iff \forall H \in OS_C. \exists H' \in OS_A. (H, H') \in \mathcal{R}$.

Theorem 1. *If* $OS_C \lhd_{\mathcal{R}} OS_A$ *and* $\mathcal{R}$ *is a simulation,* OS_C *observationally refines* OS_A.

Proof. Consider a program P and states s, s' such that $s' \in [\![P]\!](OS_C)(s)$. Then, by the definition of $[\![P]\!]$, there exist a well-formed trace $\tau \in T(P)$ and a history $H \in OS_C$ such that $\text{getHistory}(\tau) = H$ and $s' \in \text{eval}(s, \tau)$. Since $H \in OS_C$ and $OS_C \lhd_{\mathcal{R}} OS_A$ by our assumption, there exists $H' \in OS_A$ with $(H, H') \in \mathcal{R}$. Furthermore, H and H' are well-formed, because object systems contain only well-formed histories. Now, since $\mathcal{R}$ is a simulation, τ is well-formed and $\text{getHistory}(\tau) = H$, there exists a well-formed trace τ' such that (1) $\tau \sim \tau'$ and (2) $\text{getHistory}(\tau') = H'$. Note that because of Lemma 2, the first conjunct here implies that $\tau' \in T(P)$ and $s' \in \text{eval}(s, \tau')$. This and the second conjunct $\text{getHistory}(\tau') = H'$ together imply the desired $s' \in [\![P]\!](OS_A)(s)$.   □

7   Sequential Consistency, Linearizability and Refinement

Now we explain the first two main results of this paper: (1) linearizability implies observational refinement; (2) sequential consistency implies observational refinement if client operations of each thread access thread-local variables (or resources) only.

It is not difficult to obtain high-level understanding about why our results hold. Both linearizability and sequential consistency define certain relationships between two object systems, one of which is normally assumed sequential and local. Interestingly, in both cases, we can prove that these relationships are generated by lifting some *simulation* relations. From this observation follow our results, because Theorem 1 says that all such simulation-generated relationships on object systems imply observational refinements.

In the rest of this section, we will spell out the details of the high-level proof sketches just given. For this, we need to review the relations on histories used by sequential consistency and linearizability [6].

Definition 12 (Weakly Equivalent Histories). *Two histories are* **weakly equiva-**
lent, *denoted* $H \equiv H'$, *iff their projections to threads are equal:*[6] $H \equiv H' \iff \forall t. H|_t = H'|_t$.

As its name indicates, the weak equivalence is indeed a weak notion. It only says that
the two traces are both interleavings of the same sequential threads (but they could be
different interleavings).

Definition 13 (Happen-Before Order). *For each history* H, *the* **happen-before order**
$\prec_H$ *is a binary relation on object actions in* H *defined by*

$$H_i \prec_H H_j \iff \exists i', j'. \ i \leq i' < j' \leq j \wedge \mathsf{retAct}(H_{i'}) \wedge \mathsf{callAct}(H_{j'}) \wedge$$
$$\mathsf{getTid}(H_i) = \mathsf{getTid}(H_{i'}) \wedge \mathsf{getTid}(H_{j'}) = \mathsf{getTid}(H_j)$$

Here $\mathsf{retAct}(\psi)$ *holds when* ψ *is a return and* $\mathsf{callAct}(\psi)$ *holds when* ψ *is a call.*

This definition is intended to express that in the history H, the method call for H_i is
completed before the call for H_j starts. To see this intention, assume that H is well-
formed. One important consequence of this assumption is that if an object action ψ of
some thread t is followed by some return action ψ' of the same thread in the history
H (i.e., $H = ...\psi...\psi'...$), then the return for ψ itself appears before ψ' or it is ψ'.
Thus, the existence of $H_{i'}$ in the definition ensures that the return action for H_i appears
before or at $H_{i'}$ in the history H. By a similar argument, we can see that the call for
H_j appears after or at $H_{j'}$. Since $i' < j'$, these two observations mean that the return
for H_i appears before the call for H_j, which is the intended meaning of the definition.
Using this happen-before order, we define the linearizability relation $\sqsubseteq$:

Definition 14 (Linearizability Relation). *The linearizability relation is a binary re-*
lation $\sqsubseteq$ *on histories defined as follows:* $H \sqsubseteq H'$ *iff (1)* $H \equiv H'$ *and (2) there*
is a bijection $\pi : \{1, ..., |H|\} \to \{1, ..., |H'|\}$ *such that* [7] $(\forall i. H_i = H'_{\pi(i)})$ *and*
$(\forall i, j. H_i \prec_H H_j \implies H'_{\pi(i)} \prec_{H'} H'_{\pi(j)})$.

Recall that for each relation $\mathcal{R}$ on histories, its lifting $\lhd_{\mathcal{R}}$ to the relation on object
systems is defined by: $OS \lhd_{\mathcal{R}} OS' \iff \forall H \in OS. \exists H' \in OS'. (H, H') \in \mathcal{R}$. Using
this lifting, we formally specify sequential consistency and linearizability.

Definition 15. *Let* OS_A *and* OS_C *be object systems. We say that* OS_C *is* **sequentially**
consistent *wrt.* OS_A *iff* $OS_C \lhd_{\equiv} OS_A$. *We also say that* OS_C *is* **linearizable** *wrt.* OS_A
iff $OS_C \lhd_{\sqsubseteq} OS_A$.

Note that this definition does not assume the sequentiality and locality of OS_A, unlike
Herlihy and Wing's definitions. We use this more general definition here in order to em-
phasize that the core ideas of sequential consistency and linearizability lie in relations $\equiv$
and $\sqsubseteq$ on histories, not in the use of a sequential local object system (as a specification).
    We first prove the theorem that connects linearizability and observational refinement.
Our proof uses the lemma below:

---

[6] For the same definition, Herlihy and Wing use the terminology "equivalence".

[7] In this paper, we consider only those histories that arise from complete terminating computations; see the definition of $[P]$ in Section 5. Consequently, we do not have to worry about
completing or removing pending calls in histories, unlike Herlihy and Wing's definition.

Lemma 3. *Let H be a well-formed history and let i, j be indices in $\{1, \ldots, |H|\}$. Then,*

$$(\exists \tau \in \mathit{WTraces}. \, \mathsf{getHistory}(\tau) = H \ \wedge \ H_i <_\tau^+ H_j)$$
$$\implies (i < j) \wedge (\mathsf{getTid}(H_i) = \mathsf{getTid}(H_j) \vee H_i \prec_H H_j).$$

Proof. Consider a well-formed history H, indices i, j of H and a well-formed trace τ such that the assumptions of this lemma hold. Then, we have indices $i_1 < i_2 < \cdots < i_n$ of τ such that

$$H_i \ = \ \tau_{i_1} \ <_\tau \ \tau_{i_2} \ <_\tau \ \cdots \ <_\tau \ \tau_{i_{n-1}} \ <_\tau \ \tau_{i_n} \ = \ H_j. \qquad (1)$$

One conclusion $i < j$ of this lemma follows from this, because $\mathsf{getHistory}(\tau) = H$ means that the order of object actions in H are maintained in τ. To obtain the other conclusion of the lemma, let $t = \mathsf{getTid}(H_i)$ and $t' = \mathsf{getTid}(H_j)$. Suppose that $t \neq t'$. We will prove that for some $i_k, i_l \in \{i_1, \ldots, i_n\}$,

$$i_k < i_l \ \wedge \ t = \mathsf{getTid}(\tau_{i_k}) \ \wedge \ t' = \mathsf{getTid}(\tau_{i_l}) \ \wedge \ \mathsf{retAct}(\tau_{i_k}) \ \wedge \ \mathsf{callAct}(\tau_{i_l}). \qquad (2)$$

Note that this gives the conclusion we are looking for, because all object actions in τ are from H and their relative positions in τ are the same as those in H. In the rest of the proof, we focus on showing (2) for some i_k, i_l. By the definition of $\#$, an object action ψ can depend on another action φ, only when both actions are done by the same thread. Now note that the first and last actions in the chain in (1) are *object* actions by *different* threads t and t'. Thus, the chain in (1) must contain *client* operations τ_{i_x} and τ_{i_y} such that $\mathsf{getTid}(\tau_{i_x}) = t$ and $\mathsf{getTid}(\tau_{i_y}) = t'$. Let τ_{i_a} be the first client operation by the thread t in the chain and let τ_{i_b} be the last client operation by t'. Then, $i_a < i_b$. This is because otherwise, the sequence $\tau_{i_a} \, \tau_{i_a+1} \, \cdots \, \tau_{i_n}$ does not have any client operation of the thread t', while τ_{i_a} is an action of the thread t and τ_{i_n} is an action of the different thread t'; these facts make it impossible to have $\tau_{i_a} <_\tau \tau_{i_a+1} <_\tau \cdots <_\tau \tau_{i_n}$. Since τ_{i_1} is an object action by the thread t and τ_{i_a} is a client operation by the same thread, by the well-formedness of τ, there should exist some i_k between i_1 (including) and i_a such that τ_{i_k} is a return object action by the thread t. By a symmetric argument, there should be some i_l between i_b and i_n (including) such that τ_{i_l} is a call object action by t'. We have just shown that i_k and i_l satisfy (2), as desired. $\qquad \square$

Theorem 2. *The linearizability relation $\sqsubseteq$ is a simulation.*

Proof. For an action φ and a trace τ, define $\varphi \# \tau$ to mean that $\varphi \# \tau_j$ for all $j \in \{1, \ldots, |\tau|\}$. In this proof, we will use this $\varphi \# \tau$ predicate and the following facts:

Fact 1. Trace equivalence $\sim$ is symmetric and transitive.
Fact 2. If $\tau \sim \tau'$ and τ is well-formed, τ' is also well-formed.
Fact 3. If $\tau \tau'$ is well-formed, its prefix τ is also well-formed.
Fact 4. If $\varphi \# \tau'$, we have that $\tau \varphi \tau' \sim \tau \tau' \varphi$.
Fact 5. If $\tau \sim \tau'$, we have that $\tau \varphi \sim \tau' \varphi$.

Consider well-formed histories H, S and a well-formed trace τ such that $H \sqsubseteq S$ and $\mathsf{getHistory}(\tau) = H$. We will prove the existence of a trace σ such that $\tau \sim \sigma$ and getHistory$(\sigma) = S$. This gives the desired conclusion of this theorem; the only missing requirement for proving that $\sqsubseteq$ is a simulation is the well-formedness of σ, but it can be inferred from $\tau \sim \sigma$ and the well-formedness of τ by Fact 2.

Our proof is by induction on the length of S. If $|S| = 0$, H has to the empty sequence as well. Thus, we can choose τ as the required σ in this case. Now suppose that $|S| \neq 0$. That is, $S = S'\psi$ for some history S' and object action ψ. Note that since the well-formed traces are closed under prefix (Fact 3), S' is also a well-formed history. During the proof, we will use this fact, especially when applying induction on S'.

Let δ be the projection of τ to client operations (i.e., $\delta = \tau|_{\mathcal{A}_c}$). The starting point of our proof is to split τ, H, δ. By assumption, $H \sqsubseteq S'\psi$. By the definition of $\sqsubseteq$, this means that

$$\begin{aligned}
\exists H', H''. \ H = H'\psi H'' \ \wedge \ H'H'' \sqsubseteq S' \\
\wedge \ \left(\forall j \in \{1, \ldots, |H''|\}. \ \neg(\psi \prec_H H''_j) \ \wedge \ \mathsf{getTid}(\psi) \neq \mathsf{getTid}(H''_j)\right).
\end{aligned} \quad (3)$$

Here we use the bijection between indices of H and $S'\psi$, which exists by the definition of $H \sqsubseteq S'\psi$. The action ψ in $H'\psi H''$ is what is mapped to the last action in $S'\psi$ by this bijection. The last conjunct of (3) says that the thread-id of every action of H'' is different from $\mathsf{getTid}(\psi)$. Thus, $\psi \# H''$ (because an *object* action is independent of all actions by *different* threads). From this independence and the well-formedness of H, we can drive that $H'H''\psi$ is well-formed (Facts 2 and 4), and that its prefix $H'H''$ is also well-formed (Fact 3). Another important consequence of (3) is that since $\tau \in interleave(\delta, H)$, the splitting $H'\psi H''$ of H induces splittings of τ and δ as follows: there exist $\tau', \tau'', \delta', \delta''$ such that

$$\tau = \tau'\psi\tau'' \ \wedge \ \delta = \delta'\delta'' \ \wedge \ \tau' \in interleave(\delta', H') \ \wedge \ \tau'' \in interleave(\delta'', H''). \quad (4)$$

The next step of our proof is to identify one short-cut for showing this theorem. The short-cut is to prove $\psi \# \tau''$. To see why this short-cut is sound, suppose that $\psi \# \tau''$. Then, by Fact 4,

$$\tau = \tau'\psi\tau'' \sim \tau'\tau''\psi. \quad (5)$$

Since τ is well-formed, this implies that $\tau'\tau''\psi$ and its prefix $\tau'\tau''$ are well-formed traces as well (Facts 2 and 3). Furthermore, $\mathsf{getHistory}(\tau'\tau'') = H'H''$, because of the last two conjuncts of (4). Thus, we can apply the induction hypothesis to $\tau'\tau'', H'H'', S'$, and obtain σ with the property: $\tau'\tau'' \sim \sigma \ \wedge \ \mathsf{getHistory}(\sigma) = S'$. From this and Fact 5, it follows that

$$\tau'\tau''\psi \sim \sigma\psi \ \wedge \ \mathsf{getHistory}(\sigma\psi) = \mathsf{getHistory}(\sigma)\psi = S'\psi. \quad (6)$$

Now, the formulas (5) and (6) and the transitivity of $\sim$ (Fact 1) imply that $\sigma\psi$ is the required trace by this theorem. In the remainder of the proof, we will use this short-cut, without explicitly mentioning it.

The final step is to do the case analysis on δ''. Specifically, we use the nested induction on the length of δ''. Suppose that $|\delta''| = 0$. Then, $\tau'' = H''$, and by the last conjunct of (3) (the universal formula), we have that $\psi \# \tau''$; since ψ is an object action, it is independent of actions by different threads. The theorem follows from this. Now consider the inductive case of this nested induction: $|\delta''| > 0$. Note that if $\psi \# \delta''$, then

$\psi\#\tau''$, which implies the theorem. So, we are going to assume that $\neg(\psi\#\delta'')$. Pick the greatest index i of τ'' such that $\psi <_\tau^+ \tau_i''$. Let $\varphi = \tau_i''$. Because of the last conjunct of (3) and Lemma 3, τ_i'' comes from δ, not H''. In particular, this ensures that there are following further splittings of δ'', τ'' and H'': for some traces $\gamma, \gamma', \kappa, \kappa', T, T'$,

$$\delta'' = \gamma\varphi\gamma' \;\wedge\; \tau'' = \kappa\varphi\kappa' \;\wedge\; H'' = TT' \;\wedge$$
$$\kappa \in interleave(\gamma, T) \;\wedge\; \kappa' \in interleave(\gamma', T') \;\wedge\; \varphi\#\kappa'.$$

Here the last conjunct $\varphi\#\kappa'$ comes from the fact that φ is the last element of τ'' with $\psi <_\tau^+ \varphi$. Since γ' is a subsequence of κ', the last conjunct $\varphi\#\kappa'$ implies that $\varphi\#\gamma'$. Also, $\tau'\psi\kappa\varphi\kappa' \sim \tau'\psi\kappa\kappa'\varphi$ by Fact 4. Now, since $\tau = \tau'\psi\kappa\varphi\kappa'$ is well-formed, the equivalent trace $\tau'\psi\kappa\kappa'\varphi$ and its prefix $\tau'\psi\kappa\kappa'$ both are well-formed as well (Facts 2 and 3). Furthermore, $\tau'\psi\kappa\kappa' \in interleave(\delta'\gamma\gamma', H'\psi H'')$. Since the length of $\gamma\gamma'$ is shorter than δ'', we can apply the induction hypothesis of the nested induction, and get

$$\exists\sigma. \quad \tau'\psi\kappa\kappa' \sim \sigma \;\wedge\; \text{getHistory}(\sigma) = S'\psi. \tag{7}$$

We will prove that $\sigma\varphi$ is the trace desired for this theorem. Because of $\varphi\#\kappa'$ and Fact 4, $\tau = \tau'\psi\kappa\varphi\kappa' \sim \tau'\psi\kappa\kappa'\varphi$. Also, because of Fact 5 and the first conjunct of (7), $\tau'\psi\kappa\kappa'\varphi \sim \sigma\varphi$. Thus, $\tau \sim \sigma\varphi$ by the transitivity of $\sim$. Furthermore, since φ is not an object action, the second conjunct of (7) implies that getHistory($\sigma\varphi$) = getHistory(σ) = $S'\psi$. We have just shown that $\sigma\varphi$ is the desired trace. $\square$

Corollary 1. *If OS_C is linearizable wrt. OS_A, then OS_C observationally refines OS_A.*

Next, we consider sequential consistency. For sequential consistency to imply observational refinement, we need to restrict programs such that threads can access local variables only in their client operations: $\forall t, t', a, a'. (t\neq t' \wedge a \in Cop_t \wedge a' \in Cop_{t'}) \implies a\#a'$.

Lemma 4. *Suppose that all threads can access local variables only in their client operations. Then, for all well-formed histories H and indices i, j in $\{1, \ldots, |H|\}$,*

$$(\exists\tau\in WTraces. \text{getHistory}(\tau)=H \wedge H_i <_\tau^+ H_j) \implies i<j \wedge \text{getTid}(H_i)=\text{getTid}(H_j).$$

Proof. Consider a well-formed history H, indices i, j and a well-formed trace τ satisfying the assumptions of this lemma. Then, for some indices $i_1 < \ldots < i_n$ of τ,

$$H_i = \tau_{i_1} <_\tau \tau_{i_2} <_\tau \cdots <_\tau \tau_{i_{n-1}} <_\tau \tau_{i_n} = H_j. \tag{8}$$

One conclusion $i < j$ of this lemma follows from this; the assumption getHistory(τ) = H of this lemma means that the order of object actions in H are maintained in τ. To obtain the other conclusion of the lemma, we point out one important property of #: under the assumption of this lemma, $\neg(\varphi\#\varphi')$ only when getTid(φ) = getTid(φ'). (Here φ, φ' are not necessarily object actions.) To see why this property holds, we assume $\neg(\varphi\#\varphi')$ and consider all possible cases of φ and φ'. If one of φ and φ' is an object action, the definition of # implies that φ and φ' have to be actions by the same thread. Otherwise, both φ and φ' are atomic client operations. By our assumption, all threads access only local variables in their client operations, so that two client operations are independent if they are performed by different threads. This implies that φ and φ' should be actions by the same thread. Now, note that $\tau_k <_\tau \tau_l$ implies $\neg(\tau_k \# \tau_l)$, which in turn entails $\mathsf{getTid}(\tau_k) = \mathsf{getTid}(\tau_l)$ by what we have just shown. Thus, we can derive the following desired equality from (8): $\mathsf{getTid}(H_i) = \mathsf{getTid}(\tau_{i_1}) = \mathsf{getTid}(\tau_{i_2}) = \ldots = \mathsf{getTid}(\tau_{i_n}) = \mathsf{getTid}(H_j)$. □

Theorem 3. *If all threads access local variables only in their client actions, the weak equivalence $\equiv$ is a simulation.*

Proof. The proof is similar to the one for Theorem 2. Instead of repeating the common parts between these two proofs, we will explain what we need to change in the proof of Theorem 2, so as to obtain the proof of this theorem. Firstly, we should replace linearizability relation $\sqsubseteq$ by weak equivalence $\equiv$. Secondly, we need to change the formula (3) to

$$\exists H' H''. \ H = H' \psi H'' \wedge H' H'' \equiv S' \wedge \forall j \in \{1, \ldots, |H''|\}. \ \mathsf{getTid}(\psi) \neq \mathsf{getTid}(H''_j).$$

Finally, we should use Lemma 4 instead of Lemma 3. After these three changes have been made, the result becomes the proof of this theorem. □

Corollary 2. *If OS_C is sequentially consistent wrt. OS_A and all threads access local variables only in their client actions, OS_C is an observational refinement of OS_A.*

Completeness. Under suitable assumptions on programming languages and object systems, we can obtain the converse of Corollaries 1 and 2: observational refinement implies linearizability and sequential consistency. First, we assume that object systems OS contain only those histories all of whose calls have matching returns. This assumption is necessary, because observational refinement considers only terminating, completed computations. Next, we assume that threads' primitive commands include the skip statement. Finally, we consider specific assumptions for sequential consistency and linearizability, which will be described shortly.

For sequential consistency, we suppose that the programming language contains atomic assignments $x{:=}n$ of constants n to thread-local variable x and has atomic assume statements of the form $\mathtt{assume}(x{=}n)$ with thread-local variable x.[8] Note that this supposition does not require the use of any global variables, so that it is consistent with the assumption of Corollary 2. Under this supposition, observational refinement implies sequential consistency.

Theorem 4. *If OS_C observationally refines OS_A then $OS_C \lhd_\equiv OS_A$.*

The main idea of the proof is to create for every history $H \in OS_C$ a program P_H that records the interaction of every thread t with the object system using t's local variables. For the details of the proof, see the full version of this paper [3].

For linearizability, we further suppose that there is a single global variable g shared by all threads. That is, threads can assign constants to g atomically, or they can run

---

[8] Technically, this assumption also means that $T(x{:=}n)t$ and $T(\mathtt{assume}(x{=}n))t$ are singleton traces (t, a) and (t, b), where $[\![b]\!](s) \equiv$ if $(s(x){=}n)$ then $\{s\}$ else $\{\}$ and $[\![a]\!](s) \equiv \{s[x{\mapsto}n]\}$.

the statement $\texttt{assume}(g{=}n)$ for some constant n. Under this supposition, observational refinement implies linearizability.

Theorem 5. *If OS_C observationally refines OS_A, then $OS_C \lhd_{\sqsubseteq} OS_A$.*

The core idea of the proof is, again, to create for every history $H \in OS_C$ one specific program P_H. This program uses a single global variable and satisfies that for every (terminating) execution τ of P_H, the object history of τ always has the same happen-before relation as H. See the full paper [3] for the details.

8 Abstract Dependency

Although our results on observational refinements give complete characterization of sequential consistency and linearizability, they still do not explain where the relations $\equiv$ and $\sqsubseteq$ in sequential consistency and linearizability come from. In this section, we will answer this question using the dependency between actions.

The result of this section is based on one reading of a well-formed history H. In this reading, the history H means not the single trace H itself but the set of all the well-formed traces whose object actions are described by H. Formally, we let $WHist$ be the set of all the well-formed histories, and define function means : $WHist \rightarrow \mathcal{P}(WTraces)$ by means$(H) = \{\tau \in WTraces \mid \texttt{getHistory}(\tau) = H\}$.

Using means, we define a new relation on well-formed histories, which compare possible dependencies between actions in the histories.

Definition 16 (Abstract Dependency). *For each well-formed history H, the* **abstract dependency** *$<_H^{\#}$ for H is the binary relation on actions in H determined as follows:*
$$H_i <_H^{\#} H_j \iff i < j \land \exists \tau \in \texttt{means}(H). \, H_i <_\tau^+ H_j.$$

Definition 17 (Causal Complexity Relation). *The* **causal complexity relation** *$\sqsubseteq^{\#}$ is a binary relation on well-formed histories, such that $H \sqsubseteq^{\#} S$ iff there exists a bijection $\pi : \{1, \ldots, |H|\} \rightarrow \{1, \ldots, |S|\}$ satisfying (1) $\forall i \in \{1, \ldots, |H|\}. \, H_i = S_{\pi(i)}$ and (2) $\forall i, j \in \{1, \ldots, |H|\}. \, H_i <_H^{\#} H_j \implies S_{\pi(i)} <_S^{\#} S_{\pi(j)}.$*

Intuitively, $H \sqsubseteq^{\#} S$ means that S is a rearrangement of actions in H that preserves all the abstract causal dependencies in H. Note that S might contain abstract causal dependencies that are not present in H.

The result below shows when sequential consistency or linearizability coincides with causal complexity relation.

Theorem 6. *If all threads access only local variables in their client operations, then $\forall H, S \in WHist. \, H \equiv S \iff H \sqsubseteq^{\#} S.$*

Theorem 7. *Assume that for every pair (t, t') of thread-ids with $t \neq t'$, there exist client operations $a \in Cop_t$ and $a' \in Cop_{t'}$ with $\neg(a \# a')$. Under this assumption, we have the following equivalence: $\forall H, S \in WHist. \, H \sqsubseteq S \iff H \sqsubseteq^{\#} S.$*

9 Conclusions

Developing a theory of data abstraction in the presence of concurrency has been a long-standing open question in the programming language community. In this paper, we have shown that this open question can be attacked from a new perspective, by carefully studying correctness conditions proposed by the concurrent-algorithm community, using the tools of programming languages. We prove that linearizability is a sound method for proving observational refinements for concurrent objects, which is complete when threads are allowed to access shared global variables. When threads access only thread-local variables, we have shown that sequential consistency becomes a sound and complete proof method for observational refinements. We hope that our new understanding on concurrent objects can facilitate the long-delayed transfer of the rich existing theories of data-abstraction [7,8,13,10,12] from sequential programs to concurrent ones.

In the paper, we used a standard assumption on a programming language from the concurrent-algorithm community. We assumed that a programming language did not allow callbacks from concurrent objects to client programs, that all the concurrent objects were properly encapsulated [1], and that programs were running under "sequentially consistent" memory models. Although widely used by the concurrent-algorithm experts, these assumptions limit the applicability of our results. In fact, they also limit the use of linearizability in the design of concurrent data structures. Removing these assumptions and extending our results is what we plan to do next.

References

1. Banerjee, A., Naumann, D.A.: Representation independence, confinement and access control. In: POPL 2002 (2002)
2. Brookes, S.D.: A semantics for concurrent separation logic. In: Gardner, P., Yoshida, N. (eds.) CONCUR 2004. LNCS, vol. 3170, pp. 16–34. Springer, Heidelberg (2004)
3. Filipović, I., O'Hearn, P., Rinetzky, N., Yang, H.: Abstraction for concurrent objects. Technical report, Queen Mary University of London (December 2008)
4. He, J., Hoare, C.A.R., Sanders, J.W.: Data refinement refined. In: Robinet, B., Wilhelm, R. (eds.) ESOP 1986. LNCS, vol. 213. Springer, Heidelberg (1986)
5. Herlihy, M., Shavit, N.: The Art of Multiprocessor Programming. Morgan Kaufmann, San Francisco (2008)
6. Herlihy, M., Wing, J.M.: Linearizability: A correctness condition for concurrent objects. ACM TOPLAS 12(3), 463–492 (1990)
7. Hoare, C.A.R.: Proof of correctness of data representations. Acta Inf. 1, 271–281 (1972)
8. Hoare, C.A.R., He, J., Sanders, J.W.: Prespecification in data refinement. Inf. Proc. Letter 25(2), 71–76 (1987)
9. Lamport, L.: How to make a multiprocessor computer that correctly executes multiprocess programs. IEEE Trans. Computers 28(9), 690–691 (1979)
10. Mitchell, J., Plotkin, G.: Abstract types have existential types. ACM TOPLAS 10(3), 470–502 (1988)
11. Plotkin, G.: LCF considered as a programming language. TCS 5, 223–255 (1977)
12. Plotkin, G., Abadi, M.: A logic for parametric polymorphism. In: Bezem, M., Groote, J.F. (eds.) TLCA 1993. LNCS, vol. 664. Springer, Heidelberg (1993)
13. Reynolds, J.C.: Types, abstraction and parametric polymorphism. In: Mason, R.E.A. (ed.) Information Processing 1983, pp. 513–523. North-Holland, Amsterdam (1983)

Minimization Algorithm
for Symbolic Bisimilarity[*]

Filippo Bonchi[1,2] and Ugo Montanari[1]

[1] Dipartimento di Informatica, Università di Pisa
[2] Centrum voor Wiskunde en Informatica (CWI)

Abstract. The operational semantics of interactive systems is usually described by labeled transition systems. Abstract semantics is defined in terms of bisimilarity that, in the finite case, can be computed via the well-known *partition refinement algorithm*. However, the behaviour of interactive systems is in many cases infinite and thus checking bisimilarity in this way is unfeasible. *Symbolic semantics* allows to define smaller, possibly finite, transition systems, by employing symbolic actions and avoiding some sources of infiniteness. Unfortunately, the standard partition refinement algorithm does not work with symbolic bisimilarity.

1 Introduction

The operational semantics of interactive system is usually specified by labeled transition systems (LTSs). Behavioural equivalence is often defined as bisimilarity, namely the largest bisimulation. Many efficient algorithms and tools for bisimulation checking in the finite case have been developed [21,7,8]. Among these, the *partition refinement algorithm* [11,18] is the best known: first it generates the state space of the LTS (i.e., the set of reachable states); then, it creates a partition equating all the states and then, iteratively, refines this partitions by splitting non equivalent states. At the end, the resulting partition equates all and only the bisimilar states.

Most importantly, the same algorithm can be used to construct the *minimal automaton*, that is the smallest (in terms of states and transitions) LTS amongst all those bisimilar. Construction of minimal automata allows to model check efficiently for several properties by eliminating redundant states once and for all. In fact most model checking logics are *adequate w.r.t. bisimilarity*, namely a formula holds in the given system iff it holds in its minimal representative.

In practical cases, *compositionality* is also very relevant, since it is the key to master complexity. Then a fundamental property is that bisimilarity be a congruence. When this is not the case, behavioural equivalence is defined either as the *largest congruence contained into bisimilarity* [13] or as the *largest bisimulation that is also a congruence* [17]. In this paper we focus on the latter and we call it *saturated bisimilarity*. Indeed it coincides with ordinary bisimilarity on

---

[*] This work was carried out during the tenure of an ERCIM "Alain Bensoussan" Fellowship Programme and supported by the IST 2004-16004 SENSORIA.

G. Castagna (Ed.): ESOP 2009, LNCS 5502, pp. 267–284, 2009.
© Springer-Verlag Berlin Heidelberg 2009

the *saturated transition system*, that is obtained by the original LTS by adding the transition $p \xrightarrow{c,a} q$, for every context c, whenever $c(p) \xrightarrow{a} q$.

Many interesting abstract semantics are defined in this way. For example, since late and early bisimilarity of π-calculus [14] are not preserved under substitution (and thus under input prefixes), in [20] Sangiorgi introduces *open bisimilarity* as the largest bisimulation on π-calculus agents which is closed under substitutions. Other noteworthy examples are asynchronous π-calculus [1,10] and mobile ambients calculus [6,12]. The definition of saturated bisimilarity as ordinary bisimulation on the saturated LTS, while in principle operational, often makes infinite state the portion of LTS reachable by any nontrivial agent, and in any case is very inefficient, since it introduces a large number of additional states and transitions. Inspired by [9], Sangiorgi defines in [20] a symbolic transition system and symbolic bisimilarity that efficiently characterizes open bisimilarity. After this, many formalisms have been equipped with a symbolic semantics.

In [4], we have introduced a general model that describes at an abstract level both saturated and symbolic semantics. In this abstract setting, a symbolic transition $p \xrightarrow{c,\alpha}_\beta p'$ means that $c(p) \xrightarrow{\alpha} p'$ and c is a smallest context that allows p to performs such transition. Moreover, a certain *derivation relation* $\vdash$ amongst the transitions of a systems is defined: $p \xrightarrow{c_1,\alpha_1} p_1 \vdash p \xrightarrow{c_2,\alpha_2} p_2$ means that the latter transition is a logical consequence of the former. In this way, if all and only the saturated transitions are logical consequences of symbolic transitions, then saturated bisimilarity can be retrieved via the symbolic LTS.

However, the ordinary bisimilarity over the symbolic transition system differs from saturated bisimilarity. Symbolic bisimilarity is thus defined with an asymmetric shape. In the bisimulation game, when a player proposes a transition, the opponent can answer with a move with a different label. For example in the open π-calculus, a transition $p \xrightarrow{[a=b],\tau} p'$ can be matched by $q \xrightarrow{\tau} q'$. Moreover, the bisimulation game does not restart from p' and q', but from p' and $q'\{b/a\}$.

For this reason, algorithms and tools developed for bisimilarity cannot be reused for symbolic bisimilarity. Inspired by [19,15] who developed ad hoc partition refinement algorithm for open and asynchronous bisimilarity, in this paper we introduce a generical *symbolic partition refinement algorithm*, relying on the theoretical framework presented in [4]. The algorithm is based on the notion of *redundant symbolic transitions*. Intuitively, a symbolic transition $p \xrightarrow{c_2,\alpha_2}_\beta q$ is redundant if there exists another symbolic transition $p \xrightarrow{c_1,\alpha_1}_\beta p_1$ that logically implies it, that is $p \xrightarrow{c_1,\alpha_1}_\beta p_1 \vdash p \xrightarrow{c_2,\alpha_2}_\beta p_2$ and q is bisimilar to p_2. Now, if we consider the LTS having only not-redundant transitions, the ordinary notion of bisimilarity coincides with saturated bisimilarity. Thus, in principle, we could remove all the redundant transitions and then check bisimilarity with the standard partition refinement algorithm. But, how can we decide which transitions are redundant, if redundancy itself depends on bisimilarity?

Our solution consists in computing bisimilarity and redundancy *at the same time*. In the first step, the algorithm considers all the states bisimilar and all the transitions (that are potentially redundant) as redundant. At any iteration, states are distinguished according to (the current estimation of) not-redundant transitions and then not-redundant transitions are updated according to the new computed partition. The main peculiarity of the algorithm is that in the initial partition, we have to insert not only the reachable states, but also those that are needed to check redundancy. An extended version of the paper is in [5].

2   Partition Refinement and Minimal Automaton

In CCS [13], bisimilarity ($\sim$) is defined as the largest bisimulation relation, i.e., the largest relation R such that $R \subseteq \mathbf{F}(R)$ where $\mathbf{F}$ is a function such that for each relation R, $p\,\mathbf{F}(R)\,q$ iff

- if $p \xrightarrow{a} p'$ then $q \xrightarrow{a} q'$ and $p'Rq'$,
- if $q \xrightarrow{a} q'$ then $p \xrightarrow{a} p'$ and $p'Rq'$.

Since $\mathbf{F}$ is monotonic for set inclusion, $\sim = \bigcup\{R \mid R \subseteq \mathbf{F}(R)\}$ follows from standard results on fixed point theory. Moreover, $\sim$ is itself a fix point of $\mathbf{F}$, i.e., $\sim = \mathbf{F}(\sim)$. Alternatively, bisimilarity can be characterized as the limit of a decreasing chains of relations (none of them is a bisimulation) starting with the universal relation. Hereafter, we use κ to denote ordinals numbers, $\kappa + 1$ for successor of κ, λ for limits ordinals and $\mathcal{O}$ for the class of all ordinals. Formally, the *terminal sequence* is defined for each ordinal κ as follow,

$$\sim^0 = \{\mathcal{P} \times \mathcal{P}\} \qquad \sim^{\kappa+1} = \mathbf{F}(\sim^\kappa) \qquad \sim^\lambda = \bigcap_{\kappa < \lambda} \sim^\kappa$$

where $\mathcal{P}$ is the set of all CCS processes.

Bisimilarity coincides with the limit of the terminal sequence.

Proposition 1. $\sim = \bigcap_{\kappa \in \mathcal{O}} \sim^\kappa$

Given a set S, a *partition* of S is a set of *blocks*, i.e. subsets of S, that are all disjoint and whose union is S. A partition on S represents an equivalence relation, where equivalent elements belong to the same block. In the following, given a function $\mathbf{G}$ on equivalence relations, we denote by $\overline{\mathbf{G}}$ the corresponding function on partitions.

The characterization of bisimilarity through the terminal sequence suggests a procedure for checking bisimilarity of a set of initial states IS. First of all, we compute IS^*, i.e., the set of all states that are reachable from IS. Then we create the partition P^0 where all the elements of IS^* belongs to the same block. After the initialization, we iteratively refine the partitions by using the function $\overline{\mathbf{F}}$ (i.e., the function equivalent to $\mathbf{F}$ on partitions): two states p and q belong to the same block in P^{n+1}, if and only if whenever $p \xrightarrow{a} p'$ then $q \xrightarrow{a} q'$ with p' and q' in the same block of P^n and viceversa. The algorithm terminates whenever two consecutive partitions are equivalent. In such partition two states belong to the same block if and only if they are bisimilar. Notice that since $\mathbf{F}$ is monotonic, any iteration splits blocks and never fuse them. For this reason if IS^* is finite, the algorithm terminates in at most $|IS^*|$ iterations.

Algorithm 1. Partition-Refinement(IS)

Initialization

1. IS^* is the set of all processes reachable from IS,
2. $P^0 := \{IS^*\}$,

Iteration $P^{n+1} := \overline{\mathbf{F}}(P^n)$,
Termination If $P^n = P^{n+1}$ then return P^n.

Proposition 2. *If IS^* is finite, then the algorithm terminates and the resulting partition equates all and only the bisimilar state.*

The partition refinement algorithm allows not only to check bisimilarity of a set of states, but also to build the *minimal automaton* of a certain state p. Intuitively, the minimal automaton is a labeled transition systems where all the bisimilar states are identified. Hereafter, given a set A and an equivalence relation R, we write $A_{|R}$ to denote the set of equivalence classes of A w.r.t. R. Moreover, given $p \in A$, $[p]_R$ denotes the equivalence class of p w.r.t. R.

Definition 1 (Minimal Automaton). *Let $\{p\}^*$ be the set of states reachable from the state p. The minimal automaton of p (denoted by $MA(p)$) is a triple $\langle i, M, tr_M \rangle$:*

- *the initial state i is equal to $[p]_\sim$,*
- *$M = \{p\}^*_{|\sim}$ is the set of equivalence classes of $\sim$,*
- *tr_M is the transition relation defined according to the following rule.*

$$\frac{q \xrightarrow{a} r}{[q]_\sim \xrightarrow{a}_M [r]_\sim}$$

Proposition 3. *$p \sim q$ if and only if $MA(p)$ is isomorphic to $MA(q)$.*

If the set of states reachable from p is finite, we can employ the partition refinement algorithm to build the minimal automaton of p. We have just to quotient the set of reachable states $\{p\}^*$ with the partition returned by the Partition-Refinement($\{p\}$).

3   Saturated and Symbolic Semantics

In this section we recall the general framework for symbolic bisimilarity that we have introduced in [4]. As running example, we will use open Petri nets [2]. However, our theory has as special cases the abstract semantics of several formalisms such as open [20] and asynchronous [1] π-calculus.

3.1   Saturated Semantics

A *closed many-sorted unary signature* (S, Σ) consists of a set of sorts S, and an $S \times S$ sorted family $\Sigma = \{\Sigma_{s,t} \mid s, t \in S\}$ of sets of operation symbols which are closed under composition, that is if $f \in \Sigma_{s,t}$ and $g \in \Sigma_{t,u}$, then $g \circ f \in \Sigma_{s,u}$. Given $f \in \Sigma_{u,v}, g \in \Sigma_{t,u}, h \in \Sigma_{s,t}$, $f \circ (g \circ h) = (f \circ g) \circ h$ and moreover $\forall s \in S$, $\exists id_s \in \Sigma_{s,s}$ such that $\forall f \in \Sigma_{s,t}$, $id_t \circ f = f$ and $f \circ id_s = f$. A (S, Σ)-algebra $\mathbb{A}$ consists of an S sorted family $|\mathbb{A}| = \{A_s \mid s \in S\}$ of sets and a function $f_\mathbb{A} : A_s \to A_t$ for all $f \in \Sigma_{s,t}$ such that $(g \circ f)_\mathbb{A} = g_\mathbb{A}(f_\mathbb{A}(-))$ and $id_{s\mathbb{A}}$ is the identity function on A_s[1]. When $\mathbb{A}$ is clear from the context, we will write f to mean $f_\mathbb{A}$, and we will write A_s to mean the set of sort s of the family $|\mathbb{A}|$.

The first definition of the theoretical framework presented in [4] is that of *context interactive systems*. In our theory, an interactive system is a state-machine that can interact with the environment (contexts) through an evolving interface.

Definition 2 (Context Interactive System). *A context interactive system $\mathcal{I}$ is a quadruple $\langle (S, \Sigma), \mathbb{A}, O, tr \rangle$ where:*

- *(S, Σ) is a closed many-sorted unary signature,*
- *$\mathbb{A}$ is a (S, Σ)-algebra,*
- *O is a set of observations,*
- *$tr \subseteq |\mathbb{A}| \times O \times |\mathbb{A}|$ is a labeled transition relation ($p \xrightarrow{o} p'$ means $(p, o, p') \in tr$).*

Roughly speaking sorts are interfaces of the system, while operators of Σ are contexts. Every state p with interface s (i.e. $p \in A_s$) can be inserted into the context $c \in \Sigma_{s,t}$, obtaining $c_\mathbb{A}(p)$ that has interface t. Every state can evolve into a new state (possibly with different interface) producing an observation $o \in O$.

The abstract semantics of interactive systems is usually defined through behavioural equivalences. In [4] we proposed a general notion of bisimilarity that generalizes the abstract semantics of a large variety of formalisms. The idea is that two states of a system are equivalent if they are indistinguishable from an external observer that, in any moment of their execution, can insert them into some environment and then observe some transitions.

Definition 3 (Saturated Bisimilarity). *Let $\mathcal{I} = \langle (S, \Sigma), \mathbb{A}, O, tr \rangle$ be a context interactive system. Let $R = \{R_s \subseteq A_s \times A_s \mid s \in S\}$ be an S sorted family of symmetric relations. R is a* saturated bisimulation *iff, $\forall s, t \in S$, $\forall c \in \Sigma_{s,t}$, whenever pR_sq:*

- *$c_\mathbb{A}(p) \, R \, c_\mathbb{A}(q)$,*
- *if $p \xrightarrow{o} p'$, then $q \xrightarrow{o} q'$ and $p'Rq'$.*

We write $p \sim_s^S q$ iff there is a saturated bisimulation R such that pR_sq.

An alternative but equivalent definition can be given by defining the *saturated transition system* (SATTS) as follows: $p \xrightarrow{c,o}_S q$ if and only if $c(p) \xrightarrow{o} q$. Trivially the ordinary bisimilarity over SATTS coincides with $\sim^S$.

Proposition 4. $\sim^S$ *is the coarsest bisimulation congruence.*

---

[1] A closed many-sorted unary signature (S, Σ) is a category $\mathbf{C}$ and a (S, Σ)-algebra is a presheaf on $\mathbf{C}$. We adopt the above notation to be accessible to a wider audience.

3.2   Running Example: Open Petri Nets

Differently from process calculi, Petri nets have not a widely known interactive behaviour. Indeed they model concurrent systems that are closed, in the sense that they do not interact with the environment. *Open nets* [2] are P/T Petri nets that can interact by exchanging tokens on *input* and *output places*.

Definition 4 (Open Net). *An* open net *is a tuple* $N = (S, T, pre, post, l, I, O)$ *where* S *and* T *are the sets of places and transitions* $(S \cap T = \varnothing)$; $pre, post : T \to S^{\oplus}$ *are functions mapping each transition to its pre- and post-set;* $l : T \to \Lambda$ *is a labeling function* $(\Lambda$ *is a set of labels) and* $I, O \subseteq S$ *are the sets of input and output places. A* marked open net *is a pair* $\langle N, m \rangle$ *where* N *is an open net and* $m \in S^{\oplus}$ *is a marking.*

Fig.1 shows five open nets where, as usual, circles represents places and rectangles transitions (labeled with α, β). Arrows from places to transitions represent *pre*, while arrows from transitions to places represent *post*. Input places are denoted by ingoing edges, thus the only input place of N_1 is \$. To make examples easier, hereafter we only consider *open input nets*, i.e., open nets without output places. The operational semantics of marked open nets is expressed by the rules on Table 1.The rule (TR) is the standard rule of P/T nets (seen as multisets rewriting). The rule (IN) states that in any moment a token can be inserted inside an input place and, for this reason, the LTS has always an infinite number of states. Fig.1(A) shows part of the infinite transition system of $\langle N_1, a \rangle$. The abstract semantics (denoted by $\sim^{N}$) is defined in [3] as the ordinary bisimilarity over such an LTS. It is worth noting that $\sim^{N}$ can be seen as an instance of saturated semantics, where multisets over open places are contexts and transitions are only those generated by the rule (TR).

In the following we formally define $\mathcal{N} = \langle (S^{\mathcal{N}}, \Sigma^{\mathcal{N}}), \mathbb{N}, \Lambda, tr_{\mathcal{N}} \rangle$ that is the context interactive system of all open nets (labeled over the set of labels Λ).

The many-sorted signature $(S^{\mathcal{N}}, \Sigma^{\mathcal{N}})$ is formally defined as:

- $S^{\mathcal{N}} = \{ I \mid I$ is a set of places$\}$,
- $\forall I \in S^{\mathcal{N}}$, $\Sigma_{I,I}^{\mathcal{N}} = I^{\oplus}$, $id_I = \varnothing$ and $i_1 \circ i_2 = i_1 \oplus i_2$.

Intuitively sorts are sets of input places I, while operators of $\Sigma^{\mathcal{N}}$ are multisets of tokens on the input places. We say that a marked open net $\langle N, m \rangle$ has interface I if the set of input places of N is I. For example the marked open nets $\langle N_1, a \rangle$ has interface \{\$\}. Let us define the $(S^{\mathcal{N}}, \Sigma^{\mathcal{N}})$-algebra $\mathbb{N}$. For any sort I, the carrier set N_I contains all the marked open nets with interface I. Any operator $i \in \Sigma_{I,I}$ is defined as the function that maps $\langle N, m \rangle$ into $\langle N, m \oplus i \rangle$.

The transition structure $tr_{\mathcal{N}}$ (denoted by $\to_{\mathcal{N}}$) associates to a state $\langle N, m \rangle$ the transitions obtained by using the rule (TR) of Table 1. In [4], it is proved that

Table 1. Operational Semantics of marked open nets

$$
\text{(TR)} \frac{t \in T \quad l(t) = \lambda \quad m = {}^{\bullet}t \oplus c}{N, m \xrightarrow{\lambda} N, t^{\bullet} \oplus c} \qquad \text{(IN)} \frac{i \in I_N}{N, m \xrightarrow{+i} N, m \oplus i}
$$

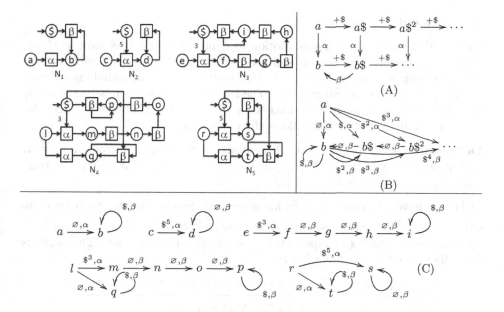

Fig. 1. The open nets N_1, N_2, N_3, N_4 and N_5.(A)Part of the infinite transition system of $\langle N_1, a\rangle$. (B)Part of the infinite saturated transition system of $\langle N_1, a\rangle$.(C)The symbolic transition systems of $\langle N_1, a\rangle$,$\langle N_2, c\rangle$,$\langle N_3, e\rangle$,$\langle N_4, l\rangle$ and $\langle N_5, r\rangle$.

saturated bisimilarity for $\mathcal{N}$ coincides with $\sim^{N}$. In the remainder of the paper we will use as running example the open nets in Fig.1. Since all the places have different names (with the exception of $), in order to make lighter the notation, we write only the marking to mean the corresponding marked net, e.g. b^2\$ means the marked net $\langle N_1, b^2$\$$\rangle$.

The marked net a (i.e., $\langle N_1, a\rangle$) represents a system that provides a service β. After the activation α, it provides β whenever the client pay one \$ (i.e., the environment insert a token into \$). The marked net c instead requires five \$ during the activation, but then provides the service β for free. The marked net e, requires three \$ during the activation. For three times, the service β is performed for free and then it costs one \$. It is easy to see that all these marked nets are not bisimilar. Indeed, a client that has only one \$ can have the service β only with a, while a client with five \$ can have the service β for six times only with c. The marked net r represents a system that offers the behaviour of both a and c, i.e. either the activation α is for free and then the service β costs one, or the activation costs five and then the service is for free. Also this marked net is different from all the others.

Now consider the marked net l. It offers the behaviour of both a and e, but it is equivalent to a, i.e. $l \sim^{N} a$. Roughly, the behaviour of e is absorbed by the behaviour of a. This is analogous to what happens in asynchronous π-calculus [1] where it holds that $a(x).(\overline{a}x \mid p) + \tau.p \sim \tau.p$.

3.3 Symbolic Semantics

Saturated bisimulation is a good notion of equivalence but it is hard to check, since it involves a quantification over all contexts. In [4], we have introduced a general notion of *symbolic bisimilarity* that coincides with saturated bisimilarity, but it avoids to consider all contexts. The idea is to define a symbolic transition system where transitions are labeled both with the usual observation and also with the minimal context that allows the transition.

Definition 5 (Symbolic Context Transition System). *A symbolic context transition system (SCTS for short) for a system $\mathcal{I} = \langle (S, \Sigma), \mathbb{A}, O, tr \rangle$ is a transition system $\beta \subseteq |\mathbb{A}| \times \Sigma \times O \times |\mathbb{A}|$.*

In [4], we have introduced a SCTS for open nets. Intuitively the symbolic transition $N, m \xrightarrow{i, \lambda}_\eta N, m'$ is possible if and only if $N, m \oplus i \xrightarrow{\lambda}_\mathcal{N} N, m'$ and i is the smallest multiset (on input places) allowing such transition. This SCTS is formally defined by the following rule.

$$\frac{t \in T \quad l(t) = \lambda \quad m = (m \cap {}^\bullet t) \oplus n \quad i \subseteq I^\oplus \quad {}^\bullet t = (m \cap {}^\bullet t) \oplus i}{N, m \xrightarrow{i, \lambda}_\eta N, t^\bullet \oplus n}$$

The marking $m \cap {}^\bullet t$ contains all the tokens of m that are needed to perform the transition t. The marking n contains all the tokens of m that are not useful for performing t, while the marking i contains all the tokens that m needs to reach ${}^\bullet t$. Note that i is exactly the *smallest* multiset that is needed to perform the transition t. Indeed if we take i_1 strictly included into i, $m \oplus i_1$ cannot match ${}^\bullet t$. As an example consider the net N_2 in Fig.1 with marking $cd\$^2$ and let t be the only transition labeled with α. We have that $cd\$^2 \cap {}^\bullet t = c\$^2$, $n = d$ and $i = \$^3$. Thus $N_2, cd\$^2 \xrightarrow{\$^3, \alpha}_\eta N_2, dd$. Fig.1(C) shows symbolic transition systems of marked open nets discussed in the previous subsection.

Definition 6 (Inference System). *An inference system $\mathcal{R}$ for a context interactive system $\mathcal{I} = \langle (S, \Sigma), \mathbb{A}, O, tr \rangle$ is a set of rules of the following format, where $s, t \in S$, $o, o' \in O$, $c \in \Sigma_{s,s'}$ and $d \in \Sigma_{t,t'}$.*

$$\frac{p_s \xrightarrow{o} q_t}{c(p_s) \xrightarrow{o'} d(q_t)}$$

The above rule states that all processes with sort s that perform a transition with observation o going into a state q_t with sort t, when inserted into the context c can perform a transition with the observation o' going into $d(q_t)$.

In the following, we write $c \xrightarrow[o']{o} d$ to mean a rule like the above. The rules $c \xrightarrow[o']{o} c'$ and $d \xrightarrow[o'']{o'} d'$ *derive* the rule $d \circ c \xrightarrow[o'']{o} d' \circ c'$ if $d \circ c$ and $d' \circ c'$ are defined. Given an inference system $\mathcal{R}$, $\Phi(\mathcal{R})$ is the set of all the rules derivable from $\mathcal{R}$ together with the identities rules ($\forall o \in O$ and $\forall s, t \in S$, $id_s \xrightarrow{o}_o id_t$).

Definition 7 (Derivations, soundness and completeness). *Let $\mathcal{I}$ be a context interactive system, β an SCTS and $\mathcal{R}$ an inference system.*

We say that $p \xrightarrow{c_1, o_1} p_1$ derives $p \xrightarrow{c_2, o_2} p_2$ in $\mathcal{R}$ (written $p \xrightarrow{c_1, o_1} p_1 \vdash_{\mathcal{R}} p \xrightarrow{c_2, o_2} p_2$)
if there exist $d, e \in \Sigma$ such that $d \xrightarrow[o_2]{o_1} e \in \Phi(\mathcal{R})$, $d \circ c_1 = c_2$ and $e_{\mathbb{A}}(p_1) = p_2$.
We say that β and $\mathcal{R}$ are sound and complete w.r.t. $\mathcal{I}$ if

$$p \xrightarrow{c, o}_s q \text{ iff } p \xrightarrow{c', o'}_{\beta} q' \text{ and } p \xrightarrow{c', o'}_{\beta} q' \vdash_{\mathcal{R}} p \xrightarrow{c, o}_s q.$$

A sound and complete SCTS could be considerably smaller than the saturated transition system, but still containing all the information needed to recover $\sim^S$. Note that the ordinary bisimilarity over SCTS (hereafter called *syntactical bisimilarity* and denoted by $\sim^W$) is usually stricter than $\sim^S$. As an example consider the marked open nets a and l. These are not syntactically bisimilar, since $l \xrightarrow{\$^3, \alpha}_\eta m$ while a cannot (Fig.1(C)). However, they are saturated bisimilar, as discussed in the previous subsection. In order to recover $\sim^S$ through the symbolic transition system we need a more elaborated definition of bisimulation.

Definition 8 (Symbolic Bisimilarity). *Let $\mathcal{I} = \langle (S, \Sigma), \mathbb{A}, O, tr \rangle$ be an interactive system, $\mathcal{R}$ be a set of rules and β be a symbolic transition system. Let $R = \{ R_s \subseteq A_s \times A_s \mid s \in S \}$ be an S sorted family of symmetric relations. R is a symbolic bisimulation iff $\forall s \in S$, whenever $p R_s q$:*

- *if $p \xrightarrow{c, o}_{\beta} p'$, then $q \xrightarrow{c_1, o_1}_{\beta} q_1'$ and $q \xrightarrow{c_1, o_1}_{\beta} q_1' \vdash_{\mathcal{R}} q \xrightarrow{c, o} q'$ and $p' R q'$.*

We write $p \sim_s^{SYM} q$ iff there exists a symbolic bisimulation R such that $p R_s q$.

Theorem 1. *Let $\mathcal{I}$ be a context interactive system, β an SCTS and $\mathcal{R}$ an inference system. If β and $\mathcal{R}$ are sound and complete w.r.t. $\mathcal{I}$, then $\sim^{SYM} = \sim^S$.*

In the remainder of this section we focus on open Petri nets. The inference system $\mathcal{R}_{\mathcal{N}}$ is defined by the following parametric rule.

$$\frac{N, m \xrightarrow{\lambda}_{\mathcal{N}} N, m'}{N, m \oplus i \xrightarrow{\lambda}_{\mathcal{N}} N, m' \oplus i}$$

The intuitive meaning of this rule is that for all possible observations λ and multiset i on input places, if a marked net performs a transition with observation λ, then the addition of i preserves this transition.

Now, consider derivations between transitions of open nets. It is easy to see that $N, m \xrightarrow{i_1, \lambda_1} N, m_1 \vdash_{\mathcal{R}_{\mathcal{N}}} N, m \xrightarrow{i_2, \lambda_2} N, m_2$ if and only if $\lambda_2 = \lambda_1$ and there exists a multiset x on input places such that $i_2 = i_1 \oplus x$ and $m_2 = m_1 \oplus x$. For all the nets N_k of our example, this just means that for all observations λ and for all multisets m, n, we have that $\langle N_k, m \rangle \xrightarrow{\$^i, \lambda}_\eta \langle N_k, n \rangle \vdash_{\mathcal{R}_{\mathcal{N}}} \langle N_k, m \rangle \xrightarrow{\$^{i+j}, \lambda} \langle N_k, n\$^j \rangle$.

In [4] we have shown that $\mathcal{R}_{\mathcal{N}}$ and η are sound and complete w.r.t. $\mathcal{N}$. For this reason, we can prove that two marked nets are bisimilar, by showing a symbolic bisimulation that relates them.

4   Saturated Terminal Sequences

In this section we introduce the terminal sequence for saturated and symbolic bisimilarity. They are almost straightforward adaptation of the terminal sequence for ordinary bisimilarity presented in Section 2. Hereafter we always implicitly refer to a context interactive system $\mathcal{I} = \langle (S, \Sigma), \mathbb{A}, O, tr \rangle$, a SCTS β and an inference system $\mathcal{R}$, such that β and $\mathcal{R}$ are sound and complete w.r.t. $\mathcal{I}$.

The *saturated terminal sequence* is defined as follows,

$$\sim_S^0 = \{A_s \times A_s \mid s \in S\} \quad \sim_S^{\kappa+1} = \mathbf{SAT}(\sim_S^\kappa) \quad \sim_S^\lambda = \bigcap_{\kappa < \lambda} \sim_S^\kappa$$

where $\mathbf{SAT}$ is a function on S indexed families of relations such that, for all $R = \{R_s \subseteq A_s \times A_s \mid s \in S\}$, $p\mathbf{SAT}(R)q$ iff

- if $p \xrightarrow{c,o}_S p'$, then $q \xrightarrow{c,o}_S q'$ and $p'Rq'$,
- if $q \xrightarrow{c,o}_S q'$, then $p \xrightarrow{c,o}_S p'$ and $p'Rq'$.

The only difference w.r.t. the terminal sequence of ordinary bisimilarity is in the fact that we consider S indexed families of relations (recall that S is the set of sorts, and A_s is carrier set of sort s of the algebra $\mathbb{A}$).

It is easy to see that $\mathbf{SAT}$ is monotonic w.r.t. (indexed) set inclusion. From classical results of fixed point theory (analogously to ordinary bisimilarity), we have that saturated bisimilarity is the limit of the saturated terminal sequence.

Proposition 5. $\sim^S = \bigcap_{\kappa \in \mathcal{O}} \sim_S^\kappa$

The following lemma is fundamental to prove the correctness of our algorithm.

Lemma 1. $\forall \kappa \in \mathcal{O}$, $\sim_S^\kappa$ is a congruence.

In Section 2, we have shown that the terminal sequence for ordinary bisimilarity provides an effective procedure for computing bisimilarity. We would like to apply the same intuition to the saturated terminal sequence but, unfortunately, the saturated transition system is usually infinite, since it considers all possible contexts. Instead of using the SATTS, we could define the *symbolic terminal sequence* relying just on the symbolic transition system. However, also this approach immediately leads to work with infinitely many states.

5   Redundant Transitions

In Section 3, we have shown that syntactical bisimilarity ($\sim^W$), i.e. the ordinary bisimilarity on the symbolic transition system, does not coincide with $\sim^S$. Here we show that this is due to the presence of *redundant transitions*. In order to better explain this phenomenon, we have to show an important property of $\vdash_\mathcal{R}$.

Lemma 2. $\forall p, q$, if $p \xrightarrow{c_1, d_1} p_1 \vdash_\mathcal{R} p \xrightarrow{c_2, d_2} e_\mathbb{A}(p_1)$, then $q \xrightarrow{c_1, d_1} q_1 \vdash_\mathcal{R} q \xrightarrow{c_2, d_2} e_\mathbb{A}(q_1)$.

Now, consider a process p that performs only the symbolic transitions $p \xrightarrow{c_1,o_1}_\beta p_1$ and $p \xrightarrow{c_2,o_2}_\beta p_2$ such that $p \xrightarrow{c_1,o_1}_\beta p_1 \vdash_\mathcal{R} p \xrightarrow{c_2,o_2} e_\mathbb{A}(p_1)$ and $p_2 \sim^S e_\mathbb{A}(p_1)$. The transition $p \xrightarrow{c_2,o_2}_\beta p_2$ is *redundant* and it makes $\sim^W$ different from $\sim^S$. Indeed, take a process q that performs only $q \xrightarrow{c_1,o_1}_\beta q_1$ such that $p_1 \sim^S q_1$. Clearly p and q are not syntactically bisimilar, because $p \xrightarrow{c_2,o_2}_\beta p_2$ while q cannot. However, $p \sim^S q$, because $q \xrightarrow{c_2,o_2}_S e_\mathbb{A}(q_1)$ (assuming that β and $\mathcal{R}$ are sound and complete and by Lemma 2) and, $p_2 \sim^S e_\mathbb{A}(p_1) \sim^S e_\mathbb{A}(q_1)$ (since $\sim^S$ is a congruence).

As an example consider the symbolic transition system of l (Fig.1). $l \xrightarrow{\varnothing,\alpha}_\eta q$ and $l \xrightarrow{\$^3,\alpha}_\eta m$. Moreover, $l \xrightarrow{\varnothing,\alpha}_\eta q \vdash_{\mathcal{R}_\mathcal{N}} l \xrightarrow{\$^3,\alpha} q\$^3$ and $q\$^3 \sim^S m$. Now consider a. $a \xrightarrow{\varnothing,\alpha}_\eta b$. Clearly $l \not\sim^W a$ but they are saturated bisimilar (Section 3).

Definition 9 (Redundant Transition). *Let $\mathcal{I} = \langle (S, \Sigma), \mathbb{A}, O, tr \rangle$ be a context interactive system, $\mathcal{R}$ be an inference system and X be an S sorted family of relations. Let $p \xrightarrow{c_1,o_1} p_1$ and $p \xrightarrow{c_2,o_2} p_2$ be two different transitions. We say that the former dominates the latter in X (written $p \xrightarrow{c_1,o_1} p_1 \prec_X p \xrightarrow{c_2,o_2} p_2$) if and only if $p \xrightarrow{c_1,o_1} p_1 \vdash_\mathcal{R} p \xrightarrow{c_2,o_2} e_\mathbb{A}(p_1)$ and $p_2 X e_\mathbb{A}(p_1)$. A transition is redundant w.r.t. X if it is dominated in X by another transition. Otherwise, it is irredundant.*

In the remainder of this section, we introduce another characterization of saturated bisimilarity that only checks irredundant symbolic transitions. The minimization algorithm that we will present in Section 6 relies on this notion.

Definition 10 (Irredundant Bisimilarity). *Let $\mathcal{I} = \langle (S, \Sigma), \mathbb{A}, O, tr \rangle$ be an interactive system, $\mathcal{R}$ be a set of rules and β be a symbolic transition system. Let $R = \{R_s \subseteq A_s \times A_s \mid s \in S\}$ be an S sorted family of symmetric relations. R is an irredundant bisimulation iff $\forall s \in S$, whenever $pR_s q$:*

– if $p \xrightarrow{c,o}_\beta p'$ is irredundant in R, then $q \xrightarrow{c,o}_\beta q'$ and $p'Rq'$.

We write $p \sim^{NR}_s q$ iff an irredundant bisimulation R such that $pR_s q$ exists.

Theorem 2 states that $\sim^{NR} = \sim^S$. However, in order to have such correspondence, we have to add a constraint to our theory. Indeed, according to the actual definition of context interactive systems, there could exist infinite descending chains like: $\cdots \prec_R p \xrightarrow{c_2,o_2} p_2 \prec_R p \xrightarrow{c_1,o_1} p_1$. In this chain, all the transitions are redundant and thus none of them is considered when checking irredundant bisimilarity.

Definition 11. *A context interactive system is well-founded w.r.t. $\mathcal{R}$ if and only if for all relations R there are no infinite descending chains of $\prec_R$.*

All the examples that we have shown in [4] are well-founded. In particular $\mathcal{N}$ is well founded w.r.t. $\mathcal{R}_\mathcal{N}$. Indeed, for all relations R, $m \xrightarrow{i_1,\lambda_1} m_1 \prec_R m \xrightarrow{i_2,\lambda_2} m_2$ only if there exists a multiset $x \neq \varnothing$ such that $x \circ i_1 = i_2$. This means that the multiset i_1 is strictly included in the multiset i_2, and since all multisets are finite, there exist only finite descending chains of $\prec_R$.

Theorem 2. *If $\mathcal{I}$ is well founded w.r.t. $\mathcal{R}$, then $\sim^{NR} = \sim^{SYM}$.*

6   A Minimization Algorithm for Symbolic Bisimilarity

In this section we introduce the terminal sequence for irredundant bisimilarity and we prove that it coincides with the saturated terminal sequence (Subsection 6.1). Relying on this, we introduce the symbolic partition refinement algorithm that checks saturated bisimilarity (Subsection 6.2). Finally, we prove the existence of minimal symbolic automata and we provide a procedure to compute them (Subsection 6.3). Hereafter, we assume that $\mathcal{I}$ is well-founded w.r.t. $\mathcal{R}$.

6.1   Irredundant Terminal Sequence

The *irredundant terminal sequence* $(\sim_{IR}^{\kappa})$ is defined as the saturated terminal sequence by replacing the function **SAT** with **IR** that is defined as follows: for all $R = \{R_s \subseteq A_s \times A_s \mid s \in S\}$, $p\mathbf{IR}(R)q$ iff

- if $p \xrightarrow{c,o}_\beta p'$ is irredundant in R, then $q \xrightarrow{c,o}_\beta q'$ and $p'Rq'$,
- if $q \xrightarrow{c,o}_\beta q'$ is irredundant in R, then $p \xrightarrow{c,o}_\beta p'$ and $p'Rq'$.

The function **IR** is clearly different from **SAT**, but they are equivalent when restricting to congruences.

Proposition 6. *Let* $R = \{R_s \subseteq A_s \times A_s \mid s \in S\}$ *be an S sorted family of symmetric relations. If R is a congruence, then* $\mathbf{SAT}(R) = \mathbf{IR}(R)$.

Since by Lemma 1 all the relations of the saturated terminal sequence are congruences, then the two terminal sequences coincide.

Theorem 3. $\forall \kappa \in \mathcal{O}, \sim_S^{\kappa} = \sim_{IR}^{\kappa}$.

6.2   Symbolic Partition Refinement

In Section 2 we have shown how the terminal sequence can be employed in order to have an effective procedure to compute bisimilarity. In this section we apply the same intuition to the irredundant terminal sequence. At the iteration n, instead of computing $\overline{\mathbf{F}}(P^n)$, we compute $\overline{\mathbf{IR}}(P^n)$: two processes p and q belong to the same block in P^{n+1}, if and only if whenever $p \xrightarrow{c,o}_\beta p'$ is not redundant in P^n then $q \xrightarrow{c,o}_\beta q'$ with p' and q' in the same block of P^n.

It is worth noting that in the computation of $\overline{\mathbf{IR}}(P^n)$ are involved also states that could be not reachable from the initial states IS. As an example consider the symbolic transition system of a and r (Fig.1(C)). The set of reachable states is $IS^* = \{a, b, r, s, t\}$. Recall that $r \xrightarrow{\varnothing,\alpha}_\eta t \vdash_{\mathcal{R}_\mathcal{N}} r \xrightarrow{\$^5,\alpha}_\eta t\$^5$. Thus, at the generic iteration $n + 1$, we need to check if the transition $j \xrightarrow{\$^5,\alpha}_\eta s$ is redundant. In order to do that we have to check if $t\$^5$ and s belong to the same block in P^n. However, the state $t\$^5$ is not reachable from $IS = \{a, r\}$.

Thus, we have to change the initialization step of our algorithm, by including in the set IS^* all the states that are needed to check redundancy. This is done,

Table 2. Closure rules

$$(\text{IS})\frac{p \in IS \quad p \in A_s}{p \in IS_s^\star} \qquad (\text{RS})\frac{p \in IS^\star \quad p \xrightarrow{c,o}_\beta q \quad q \in A_s}{q \in IS_s^\star}$$

$$(\text{RD})\frac{p \in IS^\star \quad p \xrightarrow{c_1,o_1}_\beta q_1 \quad p \xrightarrow{c_2,o_2}_\beta q_2 \quad p \xrightarrow{c_1,o_1}_\beta q_1 \vdash_\mathcal{R} p \xrightarrow{c_2,o_2} e_\mathbb{A}(q_1) \quad e_\mathbb{A}(q_1) \in A_s}{e_\mathbb{A}(q_1) \in IS_s^\star}$$

by using the closure rules in Table 2. The rule (RD) adds all the states that are needed to check redundancy. Indeed, if p can perform $p \xrightarrow{c_1,o_1}_\beta q_1$ and $p \xrightarrow{c_2,o_2}_\beta q_2$ such that $p \xrightarrow{c_1,o_1}_\beta q_1 \vdash_\mathcal{R} p \xrightarrow{c_2,o_2}_\beta e_\mathbb{A}(q_1)$, the latter could be redundant whenever $q_2 \sim^S e_\mathbb{A}(q_1)$. Thus also the state $e_\mathbb{A}(q_1)$ is needed. As an example, the closure of $IS = \{a, r\}$ is $IS^\star = \{a, b, r, s, t, t\$^1, t\$^2, t\$^3, t\$^4, t\$^5\}$ (Fig.2(B)). Usually, $IS^\star$ is not just a set, but an S indexed family of sets of states and for this reason the closure rules in Table 2 insert states in $IS^\star$ according to their sorts.

Algorithm 2. Symbolic-Partition-Refinement(IS)

Initialization

1. Compute $IS^\star$ with the rules in Table 2,
2. $P^0 := \{IS_s^\star | s \in S\}$,

Iteration $P^{n+1} := \overline{\mathbf{IR}}(P^n)$,
Termination if $P^n = P^{n+1}$ then return P^n.

Notice that in the initial partition P^0 there is one block for each sort $s \in S$. Thus P^0 equates all and the only the elements of $IS^\star$ with the same interface. Fig.2(A) shows the sequence of partitions computed by the algorithm taking as initial state $IS = \{a, r\}$. It is important to note now that in the symbolic transition system of $IS^\star$ (Fig.2(B)) the only possibly redundant transition is $r \xrightarrow{\$^5,\alpha}_\eta s$ (because $r \xrightarrow{\varnothing,\alpha}_\eta t \vdash_{\mathcal{R}_\mathcal{N}} r \xrightarrow{\$^5,\alpha}_\eta t\$^5$). Thus, in order to check redundancy, at any iteration we have only to check if $t\$^5$ and s belong to the same block. In the initial partition all the states are equivalent since they all have the same interface (recall that all the marked nets presented in Section 3 have interface $\$$). In P^1 there are three blocks. The states a and r are in the same block because the transition $r \xrightarrow{\$^5,\alpha}_\eta s$ is redundant since s and $t\$^5$ belong to the same block in P^0. In the second iteration, the state $t\$^1$ is separated from $\{t\$^2, t\$^3, t\$^4, t\$^5, s\}$ because the former can perform $\xrightarrow{\varnothing,\beta}_\eta \{r, b\}$ while all the others cannot. Note that a and r are still in the same block because s and $t\$^5$ belong to the same block in P^1. In each of the following iteration, a state $t\$^i$ is separated from s. In P^6, the state $t\$^5$ is separated from s and thus in P^7 the states a and r are divided because the transition $r \xrightarrow{\$^5,\alpha}_\eta s$ is not redundant anymore. Then P^8 is equivalent to P^7 and the algorithm returns such partition.

$$P^0 = \{a, b, r, s, t, t\$^1, t\$^2, t\$^3, t\$^4, t\$^5\}$$
$$P^1 = \{a, r\}\{b, t\}\{t\$^1, t\$^2, t\$^3, t\$^4, t\$^5, s\}$$
$$P^2 = \{a, r\}\{b, t\}\{t\$^1\}, \{t\$^2, t\$^3, t\$^4, t\$^5, s\}$$
$$P^3 = \{a, r\}\{b, t\}\{t\$^1\}, \{t\$^2\}\{t\$^3, t\$^4, t\$^5, s\}$$
$$P^4 = \{a, r\}\{b, t\}\{t\$^1\}, \{t\$^2\}\{t\$^3\}\{t\$^4, t\$^5, s\}$$
$$P^5 = \{a, r\}\{b, t\}\{t\$^1\}, \{t\$^2\}\{t\$^3\}\{t\$^4\}\{t\$^5, s\}$$
$$P^6 = \{a, r\}\{b, t\}\{t\$^1\}, \{t\$^2\}\{t\$^3\}\{t\$^4\}\{t\$^5\}\{s\}$$
$$P^7 = \{a\}\{r\}\{b, t\}\{t\$^1\}\{t\$^2\}\{t\$^3\}\{t\$^4\}\{t\$^5\}\{s\}$$
$$P^8 = \{a\}\{r\}\{b, t\}\{t\$^1\}\{t\$^2\}\{t\$^3\}\{t\$^4\}\{t\$^5\}\{s\}$$

(A)   (B)

Fig. 2. (A)The partitions computed by `Symbolic-Partition-Refinement`($\{a, r\}$).(B) The symbolic transition systems of $\{a, r\}^*$.

In order to prove the soundness of our algorithm we define the *irredundant terminal sequence for the set of initial states IS*,

$$\sim^0_{IS} = \sim^0_\beta | \; IS^* \qquad \sim^{\kappa+1}_{IS} = \mathbf{IR}(\sim^\kappa_{IS}) \qquad \sim^\lambda_{IS} = \bigcap_{\kappa < \lambda} \sim^\kappa_{IS}$$

where $R \upharpoonright A$ denotes the restriction of the relation R to the set A, IS^* is the closure of IS w.r.t. rules in Table 2.

The only difference with respect to the irredundant terminal sequence is in the first element. Here instead of taking the whole state space of $\mathcal{I}$, we restrict to IS^*. The following theorem guarantees that this is enough in order to characterize the restriction of the irredundant terminal sequence to IS^*. This is not trivial and it strongly relies on the fact that we close IS w.r.t. the rule (RD) in Table 2. Indeed whenever we remove such rule, it does not hold anymore.

Theorem 4. $\forall \kappa \in \mathcal{O}, \; \sim^\kappa_{ND} | \; IS^* = \sim^\kappa_{IS}$.

Theorem 5. *If* $\sim^\kappa_{IS} = \sim^{\kappa+1}_{IS}$, *then* $\forall k' \geq k + 1, \; \sim^\kappa_{IS} = \sim^{\kappa'}_{IS}$.

Corollary 1. *If IS^* is finite, then the algorithm terminates and the resulting partition equates all and only saturated bisimilar states.*

Since the algorithm applies to a lot of different formalisms, it is hard to provide a meaningful complexity analysis. However, we want to remark that the operation of checking redundancy is not expensive, since all the possible redundancies can be computed during the initialization (when using the rule (RD) of Table 2) and at any iteration, only those redundancies must be checked. Instead, the closure IS^* can be much larger than the set of reachable states (that is used by the ordinary partition refinement). Even worst, in our theory, nothing guarantees that if the set of reachable states (through the SCTS) is finite then also the closure IS^* is finite. However, we conjecture that this holds for many formalisms. The following proposition states that this holds in our running example.

Proposition 7. *Let $\mathcal{N}$, η and $\mathcal{R_N}$ be the context interactive system, the symbolic transition system and the inference system for open nets that we have*

$$P^0 = \{l, p, q, q\$^1, o\$, q\$^2, n, q\$^3, m\}$$
$$P^1 = \{l\}\{p, q\}\{q\$^1, o\$, q\$^2, n, q\$^3, m\}$$
$$P^2 = \{l\}\{p, q\}\{q\$^1, o\$\}\{q\$^2, n, q\$^3, m\}$$
$$P^3 = \{l\}\{p, q\}\{q\$^1, o\$\}\{q\$^2, n\}\{q\$^3, m\}$$
$$P^4 = \{l\}\{p, q\}\{q\$^1, o\$\}\{q\$^2, n\}\{q\$^3, m\}$$

Fig. 3. The partions computed by `Symbolic-Partition-Refinement({l})`

introduced in Section 3. Let $\langle N, m \rangle$ be a marked open net. If the symbolic transition system of $\langle N, m \rangle$ is finite, then also the closure w.r.t. rules in Table 2 is finite.

6.3 Minimal Symbolic Automaton

Now we introduce minimal symbolic automata, i.e. automata having only irredundant symbolic transitions. We show that they are canonical representatives for equivalence classes of saturated bisimilar states. Moreover, we provide an algorithm to compute them. Hereafter, given an S sorted family of sets $X = \{X_s \mid s \in S\}$ and an S sorted family of equivalence relations $R = \{R_s \subseteq X_s \times X_s \mid s \in S\}$, we write $X_{s \mid R}$ to mean the set of equivalence classes of X_s w.r.t. R_s and for each $p \in X$, $[p]_R$ to mean the equivalence class of p w.r.t. R.

Definition 12 (Minimal Symbolic Automaton). *Let $\mathcal{I} = \langle (S, \Sigma), \mathbb{A}, O, tr \rangle$ be a context interactive system, β a symbolic transition system and $\mathcal{R}$ an inference system. Let p be a state of $\mathcal{I}$ and $\{p\}^* = \{\{p\}_s^* \mid s \in S\}$ be the S sorted family of sets of states obtained by closing $\{p\}$ with the rules in Table 2. The minimal symbolic automaton of p (denoted by $MSA(p)$) is a triple $\langle i, M, tr_M \rangle$:*

- *the initial state i is equal to $[p]_{\sim^S}$,*
- *$M = \{M_s \subseteq \{p\}_{s \mid \sim^S}^* \mid s \in S\}$ is an S indexed family of set of equivalence classes of $\sim^S$,*
- *$tr_M \subseteq M \times \Sigma \times O \times M$ is a transition relation,*

defined according to the following two rules.

$$\frac{p \in A_s}{[p]_{\sim^S} \in M_s} \qquad \frac{[q]_{\sim^S} \in M \quad q \xrightarrow{c,o}_\beta r \text{ is irredundant in } \sim^S \quad r \in A_s}{[q]_{\sim^S} \xrightarrow{c,o}_M [r]_{\sim^S} \quad [r]_{\sim^S} \in M_s}$$

The leftmost rule states that the equivalence class of the initial state p belongs to the states of the minimal automaton. The other rule adds all the equivalence classes that are reachable from p trough symbolic irredundant transitions. Notice that in the minimal automaton for standard bisimilarity (Def.1) the set of states consisted of all the equivalence classes of reachable states, and thus in order to compute the minimal automata, we just needed to quotient the set of reachable states. For minimal symbolic automata we have also to remove all those states that are not reachable through irredundant symbolic transitions. As an example

---

Algorithm 3. Symbolic-Minimization(p)

---

1. $P :=$Symbolic-Partition-Refinement$(\{p\})$,
2. Quotient $\{p\}^*$ w.r.t. P,
3. Remove the redundant transitions,
4. Remove the states that are not reachable.

---

consider the symbolic transition system of l (Fig.1(C)). Fig.3 shows the closure $\{l\}^*$ and the partitions computed by Symbolic-Partition-Refinement$(\{l\})$. The minimal automata of l can be constructed as follows. First, we quotient the states in $\{l\}^*$ with respect to the partition P^4 returned by the algorithm.

$$\{l\} \xrightarrow{\varnothing,\alpha} \{p,q\} \xleftarrow{\varnothing,\beta} \{q\$^1,o\$\} \xleftarrow{\varnothing,\beta} \{q\$^2,n\} \xleftarrow{\varnothing,\beta} \{q\$^3,m\}$$

with the $\$^3,\alpha$ arc over the top, and $\$,\beta$ self-loop at $\{p,q\}$.

Then we remove the redundant transitions.

$$\{l\} \xrightarrow{\varnothing,\alpha} \{p,q\} \xleftarrow{\varnothing,\beta} \{q\$^1,o\$\} \xleftarrow{\varnothing,\beta} \{q\$^2,n\} \xleftarrow{\varnothing,\beta} \{q\$^3,m\}$$

Finally we take the set of states reachable from l: $\{l\} \xrightarrow{\varnothing,\alpha} \{p,q\}$ with $\$,\beta$ self-loop. This is the minimal symbolic automaton of l. Notice that it is isomorphic to the symbolic transition system of a (Fig.1(C)). This is an alternative proof of $a \sim^S l$. Indeed, for minimal symbolic automata, analogously to minimal automata, two states p and q are saturated bisimilar if and only if their minimal symbolic automata are isomorphic, where by isomorphism we mean a bijection on states that preserves sorts, transitions and initial states.

Proposition 8. $p \sim^S q$ *if and only if* $MSA(p)$ *is isomorphic to* $MSA(q)$.

7   Conclusions and Related Works

Relying on the framework of [4], we have introduced a symbolic partition refinement algorithm that allows to efficiently check saturated bisimilarity. Our approach is absolutely general and it can be applied to many formalisms. However, when considering nominal calculi where systems are able communicate names, the symbolic transition system is often infinite. Indeed, every time that a system generates a new name and extrudes it, the system goes in a new state that is different from all the previous. HD-Automata [16] are peculiar LTSs that allow to garbage collect names and avoid this other source of infiniteness. As future work, we will extend our framework to HD-Automata, so that we will be able to handle systems that generates infinitely many names. In particular we conjecture that this algorithm will generalize both [19] and [15] that provide a partition refinement algorithm for open [20] and asynchronous [1] bisimilarity.

Indeed, both our approach and [19,15] rely on *irredundant transitions*. In all these algorithms, first the closure of the set of initial states is computed by adding, not only the reachable states, but also those states that are needed to check redundancy. Then, at any iteration, only irredundant transitions are considered. In [19], the closure is called *saturated state graph* and it is computed analogously to our approach. Instead, in [15], the closure is computed by adding *negative transitions* whenever there is a possible redundancy. Roughly, if $p \overset{a}{\rightsquigarrow} q$ is a negative transition, then a transition $p \overset{a}{\rightarrow} q'$ is redundant whenever the arriving state q and q' are the same. A novel notion of bisimilarity is introduced for these kind of transition systems, but it fails to be transitive. In our context interactive systems we just rely on the algebraic structure of contexts and irredundant bisimilarity coincides with the saturated one.

Moreover, the functions Φ and Φ_A, that are used during the iteration of the algorithms in [19,15], are not monotone and, as a consequence, the convergency of the corresponding terminal sequences have to be proven by hand. Instead in our approach the function **IR** generates exactly the same sequence of saturated bisimilarity and thus convergence and coincidence with saturated bisimilarity are for free. Moreover, we have shown that the correspondence between irredundant bisimilarity and saturated bisimilarity is not by chance, but because **IR** and **SAT** behaves exactly in the same way when restricted to congruences.

References

1. Amadio, R.M., Castellani, I., Sangiorgi, D.: On bisimulations for the asynchronous π-calculus. In: Sassone, V., Montanari, U. (eds.) CONCUR 1996. LNCS, vol. 1119, pp. 147–162. Springer, Heidelberg (1996)
2. Baldan, P., Corradini, A., Ehrig, H., Heckel, R.: Compositional semantics for open Petri nets based on deterministic processes. M.S.C.S 15(1), 1–35 (2005)
3. Baldan, P., Corradini, A., Ehrig, H., Heckel, R., König, B.: Bisimilarity and behaviour-preserving reconfiguration of open petri nets. In: Mossakowski, T., Montanari, U., Haveraaen, M. (eds.) CALCO 2007. LNCS, vol. 4624, pp. 126–142. Springer, Heidelberg (2007)
4. Bonchi, F., Montanari, U.: Symbolic semantics revisited. In: Amadio, R. (ed.) FOSSACS 2008. LNCS, vol. 4962, pp. 395–412. Springer, Heidelberg (2008)
5. Bonchi, F., Montanari, U.: Minimization algorithm for symbolic bisimilarity. Technical Report TR-08-27, Department of Informatics, University of Pisa (2008)
6. Cardelli, L., Gordon, A.D.: Mobile ambients. T.C.S. 240(1), 177–213 (2000)
7. Fernandez, J.C., Mounier, L.: "on the fly" verification of behavioural equivalences and preorders. In: Larsen, K.G., Skou, A. (eds.) CAV 1991. LNCS, vol. 575, pp. 181–191. Springer, Heidelberg (1992)
8. Ferrari, G.L., Gnesi, S., Montanari, U., Pistore, M., Ristori, G.: Verifying mobile processes in the hal environment. In: Vardi, M.Y. (ed.) CAV 1998. LNCS, vol. 1427, pp. 511–515. Springer, Heidelberg (1998)
9. Hennessy, M., Lin, H.: Symbolic bisimulations. T.C.S. 138(2), 353–389 (1995)
10. Honda, K., Tokoro, M.: An object calculus for asynchronous communication. In: America, P. (ed.) ECOOP 1991. LNCS, vol. 512, pp. 133–147. Springer, Heidelberg (1991)
11. Kanellakis, P.C., Smolka, S.A.: Ccs expressions, finite state processes, and three problems of equivalence. Information and Computation 86(1), 43–68 (1990)

12. Merro, M., Zappa Nardelli, F.: Bisimulation proof methods for mobile ambients. In: Baeten, J.C.M., Lenstra, J.K., Parrow, J., Woeginger, G.J. (eds.) ICALP 2003. LNCS, vol. 2719, pp. 584–598. Springer, Heidelberg (2003)
13. Milner, R.: Communicating and Mobile Systems: the π-Calculus. Cambridge University Press, Cambridge (1999)
14. Milner, R., Parrow, J., Walker, D.: A calculus of mobile processes, i and ii. Information and Computation 100(1), 1–40 (1992)
15. Montanari, U., Pistore, M.: Finite state verification for the asynchronous pi-calculus. In: Cleaveland, W.R. (ed.) TACAS 1999. LNCS, vol. 1579, pp. 255–269. Springer, Heidelberg (1999)
16. Montanari, U., Pistore, M.: An introduction to history dependent automata. Electr. Notes Theor. Comput. Sci. 10 (1997)
17. Montanari, U., Sassone, V.: Dynamic congruence vs. progressing bisimulation for ccs. Fundamenta Informaticae 16(1), 171–199 (1992)
18. Paige, R., Tarjan, R.E.: Three partition refinement algorithms. SIAM J. Comput. 16(6), 973–989 (1987)
19. Pistore, M., Sangiorgi, D.: A partition refinement algorithm for the π-calculus. Information and Computation 164(2), 264–321 (2001)
20. Sangiorgi, D.: A theory of bisimulation for the π-calculus. Acta Informatica 33(1), 69–97 (1996)
21. Victor, B., Moller, F.: The mobility workbench - a tool for the pi-calculus. In: Dill, D.L. (ed.) CAV 1994. LNCS, vol. 818, pp. 428–440. Springer, Heidelberg (1994)

Conversation Types

Luís Caires and Hugo Torres Vieira

CITI / Departamento de Informática, FCT Universidade Nova de Lisboa, Portugal

Abstract. We present a type theory for analyzing concurrent multiparty interactions as found in service-oriented computing. Our theory introduces a novel and flexible type structure, able to uniformly describe both the internal and the interface behavior of systems, referred respectively as choreographies and contracts in web-services terminology. The notion of conversation builds on the fundamental concept of session, but generalizes it along directions up to now unexplored; in particular, conversation types discipline interactions in conversations while accounting for dynamical join and leave of an unanticipated number of participants. We prove that well-typed systems never violate the prescribed conversation constraints. We also present techniques to ensure progress of systems involving several interleaved conversations, a previously open problem.

1 Introduction

While most issues arising in the context of communication-based software systems do not appear to be new when considered in isolation, the analysis of loosely-coupled distributed systems involving type based discovery, and multiparty collaborations such as those supported by web-services technology raises many challenges and calls for new concepts, specially crafted models, and formal analysis techniques (e.g., [1,2,3,6,7,12]). In previous work [19] we introduced the Conversation Calculus (CC), a π-calculus based model for service-oriented computing that builds on the concepts of process delegation, loose-coupling, and, crucially, conversation contexts.

A key concept for the organization of service-oriented computing systems is the notion of conversation. A conversation is a structured, not centrally coordinated, possibly concurrent, set of interactions between several participants. Then, a conversation context is a medium where partners may interact in a conversation. It can be distributed in many pieces, and processes in any piece may seamlessly talk to processes in the same or any other piece of the same conversation context. Intuitively a conversation context may be seen as a virtual chat room where remote participants exchange messages according to some discipline, while simultaneously engaged in other conversations. Conversation context identities can be passed around, allowing participants to dynamically join conversations. To join an ongoing conversation, a process may perform a remote conversation access using the conversation context identifier. It is then able to participate in the conversation to which it has joined, while being able to interact back with the caller context through the access point. To discipline multiparty conversations we introduce conversation types, a novel and flexible type structure, able to uniformly describe both the internal and the interface behavior of systems, referred respectively as choreographies and contracts in web-services terminology.

We give substantial evidence that our minimal extension to the π-calculus is already effective enough to model and type sophisticated service-based systems, at a fairly high

G. Castagna (Ed.): ESOP 2009, LNCS 5502, pp. 285–300, 2009.

level of abstraction. Examples include challenging scenarios involving simultaneous multiparty conversations, with concurrency and access to local resources, and conversations with a dynamically changing and unanticipated number of participants, that fall out of scope of other approaches for modeling and typing of service-based systems.

1.1   Conversation Contexts and Conversation Types

We explain the key ideas of our development by going through a motivating example. Consider the following composition of two conversation contexts, named $Buyer$ and $Seller$, modeling a typical service collaboration:

$Buyer \blacktriangleleft [$ **new** $Seller \cdot$ startBuy $\Leftarrow$ buy!$(prod)$.price?$(v)]$ |

$Seller \blacktriangleleft [$ $PriceDB$ | **def** startBuy $\Rightarrow$ buy?$(prod)$.askPrice$^{\uparrow}$!$(prod)$.

readVal$^{\uparrow}$?(v).price!$(v)]$

Notice that in the core CC, the bounded communication medium provided by a conversation context may also be used to model a partner local context, avoiding the introduction of a primitive notion of site. The code in $Buyer$ starts a new conversation by calling service startBuy located at $Seller$ using the service instantiation idiom **new** $Seller \cdot$ startBuy $\Leftarrow$ buy!$(prod)$.price?(v). The code buy!$(prod)$.price?(v) describes the role of $Buyer$ in the conversation: a buy message is sent, and afterwards a price message should be received. Upon service instantiation, the system evolves to

$(\boldsymbol{\nu}c)($ $Buyer \blacktriangleleft [$ $c \blacktriangleleft [$ buy!$(prod)$.price?$(v)]]$ |

$Seller \blacktriangleleft [$ $PriceDB$ | $c \blacktriangleleft [$ buy?$(prod)$.askPrice$^{\uparrow}$!$(prod)$.

readVal$^{\uparrow}$?(v).price!$(v)]$ $)$

where c is the fresh name of the newly created conversation (with two pieces). The code

buy?$(prod)$.askPrice$^{\uparrow}$!$(prod)$.readVal$^{\uparrow}$?(v).price!(v)

describes the participation of $Seller$ in the conversation c: a buy message is received, and in the end, price message should be sent. In between, database $PriceDB$ located in the $Seller$ context is consulted through a pair of $\uparrow$ directed message exchanges (askPrice and readVal). Such messages are targeted to the parent conversation ($Seller$), rather than to the current conversation (c).

In our theory, message exchanges *inside* and *at* the interface of subsystems are captured by conversation types, which describe both internal and external participation of processes in conversations. The $Buyer$ and $Seller$ conversation is described by type

$$BSChat \triangleq \tau\mathrm{buy}(Tp).\tau\mathrm{price}(Tm)$$

specifying the two interactions that occur sequentially within the conversation c, first a message buy and after a message price (Tp and Tm represent basic value types).

The τ in, e.g., $\tau\mathrm{buy}(Tp)$ means that the interaction is internal. A declaration such as $\tau\mathrm{buy}(Tp)$ is like an assertion such as buy(Tp) : $Buyer \rightarrow Seller$ in a message sequence chart, or in the global types of [12], except that in our case participant identities are abstracted away, increasing flexibility. In general, the interactions described by a type such as $BSChat$ may be realized in several ways, by different participants. Technically, we specify the several possibilities by a (ternary) merge relation between types, noted $B = B_1 \bowtie B_2$, stating how a behavior B may be projected in two independent matching behaviors B_1 and B_2. In particular, we have (among others) the projection

$$BSChat = ?\, \mathtt{buy}(\mathit{Tp}).!\, \mathtt{price}(\mathit{Tm}) \bowtie !\, \mathtt{buy}(\mathit{Tp}).?\, \mathtt{price}(\mathit{Tm})$$

The type $?\, \mathtt{buy}(\mathit{Tp}).!\, \mathtt{price}(\mathit{Tm})$ will be used to type the *Buyer* participation, and the type $!\, \mathtt{buy}(\mathit{Tp}).?\, \mathtt{price}(\mathit{Tm})$ will be used to type the *Seller* participation (in conversation *BSChat*). Thus, in our first example, the conversation type *BSChat* is decomposed in a pair of "dual" conversation types, as in classical session types [10,11]; this does not need to be always the case, however. In fact, the notion of conversation builds on the fundamental concept of session but extends it along unexplored directions, as we now discuss. Consider a three-party variation (from [6]) of the example above:

Buyer ◄ [**new** *Seller* · startBuy $\Leftarrow$ buy!(*prod*).price?(*p*).details?(*d*)] |
Seller ◄ [*PriceDB* |
> **def** startBuy $\Rightarrow$ buy?(*prod*).askPrice$^\uparrow$!(*prod*).
> readVal$^\uparrow$?(*p*).price!(*p*).
> **join** *Shipper* · newDelivery $\Leftarrow$ product!(*prod*)] |
Shipper ◄ [**def** newDelivery $\Rightarrow$ product?(*p*).details!(*data*)]

The role of *Shipper* is to inform the client on the delivery details. The code is composed of three conversation contexts, representing the three partners *Buyer*, *Seller* and *Shipper*. The system progresses as in the first example: messages buy and price are exchanged between *Buyer* and *Seller* in the fresh conversation. After that, *Shipper* is asked by *Seller*, using idiom **join** *Shipper* · newDelivery $\Leftarrow \cdots$, to join the ongoing conversation (till then involving only *Buyer* and *Seller*). The system then evolves to

$$(\nu a)(\quad Buyer ◄ [\ a ◄ [\ \mathtt{details}?(d)\ ]\ ]\ |$$
$$Seller ◄ [\ a ◄ [\ \mathtt{product}!(prod)\ ]\ |\dots]\ |$$
$$Shipper ◄ [\ a ◄ [\ \mathtt{product}?(p).\mathtt{details}!(data)\ ]\ ]\ )$$

Notice that *Seller does not lose access* to the conversation after asking service *Shipper* · newDelivery to join in the current conversation a (partial session delegation). In fact, *Seller* and *Shipper* will interact later on in the very same conversation, by exchanging a product message. Finally, *Shipper* sends a message details directly to *Buyer*. In this case, the global conversation a is initially assigned type

$$BSSChat \triangleq \tau\, \mathtt{buy}(\mathit{Tp}).\tau\, \mathtt{price}(\mathit{Tm}).\tau\, \mathtt{product}(\mathit{Tp}).\tau\, \mathtt{details}(\mathit{Td})$$

We decompose type *BSSChat* in three "projections" (B_{bu}, B_{se}, and B_{sh}), by means of the *merge* $\bowtie$, first by $BSSChat = B_{bu} \bowtie B_{ss}$, and then by $B_{ss} = B_{se} \bowtie B_{sh}$, where

$$B_{bu} \triangleq ?\, \mathtt{buy}(\mathit{Tp}).!\, \mathtt{price}(\mathit{Tm}).!\, \mathtt{details}(\mathit{Td})$$
$$B_{ss} \triangleq !\, \mathtt{buy}(\mathit{Tp}).?\, \mathtt{price}(\mathit{Tm}).\tau\, \mathtt{product}(\mathit{Tp}).?\, \mathtt{details}(\mathit{Td})$$
$$B_{se} \triangleq !\, \mathtt{buy}(\mathit{Tp}).?\, \mathtt{price}(\mathit{Tm}).?\, \mathtt{product}(\mathit{Tp})$$
$$B_{sh} \triangleq !\, \mathtt{product}(\mathit{Tp}).?\, \mathtt{details}(\mathit{Td})$$

These various "local" types are merged by our type system in a compositional way, allowing e.g., service startBuy to be assigned type !startBuy($[B_{ss}]$), and the contribution of each partner in the conversation to be properly determined. At the point where the **join** operation above gets typed, the (residual) conversation type corresponding to the participation of *Seller* is typed $\tau\, \mathtt{product}(\mathit{Tp}).?\, \mathtt{details}(\mathit{Td})$. At this stage, extrusion of the conversation name a to service *Seller* · newDelivery will occur, to enable *Shipper* to join in. Notice that the global conversation *BSSChat* discipline will

nevertheless be respected, since the conversation fragment delegated to $Shipper$ is typed
! product(Tp).? details(Td) while the conversation fragment retained by $Seller$ is
typed ? product(Tp). Also notice that since conversation types abstract away from participant identities, the overall conversation type can be projected into the types of the
individual roles in several ways, allowing for different implementations of the roles of a
given conversation (cf. loose-coupling). It is even possible to type systems with an unbounded number of different participants, as needed to type, e.g., a service broker.

Our type system combines techniques from linear, behavioral, session and spatial
types (see [4,11,13,14]): the type structure features prefix $M.B$, parallel composition
$B_1 \mid B_2$, and other operators. Messages M describe external (receive ? / send !) exchanges in two views: with the *caller / parent* conversation (↑), and in the *current*
conversation (↓). They also describe internal message exchanges (τ). Key technical
ingredients in our approach to conversation types are the amalgamation of global types
and of local types (in the general sense of [12]) in the same type language, and the
definition of a merge relation ensuring, by construction, that participants typed by the
projected views of a type will behave well under composition. Merge subsumes duality,
in the sense that for each τ-free B there are types $\overline{B}, B'$ such that $B \bowtie \overline{B} = \tau(B')$,
so sessions are special cases of conversations. But merge of types allows for extra flex-
ibility on the manipulation of projections of conversation types, in an open-ended way,
as illustrated above. In particular, our approach allows fragments of a conversation type
(e.g., a choreography) to be dynamically distributed among participants, while statically
ensuring that interactions follow the prescribed discipline.

The technical contributions of this work may be summarized as follows. First, we
define the new notion of conversation type. Conversation types are a generalization of
session types to loosely-coupled, possibly concurrent, multiparty conversations, allowing mixed global / local behavioral descriptions to be expressed at the same level, while
supporting the analysis of systems with dynamic delegation of fragments of ongoing
conversations. Second, we advance new techniques to certify safety and liveness properties of service-based systems. We propose a type system for assigning conversation
types to core CC systems. Processes that get past our typing rules are ensured to be free
of communication errors, and races on plain messages (Corollary 3.6): this also implies
that well-typed systems enjoy a conversation fidelity property (i.e., all conversations
follow the prescribed protocols). Finally, we present techniques to establish progress of
systems with several interleaved conversations (Theorem 4.4), exploiting the combination of conversation names with message labels in event orderings, and, more crucially,
propagation of orderings in communications, solving a previously open problem.

Additional examples, complete definitions and detailed proofs can be found in [5].

2   The Core Conversation Calculus

In this section, we present the syntax and operational semantics of the core Conversation Calculus (CC) [19]. The core CC extends the π-calculus [16] static fragment with
the conversation construct $n \blacktriangleleft [P]$, and replaces channel based communication with
context-sensitive message based communication. For simplicity, we use here a monadic
version. The syntax of the calculus is defined in Fig. 1. We assume given an infinite set
of names Λ, an infinite set of variables $\mathcal{V}$, an infinite set of labels $\mathcal{L}$, and an infinite set

$$
\begin{array}{llll}
a, b, c, \ldots \in \Lambda & \textit{(Names)} & d \quad ::= \downarrow \mid \uparrow & \textit{(Directions)} \\
x, y, z, \ldots \in \mathcal{V} & \textit{(Variables)} & & \\
n, m, o \ldots \in \Lambda \cup \mathcal{V} & & \alpha, \beta ::= l^d!(n) & \textit{(Output)} \\
l, s \ldots \quad \in \mathcal{L} & \textit{(Labels)} & \quad \mid \ l^d?(x) & \textit{(Input)} \\
\mathcal{X}, \mathcal{Y}, \ldots \in \chi & \textit{(Process Vars)} & \quad \mid \ \textbf{this}(x) & \textit{(Conversation Awareness)}
\end{array}
$$

$$
\begin{array}{llll}
P, Q ::= \mathbf{0} & \textit{(Inaction)} & \mid \ \textbf{rec}\, \mathcal{X}.P & \textit{(Recursion)} \\
\quad \mid \ P \mid Q & \textit{(Parallel Composition)} & \mid \ \mathcal{X} & \textit{(Variable)} \\
\quad \mid \ (\nu a)P & \textit{(Name Restriction)} & \mid \ \Sigma_{i \in I}\, \alpha_i.P_i & \textit{(Prefix Guarded Choice)} \\
\quad \mid \ n \blacktriangleleft [P] & \textit{(Conversation Access)} & &
\end{array}
$$

Fig. 1. The core Conversation Calculus

of process variables χ. The static fragment is defined by the inaction $\mathbf{0}$, parallel composition $P \mid Q$, name restriction $(\nu a)P$ and recursion $\textbf{rec}\, \mathcal{X}.P$. The conversation access construct $n \blacktriangleleft [P]$, allows a process to interact, as specified by P, in conversation n.

Communication is expressed by the guarded choice construct $\Sigma_{i \in I}\, \alpha_i.P_i$, meaning that the process may select some initial action α_i and then progress as P_i. Communication actions are of two forms: $l^d!(n)$ for sending messages and $l^d?(x)$ for receiving messages. Message communication is defined by the label l and the direction d. There are two message directions: $\downarrow$ (read "here") meaning that the interaction should take place in the current conversation or $\uparrow$ (read "up") meaning that the interaction should take place in the enclosing (caller) conversation. To lighten notation we omit the $\downarrow$ in the $\downarrow$-directed messages without any ambiguity. A basic action may also be of the form $\textbf{this}(x)$, allowing a process to dynamically access the name of the current conversation. Notice that message labels (from $l \in \mathcal{L}$) are not names but free identifiers (cf. record labels or XML tags), and therefore are not subject to fresh generation, restriction or binding. Only conversation names (in Λ) may be subject to binding, and freshly generated via $(\nu a)P$. The distinguished occurrences of a, x, x and $\mathcal{X}$ are binding occurrences in $(\nu a)P$, $l^d?(x).P$, $\textbf{this}(x).P$ and $\textbf{rec}\, \mathcal{X}.P$, respectively. The sets of free $(fn(P))$ and bound $(bn(P))$ names, free variables $(fv(P))$, and free process variables $(fpv(P))$ in a process P are defined as expected. We implicitly identify α-equivalent processes.

The operational semantics of the core CC is defined by a labeled transition system. For clarity, we split the presentation in two sets of rules, one (in Fig. 3) containing the rules for the basic operators, another (in Fig. 4) grouping the rules specific to the conversations. A transition $P \xrightarrow{\lambda} Q$ states that process P may evolve to process Q by performing the action represented by the transition label λ. Transition labels (λ) and actions (σ) are defined in Fig. 2. An action τ denotes an internal communication, actions $l^d!(a)$ and $l^d?(a)$ represent communications with the environment, and $\texttt{this}$ represents a conversation identity access; these correspond to the basic actions a process may perform in the context of a given conversation. To capture the observational semantics of processes [19], transition labels register not only the action but also the conversation where the action takes place. So, a transition label λ containing $c\ \sigma$ is said to be *located at* conversation c (or just *located*), otherwise is said to be *unlocated*. In $(\nu a)\lambda$ the distinguished occurrence of a is bound with scope λ (cf., the π-calculus bound output actions). For a communication label λ we denote by $\overline{\lambda}$ the dual matching label obtaining

$$\sigma ::= \tau \mid l^d!(a) \mid l^d?(a) \mid \textbf{this} \quad \text{(Transition Labels)} \qquad \lambda ::= c\,\sigma \mid \sigma \mid (\nu a)\lambda \quad \text{(Actions)}$$

Fig. 2. Transition Labels and Actions

$$l^d!(a).P \xrightarrow{l^d!(a)} P \ (out) \qquad l^d?(x).P \xrightarrow{l^d?(a)} P\{x/a\} \ (inp) \qquad \frac{\alpha_j.P_j \xrightarrow{\lambda} Q \quad j \in I}{\Sigma_{i \in I}\, \alpha_i.P_i \xrightarrow{\lambda} Q}(sum)$$

$$\frac{P \xrightarrow{\lambda} Q \quad a = out(\lambda)}{(\nu a)P \xrightarrow{(\nu a)\lambda} Q}(opn) \qquad \frac{P \xrightarrow{\lambda} P' \quad Q \xrightarrow{\bar{\lambda}} Q'}{P \mid Q \xrightarrow{\tau} P' \mid Q'}(com) \qquad \frac{P \xrightarrow{(\nu a)\bar{\lambda}} P' \quad Q \xrightarrow{\lambda} Q'}{P \mid Q \xrightarrow{\tau} (\nu a)(P' \mid Q')}(clo)$$

$$\frac{P \xrightarrow{\lambda} Q \quad a \notin na(\lambda)}{(\nu a)P \xrightarrow{\lambda} (\nu a)Q}(res) \qquad \frac{P \xrightarrow{\lambda} Q}{P \mid R \xrightarrow{\lambda} Q \mid R}(par) \qquad \frac{P\{\mathcal{X}/\textbf{rec}\,\mathcal{X}.P\} \xrightarrow{\lambda} Q}{\textbf{rec}\,\mathcal{X}.P \xrightarrow{\lambda} Q}(rec)$$

Fig. 3. Operational Semantics: Basic Operators (π-calculus)

$$\frac{P \xrightarrow{\lambda^\uparrow} Q}{c \blacktriangleleft [P] \xrightarrow{\lambda^\downarrow} c \blacktriangleleft [Q]}(her) \qquad \frac{P \xrightarrow{\lambda^\downarrow} Q}{c \blacktriangleleft [P] \xrightarrow{c \cdot \lambda^\downarrow} c \blacktriangleleft [Q]}(loc) \qquad \frac{P \xrightarrow{a\,\lambda^\downarrow} Q}{c \blacktriangleleft [P] \xrightarrow{a\,\lambda^\downarrow} c \blacktriangleleft [Q]}(thr)$$

$$\frac{P \xrightarrow{\tau} Q}{c \blacktriangleleft [P] \xrightarrow{\tau} c \blacktriangleleft [Q]}(tau) \qquad \textbf{this}(x).P \xrightarrow{c\,\textbf{this}} P\{x/c\} \ (thi) \qquad \frac{P \xrightarrow{c\,\textbf{this}} Q}{c \blacktriangleleft [P] \xrightarrow{\tau} c \blacktriangleleft [Q]}(thl)$$

$$\frac{P \xrightarrow{\sigma} P' \quad Q \xrightarrow{c\,\bar{\sigma}} Q'}{P \mid Q \xrightarrow{c\,\textbf{this}} P' \mid Q'}(tco) \qquad \frac{P \xrightarrow{\sigma} P' \quad Q \xrightarrow{(\nu a)c\,\bar{\sigma}} Q'}{P \mid Q \xrightarrow{c\,\textbf{this}} (\nu a)(P' \mid Q')}(tcl)$$

Fig. 4. Operational Semantics: Conversation Operators

by swapping inputs with outputs, such that $\overline{l^d!(a)} = l^d?(a)$ and $\overline{l^d?(a)} = l^d!(a)$. By $na(\lambda)$ we denote the free and bound names and by $bn(\lambda)$ the bound names of λ.

Transition rules presented in Fig. 3 closely follow the ones for the π-calculus [18] and should be fairly clear to a reader familiar with mobile process calculi. For example, rule (opn) corresponds to the bound output or extrusion rule, in which a bound name a is extruded to the environment in an output message λ: we define $out(\lambda) = a$ if $\lambda = l^d!(a)$ or $\lambda = c\,l^d!(a)$ and $c \neq a$. We discuss the intuitions behind the rules for conversation contexts (Fig. 4). In (her) an $\uparrow$ directed message (to the caller conversation) becomes $\downarrow$ (in the current conversation), after passing through the conversation access boundary. We note by λ^d a transition label λ^d containing the direction d ($\uparrow, \downarrow$), and by $\lambda^{d'}$ the label obtained by replacing d by d' in λ^d (e.g., if $\lambda^\uparrow$ is $\mathtt{askPrice}^\uparrow?(a)$ then $\lambda^\downarrow$ is $\mathtt{askPrice}^\downarrow?(a)$). In (loc) an unlocated $\downarrow$ message (in the current conversation) gets explicitly located at the conversation c in which it originates. Given an unlocated label λ, we represent by $c \cdot \lambda$ the label obtained by locating λ at c (e.g., if $\lambda^\downarrow$ is $\mathtt{askPrice}^\downarrow?(p)$ then $c \cdot \lambda^\downarrow$ is $c\,\mathtt{askPrice}^\downarrow?(p)$). In (thr) an already located communication label transparently crosses some conversation boundary, and likewise for a τ label in (tau). In (thi) a $\mathtt{this}$ label reads the conversation identity, and originates a $c\,\mathtt{this}$ label. A $c\,\mathtt{this}$ labeled transition may only progress inside the c conversation, as expressed in (thl), where a $\mathtt{this}$ label matches the enclosing conversation. In (tco)

$$\textbf{def } s \Rightarrow P \triangleq s?(x).x \blacktriangleleft [P]$$

$$\textbf{new } n \cdot s \Leftarrow Q \triangleq (\nu c)(n \blacktriangleleft [s!(c)] \mid c \blacktriangleleft [Q])$$

$$\textbf{join } n \cdot s \Leftarrow Q \triangleq \textbf{this}(x).(n \blacktriangleleft [s!(x)] \mid Q)$$

Fig. 5. Service Idioms

and (tcl) an unlocated communication matches a communication located at c, originating a c this label, thus ensuring the interaction occurs in the given conversation c, as required. The reduction relation of the core CC, noted $P \rightarrow Q$, is defined as $P \xrightarrow{\tau} Q$.

Using conversation contexts and the basic message based communication mechanisms, useful programming abstractions for service-oriented systems may be idiomatically defined in the core CC, namely service definition and instantiation constructs (redundantly introduced as primitives in [19]) and also a new conversation join construct, as shown in Fig. 5. The **def** form publishes a service definition. There are two ways of using such a service definition: either by the **new** form, which establishes a fresh conversation between client and server; or by the **join** form which instead passes to the service provider the identity of the current conversation, allowing parties to ask other service providers to join in on ongoing conversations. Both usages refer the service name s and the conversation n where the service is available at, thus service definitions must be located in order to be instantiated (as e.g., methods must reside in objects).

3 Type System

In this section we formally present our type system for the core CC. As already motivated in the Introduction, our types specify the message protocols that flow between and within conversations. The syntax for the types is shown in Fig. 6. Typing judgments have the form $P :: T$, where T is a process type. Intuitively, a type judgement $P :: T$ states that if process P is placed in an environment that complies with type T, then the resulting system is safe, in a sense to be made precise below (Corollary 3.6). In general, a process type T has the form $L \mid B$, where L is a *located type* and B is a *behavioral type*. An atomic located type associates a conversation type C to a conversation name n. Conversation types C are given by $[B]$, where B specifies the message interactions that may take place in the conversation. Behavioral types B include the branch and the choice constructs ($\&_{i \in I}\{M_i.B_i\}$ and $\oplus_{i \in I}\{M_i.B_i\}$, respectively), specifying processes that can branch in either of the $M_i.B_i$ behaviors and choose between one of the $M_i.B_i$ behaviors, respectively. Prefix $M.B$ specifies a process that sends, receives, or internally exchanges a message M before proceeding with behavior B. We also have parallel composition $B_1 \mid B_2$, inaction $\mathbf{0}$, and recursion. Message types M are specified by a polarity p (either output !, input ? or internal action τ), a pair label-direction l^d, and the type C of the name communicated in the message. For typing purposes, we split the set of message labels $\mathcal{L}$ into shared $\mathcal{L}_\star$ and plain $\mathcal{L}_p$ labels (plain labeled messages will be used linearly, and shared labeled messages will be used exponentially). Notice that a message M may refer to an *internal* exchange between two partners, if it is of the form $\tau l^\downarrow(C)$. The unlocated part B of a process P type $L \mid B$ specifies the behavior of P in the current conversation (taking place in the context where P resides).

$B ::= B_1 \mid B_2 \mid 0 \mid \text{rec}\, \mathcal{X}.B \mid \mathcal{X} \mid \oplus_{i \in I}\{M_i.B_i\} \mid \&_{i \in I}\{M_i.B_i\}$ *(Behavioral)*

$M ::= p\, l^d(C)$ *(Message)* $p ::= ! \mid ? \mid \tau$ *(Polarity)* $C ::= [B]$ *(Conversation)*

$L ::= n : C \mid L_1 \mid L_2 \mid 0$ *(Located)* $T ::= L \mid B$ *(Process)*

Fig. 6. Syntax of Types

$$\text{rec}\, \mathcal{X}.T \equiv T\{\mathcal{X}/\text{rec}\, \mathcal{X}.T\}\ (1) \qquad n : [B_1 \mid B_2] \equiv n : [B_1] \mid n : [B_2]\ (2)$$

$$M.B_1 \mid B_2 <: M.(B_1 \mid B_2)\ (M \# B_2)\ (3) \qquad\qquad \downarrow B \mid \uparrow B <: B\ (4)$$

$$\frac{M_i.B_i <: M_i'.B_i'\ (i \in I)}{\oplus_{i \in I}\{M_i.B_i\} <: \oplus_{i \in I}\{M_i'.B_i'\}}(5) \qquad \frac{M_i.B_i <: M_i'.B_i'\ (i \in I) \quad I \subseteq J}{\&_{i \in J}\{M_i.B_i\} <: \&_{i \in I}\{M_i'.B_i'\}}(6)$$

Fig. 7. Selected Subtyping Rules

$$\frac{P :: L \mid B}{n \blacktriangleleft [P] :: (L \bowtie n : [\downarrow B]) \mid loc(\uparrow B)}(piece) \qquad \frac{P :: L \mid B_1 \mid x : [B_2] \quad (x \notin dom(L))}{\textbf{this}(x).P :: L \mid (B_1 \bowtie B_2)}(this)$$

$$\frac{P_i :: L \mid B_i \mid x_i : C_i \quad (x_i \notin dom(L))}{\Sigma_{i \in I}\, l_i^d?(x_i).P_i :: L \mid \oplus_{i \in I}\{!l_i^d(C_i).B_i\}}(inp) \qquad \frac{P :: L \mid B}{l^d!(n).P :: (L \bowtie n : C) \mid ?l^d(C).B}(out)$$

$$\frac{P :: T \mid a : [B] \quad (closed(B), a \notin dom(T))}{(\nu a)P :: T}(res) \quad \frac{P :: T_1 \quad Q :: T_2}{P \mid Q :: T_1 \bowtie T_2}(par) \quad \frac{}{0 :: \tau(L)}(stop)$$

$$\frac{P :: L_M \mid B\langle \mathcal{X} \rangle}{\textbf{rec}\, \mathcal{X}.P :: \star L_M \mid \text{rec}\, \mathcal{X}.B\langle \mathcal{X} \rangle}(rec) \qquad \frac{}{\mathcal{X} :: \mathcal{X}}(var) \qquad \frac{T <: T' \quad P :: T'}{P :: T}(sub)$$

Fig. 8. Typing Rules

We introduce some auxiliary notations and notions. We abbreviate both $\oplus\{M.B\}$ and $\&\{M.B\}$ with $M.B$. We write M for $M.0$, and $p\,l(C)$ for $p\,l^\downarrow(C)$. An important auxiliary notion is the *projection* $d(B)$ *in direction* d *of a behavioral type* B. It consists in the selection of all messages that have the given direction d while filtering out ones in the other direction, offering a partial view of behavior B from the d viewpoint. For instance, if $B \triangleq\ !\,buy(Tp).?\,\texttt{askPrice}^\uparrow(Tp).!\,\texttt{readVal}^\uparrow(Tm).?\,price(Tm)$ then $\downarrow(B) =\ !\,buy(Tp).?\,price(Tm)$ and $\uparrow(B) =\ ?\,\texttt{askPrice}^\uparrow(Tp).!\,\texttt{readVal}^\uparrow(Tm)$. We also write, e.g., $\uparrow B$ for $\uparrow(B)$, to lighten notation. Informally, we refer to $\downarrow B$ as the "here interface" of B, and likewise for $\uparrow B$ as the "up interface". If p is a polarity (!, ?, τ), we denote by $p(B)$ the projection type that selects all messages that have polarity p.

Types are related by the subtyping relation $<:$, for which we depict a selection of rules in Fig. 7. The subtyping rules express expected relationships of types, such as the commutative monoid rules for $(- \mid -, 0)$, congruence principles, and the split rule (2). For types T_1 and T_2 we write $T_1 \equiv T_2$ if $T_1 <: T_2$ and $T_2 <: T_1$. A key subtyping principle is (4), that allows a behavioral type to be decomposed (in the subtype) in its two projections according to the message directions $\downarrow$ and $\uparrow$. Another important subtyping principle is (3), that allows a message to be serialized (in the supertype). Notice we do not allow width subtyping in choice type (5). Essentially we can not forget some choices in the choice type, as this would allow undesired matches between choice and branch types: if the environment expected by a process does not fully reveal the choices it may take, then placing the process in such environment may lead to unexpected (not described by the type) behaviors (cf., [7], where a related issue is addressed).

We may now present our typing rules in Fig. 8. They rely on several auxiliary operations and predicates on types. The key ones are predicate *apartness* $T_1 \# T_2$ and relation *merge* $T = T_1 \bowtie T_2$. Intuitively, two types are apart when they may type subsystems that may be safely composed without undesirable interferences. Apartness is defined by checking disjointness of sets of message labels, more precisely it asserts disjointness of plain ("linear") types, and consistency of shared ("exponential") types, w.r.t. conversations. The merge relation relates two types T_1 and T_2 to some composition, so that if $T = T_1 \bowtie T_2$ then T is a particular behavioral combination of the types T_1 and T_2. Merge is defined not only in terms of spatial separation, but also, and crucially, in terms of synchronization / shuffle of behavioral traces. Notice that there might not be T such that $T = T_1 \bowtie T_2$. On the other hand, if such T exists, we use $T_1 \bowtie T_2$ to non-deterministically denote any such T (e.g., in conclusions of type rules). Intuitively, $T = T_1 \bowtie T_2$ holds if T_1 and T_2 may safely synchronize or interleave so as to produce behavioral type T. We formally define merge and apartness in the Appendix, but this informal understanding already allows us to explain the key typing rules.

Rule (*piece*) types a (piece of a) conversation. Process P expects some located behavior L, and some unlocated behavior B in the current conversation. The type in the conclusion is obtained by merging the type L with a type that describes the behavior of the new conversation piece, in parallel with the type of the toplevel conversation, the now current conversation. Essentially, the type of the projections in the two directions is collected appropriately: the "here" projection $\downarrow B$ is the behavior in conversation n, and the "up" projection $\uparrow$ of P becomes the "here" behavior at the toplevel conversation, via $loc(\uparrow B)$ which sets the direction of all messages to $\downarrow$. Rule (*this*) types the conversation awareness primitive, requiring behavior B_2 of conversation x to be a separate (in general, just partial) view of the current conversation. This allows to bind the current conversation to name x, and possibly sent to other parties that may need to join it.

In rule (*inp*) the premise states that processes P_i require some located behavior L, some current conversation behavior B_i, and some behavior at conversation x_i ($dom(L)$ denotes the set of conversation identifiers of located type L). Then, the conclusion states that the input summation process is well-typed under type L, with the behavior interface becoming the choice of the types of the continuations prefixed by the messages $! \, l_i^d(C_i)$, where the output capability $!$ corresponds to the message capability expected from the external environment (as well as the choice that also refers to the capability of performing a choice expected from the external environment). In rule (*out*) notice that the context type is a separate $\bowtie$ view of the context, which means that the type being sent may actually be some separate part of the type of some conversation, which will be (partially) delegated away. This mechanism is crucial to allow external partners to join in on ongoing conversations in a disciplined way. The behavioral interface of the output prefixed process is an input type, as an input is expected from the external environment.

In rule (*res*) we use $closed(B)$, to avoid hiding conversation names where unmatched communications still persist (necessary to ensure deadlock absence). *closed* behavioral types characterize processes that have matching receives for all sends.

$$\tau \, l^{\downarrow}(C).B \to B \qquad \frac{T_1 \to T_2}{T_1 \mid T_3 \to T_2 \mid T_3} \qquad \frac{T_1 \to T_2}{n : [T_1] \to n : [T_2]}$$

Fig. 9. Type Reduction Selected Rules

Definition 3.1. *A behavioral type B is closed, noted $closed(B)$, if the polarities of message types in B are only τ messages or outputs ! on shared labels.*

In rule (rec) we denote by $B\langle \mathcal{X} \rangle$ a behavioral type with a single occurrence of $\mathcal{X}$. We use $\star M$ as an abbreviation of $rec \, \mathcal{X}.M.\mathcal{X}$. Then, by L_M we denote a located type of the form $n_1 : [M_1] \mid \ldots \mid n_k : [M_k]$, and by $\star L_M$ we denote $n_1 : [\star M_1] \mid \ldots \mid n_k : [\star M_k]$. The rule states that the process is well typed under an environment that persistently offers messages M_i under conversations n_i, and persistently offers behavior B in the current conversation. The message types M_i must be defined with shared labels with polarity ?. We now present our main soundness results. Subject reduction is defined using a notion of reduction on types, since a reduction step at the process level may require a modification in the type. Fig. 9 shows a selection of type reduction rules.

Theorem 3.2 (Subject Reduction). *Let P be a process and T a type such that $P :: T$. If $P \to Q$ then there is T' such that $T \to T'$ and $Q :: T'$.*

Our safety result asserts that certain error processes are unreachable from well-typed processes. To define error processes we introduce static process contexts.

Definition 3.3 (Static context). *Static process contexts, noted $C[\cdot]$, are defined as:*

$$C[\cdot] ::= (\nu a)C[\cdot] \mid P \mid C[\cdot] \mid c \blacktriangleleft [C[\cdot]] \mid rec \, \mathcal{X}.C[\cdot] \mid \cdot$$

We also use $w(\lambda)$ to denote the sequence $c \, l^d$ of elements in the action label λ, for example $w((\nu a)c \, l^d!(a)) = c \, l^d$ and $w((\nu a)l^d!(a)) = l^d$.

Definition 3.4 (Error Process). *P is an error process if there is a static context C with $P = C[Q \mid R]$ and there are $Q', R', \lambda, \lambda'$ such that $Q \xrightarrow{\lambda} Q', R \xrightarrow{\lambda'} R'$ and $w(\lambda) = w(\lambda')$, $\overline{\lambda} \neq \lambda'$ and $w(\lambda)$ is not a shared label.*

A process is not an error only if for each possible immediate interaction in a plain message there is at most a single sender and a single receiver.

Proposition 3.5 (Error Freeness). *Let P be such that $P :: T$. Then P is not an error.*

By subject reduction (Theorem 3.2), we conclude that any process reachable from a well-typed process is not an error. We note by $\xrightarrow{*}$ the reflexive transitive closure of $\to$.

Corollary 3.6 (Type Safety). *Let P be a process such that $P :: T$ for some T. If there is Q such that $P \xrightarrow{*} Q$, then Q is not an error process.*

Our type safety result ensures that, in any reduction sequence arising from a well-typed process, for each plain-labeled message ready to communicate there is always at most a unique input/output outstanding synchronization. More: arbitrary interactions in shared labels do not invalidate this invariant. Another consequence of subject reduction is that any message exchange inside the process must be explained by a τM prefix in the related conversation type (via type reduction), thus implying conversation fidelity, i.e., all conversations follow the protocols prescribed by their types. In the expected polyadic extension of core CC and type system we would also exclude arity mismatch errors.

Before closing this section, we show the types of the *Buyer-Seller-Shipper* example (*BuySys*) of the Introduction, assuming the expected typing for process *PriceDB*.

$$B_{ss} \triangleq \; ! \, \mathtt{buy}(Tp).? \, \mathtt{price}(Tm).\tau \, \mathtt{product}(Tp).? \, \mathtt{details}(Td)$$

$$B_{sh} \triangleq \; ! \, \mathtt{product}(Tp).? \, \mathtt{details}(Td) \quad B_{db} \triangleq \; \tau \, \mathtt{askPrice}(Tp).\tau \, \mathtt{readVal}(Tm)$$

$$BuySys :: Seller : [\tau \, \mathtt{startBuy}([B_{ss}]).B_{db}] \; | \; Shipper : [\tau \, \mathtt{newDelivery}([B_{sh}])]$$

4   Progress

In this section, we develop an auxiliary proof system to enforce progress properties on systems. As most traditional deadlock detection methods (e.g., see [9,15,17]), we build on the construction of a well-founded ordering on events. In our case, events are message synchronizations occurring under conversations. Thus the ordering must relate pairs (conversation identifier,message label), which allows us to cope with systems with multiple interleaved conversations, and back and forth communications between two or more conversations in the same thread. Since references to conversations can be passed in message synchronization, the ordering also considers for each message the ordering associated to the conversation which is communicated in the message. These ingredients allow us to check that all events in the continuation of a prefix are of greater rank than the event of the prefix, thus guaranteeing the event dependencies are acyclic.

The proof system, for which we depict a selection of rules in Fig. 10, is presented by means of judgments of the form $\Gamma \vdash_\ell P$. The judgment $\Gamma \vdash_\ell P$ states that the communications of process P follow a well determined order, specified by Γ. In such a judgment we note by Γ an event ordering: a well-founded partial order of events. Events consist of both a pair (name,label) $((\Lambda \cup \mathcal{V}) \times \mathcal{L})$ and an event ordering abstraction, i.e., a parameterized event ordering, noted $(x)\Gamma$ (where x is a binding occurrence with scope Γ), which represents the ordering of the conversation which is to be communicated in the message. We range over events with $e, e_1, \ldots$ and denote by $n.l.(x)\Gamma$ an event where n is the conversation name, l is the message label and $(x)\Gamma$ is the event ordering abstraction. In $\Gamma \vdash_\ell P$, we use ℓ to keep track of the names of the current conversation $(\ell(\downarrow))$ and of the enclosing conversation $(\ell(\uparrow))$; if $\ell = (n, m)$ then $\ell(\uparrow) = n$ and $\ell(\downarrow) = m$. We define some operations over event orderings Γ. The event ordering $\Gamma \setminus n$ is obtained from Γ by removing all events that have n as conversation name, while

$$\frac{(\ell(d).l_i.(y)\Gamma_i' \perp \Gamma) \cup \Gamma_i'\{y/x_i\} \vdash_\ell P_i}{\Gamma \vdash_\ell \Sigma_{i \in I} \, l_i^d?(x_i).P_i}(inp) \qquad\qquad \frac{\Gamma \vdash_\ell P}{\Gamma \setminus a \vdash_\ell (\nu a)P}(res)$$

$$\frac{(\ell(d).l.(x)\Gamma' \perp \Gamma) \vdash_\ell P \quad \Gamma'\{x/n\} \subseteq (\ell(d).l.(x)\Gamma' \perp \Gamma)}{\Gamma \vdash_\ell l^d!(n).P}(out) \qquad \frac{\Gamma \vdash_{(\ell(\downarrow),n)} P}{\Gamma \vdash_\ell n \blacktriangleleft [P]}(piece)$$

Fig. 10. Selection of Proof Rules for Progress

keeping the overall ordering. By $e_1 \prec_\Gamma e_2$ we denote that e_1 is smaller than e_2 under Γ, and by $dom(\Gamma)$ we denote the set of events which are related by Γ.

Definition 4.1. *Given event e and event ordering Γ such that $e \in dom(\Gamma)$ we define $e \perp \Gamma$ as the subrelation of Γ where all events are greater than e, as follows:*

$$e \perp \Gamma \triangleq \{(e_1 \prec e_2) \mid (e_1 \prec_\Gamma e_2) \land (e \prec_\Gamma e_1)\}$$

We briefly discuss the key proof rules of Fig. 10. Rules (inp) and (out) ensure communications originating in the continuations, including the ones in the conversation being received/sent, are of a greater order. In rule (inp) the event ordering considered in the premise is such that it contains elements greater than $\ell(d).l_i.(x)\Gamma'$, the event associated with the input, enlarged with the event ordering abstraction $(x)\Gamma'$ of the event associated with the input, where the bound x is replaced by the input parameter x_i. In rule (out) the event ordering considered in the premise is such that it contains elements greater than $\ell(d).l.(x)\Gamma'$, the event associated to the output. Also the premise states that the event ordering abstraction $(x)\Gamma'$ of the event associated to the output is a subrelation of the event ordering Γ, when the parameter x is replaced by the name to be sent in the output (n). We may now present our progress results.

Theorem 4.2 (Preservation of Event Ordering). *Let P be a well typed process $P :: T$ and Γ an event ordering such that $\Gamma \vdash_\ell P$. If there is Q such that $P \to Q$ then $\Gamma \vdash_\ell Q$.*

We define finished processes so to distinguish stable from stuck processes.

Definition 4.3 (Finished Process). *P is finished if for any static context C and process Q such that $P = C[Q]$ then Q has no immediate output $(\lambda = l^d!(a))$ transitions.*

Finished processes have no reductions and also have no pending requests (outputs), hence are in a stable state, but may have some active inputs (e.g., persistent definitions).

Theorem 4.4 (Progress). *Let P be a well typed process such that $P :: T$, where $closed(T)$, and Γ an event ordering and a, b names $(a, b \notin fn(P))$ such that $\Gamma \vdash_{(a,b)} P$. If P is not a finished process then there is Q such that $P \to Q$.*

Theorem 4.4 ensures that well-typed and well-ordered processes never get stuck on an output that has no matching input. This property entails that services are always available upon request and protocols involving interleaving conversations never get stuck. In the light of these results, given we can show that the *Buyer-Seller-Shipper* example of the Introduction has such an event ordering, we can assert it enjoys the progress property. Notice that *Seller* leaves and reenters the received conversation, to consult *PriceDB*; such a scenario is not in the scope of other progress techniques for sessions.

5 Related Work

Behavioral Type Systems As most behavioral type systems (see [8,13]), we describe a conversation behavior by some kind of abstract process. However, fundamental ideas behind the conversation type structure, in particular the composition / decomposition of behaviors via merge, as captured, e.g., in the typing rule for $P \mid Q$, and used to model delegation of conversation fragments, have not been explored before.

Binary Sessions. The notion of conversation originates in that of session (introduced in [10,11]). Sessions are a medium for two-party interaction, where session participants access the session through a session endpoint. On the other hand conversations are also a single medium but for multiparty interaction, where any of the conversation participants accesses the conversation through a conversation endpoint (pieces). Session channels support single-threaded interaction protocols between the two session participants. Conversation contexts, on the other hand, support concurrent interaction protocols between multiple participants. Sessions always have two endpoints, created at session initialization. Participants can delegate their participation in a session, but the delegation is full as the delegating party loses access to the session. Conversations also initially have two endpoints. However the number of endpoints may increase (decrease) as participants join in on (leave) ongoing conversations. Participants can ask a party to join in on a conversation and not lose access to it (partial delegation). Since there are only two session participants, session types may describe the entire protocol by describing the behavior of just one of the participants (the type of the other participant is dual). Conversations types, on the other hand, describe the interactions between multiple parties so they specify the entire conversation protocol (a choreography description) that decomposes in the types of the several participants (e.g., $B_t = B_{bu} \bowtie B_{se} \bowtie B_{sh}$).

Multiparty Sessions. The goals of the works [2,12] are similar to ours. To support multiparty interaction, [12] considers multiple session channels, while [2] considers a multiple indexed session channel, both resorting to multiple communication pathways. We follow an essentially different approach, by letting a single medium of interaction support concurrent multiparty interaction via labeled messages. In [2,12] sessions are established simultaneously between several parties through a multicast session request. As in binary sessions, session delegation is full so the number of initial participants is kept invariant, unlike in conversations where parties can keep joining in. The approach of [2,12] builds on two-level descriptions of service collaborations (global and local types), first introduced in a theory of endpoint projection [6]. The global types mention the identities of the communicating partners, being the types of the individual participants projections of the global type with respect to these annotations. Our merge operation $\bowtie$ is inspired in the idea of projection [6], but we follow a different approach where "global" and "local" types are treated at the same level in the type language and types do not explicitly mention the participants identities, so that each given protocol may be realized by different sets of participants, provided that the composition of the types of the several participants produce (via $\bowtie$) the appropriate invariant. Our approach thus supports conversations with dynamically changing number of partners, ensuring a higher degree of loose-coupling. We do not see how this could be encoded in the approach of [12]. On the other hand, we believe that core CC with conversation types can express the same kind of systems as [12].

Progress in Session Types. There are a number of progress studies for binary sessions (e.g., [1,3,9]), and for multiparty sessions [2,12]. The techniques of [2,9] are nearer to ours as orderings on channels are imposed to guarantee the absence of cyclic dependencies. However they disallow processes that get back to interact in a session after interacting in another, and exclude interleaving on received sessions, while we allow processes that re-interact in a conversation and interleave received conversations.

6   Concluding Remarks

We have presented a core typed model for expressing and analyzing service and communication based systems, building on the notions of conversation, conversation context, and context-dependent communication. We believe that, operationally, the core CC can be seen as a specialized idiom of the π-calculus [18], if one considers π extended with labeled channels or pattern matching. However, for the purpose of studying communication disciplines for service-oriented computing and their typings, it is much more convenient to adopt a primitive conversation context construct, for it allows the conversation identity to be kept implicit until needed.

Conversation types elucidate the intended dynamic structure of conversations, in particular how freshly instantiated conversations may dynamically engage and dismiss participants, modeling in a fairly abstract way, the much lower level correlation mechanisms available in Web-Services technology. Conversation types also describe the information and control flow of general service-based collaborations, in particular they may describe the behavior of orchestrations and choreographies. We have established subject reduction and type safety theorems, which entail that well-typed systems follow the defined protocols. We also have studied a progress property, proving that well-ordered systems never get stuck, even when participants are engaged in multiple interleaved conversations, as is often the case in applications. Conversation types extend the notion of binary session types to multiple participants, but discipline their communication by exploiting distinctions between labeled messages in a single shared communication medium, rather than by introducing multiple or indexed more traditional session typed communication channels as, e.g., [12]. This approach allows us to unify the notions of global type and local type, and type highly dynamic scenarios of multiparty concurrent conversations not covered by other approaches. On the other hand, being more abstract and uniform, our type system does not explicitly keep track of participant identities. It would be interesting to investigate to what extent both approaches could be conciliated, for instance, by specializing our approach so as to consider extra constraints on projections on types and merges, restricting particular message exchanges to some roles.

Acknowledgments. We thank IP Sensoria, CMU-PT and anonymous referees. We also thank Mariangiola Dezani-Ciancaglini and Nobuko Yoshida for insightful discussions.

References

1. Acciai, L., Boreale, M.: A Type System for Client Progress in a Service-Oriented Calculus. In: Degano, P., De Nicola, R., Meseguer, J. (eds.) Concurrency, Graphs and Models. LNCS, vol. 5065, pp. 642–658. Springer, Heidelberg (2008)
2. Bettini, L., Coppo, M., D'Antoni, L., De Luca, M., Dezani-Ciancaglini, M., Yoshida, N.: Global Progress in Dynamically Interleaved Multiparty Sessions. In: van Breugel, F., Chechik, M. (eds.) CONCUR 2008. LNCS, vol. 5201, pp. 418–433. Springer, Heidelberg (2008)
3. Bruni, R., Mezzina, L.G.: Types and Deadlock Freedom in a Calculus of Services, Sessions and Pipelines. In: Meseguer, J., Roşu, G. (eds.) AMAST 2008. LNCS, vol. 5140, pp. 100–115. Springer, Heidelberg (2008)

4. Caires, L.: Spatial-Behavioral Types for Concurrency and Resource Control in Distributed Systems. Theoretical Computer Science 402(2-3), 120–141 (2008)

5. Caires, L., Vieira, H.T.: Conversation Types. UNL-DI-3-08, Departamento de Informática, Universidade Nova de Lisboa (2008)

6. Carbone, M., Honda, K., Yoshida, N.: Structured Communication-Centred Programming for Web Services. In: De Nicola, R. (ed.) ESOP 2007. LNCS, vol. 4421, pp. 2–17. Springer, Heidelberg (2007)

7. Castagna, G., Gesbert, N., Padovani, L.: A Theory of Contracts for Web Services. In: 35th Symposium on Principles of Programming Languages, POPL 2008, pp. 261–272. ACM, New York (2008)

8. Chaki, S., Rajamani, S.K., Rehof, J.: Types as models: Model Checking Message-Passing Programs. In: POPL 2002, pp. 45–57. ACM, New York (2002)

9. Dezani-Ciancaglini, M., de'Liguoro, U., Yoshida, N.: On Progress for Structured Communications. In: Barthe, G., Fournet, C. (eds.) TGC 2007. LNCS, vol. 4912, pp. 257–275. Springer, Heidelberg (2008)

10. Honda, K.: Types for Dyadic Interaction. In: Best, E. (ed.) CONCUR 1993. LNCS, vol. 715, pp. 509–523. Springer, Heidelberg (1993)

11. Honda, K., Vasconcelos, V.T., Kubo, M.: Language Primitives and Type Discipline for Structured Communication-Based Programming. In: Hankin, C. (ed.) ESOP 1998. LNCS, vol. 1381, pp. 122–138. Springer, Heidelberg (1998)

12. Honda, K., Yoshida, N., Carbone, M.: Multiparty Asynchronous Session Types. In: 35th Symposium on Principles of Programming Languages, POPL 2008, pp. 273–284. ACM, New York (2008)

13. Igarashi, A., Kobayashi, N.: A Generic Type System for the Pi-Calculus. Theoretical Computer Science 311(1-3), 121–163 (2004)

14. Kobayashi, N., Pierce, B.C., Turner, D.N.: Linearity and the Pi-Calculus. In: 23rd Symposium on Principles of Programming Languages, POPL 1996, pp. 358–371. ACM, New York (1996)

15. Lynch, N.: Fast Allocation of Nearby Resources in a Distributed System. In: 12th Symposium on Theory of Computing, STOC 1980, pp. 70–81. ACM, New York (1980)

16. Milner, R., Parrow, J., Walker, D.: A Calculus of Mobile Processes, Part I + II. Information and Computation 100(1), 1–77 (1992)

17. Kobayashi, N.: A New Type System for Deadlock-Free Processes. In: Baier, C., Hermanns, H. (eds.) CONCUR 2006. LNCS, vol. 4137, pp. 233–247. Springer, Heidelberg (2006)

18. Sangiorgi, D., Walker, D.: The π-calculus: A Theory of Mobile Processes. Cambridge University Press, Cambridge (2001)

19. Vieira, H.T., Caires, L., Seco, J.C.: The Conversation Calculus: A Model of Service-Oriented Computation. In: Drossopoulou, S. (ed.) ESOP 2008. LNCS, vol. 4960, pp. 269–283. Springer, Heidelberg (2008)

Appendix

In this appendix, we group the detailed definition of key technical notions, namely apartness, merge, and conformance. We denote by $Labels_{\mathcal{L}}(B)$ the set of message types with labels in $\mathcal{L}$ occurring in behavioral type B, and by $LLabels_{\mathcal{L}}(B)$ the set of directed labels (l^d) from $\mathcal{L}$ of a behavioral type B. For example, given some behavioral type B, $Labels_{\mathcal{L}_p}(B)$ is the set of all plain (from $\mathcal{L}_p$) message types ($p\, l^d(C)$) occurring in B.

Given behavioral types B_1 and B_2, we let $B_1 \asymp B_2$ state that message types with shared labels occur in both B_1 and B_2 with identical argument types.

Definition 6.1. *The conformance relation $B_1 \asymp B_2$ on behavioral types is defined as:*

$$B_1 \asymp B_2 \triangleq if \ (p_1 \ l^d(C_1)) \in Labels_{\mathcal{L}_\star}(B_1) \ and \ (p_2 \ l^d(C_2)) \in Labels_{\mathcal{L}_\star}(B_2) \ then$$
$$C_1 \equiv C_2 \ and \ either \ p_1 = p_2 = ?, \ p_1 = p_2 = \tau \ or \ p_i = ! \ and \ p_j = \tau$$

Notice that two message types defined on shared labels and polarity ! are not conformant: this allows us to disallow composition of processes that are listening on the same shared message (expecting !), thus ensuring a unique handling principle.

Definition 6.2. *The apartness relation $B_1 \# B_2$ on behavioral types is defined as:*

$$B_1 \# B_2 \triangleq B_1 \asymp B_2 \ and \ LLabels_{\mathcal{L}_p}(B_1) \cap LLabels_{\mathcal{L}_p}(B_2) = \emptyset$$

Definition 6.3. *The merge relation $B = B_1 \bowtie_u B_2$ on behavioral types is defined as:*

$$B\{? \ l^d(C)/\tau \ l^d(C)\} \mid \star \ ! \ l^d(C) = B \bowtie_u \star \ ! \ l^d(C) \qquad\qquad if \ l \in \mathcal{L}_\star \ (1)$$

$$\Pi. \oplus_{i \in I} \{\tau \ l_i^\downarrow(C_i).B_i\} = \Pi. \oplus_{i \in I} \{! \ l_i^\downarrow(C_i).B_i^+\} \bowtie_u \&_{i \in I}\{? \ l_i^\downarrow(C_i).B_i^-\} \ (2)$$
$$if \ l \in \mathcal{L}_p \ and \ \Pi \# ?l_i^\downarrow(C_i).B_i^- \ and \ B_i = B_i^- \bowtie_u B_i^+$$

$$\mathbf{rec} \ \mathcal{X}.B = \mathbf{rec} \ \mathcal{X}.B^+ \bowtie_u \mathbf{rec} \ \mathcal{X}.B^- \qquad\qquad if \ B = B^- \bowtie_u B^+ \ (3)$$

$$B_1 \mid B_2 \ = B_1^+ \mid B_2^+ \bowtie_u B_1^- \mid B_2^- \quad if \ B_1 \# B_2 \ and \ B_i = B_i^- \bowtie_u B_i^+ \ (4)$$

$$\mathcal{X} = \mathcal{X} \bowtie_u \mathcal{X} \ (5) \qquad\qquad B = B \bowtie_u \mathbf{0} \ (6) \qquad B = \mathbf{0} \bowtie_u B \ (7)$$

We denote by $\bowtie$ the congruence closure extension of $\bowtie_u$ to both located and behavioral types. In (1) we denote by $B\{? \ l^d(C)/\tau \ l^d(C)\}$ the type obtained by replacing all occurrences of $? \ l^d(C)$ by $\tau \ l^d(C)$ in B. Shared labels synchronize and leave open the possibility for further synchronizations, expecting further outputs from the environment – rule (1). Instead, plain message synchronization captures the uniquely determined synchronization on that plain label – rule (2). Also, through (2), it is possible to hoist a sequence of messages Π, where Π abbreviates $M_1.(\ldots).M_k$, by interleaving with the continuation, if Π is apart from the behavior to be placed in parallel.

Abstract Processes in Orchestration Languages[*]

Maria Grazia Buscemi[1] and Hernán Melgratti[2]

[1] IMT Lucca Institute for Advanced Studies, Italy
m.buscemi@imtlucca.it
[2] FCEyN, University of Buenos Aires, Argentina
hmelgra@dc.uba.ar

Abstract. Orchestrators are descriptions at implementation level and may contain sensitive information that should be kept private. Consequently, orchestration languages come equipped with a notion of *abstract processes*, which enable the interaction among parties while hiding private information. An interesting question is whether an abstract process accurately describes the behavior of a concrete process so to ensure that some particular property is preserved when composing services. In this paper we focus on compliance, i.e, the correct interaction of two orchestrators and we introduce two definitions of abstraction: one in terms of traces, called *trace-based abstraction*, and the other as a generalization of symbolic bisimulation, called *simulation-based abstraction*. We show that simulation-based abstraction is strictly more refined than trace-based abstraction and that simulation-based abstraction behaves well with respect to compliance.

1 Introduction

An *orchestrator* describes the execution flow of a single party in a composite service. The execution of an orchestrator takes control of service invocation, handles service answers and data flow among the different parties in the composition. Since orchestrators are descriptions at implementation level and may contain sensitive information that should be kept private to each party, orchestration comes equipped with the notion of *abstract processes*, which enable the interaction of parties while hiding private information. Essentially, abstract processes are partial descriptions intended to expose the protocols followed by the actual, concrete processes. Typically, abstract processes are used for slicing the interactions of a concrete process over a fixed set of ports. Consider the following scenario in which an organization sells goods that are produced by a different company. The process that handles order requests can be written as follows (we use CCS [15] extended with value-passing and arithmetic operations).

$$C_1 \stackrel{def}{=} order(desc).\overline{askProd}\langle desc\rangle.answProd(cost).\overline{reply}\langle cost \times 1.1\rangle$$

The process C_1 starts by accepting an order (i.e., a message on port *order*). Then, the received order is forwarded to the actual producer (message $\overline{askProd}\langle desc\rangle$) to obtain a quotation (message on port *answProd*). Finally, the client request is answered by sending the production cost incremented by a 10% (message $\overline{reply}\langle cost \times 1.1\rangle$). We

---

[*] Research supported by the EU FET-GC2 IST-2004-16004 Integrated Project SENSORIA.

G. Castagna (Ed.): ESOP 2009, LNCS 5502, pp. 301–315, 2009.

can define an abstract process that at the same time hides the sensible details of the organization (e.g., the source of the offered goods and the percentages earned) and gives enough information to the client for allowing interaction. In fact, it would be enough for a client to know that orders are placed with a message in port *order* and the quotation is received on port *reply*. For instance, we can define the following abstract process (where τ stands for a silent, hidden action) showing the interaction of C_1 with a client.

$$A_{C_1} \overset{def}{=} order(desc).\tau.\tau.\overline{reply}\langle cost \rangle$$

Abstract processes can be also used to hide particular values and internal decisions made by concrete processes. Consider the following process used for authorizing loans.

$$C_2 \overset{def}{=} request(amount, salary).\texttt{if } (salary > amount/50salary) \texttt{ then } \overline{refuse}\langle\rangle \texttt{ else } \overline{approved}\langle\rangle$$

Note that a loan is approved only when the requested amount is at most 50 times the solicitor's salary. Suppose also that the bank does not want to publicly declare this policy. This can be achieved by providing an abstract processes where some values are *opaque*, i.e., not specified. We denote opaque elements with $\square$. Then, the abstract process of C_2 can be written as follows.

$$A_{C_2} \overset{def}{=} request(amount, salary).\texttt{if } salary > \square \texttt{ then } \overline{refuse}\langle\rangle \texttt{ else } \overline{approved}\langle\rangle$$

The conditional process in A_{C_2} has to be thought of as an internal, non-deterministic choice in which the bank may decide either to approve or to refuse the application. That is, the client cannot infer from A_{C_2} the actual decision that the bank will take.

Then, the main question is whether an abstract process is a *suitable* abstraction of a concrete one or, symmetrically, when a concrete process is a *proper* instantiation of an abstract one. Suitable and proper mean that the abstraction relation should preserve some particular property about composition. In this paper we will focus on *compliance* [12], which specifies whether two partners are able to complete their interaction. So, in terms of compliance, a suitable abstraction means that whenever a pair of services are compliant, we can substitute a service with a more concrete one (according to the abstraction relation) and the composition is still compliant.

In this work we give a formal definition of compliance and propose two alternative definitions for the *abstraction* relation. Our first characterization of abstraction relies on a notion of abstraction of the traces of a process: a process P is an abstraction of a process Q with respect to a set of visible names V if the set of traces of P coincides with the set of traces of Q after the removal of all hidden names. As expected, testing whether two processes belong to this relation requires comparing infinite sets of traces. Hence, we give an efficient version of trace abstraction that only requires checking finitely-many symbolic traces and we prove that the two trace-based relations coincide.

The second notion of abstraction that we propose states that the abstract process and the concrete process must be able to simulate each other behaviors when hiding a given set of names in the concrete process. In general, this notion is not a bisimulation. For example, a process $P = \tau.\texttt{if } a = \square \texttt{ then } \overline{y}\langle a \rangle \texttt{ else } \overline{z}\langle a \rangle$ is the abstraction of a process $Q = x(u).\texttt{if } a = u \texttt{ then } \overline{y}\langle a \rangle \texttt{ else } \overline{z}\langle a \rangle$ when hiding x but, of course, P and Q are not bisimilar since P has more computations. We show that our simulation-based relation is strictly finer than trace-based abstraction. Finally, we show that this second notion of abstraction preserves compliance.

Related works. The problem of giving suitable abstractions of the behaviour of a concrete system is not new. In fact, different flavours of the same general problem have been studied in the literature ([15,2,1,6,8], just to name a few). Session types [11,7,9] and, more recently, contracts [12,5,4] provide a framework for checking whether a client is compliant with a service and whether a process can be "safely" replaced with another one (a detailed comparison among session types and contracts can be found in [13]). Our proposal shares aims with the above approaches but there are three main differences with those models. First, our abstraction relations are neither trace inclusion nor simulation. Hence, $a \leq a + b$ for $+$ an external choice does not hold in our case (roughly speaking, we do not allow abstract processes to exhibit more behaviors than their associated concrete processes). Indeed, if we hide b it holds $a + \tau \leq_{\{a\}} a + b$. Second, the main focus of contracts and session types is on the interplay between external and internal choice, while the abstraction relations we define, which specify hiding data and turning external choice and conditional statements into internal choice, have no immediate counterpart in the those models. Third, our processes include actions that not only record the type of communication but also the transmitted data and two branching structures, if-then-else and guarded choice, that do not tightly match internal and external choice in contracts or branching and choice in session types.

2   Concrete Processes

The computation model we describe is highly inspired by the composition model of WS-BPEL, which can be roughly described as follows: a composite service can be though as the parallel composition of several orchestrators that interact by exchanging XML-documents using one of the basic actions, i.e., invoke a service operation ($<$ invoke $>$), receive a message ($<$ receive $>$), and reply to a previous invocation ($<$ reply $>$). An orchestrator is a program built up from basic actions that are composed into sequences ($<$ sequence $>$), parallel flows ($<$ flow $>$), conditional statements ($<$ switch $>$), iteration blocks ($<$ while $>$), and in choice statements ($<$ pick $>$). Moreover, an orchestrator is not intended to use primitives $<$ invoke $>$, $<$ receive $>$ and $<$ reply $>$ to synchronize with itself. For this reason, we divide the presentation of the computation model in two parts: (i) the language of *concrete processes* (introduced in this section), which is intended to model the behavior of a single orchestrator; and (ii) the language of *concrete business processes* (presented in § 8) that focuses on the interaction among several orchestrators.

The remaining of this section is devoted to the presentation of the language of concrete processes, which is a version of value-passing CCS [16] with input guarded choices and conditional statements but without recursion.

2.1   Syntax

We assume an infinite denumerable set of names $\mathcal{N}$, ranged over by η, that is partitioned into a set of port names X, ranged over by $x, y, z, \ldots$, a set of data variables $\mathcal{V}$, ranged over by $u, v, \ldots$, and a set of data constants C, ranged over by $a, b, c, \ldots$. We let $m, n, \ldots$ range over $\mathcal{V} \cup C$. We write $\tilde{\eta}$ for a tuple of names. *Substitutions*, ranged over by σ, are partial maps from $\mathcal{V}$ onto $\mathcal{V} \cup C$. Domain and co-domain of σ, noted $dom(\sigma)$ and $cod(\sigma)$, are defined as usual. By $m\sigma$ we denote $\sigma(m)$ if $m \in dom(\sigma)$, and m otherwise.

Definition 1 (Concrete processes). *The set of concrete processes P is given by the following grammar:*

$$P ::= 0 \mid P|P \mid \tau.P \mid \bar{x}\langle\tilde{m}\rangle.P \mid x_1(\tilde{v_1}).P + \ldots + x_n(\tilde{v_n}).P \mid \text{if } m = n \text{ then } P \text{ else } P$$

As usual, 0 stands for the inert process, $P|P$ for the parallel composition of processes, $\tau.P$ for the process that performs a silent action and then behaves like P, $\bar{x}\langle\tilde{m}\rangle.P$ for the process that sends the message m over the port x and then becomes P. The process $x_1(\tilde{v_1}).P_1 + \ldots + x_n(\tilde{v_n}).P_n$ denotes an external choice in which some process $x_i(\tilde{v_i}).P_i$ is chosen when the corresponding guard $x_i(\tilde{v_i})$ is enabled. The conditional process if $m = n$ then P else P' behaves either as P if m and n are syntactically equivalent, or as P' otherwise. For convenience, here we restrict to equality constraints. However, more complex constraints could be "encoded" under certain conditions. Hereafter, we adopt the usual convention of omitting trailing 0's.

In $x_1(\tilde{v_1}).P_1 + \ldots + x_n(\tilde{v_n}).P_n$, the data variables v_i are bound, for all i. We use the standard notions of *free* and *bound* names of processes, noted respectively as $fn(P)$ and $bn(P)$, and α-conversion on bound names. Without loss of generality, we assume that the sets of free and bound names are disjoint and that the bound names of a process are all distinct from each other. As usual, a process P is *closed* if $fn(P) \cap \mathcal{V} = \emptyset$.

2.2 Operational Semantics

The operational semantics, as usual, is given in two steps: the definition of a *structural congruence*, which rearranges processes into adjacent positions, and a notion of *labeled transition relation* that captures computation on processes.

We define *structural congruence*, $\equiv$, as the least congruence over concrete processes closed with respect to α-conversion and satisfying the following rules:

$$P|0 \equiv P \qquad P_1|P_2 \equiv P_2|P_1 \qquad (P_1|P_2)|P_3 \equiv P_1|(P_2|P_3)$$

Let *actions* α range over *silent move*, *free input* and *free output*:

$$\alpha ::= \tau \mid x\langle\tilde{a}\rangle \mid \bar{x}\langle\tilde{a}\rangle.$$

As usual, for $\alpha \neq \tau$, $subj(\alpha)$ and $obj(\alpha)$ denote the subject and the object of α respectively. For X a process or an action, $X\sigma$ denotes the expression obtained by replacing in X each data variable $u \in fn(X)$ with $u\sigma$, possibly α-converting to avoid name capturing.

The labeled transition relation $\xrightarrow{\alpha}$ over concrete closed processes is the least relation satisfying the inference rules in Table 1. The transition rules for processes are the standard ones for value passing CCS. We only add rules (IF) and (ELSE) for handling conditional statements of processes. As mentioned before, we do not include here the standard communication rule, because our model allows synchronizations only among different orchestrators (see Section 8).

Table 1. LTS for concrete processes

$$(\text{TAU}) \quad \tau.P \xrightarrow{\tau} P \quad (\text{OUT}) \quad \bar{x}\langle \tilde{a}\rangle.P \xrightarrow{\bar{x}\langle \tilde{a}\rangle} P \quad (\text{IN}) \quad x_1(\tilde{v}_1).P_1 + \ldots + x_n(\tilde{v}_n).P_n \xrightarrow{x_i\langle \tilde{a}\rangle} P_i\{\tilde{a}/\tilde{v}_i\}$$

$$(\text{IF}) \quad \frac{P \xrightarrow{\alpha} P'}{\text{if } a = a \text{ then } P \text{ else } Q \xrightarrow{\alpha} P'} \qquad (\text{ELSE}) \quad \frac{Q \xrightarrow{\alpha} Q' \quad a \neq b}{\text{if } a = b \text{ then } P \text{ else } Q \xrightarrow{\alpha} Q'}$$

$$(\text{PAR}) \quad \frac{P \xrightarrow{\alpha} P'}{P \mid Q \xrightarrow{\alpha} P' \mid Q} \qquad (\text{STR}) \quad \frac{P \equiv Q \quad Q \xrightarrow{\alpha} Q' \quad Q' \equiv P'}{P \xrightarrow{\alpha} P'}$$

The following result shows that the labeled transition relation is well-defined. The proof is by induction on the structure of P and on the transition rules.

Proposition 1. *Let P be a closed process. If $P \xrightarrow{\alpha} Q$ then Q is a closed process.*

3 Abstract Processes

Abstract processes are defined by using the primitives of the concrete processes plus the possibility of having *opaque* definitions. An opaque element hides the precise value of an element: for instance, an opaque assignment to a data variable hides the assigned value. We denote an opaque element by the special name $\square$, and we assume $\square \notin \mathcal{N}$.

The definition of *abstract processes* is analogous to the definition of concrete processes, but making $a, b, \ldots$ range over $C \cup \{\square\}$, $m, n, \ldots$ range over $\mathcal{V} \cup C \cup \{\square\}$, and $x, y, \ldots$ range over $X \cup \{\square\}$. Hence, opaque names can appear either as subjects of input and output prefixes, values of output prefixes, or parts of conditions in if _ then _ else _ processes, but not as bound variables. We let $P, Q, R \ldots$ range over abstract processes.

The rules in Table 1 remain unchanged. We assume for the rule (IN) that every a_j can take the value $\square$ and, hence, $P_i\{\tilde{a}/\tilde{v}_i\}$ is still a process. Rules (IF) and (ELSE) consider only the cases in which the condition does not contain opaque elements. For the case of opaque values we add the rules in Table 2 and the structural congruence axioms below.

$$\square(\tilde{v}).P \equiv \tau.P\{\square/\tilde{v}\} \qquad \overline{\square}\langle \tilde{a}\rangle.P \equiv \tau.P.$$

Note that a conditional statement becomes a non-deterministic choice when at least one value in the condition is opaque, while a guarded choice becomes an internal choice

Table 2. Additional LTS rules for processes

$$(\text{CHOICE-1}) \quad \frac{P_1 \xrightarrow{\alpha} P_1' \quad \square \in \{a, b\}}{\text{if } a = b \text{ then } P_1 \text{ else } P_2 \xrightarrow{\alpha} P_1'} \qquad (\text{CHOICE-2}) \quad \frac{P_2 \xrightarrow{\alpha} P_2' \quad \square \in \{a, b\}}{\text{if } a = b \text{ then } P_1 \text{ else } P_2 \xrightarrow{\alpha} P_2'}$$

$$(\text{CHOICE-3}) \quad x_1(\tilde{v}_1).P_1 + \ldots + \square(\tilde{v}_i).P_i + \ldots + x_n(\tilde{v}_n).P_n \xrightarrow{\tau} P_i\{\tilde{\square}/\tilde{v}_i\}$$

when the subject of the input guard is the opaque name. For instance, consider the process $R \equiv \Box(v_1).P + x(v_2).Q$. A possible move for R is $R \xrightarrow{x\langle a \rangle} Q\{^a/_{v_2}\}$, where the input guard is executed. Another possibility is $R \xrightarrow{\tau} P\{^\Box/_{v_1}\}$, where R makes an internal choice.

We define the notion of traces over processes as usual. A *trace* t is a sequence of actions $\alpha_1.\cdots.\alpha_n$. The set $Tr(P)$ of traces of a process P is defined as follows:

$$Tr(P) = \{t \mid P \xrightarrow{\alpha_1} P_1 \ldots P_{n-1} \xrightarrow{\alpha_n} P_n \wedge t = \alpha_1.\cdots.\alpha_n\}.$$

4   Symbolic Semantics

This section gives a definition of the symbolic semantics of concrete and abstract processes as a symbolic labeled transition relation over processes. Labels have two components: a symbolic action λ and a Boolean condition M over the set of data variables and data constants $\mathcal{V} \cup \mathcal{C}$ that must hold for the α-transition to be enabled.

We let *symbolic actions* λ range over the *silent move, input* and *free output* and we let *conditions* M range over a language of Boolean formulas:

$$\lambda ::= \tau \mid x(\tilde{v}) \mid \bar{x}\langle \tilde{m} \rangle \qquad M ::= true \mid false \mid m = n \mid m \neq n \mid M \wedge M \mid M \vee M.$$

The notions of *free* names $fn(\cdot)$, *bound* names $bn(\cdot)$, and α-conversion over actions and conditions are as expected, considering that the occurrences of the names v_i's are bound in $x(\tilde{v})$ and that conditions have no bound names. By $M\sigma$ we mean the condition obtained by simultaneously replacing in M each data variable $v \in fn(M)$ with $v\sigma$. A condition M is *ground* if M does not contain data variables. The *evaluation* $Ev(M)$ of a ground condition M into the set $\{true, false\}$ is defined by extending in the expected homomorphical way the following clauses:

$Ev(true) = true \quad Ev(a = a) = true \qquad\qquad Ev(a = b) = true \text{ if } \{a,b\} \cap \Box \neq \emptyset$
$Ev(false) = false \quad Ev(a = b) = false \text{ if } a, b \neq \Box \quad Ev(a \neq b) = true \text{ if } \{a,b\} \cap \Box \neq \emptyset$

A substitution σ *respects* M, written $\sigma \models M$, if $M\sigma$ is ground and $Ev(M\sigma) = true$. A condition M is *consistent* if there is a substitution σ such that $\sigma \models M$. A condition M *logically entails* a condition N, written $M \Rightarrow N$, if, for every σ, $\sigma \models M$ implies $\sigma \models N$. For instance, $v = a \wedge u \neq b \wedge v = u \Rightarrow a \neq b$ and $true \Rightarrow u = a \vee u \neq a$. For λ a symbolic action and σ a substitution such that every data variable in λ belongs to $dom(\sigma)$, we write $\lambda\sigma$ to denote the following action:

$$\lambda\sigma \stackrel{def}{=} \begin{cases} \tau & \text{if } \lambda = \tau \\ \bar{x}\langle a_1, \ldots, a_k \rangle & \text{if } \lambda = \bar{x}\langle n_1, \ldots, n_k \rangle \text{ and } a_i = n_i\sigma \text{ for } i = 1, \ldots, k \\ x\langle a_1, \ldots, a_k \rangle & \text{if } \lambda = x(v_1, \ldots, v_k) \text{ and } a_i = \sigma(v_i) \text{ for } i = 1, \ldots, k \end{cases}$$

By $\lambda = \lambda'$ we denote the following condition:

$$\lambda = \lambda' \stackrel{def}{=} \begin{cases} true & \text{if } \lambda = \lambda' = \tau \text{ or } \lambda = \lambda' = x(\tilde{v}) \\ \tilde{m} = \tilde{n} & \text{if } \lambda = \bar{x}\langle \tilde{m} \rangle \text{ and } \lambda' = \bar{x}\langle \tilde{n} \rangle \\ false & \text{otherwise} \end{cases}$$

For M a condition and $D = \{M_1, \ldots, M_n\}$ a finite set of conditions, D is a M-*decomposition* if $M \Rightarrow M_1 \vee \ldots \vee M_n$. For instance, $\{u = a, u \neq a\}$ is a *true*-decomposition.

The symbolic labeled transition relation $\xrightarrow{M,\lambda}$ over concrete processes is the least relation satisfying the inference rules in Table 3. The additional symbolic rules for processes are given in Table 4. Each symbolic rule is the counterpart of a rule in Table 1. Intuitively, the condition M in the label M, λ of a transition collects the Boolean constraints on the free data variables of the source process necessary for action λ to take place. For instance, the rules for prefixes say that each prefix can be consumed unconditionally. Differently from rule (IN) in Table 1, input variables are *not* instantiated immediately (rule (S-IN)). Rules (S-IF) and (S-ELSE) make the equalities or inequalities of the conditional statements explicit. As an example, the process $P \equiv x(v).\text{if } v = a \text{ then } \bar{y}\langle v \rangle \text{ else } 0$, after a first step, can make a transition under condition that variable v is equal to a:

$$P \xrightarrow{true, x(v)} \text{if } v = a \text{ then } \bar{y}\langle v \rangle \text{ else } 0 \xrightarrow{v=a, \bar{y}\langle v \rangle} 0$$

Remark that the present rules are simpler than those given in [3] for the pi-calculus because our calculus is a value-passing CCS plus conditional statements and, thus, logical conditions do not affect channel names.

Proposition 2. *Let P be a closed process.*

- *If $P \xrightarrow{\alpha} Q$ then there exist R, M, λ, and $\sigma \models M$ s.t. $P \xrightarrow{M,\lambda} R$, $\alpha = \lambda\sigma$ and $Q = R\sigma$.*
- *If $P \xrightarrow{M,\lambda} Q$ then there exists $\sigma \models M$ such that $P \xrightarrow{\alpha} Q\sigma$ and $\alpha = \lambda\sigma$.*

5 Notion of Abstraction

This section informally presents our notion of abstraction by introducing the ideas that are formalized in the following sections. The abstraction relation is parametric with respect to the names that should be shown by the abstract process. For instance, given the concrete process $P \equiv \bar{x}\langle a \rangle . \bar{y}\langle b, c \rangle$ and the set $V = \{y, a, b\}$ of visible names, we require the abstract process (i) to show every interaction that takes place over channel y, (ii) to hide every interaction occurring over a channel different from y, (iii) to show every occurrence of the data values a and b in visible interactions and (iv) to hide every occurrence of a data value different form a and b. Hence, we expect the abstraction of P to be $Q \equiv \tau.\bar{y}\langle b, \square \rangle$. Note that the output action on the hidden channel x is mimicked by the silent movement τ (independently from the fact that a is a visible name) and the output $\bar{y}\langle b, c \rangle$ over the channel y is represented in the abstraction as $\bar{y}\langle b, \square \rangle$, where the hidden value c has been replaced by the opaque element.

A side-effect of hiding concrete elements is the introduction of non-determinism at the abstract level. This may happen either because decisions become opaque or because input guarded choices become internal choices, as shown by the following example.

Example 1. Consider the following two processes

$$P \equiv x(u).\text{if } u = a \text{ then } \bar{y}\langle b \rangle \text{ else } \bar{z}\langle c \rangle \qquad Q \equiv x(u).\text{if } u = \square \text{ then } \bar{y}\langle b \rangle \text{ else } \bar{z}\langle c \rangle$$

We expect Q to be an abstraction of P when a is a hidden name.

Table 3. Symbolic LTS for concrete processes

(S-TAU)   (S-OUT)   (S-IN)

$$\tau.P \xrightarrow{true,\tau} P \qquad \bar{x}\langle \tilde{m}\rangle.P \xrightarrow{true,\bar{x}\langle \tilde{m}\rangle} P \qquad x_1(\tilde{v}_1).P_1 + \ldots + x_n(\tilde{v}_n).P_n \xrightarrow{true,x_i(\tilde{v}_i)} P_i$$

(S-PAR) $\dfrac{P \xrightarrow{M,\lambda} P' \quad bn(\lambda) \cap fn(Q) = \emptyset}{P \mid Q \xrightarrow{M,\lambda} P' \mid Q}$ (S-IF) $\dfrac{P \xrightarrow{M,\lambda} P' \quad m = n \wedge M \text{ consistent}}{\text{if } m = n \text{ then } P \text{ else } Q \xrightarrow{m=n\wedge M,\lambda} P'}$

(S-STR) $\dfrac{P \equiv Q \quad Q \xrightarrow{M,\lambda} Q' \quad Q' \equiv P'}{P \xrightarrow{M,\lambda} P'}$ (S-ELSE) $\dfrac{Q \xrightarrow{M,\lambda} Q' \quad m \neq n \wedge M \text{ consistent}}{\text{if } m = n \text{ then } P \text{ else } Q \xrightarrow{m\neq n\wedge M,\lambda} Q'}$

Table 4. Additional symbolic rules for processes

(S-CHOICE-1)   (S-CHOICE-2)

$$\dfrac{P \xrightarrow{M,\lambda} P' \quad \Box \in \{m,n\}}{\text{if } m = n \text{ then } P \text{ else } Q \xrightarrow{M,\lambda} P'} \qquad \dfrac{Q \xrightarrow{M,\lambda} Q' \quad \Box \in \{m,n\}}{\text{if } m = n \text{ then } P \text{ else } Q \xrightarrow{M,\lambda} Q'}$$

(S-CHOICE-3) $\quad x_1(\tilde{v}_1).P_1 + \ldots + \Box(\tilde{v}_i).P_i + \ldots + x_n(\tilde{v}_n).P_n \xrightarrow{true,\tau} P_i$

In addition, non-determinism is a valid abstraction only when either alternative is actually present in the concrete process, namely abstraction must reflect real choices. For instance, let P below be a concrete process and R be a process obtained from P by turning the conditional statement into a non-deterministic choice:

$$P' \equiv \text{if } a = a \text{ then } P_1 \text{ else } P_2 \quad R \equiv \text{if } \Box = \Box \text{ then } P_1 \text{ else } P_2$$

We expect R not to be an abstraction of P', since $a = a$ is always true and P' can never evolve to P_2. In fact, a suitable abstraction of P' is simply P_1.

6   Trace-Based Abstraction

We present a relation of abstraction based on *symbolic traces*. Roughly, for V a set of ports and data names that must be kept visible, a process P is an abstraction of a process Q with respect to V if the set of traces of P coincides with the set of concrete traces derived by the symbolic traces of Q "up to" the names not in V.

Definition 2 (symbolic traces). *A symbolic trace s is a sequence of symbolic actions $\lambda_1. \cdots .\lambda_n$. The set $STr(P)$ of symbolic traces of a process P is defined as follows:*

$$STr(P) = \{ \langle M,s\rangle \mid P \xrightarrow{M_1,\lambda_1} P_1 \ldots P_{n-1} \xrightarrow{M_n,\lambda_n} P_n \text{ and } M = M_1 \wedge \ldots \wedge M_n \text{ and}$$
$$s = \lambda_1. \cdots .\lambda_n \text{ and } bn(\lambda_i) \cap bn(\lambda_j) = \emptyset \text{ for all } i \text{ and } j \text{ s.t. } i \neq j \}$$

For $s = \lambda_1. \cdots .\lambda_n$ and σ such that every data variable in s belongs to $dom(\sigma)$, $s\sigma$ stands for $\lambda_1\sigma. \cdots .\lambda_n\sigma$. For instance, if $s = x(u).z(v).\bar{y}\langle v\rangle$ and $\sigma = \{a/u, b/v\}$, $s\sigma = x\langle a\rangle.z\langle b\rangle.\bar{y}\langle b\rangle$. Given a process, we can recover its concrete traces by instantiating its symbolic traces, as stated by the following definition.

Definition 3 (derived concrete traces). *The set $DCTr(P)$ of derived concrete traces of a process P is defined as follows:*

$$DCTr(P) = \{s\sigma \mid \langle M, s \rangle \in STr(P) \text{ and } \sigma \models M \text{ and } s\sigma \text{ is a trace}\}.$$

Consider the process $P \equiv x(v).\text{if } v = a \text{ then } \bar{y}\langle v \rangle \text{ else } \bar{z}\langle v \rangle$ shown in Ex. 1. The sets of symbolic traces and of derived concrete traces of P are as follows.

$$STr(P) = \{\langle \mathit{true}, x(v) \rangle, \langle v = a, x(v).\bar{y}\langle v \rangle \rangle, \langle v \neq a, x(v).\bar{z}\langle v \rangle \rangle\}$$
$$DCTr(P) = \{x\langle a \rangle, x\langle b \rangle, \cdots, x\langle a \rangle.\bar{y}\langle a \rangle, x\langle b \rangle.\bar{z}\langle b \rangle, x\langle c \rangle.\bar{z}\langle c \rangle, \ldots\}.$$

Note that $DCTr(P)$ is equal to the set $Tr(P)$ of traces of P (shown in Ex. 1). The following proposition formally states the equivalence of these two alternative characterizations of the concrete traces of a process.

Proposition 3. *Let P be a closed process. The sets $Tr(P)$ and $DCTr(P)$ coincide.*

As stated before, an abstract process hides names used by the concrete process. The following definitions describe the effect of hiding names in conditions, actions, and symbolic traces. Hereafter, V stands for a set of names that are kept visible.

We write $M_{|V}$ for the abstraction of a condition M with respect to a set V. The effect of the abstraction $M_{|V}$ is defined inductively as expected, once it is set that:

$$(m = n)_{|V} = \mathit{true} \text{ if } \{m, n\} \setminus V \neq \emptyset \qquad (m \neq n)_{|V} = \mathit{true} \text{ if } \{m, n\} \setminus V \neq \emptyset$$

Note that the operator $_{|V}$ makes a condition weaker, since all constraints involving hidden names are removed. For instance, given the condition $M \equiv (v = a \wedge v = w \wedge u \neq b)$, the abstraction of M when hiding a is $M_{|\{v,w,u,b\}} \equiv (\mathit{true} \wedge v = w \wedge u \neq b)$.

The abstraction of a symbolic action λ with respect to a set V, written $\lambda_{|V}$, is defined by the following expression, with $\{\Box/m_1, \ldots, \Box/m_n\}$ a partial map from $\mathcal{V} \cup C$ to $\{\Box\}$.

$$\lambda_{|V} = \begin{cases} \lambda\{\Box/m_1, \ldots, \Box/m_n\} & \text{if } subj(\lambda) \in V \text{ and } m_i \in (obj(\lambda) \setminus V), \text{ for } i = 1, \ldots, n \\ \tau & \text{if } subj(\lambda) \notin V \text{ or } \lambda = \tau \end{cases}$$

Abstraction on actions is naturally extended to sequences of symbolic actions as below.

$$s_{|V} = \begin{cases} \lambda_{|V} & \text{if } s = \lambda \\ \tau s'_{|V \setminus \tilde{u}} & \text{if } s = x(\tilde{u}) s' \text{ and } x \notin V \\ x(\tilde{u}) s'_{|V \cup \tilde{u}} & \text{if } s = x(\tilde{u}) s' \text{ and } x \in V \\ \lambda_{|V} s'_{|V} & \text{if } s = \lambda s' \text{ and } \lambda \neq x(\tilde{u}) \end{cases}$$

Note that any input action over a hidden channel (second line in the above definition) is mapped to a silent action and all received names are considered hidden when abstracting the remaining part of the trace. Differently, when abstracting an input action over a visible name (third line in the above definition) all received names are considered visible for the rest of the trace. For instance, when considering the trace $s = x(u).y(v).\bar{z}\langle u, v \rangle$ and the set $V = \{x, z\}$ of visible names, the abstraction of s when considering V is

$s_{|V} = x(u).\tau.\bar{z}\langle u, \Box \rangle$. The set of abstract symbolic traces of P is obtained as the abstraction of any symbolic trace of P:

$$STr(P)_{|V} = \{\langle M_{|V}, s_{|V}\rangle \mid \langle M, s\rangle \in STr(P)\}$$

Since $STr(P)_{|V}$ is a set of symbolic traces, we can define the set of the associated concrete traces. We call this set the abstraction of the derived concrete traces of a process P with respect to a set V, written $DCTr(P)_{|V}$ and defined as follows.

$$DCTr(P)_{|V} = \{s\sigma \mid \langle M, s\rangle \in STr(P)_{|V} \text{ and } \sigma \models M \text{ and } s\sigma \text{ is a trace}\}.$$

Consider the process $P = x(v).\text{if } v = a \text{ then } \bar{y}\langle v\rangle \text{ else } \bar{z}\langle v\rangle$ introduced in Ex. 1. The abstraction of $STr(P)$ when hiding a and the corresponding derived concrete traces are:

$$STr(P)_{|\{x,y,z\}} = \{\langle true, x(v)\rangle, \langle true, x(v).\bar{y}\langle v\rangle\rangle, \langle true, x(v).\bar{z}\langle v\rangle\rangle\}$$
$$DCTr(P)_{|\{x,y,z\}} = \{x\langle a\rangle, x\langle b\rangle, \cdots, x\langle a\rangle.\bar{y}\langle a\rangle, x\langle a\rangle.\bar{z}\langle a\rangle, x\langle b\rangle.\bar{y}\langle b\rangle, x\langle b\rangle.\bar{z}\langle b\rangle, \ldots\}.$$

Note that the set $DCTr(P)_{|\{x,y,z\}}$ coincides with the set of concrete traces of $Q \equiv x(v).\text{if } v = \Box \text{ then } \bar{y}\langle v\rangle \text{ else } \bar{z}\langle v\rangle$ shown in Ex. 1, which is a suitable abstraction of P when hiding a. Below we formally define the notion of trace abstraction.

Definition 4. *A closed process Q is a* trace abstraction *of a closed process P with respect to a set $V \subseteq \mathcal{N}$ such that $fn(Q) \subseteq V$, written $Q \ltimes^V P$, if $Tr(Q) = DCTr(P)_{|V}$.*

As mentioned before, the equation $Tr(Q) = DCTr(P)_{|V}$ holds for P and Q as defined in Ex. 1 and for $V = \{x,y,z\}$. Therefore, $Q \ltimes^V P$ for $V = \{x,y,z\}$.

Remark 1. The abstraction condition cannot be obtained directly by abstracting concrete traces, i.e., condition $Tr(Q) = DCTr(P)_{|V}$ is different from requiring either $Tr(Q) = Tr(P)_{|V}$ or $Tr(Q)_{|V} = Tr(P)_{|V}$, where $Tr(P)_{|V}$ stands for the set obtained by abstracting every trace in $Tr(P)$ with respect to V. For instance, when considering the processes P and Q of Ex. 1, their sets of concrete traces are as follows

$$Tr(P) = \{x\langle a\rangle, x\langle b\rangle, \cdots, x\langle a\rangle.y\langle a\rangle, x\langle b\rangle.z\langle b\rangle, x\langle c\rangle.z\langle c\rangle, \ldots\}$$
$$Tr(Q) = \{x\langle a\rangle, x\langle b\rangle, \cdots, x\langle a\rangle.y\langle a\rangle, x\langle a\rangle.z\langle a\rangle, x\langle b\rangle.y\langle b\rangle, x\langle b\rangle.z\langle b\rangle, \ldots\}$$

and their direct abstractions as below.

$$Tr(P)_{|V} = \{x\langle \Box\rangle, x\langle b\rangle, \cdots, x\langle \Box\rangle.y\langle \Box\rangle, x\langle b\rangle.z\langle b\rangle, x\langle c\rangle.z\langle c\rangle, \ldots\}$$
$$Tr(Q) \quad = \{x\langle \Box\rangle, x\langle b\rangle, \cdots, x\langle \Box\rangle.y\langle \Box\rangle, x\langle \Box\rangle.z\langle \Box\rangle, x\langle b\rangle.y\langle b\rangle, x\langle b\rangle.z\langle b\rangle, \ldots\}$$

Checking the abstraction relation introduced before is hard, since it requires to compare infinite sets of traces. Because of this, we provide an alternative characterization of trace abstraction that requires to consider finitely-many symbolic traces.

We start by introducing some auxiliary notions that will allow us to compare sets of symbolic traces. Consider the sets $S_1 = \{\langle true, s\rangle\}$ and $S_2 = \{\langle u = a, s\rangle, \langle u \neq a, s\rangle\}$. They describe the same behavior since, for any substitution $\sigma \models true$, either $\sigma \models u = a$ or $\sigma \models u \neq a$. Hence, the set of concrete traces derived from S_1 and S_2 coincide. The following definition formally states when two sets of symbolic traces describe the same behavior.

Definition 5. *Let S_1 and S_2 be sets of pairs of conditions and symbolic traces. We write $S_1 \sqsubseteq S_2$ iff for all $\langle M, s \rangle$ in S_1 there exists an M-decomposition D such that for all N in D there exists $\langle N', s' \rangle$ in S_2 such that $N \Rightarrow N' \sigma_\alpha$ and $s = s' \sigma_\alpha$ for some renaming σ_α of the bound names of s'. We write $S_1 \stackrel{*}{=} S_2$ when both $S_1 \sqsubseteq S_2$ and $S_2 \sqsubseteq S_1$ hold.*

We define below an alternative (and more efficient) characterization of abstraction in terms of symbolic traces.

Definition 6. *(trace abstraction) A process P is a* symbolic trace abstraction *of a process Q with respect to a set $V \subseteq \mathcal{N}$ s.t. $fn(P) \subseteq V$, written $P \ltimes^V_s Q$, if $STr(P) \stackrel{*}{=} STr(Q)_{|V}$.*

We remark that the above definition extends the definition of abstraction over processes that are not necessarily closed. The following proposition ensures that symbolic trace abstraction coincides with trace abstraction when restricting to closed processes.

Proposition 4. *Let P and Q be two closed processes. $P \ltimes^V_s Q$ iff $P \ltimes^V Q$.*

7 Abstraction as a Generalized Symbolic Bisimulation

A main challenge of defining a simulation-based abstraction relation is that the application of substitutions when executing concrete processes makes the evaluation of branching statements deterministic while such statements should match non-deterministic choices. As a solution, we propose an abstraction based on a generalization of symbolic bisimulation [10,3]. Symbolic bisimulation is defined on top of a symbolic transition system. Informally, to verify whether two processes P and Q are bisimilar with respect to a given Boolean condition M it is required to find, for each symbolic move of P labeled with $\langle N, \lambda \rangle$, a partition of $N \wedge M$ such that each subcase entails a corresponding symbolic move of Q, and vice-versa for Q and P. First, we give an auxiliary definition that will be used in the subsequent characterization of abstraction.

Definition 7 (visible names). *Given a set of visible names V and a symbolic action λ, the set of visible received names of λ, written $vn(\lambda)_V$, is defined as follows:*

$$vn(\lambda)_V \stackrel{\text{def}}{=} \begin{cases} \tilde{u} \text{ if } \lambda = x(\tilde{u}) \text{ and } x \in V \\ \emptyset \text{ otherwise} \end{cases}$$

We will omit the subscript V when it is clear from the context.

Definition 8 (simulation-based abstraction). *The family $\mathcal{R} = \{\mathcal{R}^V_M\}_M$ of process relations is a* family of simulation-based abstraction relations, *indexed over the set of conditions M, iff for all M and $P\mathcal{R}^V_M Q$:*

1. *If $Q \stackrel{N,\lambda}{\longrightarrow} Q'$ and $bn(\lambda) \cap fn(P,Q,M) = \emptyset$ then there exists a $M \wedge N$-decomposition D s.t. $\forall M' \in D$ there exists $P \stackrel{N',\lambda'}{\longrightarrow} P'$, with $M' \Rightarrow N' \wedge \lambda_{|V} = \lambda'$ and $P'\mathcal{R}^{V \cup vn(\lambda)}_{M'} Q'$.*

2. *if $P \stackrel{N,\lambda}{\longrightarrow} P'$ and $bn(\lambda) \cap fn(P,Q,M) = \emptyset$ then there exists a $M \wedge N$-decomposition D s.t. $\forall M' \in D$ there exists $Q \stackrel{N',\lambda'}{\longrightarrow} Q'$ with $M' \Rightarrow N'_{|V} \wedge \lambda = \lambda'_{|V}$ and $P'\mathcal{R}^{V \cup vn(\lambda')}_{M'} Q'$.*

A process P is a simulation-based abstraction *of a process Q with respect to a set $V \subseteq \mathcal{N}$, written $P \propto^V Q$, if there is an abstraction relation $\mathcal{R}^V_{true}$ s.t. $P \mathcal{R}^V_{true} Q$, with $fn(P) \subseteq V$.*

Condition 1 above states that the abstraction P simulates the concrete process Q up to hidden names. Note that we require $\lambda_{|V} = \lambda'$ instead of the standard definition of symbolic bisimulation that imposes the exact matching of action labels. Condition 2 states that the (concrete) process Q can simulate its abstraction P if we forget about the constraints involving hidden values. That is, if P proposes a move with label $\langle N, \lambda \rangle$ we allow Q to mimic the behavior for a more restrictive condition N'. (Actually, N' may contain several additional constraints involving hidden names.) Note that this makes the abstraction relation not symmetric. For instance, consider the two processes below:

$$P \equiv \text{if } v = \square \text{ then } \bar{y}\langle v \rangle \text{ else } \bar{z}\langle v \rangle \quad Q \equiv \text{if } v = a \text{ then } \bar{y}\langle v \rangle \text{ else } \bar{z}\langle v \rangle.$$

It holds that $P \propto^V Q$ for $V = \{v, y, z\}$. Indeed, when considering the transition $P \xrightarrow{true, \bar{y}\langle v \rangle} 0$, we can take $Q \xrightarrow{v=a, \bar{y}\langle v \rangle} 0$ since $true \Rightarrow (v = a)_{|V} \wedge \bar{y}\langle v \rangle = \bar{y}\langle v \rangle_{|V}$. Conversely, $P \not\propto^V Q'$ for $Q' \equiv \text{if } a = a \text{ then } \bar{y}\langle v \rangle \text{ else } \bar{y}\langle v \rangle$ because $P \xrightarrow{true, \bar{z}\langle v \rangle} 0$ but $Q' \not\xrightarrow{M, \bar{z}\langle v \rangle}$.

We remark that the relation $\propto$ is a simulation (since the abstract process simulates the concrete one) but, in general, is not either a bisimulation or a similarity.

Remark 2. The abstraction relation generalizes symbolic early bisimulation [3,10]. If we restrict to concrete processes, i.e., all names are visible (hence $V = \mathcal{N}$), then $\propto^{\mathcal{N}} = \approx_e$. Indeed, the abstraction operator $_{-|V}$ is the identity when $V = \mathcal{N}$.

The following result states that simulation-based abstraction is finer than trace-based abstraction.

Theorem 1. $\propto^V \subset \ltimes^V$.

8   Composition of Orchestrators

This section addresses the problem of composing orchestrators, and the properties that are ensured by the abstraction relation. Basically, an orchestrator is a concrete process P plus the declaration of the operations it provides, which is a set $I \subseteq X$ of channel names, and a declaration of the operations it invokes, which is a set $O \subseteq X$.

Definition 9 (business processes). *The set of business processes B is defined by the following grammar:*

$$B ::= (I, O)P \mid B \| B$$

We usually abbreviate $B = (I_1, O_1)P_1 \| \cdots \| (I_n, O_n)P_n$ with $B = \|_{i \le n}(I_i, O_i)P_i$. We say that a business process $B = \|_{i \le n}(I_i, O_i)P_i$ is *well-formed* iff the three conditions below hold:

1. For all i, if $x \in fn(P_i)$ and x occurs as subject of an input prefix of P_i, then $x \in I_i$. Similarly, if $x \in fn(P_i)$ and x occurs as subject of an output prefix of P_i then $x \in O_i$.
2. $I_i \cap I_j = \emptyset$ for all $i \neq j$.
3. For all i, $I_i \cap O_i = \emptyset$

Table 5. LTS for business processes

$$(\text{B-TAU}) \quad \frac{P \xrightarrow{M,\tau} P'}{(I,O)P \xrightarrow{M,\tau} (I,O)P'} \qquad\qquad (\text{B-OUT}) \quad \frac{P \xrightarrow{M,\bar{x}\langle\tilde{m}\rangle} P' \quad x \in O}{(I,O)P \xrightarrow{M,\bar{x}\langle\tilde{m}\rangle} (I,O)P'}$$

$$(\text{B-IN}) \quad \frac{P \xrightarrow{M,x(\tilde{v})} P' \quad x \in I}{(I,O)P \xrightarrow{M,x(\tilde{v})} (I,O)P'} \quad (\text{B-COMM}) \quad \frac{B_1 \xrightarrow{M,\bar{x}\langle\tilde{m}\rangle} B_1' \quad B_2 \xrightarrow{N,x(\tilde{v})} B_2' \quad M \wedge N \text{ consistent}}{B_1 \| B_2 \xrightarrow{M \wedge N,\tau} B_1' \| B_2' \{\tilde{m}/\tilde{v}\}}$$

$$(\text{B-PAR}) \quad \frac{B_1 \xrightarrow{M,\lambda} B_1' \quad bn(\lambda) \cap fn(B_2) = \emptyset}{B_1 \| B_2 \xrightarrow{M,\lambda} B_1' \| B_2} \qquad (\text{B-STR}) \quad \frac{B \equiv C \quad C \xrightarrow{M,\lambda} C' \quad C' \equiv B'}{B \xrightarrow{M,\lambda} B'}$$

The first condition requires every orchestrator P_i to correctly declare the operations it provides and the operations it invokes. The second condition imposes operations provided by different orchestrators to be named differently. Last condition forbids self-communications in orchestrators. Hereafter, we will assume all business processes to be well-formed. The operational semantics of business processes is defined up-to the structural congruence $\equiv$ over business processes, which is the least congruence over business processes closed with respect to the commutative and associative laws for $\|$ and the structural rules for concrete processes.

Definition 10. *The symbolic labeled transition relation $\xrightarrow{M,\lambda}$ over business processes is the least relation satisfying the inference rules in Table 5.*

Rules (B-TAU), (B-IN), (B-OUT) lift silent, input and output actions performed by the process P to corresponding actions of the business process $(I,O)P$. The other rules are standard.

8.1 Composition Compliance and Abstraction

We now study the notion of compliance among orchestrators and its relation with abstraction. Different notions of compliance have been proposed in the literature (notably weak termination in the context of Workflow Nets [14]). We adopt here the proposal of [14], which requires both the client and the server to complete in every possible interaction. The following definition introduces the notion of compliance up-to a set of visible names.

Definition 11 (business process compliance up-to V). *We say that two business processes $B_1 = (I_1,O_1)P$ and $B_2 = (I_2,O_2)Q$ are compliant with respect to a condition M and a set of visible names V s.t. $I_1 \cap O_2 \subseteq V$, $O_1 \cap I_2 \subseteq V$, written $B_1 \bowtie_M^V B_2$, whenever $B_1 \| B_2$ is well-formed and either $P \equiv Q \equiv 0$ or all the following conditions hold*

- *if $B_1 \xrightarrow{N,\bar{x}\langle\tilde{m}\rangle} B_1'$ and $x \in V$ and $M \wedge N$ consistent, then $B_2 \xrightarrow{N',x(\tilde{v})} B_2'$ and $M \wedge N \wedge N'$ consistent and $B_1' \bowtie_{M \wedge N \wedge N'}^V B_2' \{\tilde{m}/\tilde{v}\}$*
- *if $B_1 \xrightarrow{N,x(\tilde{v})} B_1'$ and $x \in V$ and $M \wedge N$ consistent, then $B_2 \xrightarrow{N',\bar{x}\langle\tilde{m}\rangle} B_2'$ and $M \wedge N \wedge N'$ consistent and $B_1' \{\tilde{m}/\tilde{v}\} \bowtie_{M \wedge N \wedge N'}^V B_2'$*

- if $B_1 \xrightarrow{N,\lambda} B_1'$ and $(\lambda = \tau$ or $subj(\lambda) \notin V)$ and $M \wedge N$ consistent, then $B_1' \bowtie^V_{M \wedge N} B_2$
- if $B_2 \xrightarrow{N,\lambda} B_2'$ and $(\lambda = \tau$ or $subj(\lambda) \notin V)$ and $M \wedge N$ consistent, then $B_1 \bowtie^V_{M \wedge N} B_2'$

We write $B_1 \bowtie^V B_2$ to denote $B_1 \bowtie^V_{true} B_2$, and $B_1 \bowtie B_2$ for $B_1 \bowtie^{\mathcal{N}} B_2$.

Note that above relation requires V to include all channels through which B_1 and B_2 may synchronize. Then, the notion of compliance up-to V ensures that the interaction among two business processes B_1 and B_2 completes provided with the fact that any other action involving the synchronization of either B_1 or B_2 with a third party will take place at the right moment. Furthermore, remark that the above relation is asymmetric. For instance, for $B_1 = (\emptyset, \{x\})\bar{x}\langle c\rangle.\bar{x}\langle a\rangle$ and $B_2 = (\{x\}, \emptyset)x(v).\text{if } v = \square \text{ then } x(z) \text{ else } y(z)$, it holds $B_1 \bowtie B_2$ but not the converse $B_2 \bowtie B_1$.

Next result ensures "safe replacement", i.e. that substituting an abstract process P with a more concrete one R, i.e. $P \propto^V R$ for some set of visible names V, we still obtain a compliant composition if we ignore the interactions that take place over channels that are not in the abstraction, namely that are not in V.

Theorem 2. *If $P_1 \propto^V Q$ and $(I_1, O_1)P_1 \bowtie (I_2, O_2)P_2$, then $(I, O)Q \bowtie^V (I_2, O_2)P_2$.*

9   Future Work

In this paper we have studied a notion of abstraction for orchestration languages. It would be interesting to extend our approach by including recursion. Although being less expressive, several models of orchestration consider finite fragments of process calculi because they allow for the description of usual scenarios: most instances of business interactions are finite in practice. Nevertheless, our main contribution, i.e., the definition of abstraction as symbolic bisimulation and the composition result extend to a recursive form of process like `rec K in P` with the usual operational semantics: (i) the definition of abstraction remains unchanged, since it is given in terms of transitions independently from the form of the process, (ii) abstractions will preserve all non terminating computations of the concrete process, because the abstraction relation requires the abstract process to exhibit "at least the same computations as the concrete processes", hence (iii) the substitution of an abstraction by a concrete process in a compliant composition will preserve termination. Extending the results presented in §6 would be more involved since we would lose the property of having finite sets of finite symbolic traces.

We also plan a formal study of the relationship with session types and contracts. As remarked in the introduction, even if these approaches have similarities with ours, a precise comparison seems not to be immediate.

References

1. Alur, R., Henzinger, T., Kupferman, O., Vardi, M.: Alternating refinement relations. In: Sangiorgi, D., de Simone, R. (eds.) CONCUR 1998. LNCS, vol. 1466, pp. 163–178. Springer, Heidelberg (1998)
2. Arun-Kumar, S., Natarajan, V.: Conformance: A precongruence close to bisimilarity. In: STRICT. Springer Workshops in Computer Series, pp. 148–165. Springer, Heidelberg (1995)

3. Boreale, M., De Nicola, R.: A symbolic semantics for the pi-calculus. Information and Computation 126(1), 34–52 (1996)
4. Bravetti, M., Zavattaro, G.: Towards a unifying theory for choreography conformance and contract compliance. In: Lumpe, M., Vanderperren, W. (eds.) SC 2007. LNCS, vol. 4829, pp. 34–50. Springer, Heidelberg (2007)
5. Castagna, G., Gesbert, N., Padovani, L.: A theory of contracts for web services. In: Necula, G.C., Wadler, P. (eds.) POPL 2008, pp. 261–272. ACM, New York (2008)
6. de Alfaro, L., Henzinger, T.: Interface theories for component-based design. In: Henzinger, T.A., Kirsch, C.M. (eds.) EMSOFT 2001. LNCS, vol. 2211, pp. 148–165. Springer, Heidelberg (2001)
7. Dezani-Ciancaglini, M., Mostrous, D., Yoshida, N., Drossopoulou, S.: Session Types for Object-Oriented Languages. In: Thomas, D. (ed.) ECOOP 2006. LNCS, vol. 4067, pp. 328–352. Springer, Heidelberg (2006)
8. Fournet, C., Hoare, C.A.R., Rajamani, S., Rehof, J.: Stuck-free conformance. In: Alur, R., Peled, D.A. (eds.) CAV 2004. LNCS, vol. 3114, pp. 242–254. Springer, Heidelberg (2004)
9. Gay, S., Hole, M.: Subtyping for session types in the pi calculus. Acta Informatica 42(2), 191–225 (2005)
10. Hennessy, M., Lin, H.: Symbolic bisimulations. Theoretical Computer Science 138, 353–389 (1995)
11. Honda, K.: Types for dyadic interaction. In: Best, E. (ed.) CONCUR 1993. LNCS, vol. 715, pp. 509–523. Springer, Heidelberg (1993)
12. Laneve, C., Padovani, L.: The must preorder revisited. In: Caires, L., Vasconcelos, V.T. (eds.) CONCUR 2007. LNCS, vol. 4703, pp. 212–225. Springer, Heidelberg (2007)
13. Laneve, C., Padovani, L.: The pairing of contracts and session types. In: Degano, P., De Nicola, R., Meseguer, J. (eds.) Concurrency, Graphs and Models. LNCS, vol. 5065, pp. 681–700. Springer, Heidelberg (2008)
14. Massuthe, P., Schmidt, K.: Operating guidelines - an automata-theoretic foundation for the service-oriented architecture. In: QSIC, pp. 452–457. IEEE Computer Society, Los Alamitos (2005)
15. Milner, R.: A Calculus of Communicating Systems. LNCS, vol. 92. Springer, Heidelberg (1980)
16. Milner, R.: Communication and Concurrency. Prentice Hall International, Englewood Cliffs (1989)

Global Principal Typing in Partially Commutative Asynchronous Sessions

Dimitris Mostrous[1], Nobuko Yoshida[1], and Kohei Honda[2]

[1] Department of Computing, Imperial College London
[2] Department of Computer Science, Queen Mary, University of London

Abstract. We generalise a theory of multiparty session types for the π-calculus through asynchronous communication subtyping, which allows partial commutativity of actions with maximal flexibility and safe optimisation in message choreography. A sound and complete algorithm for the subtyping relation, which can calculate conformance of optimised end-point processes to an agreed global specification, is presented. As a complementing result, we show a type inference algorithm for deriving the principal global specification from end-point processes which is minimal with respect to subtyping. The resulting theory allows a programmer to choose between a top-down and a bottom-up style of communication programming, ensuring the same desirable properties of typable processes.

1 Introduction

Programs which communicate by asynchronous message passing are abundant in critical computing scenes, from a simple web-service application between two parties to a global financial network hosting thousands of nodes and billions of messages per year. The design of such programs, which may be developed in geographically disparate sites, demands a clear high-level specification of their conversation structure, against which participating programs can be validated (*conformance*). Further such specifications may change during development (*refinement*), and might even need to be synthesised from individual endpoint programs, against which updated programs can be further validated (*synthesis of global specifications*).

This paper develops a new theory of multiparty session types [1, 2, 4, 5, 13, 23], which can handle uniformly these three concerns by seamlessly integrating the *top-down* and *bottom-up* strategies for the development of communication-centred software. The methodology for distributed programming put forward in [1, 13] centres on the concept of a *global type* which plays the role of type signature for distributed communications, presenting an abstract high-level description of the protocol that all the participants have to honour when an actual conversation takes place. Building on this framework, we propose the following two strategies for communication programming:

Top-Down Approach: Once this signature G is agreed upon by all parties as a global protocol, a local protocol from each party's viewpoint (*local type* T_i) is generated as a projection of G to each party. Then each local type T_i can be *locally refined* to, say, T_i', possibly giving a more *optimised* protocol, realised as a program, say, P_i. If all the resulting local programs $P_1, .., P_n$ can be type-checked against refined $T_1', .., T_n'$, then they

G. Castagna (Ed.): ESOP 2009, LNCS 5502, pp. 316–332, 2009.

are automatically guaranteed to interact properly, without communication mismatch or getting stuck inside a session, precisely following the intended scenario.

Bottom-Up Approach: In this case the programmers may work based on an informal understanding of shared conversation structures, which, after appropriate development, will get reified into a formal global protocol by synthesis of local behaviours of all endpoint programs: first, a type T_i is inferred from each program P_i, then a new global specification is synthesised from $T_1, .., T_n$. If this specification is validated to satisfy certain conditions, $P_1, .., P_n$ are guaranteed to interact properly. This process can be repeated incrementally, using a succession of synthesised types as *globally refined* protocols.

This paper presents a general and rigorous foundation for these two approaches and their seamless integration, based on multiparty session types. For the automatic refinement, we introduce *asynchronous communication subtyping* over local types, which allows permutation of actions to increase efficiency, while ensuring type-soundness and communication-safety. As an example, suppose we are using an asynchronous communication transport where the message order is preserved but the sending is non-blocking, as in TCP. Let us assume the following three simple processes:

$$P_1 \overset{\text{def}}{=} t?(y_1); s!\langle 5\rangle; s!\langle\text{apple}\rangle; Q_1 \quad P_2 \overset{\text{def}}{=} b?(y_2); t!\langle 7\rangle; Q_2 \quad P_3 \overset{\text{def}}{=} s?(z_1); s?(z_2); Q_3$$

where $s?(y)$ is an input and $s!\langle 5\rangle$ is an output via channel s; and ";" is sequential composition. Then first P_2 gets the value at b; then P_2 sends 7 to P_1; finally P_1 sends 5 and "apple" to P_3 preserving the order. We note that P_3 is blocked until b is fired at P_2. To execute P_3 ahead, P_1 might be locally optimised since y_1 does not bind the subsequent outputs at s. We can similarly optimise P_2. The resulting processes given below still preserve linearity and proper communication structures.

$$P_1' \overset{\text{def}}{=} s!\langle 5\rangle; s!\langle\text{apple}\rangle; t?(y_1); Q_1 \quad P_2' \overset{\text{def}}{=} t!\langle 7\rangle; b?(y_2); Q_2 \quad P_3 \overset{\text{def}}{=} s?(z_1); s?(z_2); Q_3$$

Asynchronous communication subtyping specifies safe permutations of actions, by which we can refine a local protocol to maximise asynchrony without violating the global protocol. For example, in the above case, P_1' is given local type $s!\langle\text{nat}\rangle; s!\langle\text{string}\rangle; t?\langle\text{nat}\rangle; T$ which is a subtype of $t?\langle\text{nat}\rangle; s!\langle\text{nat}\rangle; s!\langle\text{string}\rangle; T$ projected from the global type. Hence optimisations can be checked locally. The idea of this subtyping is intuitive, but it requires delicate formal formulations due to the presence of recursive types and branching/selection session types, whose combinations are vital for typing many practical protocols [12, 22]. This subtlety is because type-permutations *affect the structures of session types*, which makes straightforward constructions following the preceding literature [10, 20] inapplicable. Intuitively, because partial commutativity is defined between *a sequence of actions*, it may require *more than one unfolding* of recursive types to find a match. However, this calculation can be made automatic by an *algorithmic subtyping* which completely characterises the semantic notion of subtyping and can be used to effectively (in)validate conformance of an optimised local type to a global type.

For the bottom-up strategy, we formulate *principal global typing* by which we can synthesise the most general global type from untyped endpoint programs, or can check they can have no global type, i.e. their protocols are incompatible. The framework uses graph-shaped global types which generalise the original syntactic global types, extending typability. Asynchronous communication subtyping plays a central role in the synthesis process. We demonstrate the use of the theory for the two strategies by providing correctness arguments for the development of a distributed parallel algorithm. A full version, containing more examples and detailed proofs, is available from `http://www.doc.ic.ac.uk/~mostrous/asyncsub`.

2 Asynchronous Multiparty Sessions

Syntax. We use the π-calculus for multiparty sessions from [13], omitting polyadicity and delegation for simplicity. We use the following base sets: *shared names* or *names*, written $a,b,x,y,z,\ldots$; *session channels* or *channels*, written $s,t,\ldots$; *labels* (functioning like labels in labelled records), written $l,l',\ldots$; and *process variables*, written $X,Y,\ldots$. For hiding, we use n for either a single shared name or a vector of session channels. Then *processes* $(P,Q\ldots)$ and *expressions* $(e,e',\ldots)$ are given below:

P	::=	$\overline{a}_{[2..n]}(\tilde{s}).P$	request			$P \mid Q$	parallel
		$a_{[p]}(\tilde{s}).P$	acceptance			$\mathbf{0}$	inaction
		$s!\langle e\rangle;P$	sending			$(\nu n)P$	hiding
		$s?(x);P$	reception			$\text{def } D \text{ in } P$	recursion
		$s \triangleleft l;P$	selection			$X\langle \tilde{e}\tilde{s}\rangle$	process call
		$s \triangleright \{l_i: P_i\}_{i\in I}$	branching			$s:\tilde{h}$	message queue
		$\text{if } e \text{ then } P \text{ else } Q$	conditional		h ::=	$l \mid v$	message values
e	::=	$v \mid e \text{ and } e' \mid \text{not } e \cdots$	expressions		D ::=	$\{X_i(\tilde{x}_i\tilde{s}_i) = P_i\}_{i\in I}$	declaration
v	::=	$a \mid \text{true} \mid \text{false} \cdots$	values				

$\overline{a}_{[2..n]}(\tilde{s}).P$ initiates, through a shared name a, a new session with other participants, each of shape $a_{[p]}(\tilde{s}).Q$ with $2 \leq p \leq n$. The (bound) s_i in vector $\tilde{s}$ are session channels used in the session. We call p, q,... (natural numbers) the *participants* of a session. Session communications (which take place inside an established session) are performed by the sending and receiving of a value; and by selection and branching (the former chooses one of the branches offered by the latter). $s:\tilde{h}$ is a *message queue* representing ordered messages in transit $\tilde{h}$ with destination s (which may be considered as a network pipe in a TCP-like transport). The rest of the syntax is standard from [13]. We often omit $\mathbf{0}$, and unimportant arguments of sending/receiving, e.g. $s!\langle\rangle$ and $s?();P$.

Operational semantics. Some selected rules of reduction $P \to P'$ are given below:

$$\overline{a}_{[2..n]}(\tilde{s}).P_1 \mid a_{[2]}(\tilde{s}).P_2 \mid \cdots \mid a_{[n]}(\tilde{s}).P_n \to (\nu\tilde{s})(P_1 \mid P_2 \mid ... \mid P_n \mid s_1:\emptyset \mid ... \mid s_m:\emptyset)$$

$$s!\langle e\rangle;P \mid s:\tilde{h} \to P \mid s:\tilde{h}\cdot v \quad (e\downarrow v) \qquad s?(x);P \mid s:v\cdot\tilde{h} \to P[v/x] \mid s:\tilde{h}$$

$$s \triangleleft l;P \mid s:\tilde{h} \to P \mid s:\tilde{h}\cdot l \qquad s \triangleright \{l_i: P_i\}_{i\in I} \mid s:l_j\cdot\tilde{h} \to P_j \mid s:\tilde{h} \quad (j\in I)$$

The first rule describes the initiation of a new session among n participants that synchronise over the shared name a. After the initiation, they will share the private m fresh session channels s_i and the associated m empty queues ($\emptyset$ denotes the empty string). The output rules enqueue a value and a label, respectively ($e\downarrow v$ denotes the evaluation of e to v). The input rules perform the complementary operations. Processes are considered modulo structural equivalence, $\equiv$, defined by the standard rules [13].

Global types. A *global type*, written $G, G', ..$, describes the whole conversation scenario of a multiparty session as a type signature [13].

Global G	$::=$	$p \to p': k \langle U \rangle; G'$	values	$\mid \mu t.G$	recursive
	$\mid$	$p \to p': k \{l_j: G_j\}_{j \in J}$	branching	$\mid t$	variable
	$\mid$	G, G'	parallel	$\mid end$	end
Value U	$::=$	$bool \mid nat \mid \cdots \mid G$			

Type $p \to p': k \langle U \rangle; G'$ says that participant p sends a message of type U to channel k (represented as a finite natural number) received by participant p' and then interactions described in G' take place. *Value types* range over U, and are either global types for shared names, or base values. Type $p \to p': k \{l_j: G_j\}_{j \in J}$ says that participant p invokes one of the l_i labels on channel k (at participant p'), then interactions described in G_j take place. Type $\mu t.G$ is for recursive protocols, assuming type variables $(t, t', ...)$ are guarded in the standard way, i.e. they only occur under values or branches. We assume G in value types is closed, i.e. without free type variables. Type end represents the termination of a session. We often omit end and identify "G, end" and "end, G" with G. We stipulate that each channel can only be used among two parties (but maybe repeatedly), one party using it for input/branching while the other party for output/selection.[1]

Local types. Local session types type-abstract sessions from each endpoint's view.

Local T	$::=$	$k! \langle U \rangle; T$	send	$\mid k \& \{l_i: T_i\}_{i \in I}$ branching
	$\mid$	$k? \langle U \rangle; T$	receive	$\mid \mu t.T \mid t$ recursion
	$\mid$	$k \oplus \{l_i: T_i\}_{i \in I}$	selection	$\mid end$ end

Type $k! \langle U \rangle$ expresses the sending to k of a value of type U. Type $k? \langle U \rangle$ is its dual input. Type $k \oplus \{l_i: T_i\}_{i \in I}$ represents the transmission to k of a label l_i chosen in the set $\{l_i \mid i \in I\}$, followed by the communications described by T_i. Type $k \& \{l_i: T_i\}_{i \in I}$ is its dual. The remaining types are standard. We say a type is *guarded* if it is neither a recursive type nor a type variable. (An occurrence of) a type constructor *not* under a recursive prefix in a recursive type is called *top-level action* (for example, $k_1! \langle U_1 \rangle$ and $k_2! \langle U_2 \rangle$ in $k_1! \langle U_1 \rangle; k_2! \langle U_2 \rangle; \mu t.k_3! \langle U_3 \rangle; t$ are top-level, but $k_3! \langle U_3 \rangle$ in the same type is not). k is *the head of* T if k appears at the left-most occurrence of the top-level actions in T (e.g. $k_1! \langle U_1 \rangle$ is the head of the above type). The relation between global and local types is formalised by *projection*, written $G \upharpoonright p$ (called *projection of G onto* p), defined as in [13]. For example, $(p \to p': k \langle U \rangle; G') \upharpoonright p = k! \langle U \rangle; (G' \upharpoonright p)$, $(p \to p': k \langle U \rangle; G') \upharpoonright p' = k? \langle U \rangle; (G' \upharpoonright p')$ and $(p \to p': k \langle U \rangle; G') \upharpoonright q = (G' \upharpoonright q)$. We write *Type* for the collection of all closed local types.

3 Asynchronous Partially Commutative Sessions

3.1 Asynchronous Communication Subtyping: Top-Level Actions

This section introduces and studies a basic theory of asynchronous session subtyping. Figure 1 defines the axioms for partial permutation of top-level actions for closed types,

---

[1] This condition dispenses with the need for linearity-check to ensure well-formedness [1].

$$\text{(OI)} \qquad k!\langle U\rangle;k'?\langle U'\rangle;T \;\ll\; k'?\langle U'\rangle;k!\langle U\rangle;T$$

$$\text{(OB)} \qquad k!\langle U\rangle;k'\&\{l_j:T_j\}_{j\in J} \;\ll\; k'\&\{l_j:k!\langle U\rangle;T_j\}_{j\in J}$$

$$\text{(SI)} \qquad k\oplus\{l_j:k'?\langle U\rangle;T_j\}_{j\in J} \;\ll\; k'?\langle U\rangle;k\oplus\{l_j:T_j\}_{j\in J}$$

$$\text{(SB)} \qquad k\oplus\{l_i:k'\&\{l'_j:T_{ij}\}_{j\in J}\}_{i\in I} \;\ll\; k'\&\{l'_j:k\oplus\{l_i:T_{ij}\}_{i\in I}\}_{j\in J}$$

$$\text{(OO)} \qquad k!\langle U\rangle;k'!\langle U'\rangle;T \;\ll\; k'!\langle U'\rangle;k!\langle U\rangle;T$$

$$\text{(II)} \qquad k?\langle U\rangle;k'?\langle U'\rangle;T \;\ll\; k'?\langle U'\rangle;k?\langle U\rangle;T$$

$$\text{(SO)} \qquad k\oplus\{l_i:k'!\langle U\rangle;T_i\}_{i\in I} \;\ll\; k'!\langle U\rangle;k\oplus\{l_i:T_i\}_{i\in I}$$

$$\text{(OS)} \qquad k'!\langle U\rangle;k\oplus\{l_i:T_i\}_{i\in I} \;\ll\; k\oplus\{l_i:k'!\langle U\rangle;T_i\}_{i\in I}$$

$$\text{(SS)} \qquad k\oplus\{l_i:k'\oplus\{l'_j:T_{ij}\}_{j\in J}\}_{i\in I} \;\ll\; k'\oplus\{l'_j:k\oplus\{l_i:T_{ij}\}_{i\in I}\}_{j\in J}$$

$$\text{(Tr)} \;\frac{T_1\ll T_2 \quad T_2\ll T_3}{T_1\ll T_3} \qquad \text{(CO)} \;\frac{T\ll T'}{k!\langle U\rangle;T\ll k!\langle U\rangle;T'} \qquad \text{(CI)} \;\frac{T\ll T'}{k?\langle U\rangle;T\ll k?\langle U\rangle;T'}$$

$$\text{(CB)} \;\frac{\forall i\in I.\; T_i\ll T'_i}{k\&\{l_i:T_i\}_{i\in I}\ll k\&\{l_i:T'_i\}_{i\in I}} \qquad \text{(CS)} \;\frac{\forall i\in I.\; T_i\ll T'_i}{k\oplus\{l_i:T_i\}_{i\in I}\ll k\oplus\{l_i:T'_i\}_{i\in I}} \qquad \begin{array}{l}\text{(E) end}\ll\text{end}\\[4pt]\text{(M) }\mu t.T\ll \mu t.T\end{array}$$

Fig. 1. Action Asynchronous Subtyping Rules ((BI, IB, BB) are omitted)

denoted $\ll$. We assume $k\neq k'$ for all the axioms. $T\ll T'$ is read: T is an *action-asynchronous subtype* of T', and means T is more asynchronous than (or more optimised than) T'. We write $T\gg T'$ for $T'\ll T$.

A partial permutation is applied only to finite parts of the top-level actions (*without* unfolding recursive types); see Proposition 7. Note that we *cannot* exchange an input and output in the reverse direction of (OI) even for different channels. Consider: $P = s?();r!\langle\rangle$ and $Q = s!\langle\rangle;r?()$. These processes interact correctly. If we permute the output and input of Q, we get $Q' = r?();s!\langle\rangle$. Then the parallel composition $(P\mid Q')$ causes deadlock, losing progress. For the same reason, the reverse direction of (OB, SI, SB) is not allowed. By combining these input and output permutation rules, we can achieve a flexible local refinement for communications. For example, suppose $R = s?(x);r?(y);t!\langle 1\rangle;t'!\langle y\rangle$ typed by $T_R = s?\langle\text{file}\rangle;r?\langle\text{bool}\rangle;t!\langle\text{nat}\rangle;t'!\langle\text{bool}\rangle;\text{end}$. We might wish to receive the (small) value via r first, and immediately forward to t', then receive the (larger) file at s in the end: we can obtain $S = r?(y);t'!\langle y\rangle;t!\langle 1\rangle;s?(x)$ typed by $T_S = r?\langle\text{bool}\rangle;t'!\langle\text{bool}\rangle;t!\langle\text{nat}\rangle;s?\langle\text{file}\rangle;\text{end}$, transformed from T_R (i.e. $T_S\ll T_R$) by using a combination of (OO, OI, II).

3.2 Asynchronous Communication Subtyping: Recursive Types

For handling recursive types in asynchronous subtyping, we extend the coinductive method in [20, § 2.3] and [10, § 3.3]. In particular, we need to modify the unfolding function for recursive types since $\ll$ might be applicable to *a sequence of types* after unfolding of recursions under guarded prefixes. The resulting definition integrates $\ll$ with the traditional session subtyping [10, 13]. For any recursive type T, unfold$^n(T)$ is the result of inductively unfolding the first recursion (even under guarded types) up to a fixed level of nesting.

Definition 1 (*n*-time unfolding)

$\text{unfold}^0(T) = T$ for all T $\text{unfold}^{1+n}(T) = \text{unfold}^1(\text{unfold}^n(T))$

$\text{unfold}^1(k!\langle U\rangle;T) = k!\langle U\rangle;\text{unfold}^1(T)$ $\text{unfold}^1(k \oplus \{l_i : T_i\}_{i\in I}) = k \oplus \{l_i : \text{unfold}^1(T_i)\}_{i\in I}$

$\text{unfold}^1(k?\langle U\rangle;T) = k?\langle U\rangle;\text{unfold}^1(T)$ $\text{unfold}^1(k\&\{l_i : T_i\}_{i\in I}) = k\&\{l_i : \text{unfold}^1(T_i)\}_{i\in I}$

$\text{unfold}^1(\mu\mathbf{t}.T) = T[\mu\mathbf{t}.T/\mathbf{t}]$ $\text{unfold}^1(\mathbf{t}) = \mathbf{t}$ $\text{unfold}^1(\text{end}) = \text{end}$

We also use $\text{unfold}^n(U)$ which is defined as $\text{unfold}^n(T)$ above. [2]

For example, $\text{unfold}^2(k?\langle U\rangle;\mu\mathbf{t}.k'!\langle U'\rangle;\mathbf{t}) = k?\langle U\rangle;k'!\langle U'\rangle;k'!\langle U'\rangle;\mu\mathbf{t}.k'!\langle U'\rangle;\mathbf{t}$. Note that, because our recursive types are contractive, $\text{unfold}^n(T)$ terminates. We can now introduce the central notion of asynchronous communication subtyping.

Definition 2. A relation $\mathfrak{R} \in \textit{Type} \times \textit{Type}$ is an asynchronous type simulation if $(T_1, T_2) \in \mathfrak{R}$ implies the following conditions:

- If $T_1 = \text{end}$, then $\text{unfold}^n(T_2) = \text{end}$.
- If $T_1 = k!\langle U_1\rangle;T_1'$, then $\text{unfold}^n(T_2) \gg k!\langle U_2\rangle;T_2'$, $(T_1', T_2') \in \mathfrak{R}$ and $(U_1, U_2) \in \mathfrak{R}$.
- If $T_1 = k?\langle U_1\rangle;T_1'$, then $\text{unfold}^n(T_2) \gg k?\langle U_2\rangle;T_2'$, $(T_1', T_2') \in \mathfrak{R}$ and $(U_2, U_1) \in \mathfrak{R}$.
- If $T_1 = k \oplus \{l_i : T_{1i}\}_{i\in I}$, then $\text{unfold}^n(T_2) \gg k \oplus \{l_j : T_{2j}\}_{j\in J}$ and $I \subseteq J$ and $\forall i \in I.(T_{1i}, T_{2i}) \in \mathfrak{R}$.
- If $T_1 = k\&\{l_i : T_{1i}\}_{i\in I}$, then $\text{unfold}^n(T_2) \gg k\&\{l_j : T_{2j}\}_{j\in J}$ and $J \subseteq I$ and $\forall j \in J.(T_{1j}, T_{2j}) \in \mathfrak{R}$.
- If $T_1 = \mu\mathbf{t}.T$, then $(\text{unfold}^1(T_1), T_2) \in \mathfrak{R}$.

where a type simulation of $(U_1, U_2) \in \mathfrak{R}$ is defined as the standard bisimulation (since U is invariant).[3] The coinductive subtyping relation $T_1 \leqslant_c T_2$ (read: T_1 is an *asynchronous subtype* of T_2) is defined when there exists a type simulation $\mathfrak{R}$ with $(T_1, T_2) \in \mathfrak{R}$.

An output of T_1 can be simulated after applying asynchronous optimisation $\gg$ to the unfolded T_2. We also need to ensure object type U_1 is a subtype of U_2. For the input, we ensure U_2 is a subtype of U_1. The definitions of selection and branching subsume the traditional session branching/selection subtyping.[4] In selection a label appearing in T_1 must be included in T_2; dually, in branching a subtype T_1 must cover all branches declared in T_2. For a value type, $U_1 \leqslant_c U_2$ implies $U_2 \leqslant_c U_1$ by definition. We show examples to justify our subtyping.

Example 3. Below we write $k!$ for $k!\langle U\rangle$ and $k?$ for $k?\langle U\rangle$, omitting U.

1. Let $T_1 = \mu\mathbf{t}.k?;k'!;\mathbf{t}$, $T_2 = \mu\mathbf{t}.k'!;k?;\mathbf{t}$. Then we can prove $T_2 \leqslant_c T_1$ using the simulation $\mathfrak{R} = \{(T_2, T_1), (k'!;k?;T_2, T_1), (k?;T_2, k?;T_1)\}$. T_2 represents more optimal communications than T_1 since it can output messages at k' without waiting.
2. Let $T_2' = k'!;T_1$ which means first sending a signal at k' then repeating input-output actions. Then $T_2' \leqslant_c T_1$ by taking $\mathfrak{R} = \{(T_2', T_1), (T_1, k?;T_1), (k?;T_2', k?;T_1)\}$ as a simulation closure. Note also $T_2 \leqslant_c T_2'$ and $T_2' \leqslant_c T_2$.

---

[2] In [10], $\text{unfold}(T)$ repeatedly unfolds consecutive top-level recursion until a guarded type is obtained. In our definition, $\text{unfold}^1(T)$ expands a single recursion, not only top-level but also under guarded types.

[3] Note that G is invariant like standard channel types $\hat{[}\tilde{T}]$ [10].

[4] We follow the subtyping relation in [7, 13] whose ordering is reversed from [10] since in our judgement the session environment is declared on the right-hand side of a process.

3. Let $T_4' = k_1!;k_2!;T_3$ with $T_3 = \mu t.k_3?;k_1!;k_4?;k_2!;t$ and $T_4 = \mu t.k_1!;k_3?;k_2!;k_4?;t$. These types are extended from T_2',T_1 and T_2 with two signal messages at the top level. Then $T_4' \leqslant_c T_3$. To simulate T_4', we require nested unfold for T_3. More exactly, the intermediate type $k_1!;k_4?;k_2!;T_3$ can be simulated by $k_4?;T_3$ if T_3 unfolds and $k_1!$ under recursion appears at the top-level. Similarly for $T_4' \leqslant_c T_4$.
4. Take $T_5 = \mu t_1.k_1!;\mu t_2.k_1!;\&\{l_1 : k_2?;k_1!;t_1, \, l_2 : k_1!;t_2\}$ and let $T_6 = \mu t_1.\mu t_2.\&\{l_1 : k_2?;k_1!;t_1, \, l_2 : k_1!;t_2\}$. Then $T_5 \leqslant_c T_6$. This example is proved similarly to (3).

Note that none of the above subtyping relations, except $T_2 \leqslant_c T_2'$ and $T_2' \leqslant_c T_2$, can be derived without including $\ll$ in the typed simulation.

Before we prove that $\leqslant_c$ is a preorder, we show that there are connecting simulations relating the components of two subtyping relations. We write $T_1 \, \mathfrak{R}_1 \, T_2$ for $(T_1,T_2) \in \mathfrak{R}_1$.

Lemma 4. *If $T_1 \, \mathfrak{R}_1 \, T_2$ and $T_2 \, \mathfrak{R}_2 \, T_3$ for type simulations $\mathfrak{R}_1$ and $\mathfrak{R}_2$ then there exists a type simulation $\mathfrak{R}_3$ such that if $\text{unfold}^n(T_2) \gg T_2'$, then $T_2' \, \mathfrak{R}_3 \, T_3$.*

Definition 5 (Transitivity connection). For simulations $\mathfrak{R}_1$ and $\mathfrak{R}_2$, we say $\mathfrak{R}_3$ (from the condition in Lemma 4) is a transitivity connection of $T_1 \, \mathfrak{R}_1 \, T_2$ and $T_2 \, \mathfrak{R}_2 \, T_3$. We write $\mathbf{trc}(T_1 \, \mathfrak{R}_1 \, T_2 \, \mathfrak{R}_2 \, T_3)$ for $\mathfrak{R}_3$. We define $\mathbf{trc}(\mathfrak{R}_1,\mathfrak{R}_2)$ as the smallest relation such that if $(T_1,T_2) \in \mathfrak{R}_1$ and $(T_2,T_3) \in \mathfrak{R}_2$, then $\mathbf{trc}(T_1 \, \mathfrak{R}_1 \, T_2 \, \mathfrak{R}_2 \, T_3) \subseteq \mathbf{trc}(\mathfrak{R}_1,\mathfrak{R}_2)$.

From the definition, $\mathbf{trc}(\mathfrak{R}_1,\mathfrak{R}_2)$ only contains type simulations, and as the union of these it is also a type simulation. Note that the smallest relation exists, by set inclusion of relation pairs, containing all the transitivity connections of elements in $\mathfrak{R}_1/\mathfrak{R}_2$. For example, $\mathfrak{R}_3 = \mathbf{trc}(T_1 \, \mathfrak{R}_1 \, T_2 \, \mathfrak{R}_2 \, T_3)$ does not contain $(k!\langle U\rangle;\text{end}, k?\langle U\rangle;\text{end})$, which cannot be a member of any type simulation; and by set inclusion, it is smaller than $\mathfrak{R}_3 \cup (k!\langle U\rangle;\text{end}, k?\langle U\rangle;\text{end})$.

Theorem 6. *The relation $\leqslant_c$ is a preorder.*

Proof. Using as standard the relation $\{(T,T) \mid T \in Type\}$, we prove $\leqslant_c$ is reflexive. For transitivity of $\leqslant_c$, suppose $T_1 \leqslant_c T_2 \leqslant_c T_3$ and let $\mathfrak{R}_1$ and $\mathfrak{R}_2$ be type simulations with $(T_1,T_2) \in \mathfrak{R}_1$ and $(T_2,T_3) \in \mathfrak{R}_2$. To show $T_1 \leqslant_c T_3$ we need to find a type simulation $\mathfrak{R}$ such that $(T_1,T_3) \in \mathfrak{R}$. Define $\mathfrak{R}$ as $(\mathfrak{R}_1 \cdot \mathfrak{R}_2) \cup (\mathfrak{R}_1 \cdot \mathbf{trc}(\mathfrak{R}_1,\mathfrak{R}_2))$. Clearly $(T_1,T_3) \in \mathfrak{R}$, and it remains to show that $\mathfrak{R}$ is a type simulation. For any $(T,T'') \in \mathfrak{R}$, there are two cases (relations above), and six subcases (simulation rules). For $(U,U') \in \mathfrak{R}$, the result is easy as U types are invariant. We only show one of the most interesting cases.

Suppose $(T,T'') \in \mathfrak{R}_1 \cdot \mathfrak{R}_2$ and $T = k!\langle U_1\rangle;T_1$. Then there exists $(T,T') \in \mathfrak{R}_1$ and $(T',T'') \in \mathfrak{R}_2$. By the definition of type simulation, we have $\text{unfold}^n(T') \gg k!\langle U_1'\rangle;T_1'$ and $(U_1,U_1') \in \mathfrak{R}_1$ and $(T_1,T_1') \in \mathfrak{R}_1$. Let $\mathbf{trc}(T \, \mathfrak{R}_1 \, T' \, \mathfrak{R}_2 \, T'') = \mathfrak{R}_3 \subseteq \mathbf{trc}(\mathfrak{R}_1,\mathfrak{R}_2)$, then by Lemma 4 we obtain $(k!\langle U_1'\rangle;T_1',T'') \in \mathfrak{R}_3$, and by the definition of simulation we have $\text{unfold}^m(T'') \gg k!\langle U_1''\rangle;T_1''$ and $(U_1',U_1'') \in \mathfrak{R}_3$ and $(T_1',T_1'') \in \mathfrak{R}_3$. Finally, by the definition of $\mathfrak{R}_1 \cdot \mathbf{trc}(\mathfrak{R}_1,\mathfrak{R}_2)$, $(U_1,U_1'') \in \mathfrak{R}$ and $(T_1,T_1'') \in \mathfrak{R}$ as required. Other cases are similar.   □

3.3   Algorithmic Asynchronous Subtyping

The algorithmic subtyping of session types is studied in [10, § 5.1]. Due to the incorporation of asynchronous permutation and n-time unfolding in the type simulation, we need the bound of unfolding for constructing a terminating algorithm. We first list some selected rewriting rules $\overset{k}{\mapsto}$ which move the types with channel k to the head applying the rules of $\gg$ in Figure 1 in the reverse direction.

(OI) $k'?\langle U'\rangle;k!\langle U\rangle;T \overset{k}{\mapsto} k!\langle U\rangle;k'?\langle U'\rangle;T$ (Tr) $\dfrac{T_1 \overset{k}{\mapsto} T_2 \quad T_2 \overset{k}{\mapsto} T_3}{T_1 \overset{k}{\mapsto} T_3}$

(CO) $\dfrac{T \overset{k}{\mapsto} T'}{k'!\langle U\rangle;T \overset{k}{\mapsto} k'!\langle U\rangle;T'}$ (CB) $\dfrac{T_j \overset{k}{\mapsto} T'_j}{k'\&\{l_1:T_1,..,l_j:T_j,..\} \overset{k}{\mapsto} k'\&\{l_1:T_1,..,l_j:T'_j,..\}}$

We omit the similar rules for (OB–SS), (CI,CS), which are defined similarly to (OI) and (CO,CB). Note that we do not define $\overset{k}{\mapsto}$ for (E) and (M). (CO,CB) are for congruency. For a simple example, let $T_0 = k \oplus \{l_1 : k_1?\langle U_1\rangle;k_2!\langle U_2\rangle;\mathsf{end}, l_2 : k_2!\langle U_2\rangle;\mathsf{end}\}$. Then $T_0 \overset{k_2}{\mapsto} k \oplus \{l_1 : k_2!\langle U_2\rangle;k_1?\langle U_1\rangle;\mathsf{end}, l_2 : k_2!\langle U_2\rangle;\mathsf{end}\} \overset{k_2}{\mapsto}$ $k_2!\langle U_2\rangle;k \oplus \{k_1?\langle U_1\rangle;\mathsf{end}, l_2 : \mathsf{end}\}$ by (CS,OS). We can easily show $\overset{k}{\mapsto}$ is confluent and terminates, and $T \overset{k}{\mapsto} T'$ implies $T' \ll T$. We can also prove if $T \ll T'$, then we always have $T' \overset{k_1}{\mapsto} \cdot \overset{k_2}{\mapsto} \cdots \overset{k_n}{\mapsto} T$ where $k_1 k_2 .. k_n$ are a (possibly empty) subsequence of channels occurring at the top-level in T with this order (e.g., $k_1 k_2 k_3 k_4$ if $k_1!;k_2 \oplus \{l_1 : k_3!, l_2 : k_4!\}$). Hence:

Proposition 7. *Given T and T', $T \ll T'$ is decidable.*

The derivability of judgement $\Sigma \vdash T \leqslant T'$ is defined in Figure 2 where Σ is a sequence of assumed instances of the subtyping relation. We use n-hole type contexts ($\mathscr{T}, \mathscr{T}',...$) where $[\ ]^{h\in H}$ denotes a hole with index h.

$$\mathscr{T} ::= [\ ]^{h\in H} \mid k!\langle U\rangle;\mathscr{T} \mid k?\langle U\rangle;\mathscr{T} \mid k \oplus \{l_i : \mathscr{T}_i\}_{i\in I} \mid k\&\{l_i : \mathscr{T}_i\}_{i\in I}$$

For example, with $H = \{1,2\}$ and $\mathscr{T} = k \oplus \{l_1 : k_1?\langle U_1\rangle;[\ ]^{1\in H}, l_2 : [\ ]^{2\in H}\}$, we have $\mathscr{T}[T_i]^{i\in H} = k \oplus \{l_1 : k_1?\langle U_1\rangle;T_1, l_2 : T_2\}$. A hole in $\mathscr{T}$ does not appear under recursion since $\ll$ permutes top-level actions only. We also use (1) function $\mathsf{top}(T)$ which returns the channel at the head of T and (2) function $\mathsf{depth}\langle k,T\rangle$ to calculate how many unfoldings are needed for k to appear at the top-level. If k does not appear in T, $\mathsf{depth}\langle k,T\rangle$ is undefined. When $\mathsf{depth}\langle k,T\rangle$ is defined, $\mathsf{depth}\langle k,T\rangle$ is finite.

$\mathsf{top}(\mathsf{end}) = \bullet$ $\mathsf{top}(k?\langle U\rangle;T) = \mathsf{top}(k!\langle U\rangle;T) = \mathsf{top}(k\&\{l_i : T_i\}_{i\in I}) = \mathsf{top}(k \oplus \{l_i : T_i\}_{i\in I}) = k$
$\mathsf{depth}\langle k,T\rangle = 0$ if $\mathsf{top}(T) = k$ $\mathsf{depth}\langle\bullet,\mathsf{end}\rangle = 0$
$\mathsf{depth}\langle k,k'?\langle U\rangle;T\rangle = \mathsf{depth}\langle k,k'!\langle U\rangle;T\rangle = \mathsf{depth}\langle k,T\rangle$ $k \neq k'$
$\mathsf{depth}\langle k,k'\&\{l_i : T_i\}_{i\in I}\rangle = \mathsf{depth}\langle k,k' \oplus \{l_i : T_i\}_{i\in I}\rangle = \max_{i\in I}(\mathsf{depth}\langle k,T_i\rangle)$ $k \neq k'$
$\mathsf{depth}\langle k,\mu t.T\rangle = \mathsf{depth}\langle k,T[\mu t.T/t]\rangle + 1$ $\mathsf{depth}\langle\bullet,\mu t.T\rangle = \mathsf{depth}\langle\bullet,T[\mu t.T/t]\rangle + 1$

In Figure 2, [ASMP,END] are standard. In [OUT], we fix the subtype and apply $\overset{k}{\mapsto}$ to place $k!\langle U\rangle$ to the top level. Then we check the tail of the result of rewriting $\mathscr{T}[T'_{2h}]^{h\in H}$ is a supertype of T_1 (the rule subsumes the case $k!\langle U\rangle$ already at the top level). Rule [SEL] is similarly defined. Rule [RECL] is standard. Rule [RECR] unfolds T' until a type with the same channel as the top of T appears at the top-level. The rule for input/branching is defined like [OUT]/[SEL], respectively.

$$[\text{ASMP}]\frac{T \leqslant T' \in \Sigma}{\Sigma \vdash T \leqslant T'} \quad [\text{END}]\frac{-}{\Sigma \vdash \text{end} \leqslant \text{end}}$$

$$[\text{OUT}]\frac{\Sigma \vdash U_1 \leqslant U_2 \quad \Sigma \vdash T_1 \leqslant \mathscr{T}[T'_{2h}]^{h \in H} \quad \mathscr{T}[k!\langle U_2 \rangle; T_{2h}]^{h \in H} \xrightarrow{k} k!\langle U_2 \rangle; \mathscr{T}[T'_{2h}]^{h \in H}}{\Sigma \vdash k!\langle U_1 \rangle; T_1 \leqslant \mathscr{T}[k!\langle U_2 \rangle; T_{2h}]^{h \in H}}$$

$$[\text{SEL}]\frac{\forall i \in I.\Sigma \vdash T_i \leqslant \mathscr{T}[T''_{ih}]^{h \in H} \quad \mathscr{T}[k \oplus \{l_i : T'_{ih}\}_{i \in J}]^{h \in H} \xrightarrow{k} k \oplus \{l_i : \mathscr{T}[T''_{ih}]^{h \in H}\}_{i \in J} \quad I \subseteq J}{\Sigma \vdash k \oplus \{l_i : T_i\}_{i \in I} \leqslant \mathscr{T}[k \oplus \{l_i : T'_{ih}\}_{i \in J}]^{h \in H}}$$

$$[\text{RECL}]\frac{\Sigma, \mu t.T \leqslant T' \vdash \text{unfold}^1(\mu t.T) \leqslant T'}{\Sigma \vdash \mu t.T \leqslant T'} \quad [\text{RECR}]\frac{n = \text{depth}\langle \text{top}(T), T' \rangle \quad n \geq 1}{\Sigma, T \leqslant T' \vdash T \leqslant \text{unfold}^n(T')}{\Sigma \vdash T \leqslant T'}$$

Fig. 2. Algorithmic Subtyping Rules

The rules give an algorithm for checking *the algorithmic subtyping relation* $\leqslant$ (by reading these rules from upwards). As usual, [ASMP] should always be used if it is applicable, and when both [RECL] and [RECR] are applicable, [RECL] is used in preference to [RECR]. Similarly, other rules are applied in preference to [RECR], which can only be applied if the top of T does not appear at the top level of T'. As an example, let $T_1 = k \oplus \{l_1 : k_1?\langle U_1 \rangle; \text{end}\}$. Then we can derive $k_2!\langle U_2 \rangle; T_1 \leqslant T_0$ (T_0 is given above) by using [OUT]. At the top level, the algorithm is applied to the initial goal $\emptyset \vdash T \leqslant T'$ (which we often write $T \leqslant T'$).

Lemma 8. *1. The subtyping algorithm always terminates.*
2. If $T \leqslant_c T'$ then the algorithm does not return false when applied to $\Sigma \vdash T \leqslant T'$.

The proof uses techniques related to those developed in [10]; the main differences are, for the proof of (1), we have to take the subterms up to $\ll$ with the finite number of unfolding when we argue the size of Σ cannot increase without bound. However since $\ll$ does not change the size of the judgement (defined in [10, Lemma 10]), we can prove (1). The proof of (2) is standard from (1).

Theorem 9 (Soundness and Completeness of the Algorithmic Subtyping). *For all closed types T and T', $T \leqslant_c T'$ if and only if $T \leqslant T'$.*

The if-direction is by Lemma 8 (2) and the only-if direction by constructing a relation following [10, Theorem 4].

3.4 Local Asynchronous Commutative Session Typing

The type judgement for end-point processes is of the shape $\Gamma \vdash P \triangleright \Delta$ which reads: "under the environment Γ, process P has typing Δ" where environments are defined as:

$$\Gamma ::= \emptyset \mid \Gamma, u : U \mid \Gamma, X : \tilde{U}\tilde{T} \qquad \Delta ::= \emptyset \mid \Delta, \tilde{s} : \{T_p @ p\}_{p \in I}$$

A *sorting* ($\Gamma, \Gamma', ..$) is a finite map from names to value types and from process variables to sequences of value types and session types. *Typing* ($\Delta, \Delta', ..$) records linear usage of session channels. $T @ p$ is called *located type* which means T is a session type of the participant p. In multiparty sessions, it assigns a family of located types to a vector of session channels. The typing system is identical with [13]: we only have to add the subsumption rule: i.e. $\Gamma \vdash P \triangleright \Delta$ and $\Delta \leqslant \Delta'$ then $\Gamma \vdash P \triangleright \Delta'$ where $\Delta \leqslant \Delta'$ is defined by pointwise application of $\leqslant$.

Theorem 10 (Subject Congruence and Reduction). $\Gamma \vdash P \triangleright \emptyset$ and $P \equiv Q$ imply $\Gamma \vdash Q \triangleright \emptyset$; and $\Gamma \vdash P \triangleright \emptyset$ and $P \longrightarrow Q$ imply $\Gamma \vdash Q \triangleright \emptyset$.

The proof follows the same routine as in [13], but we must take care that all permutations defined by $\ll$ do not affect the input-output causal dependencies of the global types. We can also obtain the other three key proprieties, communication-safety, session-fidelity and progress as stated in [13, § 5]. The rest of the paper can be read without knowing the details of a typing system.

4 Principal Global Typing through Graph-Based Types

Why graph-based types. Let $P \stackrel{\text{def}}{=} a[\mathsf{p}](\tilde{s}).s_1!\langle 3 \rangle; s_2?(x)$ and $Q \stackrel{\text{def}}{=} \bar{a}[\mathsf{p}](\tilde{s})$. $s_2!\langle \text{true} \rangle; s_1?(y)$ where P is a participant named by p and Q is an initiator named by q. Then P and Q are typable under essentially only two global types, $G = \mathsf{p} \to \mathsf{q} : k\langle\text{int}\rangle; \mathsf{q} \to \mathsf{p} : h\langle\text{bool}\rangle;$ end and $G' = \mathsf{q} \to \mathsf{p} : h\langle\text{bool}\rangle; \mathsf{p} \to \mathsf{q} : k\langle\text{int}\rangle;$ end. Note the projection of G to p is $\leqslant$-minimal for P (i.e. other local types of P can be derived by subsumption): but this is not true for its projection to q. Similarly G' does not give a minimal type for P. Thus there is no "best" global type for $P|Q$: this is because interactions between P and Q take place in a criss-crossing way: the syntax of global types, which can only represent tree-like causality, is too rigid to represent such a situation.

Local and global graphs. A *local graph* is a (finite or infinite) directed graph where each node, called *action*, is labelled by one of $k?\langle U \rangle$ (input), $k!\langle U \rangle$ (output), $k\&[l_i]_{i\in I}$ (branching), $k \oplus [l_i]_{i\in I}$ (selection) and $k \oplus l$ (label-output [1]); and, for edges: (1) each edge from $k\&[l_i]_{i\in I}$ or $k \oplus [l_i]_{i\in I}$ is labelled by one of $\{l_i\}$; and (2) $k \oplus l$ (resp. $k!\langle U \rangle$) has a unique outgoing edge, and its target is always an output/selection/label-output at k. A *global graph for participants* $\{\mathsf{p}_1,..,\mathsf{p}_n\}$, written $\mathscr{G}, \mathscr{G}',\ldots$, is a disjoint union of an $\{\mathsf{p}_1,..,\mathsf{p}_n\}$-indexed family of local graphs. Given $\mathscr{G}$ for $\{\mathsf{p}_1,..,\mathsf{p}_n\}$, its p_i-*component* is the local graph in $\mathscr{G}$ indexed by p_i. A node is *active* if it has no incoming edges.

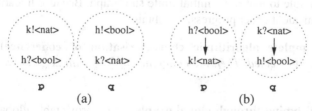

(a)   (b)

In (a) above, we show a global graph for P and Q given above, consisting of two local graphs (balloons labelled by p and q), each with an output, an input and no edges. If we add an edge from input to output in each local graph, we get the global graph (b) for $a[\mathsf{p}](\tilde{s}).s_2?(x);s_1!\langle 3 \rangle$ and $\bar{a}[\mathsf{p}](\tilde{s}).s_1?(y);s_2!\langle \text{true} \rangle$, which now deadlocks.

Linearity, progress and coherence. We equip global graphs with a notion of reduction which abstracts that of processes. Below we write $\mathscr{E}[\,\cdot\,]..[\,\cdot\,]$ for a global graph with one or more holes, each of which is to be filled with a sub-graph of a local graph, such that all holes are active, i.e. have no incoming edges.

$$\mathscr{E}[k?\langle U\rangle][k!\langle U\rangle] \longrightarrow \mathscr{E}[\mathbf{0}] \qquad \mathscr{E}[k\&[l_i:\mathscr{G}_i]_{i\in I}][k\oplus l_j] \longrightarrow \mathscr{E}[\mathscr{G}_j][\mathbf{0}] \quad (j\in I)$$
$$\mathscr{E}[k\oplus[l_i:\mathscr{G}_i]_{i\in I}] \longrightarrow \mathscr{E}[k\oplus l_i;\mathscr{G}_i]$$

Above $\mathbf{0}$ is the empty graph. In each rule, the replacement in the hole(s) entails taking off *both* the old graph *and* all the outgoing edge(s) from it and filling the hole with the new graph. A reduction by the first two rules is called *communication at k*. In the second rule, $k\&[l_i:\mathscr{G}_i]_{i\in I}$ is the disjoint union of $k\&[l_i]_{i\in I}$ and $\{\mathscr{G}_i\}_{i\in I}$ together with, for each $i\in I$, l_i-labelled edges from $k\&[l_i]_{i\in I}$ to all the active actions in $\mathscr{G}_i$. In the third (from [1]), $k\oplus[l_i:\mathscr{G}_i]_{i\in I}$ is as $k\&[l_i:\mathscr{G}_i]_{i\in I}$ while $k\oplus l_i;\mathscr{G}_i$ is the disjoint union of $k\oplus l_i$ and $\mathscr{G}_i$ with edges from the former to the active output/selection/label-outputs at k in $\mathscr{G}_i$. A global graph $\mathscr{G}$ is *linear* when for each $\mathscr{G}'$ such that $\mathscr{G}\longrightarrow^*\mathscr{G}'$, if $\mathscr{G}'$ has two active actions at k, a reduction at k is possible, and no other active action shares k. A global graph $\mathscr{G}$ has *progress* when for each $\mathscr{G}'$ such that $\mathscr{G}\longrightarrow^*\mathscr{G}'$, either $\mathscr{G}'$ reduces or it is empty. Finally we say $\mathscr{G}$ is *coherent* when it is linear and has progress.

Coherent global graphs from local types. A local graph is constructed from a local type as the latter's regular tree representations. Given $\Delta=\{T_i@\mathsf{p}_i\}_{i\in I}$, this immediately gives the global graph for $\{\mathsf{p}_i\}_{i\in I}$, which we write $[\![\Delta]\!]$. The coherence of $[\![\Delta]\!]$ is decidable, as we outline below.

We first check Δ is *well-directed* in the sense that each channel in Δ is used by two and only two participants and moreover one of them uses it only for input/branching and the other only for output/selection/label-output, which can be checked by going through Δ once. For well-directed Δ, there is an algorithm to ensure linearity of $[\![\Delta]\!]$, by checking if each pair of participants in Δ are compatible in their type structures, closely following the algorithmic subtyping in § 3.2.

Through the validation of compatibility of Δ, we can equip $[\![\Delta]\!]$ with the additional *communication edges*, from each output/selection/label-output to its potentially interacting action(s), representing potential redexes. Using this added set of edges, we reduce the progress of $[\![\Delta]\!]$ to the acyclicity of its paths consisting of its local and communication edges, completely characterising progress under linearity. The acyclicity of $[\![\Delta]\!]$ is then reducible to that of its initial finite sub-graph. Because linearity and compatibility are equivalent under progress, we obtain:

Theorem 11 (complete algorithmic characterisation of coherence). *Let $\Delta=\{T_i@\mathsf{p}_i\}_{i\in I}$ be well-directed. Then the coherence of $[\![\Delta]\!]$ with Δ given as input is decidable.*

Principal global typing through global graphs. Any projectable global type G for participants say $\{\mathsf{p}_i\}_{i\in I}$ is equivalent to its projections $\Delta=\{(G\upharpoonright\mathsf{p}_i)@\mathsf{p}_i\}_{i\in I}$, and because such Δ is immediately compatible and acyclic, we can regard G as a coherent global graph. This motivates the use of coherent global graphs instead of global types in the type discipline, presenting $[\![\Delta]\!]$ as Δ itself.[5] By replacing global types with coherent global graphs in types and typing rules, we obtain a new type discipline. We write $\Gamma \vdash_g P \triangleright \Delta$ for typability in this new discipline (subsumption is consistent because if $[\![\Delta]\!]$ is coherent and Δ' is point-wise $\leqslant$-smaller than Δ then $[\![\Delta']\!]$ is also coherent). By identifying $\mathscr{G}$ as the corresponding coherent global graph, $\Gamma \vdash P \triangleright \Delta$ implies $\Gamma \vdash_g P \triangleright \Delta$. Further, since linearity and progress of $[\![\Delta]\!]$ are reflected onto the dynamics of typed processes (precisely following the arguments in [13]), the typability in $\vdash_g$ ensures communication safety and progress.

For the principal typing property, we add the $\leqslant$-least element $\bot$ to the set of local types; $\bot$ is also used as local graph occurring in global graphs (where intuitively $\bot$ denotes a placeholder for a local behaviour). The coherence and other notions for global graphs are defined ignoring $\bot$. Without loss of practical generality we assume each shared name say a has a fixed *arity* which is the number of participants for a potential session established through a; and that processes are type-annotated on bound variables and free object names in the standard way. Through local type inference [6, 15] using the point-wise join of coherent global types (calculated as in algorithmic subtyping), together with Theorem 11, we obtain a principal global typing property. Below we write $\Gamma' \leqslant \Gamma$ for $\mathrm{dom}(\Gamma') \subset \mathrm{dom}(\Gamma)$ and $\Gamma'(a) \leqslant \Gamma(a)$ for each $a \in \mathrm{dom}(\Gamma')$. We say P is *closed* if it has no free session channels nor free variables.

Theorem 12 (principal global typing). *Let P be closed.* (1) *The typability of P with respect to $\vdash_g$ is decidable.* (2) *If P is typable then P has a principal global typing Γ_0 in the sense that $\Gamma_0 \vdash_g P \triangleright \emptyset$ holds and moreover $\Gamma \vdash_g P \triangleright \emptyset$ implies $\Gamma_0 \leqslant \Gamma$.*

5   Application: Double-Buffering Algorithm

This section illustrates the use of our type theory using the *double-buffering algorithm* [21], a basic distributed algorithm widely used in stream/media processing and high-performance and multicore computing, presenting how the two strategies discussed in Introduction can be applied through the theories presented in the previous sections.

The purpose of the double-buffering algorithm is to transform a large amount of data, where a series of chunks of data are transferred from a source (Source) to a transformer (called Kernel), gets processed there and delivered to a sink (Sink). Under potential temporal variations in processing and communication time, it is necessary to synchronise among these three parties through message passing. However a naive, and obviously safe, protocol leads to a highly sequential, non-optimal distributed algorithm. Thus it is beneficial to increase asynchrony of local programs without violating the shared protocol. We show the outline of an application of our theories to achieve this goal, starting from a sequential and safe global protocol to optimised local protocols through asynchronous communication subtyping, with a formal safety guarantee.

---

[5] To be precise, we regard Δ up to the type isomorphism corresponding to $\leqslant$; and we take off, from each branching type, its branches (if any) which never get invoked in any reduction path: such "garbage" branches are precisely identified during the validation of coherence.

Global Type : G =
$\mu t.($
 $K \to So : r_1 \langle\rangle;$ $K \to So : r_2 \langle\rangle;$
 $So \to K : s_1 \langle U\rangle;$ $So \to K : s_2 \langle U\rangle;$
 $Si \to K : t_1 \langle\rangle;$ $Si \to K : t_2 \langle\rangle;$
 $K \to Si : u_1 \langle U\rangle;$ $K \to Si : u_2 \langle U\rangle; t)$

Projected Local Type of Kernel :
$T =$
$\mu t.r_1! \langle\rangle; s_1? \langle U\rangle; t_1? \langle\rangle; u_1! \langle U\rangle;$
 $r_2! \langle\rangle; s_2? \langle U\rangle; t_2? \langle\rangle; u_2! \langle U\rangle; t$

Local Type of Kernel :
$T^\star =$
$r_1! \langle\rangle; r_2! \langle\rangle;$
 $\mu t.s_1? \langle U\rangle; t_1? \langle\rangle; u_1! \langle U\rangle; r_1! \langle\rangle;$
  $s_2? \langle U\rangle; t_2? \langle\rangle; u_2! \langle U\rangle; r_2! \langle\rangle; t$

Source:
$a[1](r_1 r_2 s_1 s_2 t_1 t_2 u_1 u_2).$
$\mu X.($
 .. // assign data to $y[1..n]$
 $r_1?(); s_1!\langle y[1..n]\rangle);$
 .. // assign data to $y[1..n]$
 $r_2?() ; s_2!\langle y\rangle; X)$

Sink:
$a[2](r_1 r_2 s_1 s_2 t_1 t_2 u_1 u_2).$
$\mu X.($
 $t_1!\langle\rangle; u_1?(z);$
 .. // print $z[1..n]$
 $t_2!\langle\rangle; u_2?(z);$
 .. // print $z[1..n]$
 $X)$

Kernel:
$\overline{a}[1,2](r_1 r_2 s_1 s_2 t_1 t_2 u_1 u_2).$
$r_1!\langle\rangle; r_2!\langle\rangle;$
$\mu X.($
 $s_1?(x_A);$
 .. // repeat:
 .. // $x_A[i] ::= x_A[i] \oplus key$
 .. // $key ::= x_A[i]$
 $t_1?(); u_1!\langle x_A\rangle; r_1!\langle\rangle;$
 $s_2?(x_B);$
 .. // repeat:
 .. // $x_B[i] = x_B[i] \oplus key$
 .. // $key = x_B[i]$
 $t_2?(); u_2!\langle x_B\rangle; r_2!\langle\rangle; X$
$)$

Fig. 3. Double-Buffering Algorithm: Processes and Types

Top-down approach (1): global type. The development of programs starts from the global type G on the left-most column in Figure 3. So, K and Si denote participant names for Source, Kernel and Sink. U denotes a large int-array type. Assuming Kernel will use two channels and the associated arrays for potential parallelism, the global type G starts from a recursion, describing an infinite loop. In the loop, Kernel first notifies Source via $r_{1,2}$ that it is ready to receive data in its two channels ($s_{1,2}$, with signal at r_i saying s_i is ready); Source complies, sending two chunks of data sequentially via $s_{1,2}$. Then Kernel (internally processes data and) waits for Sink to inform (via $t_{1,2}$) that Sink is ready to receive data via $u_{1,2}$: upon receiving the signals, Kernel sends the two chunks of processed data to Sink. This protocol is sequential but is safe and deadlock-free.

Top-down approach (2): local type and its refinement. Just below the global type G, Figure 3 gives the local type T of Kernel as directly projected from the global type. Our purpose is to refine T so that (1) the new local protocol is more asynchronous, allowing overlap of communication and computation [9, 11]; and (2) it still conforms to G — Kernel with the new optimised protocol will safely interact with Source and Sink who conform to the original global type G. For this purpose the developer may come up with a more asynchronous $T^\star$, given in Figure 3 after T. In this refined protocol, Kernel notifies Source via both $r_{1,2}$, but only once before entering the loop, allowing Source to start its work. Now inside the loop, the refined protocol dictates Kernel first receives data via its first channel s_1 with Source, processes the data and sends out the result to Sink via its first channel u_1 with Sink and *immediately notifies Source via r_1 that it's ready in its first channel*, allowing Source to start sending data early. Kernel then repeats the same work for its second channels with Source and Sink. In this way, Kernel can process data it has already received in one channel while it is receiving data in the other, noting it can take time for large data to sent, transferred and received.

 We now show this optimised local protocol is safe w.r.t. other participants conforming to G, through the asynchronous communication subtyping. The justification uses nested unfolding. We start from unfolding T once to match r_1, r_2 of $T^\star$ as $\text{unfold}^1(T) = r_1!\langle\rangle; s_1?\langle U\rangle; t_1?\langle\rangle; u_1!\langle U\rangle; r_2!\langle\rangle; s_2?\langle U\rangle; t_2?\langle\rangle; u_2!\langle U\rangle; T$. Then $r_1!\langle\rangle$ matches $T^\star$. To simulate $r_2!\langle\rangle$ of $T^\star$, $r_2!\langle\rangle$ is permuted by $\ll$. Let $T^\star = r_1!\langle\rangle; r_2!\langle\rangle; T_R^\star$. Thus $\text{unfold}^1(T_R^\star)$ must be simulated by $T' = s_1?\langle U\rangle; t_1?\langle\rangle; u_1!\langle U\rangle; s_2?\langle U\rangle; t_2?\langle\rangle; u_2!\langle U\rangle; T$. However to simulate $r_1!\langle\rangle$ in $\text{unfold}^1(T_R^\star)$, T *must be unfolded again* since the types in the guarded position of T' do *not* include $r_1!\langle\rangle$. By [RECR], it now suffices to solve the following:

$$r_1!\langle\rangle; s_2?\langle U\rangle; t_2?\langle\rangle; u_2!\langle U\rangle; r_2!\langle\rangle; T_R^\star \leqslant s_2?\langle U\rangle; t_2?\langle\rangle; u_2!\langle U\rangle; \text{unfold}^1(T).$$

For this we apply [IN,OUT] of $\leqslant$ with $\ll$, reaching the assumption in Σ in [ASMP].

Top-down approach (3): code development. Figure 3 depicts the skeleton of the three (final) programs which conform to the global type. All participants initiate the session at a in the first line. We only illustrate the behaviour of Kernel, considering a simple transformation for stream encryption. Kernel, after initialising its variables including the initial key value, signals to Source that its buffers are both empty, via r_1 and r_2: then enters the main loop, where it does the following: it first receives the datum at x_A via s_1, goes through the buffer taking the XOR element-wise with key, after which it waits for Sink's cue via t_1 (which may have already arrived asynchronously), and finally sends out the buffer content to Sink via u_1, and tells Source it's ready at A via r_1: then similarly works for the second buffer (given in the next column). Unlike Source and Sink, the behaviour of Kernel does not conform to the projection of G to Kernel (T): however $T^\star$ does type-abstract its behaviour directly and because $T^\star \leqslant T$ by the argument above, Kernel does type-check under T with subsumption, hence under G.

Integration with bottom-up approach. The development process described above can be effectively and seamlessly integrated with the "bottom-up" strategy discussed in Introduction through the type inference (synthesis) of global types in § 4, which allows developers to directly refine programs and to synthesise a new global protocol reflecting the refinement, incrementally validating compatibility. This added flexibility is useful since, in actual development, programmers may often directly work on programs rather than starting from refinement of local protocols.

Further examples showing the applicability of permutation of branching/selections to parallel algorithms [14] can be found in the full version.

6   Related Work

Branching/selection subtyping in session types is first studied in [10] for binary session types. We use their syntactic approach for defining a type-simulation, but a significant extension from their technique is needed due to the incorporation of $\ll$ and nested unfoldings, which makes the proof of transitivity delicate and challenging. An initial idea of asynchronous communication subtyping for binary sessions is presented in an unpublished manuscript [18], where the treatment for recursive types and branching/selection types is left open. A recent work in a technical report [17] demonstrates a subtyping rule similar to our (OI) rule is useful for an object calculus with asynchronous binary sessions, with an iso-recursive system. It is an interesting future work to extend to the HOπ-calculus [16] where a careful formulation for the algorithmic subtyping would be required in the presence of arrow types. The top-down approach in multiparty session types is first studied in [13], but a local refinement (asynchronous subtyping) is not proposed there. The problem of synthesising a global specification from endpoint behaviours has been a lingering question since the inception of the notion of global descriptions for business protocols [24], being posed as an open problem in [1, 2, 13]. Inference of principal types is studied in [15] for binary session types (note in binary sessions the issue of global synthesis does not arise). The present work gives clear and general solutions to these extant technical problems.

In the context of multiparty session types, a typing system for a strong progress property is studied in [1]. Asynchronous communication subtyping can be smoothly applied to [1]. For delegations, the main definitions of $\ll$, $\leqslant_c$ and $\leqslant$ stay as the same, but proofs need to be revised to treat nesting types; and for the principal typing, $\perp$ should be added into a carried type in global graphs. The study of formal theories of contracts are studied in [8] using CCS-like processes as a type representation. The work [19] extends [8] with the treatment of asynchronous behaviours using orchestrators, through the use of bounded buffers that control message flows between a client and servers. Our own system in [7] developed a theory in which a global specification arises as a programming language itself.

Conformance and refinement based on agreement of service specifications is studied in [3], using a synchronous CCS-based calculus as a contract language, and testing-preorders to check subcontract compliance. Neither type-checking of end-point processes using projected contracts (in our case, Theorem 9) nor a bottom-up strategy is presented there. The work [5] proposes a distributed calculus with sessions, incorporating the merging of running sessions. Another work [23] presents a calculus for service orientations by extending the π-calculus with context-sensitive interactions, equipped with service and request primitives and local exceptions. These preceding works do not treat the main technical problems addressed in the present work – the asynchronous communication subtyping, type-based local refinement/conformance, and a derivation of the minimum global types, backed-up by the efficient type-checking and inference algorithms, ensuring strong safety properties based on the session type discipline.

Acknowledgements. We thank the reviewers for their useful comments, Gary Brown and Steve Ross-Talbot for discussions on the potential applications of the presented framework for software development, and Matthew Rawlings for discussions on the practical significance of asynchrony in financial protocols. We generalised $\ll$ with input commutativity following a suggestion by Raymond Hu. The work is partially supported by EPSRC GR/T03208, GR/T03215, EP/F002114, EP/F003757 and IST2005-015905 MOBIUS.

References

1. Bettini, L., et al.: Global progress in dynamically interleaved multiparty sessions. In: van Breugel, F., Chechik, M. (eds.) CONCUR 2008. LNCS, vol. 5201, pp. 418–433. Springer, Heidelberg (2008)
2. Bonelli, E., Compagnoni, A.: Multipoint Session Types for a Distributed Calculus. In: Barthe, G., Fournet, C. (eds.) TGC 2007. LNCS, vol. 4912, pp. 240–256. Springer, Heidelberg (2008)
3. Bravetti, M., Zavattaro, G.: A theory for strong service compliance. In: Murphy, A.L., Vitek, J. (eds.) COORDINATION 2007. LNCS, vol. 4467, pp. 96–112. Springer, Heidelberg (2007)
4. Bravetti, M., Zavattaro, G.: Towards a unifying theory for choreography conformance and contract compliance. In: Lumpe, M., Vanderperren, W. (eds.) SC 2007. LNCS, vol. 4829, pp. 34–50. Springer, Heidelberg (2007)
5. Bruni, R., Lanese, I., Melgratti, H., Tuosto, E.: Multiparty Sessions in SOC. In: Lea, D., Zavattaro, G. (eds.) COORDINATION 2008. LNCS, vol. 5052, pp. 67–82. Springer, Heidelberg (2008)
6. Carbone, M., Honda, K., Yoshida, N.: A theoretical basis of communication-centered concurrent programming. To appear as a WS-CDL working report, www.dcs.qmul.ac.uk/~carbonem/cdlpaper/workingnote.pdf
7. Carbone, M., Honda, K., Yoshida, N.: Structured communication-centred programming for web services. In: De Nicola, R. (ed.) ESOP 2007. LNCS, vol. 4421, pp. 2–17. Springer, Heidelberg (2007)
8. Castagna, G., Gesbert, N., Padovani, L.: A theory of contracts for web services. In: POPL, pp. 261–272 (2008)
9. Culler, D., et al.: Logp: towards a realistic model of parallel computation. SIGPLAN Not. 28(7), 1–12 (1993)
10. Gay, S., Hole, M.: Subtyping for Session Types in the Pi-Calculus. Acta Informatica 42(2/3), 191–225 (2005)
11. Gschwind, M.: The cell broadband engine: Exploiting multiple levels of parallelism in a chip multiprocessor. International Journal of Parallel Programming 35(3), 233–262 (2007)
12. Honda, K., Vasconcelos, V.T., Kubo, M.: Language primitives and type disciplines for structured communication-based programming. In: Hankin, C. (ed.) ESOP 1998. LNCS, vol. 1381, pp. 122–138. Springer, Heidelberg (1998)
13. Honda, K., Yoshida, N., Carbone, M.: Multiparty Asynchronous Session Types. In: POPL 2008, pp. 273–284. ACM, New York (2008)
14. Mattson, T., Sanders, B., Massingill, B.: Patterns for Parallel Programming. Addison Wesley, Reading (2005)
15. Mezzina, L.G.: How to infer finite session types in a calculus of services and sessions. In: Lea, D., Zavattaro, G. (eds.) COORDINATION 2008. LNCS, vol. 5052, pp. 216–231. Springer, Heidelberg (2008)
16. Mostrous, D., Yoshida, N.: Two Sessions Typing Systems for Higher-Order Mobile Processes. In: Della Rocca, S.R. (ed.) TLCA 2007. LNCS, vol. 4583, pp. 321–335. Springer, Heidelberg (2007)
17. Mostrous, D., Yoshida, N.: A Session Object Calculus for Structured Communication-Based Programming. Technical report, Imperial College London (2008), www.doc.ic.ac.uk/~mostrous
18. Neubauer, M., Thiemann, P.: Session Types for Asynchronous Communication. Universität Freiburg (2004)
19. Padovani, L.: Contract-directed synthesis of simple orchestrators. In: van Breugel, F., Chechik, M. (eds.) CONCUR 2008. LNCS, vol. 5201, pp. 131–146. Springer, Heidelberg (2008)

20. Pierce, B., Sangiorgi, D.: Typing and subtyping for mobile processes. Journal of Mathematical Structures in Computer Science 6(5), 409–454 (1996)
21. Sancho, J.C., Kerbyson, D.J.: Analysis of Double Buffering on two Different Multicore Architectures: Quad-core Opteron and the Cell-BE. In: International Parallel and Distributed Processing Symposium (IPDPS), April 14–18. IEEE, Los Alamitos (2008)
22. Takeuchi, K., Honda, K., Kubo, M.: An interaction-based language and its typing system. In: Halatsis, C., Philokyprou, G., Maritsas, D., Theodoridis, S. (eds.) PARLE 1994. LNCS, vol. 817, pp. 398–413. Springer, Heidelberg (1994)
23. Vieira, H.T., Caires, L., Seco, J.C.: The conversation calculus: A model of service-oriented computation. In: Drossopoulou, S. (ed.) ESOP 2008. LNCS, vol. 4960, pp. 269–283. Springer, Heidelberg (2008)
24. Web Services Choreography Working Group. Web Services Choreography Description Language, http://www.w3.org/2002/ws/chor/

Tisa: A Language Design and Modular Verification Technique for Temporal Policies in Web Services*

Hridesh Rajan[1], Jia Tao[1], Steve Shaner[1], and Gary T. Leavens[2]

[1] Iowa State University, Ames, Iowa, USA
{hridesh,jtao,smshaner}@iastate.edu
[2] University of Central Florida, Orlando, Florida, USA
leavens@eecs.ucf.edu

Abstract. Web services are distributed software components, that are decoupled from each other using interfaces with specified functional behaviors. However, such behavioral specifications are insufficient to demonstrate compliance with certain temporal non-functional policies. An example is demonstrating that a patient's health-related query sent to a health care service is answered only by a doctor (and not by a secretary). Demonstrating compliance with such policies is important for satisfying governmental privacy regulations. It is often necessary to expose the internals of the web service implementation for demonstrating such compliance, which may compromise modularity. In this work, we provide a language design that enables such demonstrations, while hiding majority of the service's source code. The key idea is to use greybox specifications to allow service providers to selectively hide and expose parts of their implementation. The overall problem of showing compliance is then reduced to two subproblems: whether the desired properties are satisfied by the service's greybox specification, and whether this greybox specification is satisfied by the service's implementation. We specify policies using LTL and solve the first problem by model checking. We solve the second problem by refinement techniques.

1 Introduction

Web services promote abstraction, loose coupling and interoperability of clients and services [1]. The key idea of web services is to introduce a published interface (often a description written in an XML-based language such as WSDL [2]), for communication between services and clients [1]. By allowing components to be decoupled using a specified interface, web services enable platform-independent integration.

Behavioral Contracts for Web Services. A behavioral contract for a web service specifies, for each of the web service's methods the relationships between its inputs and outputs. Such a contract treats the implementation of the service as a black box, hiding all the service's internal states from its clients. The benefit of this encapsulation is that clients do not depend upon the service's changeable design decisions. To illustrate, consider a healthcare service that allows patients to make appointments and ask prescription and health-related questions from healthcare practitioners [3].

---

* Rajan and Tao were supported in part by the NSF grant CNS 06-27354. Rajan, Shaner and Leavens were supported in part by the NSF grant CNS 08-08913.

G. Castagna (Ed.): ESOP 2009, LNCS 5502, pp. 333–347, 2009.

An example JML-like contract [4] for such a service follows.

```
service Patient {
    /*@ requires pId >= 0; ensures result >=0; @*/
    int query(int pId, int msg);
    /*@ requires qId >= 0; ensures result >=0; @*/
    int retrieve(int qId);
}
```

The service description in this contract is written in a form similar to our language, Tisa, to make comparisons easier. It specifies that a service named Patient makes two web-methods available: query and retrieve. The query method takes a patient identifier and a message as arguments. The message is represented as an integer for simplicity (think of it as an index into a table of pre-defined questions, such as "does the test show I have AIDS?"). The precondition of calling this web-method is that the patient identifier is positive; the postcondition is that it returns a positive result. The retrieve method takes a query identifier as argument; its precondition is that this identifier must be positive. Its postcondition is that the result is also positive. These contracts could be checked by observing the interface of the web-methods [5,6,7,8,9].

Demonstrating Compliance to Temporal Policies. Let us now consider the following policy inspired from Barth *et al.*'s work [3]: "a health question about a patient should only be answered by the doctor", "furthermore such answers should only be disclosed to the concerned patients". We will refer to these as "HIPAA policies" as they are similar to regulations in the US health insurance portability and accountability act (HIPAA). The behavioral contract above is insufficient for demonstrating compliance with the HIPAA policies, as it does not provide sufficient details about the internal state of the service. For example, the entity that is finally receiving the query is hidden by query's contract. Demonstrating compliance to such policies is important. In our example, a patient may feel much better about their queries regarding an AIDS test result, if such compliances were demonstrated by the service.

Compliance and Modularity at Conflict. Alternatively suppose the implementation of the two web-methods query and retrieve were available, including the component services that they use. Then demonstrating compliance to the two HIPAA policies would be equivalent to ensuring that the implementation avoids non-compliant states. However, by making code for these methods available, clients might write code that depends on implementation design decisions. As a result, changing these design decisions will become harder, as these changes could break client's code [10].

We thus believe that, for web services, modularity [10] and verification of temporal policies are fundamentally in conflict. To make the service implementation evolvable, modularity requires hiding the design decisions that are likely to change. But to demonstrate compliance to key temporal policies, internal states need to be exposed.

A Language Design and Verification Logic. To reconcile these requirements, we propose a technique based on greybox specifications [11] that exposes only some internal states. This technique enables web service providers to demonstrate compliance to temporal policies, such that above, by exposing only parts of their implementation. A client can verify that the service complies with the desired policies by inspecting a greybox

```
 1 service Secretary {
 2 int query(int pId, int msg) {
 3   preserve pId > 0 && msg > 0;
 4   if (msg >= 2) {
 5     query(pId,msg)@Doctor
 6   }
 7   else {
 8     /* Appointment? */
 9     establish result > 0
10   }
11 }
12 int retrieve(int qId) {
13   requires qId > 0 ensures result > 0
14 }
15 }
```

```
16 service Doctor {
17 int query(int pId, int msg) { /* Re: Test */
18   requires pId > 0 && msg >= 2 ensures result > 0
19 }
20 int retrieve(int qId) {
21   requires qId > 0 ensures result > 0
22 }
23 }
24 service Patient {
25 int query(int pId, int msg) {
26   query(pId, msg)@Secretary;
27 }
28 int retrieve(int qId) {
29   preserve qId > 0;
30   if ((qId/1000)==1) { retrieve(qId)@Secretary}
31   else if ((qId/1000)==2) { retrieve(qId)@Doctor}
32 } }
```

Fig. 1. An Example Greybox Specification

specification. Providers can also choose to hide many implementation details, so the service's implementation can evolve as long as it refines the specification [12,13].

To illustrate, consider the greybox specification shown in Figure 1. This example has three services. In each service the methods are web-methods that may be called by clients and other services. Specification expressions of the form **preserve** e, **establish** e, and **requires** e_1 **ensures** e_2 are used within these methods to hide internal details. The code that is not hidden by specification expressions is exposed. Calls to web-methods are written using an at-sign (@), such as query(pId, msg)@Secretary. For simplicity, Tisa only allows integers to be passed as arguments in such remote calls, thus we encode questions using integers: 1 for appointments, 2 for prescriptions, and higher numbers for health-related questions. Contrary to standard black box specifications, internal states of the service, including calls to other services are exposed. By analyzing lines 26 and 4–6 (in that order) one could conclude that "health questions by patients are answered by the doctor." Demonstrating compliance to temporal policies thus becomes possible. Note that this specification only exposes selected details about the implementation. For example, the specification of retrieve on line 13 hides all details of how this service responds to appointment questions. Therefore, it hides the design decisions made in the implementation of creating, storing, and forwarding responses.

Contributions. An important contribution is the identification of the conflict between verification of temporal policies and modularity in web services. We show how to resolve this conflict using greybox specifications. Our language, *Tisa*, supports specification of policies specified in a variant of linear temporal logic [14], greybox specification [11] and a simple notion of refinement [12,13,15] for modular reasoning about correctness of implementations with respect to such policies. As usual, implementations are hidden, but policies and greybox specifications are public. To demonstrate these claims, we present two preliminary verification techniques: one checks if a greybox specification satisfies a temporal policy, the second checks whether a service implementation refines its greybox specification. (The first technique could be used by the clients to select a service whose specification satisfies their desired policies.) We also show soundness:

```
program ::= decl* client
decl ::= classdecl | servicedecl
classdecl ::= class c extends d { field* meth* }
servicedecl ::= service w { field* meth* }
client ::= client w { e }
field ::= t f ;
meth ::= t m (form*) { e }
form ::= t var, where var≠this and var≠thisSite
t ::= c | int
e ::= n | e == e | e != e | e > e | e < e | e >= e | e <= e
    | e + e | e - e | e * e | ! e | e && e | e '||' e | isNull (e)
    | if (e) { e } else { e } | new c () | var
    | null | e.m (e*) | e.f | e.f = e | cast c e | form = e; e
    | e; e | w | m (e*) @e | refining spec { e }
```

$n \in \mathcal{N}$, the set of numeric, integer literals
$c, d \in$ {Object, Site} $\cup \mathcal{C}$,
    $\mathcal{C}$ is the set of class names
$f \in \mathcal{F}$, the set of field names
$m \in \mathcal{M}$, the set of method names
$var \in$ {this, thisSite} $\cup \mathcal{V}$,
    $\mathcal{V}$ is the set of variable names
$w \in \mathcal{W} \subseteq \mathcal{C}$,
    $\mathcal{W}$ is the set of web service names

Fig. 2. Abstract syntax, based on [25, Figure 3.1, 3.7]

that the composition of these two verification techniques, applied modularly by clients and all service providers, implies that the web service implementation satisfies the specified temporal policies. In practice, some additional technique, such as proof-carrying code [16], or a hardware-based root of trust [17,18] would be needed to satisfy clients that web services in fact satisfy their specifications.

2   Tisa Language Design

In this section, we describe Tisa, an object-oriented (OO) language that incorporates ideas from existing work on specification languages, web services authentication languages and modeling languages. In particular, Tisa's design is inspired by Argus [19] and the work of Gordon and Pucella [20]. (Furthermore, some of our descriptions of the language syntax are adapted from Ptolemy [21].) Tisa is a distributed programming language with statically created web services and a single client, each of which has its own address space. Web services are named and declare web-methods, which can be called by the client and by other services. As a small, core language, the technical presentation of Tisa shares much in common with MiniMAO$_1$ [22], a variant of Featherweight Java [23] and Classic Java [24]. Tisa has classes, objects, inheritance, and subtyping, but it does not have **super**, interfaces, exception handling, built-in value types, privacy modifiers, or abstract methods. Furthermore, other features of web-service description languages (WSDLs) such as composite data types for exchanging messages between services, messages, ports, one-way vs. request-response operations, etc, are omitted to avoid complications in Tisa's theory. However, most of these are syntactic sugars that can be desugared to existing constructs in Tisa. Tisa features new mechanisms for declaring policies and greybox specifications. Our description starts with its programming features, and then describes its specification features.

2.1   Program Syntax

The syntax of Tisa executable programs is shown in Figure 2 and explained below. A Tisa program consists of zero or more declarations, and a client (see Figure 3). Declarations are either class declarations or web service declarations.

```
1 class Query extends Object {              32 service Doctor {
2 int pId; int msg; int qId;                33  Queue topQ; Queue medQ; Queue lowQ;
3 }                                          34  int query(int pId, int msg) {
4 class Queue extends Object { //...         35   refining requires pId > 0 && msg >= 2
5 int add(int pId, int msg, int qId){        36    ensures result > 0 {
6  /* add to inner list */; qId              37    ticket = ticket + 1;
7 } }                                        38    if (msg > 500) {
8 service Secretary {                        39     topQ.add(pId, msg, ticket + 2000)
9 Queue queryQ; Hashtable responses;         40    } else if (msg > 250) {
10 int ticket; Log log;                      41     medQ.add(pId, msg, ticket + 2000)
11 int query(int pId, int msg) {             42    } else {
12  refining preserve pId > 0 && msg > 0 {43   lowQ.add(pId, msg, ticket + 2000)
13   log.recordCurrentTime()                 44    };
14  };                                       45    q.qId
15  if (msg >= 2) {                          46 } }
16   query(pId, msg)@Doctor                  47 /* retrieve similar to Secretary's */
17  } else { /* Re: Appointment */           48 }
18   refining establish result > 0 {         49 service Patient {
19    ticket = ticket + 1;                   50 int query(int pId, int msg) {
20    queryQ.add(pId, msg, ticket + 1000)    51  query(pId, msg)@Secretary
21 } } }                                     52 }
22 int respond(int qId,int pId,int msg){     53 int retrieve(int qId) {
23  /* Encode patient's information */       54  if ((qId/1000) == 1) {
24  responses.add(qId, pId*1000 + msg);      55   retrieve(qId)@Secretary
25  queryQ.remove(qId)                       56  } else if((qId/1000) == 2) {
26 }                                         57   retrieve(qId)@Doctor
27 int retrieve(int qId) {                   58 } } }
28  refining requires qId > 0               59 client User{
29   ensures result > 0 {                    60 int qid = query(101,3)@Patient;
30   responses.get(qId)                      61 retrieve(qid)@Patient
31 } } }                                     62 }
```

Fig. 3. An Example Tisa Implementation

Each web service has a name (w) representing that web service; thus web service names can be thought of as web sites. (The mapping of web services to actual computers is not specified in the language itself.) A web service can be thought of as a singleton object; however, each web service has a separate address space and its methods can only be called using a remote procedure call.

An example web service declaration for the service Patient appears on lines 49–62 in Figure 3. This service contains two web-methods declaration, named query and retrieve. The web-method query takes a patient Id and message as arguments and returns a unique query Id generated according to the input arguments. The web-method retrieve takes query Id as an argument and returns an answer message which encodes a patient Id. A client declares a name and runs an expression that is the main expression of the program. We next explain class declarations and expressions.

Class Declarations.   Class declarations may not be nested. Each class has a name (c) and names its superclass (d), and may declare finite number of fields (*field**) and methods (*meth**). Field declarations are written with a class name, giving the field's type, followed by a field name. Methods also have a C++ or Java-like syntax, although their body is an expression.

Expressions.   Tisa is an expression language. Thus the syntax for expressions includes integer literals, various standard integer and logical operations, several standard OO expressions and also some expressions that are specific to web services. The logical

$specification ::= servicespec*$
$servicespec ::= \textbf{service } w \; \{ \; wmspec* \; \}$
$wmspec ::= t \; m \; (form*) \; \{ \; se \; \}$
$form ::= t \; var, \text{ where } var \neq \textbf{thisSite}$
$spec ::= \textbf{requires } sp \textbf{ ensures } sp$

$se ::= sp \mid spec \mid se; \; se \mid form = se; \; se \mid m \, (sp*) \, @sp$
$\quad \mid \textbf{if } (sp) \; \{ \; se \; \} \; \textbf{else } \{ \; se \; \}$
$sp ::= n \mid sp == sp \mid sp \; != sp \mid sp > sp \mid sp < sp \mid sp >= sp \mid sp <= sp$
$\quad \mid sp + sp \mid sp - sp \mid sp * sp \mid \; ! \; sp \mid sp \; \&\& \; sp \mid sp \text{'} \mid \text{'} sp$
$\quad \mid var \mid w$

Fig. 4. Syntax for Writing Specifications in Tisa

operations operate on integers, with 0 representing false, and all other integer values representing true. An **if** (e_1) $\{ e_2 \}$ **else** $\{ e_3 \}$ expression tests if e_1 is non-zero; if so it returns the value of e_2, otherwise it returns the value of e_3.

The standard OO expressions include object construction (**new** c ( )), variable deference (*var*, including **this**), field dereference ($e.f$), **null**, cast (cast $t \; e$), assignment to a field ($e_1.f = e_2$), sequencing ($e_1; \; e_2$), casts and a definition block ($t \; var = e_1; \; e_2$). The other OO expressions are standard [25,22].

There are three new expressions: web service names, web-method calls, and refining statements. Web service names of form w are constants. A *web-method call* has the form ($m \, (e*) \, @e_w$), where the expression following the at-sign (e_w) denotes the name of the web service name that will execute the web-method call named m with formals $e*$. A **refining** statement, of the form **refining** $spec$ $\{ \; e \; \}$, is used in implementing Tisa's greybox specifications (see below). It executes the expression e, which is supposed to satisfy the specification $spec$.

2.2 Specification Constructs

The syntax for writing specifications in Tisa is shown in Figure 4. In this figure, all nonterminals that are used but not defined are the same as in Figure 2. Specifications consist of several service specifications (*servicespec*). (Since we only permit integers to be sent to and returned from web-method calls, we omit class declarations from specifications.) A service specification may contain finite number of web-method specifications (*wmspec*). All fields are hidden, so field declarations are not allowed in a service specification. The body of a web-method specification contains a side-effect free expression (*se*). Many expressions from Figure 2 also appear as such side-effect free expressions, but not field-related operations, method calls, and **isNull**. Web-method call expressions are allowed and so are local variable definition expressions.

The main new feature of specifications, borrowed from the refinement calculus and the greybox approach, is the specification expression (*spec*). Such an expression hides (abstracts from) a piece of code in a correct implementation. The most general form of specification expression is **requires** sp_1 **ensures** sp_2, where sp_1 is a precondition expression and sp_2 is a postcondition. Such a specification expression hides program details by specifying that a correct implementation contains a **refining** expression whose body expression, when started in a state that satisfies sp_1, will terminate in a state that satisfies sp_2 [15].

In examples we use two sugared forms of specification expression. The expression **preserve** sp is sugar for **requires** sp **ensures** sp and **establish** sp is sugar for **requires** 1 **ensures** sp.

An example greybox specification of the web service Patient appears in Figure 1. The specification of the web-method query appears on line 26, and specifies (and thus exposes) all the code for that method. The specification of `retrieve` hides a bit more in its **preserve** expression (line 29). But it also exposes code that makes a web-method call `retrieve` to the `Secretary` or `Doctor`. With these greybox specifications, enough details are exposed about what the service does when invoking other services, which makes it feasible to show compliance to the HIPAA policies.

2.3   Constructs for Specifying Policies

Our simple policy specification language is similar to Linear Temporal Logic [14].

$$\Phi(specification) ::= \mathcal{P}(specification) \mid \neg \phi \mid \phi_1 \wedge \phi_2 \mid \phi_1 \, \mathbf{U} \, \phi_2 \mid \mathbf{X} \, \phi$$

The language specifies histories that are sequences of web method calls. For a given *specification*, a policy can be an atomic proposition in $\mathcal{P}(specification)$; a negation of a policy or boolean combination of policies. For simplicity here we take the set of legal propositions $\mathcal{P}(specification)$ to be all legal web-method calls in the given specification. This set can be statically computed from the specification against which the policy is to be verified by traversing the abstract syntax tree of the specification up to the depth of web-method specifications. The operator $\mathbf{U}$ is read as "until" and $\mathbf{X}$ as "next." $\phi_1 \mathbf{U} \phi_2$ states that policy ϕ_2 must be satisfied after policy ϕ_1 is satisfied along all executions of the service. $\mathbf{X}\phi$ states that policy ϕ must be satisfied in the next state (i.e., at the next web method call). We also use the following common abbreviations:

$$\begin{array}{lll} \phi_1 \vee \phi_2 \equiv \neg(\neg\phi_1 \wedge \neg\phi_2) & \phi_1 \rightarrow \phi_2 \equiv \neg\phi_1 \vee \phi_2 & true \equiv \phi \vee \neg\phi \\ false \equiv \neg true & \mathbf{F}\,\phi \equiv true\,\mathbf{U}\,\phi & \mathbf{G}\,\phi \equiv \neg\mathbf{F}\,\neg\phi \end{array}$$

The constant *true* means that the service does not have any obligation. The operator $\mathbf{F}$ is read as "eventually" and $\mathbf{G}$ as "always". Below we present two sample policies for our healthcare service example.

$\phi_1 = \mathbf{G}(\mathtt{query@Patient} \wedge (\mathbf{XF}(\mathtt{query@Secretary} \vee \mathbf{XF}\mathtt{query@Doctor})))$
$\phi_2 = \mathbf{G}(\mathtt{retrieve@Patient} \wedge \mathbf{XF}\mathtt{retrieve@Doctor} \rightarrow \neg \mathbf{XF}\mathtt{retrieve@Secretary})$

The policy ϕ_1 states that whenever there is a web-method call `query@Patient`, there is eventually a web-method call `query` at one of the sites `Secretary` or `Doctor`. This policy says that a query is eventually delivered to one of the healthcare providers. The policy ϕ_2 encodes the constraint that a health answer that comes from doctors goes directly to the patient, and is never forwarded to secretaries. In terms of the service specification, if there is a web-method call `retrieve@Patient` and it is followed by a web-method call `retrieve@Doctor`, then there is never a web-method call `retrieve` at the site `Secretary` in the same trace.

2.4   Dynamic Semantics of Tisa's Constructs

This section defines a small step operational semantics for Tisa programs (adapted from Clifton's work [25]). In the semantics, all declarations are formed into a single class table that maps class names and web service names to class and service declarations, respectively. However, despite this global view of declarations, the model of storage is distributed, with each web service having an independent store.

Evaluation relation: $\hookrightarrow: \Gamma \to \Gamma$

(WEB METHOD CALL)
$$\Pi = \{var_i : \mathbf{var}\ t_i \mid 1 \le i \le n\} \uplus \{\mathbf{this} : \mathbf{var}\ c_2\} \uplus \{\mathbf{thisSite} : \mathbf{var}\ \mathtt{Site}\} \qquad \nu = \mathbf{frame}\ \rho\ \Pi$$
$$\rho = \{var_i \mapsto v_i \mid 1 \le i \le n\} \oplus (\mathbf{this} \mapsto loc) \oplus (\mathbf{thisSite} \mapsto w)$$
$$(loc, c_2, t\ m(t_1 var_1, \dots t_n var_n)\{e\}) = find(w, m)$$
$$\overline{\langle \mathbb{E}[m(v_1, \dots, v_n)@w], J, S \rangle \hookrightarrow \langle \mathbb{E}[\mathbf{under}\ e], \nu + J, S \rangle}$$

(REFINING)
$$\frac{n \ne 0}{\langle \mathbb{E}[\mathbf{refining\ requires}\ n\ \mathbf{ensures}\ e'\ \{e''\}], J, S \rangle \hookrightarrow \langle \mathbb{E}[\mathbf{evalbody}\ e''e'], J, S \rangle}$$

(EVALBODY)
$$\rho = envOf(\nu) \qquad \Pi = tenvOf(\nu) \qquad w = thisSite(\nu) \qquad t = typeOf(v, S, w)$$
$$\rho' = \Pi \uplus \{\mathbf{result} : v\} \qquad \Pi' = \Pi \uplus \{\mathbf{result} : \mathbf{var}\ t\} \qquad \nu' = \mathbf{frame}\ \rho'\ \Pi'$$
$$\overline{\langle \mathbb{E}[\mathbf{evalbody}\ v\ e'], \nu + J, S \rangle \hookrightarrow \langle \mathbb{E}[\mathbf{under\ evalpost}\ v\ e'], \nu' + \nu + J, S \rangle}$$

(EVALPOST)   (UNDER)
$$\frac{n \ne 0}{\langle \mathbb{E}[\mathbf{evalpost}\ v\ n], J, S \rangle \hookrightarrow \langle \mathbb{E}[v], J, S \rangle} \qquad \begin{array}{l} \langle \mathbb{E}[\mathbf{under}\ v], \nu + J, S \rangle \\ \hookrightarrow \langle \mathbb{E}[v], J, S \rangle \end{array}$$

Fig. 5. Operational semantics of Tisa. Standard OO rules are omitted.

The operational semantics relies on four expressions, not part of Tisa's surface syntax, to record final or intermediate states of the computation. The *loc* expression represents locations in the store. The **under** expression is used as a way to mark when the evaluation stack needs popping. The **evalbody** and **evalpost** are used in evaluation of specification expressions. The three exceptions NullPointerException, ClassCastException, and SpecException record various problems orthogonal to the type system.

A configuration in the semantics contains an expression (e), an evaluation stack (J), and a store (S). The current web service name is maintained in the evaluation stack under the name **thisSite**. The auxiliary function *thisSite* extracts the current web service name from a stack frame. Stacks are an ordered list of frames, each frame recording the static environment, ρ, and a type environment. (The type environment, Π, is only used in the type soundness proof.) The static environment ρ maps identifiers to values. A value is a number, a web service name (site), a location, or **null**. Stores are maps from locations to storable values, which are object records. Object records have a class and also a map from field names to values.

The semantics is presented as a set of evaluation contexts $\mathbb{E}$ and an one-step reduction relation [26] that acts on the position in the overall expression identified by the evaluation context as shown in Figure 5. Standard OO rules are presented in our technical report [27]. The key rule is (WEB METHOD CALL), which uses the auxiliary function *find* to retrieve the body of the web method from a class table CT implicitly used by the semantics. It creates the frame for execution of the web method with necessary static environment and type environment and starts execution of the web method body. The **under** e expression is used in the resulting configuration to mark that the stack should be popped when the evaluation of e is finished.

Evaluation of a **refining** expression involves 3 steps. First the precondition is evaluated (due to the context rules). If the precondition is non-zero (i.e., true), then the next configuration is **evalbody** $e''\ e'$, where e'' is the body and e' is the postcondition (regarded as an expression). The body is then evaluated; if it yields a value v, then the next configuration is **under** evalpost v e', with a new stack frame that binds **result** to v pushed on the stack. The type of **result** in the type environment Π' is determined by the auxiliary function *typeOf*. Finally, the (EVALPOST) rule checks that the postcondition is true and uses the body's value as the value of the expression.

3 Verification of Policies in Tisa

A key contribution of our work is to decouple, with Tisa's language design, the verification of whether a policy is satisfied by a web service implementation into two verification tasks that can proceed modularly and independently. The first task is to verify whether a policy is satisfied by the service specification. The second task is to verify whether the service specification is satisfied by the service implementation. Three benefits follow from this modular approach. First, the service implementation need not be visible to clients, as a client uses the specification to determine whether their desired policies hold. Thus, our approach achieves modularity for service implementations. Second, regardless of the number of clients, the second verification task must only be done once; thus our approach is likely to be scalable for web service providers. Last but not the least, policy verification is performed on the (generally smaller) specification. Thus, our approach has efficiency benefits for policy verification.

Determining whether a policy is satisfied by the specification can be reduced to a standard model checking problem [14]. We claim no contribution here; rather, the novelty of our approach is in a combination of these two techniques, enabled by a careful language design. To show the feasibility of applying ideas from model checking [14] and refinement calculus [12,13] to our problem, in the rest of this section we describe our techniques for verifying policies and refinement.

3.1 Verifying Policies

We adopt the standard automata-theoretic approach for verifying linear temporal logic formulas proposed by Vardi and Wolper [28] to verify policies in Tisa. Following Vardi and Wolper [28], a policy $\phi \in \Phi(\mathcal{S})$ is viewed as a finite-state acceptor and a specification $\mathcal{S}$ as a finite-state generator of expression execution histories. Thus the specification $\mathcal{S}$ satisfies policy ϕ if every (potentially infinite) history generated by $\mathcal{S}$ is accepted by ϕ, in other words, if $\mathcal{S} \cap \neg\phi$ is empty.

Figure 6 shows main parts of an algorithm for constructing a finite-state machine $\mathcal{F}(\mathcal{S}) = (\mathcal{Z}, z_0, R, \Delta)$ from a Tisa specification $\mathcal{S}$. Here, Z is a finite set of states, z_0 is the initial state, R is a total accessibility relation, $\Delta : Z \rightarrow 2^{\mathcal{P}(\mathcal{S})}$, which determines how truth values are assigned to propositions in each state [28, pp. 5]. All rules make use of unions for joining set of states (Z) and disjoint union ($\uplus$) for joining propositions. Rules for standard OO expressions are omitted.

The (IF EXP FSM) rule demonstrates creation of non-deterministic transitions in the state machine. It computes the FSMs corresponding to the true branch and the false branch of the **if** expression with initial states z' and z'' and joins these two FSMs to make a new FSM with initial state z. Corresponding to the state z', which corresponds

Production relation: $NT \vdash se \rightsquigarrow (Z, z_0, R, \Delta), NT$ where $NT \in \mathcal{NT} = \mathcal{W} \times \mathcal{M} \rightarrow Z$

(IF EXP FSM)

$$\frac{\begin{array}{c} NT \vdash se' \rightsquigarrow (Z', z', R', \Delta'), NT' \quad NT' \vdash se'' \rightsquigarrow (Z'', z'', R'', \Delta''), NT'' \quad Z = Z' \cup Z'' \cup \{z\} \\ \Delta = \Delta' \uplus \Delta'' \uplus \{(z', \{sp\}), (z'', \{!sp\})\} \quad R = R' \cup R'' \cup \{(z, z'), (z, z'')\} \end{array}}{NT \vdash \textbf{if } (sp) \ \{se'\} \ \textbf{else} \ \{se''\} \rightsquigarrow (Z, z, R, \Delta), NT''}$$

(WEB METHOD CALL FSM 1)

$$\frac{\begin{array}{c} \neg(\exists z :: NT(w, m) = z) \\ NT' = NT \cup ((w, m), z) \quad m(t_1, \ldots t_n)\{se\} = find(w, m) \quad NT' \vdash se \rightsquigarrow (Z', z', R', \Delta'), NT'' \\ Z = Z' \cup \{z\} \quad \Delta = \Delta' \uplus \{(z', \{m@w\})\} \quad R = R' \cup \{(z, z')\} \end{array}}{NT \vdash m(v_1, \ldots, v_n)@w \rightsquigarrow (Z, z, R, \Delta), NT''}$$

(WEB METHOD CALL FSM 2)

$$\frac{z = NT(w, m)}{NT \vdash m(v_1, \ldots, v_n)@w \rightsquigarrow (\{z\}, z, \{\}, \{\}), NT}$$

(SPEC EXP FSM)

$$\frac{\begin{array}{c} Z = \{z_1, z_2, z_3, z_4\} \quad R = \{(z, z_1), (z, z_2), (z_1, z_3), (z_1, z_4), (z_3, z')\} \\ \Delta_{pre} = \{(z_1, \{sp_1\}), (z_2, \{!sp_1\})\} \quad \Delta = \Delta_{pre} \uplus \{(z_3, \{sp_1, sp_2\}), (z_4, \{sp_1, !sp_2\})\} \end{array}}{NT \vdash \textbf{requires } sp_1 \ \textbf{ensures} \ sp_2 \rightsquigarrow (Z, z, R, \Delta), NT}$$

Fig. 6. Finite-state machine construction, built from expressions in a specification

to the true branch, the proposition sp is added to Δ, which corresponds to the conditional expression evaluating to the truth value true. Similarly for the state z'', which corresponds to the false branch, the proposition $!sp$ is added to Δ, which corresponds to the conditional expression evaluating to the truth value false.

The (SPEC EXP FSM) rule models the cases for satisfaction of precondition and postcondition. The (WEB METHOD CALL FSM) rules make use of a table NT that maps pairs of web service names and method names (w, m) to states. This table is used to account for recursion in web-method calls. Finally, the finite-state machine for a service specification is created by first creating finite-state machines for each of its web-method specifications as if it is being called and by joining them using an extra state that becomes the new initial state.

Given the FSM $\mathcal{F}(S)$ we construct a Büchi automaton [29], $\mathcal{B}(\neg\phi)$ for the policy $\phi \in \Phi(S)$ as shown by Vardi and Wolper [28]. Specification S satisfies the policy ϕ if $\mathcal{F}(S) \cap \mathcal{B}(\neg\phi)$ is empty.

3.2 Verifying Refinement

Our technique for checking whether a program refines a specification in Tisa is similar to the work of Shaner, Leavens and Naumann [15]. An implementation refines a specification if it meets two criteria: first, that the code and specification are structurally similar and second, that the body of every **refining** expression obeys the specification it is refining. By structural similarity we mean that for every non-specification expression in the specification, the implementation has the identical expression at that position in the code. This is checked in a top-down manner as shown in Figure 7. The operational semantics rules (REFINING), (EVALBODY) and (EVALPOST) ensure that the body of every **refining** expression obeys the specification it is refining.

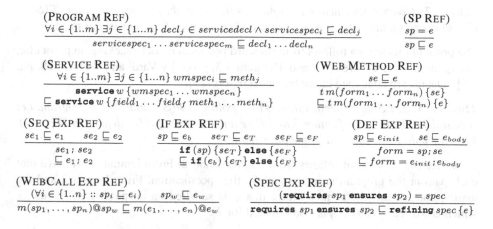

$$(\textsc{Program Ref})$$
$$\frac{\forall i \in \{1..m\}\; \exists j \in \{1...n\}\; decl_j \in servicedecl \wedge servicespec_i \sqsubseteq decl_j}{servicespec_1 \ldots servicespec_m \sqsubseteq decl_1 \ldots decl_n}$$

$$(\textsc{SP Ref})$$
$$\frac{sp = e}{sp \sqsubseteq e}$$

$$(\textsc{Service Ref})$$
$$\frac{\forall i \in \{1..m\}\; \exists j \in \{1...n\}\; wmspec_i \sqsubseteq meth_j}{\mathbf{service}\, w\, \{wmspec_1 \ldots wmspec_n\} \sqsubseteq \mathbf{service}\, w\, \{field_1 \ldots field_f\, meth_1 \ldots meth_n\}}$$

$$(\textsc{Web Method Ref})$$
$$\frac{se \sqsubseteq e}{t\, m(form_1 \ldots form_n)\, \{se\} \sqsubseteq t\, m(form_1 \ldots form_n)\, \{e\}}$$

$$(\textsc{Seq Exp Ref})$$
$$\frac{se_1 \sqsubseteq e_1 \qquad se_2 \sqsubseteq e_2}{se_1;\, se_2 \sqsubseteq e_1;\, e_2}$$

$$(\textsc{If Exp Ref})$$
$$\frac{sp \sqsubseteq e_b \qquad se_T \sqsubseteq e_T \qquad se_F \sqsubseteq e_F}{\mathbf{if}\, (sp)\, \{se_T\}\, \mathbf{else}\, \{se_F\} \sqsubseteq \mathbf{if}\, (e_b)\, \{e_T\}\, \mathbf{else}\, \{e_F\}}$$

$$(\textsc{Def Exp Ref})$$
$$\frac{sp \sqsubseteq e_{init} \qquad se \sqsubseteq e_{body}}{form = sp;\, se \sqsubseteq form = e_{init};\, e_{body}}$$

$$(\textsc{WebCall Exp Ref})$$
$$\frac{(\forall i \in \{1..n\} :: sp_i \sqsubseteq e_i) \qquad sp_w \sqsubseteq e_w}{m(sp_1, \ldots, sp_n)@sp_w \sqsubseteq m(e_1, \ldots, e_n)@e_w}$$

$$(\textsc{Spec Exp Ref})$$
$$\frac{(\mathbf{requires}\, sp_1\, \mathbf{ensures}\, sp_2) = spec}{\mathbf{requires}\, sp_1\, \mathbf{ensures}\, sp_2 \sqsubseteq \mathbf{refining}\, spec\, \{e\}}$$

Fig. 7. Inference rules for proving Tisa refinement

3.3 Soundness of Verification Technique

The proof of soundness of our verification technique uses the following three definitions.

Definition 1 (A Path for S). *Let S be a specification and $\mathcal{F}(S) = (\mathcal{Z}, z_0, R, \Delta)$ be the FSM for S constructed using algorithm shown in Figure 6. A path t for S is a (possibly infinite) sequence of pairs $(z_i, \Delta(z_i))$ starting with pair $(z_0, \Delta(z_0))$, where for each $i \geq 0$, $z_i \in Z$ and $(z_i, z_{i+1}) \in R$.*

Definition 2 (A Path for P). *Let P be a program and $\mathcal{CFG}(P) = (Z', z'_0, R', \Delta')$ be an annotated control flow graph for P, where Z' is the set of nodes representing expressions in program, R' is the control flow relation between nodes, and $\Delta' : Z' \rightarrow 2^{\mathcal{P}(P)}$ is such that for each $z'_i \in Z'$, if it represents a web-method call expression $m(..)@w$ then $(z'_i, \{m@w\}) \in \Delta'$. A path t' for P is a (possibly infinite) sequence of pairs $(z'_i, \Delta(z'_i))$ starting with pair $(z'_0, \Delta(z'_0))$, where for each $i \geq 0$, $z'_i \in Z$ and $(z'_i, z'_{i+1}) \in R'$.*

Definition 3 (Path Refinement). *Let t be a path for S and t' be a path for P. Then t is refined by t', written $t \sqsubseteq t'$, just when one of the following holds:*

- *$t \equiv t'$ i.e., for each $i \geq 0$, $(z_i, \delta_i) \in t$ and $(z'_i, \delta'_i) \in t'$ implies $z_i = z'_i$ and $\delta_i = \delta'_i$,*
- *$t = (z, \delta) + t_1$ and $t' = (z', \delta') + t'_1$ and $\delta \Rightarrow \delta'$ and $t_1 \sqsubseteq t'_1$,*
- *$t = (z, \delta) + t_1$ and $t' = (z'_1, \delta'_1) + \ldots + (z'_n, \delta'_n) + t'_1$ and $\delta \Rightarrow (\delta'_1 \uplus \ldots \uplus \delta'_n)$ and $t_1 \sqsubseteq t'_1$, or*
- *$t = t_1 + t_2$ and $t' = t'_1 + t'_2$ and $t_1 \sqsubseteq t'_1$ and $t_2 \sqsubseteq t'_2$.*

Lemma 1. *Let $P \in program$ and $S \in specification$ be given. If P refines S, then for each path t' for P there exists a path t for S such that $t \sqsubseteq t'$.*

Proof Sketch: The proof for this lemma follows from structural induction on the refinement rules shown in Figure 7. Details are contained in our technical report [27].

Lemma 2. *Given a specification S and a policy $\phi \in \Phi(S)$, the automaton $\mathcal{F}(S) \cap \mathcal{B}(\neg\phi)$ accepts a language, which is empty when the specification satisfies the policy.*

The proof of this lemma follows from standard proofs in model checking, in particular, from Lemma 3.1, Theorem 2.1 and Theorem 3.3. given by Vardi and Wolper [28, pp. 4,6]. Details are contained in our technical report [27].

Theorem 1. *Let S be a specification, ϕ be a policy in $\Phi(S)$, and P be a program. Let ϕ be satisfied by the specification S and P be a refinement of S (as defined in Figure 7). Then the policy ϕ is satisfied by the program P.*

Proof Sketch: The proof follows from lemma 1 and 2. From lemma 1, we have that each path in the program refines a path in the specification. From lemma 2 and the assumptions of this theorem, we have that ϕ is satisfied on all paths in S. Thus, ϕ, which is written over $\mathcal{P}(S)$, is also satisfied for P.

4   Related Work

In this section, we discuss techniques that are closely related to our approach.

Greybox specifications. We are not the first to consider greybox specifications [11] as a solution for verification problems. Barnett and Schulte [30,31] have considered using greybox specifications written in AsmL [32] for verifying contracts for .NET framework. Wasserman and Blum [33] also use a restricted form of greybox specifications for verification. Tyler and Soundarajan [34] and most recently Shaner, Leavens, and Naumann [15] have used greybox specifications for verification of methods that make mandatory calls to other dynamically-dispatched methods. Compared to these related ideas, to the best of our knowledge our work is the first to consider greybox specifications as a mechanism to decouple verification of web services without exposing all of their implementation details. Secondly, most of these, e.g. Shaner, Leavens, and Naumann [15] use the refinement of Hoare logic as their underlying foundation. This was insufficient to tackle the problem that we address, which required showing refinement of (a variant of) linear temporal logic. Thus adaptation of much of their work was not possible, although we were able to adapt the notion of structural refinement.

Specification and Verification Techniques for Web Services. The technique proposed by Bravetti and Zavattaro [35] for determining whether the behavioral contract of a service correctly refines its desired requirements in a composition of web-services is closely related and complementary to this work. The main difference between this work and the current work is that we verify refinement of greybox specifications by service implementations that allows us to reason about temporal policies, while hiding much of the implementation. However, we foresee a combination of our work and Bravetti and Zavattaro's work for determining fitness of a service implementation in a desired composition of web-services.

Some approaches have recently been proposed to verify contracts for web services, as seen in the works of Acciai and Boreale [36], Kuo *et al.* [8], Baresi *et al.* [6], Barbon *et al.* [5], etc. These ideas focus on verifying the behavioral contracts as defined by the externally visible interface of the web services, whereas our work provides a principled, modular technique for verifying such policies that require inspecting the web service implementation to a limited extent.

Castagna, Gesbert and Padovani present a formalism for specifying web services based on the notion of "filtering" the possible behaviors of an existing web service to conform to the behavior of some contract [7]. These filters take the form of coercions that limit when and how an available service may be consumed. These coercions permits contract subtyping and support reasoning in a language-independent way about the sequence of reads and writes performed between service clients and providers. Their contracts are intended to constrain the usage scenarios of a web service, whereas the present work describes a modular way to specify the observable behaviors that occur inside service implementations.

Bartoletti et al. [37] provide a formalization of web service composition in order to reason about the security properties provided by connected services. While they ignore policy language details, our work shows how the amount of overhead used to relate specifications to policies depends on the level of detail in the policy language. Furthermore, we believe greybox reasoning grants real benefits in readability and modularity over their type system. We view later work developing executable specifications for design of web services [38] as possible future work for Tisa.

Another approach [39] proposes an architecture to enforce these access policies at component web services, but again the work is tightly coupled to the WS-SensFlow and Axis implementations. Srivatsa et al. [40] propose an Access Control system for composite services which does not take care of the Trust in the resulting service oriented architecture. Skalka and Wang [41] introduced a trust but verify framework which is an access control system for web services, but they do not provide temporal reasoning for the verification of policies. By recording the sequence of program events in temporal order, Skalka and Smith [42] are able to verify the policies such as whether the events were happened in a reasonable order, but the mechanism does not support decoupling the model and the implementation. Other approaches [43,44] either do not have a formal model supporting them or are tightly coupled with implementations.

Future Work and Conclusions

We have designed Tisa to be a small core language to clearly communicate how it allows users to balance compliance and modularity in web service specification. However, our desire for simplicity and clarity led us to leave for future work many practical and useful extensions. The most important future work in the area of Tisa's semantics is to investigate refinement of information flow properties. It would also be interesting to investigate the utility of Tisa's specification forms for reasoning about the composition of web services.

Verifying web services is an important problem [7,5,6,8,9], which is crucial for wider adoption of this improved modularization technique that enables new integration possibilities. There are several techniques for verifying web-services using behavioral interfaces, but none facilitates verification that requires access to internal states of the service. To that end, the key contribution of this work is to identify the conflict between verification of temporal properties and modularity requirements in web services. Our language design, Tisa, addresses these challenges. It allows service providers to demonstrate compliance to policies expressed in an LTL-like language [14]. We also showed that policies in Tisa can be verified by clients using just the specification. Furthermore, refinement of specifications by program ensures that conclusion drawn from verifying policies are valid for Tisa programs. Another key benefit of Tisa is that its greybox specifications [11] allow service providers to encapsulate changeable implementation details by hiding them using a combination of *spec* and **refining** expressions. Thus, Tisa provides significant modularity benefits while balancing the verification needs.

References

1. Papazoglou, M.P., Georgakopoulos, D.: Service-oriented computing: Introduction. Commun. ACM 46(10), 24–28 (2003)
2. Christensen, E., Curbera, F., Meredith, G., Weerawarana, S.: Web services description language (WSDL) 1.1. Technical report, World Wide Web Consortium (March 2001)
3. Barth, A., Mitchell, J., Datta, A., Sundaram, S.: Privacy and utility in business processes. In: CSF 2007, pp. 279–294 (2007)
4. Leavens, G.T., Baker, A.L., Ruby, C.: Preliminary design of JML: a behavioral interface specification language for Java. SIGSOFT Softw. Eng. Notes 31(3), 1–38 (2006)
5. Barbon, F., Traverso, P., Pistore, M., Trainotti, M.: Run-time monitoring of instances and classes of web service compositions. In: ICWS 2006, pp. 63–71 (2006)
6. Baresi, L., Ghezzi, C., Guinea, S.: Smart monitors for composed services. In: ICSOC 2004, pp. 193–202 (2004)
7. Castagna, G., Gesbert, N., Padovani, L.: A theory of contracts for web services. In: POPL 2008, pp. 261–272 (2008)
8. Kuo, D., Fekete, A., Greenfield, P., Nepal, S., Zic, J., Parastatidis, S., Webber, J.: Expressing and reasoning about service contracts in service-oriented computing. In: ICWS 2006, pp. 915–918 (2006)
9. Wada, H., Suzuki, J., Oba, K.: Modeling non-functional aspects in service oriented architecture. In: IEEE International Conference on Services Computing (SCC 2006), pp. 222–229 (2006)
10. Parnas, D.L.: On the criteria to be used in decomposing systems into modules 15(12), 1053–1058 (1972)
11. Büchi, M., Weck, W.: The greybox approach: When blackbox specifications hide too much. Technical Report 297, Turku Center for Computer Science (August 1999)
12. Back, R.J.R., von Wright, J.: Refinement calculus, part i: sequential nondeterministic programs. In: REX workshop, pp. 42–66 (1990)
13. Morris, J.M.: A theoretical basis for stepwise refinement and the programming calculus. Sci. Comput. Program. 9(3), 287–306 (1987)
14. Edmund, M., Clarke, J., Grumberg, O., Peled, D.A.: Model checking. MIT Press, Cambridge (1999)
15. Shaner, S.M., Leavens, G.T., Naumann, D.A.: Modular verification of higher-order methods with mandatory calls specified by model programs. In: OOPSLA 2007, pp. 351–368 (2007)
16. Necula, G.C.: Proof-carrying code. In: POPL 1997, pp. 106–119 (1997)
17. Rajan, H., Hosamani, M.: Tisa: Towards trustworthy services in a service-oriented architecture. IEEE Transactions on Services Computing (SOC) 1(2) (2008)
18. Hosamani, M., Narayanappa, H., Rajan, H.: How to trust a web service monitor deployed in an untrusted environment? In: NWESP 2007: Proceedings of the Third International Conference on Next Generation Web Services Practices, pp. 79–84 (2007)
19. Liskov, B., Scheifler, R.: Guardians and actions: Linguistic support for robust, distributed programs. TOPLAS 5(3), 381–404 (1983)

20. Gordon, A.D., Pucella, R.: Validating a web service security abstraction by typing. Formal Aspects of Computing 17(3), 277–318 (2005)

21. Rajan, H., Leavens, G.T.: Ptolemy: A language with quantified typed events. In: Vitek, J. (ed.) ECOOP 2008. LNCS, vol. 5142, pp. 155–179. Springer, Heidelberg (2008)

22. Clifton, C., Leavens, G.T.: MiniMAO$_1$: Investigating the semantics of proceed. Science of Computer Programming 63(3), 321–374 (2006)

23. Igarashi, A., Pierce, B., Wadler, P.: Featherweight Java: A minimal core calculus for Java and GJ. In: OOPSLA 1999, pp. 132–146 (1999)

24. Flatt, M., Krishnamurthi, S., Felleisen, M.: A programmer's reduction semantics for classes and mixins. In: Formal Syntax and Semantics of Java, pp. 241–269 (1999)

25. Clifton, C.: A design discipline and language features for modular reasoning in aspect-oriented programs. Technical Report 05-15, Iowa State University (Jul 2005)

26. Wright, A.K., Felleisen, M.: A syntactic approach to type soundness. Information and Computation 115(1), 38–94 (1994)

27. Rajan, H., Tao, J., Shaner, S.M., Leavens, G.T.: Reconciling trust and modularity in web services. Technical Report 08-07, Dept. of Computer Sc., Iowa State U. (July 2008)

28. Vardi, M.Y., Wolper, P.: An automata-theoretic approach to automatic program verification. In: Proceedings of the First Symposium on Logic in Computer Science, pp. 322–331 (1986)

29. Buchi, J.: On a decision method in restricted second order arithmetic. In: Proc. Internat. Congr. Logic, Method. and Philos. Sci., pp. 1–12 (1960)

30. Barnett, M., Schulte, W.: Runtime verification of .net contracts. Journal of Systems and Software 65(3), 199–208 (2003)

31. Barnett, M., Schulte, W.: Spying on components: A runtime verification technique. In: Workshop on Specification and Verification of Component-Based Systems (2001)

32. Barnett, M., Schulte, W.: The ABCs of specification: AsmL, Behavior, and Components. Informatica 25(4), 517–526 (2001)

33. Wasserman, H., Blum, M.: Software reliability via run-time result-checking. J. ACM 44(6), 826–849 (1997)

34. Tyler, B., Soundarajan, N.: Black-box testing of grey-box behavior. In: Petrenko, A., Ulrich, A. (eds.) FATES 2003. LNCS, vol. 2931, pp. 1–14. Springer, Heidelberg (2004)

35. Bravetti, M., Zavattaro, G.: Towards a unifying theory for choreography conformance and contract compliance. In: Lumpe, M., Vanderperren, W. (eds.) SC 2007. LNCS, vol. 4829, pp. 34–50. Springer, Heidelberg (2007)

36. Acciai, L., Boreale, M.: XPi: A typed process calculus for XML messaging. Science of Computer Programming 71(2), 110–143 (2008)

37. Bartoletti, M., Degano, P., Ferrari, G.L.: Types and effects for secure service orchestration. In: CSFW, pp. 57–69 (2006)

38. Bartoletti, M., Degano, P., Ferrari, G.L., Zunino, R.: Semantics-based design for secure web services. IEEE Trans. Software Eng. 34(1), 33–49 (2008)

39. Wei, J., Singaravelu, L., Pu, C.: Guarding sensitive information streams through the jungle of composite web services. In: ICWS 2007, pp. 455–462 (2007)

40. Srivatsa, M., Iyengar, A., Mikalsen, T., Rouvellou, I., Yin, J.: An access control system for web service compositions. In: ICWS 2007, pp. 1–8 (2007)

41. Skalka, C., Wang, X.S.: Trust but verify: authorization for web services. In: SWS, pp. 47–55 (2004)

42. Skalka, C., Smith, S.F.: History effects and verification. In: Chin, W.-N. (ed.) APLAS 2004. LNCS, vol. 3302, pp. 107–128. Springer, Heidelberg (2004)

43. Biskup, J., Carminati, B., Ferrari, E., Muller, F., Wortmann, S.: Towards secure execution orders for composite web services. In: ICWS 2007, pp. 489–496 (2007)

44. Vorobiev, A., Han, J.: Specifying dynamic security properties of web service based systems. In: SKG 2006, p. 34 (2006)

Automatic Parallelization with Separation Logic

Mohammad Raza, Cristiano Calcagno, and Philippa Gardner

Department of Computing, Imperial College London
180 Queen's Gate, London SW7 2AZ, UK
{mraza,ccris,pg}@doc.ic.ac.uk

Abstract. Separation logic is a recent approach to the analysis of pointer programs in which resource separation is expressed with a logical connective in assertions that describe the state at any given point in the program. We extend this approach to express properties of memory separation between *different* points in the program, and present an algorithm for determining independences between program statements which can be used for parallelization.

1 Introduction

Automatic parallelization techniques are generally based on a detection of independence between statements in a program, in the sense that two statements accessing separate resources can be executed in parallel. Such techniques have been extensively studied and successfully applied for programs with simple data types and arrays, but there has been limited progress for programs that manipulate pointers and dynamic data structures [8,9,12]. Separation logic is a recent approach to the study of pointer programs [15] in which the separation of resource is expressed with the logical connective '$*$'. This approach has been implemented in many program analysis tools for the purposes of shape analysis and safety verification [17,4,1]. However, these analyses cannot be used for program parallelization, because the $*$ connective only expresses separation of memory at a single program point and therefore cannot determine independences between statements in a program. In this paper we extend the separation logic approach to express memory separation properties throughout a program's lifetime.

The basic idea is to extend separation logic formulae with *labels*, which are used to keep track of memory regions through an execution. Symbolic execution based on separation logic [2,5] is extended so that occurrences of the same label, even in different formulae referring to different program points, refer to the same memory locations throughout the execution. However, the symbolic execution mechanism is such that memory locations cannot always be represented by the same label through an entire execution: fresh labels have to be introduced during the execution to replace existing labels and the new labels may represent memory regions that overlap with old ones. For this reason, we keep an *intersection log* which relates labels that may represent possibly overlapping memory regions. To keep track of the memory locations that are accessed by a command, we keep a *footprint log* which records the labels of the part of the call-site formula that the command depends on. These labels are clearly determined for primitive commands. For procedure calls and while loops, the labels are determined

G. Castagna (Ed.): ESOP 2009, LNCS 5502, pp. 348–362, 2009.
© Springer-Verlag Berlin Heidelberg 2009

by a frame inference method [2] that keeps track of the labels by using a form of *label respecting* entailment between formulae.

Our approach fits in the line of work of using static analysis to detect independent statements in programs that manipulate pointer data structures [9,7,10,12,13]. Our departure point is the use of separation logic-based shape analysis. A logic-based approach is also advocated in [10], where *aliasing axioms* and theorem proving are used to detect independence. However, this method has difficulty handling structural modifications to the data structure, which do not cause problems in our case. Our method also does not rely on *reachability* properties of data structures, as in [9]. Such approaches encounter difficulties with data structure 'segments', such as non-nil-terminated list segments, and the situation is even worse when there is internal sharing within the data structure, as in the case of doubly linked lists. Our approach does not suffer from these inherent limitations as it is based on detecting the *footprints* of statements, that is, the cells that are actually accessed rather than all the ones that may possibly be accessed. We illustrate this on a program that converts a singly linked list segment into a doubly linked segment. A somewhat different approach to parallelization is proposed in [16], where *commutativity analysis* is used for identifying operations that produce the same output regardless of the order of execution. This method works together with an independence analysis, and works better depending on the strength of the independence analysis, and it will therefore be interesting to explore its combination with our method in future work.

In this paper we illustrate our method in a restricted setting adapted from [2], working with simple list and tree formulae. Our proposed method is engineered so that it can be applied as a post-processing phase starting from the output of an existing shape analysis based on separation logic, and requires only minor changes to existing symbolic execution engines. We begin in the next section by introducing labelled symbolic heaps, which are standard symbolic heap formulae extended with labels. In the next section we describe the programming language we work with and an intermediate language which is actually used in the analysis. We then describe the extended symbolic execution algorithm for determining independences, and discuss examples. In the following section we describe the frame inference method that keeps track of the labels in the inferred frame axiom. In the final section we demonstrate the soundness of the method with respect to an action trace semantics of programs.

2   Labelled Symbolic Heaps

The concrete heap model is based on a set of fields Fields, and disjoint sets Loc of locations and Val of non-addressable values, with nil $\in$ Val. We assume a finite set Var of program variables and an infinite set Var' of primed variables. Primed variables will not be used in programs, only within the symbolic heaps where they will be implicitly existentially quantified. We then set Heaps = Loc $\rightharpoonup_{fin}$ (Fields $\rightarrow$ Val $\cup$ Loc) and Stacks = (Var $\cup$ Var') $\rightarrow$ Val $\cup$ Loc. We work with a class of separation logic formulae called *symbolic heaps*, as described in [2,5], except that we introduce *labels*, $l \in$ Lab, on the spatial assertions in symbolic heaps.

$$
\begin{array}{ll}
x, y, .. \in \texttt{Var} & \text{program variables} \\
x', y', .. \in \texttt{Var}' & \text{primed variables} \\
l, k.. \in \texttt{Lab} & \text{labels} \\
f_1, f_2, .. \in \texttt{Fields} & \text{fields}
\end{array}
$$

$$
\begin{array}{ll}
E, F ::= \texttt{nil} \mid x \mid x' & \text{expressions} \\
\rho ::= f_1 : E_1, ..., f_k : E_k & \text{record expressions} \\
\Pi ::= \texttt{true} \mid E = E \mid E \neq E \mid \Pi \wedge \Pi & \text{pure assertions} \\
S ::= E \mapsto [\rho] \mid \texttt{ls}(E, F) \mid \texttt{dls}(E_f, E_b, F_f, F_b) \mid \texttt{tree}(E) & \text{simple spatial assertions} \\
\Sigma ::= \texttt{emp} \mid \langle S \rangle_l \mid \Sigma * \Sigma & \text{labelled spatial assertions} \\
\texttt{SH} ::= \Pi \mid \Sigma & \text{symbolic heaps}
\end{array}
$$

The simple spatial assertions we consider in this paper are for list segments, doubly linked list segments and binary trees, the formal semantics of which are given below. Every simple spatial assertion (conjunct) in a symbolic heap has a label, which shall be used to keep track of the part of the heap that the conjunct is describing. The *empty label* $\bullet \in \texttt{Lab}$ shall be used in situations where the label is unspecified. Except for the empty label, we require that every label has at most a unique occurrence in a symbolic heap. We let $L(\Pi \mid \Sigma)$ denote the set of labels in the symbolic heap $\Pi \mid \Sigma$.

Labels shall be interpreted in the context of a symbolic execution rather than on a single symbolic heap. This is because they shall be used to relate the states at different points through the execution of a program, and thus do not hold meaning on an individual state. The interpretation of symbolic heaps is therefore the standard one (ignoring the labels), given by a forcing relation $s, h \models A$ where $s \in \texttt{Stacks}$, $h \in \texttt{Heaps}$, and A is a pure assertion, spatial assertion, or symbolic heap. We write $h = h_0 * h_1$ to indicate that the domains of h_0 and h_1 are disjoint, and h is their graph union. We assume the fields $n, b, l, r \in \texttt{Fields}$, where n is the next field for list segments, b is the back field for doubly linked segments, and l and r are the left and right fields for trees.

$$
[\![x]\!]s = s(x) \quad [\![x']\!]s = s(x') \quad [\![\texttt{nil}]\!]s = \texttt{nil}
$$

$$
\begin{array}{lll}
s, h \models E_1 = E_2 & \text{iff} & [\![E_1]\!]s = [\![E_2]\!]s \\
s, h \models E_1 \neq E_2 & \text{iff} & [\![E_1]\!]s \neq [\![E_2]\!]s \\
s, h \models \texttt{true} & & \text{always} \\
s, h \models \Pi_0 \wedge \Pi_1 & \text{iff} & s, h \models \Pi_0 \text{ and } s, h \models \Pi_1 \\
s, h \models \langle E_0 \mapsto [f_1 : E_1, ..., f_k : E_k] \rangle_l & \text{iff} & h = [[\![E_0]\!]s \to r] \text{ where } r(f_i) = [\![E_i]\!]s \text{ for } i \in 1..k \\
s, h \models \langle \texttt{ls}(E, F) \rangle_l & \text{iff} & \text{there is a linked list segment from } E \text{ to } F \\
s, h \models \langle \texttt{dls}(E_f, E_b, F_f, F_b) \rangle_l & \text{iff} & \text{there is a doubly linked list segment from } E_f \text{ to } F_f \\
& & \text{with initial and final back pointers } E_b \text{ and } F_b \\
s, h \models \langle \texttt{tree}(E) \rangle_l & \text{iff} & \text{there is a tree at } E \\
s, h \models \texttt{emp} & \text{iff} & h = \emptyset \\
s, h \models \Sigma_0 * \Sigma_1 & \text{iff} & \exists h_0 h_1 . h = h_0 * h_1 \text{ and } s, h_0 \models \Sigma_0 \text{ and } s, h_1 \models \Sigma_1 \\
s, h \models \Pi \mid \Sigma & \text{iff} & \exists v. s(x' \mapsto v), h \models \Pi \text{ and } s(x' \mapsto v), h \models \Sigma \\
& & \text{where } x' \text{ is the collection of primed variables in } \Pi | \Sigma
\end{array}
$$

The formal semantics of the data structure formulae is given as the least predicates satisfying the following inductive definitions:

$$\mathtt{ls}(E,F) \Leftrightarrow (E = F \wedge \mathtt{emp}) \vee (E \neq F \wedge \exists y.E \mapsto [n : y] * \mathtt{ls}(y, F))$$
$$\mathtt{dls}(E_f, E_b, F_f, F_b) \Leftrightarrow (E_f = F_f \wedge E_b = F_b \wedge \mathtt{emp}) \vee$$
$$(E_f \neq F_f \wedge E_b \neq F_b \wedge \exists y.E_f \mapsto [n : y, b : E_b] * \mathtt{dls}(y, E_f, F_f, F_b))$$
$$\mathtt{tree}(E) \Leftrightarrow (E = \mathtt{nil} \wedge \mathtt{emp}) \vee (\exists x, y.E \mapsto [l : x, r : y] * \mathtt{tree}(x) * \mathtt{tree}(y))$$

3 Programming Language

We consider a standard programming language with procedures.

$b ::= E = E \mid E \neq E$		boolean expressions
$A ::= x := E \mid x := E \to f \mid E_1 \to f := E_2 \mid \mathtt{new}(x)$		atomic commands
$c ::= i : A \mid i : f(\overrightarrow{E_1}; \overrightarrow{E_2}) \mid i : \mathtt{if}\ b\ c_1\ c_2 \mid i : \mathtt{while}\ b\ c \mid c_1; c_2$		indexed commands $(i \in I)$
$p ::= . \mid f(\overrightarrow{x}; \overrightarrow{y})\ \{\mathtt{local}\ \overrightarrow{z}; c\}; p$		programs

A program is given by a number of procedure definitions. We assume that every command $i : c$ in a procedure body has a unique index i from some set of indices I. We let $I(c)$ be the set of indices of all command statements in c. In a procedure with header $f(\overrightarrow{x}; \overrightarrow{y})$, $\overrightarrow{x} = x_1, .., x_n$ are the variables not modified in the body, and $\overrightarrow{y} = y_1, .., y_m$ are the variables that are. We assume that all variables occurring free in the body are declared in the header. We define $\mathtt{free}(c)$ and $\mathtt{mod}(c)$ sets as the set of free and modified variables of c. For atomic commands these are defined as usual. For procedures we have $\mathtt{free}(f(\overrightarrow{x}; \overrightarrow{y})) = \{\overrightarrow{x}, \overrightarrow{y}\}$ and $\mathtt{mod}(f(\overrightarrow{x}; \overrightarrow{y})) = \{\overrightarrow{y}\}$.

For a given program, we assume that we have separation logic specifications for the procedure calls and loop invariants for the while loops. These may be obtained from an interprocedural shape analysis based on separation logic, such as that described in [4], or could be given as annotations by hand [3]. Formally, a specification is represented by a *spec table*, $\mathcal{T} : \mathtt{SH} \rightharpoonup \mathcal{P}(\mathtt{SH})$, which is a partial function from symbolic heaps to sets of symbolic heaps. A spec table $\mathcal{T}$ for a command represents the set of Hoare triples in which, for every $P \in dom(\mathcal{T})$, there is a triple with pre-condition P and post-condition $\bigvee_{Q \in \mathcal{T}(P)} Q$. In the case of while loops, the loop invariant may be given as a set of symbolic heaps, the intended formula being the disjunction of all the symbolic heaps in this set. For a while loop $\mathtt{while}\ b\ c$ with invariant S, we obtain the spec table as the partial function that is only defined on symbolic heaps $\Pi \mid \Sigma \in S$, and maps each of these inputs to the set $\{\neg b \wedge \Pi \mid \Sigma \mid \Pi \mid \Sigma \in S\}$. Given these specifications, for our analysis we shall consider an intermediate language for commands in which procedure calls and while loops are replaced by *specified* commands, $\mathtt{com}[\mathcal{T}]$, where $\mathcal{T}$ is a spec table.

$$c ::= i : A \mid i : \mathtt{com}[\mathcal{T}] \mid i : \mathtt{if}\ b\ c_1\ c_2 \mid c_1; c_2$$

A $\mathtt{com}[\mathcal{T}]$ command is some command which satisfies the specification given by $\mathcal{T}$. We assume that all symbolic heaps in the spec tables of specified commands have empty labels. Atomic and specified commands may be referred to as *basic* commands, and may be denoted by $i : B$. For any command c, we let $I_b(c)$ be the set of indices of all basic commands in c.

4   Independence Detection

In this section we describe the algorithm for determining when two statements in a given program are independent in the sense that they do not access a common heap location in any possible execution. The basic idea is to perform a symbolic execution [2] with labelled symbolic heaps, in which the labels keep track of regions of memory through the execution. The symbolic *footprint* of every program statement is recorded as the set of labels which represent the memory regions that are accessed in the execution of that statement. In order to determine independences between footprints, an *intersection* relation between labels needs to be maintained, which relates any two labels that represent possibly overlapping regions of memory.

Formally, we define a symbolic state as a triple $(\Pi \mid \Sigma, \mathcal{F}, \mathcal{I})$, where $\Pi \mid \Sigma$ is a labelled symbolic heap, $\mathcal{F}$ is a **footprint log**, and $\mathcal{I}$ is an **intersection log**. The footprint log is as a partial function $\mathcal{F} : I \rightharpoonup \mathcal{P}(\mathtt{Lab})$ which maps indices of commands to sets of labels which represent their footprint, and is updated for every command index when the command is encountered during symbolic execution. The intersection log $\mathcal{I} \in \mathcal{P}(\mathcal{P}_2(\mathtt{Lab}))$ is a set of unordered pairs of labels which determines a relation between labels that represent possibly overlapping regions of the heap.

4.1   Symbolic Execution Rules

Symbolic execution is based on a set of *operational* and *rearrangement* rules which determine the transformation of the symbolic states through the execution. The rules are displayed in figure 1, where they should be read from top to bottom, and they employ some expressions which we define below. The operational rules describe, for each kind of command, the effect of the command on the symbolic heap on which it executes safely. The footprint log is updated for the index of the command with the labels of the accessed portion of the symbolic heap, and the intersection log is updated when fresh labels are introduced that may possibly intersect with old ones. The first four rules are those for the atomic commands, where the footprint log is updated with the label of the accessed cell. The rules for mutation and lookup use the following definitions:

$$
mutate(\rho, f, F) = \begin{cases} f : F, \rho' & \text{if } \rho = f : E, \rho' \\ f : F, \rho & \text{if } f \notin \rho \end{cases} \qquad lookup(\rho, f) = \begin{cases} E & \text{if } \rho = f : E, \rho' \\ x \; fresh & \text{if } f \notin \rho \end{cases}
$$

In the case of allocation, a fresh label is introduced for the newly allocated cell, but the intersection log is unchanged as the new label does not intersect with any old ones.

The last operational rule is for the specified commands. In this case the pre- and post- conditions in the command's spec table determine the transformation of the symbolic heap. However, the assertion at the call-site may be larger than the command pre-condition, since the pre-condition only describes the part of the heap that is accessed by the command. For this reason, the *frame assertion* needs to be discovered, which is the part of the call-site heap that is not in the pre-condition of the command. We describe the frame inference method in detail in section 6. For now, we use the expression $frame(\Pi \mid \Sigma, \Pi_1 \mid \Sigma_1)$ to denote the frame assertion obtained for call-site assertion $\Pi \mid \Sigma$ and pre-condition $\Pi_1 \mid \Sigma_1$. The transformed symbolic heap is obtained by the conjunction of the frame assertion with the post-condition. The frame inference method ensures that the frame assertion preserves its labels from the call-site assertion. The post-condition assertion, which has all empty labels in the spec table, is assigned fresh non-empty labels with the expression $\mathit{freshlabs}(\Sigma_2, \Sigma_2')$, which means that Σ_2' is the formula Σ_2 with fresh non-empty labels on all simple conjuncts.

As an example, consider the case where the call-site state is $(\langle x \mapsto [l : y, r : z] \rangle_1 * \langle \mathtt{tree}(y) \rangle_2 * \langle \mathtt{tree}(z) \rangle_3, \mathcal{F}, \mathcal{I})$ and the specified command is a call to a procedure which rotates a tree at y, having a spec table with pre- and post- condition $\langle \mathtt{tree}(y) \rangle_{\bullet}$. In this case the inferred frame assertion is $\langle x \mapsto [l : y, r : z] \rangle_1 * \langle \mathtt{tree}(z) \rangle_3$. The fresh label 4 may be assigned to the post-condition, giving the transformed symbolic heap to be $\langle x \mapsto [l : y, r : z] \rangle_1 * \langle \mathtt{tree}(y) \rangle_4 * \langle \mathtt{tree}(z) \rangle_3$.

The footprint labels of the specified command are determined by the labels of the pre- and post- condition assertions. In the example, the footprint of the procedure call will be $\{2, 4\}$. Since fresh labels are introduced in the post-condition, the intersection log should be updated with the information of which labels the new labels may possibly intersect with. In the rule, we use the expression $\mathit{relFresh}(L_1, L_2, \mathcal{I})$ to update the intersection log $\mathcal{I}$ when a fresh set of labels L_1 is introduced in such a way that any label in L_1 may possibly intersect with any label in the set L_2, or with any label that intersects with some label in L_2 according to $\mathcal{I}$.

$$\mathit{relFresh}(L_1, L_2, \mathcal{I}) = \mathcal{I} \cup \{\{l_1, l\} \mid l_1 \in L_1 \wedge (l \in L_2 \vee \exists l' \in L_2. \{l, l'\} \in \mathcal{I})\}$$

In our example, if $\mathcal{I} = \{\{1, 5\}, \{2, 5\}, \{3, 5\}\}$ then the transformed intersection log is given by $\mathit{relFresh}(\{4\}, \{2\}, \mathcal{I}) = \{\{1, 5\}, \{2, 5\}, \{3, 5\}, \{4, 2\}, \{4, 5\}\}$, meaning that the fresh label 4 possibly intersects with 2 and everything that 2 was already possibly intersecting with in $\mathcal{I}$. Note that this example shows that the relation determined by the intersection log is not transitive. The intended relation is of course reflexive and symmetric, and this is taken into account in the independence detection algorithm.

The rearrangement rules are needed to make an expression E explicit in the symbolic heap so that an operational rule for a command that accesses the heap cell at E can be applied. Apart from the first simple substitution rule, these are basically unfolding rules for each of the inductively defined data structure predicates, where fresh labels in the unfolding are related to the original label using $\mathit{relFresh}$.

4.2   Independence Detection Algorithm

The independence detection algorithm is given in Figure 2. Given a command c with a set of preconditions Pre, the $\mathit{getInd}(c, Pre)$ function returns a set $Ind \subseteq \mathcal{P}_2(I_b(c))$ such that $\{i, j\} \in Ind$ implies that the basic statements with indices i and j are independent. For a conditional $i : \mathtt{if}\ b\ c_1\ c_2$, we can test independence with a statement $j : c$ by testing independence between $j : c$ and all the basic statements in the conditional. The $\mathit{track}(S, c)$ function takes a command c and a set S of initial symbolic states, applies the execution rules from Figure 1, and returns the set of all possible output symbolic

Operational rules

$$\frac{(\Pi \,\vert\, \Sigma, \mathcal{F}, \mathcal{I})}{(x = E[x'/x] \wedge (\Pi \,\vert\, \Sigma)[x'/x], \mathcal{F}[i \to \emptyset], \mathcal{I})} \quad i : x := E, x' \, fresh$$

$$\frac{(\Pi \,\vert\, \Sigma * \langle E \mapsto [\rho] \rangle_l, \mathcal{F}, \mathcal{I})}{(x = F[x'/x] \wedge (\Pi \,\vert\, \Sigma * \langle E \mapsto [\rho] \rangle_l)[x'/x], \mathcal{F}[i \to \{l\}], \mathcal{I})} \quad i : x := E \to f, x' \, fresh, lookup(\rho, f) = F$$

$$\frac{(\Pi \,\vert\, \Sigma * \langle E \mapsto [\rho] \rangle_l, \mathcal{F}, \mathcal{I})}{(\Pi \,\vert\, \Sigma * \langle E \mapsto [\rho'] \rangle_l, \mathcal{F}[i \to \{l\}], \mathcal{I})} \quad i : E \to f := F, mutate(\rho, f, F) = \rho'$$

$$\frac{(\Pi \,\vert\, \Sigma, \mathcal{F}, \mathcal{I})}{((\Pi \,\vert\, \Sigma)[x'/x] * \langle x \mapsto [] \rangle_l, \mathcal{F}[i \to \{l\}], \mathcal{I})} \quad i : \texttt{new}(x), x' \, fresh, l \, fresh$$

$$\frac{(\Pi \,\vert\, \Sigma, \mathcal{F}, \mathcal{I})}{(\Pi \wedge \Pi_2 \,\vert\, \Sigma_2' * \Sigma_F, \mathcal{F}[i \to L(\Sigma_2') \cup (L(\Sigma) \setminus L(\Sigma_F))], relFresh(L(\Sigma_2'), L(\Sigma) \setminus L(\Sigma_F), \mathcal{I}))} \;\dagger$$

$$\dagger \; i : \texttt{com}[\mathcal{T}], \Pi_2 \,\vert\, \Sigma_2 \in \mathcal{T}(\Pi_1 \,\vert\, \Sigma_1), \Sigma_F = frame(\Pi \,\vert\, \Sigma, \Pi_1 \,\vert\, \Sigma_1), freshlabs(\Sigma_2, \Sigma_2')$$

Rearrangement rules

$$\frac{(\Pi \,\vert\, \Sigma * \langle F \mapsto [\rho] \rangle_l, \mathcal{F}, \mathcal{I})}{(\Pi \,\vert\, \Sigma * \langle E \mapsto [\rho] \rangle_l, \mathcal{F}, \mathcal{I})} \quad \Pi \vdash E = F$$

$$\frac{(\Pi \,\vert\, \Sigma * \langle \texttt{ls}(F, F') \rangle_l, \mathcal{F}, \mathcal{I})}{(\Pi \,\vert\, \Sigma * \langle E \mapsto [n : x'] \rangle_{l_1} * \langle \texttt{ls}(x', F') \rangle_{l_2}, \mathcal{F}, relFresh(\{l_1, l_2\}, \{l\}, \mathcal{I}))} \;\dagger$$

$$\dagger \; \Pi \,\vert\, \Sigma * \texttt{ls}(F, F') \vdash F \neq F' \wedge E = F \text{ and } x' \text{ fresh and } l_1, l_2 \text{ fresh}$$

$$\frac{(\Pi \,\vert\, \Sigma * \langle \texttt{dls}(F, F_b, F', F_b') \rangle_l, \mathcal{F}, \mathcal{I})}{(\Pi \,\vert\, \Sigma * \langle E \mapsto [n : x', b : F_b] \rangle_{l_1} * \langle \texttt{dls}(x', E, F', F_b') \rangle_{l_2}, \mathcal{F}, relFresh(\{l_1, l_2\}, \{l\}, \mathcal{I}))} \;\dagger$$

$$\dagger \; \Pi \,\vert\, \Sigma * \texttt{dls}(F, F_b, F', F_b') \vdash F \neq F' \wedge E = F \text{ and } x' \text{ fresh and } l_1, l_2 \text{ fresh}$$

$$\frac{(\Pi \,\vert\, \Sigma * \langle \texttt{dls}(F, F_b, F', F_b') \rangle_l, \mathcal{F}, \mathcal{I})}{(\Pi \,\vert\, \Sigma * \langle \texttt{dls}(F, F_b, E, x') \rangle_{l_1} * \langle E \mapsto [n : F', b : x'] \rangle_{l_2}, \mathcal{F}, relFresh(\{l_1, l_2\}, \{l\}, \mathcal{I}))} \;\dagger$$

$$\dagger \; \Pi \,\vert\, \Sigma * \texttt{dls}(F, F_b, F', F_b') \vdash F \neq F' \wedge E = F_b' \text{ and } x' \text{ fresh and } l_1, l_2 \text{ fresh}$$

$$\frac{(\Pi \,\vert\, \Sigma * \langle \texttt{tree}(F) \rangle_l, \mathcal{F}, \mathcal{I})}{(\Pi \,\vert\, \Sigma * \langle E \mapsto [l : x', r : y'] \rangle_{l_1} * \langle \texttt{tree}(x') \rangle_{l_2} * \langle \texttt{tree}(y') \rangle_{l_3}, \mathcal{F}, relFresh(\{l_1, l_2, l_3\}, \{l\}, \mathcal{I}))} \;\dagger$$

$$\dagger \; \Pi \,\vert\, \Sigma * \texttt{tree}(F) \vdash F \neq \texttt{nil} \wedge E = F \text{ and } x', y' \text{ fresh and } l_1, l_2, l_3 \text{ fresh}$$

Fig. 1. Rules for symbolic execution with footprint tracking

states. The footprint and intersection logs from all of these states are used by the $getInd$ function to find the independences. Once we have detected heap independences, we can use the `free` and `mod` sets of commands to determine stack independences, and then apply standard parallelization techniques such as those discussed in [7,9].

$track(S, c) =$
  if c is empty then **return** S
  else let $c = i : c'; c''$
    $S' := \emptyset$
    for all $(\Pi \mid \Sigma, \mathcal{F}, \mathcal{I}) \in S$
      if c' is atomic command A and $(\Pi \mid \Sigma, \mathcal{F}, \mathcal{I})$ matches premise
        of operational rule for A then add the conclusion to S'
      elseif c' is atomic command A accessing heap cell E and
        $(\Pi \mid \Sigma, \mathcal{F}, \mathcal{I})$ matches premise of a rearrangement rule for E
        then add the conclusion to S'
      elseif $c' = \text{com}[\mathcal{T}]$ then
        for all $P \in dom(\mathcal{T})$ for which frame inference succeeds
          for all $Q \in \mathcal{T}(P)$
            add the conclusions of operational rule for $\text{com}[\mathcal{T}]$ to S'
      elseif $c' = \text{if } b\ c_1\ c_2$ then
        $S_1 := track((b \wedge \Pi \mid \Sigma, \mathcal{F}, \mathcal{I}), c_1)$
        $S_2 := track((\neg b \wedge \Pi \mid \Sigma, \mathcal{F}, \mathcal{I}), c_2)$
        $S' := S' \cup S_1 \cup S_2$
      else return fail
    return $track(S', c'')$

$getInd(c, Pre) =$
  $S := \emptyset$
  for all $\Pi \mid \Sigma \in Pre$
    assign fresh non-empty labels in $\Pi \mid \Sigma$
    $\mathcal{F} := \emptyset$
    $\mathcal{I} := \emptyset$
    $S := S \cup track(\{(\Pi \mid \Sigma, \mathcal{F}, \mathcal{I})\}, c)$
  $Ind := \{i, j \mid i, j \in I_b(c)\}$
  for all $i, j \in I_b(c)$
    for all $(\Pi \mid \Sigma, \mathcal{F}, \mathcal{I}) \in S$
      if there exist $l \in \mathcal{F}(i)$ and $k \in \mathcal{F}(j)$
        such that $l = k$ or $\{l, k\} \in \mathcal{I}$
        then remove $\{(i, j)\}$ from Ind
  return Ind

Fig. 2. Independence Detection Algorithm

5   Examples

We begin by illustrating our algorithm on a tree rotation program which is based on the main example from [9]. We have the procedure $rotateTree(x;)\ \{local\ x_1, x_2; c\}$, where the body c is shown in figure 3. The procedure takes a tree at x and rotates it by recursively swapping its left and right subtrees. Given the spec table with a single pre-condition $\langle tree(x) \rangle_{\bullet}$ and single post-condition $\langle tree(x) \rangle_{\bullet}$, the execution of the independence detection algorithm is shown in figure 3. At the end of the execution, for final footprint log $\mathcal{F}_6$, we have $\mathcal{F}_6(i_6) = \{3, 5\}$ and $\mathcal{F}_6(i_7) = \{4, 6\}$. Since these labels do not intersect according to the final intersection log $\mathcal{I}_3$, we have that the two recursive calls i_6 and i_7 are independent, and therefore may be executed in parallel. Similar examples are given by other divide-and-conquer programs, such as $copyTree$ and $mergeSort$ on linked lists, in which our algorithm determines the recursive calls to be independent.

Previous approaches to independence detection such as [9] have been based on *reachability* properties of certain pointer data structures, e.g., statements referring to the left and right subtrees of a tree can be determined to be independent since no heap location is reachable from both of them. The limitations of this approach can be seen even on simple list segment programs, where reachability analysis is unable to guarantee independence since the list segment may in fact be part of a larger cyclic data structure. Worse is the situation where there is internal sharing within the data structure, such as in the case of doubly linked lists. In contrast, our approach does not suffer

$(\langle \text{tree}(\text{x}) \rangle_1, \emptyset, \emptyset)$

$i_1 :$ if$(x \neq \text{nil})\{$

$\quad (\text{x} \neq \text{nil} \,|\, \langle \text{tree}(\text{x}) \rangle_1, \emptyset, \emptyset)$

$\quad (\text{x} \neq \text{nil} \,|\, \langle \text{x} \mapsto [1:\text{x}', \text{r}:\text{y}'] \rangle_2 * \langle \text{tree}(\text{x}') \rangle_3 * \langle \text{tree}(\text{y}') \rangle_4, \emptyset, \mathcal{I}_1)$

$i_2 : \quad x_1 := x \to l;$

$\quad (\text{x}_1 = \text{x}' \wedge \text{x} \neq \text{nil} \,|\, \langle \text{x} \mapsto [1:\text{x}', \text{r}:\text{y}'] \rangle_2 * \langle \text{tree}(\text{x}') \rangle_3 * \langle \text{tree}(\text{y}') \rangle_4, \mathcal{F}_1 = i_2 \to \{2\}, \mathcal{I}_1)$

$i_3 : \quad x_2 := x \to r;$

$\quad (\text{x}_2 = \text{y}' \wedge \text{x}_1 = \text{x}' \wedge \text{x} \neq \text{nil} \,|\, \langle \text{x} \mapsto [1:\text{x}', \text{r}:\text{y}'] \rangle_2 * \langle \text{tree}(\text{x}') \rangle_3 * \langle \text{tree}(\text{y}') \rangle_4, \mathcal{F}_2 = \mathcal{F}_1[i_3 \to \{2\}], \mathcal{I}_1)$

$i_4 : \quad x \to l := x_2;$

$\quad (\text{x}_2 = \text{y}' \wedge \text{x}_1 = \text{x}' \wedge \text{x} \neq \text{nil} \,|\, \langle \text{x} \mapsto [1:\text{x}_2, \text{r}:\text{y}'] \rangle_2 * \langle \text{tree}(\text{x}') \rangle_3 * \langle \text{tree}(\text{y}') \rangle_4, \mathcal{F}_3 = \mathcal{F}_2[i_4 \to \{2\}], \mathcal{I}_1)$

$i_5 : \quad x \to r := x_1;$

$\quad (\text{x}_2 = \text{y}' \wedge \text{x}_1 = \text{x}' \wedge \text{x} \neq \text{nil} \,|\, \langle \text{x} \mapsto [1:\text{x}_2, \text{r}:\text{x}_1] \rangle_2 * \langle \text{tree}(\text{x}') \rangle_3 * \langle \text{tree}(\text{y}') \rangle_4, \mathcal{F}_4 = \mathcal{F}_3[i_5 \to \{2\}], \mathcal{I}_1)$

$i_6 : \quad rotate\,Tree(x_1;);$

$\quad (\text{x}_2 = \text{y}' \wedge \text{x}_1 = \text{x}' \wedge \text{x} \neq \text{nil} \,|\, \langle \text{x} \mapsto [1:\text{x}_2, \text{r}:\text{x}_1] \rangle_2 * \langle \text{tree}(\text{x}_1) \rangle_5 * \langle \text{tree}(\text{y}') \rangle_4, \mathcal{F}_5 = \mathcal{F}_4[i_6 \to \{3, 5\}], \mathcal{I}_2)$

$i_7 : \quad rotate\,Tree(x_2;);$

$\quad (\text{x}_2 = \text{y}' \wedge \text{x}_1 = \text{x}' \wedge \text{x} \neq \text{nil} \,|\, \langle \text{x} \mapsto [1:\text{x}_2, \text{r}:\text{x}_1] \rangle_2 * \langle \text{tree}(\text{x}_1) \rangle_5 * \langle \text{tree}(\text{x}_2) \rangle_6, \mathcal{F}_6 = \mathcal{F}_5[i_7 \to \{4, 6\}], \mathcal{I}_3)$

$\quad \}$

where $\mathcal{I}_1 = \{\{1, 2\}, \{1, 3\}, \{1, 4\}\}, \mathcal{I}_2 = \mathcal{I}_1 \cup \{\{5, 3\}, \{5, 1\}\}, \mathcal{I}_3 = \mathcal{I}_2 \cup \{\{6, 4\}, \{6, 1\}\}$

Fig. 3. Independence detection for *rotate Tree*

from these inherent limitations since it is based on detecting the *footprints* of statements. We illustrate this with the example in figure 4. In this case we have the procedure $setBack(x, y, z;)\{local\ x_1; c\}$, which transforms a singly linked list segment from x to y into a doubly linked segment by recursively traversing the segment and setting the back pointers. The body c is shown in the figure. The parameter z is the back pointer to be set for the head element. In this case we have the spec table with a single pre-condition $\langle \text{ls}(x, y) \rangle_\bullet$ and single post-condition $\langle \text{dls}(x, z, y, z') \rangle_\bullet$, where z' is the existentially quantified pointer to the last element. As can be seen in figure 4, our algorithm detects the recursive call at i_4 to be independent of the statement i_3, and they can hence be executed in parallel. A reachability-based approach will fail to determine this independence even though the statements are accessing disjoint locations.

6   Frame Inference with Label Respecting Entailment

We have discussed how, in the case of the operational rule for specified commands, there is a need to infer the *frame assertion* in order to match the call-site assertion to the command's pre-condition. Given a call-site assertion $\Pi \,|\, \Sigma$ and command pre-condition $\Pi_1 \,|\, \Sigma_1$, the objective is to find a frame assertion Σ_F such that $\Pi \,|\, \Sigma \vdash \Pi_1 \,|\, \Sigma_1 * \Sigma_F$. We adapt the frame inference method of [2], which uses a proof theory for entailments between symbolic heaps. However, in our case, as well as inferring the formula, we also require that the frame assertion should correctly preserve its labels from the original call-site assertion since these are used to determine the footprint labels of the specified command. For this purpose we introduce the notion of *label respecting* entailment.

$$(\langle \mathtt{ls(x,y)} \rangle_1, \emptyset, \emptyset)$$

$i_1 :$ if$(x \neq y)\{$

$\qquad (\mathtt{x} \neq \mathtt{y} | \langle \mathtt{ls(x,y)} \rangle_1, \emptyset, \emptyset)$

$\qquad (\mathtt{x} \neq \mathtt{y} | \langle \mathtt{x} \mapsto [\mathtt{n : x'}] \rangle_2 * \langle \mathtt{ls(x',y)} \rangle_3, \emptyset, \mathcal{I}_1)$

$i_2 : \quad x_1 := x \rightarrow n;$

$\qquad (\mathtt{x_1 = x'} \wedge \mathtt{x} \neq \mathtt{y} | \langle \mathtt{x} \mapsto [\mathtt{n : x'}] \rangle_2 * \langle \mathtt{ls(x',y)} \rangle_3, \mathcal{F}_1 = i_2 \rightarrow \{2\}, \mathcal{I}_1)$

$i_3 : \quad x \rightarrow b := z;$

$\qquad (\mathtt{x_1 = x'} \wedge \mathtt{x} \neq \mathtt{y} | \langle \mathtt{x} \mapsto [\mathtt{n : x', b : z}] \rangle_2 * \langle \mathtt{ls(x',y)} \rangle_3, \mathcal{F}_2 = \mathcal{F}_1[i_3 \rightarrow \{2\}], \mathcal{I}_1)$

$i_4 : \quad setBack(x_1, y, x)$

$\qquad (\mathtt{x_1 = x'} \wedge \mathtt{x} \neq \mathtt{y} | \langle \mathtt{x} \mapsto [\mathtt{n : x', b : z}] \rangle_2 * \langle \mathtt{dls(x_1, x, y, z')} \rangle_4, \mathcal{F}_3 = \mathcal{F}_2[i_4 \rightarrow \{3,4\}], \mathcal{I}_2)$

$\qquad \}$

where $\mathcal{I}_1 = \{\{2,1\},\{3,1\}\}$ and $\mathcal{I}_2 = \mathcal{I}_1 \cup \{\{4,3\},\{4,1\}\}$

Fig. 4. Independence detection for *setBack*

The standard meaning of an entailment $\Pi_1 | \Sigma_1 \vdash \Pi_2 | \Sigma_2$ between two symbolic heaps is given as $\forall s, h.\ s, h \models \Pi_1 | \Sigma_1$ implies $s, h \models \Pi_2 | \Sigma_2$. For label respecting entailment, we have the additional constraint that a label appearing on both sides of the entailment 'refers to the same heap locations' on both sides. The formal definition of this form of entailment is based on the following property of labelled symbolic heaps.

Lemma 1. *If* $s, h \models \Pi | \Sigma * \langle S \rangle_l$ *and* $l \neq \bullet$, *then there is a unique* h' *such that* $h = h' * h''$ *and* $s, h' \models \Pi | \langle S \rangle_l$. *In this case we define* $subheap(s, h, \Pi | \Sigma * \langle S \rangle_l, l) = h'$, *and it is undefined otherwise.*

Definition 1 (Label respecting entailment). *The entailment* $\Pi_1 | \Sigma_1 \vdash \Pi_2 | \Sigma_2$ *holds iff for all* $s, h,\ s, h \models \Pi_1 | \Sigma_1$ *implies* $s, h \models \Pi_2 | \Sigma_2$, *and if* $l \in L(\Sigma_1)$ *and* $l \in L(\Sigma_2)$ *and* $l \neq \bullet$ *then* $subheap(s, h, \Pi_1 | \Sigma_1, l) = subheap(s, h, \Pi_2 | \Sigma_2, l)$.

We have adapted the proof theory for entailments from [2] for label respecting entailment in figure 5. We omit the normalization rules and rules for the tree and doubly linked segment predicates as they adapt in a very similar manner. In the figure, the expression $op(E)$ is an abbreviation for $E \mapsto [\rho]$, $ls(E, F)$, $dls(E, E_b, F, F_b)$ or $tree(E)$. The guard $G(op(E))$ asserts that the heap is non-empty, and is defined as

$$G(E \mapsto [\rho]) \triangleq \mathtt{true} \qquad G(ls(E, F)) \triangleq E \neq F \qquad G(tree(E)) \triangleq E \neq \mathtt{nil}$$

$$G(dls(E, E_b, F_f, F_b)) \triangleq E \neq F_f \qquad G(dls(F_f, F_b, E_f, E)) \triangleq E \neq F_b$$

The label respecting aspect of these rules can be best appreciated by considering the way in which the frame inference method works. Assume we are given a call-site assertion $\Pi | \Sigma$ and procedure pre-condition $\Pi_1 | \Sigma_1$. To find Σ_F such that $\Pi | \Sigma \vdash \Pi_1 | \Sigma_1 * \Sigma_F$, we apply the proof rules upwards starting from the entailment $\Pi | \Sigma \vdash \Pi_1 | \Sigma_1$, as instructed by the following theorem which we inherit from [2].

Theorem 1. *Suppose that we have an incomplete proof:*

$$\Pi' | \Sigma_F \vdash \mathtt{true} | \mathtt{emp}$$
$$\vdots$$
$$\Pi | \Sigma \vdash \Pi_1 | \Sigma_1$$

Then there is a complete proof of the label respecting entailment $\Pi | \Sigma \vdash \Pi_1 | \Sigma_1 * \Sigma_F$.

$$\frac{}{\Pi \,|\, \text{emp} \vdash \text{true} \,|\, \text{emp}} \qquad \frac{\Pi \,|\, \Sigma \vdash \Pi' \,|\, \Sigma'}{\Pi \,|\, \Sigma \vdash \Pi' \wedge E = E \,|\, \Sigma'}$$

$$\frac{\Pi \wedge P \,|\, \Sigma \vdash \Pi' \,|\, \Sigma'}{\Pi \wedge P \,|\, \Sigma \vdash \Pi' \wedge P \,|\, \Sigma'} \qquad \frac{\langle S \rangle_l \vdash \langle S' \rangle_k \quad \Pi \,|\, \Sigma \vdash \Pi' \,|\, \Sigma'}{\Pi \,|\, \langle S \rangle_l * \Sigma \vdash \Pi' \,|\, \langle S' \rangle_k * \Sigma'} \quad l, k \in \{\bullet\} \cup \text{Lab} \setminus (L(\Sigma) \cup L(\Sigma'))$$

$$\frac{\Pi \,|\, \Sigma \vdash \Pi' \,|\, \Sigma'}{\langle S \rangle_l \vdash \langle S \rangle_k \quad \Pi \,|\, \Sigma \vdash \Pi' \,|\, \langle \text{ls}(E, E) \rangle_l * \Sigma'} \quad l \in \{\bullet\} \cup \text{Lab} \setminus L(\Sigma')$$

$$\frac{\Pi \wedge E_1 \neq E_3 \,|\, \langle E_1 \mapsto E_2 \rangle_{l_1} * \Sigma \vdash \Pi' \,|\, \langle E_1 \mapsto E_2 \rangle_{l_2} * \langle \text{ls}(E_2, E_3) \rangle_{l_3} * \Sigma'}{\Pi \wedge E_1 \neq E_3 \,|\, \langle E_1 \mapsto E_2 \rangle_{l_1} * \Sigma \vdash \Pi' \,|\, \langle \text{ls}(E_1, E_3) \rangle_{l_4} * \Sigma'} \quad l_4 \in \{\bullet\} \cup \text{Lab} \setminus (L(\Sigma) \cup L(\Sigma') \cup \{l_1, l_2, l_3\})$$

$$\frac{\Pi \,|\, \langle \text{ls}(E_1, E_2) \rangle_{l_1} * \Sigma \vdash \Pi' \,|\, \langle \text{ls}(E_1, E_2) \rangle_{l_2} * \langle \text{ls}(E_2, \text{nil}) \rangle_{l_3} * \Sigma'}{\Pi \,|\, \langle \text{ls}(E_1, E_2) \rangle_{l_1} * \Sigma \vdash \Pi' \,|\, \langle \text{ls}(E_1, \text{nil}) \rangle_{l_4} * \Sigma'} \quad l_4 \in \{\bullet\} \cup \text{Lab} \setminus (L(\Sigma) \cup L(\Sigma') \cup \{l_1, l_2, l_3\})$$

$$\frac{\Pi \wedge \text{G}(\text{op}(E_3)) \,|\, \langle \text{ls}(E_1, E_2) \rangle_{l_1} * \langle \text{op}(E_3) \rangle_{l_2} * \Sigma \vdash \Pi' \,|\, \langle \text{ls}(E_1, E_2) \rangle_{l_3} * \langle \text{ls}(E_2, E_3) \rangle_{l_4} * \Sigma'}{\Pi \wedge \text{G}(\text{op}(E_3)) \,|\, \langle \text{ls}(E_1, E_2) \rangle_{l_1} * \langle \text{op}(E_3) \rangle_{l_2} * \Sigma \vdash \Pi' \,|\, \langle \text{ls}(E_1, E_3) \rangle_{l_5} * \Sigma'} \quad \dagger$$

$$\dagger \; l_5 \in \{\bullet\} \cup \text{Lab} \setminus (L(\Sigma) \cup L(\Sigma') \cup \{l_1, l_2, l_3, l_4\})$$

Fig. 5. Rules for label respecting entailment

When applying the label-respecting proof rules upwards, labels can only be removed from the left hand side of an entailment. Hence Σ_F will retain its labels from the call-site assertion $\Pi \,|\, \Sigma$. By theorem 1, the entailment $\Pi \,|\, \Sigma \vdash \Pi_1 \,|\, \Sigma_1 * \Sigma_F$ is label respecting, and so we have that the labels common to the call-site assertion and the frame assertion refer to the same heap locations. Notice that when applying this method in practice, since we are only concerned about preserving the labels in the frame assertion, we do not care about the labels on the right hand side of the entailments as we go up the proof. They can hence be chosen to be the empty label when applying the rules upwards. As a simple illustration, in the case where the call-site assertion is $\langle x \mapsto [l : y, r : z] \rangle_1 * \langle \text{tree}(y) \rangle_2 * \langle \text{tree}(z) \rangle_3$ and the command pre-condition is $\langle \text{tree}(y) \rangle_\bullet$, the following derivation gives us the correctly labelled frame assertion:

$$\frac{\langle x \mapsto [l : y, r : z] \rangle_1 * \langle \text{tree}(z) \rangle_3 \vdash \text{emp}}{\langle x \mapsto [l : y, r : z] \rangle_1 * \langle \text{tree}(y) \rangle_2 * \langle \text{tree}(z) \rangle_3 \vdash \langle \text{tree}(y) \rangle_\bullet}$$

7   Soundness

We demonstrate the soundness of our algorithm in detecting independences, a property which is necessary if we are to use the algorithm to safely parallelize a program. For this we adapt an action trace semantics of programs from [6]. The action traces are composed of primitive actions α:

$$\alpha ::= x := E \mid x := E \to f \mid E_1 \to f := E_2 \mid \text{new}_l(x) \mid \text{assume}(b) \quad \text{where } l \in Loc$$

The $\text{assume}(b)$ action is used to implement conditionals, as shown in the trace semantics of commands below. It filters out states which do not satisfy the boolean b. The $\text{new}_l(x)$ command allocates the location l if it is not already allocated. We choose this

α	$[\![\alpha]\!](s,h),\ loc(\alpha,s,h)$	
$x := E$	$\{s[x\mapsto [\![E]\!]s], h\}, \emptyset$	
$x := E \to f$	$\{s[x\mapsto v], h\}, \{l\}$	if $[\![E]\!]s = l,\ l \in$ Loc and $h(l)(f) = v$
	$\top, \emptyset$	otherwise
$E_1 \to f := E_2$	$\{s, h[l\mapsto r]\}, \{l\}$	if $[\![E_1]\!]s = l,\ [\![E_2]\!]s = v,\ l \in$ Loc and $r = h(l)[f \to v]$
	$\top, \emptyset$	otherwise
$\mathtt{new}_l(x)$	$\{s, h * l \mapsto r\}, \{l\}$	if $l \in$ Loc$\setminus dom(h)$ and $r(f) = \mathtt{nil}$ for all $f \in$ Fields
	$\emptyset, \emptyset$	otherwise
$\mathtt{assume}(b)$	$\{s,h\}, \emptyset$	if $[\![b]\!]s$
	$\emptyset, \emptyset$	otherwise

Fig. 6. Denotational semantics and location sets of primitive actions

instead of a non-deterministic allocation primitive (which is usually used in separation logic works) as keeping traces deterministic will be useful for our purposes.

Semantically, the primitive actions correspond to total functions that are of the form Stacks $\times$ Heaps $\to \mathcal{P}($Stacks $\times$ Heaps$)^{\top}$. The $\top$ element represents a faulting execution, that is, dereferencing a null pointer or an unallocated region of the heap. For a primitive action α and a state $(s,h) \in$ Stacks $\times$ Heaps, we define the **location set** $loc(\alpha, s, h)$ as the set of locations that are accessed by α when executed on the state (s,h). The denotational semantics and location sets of the primitive actions is given in figure 6.

Definition 2 (Action trace). *An action trace τ is a finite sequential composition of atomic actions,* $\tau ::= \alpha; \cdots ; \alpha$

Denotational semantics of action traces is given by the sequential composition of actions, which is defined as

$$[\![\alpha_1; \alpha_2]\!](s,h) = \begin{cases} \bigcup_{(s',h')\in[\![\alpha_1]\!](s,h)} [\![\alpha_2]\!](s',h') & \text{if } [\![\alpha_1]\!](s,h) \neq \top \\ \top & \text{otherwise} \end{cases}$$

Note that every trace τ is deterministic in that for any state (s,h), $[\![\tau]\!](s,h)$ either faults or has at most a single outcome $\{(s',h')\}$.

$$T(x := E) = \{x := E\} \qquad T(x := [E]) = \{x := [E]\}$$

$$T([E_1] := [E_2]) = \{[E_1] := [E_2]\} \qquad T(\mathtt{new}(x)) = \{\mathtt{new}_l(x) \mid l \in \mathtt{Loc}\}$$

$$T(\mathtt{com}(T)) \subseteq \{\tau \mid \forall P \in dom(T). \forall (s,h) \in [\![P]\!]. \exists Q \in T(P).\ [\![\tau]\!](s,h) \subseteq [\![Q]\!]\}$$

$$T(c_1; c_2) = \{\tau_1; \tau_2 \mid \tau_1 \in T(c_1), \tau_2 \in T(c_2)\}$$

$$T(\mathtt{if}\ b\ c_1\ c_2) = \{\mathtt{assume}(b); \tau_1 \mid \tau_1 \in T(c_1)\} \cup \{\mathtt{assume}(\neg b); \tau_2 \mid \tau_2 \in T(c_2)\}$$

Fig. 7. Action trace semantics of commands

The action trace semantics of commands of our programming language is given in figure 7. Just as our commands are indexed, we assign unique indices to the primitive actions in every action trace of every command as follows. For each atomic command $i : A$, every trace is a single primitive action α, and we index this as $(i, 1) : \alpha$. For each specified command $i : \mathtt{com}(\mathcal{T})$, every trace $\alpha_1; ...; \alpha_n$ is indexed as $(i, 1) : \alpha_1; ...; (i, n) : \alpha_n$. For sequential composition the indices are obtained from the component commands. For a conditional $i : \mathtt{if}\ b\ c_1\ c_2$, we index the assume actions as $(i, 1) : \mathtt{assume}(b)$ and $(i, 1) : \mathtt{assume}(\neg b)$ and the other indices are obtained from the component commands. We shall write $(i, j) : \alpha \in \tau$ to mean that $\tau = \tau'; (i, j) : \alpha; \tau''$ for some τ' and τ''.

Definition 3 (Index subtrace). *For a trace τ and a command index i, we define $\tau|_i$ to be the subtrace of τ containing all the actions of the form $(i, j) : \alpha$. If there are no such actions in τ then $\tau|_i$ is undefined.*

Lemma 2. *For a command c, every trace $\tau \in T(c)$ is of the form $\tau|_{i_1}; ...; \tau|_{i_n}$, where $i_1, ..., i_n \in I(c)$.*

We define the locations accessed by an atomic action in the execution of a trace.

Definition 4 (Location set of an action in a trace). *The location set of an action $(i, j) : \alpha$ in a trace τ from initial state (s, h) is defined as*

$$loc((i, j) : \alpha, \tau, s, h) = \begin{cases} loc(\alpha, s', h') & \text{if } \tau = \tau_1; (i, j) : \alpha; \tau_2 \text{ and } [\![\tau_1]\!](s, h) = \{(s', h')\} \\ \emptyset & \text{otherwise} \end{cases}$$

We extend the definition of locations accessed by an action to the locations accessed by a subtrace of τ.

Definition 5 (Location set of a subtrace). *The location set of subtrace τ' of τ from initial state (s, h) is defined as $loc(\tau', \tau, s, h) = \bigcup\limits_{(i,j):\alpha \in \tau'} loc((i, j) : \alpha, \tau, s, h)$*

We now give the formal definition of independence between two basic statements in a progam, for a given pre-condition.

Definition 6 (Independence). *Given a command c and a pre-condition given by a set of symbolic heaps Pre, for two basic commands with indices i and i' in c, we say that command i is **independent** of command i', written $indep(i, i', c, Pre)$, iff for all $\Pi \mid \Sigma \in Pre$ and for all $(s, h) \in [\![\Pi \mid \Sigma]\!]$, we have for every $\tau \in T(c)$ such that $\tau|_i$ and $\tau|_{i'}$ are defined, that $loc(\tau|_i, \tau, s, h) \cap loc(\tau|_{i'}, \tau, s, h) = \emptyset$.*

Given the trace model developed above, we can now formally state the soundness property of the independence detection algorithm given in figure 2.

Theorem 2. *For a command c and a pre-condition set Pre, if for two basic commands with indices i and i' in c we have $\{i, i'\} \in getInd(c, Pre)$, then $indep(i, i', c, Pre)$.*

The complete proof of this result can be found in the technical report [14], and we give here an outline. The algorithm of figure 2 works by applying the operational and rearrangement rules of figure 1 through the program, possibly branching on disjunctive outcomes and conditionals. We can therefore think of it as determining a set of *symbolic execution traces*. A symbolic execution trace, $\mathcal{S}$, is a sequence of symbolic states related by applications of operational or rearrangement rules, beginning with some initial state ψ_I in the pre-condition and ending with some ψ_F in the final set of symbolic states that is used to test independences.

The concrete and symbolic executions are related by a notion of satisfaction between an action trace and a symbolic execution trace. An action trace τ satisfies a symbolic execution trace $\mathcal{S}$ if it is of the form $\tau|_{i_1}; ...; \tau|_{i_n}$, where $i_1, ..., i_n$ are the command indices for the operational rules that generate $\mathcal{S}$, and every intermediate concrete state in τ (after the execution of each index subtrace) satisfies the symbolic heap in the corresponding symbolic states. Thus this notion of satisfaction depends only on the symbolic heap component of symbolic states and not on the footprint and intersection logs. By soundness of standard symbolic execution [2], we have that every concrete trace of the program satisfies *some* symbolic execution trace generated by the algorithm.

This relation connecting concrete and symbolic executions is then used to interpret the labels in the symbolic heaps and the footprint and intersection logs. The underlying idea is that, given a concrete initial state (s, h) and an action trace τ satisfying a symbolic execution trace $\mathcal{S}$, every label l occurring in any of the symbolic states in $\mathcal{S}$ corresponds to a *fixed* set of heap locations throughout the entire concrete execution of τ from (s, h). This location set, denoted $labloc(l, \mathcal{S}, \tau, s, h)$, is used to reason about the heap locations that the labels in the footprint and intersection logs represent. We show that for any two subtraces $\tau|_i$ and $\tau|_{i'}$ of τ, if the footprint labels of i and i' in the final footprint log of $\mathcal{S}$ do not intersect according to the final intersection log of $\mathcal{S}$, then the two subtraces access disjoint locations, that is, $loc(\tau|_i, \tau, s, h) \cap loc(\tau|_{i'}, \tau, s, h) = \emptyset$.

The algorithm determines two commands with indices i and i' to be independent if they have non-intersecting footprint labels according to each of the final symbolic states generated by the algorithm. Since every action trace satisfies some symbolic execution trace, we have that in every action trace of the program, the subtraces of i and i' access disjoint locations, which means that i and i' are independent by definition 6.

8   Conclusion and Future Work

In this work we have focussed on laying the foundations of our extended separation logic framework for independence detection. We plan to extend the method we describe to the more complex data structures handled by separation logic shape analyses [1], to integrate our method with the existing *space invader* tool for shape analysis [17,4], and conduct practical experiments, conceivably exploiting the scalability of this tool to large programs. A notable aspect of this integration is that, while our framework relies on the atomic predicates being precise, sometimes imprecise predicates, e.g. 'possibly cyclic list', are used in shape analyses. However, these predicates are 'boundedly imprecise', so that case analysis can be performed to obtain finite disjunctions of precise predicates from imprecise ones. Another direction for future work is to improve the precision of label tracking by incorporating it into the shape analysis phase itself, which would involve taking the footprint and intersection logs through the abstraction and fixpoint calculations. Following this, we intend to investigate the application of our method to other kinds of program optimizations.

Acknowledgements. We thank the anonymous referees for very helpful comments. Raza acknowledges support of an ORS award and EPSRC grant "Smallfoot: static assertion checking for C programs". Gardner acknowledges support of a Microsoft Research Cambridge/Royal Academy of Engineering Senior Research Fellowship. Calcagno acknowledges support of an EPSRC advanced fellowship.

References

1. Berdine, J., Calcagno, C., Cook, B., Distefano, D., OHearn, P., Wies, T., Yang, H.: Shape Analysis for Composite Data Structures. In: Damm, W., Hermanns, H. (eds.) CAV 2007. LNCS, vol. 4590, pp. 178–192. Springer, Heidelberg (2007)
2. Berdine, J., Calcagno, C., O'Hearn, P.W.: Symbolic Execution with Separation Logic. In: Yi, K. (ed.) APLAS 2005. LNCS, vol. 3780, pp. 52–68. Springer, Heidelberg (2005)
3. Berdine, J., Calcagno, C., O'Hearn, P.W.: Smallfoot: Automatic modular assertion checking with separation logic. In: 4th FMCO (2006)
4. Calcagno, C., Distefano, D., O'Hearn, P., Yang, H.: Compositional Shape Analysis. In: POPL (2009)
5. Distefano, D., O'Hearn, P., Yang, H.: A Local Shape Analysis based on Separation Logic. In: Hermanns, H., Palsberg, J. (eds.) TACAS 2006. LNCS, vol. 3920, pp. 287–302. Springer, Heidelberg (2006)
6. Calcagno, C., O'Hearn, P., Yang, H.: Local Action and Abstract Separation Logic. In: LICS (2007)
7. Ghiya, R., Hendren, L.J., Zhu, Y.: Detecting Parallelism in C programs with recursive data structures. In: Koskimies, K. (ed.) CC 1998. LNCS, vol. 1383. Springer, Heidelberg (1998)
8. Gupta, R., Pande, S., Psarris, K., Sarkar, V.: Compilation Techniques for Parallel Systems. In: Parallel Computing (1999)
9. Hendren, L.J., Nicolau, A.: Parallelizing programs with recursive data structures. In: IEEE Transactions on Parallel and Distributed Systems (1990)
10. Hummel, J., Hendren, L.J., Nicolau, A.: A general data dependence test for dynamic, pointer-based data structures. In: PLDI (1994)
11. Hoare, T., O'Hearn, P.: Separation Logic Semantics of Communicating Processes. In: FICS (2008)
12. Horwitz, S., Pfeiffer, P., Reps, T.W.: Dependence analysis for poiner variables. In: PLDI (1989)
13. Marron, M., Stefanovic, D., Kapur, D., Hermenegildo, M.: Identification of Heap-Carried Data Dependence Via Explicit Store Heap Models. In: LCPC (2008)
14. Raza, M., Calcagno, C., Gardner, P.: Automatic Parallelization with Separation Logic. Imperial College Technical Report DTR08-16 (2008)
15. Reynolds, J.C.: Separation logic: A logic for shared mutable data structures. In: 17th LICS (2002)
16. Rinard, M.C., Diniz, P.C.: Commutativity Analysis: A New Analysis Technique for Parallelizing Compilers. In: ACM Transactions on Programming Languages and Systems (1997)
17. Yang, H., Lee, O., Berdine, J., Calcagno, C., Cook, B., Distefano, D., O'Hearn, P.: Scalable Shape Analysis for Systems Code. In: Gupta, A., Malik, S. (eds.) CAV 2008. LNCS, vol. 5123, pp. 385–398. Springer, Heidelberg (2008)

Deny-Guarantee Reasoning

Mike Dodds[1], Xinyu Feng[2], Matthew Parkinson[1], and Viktor Vafeiadis[3]

[1] University of Cambridge, UK
[2] Toyota Technological Institute at Chicago, USA
[3] Microsoft Research Cambridge, UK

Abstract. Rely-guarantee is a well-established approach to reasoning about concurrent programs that use parallel composition. However, parallel composition is not how concurrency is structured in real systems. Instead, threads are started by 'fork' and collected with 'join' commands. This style of concurrency cannot be reasoned about using rely-guarantee, as the life-time of a thread can be scoped dynamically. With parallel composition the scope is static.

In this paper, we introduce deny-guarantee reasoning, a reformulation of rely-guarantee that enables reasoning about dynamically scoped concurrency. We build on ideas from separation logic to allow interference to be dynamically split and recombined, in a similar way that separation logic splits and joins heaps. To allow this splitting, we use *deny* and *guarantee* permissions: a deny permission specifies that the environment cannot do an action, and guarantee permission allow us to do an action. We illustrate the use of our proof system with examples, and show that it can encode all the original rely-guarantee proofs. We also present the semantics and soundness of the deny-guarantee method.

1 Introduction

Rely-guarantee [10] is a well-established compositional proof method for reasoning about concurrent programs that use parallel composition. Parallel composition provides a structured form of concurrency: the lifetime of each thread is statically scoped, and therefore interference between threads is also statically known. In real systems, however, concurrency is not structured like this. Instead, threads are started by a 'fork' and collected with 'join' commands. The lifetime of such a thread is dynamically scoped in a similar way to the lifetime of heap-allocated data.

In this paper, we introduce *deny-guarantee* reasoning, a reformulation of rely-guarantee that enables reasoning about such dynamically scoped concurrency. We build on ideas from separation logic to allow interference to be dynamically split and recombined, in a similar way that separation logic splits and joins heaps.

In rely-guarantee, interference is described using two binary relations: the *rely*, R, and the *guarantee*, G. Specifications of programs consist of a precondition, a postcondition and an interference specification. This setup is sufficient to reason about lexically-scoped parallel composition, but not about dynamically-scoped threads. With dynamically-scoped threads, the interference at the end of the program may be quite different from the interference at the beginning of the program, because during execution other threads may have been forked or joined. Therefore, just as in Hoare logic

G. Castagna (Ed.): ESOP 2009, LNCS 5502, pp. 363–377, 2009.
© Springer-Verlag Berlin Heidelberg 2009

a program's precondition and postcondition may differ from each other, so in deny-guarantee logic a thread's pre-interference and post-interference specification may differ from each other.

Main results. The main contributions of this paper are summarized below:

- We introduce deny-guarantee logic and apply it to an example (see §3 and §4).
- We present an encoding of rely-guarantee into deny-guarantee, and show that every rely-guarantee proof can be translated into a deny-guarantee proof (see §5).
- We prove that our proof rules are sound (see §6).
- We have formalized our logic and all the proofs in Isabelle [4].

For clarity of exposition, we shall present deny-guarantee in a very simple setting where the memory consists only of a pre-allocated set of global variables. Our solution extends easily to a setting including memory allocation and deallocation (see §7).

Related work. Other work on concurrency verification has generally ignored fork/join, preferring to concentrate on the simpler case of parallel composition. This is true of all of the work on traditional rely-guarantee reasoning [10, 11]. This is unsurprising, as the development of deny-guarantee depends closely on the abstract characterization of separation logic [3]. However, even approaches such as SAGL [5] and RGSep [12] which combine rely-guarantee with separation logic omit fork/join from their languages.

There exist already some approaches to concurrency that handle fork. Feng *et al.* [6] and Hobor *et al.* [9] both handle fork. However, both omit join with the justification that it can be handled by synchronization between threads. However, this approach is not compositional: it forces us to specify interference globally. Gotsman *et al.* [7] propose an approach to locks in the heap which includes both fork and join. However, this is achieved by defining an invariant over protected sections of the heap, which makes compositional reasoning about inter-thread interference impossible (see the next section for an example of this). Haack and Hurlin [8] have extended Gotsman *et al.*'s work to reason about fork and join in Java, where a thread can be joined multiple times.

2   Towards Deny-Guarantee Logic

Consider the very simple program given in Fig. 1. If we run the program in an empty environment, then at the end, we will get x = 2. This happens because the main thread will block at line L3 until thread t1 terminates. Hence, the last assignment to x will either be that of thread t2 or of the main thread, both of which write the value 2 into x. We also know that the error in the forked code on L1 and L2 will never be reached.

```
L0: x := 0;
L1: t1 := fork(if(x==1) error;
                x := 1);
L2: t2 := fork(x := 2;
                if (x==3) error);
L3: join t1;
L4: x := 2;
L5: join t2;
```

Fig. 1. Illustration of fork/join

Now, suppose we want to prove that this program indeed satisfies the postcondition x = 2. Unfortunately, this is not possible with existing compositional proof methods.

Invariant-based techniques (such as Gotsman *et al.* [7]) cannot handle this case, because they cannot describe interference. Unless we introduce auxiliary state to specify a more complex invariant, we cannot prove the postcondition, as it does not hold throughout the execution of the program.

Rely-guarantee can describe interference, but still cannot handle this program. Consider the parallel rule:

$$\frac{R_1, G_1 \vdash \{P_1\} \, C_1 \, \{Q_1\} \quad G_1 \subseteq R_2 \quad R_2, G_2 \vdash \{P_2\} \, C_2 \, \{Q_2\} \quad G_2 \subseteq R_1}{R_1 \cap R_2, G_1 \cup G_2 \vdash \{P_1 \wedge P_2\} \, C_1 \parallel C_2 \, \{Q_1 \wedge Q_2\}}$$

In this rule, the interference is described by the rely, R, which describes what the environment can do, and the guarantee, G, which describes what the code is allowed to do. The rely and guarantee do not change throughout the execution of the code, they are 'statically scoped' interference, whereas the scope of the interference introduced by fork and join commands is dynamic.

Separation logic solves this kind of problem for dynamically allocated memory, also known as the heap. It uses the star operator to partition the heap into heap portions and to pass the portions around dynamically. The star operator on heaps is then lifted to assertions about heaps. In this work, we shall use the star operator to partition the *interference* between threads, and then lift it to assertions about the interference.

Let us assume we have an assertion language which can describe interference. It has a separation-logic-like star operation. We would like to use this star to split and join interference, so that we can use simple rules to deal with fork and join:

$$\frac{\{P_1\} \, C \, \{P_2\} \quad \dots}{\{P * P_1\} \, x := \textbf{fork} \, C \, \{P * \mathsf{Thread}(x, P_2)\}} \text{(FORK)} \qquad \frac{\dots}{\{P * \mathsf{Thread}(E, P')\} \, \textbf{join} \, E \, \{P * P'\}} \text{(JOIN)}$$

The FORK rule simply removes the interference, P_1, required by the forked code, C, and returns a token $\mathsf{Thread}(x, P_2)$ describing the final state of the thread. The JOIN rule, knowing the thread E is dead, simply takes over its final state[1].

Now, we will consider how we might prove our motivating example. Let us imagine we have some assertions that both allow us to do updates to the state, and forbid the environment from doing certain updates. We provide the full details in §4, and simply present the outline (Fig. 2) and an informal explanation of the permissions here. The first thread we fork can be verified using the T_1 and $x \neq 1$, where T_1 allows us to update x to be 1, and prevents any other thread updating x to be 1. Next, we use G_2 which allows us to update x to be 2; and D_3 which prevents the

```
{T_1 * G_2 * D_3 * L * x ≠ 1}
   t1 := fork (if(x==1) error;
               x := 1);
{G_2 * D_3 * L * Thread(t1,T_1)}
   t2 := fork (x := 2;
               if(x==3) error );
{L * Thread(t1,T_1) * Thread(t2,G_2 * D_3)}
   join t1;
{T_1 * L * Thread(t2,G_2 * D_3)}
   x := 2;
{T_1 * L * Thread(t2,G_2 * D_3) * x = 2}
   join t2
{T_1 * G_2 * D_3 * L * x = 2}
```

Fig. 2. Proof outline

---

[1] As in the pthread library, we allow a thread to be joined only once. We could also adapt the work of Haack and Hurlin [8] to our deny-guarantee setting to handle Java-style join.

environment from updating x to be 3. These two permissions are sufficient to verify the second thread. Finally, L is a leftover permission which prevents any other thread updating x to be any value other than 1 or 2. When we get to the assignment, we have $T_1 * L$ which forbids the environment performing any update except assigning x with 2. Hence, we know that the program will terminate with x = 2.

Now, we consider how to build a logic to represent the permission on interference used in the proof outline. Let us consider the information contained in a rely-guarantee pair. For each state change it has one of four possibilities presented in Fig. 3: *guar* permission, allowed by both the thread and the environment (me,env); 1 permission, allowed by the thread, and not allowed for the environment (me,¬env); 0 permission, not allowed by the thread, but allowed by the environment (¬me,env); and *deny* permission, not allowed by the thread or the environment (¬me,¬env).

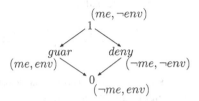

Fig. 3. Possible interference

To allow inter-thread reasoning about interference, we want to split full permissions 1 into either *deny* permissions or *guar* permissions. We also want to further split *deny*, or *guar*, permissions into smaller *deny* or *guar* permissions respectively. The arrows of Fig. 3 show the order of permission strength captured by splitting. If a thread has a *deny* on a state change, it can give another thread a *deny* and keep one itself while preserving the fact that the state change is prohibited for itself and the environment. The same holds for *guar*.

To preserve soundness, we cannot allow unrestricted copying of permissions – we must treat them as *resources*. Following Boyland [2] and Bornat et al. [1] we attach weights to splittable resources. In particular we use fractions in the interval (0,1). For example, we can split an $(a+b)deny$ into an $(a)deny$ and a $(b)deny$, and similarly for *guar* permissions. We can also split a full permission 1 into $(a)deny$ and $(b)deny$, or $(a)guar$ and $(b)guar$, where $a+b=1$.

In the following sections we will show how these permissions can be used to build deny-guarantee, a separation logic for interference.

Aside. Starting with the parallel composition rules of rely-guarantee and of separation logic, you might wonder if we can define our star as $(R_1, G_1) * (R_2, G_2) = (R_1 \cap R_2, G_1 \cup G_2)$ provided $G_1 \subseteq R_2$ and $G_2 \subseteq R_1$, and otherwise it is undefined. Here we have taken the way rely-guarantee combines the relations, and added it to the definition of $*$.

This definition, however, does not work. The star we have defined is not *cancellative*, a condition that is required for proving that separation is sound [3]. Cancellativity says that for all x, y and z, if $x * y$ is defined and $x * y = x * z$, then $y = z$. Intuitively, the problem is that $\cap$ and $\cup$ lose information about the overlap.

3   The Logic

Language. The language is defined in Fig. 4. This is a standard language with two additional commands for forking a new thread and for joining with an existing thread.

(Expr) $E ::= x \mid n \mid E + E \mid E - E \mid \ldots$

(BExp) $B ::= \text{true} \mid \text{false} \mid E = E \mid E \neq E \mid \ldots$

(Stmts) $C ::= x := E \mid \textbf{skip} \mid C; C \mid \textbf{if } B \textbf{ then } C \textbf{ else } C \mid \textbf{while } B \textbf{ do } C \mid x := \textbf{fork } C \mid \textbf{join } E$

Fig. 4. The Language

Informally, the $x := \textbf{fork } C$ command allocates an unused thread identifier t, creates a new thread with thread identifier t and body C, and makes it run in parallel with the rest of the program. Finally, it returns the thread identifier t by storing it in x. The command **join** E blocks until thread E terminates; it fails if E is not a valid thread identifier. For simplicity, we assume each primitive operation is atomic. The formal operational semantics is presented in §6.

Deny-Guarantee Permissions. The main component of our logic is the set of deny-guarantee permissions, PermDG. A deny-guarantee permission is a function that maps each action altering a single variable[2] to a certain deny-guarantee fraction:

$$
\begin{aligned}
\text{Vars} &\overset{\text{def}}{=} \{x, y, z, \ldots\} \\
n \in \text{Vals} &\overset{\text{def}}{=} \mathbb{Z} \\
\sigma \in \text{States} &\overset{\text{def}}{=} \text{Vars} \to \text{Vals} \\
a \in \text{Actions} &\overset{\text{def}}{=} \{\sigma[x \mapsto n], \sigma[x \mapsto n'] \mid \sigma \in \text{States} \wedge n \neq n'\} \\
f \in \text{FractionDG} &\overset{\text{def}}{=} \{(\text{deny}, \pi) \mid \pi \in (0, 1)\} \cup \{(\text{guar}, \pi) \mid \pi \in (0, 1)\} \cup \{0, 1\} \\
pr \in \text{PermDG} &\overset{\text{def}}{=} \text{Actions} \to \text{FractionDG}
\end{aligned}
$$

We sometimes write deny-guarantee fractions in FractionDG in shorthand, with $\pi\textbf{d}$ for (deny, π), and $\pi\textbf{g}$ for (guar, π).

The fractions represent a permission or a prohibition to perform a certain action. The first two kinds of fractions are symmetric: (deny, π) says that nobody can do the action; (guar, π) says that everybody can do the action. The last two are not: 1 represents full control over the action (only I can do the action), whereas 0 represents no control over an action (others can do it, but I cannot).

From a deny-guarantee permission, pr, we can extract a pair of rely-guarantee conditions. The rely contains those actions permitted to the environment, while the guarantee contains those permitted to the thread (see Fig. 3).

$$[\![\_]\!] \in \text{PermDG} \to \mathcal{P}(\text{Actions}) \times \mathcal{P}(\text{Actions})$$

$$
\begin{aligned}
[\![pr]\!] \overset{\text{def}}{=} (&\{a \mid pr(a) = (\text{guar}, \_) \vee pr(a) = 0\}, \\
&\{a \mid pr(a) = (\text{guar}, \_) \vee pr(a) = 1\})
\end{aligned}
$$

As shorthand notations, we will use $pr.R$ and $pr.G$ to represent the first and the second element in $[\![pr]\!]$ respectively.

---

[2] We do not consider updates to simultaneous locations as it complicates the presentation.

$$\sigma, pr, \gamma \models B \quad\quad \Longleftrightarrow \quad ([\![B]\!]_\sigma = \mathrm{tt}) \wedge (\forall a.\, pr(a) = 0) \wedge (\gamma = \emptyset)$$

$$\sigma, pr, \gamma \models pr' \quad\quad \Longleftrightarrow \quad (\gamma = \emptyset) \wedge (pr = pr')$$

$$\sigma, pr, \gamma \models \mathsf{full} \quad\quad \Longleftrightarrow \quad (\gamma = \emptyset) \wedge (\forall a.\, pr(a) = 1)$$

$$\sigma, pr, \gamma \models \mathsf{Thread}(E, P) \quad \Longleftrightarrow \quad \gamma = [[\![E]\!]_\sigma \mapsto P]$$

$$\sigma, pr, \gamma \models P_1 * P_2 \quad\quad \Longleftrightarrow \quad \exists pr_1, pr_2, \gamma_1, \gamma_2.\; pr = pr_1 \oplus pr_2 \wedge \gamma = \gamma_1 \uplus \gamma_2$$
$$\wedge\, (\sigma, pr_1, \gamma_1 \models P_1) \wedge (\sigma, pr_2, \gamma_2 \models P_2)$$
$$\text{where } \uplus \text{ means the union of disjoint sets.}$$

$$\sigma, pr, \gamma \models P_1 \twoheadrightarrow P_2 \quad\quad \Longleftrightarrow \quad \forall pr_1, pr_2, \gamma_1, \gamma_2.\; pr_2 = pr \oplus pr_1 \wedge \gamma_2 = \gamma \uplus \gamma_1$$
$$\wedge\, (\sigma, pr_1, \gamma_1 \models P_1) \text{ implies } (\sigma, pr_2, \gamma_2 \models P_2)$$

Fig. 5. Semantics of Assertions

Note that the deny and guar labels come with a fractional coefficient. These coefficients are used in defining the addition of two deny-guarantee fractions.

$$0 \oplus x \overset{\mathrm{def}}{=} x \oplus 0 \overset{\mathrm{def}}{=} x$$

$$(\mathsf{deny}, \pi) \oplus (\mathsf{deny}, \pi') \overset{\mathrm{def}}{=} \text{if } \pi + \pi' < 1 \text{ then } (\mathsf{deny}, \pi + \pi')$$
$$\text{else if } \pi + \pi' = 1 \text{ then } 1 \text{ else undef}$$

$$(\mathsf{guar}, \pi) \oplus (\mathsf{guar}, \pi') \overset{\mathrm{def}}{=} \text{if } \pi + \pi' < 1 \text{ then } (\mathsf{guar}, \pi + \pi')$$
$$\text{else if } \pi + \pi' = 1 \text{ then } 1 \text{ else undef}$$

$$1 \oplus x \overset{\mathrm{def}}{=} x \oplus 1 \overset{\mathrm{def}}{=} \text{if } x = 0 \text{ then } 1 \text{ else undef}$$

The addition of two deny-guarantee permissions, $pr = pr_1 \oplus pr_2$, is defined so that for all $a \in \mathsf{Actions}$, $pr(a) = pr_1(a) \oplus pr_2(a)$. The permission inverse inv is defined so that $\mathsf{inv}(1) = 0$, $\mathsf{inv}(0) = 1$, $\mathsf{inv}(\mathsf{guar}, \pi) = (\mathsf{guar}, 1 - \pi)$, and $\mathsf{inv}(\mathsf{deny}, \pi) = (\mathsf{deny}, 1 - \pi)$.

It is easy to show that addition is commutative, associative, cancellative, and has 0 as a unit element. This allows us to define a separation logic over PermDG.

Assertions and Judgements. The assertions are defined below.

$$P, Q ::= B \mid pr \mid \mathsf{full} \mid \mathsf{false} \mid \mathsf{Thread}(E, P) \mid P \Rightarrow Q \mid P * Q \mid P \twoheadrightarrow Q \mid \exists x.\, P$$

An assertion P is interpreted as a predicate over a program state σ, a permission token pr, and a thread queue γ. A thread queue, as defined below, is a finite partial function mapping thread identifiers to the postcondition established by the thread when it terminates.

$$t \in \mathsf{ThreadIDs} \overset{\mathrm{def}}{=} \mathbb{N} \quad\quad\quad \gamma \in \mathsf{ThreadQueues} \overset{\mathrm{def}}{=} \mathsf{ThreadIDs} \rightharpoonup_{\mathrm{fin}} \mathsf{Assertions}$$

Semantics of assertions is defined in Fig. 5.

The judgments for commands are in the form of $\{P\}\, C\, \{Q\}$. As in Hoare Logic, a command is specified by a precondition (P) and a postcondition (Q). Informally, it means that if the precondition, P, holds in the initial configuration and the environment

$$\frac{P_1 \text{ precise} \quad \{P_1\} \, C \, \{P_2\} \quad x \notin \text{fv}(P_1 * P_3) \quad \text{Thread}(x, P_2) * P_3 \Rightarrow P_4 \quad \text{allowed}([\![x := *]\!], P_3)}{\{P_1 * P_3\} \, x := \textbf{fork}_{[P_1, P_2]} \, C \, \{P_4\}} \text{ (FORK)}$$

$$\frac{}{\{P * \text{Thread}(E, P')\} \, \textbf{join} \, E \, \{P * P'\}} \text{ (JOIN)} \qquad \frac{P_1 \Rightarrow P_1' \quad \{P_1'\} \, C \, \{P_2'\} \quad P_2' \Rightarrow P_2}{\{P_1\} \, C \, \{P_2\}} \text{ (CONS)}$$

$$\frac{\{P\} \, C \, \{P'\} \quad \text{stable}(P_0)}{\{P * P_0\} \, C \, \{P' * P_0\}} \text{ (FRAME)} \qquad \frac{P \Rightarrow [E/x]P' \quad \text{allowed}([\![x := E]\!], P)}{\{P\} \, x := E \, \{P'\}} \text{ (ASSN)}$$

Fig. 6. Proof Rules

adheres to its specification, then the command C is safe to execute; moreover every forked thread will fulfil its specification and if C terminates, the final configuration will satisfy Q. A formal definition of the semantics is presented in §6.

The main proof rules are shown in Fig. 6. The proof rules are covered by a general side-condition requiring that any assertion we write in a triple is *stable*. Intuitively this means that the assertion still holds under any interference from the environment, as expressed in the deny. Requiring stability for every assertion in a triple removes the need for including explicit stability checks in the proof rules, simplifying the presentation.

Definition 1 (Stability). *An assertion P is* stable *(written* stable(P)*) if and only if, for all σ, σ', pr and γ, if $\sigma, pr, \gamma \models P$ and $(\sigma, \sigma') \in pr.R$, then $\sigma', pr, \gamma \models P$.*

The fork and assign rules include allowed-statements, which assert that particular rewrites are permitted by deny-guarantee assertions. Rewrites are given as relations over states. In the rules, we write $[\![x := E]\!]$ for the relation over states denoted by assigning E to x, where E can be $*$ for non-deterministic assignment.

Definition 2 (Allowed). *Let K be a relation over states. Then* allowed(K, P) *holds if and only if, for all σ, σ', pr and γ, if $\sigma, pr, \gamma \models P$ and $(\sigma, \sigma') \in K$, then $(\sigma, \sigma') \in pr.G$.*

The assignment rule is an adaptation of Hoare's assignment axiom for sequential programs. In order to deal with concurrency, it checks that the command has enough permission (pr) to update the shared state.

The fork and join rules modify the rules given in [7]. The fork rule takes a precondition and converts it into a Thread-predicate recording the thread's expected postcondition. The rule checks that any pr satisfying the context P_3 is sufficient to allow assignment to the thread variable x. It requires that the variable x used to store the thread identifier is not in $\text{fv}(P_1 * P_3)$, the free variables for the precondition. As with Gotsman et al. [7], the rule also requires that the precondition P_1 is precise.

The join rule takes a thread predicate and replaces it with the corresponding postcondition. The frame and consequence rules are modified from standard separation-logic rules. Other rules are identical to the standard Hoare logic rules.

```
1   {T₁ * G₂ * G₂ * D₃ * D₃ * L' * x ≠ 1}
2       t1 := fork[T₁*(x≠1),T₁] (if(x==1) error; x := 1)
3   {G₂ * G₂ * D₃ * D₃ * L' * Thread(t1,T₁)}
4       t2 := fork[G₂*D₃,G₂*D₃] (x := 2; if(x==3) error)
5   {G₂ * D₃ * L' * Thread(t1,T₁) * Thread(t2,G₂*D₃)}
6       join t1;
7   {T₁ * G₂ * D₃ * L' * Thread(t2,G₂*D₃)}
8       x := 2;
9   {T₁ * G₂ * D₃ * L' * Thread(t2,G₂*D₃) * x = 2}
10      join t2;
11  {T₁ * G₂ * G₂ * D₃ * D₃ * L' * x = 2}
```

where $T_1 \overset{\text{def}}{=} [x: \mathbb{Z} \rightsquigarrow 1]_1$, $G_2 \overset{\text{def}}{=} [x: \mathbb{Z} \rightsquigarrow 2]_{\frac{1}{2}g}$, $D_3 \overset{\text{def}}{=} [x: \mathbb{Z} \rightsquigarrow 3]_{\frac{1}{2}d}$,

and $L' \overset{\text{def}}{=} [x: \mathbb{Z} \rightsquigarrow \{1,2,3\}]_1 \twoheadrightarrow \text{full}$

Fig. 7. Proof outline of the fork / join example

4   Two-Thread Example

In §2 we said that the program shown in Fig. 1 cannot be verified in conventional rely-guarantee reasoning. We now show that deny-guarantee allows us to verify this example. The proof outline is given in Fig. 7.

We use the following notation to represent permissions. Here $x \in \text{Vars}$, $A, B \subseteq \text{Vals}$ and $f \in \text{FractionDG}$.

$$x: A \rightsquigarrow B \overset{\text{def}}{=} \{(\sigma[x \mapsto v], \sigma[x \mapsto v']) \mid \sigma \in \text{State} \land v \in A \land v' \in B \land v \neq v'\}$$

$$[X]_f \overset{\text{def}}{=} \lambda a. \begin{cases} f & \text{if } a \in X \\ 0 & \text{otherwise} \end{cases}$$

Lemma 3 (Permission splitting).

$$[x: A \rightsquigarrow B \uplus B']_f \iff [x: A \rightsquigarrow B]_f * [x: A \rightsquigarrow B']_f$$
$$[x: A \rightsquigarrow B]_{f \oplus f'} \iff [x: A \rightsquigarrow B]_f * [x: A \rightsquigarrow B]_{f'}$$

Lemma 4 (Permission subtraction). *If P is precise and satisfiable, then $(P \twoheadrightarrow \text{full}) * P \iff \text{full}$.*

Proof. Holds because $(P \twoheadrightarrow Q) * P \iff Q \land (P * \text{true})$ and $\text{full} \Rightarrow P * \text{true}$ hold for any precise and satisfiable P and any Q.   □

The fork / join program has precondition $\{\text{full} * x \neq 1\}$, giving the full permission, 1, on every action. The permission $[x: \mathbb{Z} \rightsquigarrow \{1,2,3\}]_1$ permits any rewrite of the variable x to the value 1, 2 or 3, and prohibits all other rewrites. By Lemma 4,

$$\text{full} \iff ([x: \mathbb{Z} \rightsquigarrow \{1,2,3\}]_1 \twoheadrightarrow \text{full}) * [x: \mathbb{Z} \rightsquigarrow \{1,2,3\}]_1$$

By Lemma 3 can split $[x : \mathbb{Z} \rightsquigarrow \{1,2,3\}]_1$ as follows

$$[x : \mathbb{Z} \rightsquigarrow \{1,2,3\}]_1 \iff [x : \mathbb{Z} \rightsquigarrow 1]_1 * [x : \mathbb{Z} \rightsquigarrow 2]_1 * [x : \mathbb{Z} \rightsquigarrow 3]_1$$
$$\iff T_1 * G_2 * G_2 * D_3 * D_3$$

where T_1, G_2 and D_3 are defined in Fig. 7. We define L' as $([x : \mathbb{Z} \rightsquigarrow \{1,2,3\}]_1 \twoheadrightarrow \text{full})$ (the L used in the proof sketch in Fig. 2 is $L' * G_2 * D_3$). Consequently, we can derive the precondition $\{T_1 * G_2 * G_2 * D_3 * D_3 * L' * x \neq 1\}$

The specification for thread t1 is shown below. Note that $x \neq 1$ is stable because T_1 prevents the environment from writing 1 into x. The post-condition does not include $x = 1$, because T_1 does not prohibit the environment from writing other values into x.

$$\{T_1 * x \neq 1\} \quad \texttt{if(x==1) error; x := 1;} \quad \{T_1\}$$

The specification for thread t2 is shown below. The assertion $x \neq 3$ is stable because the permission D_3 is a deny prohibiting the environment from writing 3 in x. Note that a deny is used rather than full permission because another instance of D_3 is needed to ensure stability of the assertion on line 9, before the main thread joins t2.

$$\{G_2 * D_3\} \quad \texttt{x := 2;} \quad \{G_2 * D_3 * x \neq 3\} \quad \texttt{if(x==3) error} \quad \{G_2 * D_3\}$$

The specifications for t1 and t2 allow us to apply the fork rule (lines 2 and 4). We then join the thread t1 and recover the permission T_1 (line 6). Then we apply the assignment rule for the assignment x := 2 (line 8).

The post-condition $x = 2$ on line 9 is stable because $T_1 * L'$ gives the exclusive permission, 1, on every rewrite except rewrites of x with value 2 or 3, and the deny D_3 prohibits rewrites of x with value 3. Consequently the only permitted interference from the environment is to write 2 into x, so $x = 2$ is stable.

Finally we apply the join rule, collect the permissions held by the thread t2, and complete the proof.

5 Encoding Rely-Guarantee Reasoning

In this section, we show that the traditional rely-guarantee reasoning can be embedded into our deny-guarantee reasoning. First, we present an encoding of parallel composition using the fork and join commands, and derive a proof rule. Then, we prove that every rely-guarantee proof for programs using parallel composition can be translated into a corresponding deny-guarantee proof.

5.1 Adding Parallel Composition

We encode parallel composition into our language by the following translation:

$$C_1 \parallel_{(x,P_1,Q_1)} C_2 \overset{\text{def}}{=} \ x := \textbf{fork}_{[P_1,Q_1]} \ C_1; \ C_2; \ \textbf{join} \ x$$

Here the annotations P_1, Q_1 are required to provide the translation onto the **fork**, which requires annotations. x is an intermediate variable used to hold the identifier for thread

C_1. We assume that x is a fresh variable that is not used in C_1 or C_2. The parallel composition rule for deny-guarantee is as follows:

$$\frac{\{P_1\}\, C_1\, \{Q_1\} \quad \{P_2\}\, C_2\, \{Q_2\} \quad \text{x} \notin \text{fv}(P_1,P_2,C_1,C_2,Q_1,Q_2) \quad P_1 \text{ precise}}{\{P_1 * P_2 * \text{full}(\text{x})\}\, C_1\, \|_{(\text{x},P_1,Q_1)}\, C_2\, \{Q_1 * Q_2 * \text{full}(\text{x})\}} \quad \text{(PAR)}$$

Modulo the side-conditions about x and precision, and the full(x) star-conjunct, this is the same rule as in separation logic. The assertion full(x) stands for the full permission on the variable x; that is, we have full permission to assign any value to x.

$$\text{full}(\text{x})(\sigma,\sigma') \overset{\text{def}}{=} \text{ if } \sigma[x \mapsto v] = \sigma' \wedge v \neq \sigma(x) \text{ then } 1, \text{ else } 0$$

We extend this notation to sets of variables: $\text{full}(\{\text{x}_1,\ldots,\text{x}_n\}) \overset{\text{def}}{=} \text{full}(\text{x}_1) \oplus \ldots \oplus \text{full}(\text{x}_n)$.

Precision is required as the underlying **fork** rule requires it. This makes this rule weaker than if we directly represented the parallel composition in the semantics.

Lemma 5. *The parallel composition rule can be derived from the rules given in Fig. 6.*

Proof. The proof has the following outline.

$$\{P_1 * P_2 * \text{full}(\text{x})\}$$
$$\text{x} := \textbf{fork}_{[P_1,Q_1]}\, C_1$$
$$\{\text{Thread}(\text{x},Q_1) * P_2 * \text{full}(\text{x})\}$$
$$C_2$$
$$\{\text{Thread}(\text{x},Q_1) * Q_2 * \text{full}(\text{x})\}$$
$$\textbf{join x}$$
$$\{Q_1 * Q_2 * \text{full}(\text{x})\}$$

The first step uses the first premise, and the frame and fork rules. The second step uses the second premise and the frame rule. The final step uses the frame and join rules.

5.2 Translation

Now let us consider the translation of rely-guarantee proofs into the deny-guarantee framework. The encoding of parallel composition into **fork** and **join** introduces extra variables, so we partition variables in constructed fork-join programs into two kinds: Vars, the original program variables, and TVars, variables introduced to carry thread identifiers. We will assume that the relies and guarantees from the original proof assume that the TVars are unchanged.

In §3, we showed how to extract a pair of rely-guarantee conditions from permissions $pr \in \text{PermDG}$. Conversely, we can encode rely-guarantee pairs into sets of PermDG permissions as follows:

$$[\![\_]\!] \quad \in \mathcal{P}(\text{Actions}) \times \mathcal{P}(\text{Actions}) \to \mathcal{P}(\text{PermDG})$$

$$[\![R,G]\!] \overset{\text{def}}{=} \{\langle R,G \rangle_F \mid F \in \text{Actions} \to (0,1)\}$$

$$\langle R,G \rangle_F \overset{\text{def}}{=} \lambda a. \begin{cases} (\text{guar}, F(a)) & a \in R \wedge a \in G \\ 0 & a \in R \wedge a \notin G \\ 1 & a \notin R \wedge a \in G \\ (\text{deny}, F(a)) & a \notin R \wedge a \notin G \end{cases}$$

First, we show that our translation is non-empty: each pair maps to something:

Lemma 6 (Non-empty translation). $\forall R, G. \; [\![R, G]\!] \neq \emptyset$

By algebraic manipulation, we can show that the definition above corresponds to the following more declarative definition:

Lemma 7. $[\![R, G]\!] = \{pr \mid [\![pr]\!] = (R, G)\}$

Moreover, as R and G assume that the TVars are unchanged, the following lemma holds:

Lemma 8. *If* $pr \in [\![R, G]\!]$, *and* $X \subseteq$ TVars, *then* $full(X) \oplus pr$ *is defined.*

Now, we can translate rely-guarantee judgements into a non-empty set of equivalent triples in deny-guarantee. Non-emptiness follows from Lemmas 6 and 8.

Definition 9 (Triple translation).

$$[\![R, G \vdash_{RG} \{P\} \, C \, \{Q\}]\!]_X \stackrel{\text{def}}{=} \forall pr \in [\![R, G]\!].\exists C'. \; \vdash \{P * pr * full(X)\} \; C' \; \{Q * pr * full(X)\}$$
$$\wedge \; C = erase(C')$$

where the set $X \subseteq$ TVars *carries the set of identifiers used in the parallel compositions, and* $erase(C')$ *is* C' *with all annotations removed from parallel compositions.*

Note that the judgement $R, G \vdash_{RG} \{P\} \, C \, \{Q\}$ in traditional rely-guarantee reasoning does not need annotations in C. The C is a cleaned-up version of some annotated statement C'. We elide the standard rely-guarantee rules here. This translation allows us to state the following theorem:

Theorem 10 (Complete embedding). *If* $R, G \vdash_{RG} \{P\} \, C \, \{Q\}$ *is derivable according to the rely-guarantee proof rules, then* $[\![R, G \vdash_{RG} \{P\} \, C \, \{Q\}]\!]_X$ *holds.*

In other words, given a proof in rely-guarantee, we can construct an equivalent proof using deny-guarantee. We prove this theorem by considering each rely-guarantee proof rule separately, and showing that the translated versions of the rely-guarantee proof rules are sound in deny-guarantee. Below we give proofs of the two most interesting rules: the rule of parallel composition and of weakening. For each of these, we first need a corresponding helper lemma for the translation of the rely-guarantee conditions. These helper lemmas follow from the definitions of PermDG and $[\![R, G]\!]$.

Lemma 11 (Composition). *If* $G_1 \subseteq R_2$, $G_2 \subseteq R_1$, *and* $pr \in [\![R_1 \cap R_2, G_1 \cup G_2]\!]$, *then there exist* pr_1, pr_2 *such that* $pr = pr_1 \oplus pr_2$ *and* $pr_1 \in [\![R_1, G_1]\!]$ *and* $pr_2 \in [\![R_2, G_2]\!]$.

Lemma 12 (Soundness of translated parallel rule).
If $G_2 \subseteq R_1$, $G_1 \subseteq R_2$, $[\![R_1, G_1 \vdash_{RG} \{P_1\}C_1\{Q_1\}]\!]_X$ *and* $[\![R_2, G_2 \vdash_{RG} \{P_2\}C_2\{Q_2\}]\!]_Y$, *then* $[\![R_1 \cap R_2, G_1 \cup G_2 \vdash_{RG} \{P_1 \wedge P_2\}C_1 \parallel C_2\{Q_1 \wedge Q_2\}]\!]_{\{x\} \uplus X \uplus Y}$.

Lemma 13 (Weakening). *If* $R_2 \subseteq R_1$, $G_1 \subseteq G_2$, *and* $pr \in [\![R_2, G_2]\!]$ *then there exist permissions* pr_1, pr_2 *such that* $pr = pr_1 \oplus pr_2$ *and* $pr_1 \in [\![R_1, G_1]\!]$.

Lemma 14 (Soundness of translated weakening rule). *If* $R_2 \subseteq R_1$, $G_1 \subseteq G_2$, *and* $[\![R_1, G_1 \vdash_{RG} \{P\}C\{Q\}]\!]_X$, *then* $[\![R_2, G_2 \vdash_{RG} \{P\}C\{Q\}]\!]_X$.

6 Semantics and Soundness

The operational semantics of the language is defined in Fig. 8. The semantics is divided into two parts: the local semantics and the global semantics. The local semantics is closely related to the interpretation of the logical judgements, while the global semantics can easily be erased to a machine semantics. This erasure and other additional definitions and proofs can be found in the associated technical report [4].

Local Semantics. The local semantics represents the view of execution from a single thread. It is defined using the constructs described in §3. The commands all work with an abstraction of the environment: γ abstracts the other threads, and carries their final states; and pr abstracts the interference from other threads and the interference that it is allowed to generate. The semantics will result in **abort** if it does not respect the abstraction.

The first two rules, in Fig. 8, deal with assignment. If the assignment is allowed by pr, then it executes successfully, otherwise the program aborts signalling an error. The next two rules handle the joining of threads. If the thread being joined with is in γ, then that thread's terminal pr' and γ' are added to the current thread before the current thread continues executing. We annotate the transition with **join** (t, pr', γ'), so the semantics can be reused in the global semantics. If the thread identifier is not in γ, we signal an error as we are joining on a thread that we do not have permission to join. The next two rules deal with forking new threads. If part of the state satisfies P then we remove that part of the state, and extend our environment with a new thread that will terminate in a state satisfying Q. If there is no part of the state satisfying P, then we will raise an error as we do not have the permission to give to the new thread. The remaining local rules deal with sequential composition.

In the next section of Fig. 8, we define $\overset{r}{\leadsto}$, which represents the environment performing an action. We also define $\leadsto^*$ as the transitive and reflexive closure of the operational semantics extended with the environment action.

Given this semantics, we say a local thread is safe if it will not reach an error state.

Definition 15. $\vdash (C, \sigma, pr, \gamma)$ *safe* $\iff \neg((C, \sigma, pr, \gamma) \leadsto^*$ *abort*$)$

We can give the semantics of the judgements from earlier in terms of this local operational semantics.

Definition 16 (Semantics of a triple). $\models \{P\}C\{Q\}$ *asserts that, if* $\sigma, pr, \gamma \models P$, *then*

- *(1)* $\vdash (C, \sigma, pr, \gamma)$ *safe; and*
- *(2) if* $(C, \sigma, pr, \gamma) \leadsto^*$ (**skip**$, \sigma', pr', \gamma')$, *then* $\sigma', pr', \gamma' \models Q$.

As the programs carry annotations for each **fork**, we need to define programs that are well-annotated, that is, the code for each fork satisfies its specification.

Definition 17 (Well-annotated command). *We define a command as well-annotated,* $\vdash C$ *wa, as follows*

$$\vdash \mathbf{fork}_{[P,Q]}\, C\ \textsf{wa} \iff \models \{P\}C\{Q\} \wedge \vdash C\ \textsf{wa}$$
$$\vdash \mathbf{skip}\ \textsf{wa} \iff always$$
$$\vdash C_1; C_2\ \textsf{wa} \iff \vdash C_1\ \textsf{wa} \wedge \vdash C_2\ \textsf{wa}$$

$$\cdots$$

Local semantics

$$\frac{[E]_\sigma = n \quad (\sigma, \sigma[x \mapsto n]) \in pr.G}{(x := E, \sigma, pr, \gamma) \rightsquigarrow (\mathbf{skip}, \sigma[x \mapsto n], pr, \gamma)} \qquad \frac{[E]_\sigma = n \quad (\sigma, \sigma[x \mapsto n]) \notin pr.G}{(x := E, \sigma, pr, \gamma) \rightsquigarrow \mathbf{abort}}$$

$$\frac{[E]_\sigma = t \quad \gamma(t) = Q \quad \sigma, pr', \gamma' \models Q}{(\mathbf{join}\ E, \sigma, pr, \gamma) \overset{\mathbf{join}\ (t, pr', \gamma')}{\rightsquigarrow} (\mathbf{skip}, \sigma, pr \oplus pr', (\gamma \setminus t) \uplus \gamma')} \qquad \frac{[E]_\sigma = t \quad t \notin dom(\gamma)}{(\mathbf{join}\ E, \sigma, pr, \gamma) \rightsquigarrow \mathbf{abort}}$$

$$\frac{t \notin dom(\gamma) \quad \sigma, pr', \gamma' \models P \quad pr = pr' \oplus pr'' \quad \gamma = \gamma' \uplus \gamma'' \quad (\sigma, \sigma[x \mapsto t]) \in pr.G}{(x := \mathbf{fork}_{[P,Q]}\ C, \sigma, pr, \gamma) \overset{\mathbf{fork}\ (t, C, pr', \gamma')}{\rightsquigarrow} (\mathbf{skip}, \sigma[x \mapsto t], pr'', \gamma''[t \mapsto Q])}$$

$$\frac{\sigma, pr, \gamma \not\models P * \mathbf{true}}{(x := \mathbf{fork}_{[P,Q]}\ C, \sigma, pr, \gamma) \rightsquigarrow \mathbf{abort}} \qquad \frac{(\sigma, \sigma[x \mapsto t]) \notin pr.G}{(x := \mathbf{fork}_{[P,Q]}\ C, \sigma, pr, \gamma) \rightsquigarrow \mathbf{abort}}$$

$$\frac{(C, \sigma, pr, \gamma) \rightsquigarrow (C', \sigma', pr', \gamma')}{(C; C'', \sigma, pr, \gamma) \rightsquigarrow (C'; C'', \sigma', pr', \gamma')} \qquad (\mathbf{skip}; C, \sigma, pr, \gamma) \rightsquigarrow (C, \sigma, pr, \gamma)$$

$$\frac{(C, \sigma, pr, \gamma) \rightsquigarrow \mathbf{abort}}{(C; C', \sigma, pr, \gamma) \rightsquigarrow \mathbf{abort}}$$

Interference

$$\frac{(\sigma, \sigma') \in pr.R}{(C, \sigma, pr, \gamma) \overset{r}{\rightsquigarrow} (C, \sigma', pr, \gamma)} \qquad \frac{\forall (t \mapsto C, pr, \gamma) \in \delta. \ (\sigma, \sigma') \in pr.R}{(\sigma, \delta) \overset{r}{\Longmapsto} (\sigma', \delta)}$$

Global semantics

$$\frac{(C, \sigma, pr, \gamma) \rightsquigarrow (C', \sigma', pr', \gamma') \quad (\sigma, \delta) \overset{r}{\Longmapsto} (\sigma', \delta')}{(\sigma, [t \mapsto C, pr, \gamma] \uplus \delta) \Longmapsto (\sigma', [t \mapsto C', pr', \gamma'] \uplus \delta')}$$

$$\frac{(C, \sigma, pr, \gamma) \overset{\mathbf{fork}\ (t_2, C_2, pr_2, \gamma_2)}{\rightsquigarrow} (C', \sigma', pr', \gamma') \quad (\sigma, \delta) \overset{r}{\Longmapsto} (\sigma', \delta')}{(\sigma, [t_1 \mapsto C, pr, \gamma] \uplus \delta) \Longmapsto (\sigma', [t \mapsto C', pr', \gamma'] \uplus [t_2 \mapsto C_2, pr_2, \gamma_2] \uplus \delta')}$$

$$\frac{(C, \sigma, pr, \gamma) \overset{\mathbf{join}\ (t_2, pr_2, \gamma_2)}{\rightsquigarrow} (C', \sigma', pr', \gamma') \quad (\sigma, \delta) \overset{r}{\Longmapsto} (\sigma', \delta')}{(\sigma, [t_1 \mapsto C, pr, \gamma] \uplus [t_2 \mapsto \mathbf{skip}, pr_2, \gamma_2] \uplus \delta) \Longmapsto (\sigma', [t \mapsto C', pr', \gamma'] \uplus \delta')}$$

$$\frac{(C, \sigma, pr, \gamma) \rightsquigarrow \mathbf{abort}}{(\sigma, [t \mapsto C, pr, \gamma] \uplus \delta) \Longmapsto \mathbf{abort}} \qquad \frac{(C, \sigma, pr, \gamma) \overset{r}{\rightsquigarrow} (C, \sigma', pr', \gamma') \quad \neg(\exists \delta'. (\sigma, \delta) \overset{r}{\Longmapsto} (\sigma', \delta'))}{(\sigma, [t \mapsto C, pr, \gamma] \uplus \delta) \Longmapsto \mathbf{abort}}$$

$$\frac{(C, \sigma, pr, \gamma) \overset{\mathbf{join}\ (t_2, pr_3, \gamma_3)}{\rightsquigarrow} (C', \sigma', pr', \gamma') \quad \neg((C, \sigma, pr, \gamma) \overset{\mathbf{join}\ (t_2, pr_2, \gamma_2)}{\rightsquigarrow} (C', \sigma', pr', \gamma'))}{(\sigma, [t_1 \mapsto C, pr, \gamma] \uplus [t_2 \mapsto \mathbf{skip}, pr_2, \gamma_2] \uplus \delta) \Longmapsto \mathbf{abort}}$$

Fig. 8. Operational Semantics

Given these definitions we can now state soundness of our logic with respect to the local semantics.

Theorem 18 (Local soundness). *If* $\vdash \{P\}C\{Q\}$*, then* $\models \{P\}C\{Q\}$ *and* $\vdash C$ **wa**.

Global Semantics. Now we will consider the operational semantics of the whole machine, that is, for all the threads. This semantics is designed as a stepping stone between the local semantics and the concrete machine semantics. We need an additional abstraction of the global thread-queue.

$$\delta \in \mathsf{GThrdQ} \stackrel{\mathsf{def}}{=} \mathsf{ThreadIDs} \rightharpoonup_{\mathrm{fin}} \mathsf{Stmts} \times \mathsf{PermDG} \times \mathsf{ThreadQueues}$$

In the third part of Fig. 8, we present the global operational semantics. The first rule progresses one thread, and advances the rest with a corresponding environment action. The second rule deals with removing a thread from a machine when it is successfully joined. Here the label ensures that the local semantics uses the same final state for the thread as it actually has. The third rule creates a new thread. Again the label carries the information required to ensure the local thread semantics has the same operation as the global machine.

The three remaining rules deal with the cases when something goes wrong. The first rule says that if the local semantics can fault, then the global semantics can also. The second raises an error if a thread performs an action that cannot be accepted as a legal environment action by other threads. The final rule raises an error if a thread has terminated and another thread tries to join on it, but cannot join with the right final state.

We can prove the soundness of our logic with respect to this global semantics.

Theorem 19 (Global soundness). *If* $\vdash \{P\}C\{Q\}$ *and* $\sigma, 1, \emptyset \models P$*, then*

- $\neg((\sigma, [t \mapsto C, 1, \emptyset]) \Longrightarrow^* \textbf{abort})$*; and*
- *if* $(\sigma, [t \mapsto C, 1, \emptyset]) \Longrightarrow^* (\sigma', [t \mapsto \textbf{skip}, pr, \gamma])$ *then* $\sigma', pr, \gamma \models Q$.

This says, if we have proved a program and it does not initially require any other threads, then we can execute it without reaching **abort**, and if it terminates the final state will satisfy the postcondition.

7   Conclusions and Future Developments

In this paper we have demonstrated that deny-guarantee enables reasoning about programs using dynamically scoped threads, that is, programs using fork to create new threads and join to wait for their termination. Rely-guarantee cannot reason about this form of concurrency. Our extension borrows ideas from separation logic to enable an interference to be split dynamically with a logical operation, *.

We have applied the deny-guarantee method to a setting with only a pre-allocated set of global variables. However, deny-guarantee extends naturally to a setting with memory allocation and deallocation.

Deny-guarantee can be applied to separation logic in much the same way as rely-guarantee, because the deny-guarantee approach is largely orthogonal to the presence of the heap. Deny-guarantee permissions can be made into *heap permissions* by defining actions as binary relations over heaps, rather than over states with fixed global variables.

The SAGL [5] and RGSep [12] approaches can be easily extended to a setting with fork and join by using heap permissions in place of relies and guarantees.

Finally, deny-guarantee may allow progress on the problem of reasoning about dynamically-allocated locks in the heap. Previous work in this area, such as [7] and [9], has associated locks with invariants. With deny-guarantee we can associate locks with heap permissions, and make use of compositional deny-guarantee reasoning. However, considerable challenges remain, in particular the problems of recursive stability checking and of locks which refer to themselves (Landin's 'knots in the store'). We will address these challenges in future work.

Acknowledgements. We should like to thank Alexey Gotsman, Tony Hoare, Tom Ridge, Kristin Rozier, Sam Staton, John Wickerson and the anonymous referees for comments on this paper. We acknowledge funding from EPSRC grant EP/F019394/1 (Parkinson and Dodds) and a Royal Academy of Engineering / EPSRC fellowship (Parkinson).

References

[1] Bornat, R., Calcagno, C., O'Hearn, P., Parkinson, M.: Permission accounting in separation logic. In: POPL 2005, pp. 259–270. ACM Press, New York (2005)

[2] Boyland, J.: Checking interference with fractional permissions. In: Cousot, R. (ed.) SAS 2003. LNCS, vol. 2694, pp. 55–72. Springer, Heidelberg (2003)

[3] Calcagno, C., O'Hearn, P.W., Yang, H.: Local action and abstract separation logic. In: LICS 2007, pp. 366–378. IEEE Computer Society, Los Alamitos (2007)

[4] Dodds, M., Feng, X., Parkinson, M., Vafeiadis, V.: Deny-guarantee reasoning (extended version and formalization in Isabelle). Technical Report UCAM-CL-TR-736, University of Cambridge (2009),
http://www.cl.cam.ac.uk/techreports/UCAM-CL-TR-736.html

[5] Feng, X., Ferreira, R., Shao, Z.: On the relationship between concurrent separation logic and assume-guarantee reasoning. In: De Nicola, R. (ed.) ESOP 2007. LNCS, vol. 4421, pp. 173–188. Springer, Heidelberg (2007)

[6] Feng, X., Shao, Z.: Modular verification of concurrent assembly code with dynamic thread creation and termination. In: ICFP 2005, pp. 254–267. ACM Press, New York (2005)

[7] Gotsman, A., Berdine, J., Cook, B., Rinetzky, N., Sagiv, M.: Local reasoning for storable locks and threads. In: Shao, Z. (ed.) APLAS 2007. LNCS, vol. 4807, pp. 19–37. Springer, Heidelberg (2007)

[8] Haack, C., Hurlin, C.: Separation logic contracts for a java-like language with fork/join. In: Meseguer, J., Roşu, G. (eds.) AMAST 2008. LNCS, vol. 5140, pp. 199–215. Springer, Heidelberg (2008)

[9] Hobor, A., Appel, A.W., Nardelli, F.Z.: Oracle semantics for concurrent separation logic. In: Drossopoulou, S. (ed.) ESOP 2008. LNCS, vol. 4960, pp. 353–367. Springer, Heidelberg (2008)

[10] Jones, C.B.: Tentative steps toward a development method for interfering programs. ACM Trans. Program. Lang. Syst. 5(4), 596–619 (1983)

[11] Jones, C.B.: Annotated bibliography on rely/guarantee conditions (2007),
http://homepages.cs.ncl.ac.uk/cliff.jones/ftp-stuff/rg-hist.pdf

[12] Vafeiadis, V., Parkinson, M.: A marriage of rely/guarantee and separation logic. In: Caires, L., Vasconcelos, V.T. (eds.) CONCUR 2007. LNCS, vol. 4703, pp. 256–271. Springer, Heidelberg (2007)

A Basis for Verifying Multi-threaded Programs

K. Rustan M. Leino[0] and Peter Müller[1]

[0] Microsoft Research, Redmond, WA, USA
leino@microsoft.com
[1] ETH Zurich, Switzerland
peter.mueller@inf.ethz.ch

Abstract. Advanced multi-threaded programs apply concurrency concepts in so-phisticated ways. For instance, they use fine-grained locking to increase paral-lelism and change locking orders dynamically when data structures are being reorganized. This paper presents a sound and modular verification methodology that can handle advanced concurrency patterns in multi-threaded, object-based programs. The methodology is based on implicit dynamic frames and uses frac-tional permissions to support fine-grained locking. It supports concepts such as multi-object monitor invariants, thread-local and shared objects, thread pre- and postconditions, and deadlock prevention with a dynamically changeable locking order. The paper prescribes the generation of verification conditions in first-order logic, well-suited for scrutiny by off-the-shelf SMT solvers. A verifier for the methodology has been implemented for an experimental language, and has been used to verify several challenging examples including hand-over-hand locking for linked lists and a lock re-ordering algorithm.

0 Introduction

Mainstream concurrent programs use multiple threads and synchronization through locks or monitors. To increase parallelism and to reduce the locking overhead, they apply these concurrency concepts in sophisticated ways. They use fine-grained lock-ing to permit several threads to access a data structure concurrently. They distinguish between thread-local and shared objects to avoid unnecessary locking of thread-local objects, and they allow objects to transition from thread-local to shared and back. They dynamically change locking orders, which are used to prevent deadlocks, when data structures are being reorganized. They distinguish between read and write accesses to permit concurrent reading but ensure exclusive writing. Several other such concurrency patterns are described in the literature [16,9].

These patterns improve the performance and flexibility of programs, but also com-plicate reasoning. For instance, fine-grained locking often requires that several locks be acquired before a field can be updated safely. Omitting one of the locks potentially leads to inconsistent data structures. Consider for example a sorted linked list, where each node has to maintain a monitor invariant such as $next \neq \textbf{null} \Rightarrow val \leq next.val$. Updating a field $n.val$ potentially breaks the invariant of n and n's predecessor in the list. Consequently, the monitors of both objects have to be acquired before updating $n.val$, and the monitor invariants of both monitors have to be checked when they are released. This problem does not occur with coarse-grained locking, where invariants

G. Castagna (Ed.): ESOP 2009, LNCS 5502, pp. 378–393, 2009.
© Springer-Verlag Berlin Heidelberg 2009

over several objects can be associated with the (single) lock for the whole data structure. Other advanced concurrency patterns also lead to subtle correctness conditions, which is one of the reasons why concurrent programs are so difficult to get right.

A standard verification technique for concurrent programs is to proceed in two steps. First, the code is divided into atomic sections. Second, sequential reasoning is used within each atomic section and rely-guarantee reasoning [14,20] between atomic sections. Advanced concurrency patterns complicate especially the first step because atomicity is not always achieved by acquiring a single lock; instead, the permission to access a field may be justified by thread-locality, by acquiring one or more locks, or by sharing fields just among readers.

In this paper, we present a verification methodology for multi-threaded, object-based programs that handles all of these complications. It verifies the absence of data races and deadlocks, and that implementations satisfy their contracts. We build on Smans et al.'s implicit dynamic frames [18] and extend them to concurrent programs. Contracts such as monitor invariants specify access permissions along with conditions on variables. Evaluating these contracts transfers these access permissions, for instance from a monitor to the thread that acquires the monitor. To support fine-grained locking and concurrent reading, we use Boyland's fractional permissions [4], which allow us to split the access permission for a field among several monitors or threads. The permission accounting is similar to previous work on concurrent separation logic [2,8], but our approach generates verification conditions in first-order logic, well-suited for off-the-shelf SMT solvers such as Z3 [6]. Finally, our methodology permits not a fixed but a changeable locking order among monitors. We have implemented a verifier for our methodology for an experimental language called Chalice, and have used it to verify automatically several challenging examples including hand-over-hand locking for linked lists and a lock re-ordering algorithm.

Outline. The next three sections present our verification methodology informally: Section 1 explains permissions, Section 2 discusses shared objects and thread synchronization, and Section 3 shows how we prevent deadlocks. The formal encoding including proof obligations is presented in Section 4. We discuss related work in Section 5 and conclude in Section 6.

1   Permissions

A thread may access a heap location only if it has the permission to do so. Abstractly, a *permission* is a percentage between 0 and 100%, inclusive. A permission of 100% means the thread has exclusive access to the location, which in particular means it is allowed to write the location. Any non-zero permission means the thread is allowed to read the location. Our methodology ensures that for each location, the sum of permissions held by the various threads is between 0 and 100%, inclusive; what remains up to 100% is held by the system or by an un-acquired monitor.

Specification of Access Permissions. To support modular verification, we specify for each method in its precondition the permissions that it requires from its caller, and

```
class Cell {
  int val ;

  Cell Clone()
    requires rd(this.val) ;
    ensures acc(result.val) ∧ rd(this.val) ;
  {
    Cell tmp := new Cell ;
    tmp.val := this.val ;
    return tmp ;
  }
}
```

Fig. 0. A simple example with read and write permissions

in its postcondition the permissions that it returns to its caller. The *full permission* of 100% for a field f of an object o is denoted by $acc(o.f)$. A *fractional permission* of n% is denoted by $acc(o.f, n)$; that is, $acc(o.f)$ is a shorthand for $acc(o.f, 100)$. Finally, $rd(o.f)$ denotes one *infinitesimal permission* ε, $rd(o.f, k)$ denotes k such permissions, and $rd(o.f, *)$ denotes an inexhaustible supply of ε permissions.

For instance, method *Clone* in Fig. 0 requires read permission for the location this.*val*. For a call to $o.Clone()$, the executing thread must possess a non-zero permission for $o.val$. With implicit dynamic frames, frame axioms for methods are expressed implicitly through the specification of access permissions in pre- and postconditions. Instead of providing a separate frame axiom that describes changes of permissions, the evaluation of an assertion changes the permissions. Upon a call to $o.Clone()$, the caller is deprived of the permission required by the precondition, that is, an ε-permission for $o.val$, which is transferred to the callee. Therefore, in the callee method, one may assume that the current thread has at least an ε-permission for $o.val$. However, after the call, the caller may assume this permission only if it is explicitly returned by the method through an appropriate postcondition. This is the case in our example, where the postcondition provides full permission for **result**.*val* and read permission for **this**.*val*. If one omitted $rd(\text{this}.val)$ from *Clone*'s postcondition, the caller would not re-gain the permission it had before the call; the executing thread would lose an ε-permission for $o.val$, which would be retained by the system. From then on, no thread could ever obtain full permission for $o.val$, and the location would be immutable.

This form of permission transfer is similar to reasoning in linear logic or capability systems [19]. In particular, the predicate $acc(x) \land acc(x)$ is equivalent to false, just like $x \mapsto \_ * x \mapsto \_$ is false in separation logic.

Since method calls change the permissions that may be assumed for the executing thread, it is often useful to think of permissions as being held by method executions rather than by threads. The situation is analogous for loops, where the loop invariant specifies the permissions required and provided by a loop iteration.

Since the evaluation of specifications leads to a transfer of permissions, it must be possible to infer from a specification which permissions to transfer. Therefore, the acc and rd predicates may occur only in positive positions, and not under a quantifier.

Obtaining and Using Permissions. A thread can obtain permissions in four ways: First, when a thread creates a new object o, it obtains full permission for all fields of o. This exclusive access is justified because o is thread-local until it is explicitly shared with other threads, as we explain below. Second, when a thread acquires the monitor of an object o, it obtains the permissions held by the monitor. The monitor obtained these permissions from the thread that initially shared the object. They are then transferred between the monitor and a thread each time the monitor is acquired or released. Third, when a new thread is forked for an object o, it obtains the permissions required by the precondition of o's Run method. The forking thread is deprived of these permissions. Fourth, when a thread is joined, the joining thread obtains the permissions provided by the postcondition of the Run method of the joined thread, which has then terminated.

Permissions are used to access locations. Each read access to a location $o.f$ generates a proof obligation that the current thread possesses a non-zero permission for $o.f$. Each write access to $o.f$ generates a proof obligation that the current thread possesses full permission for $o.f$.

In method $Clone$ (Fig. 0), the read access to **this**.val is permitted because the precondition guarantees that the executing thread has a non-zero permission for this location. The write access to $tmp.val$ is permitted because after tmp's creation, the executing thread has full permission. An attempt to modify **this**.val would fail because $Clone$'s precondition does not allow one to prove that the executing thread has full permission for this location.

2   Shared Objects

It is possible to share objects between threads. To make a thread-local object available for sharing, the object is first given to the system, which then synchronizes accesses using monitors to ensure a suitable level of mutual exclusion. It is also possible for a shared object to be un-shared, that is, to become thread-local after a period of being shared. In this section, we describe sharing and synchronization, and how they affect access permissions.

Monitors. Objects can be used as *monitors*—locks that protect a set of locations and an invariant [5,10]. While an object is shared, a thread can acquire it using the **acquire** statement and then release it using the **release** statement. We say that a thread *holds a monitor* if it has acquired, but not yet released the monitor.

The system manages a shared object under a specified *monitor invariant*, declared in the object's class with an **invariant** declaration. Our methodology ensures that the monitor invariant of an object o holds whenever o is shared and o's monitor is not held by any thread. This can be proved by making the monitor invariant a precondition of the share and release operations and a postcondition of the acquire operation.

Like method contracts, monitor invariants specify access permissions along with conditions on variables. For shared objects, these permissions are held by the monitor whenever it is not held by a thread. When a thread acquires the monitor, the permissions are transferred to the acquiring thread, and they are transferred back to the monitor upon release.

```
class Node {
    int val ;
    Node next ;
    int sum ;

    invariant acc(next) ∧ rd(val) ;
    invariant next ≠ null ⇒ rd(next.val) ∧ val ≤ next.val ;
    invariant acc(sum, 50) ∧ (next = null ⇒ sum = 0) ;
    invariant next ≠ null ⇒ acc(next.sum, 50) ∧ sum = next.val + next.sum ;
    invariant acc(μ, 50) ∧ (next ≠ null ⇒ acc(next.μ, 50) ∧ μ ⊏ next.μ) ;
}
```

Fig. 1. Nodes of a sorted linked list

We illustrate monitor invariants using the linked-list implementation in Fig. 1. Every node of the list stores an integer value, a reference to the next node in the list, and the sum of all values stored in all the successors of the current node. Here, we discuss the first four invariants of class $Node$; the fifth invariant has to do with sharing and the locking order and is discussed later.

The first monitor invariant expresses that the monitor possesses full permission for **this**.$next$ and read permission for **this**.val. (We omit the receiver **this** in programs and when it is clear from the context.) Consequently, when a thread acquires the monitor of a node n, it may read and write $n.next$ and read $n.val$. Having at least read permission for these locations allows them to be mentioned in the monitor invariant. For instance, the second invariant states that if there is a successor node, then the present monitor also has read permission for the val field of the successor and that the two nodes are sorted according to their values.

It is important to understand that the monitor invariant of an object o may depend on a location $x.f$ only if o's monitor has (at least) read permission for $x.f$. If this is not the case, the invariant is rejected by the verifier. This requirement is necessary for soundness. For instance, if the invariant of $Node$ did not require $rd(val)$, then it might be possible for some thread to obtain full permission for $n.val$ without acquiring n's monitor. The full permission could then be used to modify $n.val$ and break n's second invariant. When n's monitor is later acquired by another thread, that thread would assume the invariant even though it does not hold, which is unsound.

The third invariant expresses that the monitor holds a fractional permission of 50% for **this**.sum. Therefore, the invariant is allowed to depend on this location. The fourth invariant states that if there is a successor node, then the present monitor also holds a 50%-permission for the successor's sum location and may, thus, depend on it in its invariant. Using 50%-permissions enables a thread to get full permission for $n.sum$ by acquiring the monitors of n and n's predecessor. It is indeed necessary to acquire both monitors before updating this location because a modification potentially affects the (third) monitor invariant of n as well as the (fourth) monitor invariant of n's predecessor. So both invariants must be checked after an update of $n.sum$, which happens when the monitors are released.

```
class List {
    Node head ;      // sentinel node
    int sum ;

    invariant acc(head) ∧ head ≠ null ;
    invariant rd(head.val) ∧ head.val = −1 ;
    invariant acc(sum, 20) ∧ acc(head.sum, 50) ∧ sum = head.sum ;
    invariant rd(μ) ∧ acc(head.μ, 50) ∧ μ ⊑ head.μ ;

    void Init()
        requires acc(head) ∧ acc(sum) ;
        requires acc(μ) ∧ μ = ⊥ ;
        ensures acc(sum, 80) ∧ sum = 0 ;
        ensures rd(μ) ∧ maxlock ⊑ μ ;
    {
        Node t := new Node ; t.val := − 1 ; t.next := null ; t.sum := 0 ;
        share t between maxlock and  ;
        head := t ; sum := 0 ;
        share this between maxlock and t ;
    }

    void Insert(int x)
        requires acc(sum, 80) ∧ 0 ≤ x ∧ rd(μ) ∧ maxlock ⊑ μ ;
        ensures acc(sum, 80) ∧ sum = old(sum) + x ∧ rd(μ) ∧ maxlock ⊑ μ ;
    {
        acquire this ; sum := sum + x ;
        Node p := head ; acquire p ; p.sum := p.sum + x ;
        release this ;
        while (p.next ≠ null ∧ p.next.val < x)
        invariant p ≠ null ∧ acc(p.next) ∧ acc(p.sum, 50) ∧ acc(p.μ, 50) ;
        invariant rd(p.val) ∧ p.val ≤ x ∧ p.held ∧ maxlock = p.μ ;
        invariant p.next = null ⇒ p.sum = x ;
        invariant p.next ≠ null ⇒
            rd(p.next.val) ∧ p.val ≤ p.next.val ∧ acc(p.next.μ, 50) ∧ p.μ ⊑ p.next.μ ∧
            acc(p.next.sum, 50) ∧ p.sum = p.next.val + p.next.sum + x ;
        lockchange p ;
        {
            Node nx := p.next ; acquire nx ; nx.sum := nx.sum + x ;
            release p ; p := nx ;
        }
        Node t := new Node ; t.val := x ; t.next := p.next ;
        if (t.next = null) { t.sum := 0 ; } else { t.sum := p.next.val + p.next.sum ; }
        share t between p and p.next ;
        p.next := t ;
        release p ;
    }
}
```

Fig. 2. Main class of the sorted linked list. The **while** statement in method *Insert* includes a loop invariant and a **lockchange** clause that says how a loop iteration may affect what locks the thread holds.

Fig. 2 shows the implementation of the main class of the linked list. According to the third monitor invariant, the monitor of a *List* object l holds a 20%-permission for $l.sum$, which allows the monitor invariant to depend on the location. Threads may hold parts of the remaining 80% and read the location without acquiring l's monitor. But only a thread that holds exactly 80% can obtain write permission for $l.sum$ by acquiring the monitor. The exact percentages for the fractional permissions here are arbitrary; we could as well have chosen 50% or any other non-zero percentage.

Just like the monitor of a *Node* object holds a 50%-permission for the *sum* location of the next node, the monitor of a *List* object l holds a 50%-permission for the *sum* location of the first node $l.head$. Therefore, to obtain write permission for $l.head.sum$, a thread has to acquire not only the monitor of $l.head$ but also the monitor of l, which protects *List*'s third monitor invariant.

Method *Insert* of class *List* inserts a new value into the list. It uses fine-grained hand-over-hand locking to traverse the list. This locking strategy ensures that once the method finds the appropriate place to insert the new element, it holds the lock of the new node's predecessor. Moreover, it enables us to update the *sum* field while traversing the list. Hand-over-hand locking becomes possible by our use of fractional permissions in the monitor invariant of *Node*.

Sharing and Unsharing. Every object is either thread-local or shared. An object is thread-local upon creation. A thread-local object o is shared by the **share** o statement; conversely, a shared object o is made thread-local by the **unshare** o statement.

Sharing an object o transfers the permissions required by o's monitor invariant from the current thread to o's monitor. That is, the **share** o statement checks that o is a thread-local object, after which it makes o shared. It then checks that o's monitor invariant holds, in particular, that the current thread holds all the permissions required by o's monitor invariant. Finally, it deprives the current thread of these permissions.

Conversely, **unshare** o checks that o is a shared object, after which it makes o thread-local. Whereas **share** o requires o to be thread-local, which implies its monitor is not held by any thread, **unshare** o requires o's monitor to be held by the current thread and then releases the monitor of o.

Note that **unshare** o does not necessarily give the current thread full permissions for o's fields. The thread obtains only the permissions held by o's monitor, but other threads might still hold permissions. Therefore, thread-locality of o means only that no thread can acquire o's monitor, but other threads might still access o's fields.

Method *Init* of class *List* (Fig. 2) illustrates sharing. The method plays the role of a constructor, that is, it is expected to be called on newly allocated *List* objects. Hence, it requires write permissions for the *head* and *sum* fields of its receiver. The second precondition requires that the receiver be thread-local, as we discuss later. The method creates and initializes a new *Node* object t. Since t is thread-local and since $t.next$ is null, the current thread possesses all the permissions required by t's monitor invariant (Fig. 1). Therefore, the **share** t statement verifies (we will explain the **between** clause in the next section). The **share this** statement verifies because the current thread possesses all the permissions required by the monitor invariant of **this**. In particular, when t is being shared, the current thread retains a read permission for $t.val$ (since *Node*'s monitor invariant requires only an ε-permission) and a 50%-permission for $t.sum$ (since $Node$ requires only a 50%-permission). $Init$ satisfies its first post-condition because the current thread retains an 80%-permission for $\mathbf{this}.sum$ when $\mathbf{this}$ is being shared (since $List$'s invariant requires only 20%), and because sum is set to zero by the method. We will discuss the second postcondition in the next section.

It is interesting to trace the permissions for $t.val$. After creating t, the current thread possesses full permission for this location. Sharing t transfers an ε-permission to t's monitor, such that the current thread retains $100\% - \varepsilon$. Consequently, by acquiring t's monitor, the thread could now re-gain write permission for $t.val$. Later, when $\mathbf{this}$ is being shared, another ε-permission is transferred to the monitor of $\mathbf{this}$, which leaves the current thread with $100\% - 2 \cdot \varepsilon$. However, when the $Init$ method terminates, this remaining permission is not transferred to the caller. Therefore, it is effectively lost for all threads, and $t.val$ is from then on immutable.

3 Deadlock Prevention

To prevent deadlocks, locks must be acquired in ascending order, according to a user-defined locking order. In this section, we show how this order is defined, how it is enforced, and how programs can set and change an object's position in the order.

Locking Order. To allow the locking order to be changed dynamically, we store each object's position in a predefined field μ. The type of μ is a lattice in which for any two distinct, ordered elements u and v, there is some element w strictly in between them. This requirement ensures that it is always possible to place an object between any two existing objects in the locking order. We use $u \sqsubset v$ to denote that u is strictly less than v in the lattice. The bottom element of the lattice is denoted by $\bot$.

As for other fields, accesses to μ require the appropriate permissions. However, μ may be modified only through the **share** statement and the **reorder** statement described below. The μ field may be used in specifications. For instance, the last invariant of class $Node$ (Fig. 1) specifies the locking order between a node and its successor. To do so, it requires 50%-permissions for the μ fields of both nodes and orders $\mathbf{this}$ before its successor. Consequently, the monitors of the nodes have to be acquired in the order of the nodes in the list. Similarly, the last invariant of $List$ (Fig. 2) orders $\mathbf{this}$ before the first node; so the $List$ object must be acquired before its nodes.

We use the μ field also to encode whether an object is thread-local or shared. An object o is thread-local if and only if $o.\mu = \bot$. For instance, the second precondition of method $Init$ (Fig. 2) requires that the receiver be thread-local, and the second postcondition ensures that it is shared (since for all u, $u \sqsubset \mu$ implies $o.\mu \neq \bot$).

Acquiring Monitors. To check that a thread acquires monitors in the specified order, we have to keep track of the monitors held by each thread. We use the expression $\mathbf{maxlock} \sqsubset u$ to express that u is greater than $o.\mu$ for each object o currently locked by the current thread. Since this expression implicitly reads $o.\mu$ for all objects held by the current thread, we ensure that $o.\mu$ may be changed only by the thread that holds o, see below.

The proof obligation for **acquire** o ensures that monitors are acquired in ascending order, that is, that the current thread has read permission for $o.\mu$ and that o is strictly above all objects already held by the current thread. Note that because of this proof obligation, it is (allowed but) not sensible to require full permission for **this**.μ in the monitor invariant of an object o: when o is being shared, its monitor would obtain full permission to $o.\mu$; so no thread could possess read permission for $o.\mu$ and, thus, no thread could ever acquire o's monitor.

Determining the Locking Order. The locking order is specified and changed by the **between** $\overline{p}$ **and** $\overline{s}$ clause of the **share** o and **reorder** o statements, for any (possibly empty) lists of expressions $\overline{p}$ and $\overline{s}$. It assigns a value to $o.\mu$ that is strictly above all the lower bounds $p_i.\mu$ and strictly below all the upper bounds $s_j.\mu$. The operations require the current thread to have write permission for $o.\mu$ and read permission for all $p_i.\mu$ and $s_j.\mu$ and require each lower bound $p_i.\mu$ to be strictly below each upper bound $s_j.\mu$. Whereas the **share** statement places a thread-local object in the locking order, **reorder** o is used to change the position of a shared object o, which must be held by the current thread to prevent one thread from confusing another thread's **maxlock** value.

In *List*'s *Init* method (Fig. 2), the new (thread-local) *Node* object t is ordered above **maxlock**, which lets **share this** order the (thread-local) **this** object between **maxlock** and t, as required by the last postcondition of *Init* and *List*'s last monitor invariant, respectively. Since we are not interested in ordering t below any particular object, the second expression list of the **share** t statement is empty.

It is an important feature of our verification methodology that the μ field of an object can be assigned to more than once, that is, the locking order can be changed during program execution. In our example, the monitor invariant of *Node* (Fig. 1) requires 50%-permissions for **this**.μ and $next.\mu$. Therefore, it is possible for a thread to acquire the monitors of nodes n and $n.next$, and thus, obtain full permission for $n.next.\mu$. Consequently, the thread can change the place of $n.next$ in the locking order. We used this feature to implement an association list that re-orders its nodes after each lookup to ensure that frequently-used elements appear toward the head of the list. List reversal and balanced trees are other common examples that require a dynamic change of the locking order.

4   Technical Treatment

In this section, we explain how our methodology is encoded in the program verifier. We define the proof rules for the most interesting statements by translating them to a simple guarded-command language, whose weakest precondition semantics is obvious. In this translation, we use **assert** statements to denote proof obligations and **assume** statements to state assumptions that may be used to prove the assertions. The heap is encoded as a two-dimensional array that maps objects and field names to values. The current heap is denoted by the global variable *Heap*.

Encoding of Permissions. A permission has the form (p, n) where p is a percentage between 0 and 100, and n is either an integer or one of the special values $-\infty$ or $+\infty$. These special values are used to represent an inexhaustible supply of ε permissions, as expressed by the predicate $rd(o.f, *)$. We use integral percentages rather than the mathematically more appealing fractions, due to a limitation in many popular SMT solvers in their handling of both integers and rationals. Intuitively, we define the value of a permission (p, n) as $p + n \cdot \varepsilon$, where ε is a positive infinitesimal.

Percentages are a simple way to encode fractions of a definite size, which are for instance needed to split permissions over a statically-known number of monitors or threads. Infinitesimals allow one to split permissions between arbitrarily many monitors and threads, for instance, to allow a statically-unknown number of concurrent readers.

A permission (p, n) is called:

- full permission if $p + n \cdot \varepsilon = 100$, that is, $p = 100 \wedge n = 0$;
- some permission if $p + n \cdot \varepsilon > 0$, that is, $p > 0 \vee n > 0$;
- no permission if $p + n \cdot \varepsilon = 0$, that is, $p = 0 \wedge n = 0$.

Other combinations of p and n do not occur. Note that our encoding does not reflect that ε is an infinitesimal. It simply counts the number of such ε's (or "tokens").

We assume the following operations on permissions: incrementing (denoted by $+$) and decrementing (denoted by $-$) by a percentage or by a possibly inexhaustible number of infinitesimal permissions ε, and comparison ($=, <, \leq$). The definitions of these operations are straightforward and, therefore, omitted.

To keep track of the permissions it holds, each thread t has a (thread-local) variable $\mathcal{P}_t$ that maps every location to t's permission for that location. Since specifications are given with respect to one thread (the current thread, denoted by tid) and, likewise, verification conditions are prescribed for each thread, we usually refer only to one variable $\mathcal{P}_{tid}$, so we drop the subscript tid.

It is convenient to introduce shorthands for the two most common permission requirements. $CanRead(o.f)$ and $CanWrite(o.f)$ express that the current thread holds some permission and full permission for location $o.f$, respectively:

$$CanRead(o.f) \equiv o \neq \mathbf{null} \wedge \mathbf{let}\ (p, n) = \mathcal{P}_{tid}[o, f]\ \mathbf{in}\ p > 0 \vee n > 0$$
$$CanWrite(o.f) \equiv o \neq \mathbf{null} \wedge \mathbf{let}\ (p, n) = \mathcal{P}_{tid}[o, f]\ \mathbf{in}\ p = 100 \wedge n = 0$$

Object Creation. For any class C and local variable x, the allocation statement is given the following semantics:

```
x := new C;  ≡
   havoc x;
   assume x ≠ null ∧ (∀f • P[x,f] = (0,0) ∧ Heap[x,f] = zero );
   #foreach f { P[x,f] := (100,0); }
```

The **havoc** x statement assigns an arbitrary value to x, which is then constrained by the following **assume** statement. *zero* denotes the zero-equivalent value for each type, in particular, $\bot$ for the locking order. Note that this semantics is simplified. In particular, we do not express here that the new object is an instance of class C or that the f in the **#foreach** statement is a field of class C, because these are not relevant for our discussion. **#foreach** loops can be statically expanded by the translator.

Field Access. Reading and writing locations first checks that the thread has the appropriate permission:

$x := o.f; \quad \equiv$
    assert $CanRead(o.f)$;
    $x := Heap[o, f]$;

$o.f := x; \quad \equiv$
    assert $CanWrite(o.f)$;
    $Heap[o, f] := x$;

Monitors. Each thread keeps track of the monitors it holds. For that purpose, we introduce a thread-local boolean field *held*. As with $\mathcal{P}$, this field would be subscripted with the thread, but since we only refer to the field for the current thread, we drop the subscripts. That is, $Heap[o, held]$ denotes whether the monitor of object o is held by the current thread. Since *held* is thread-local, it is not subject to permission checks; each thread always has full permission for its *held* fields.

The expression **maxlock** is encoded using quantifiers over the objects whose monitors are held by the current thread. For instance, **maxlock** $\sqsubset u$ is encoded as $(\forall p \bullet Heap[p, held] \Rightarrow Heap[p, \mu] \sqsubset u)$.

Permission Transfer. Several statements of our programming language transfer permissions between threads and monitors (for instance, **acquire**), two threads (for instance, **fork**, see below), or between two method executions of the same thread (method call). We model this permission transfer by two operations, Exhale and Inhale, which describe the transfer from the current thread's perspective.

Roughly speaking, Exhale$[\![E]\!]$ checks that expression E holds, in particular, that the current thread holds the permissions required by E, and then takes away these permissions. Inhale$[\![E]\!]$ assumes E and transfers the permissions required by E to the current thread. If the current thread obtains some permission for a location $o.f$ for which it previously had no permission, Inhale assigns an arbitrary value to $o.f$, which models the fact that another thread might have modified the location since the current thread last accessed it. The definitions for both operations are shown in Fig. 3.

Acquiring and Releasing Monitors. The precondition of **acquire** o requires object o to be ordered above all objects already held by the acquiring thread. This proof obligation also ensures that o is shared, because our encoding is consistent with a model where every thread holds an anonymous sentinel monitor; in particular, it is not possible to refute $Heap[\bot, held] = true$. To ensure mutual exclusion, the execution of the **acquire** statement suspends until no other thread holds o's monitor. The Inhale operations expresses that the acquiring thread may assume the monitor invariant of o, denoted by $J(o)$, and that it obtains the permissions held by o's monitor.

The **release** o statement requires o's monitor to be held by the current thread. Using the Exhale operation, it then asserts o's monitor invariant and transfers permissions back to the monitor:

acquire $o; \quad \equiv$
    assert $CanRead(o.\mu)$;
    assert $(\forall p \bullet Heap[p, held] \Rightarrow Heap[p, \mu] \sqsubset Heap[o, \mu])$;
    $Heap[o, held] := $ **true**;
    Inhale$[\![J(o)]\!]$

release $o; \quad \equiv$
    assert $o \neq null$;
    assert $Heap[o, held]$;
    Exhale$[\![J(o)]\!]$
    $Heap[o, held] := $ **false**;

$\text{Exhale}[\![acc(E.f, r)]\!] \equiv$
  assert $\mathcal{P}[\text{Tr}[\![E]\!], f] \geq \text{Tr}[\![r]\!]$;
  $\mathcal{P}[\text{Tr}[\![E]\!], f] := \mathcal{P}[\text{Tr}[\![E]\!], f] - \text{Tr}[\![r]\!]$;

$\text{Inhale}[\![acc(E.f, r)]\!] \equiv$
  if $(\mathcal{P}[\text{Tr}[\![E]\!], f] = (0, 0))$
    havoc $Heap[\text{Tr}[\![E]\!], f]$;
  $\mathcal{P}[\text{Tr}[\![E]\!], f] := \mathcal{P}[\text{Tr}[\![E]\!], f] + \text{Tr}[\![r]\!]$;

$\text{Exhale}[\![rd(E.f)]\!] \equiv$
  assert $\mathcal{P}[\text{Tr}[\![E]\!], f] \geq \varepsilon$;
  $\mathcal{P}[\text{Tr}[\![E]\!], f] := \mathcal{P}[\text{Tr}[\![E]\!], f] - \varepsilon$;

$\text{Inhale}[\![rd(E.f)]\!] \equiv$
  if $(\mathcal{P}[\text{Tr}[\![E]\!], f] = (0, 0))$
    { **havoc** $Heap[\text{Tr}[\![E]\!], f]$; }
  $\mathcal{P}[\text{Tr}[\![E]\!], f] := \mathcal{P}[\text{Tr}[\![E]\!], f] + \varepsilon$;

$\text{Exhale}[\![P \wedge Q]\!] \equiv$
  $\text{Exhale}[\![Q]\!]$;
  $\text{Exhale}[\![P]\!]$;

$\text{Inhale}[\![P \wedge Q]\!] \equiv$
  $\text{Inhale}[\![P]\!]$;
  $\text{Inhale}[\![Q]\!]$;

$\text{Exhale}[\![P \Rightarrow Q]\!] \equiv$
  if $(\text{Tr}[\![P]\!])$ { $\text{Exhale}[\![Q]\!]$; }

$\text{Inhale}[\![P \Rightarrow Q]\!] \equiv$
  if $(\text{Tr}[\![P]\!])$ { $\text{Inhale}[\![Q]\!]$; }

Otherwise:

$\text{Exhale}[\![E]\!] \equiv$
  assert $\text{Tr}[\![E]\!]$;

Otherwise:

$\text{Inhale}[\![E]\!] \equiv$
  assume $\text{Tr}[\![E]\!]$;

Fig. 3. $\text{Exhale}[\![E]\!]$ and $\text{Inhale}[\![E]\!]$ are defined by structural induction over expression E. The function Tr translates source expressions to our intermediate language. We assume here that acc and rd expressions only occur on the outermost level of conjuncts and consequences of implications. Therefore, Tr never encounters these expressions. $\text{Exhale}[\![E]\!]$ also asserts that E is well-defined, in particular, that the current thread possesses the permissions needed for the field accesses in E. We omit these checks and related technicalities for simplicity.

Finally, the **reorder** statement requires write permission for $o.\mu$, that o is held by the current thread, and that any lower bound $p_i.\mu$ is below any upper bound $s_j.\mu$. It then chooses an appropriate value w for $o.\mu$ and assigns it. Recall from Section 3 that the lattice of positions in the locking order guarantees that for any two distinct, ordered elements u and v, there is some element w strictly in between them. Therefore, it is always possible to choose an appropriate value for $o.\mu$:

reorder o **between** $\overline{p}$ **and** $\overline{s}$; $\equiv$
  assert $CanWrite(o, \mu) \wedge Heap[o, held]$;
  #**foreach** $p_i \in \overline{p}, s_j \in \overline{s}$ {
    assert $p_i = null \vee s_j = null \vee$
      $(CanRead(p_i.\mu) \wedge CanRead(s_j.\mu) \wedge Heap[p_i, \mu] \sqsubset Heap[s_j, \mu])$;
  }
  havoc w;
  #**foreach** $p_i \in \overline{p}$ { **assume** $p_i = null \vee Heap[p_i, \mu] \sqsubset w$; };
  #**foreach** $s_j \in \overline{s}$ { **assume** $s_j = null \vee w \sqsubset Heap[s_j, \mu]$; };
  $Heap[o, \mu] := w$;

$(*)$

Sharing and Unsharing. An object o can be shared if the current thread has write permission for $o.\mu$ and if the object is not shared already. Like for **release**, the Exhale operation is used to check that the current thread has the permissions required by o's monitor invariant $J(o)$ and transfers them to the monitor.

The **unshare** o statement releases o and at the same time makes it unavailable for sharing by setting $o.\mu$ to $\perp$. Since it changes $o.\mu$, the **unshare** statement requires full permission for $o.\mu$. This requirement also ensures mutual exclusion with the **acquire** o statement, which requires read permission for $o.\mu$.

$$\begin{array}{ll}
\textbf{share } o \textbf{ between } \overline{p} \textbf{ and } \overline{s}; \quad\equiv & \textbf{unshare } o; \quad\equiv \\
\quad \textbf{assert } CanWrite(o, \mu); & \quad \textbf{assert } CanWrite(o, \mu); \\
\quad \textbf{assert } Heap[o, \mu] = \perp; & \quad \textbf{assert } Heap[o, held]; \\
\quad /\!/ \text{ see } (*) \text{ of } \textbf{reorder} & \quad Heap[o, held] := \textbf{false}; \\
\quad \mathsf{Exhale}[\![J(o)]\!] & \quad Heap[o, \mu] := \perp;
\end{array}$$

Thread Creation and Termination. Every object o can give rise to a computation, which is performed in a separate thread as if, in Java, every object were an instance of class $Thread$. The **fork** o statement starts such a computation by executing o's Run method. Like in Java, we do not permit several overlapping computations on the same object, which allows us in particular to identify a thread through the object on which it was forked. To prevent overlaps, we introduce a boolean field $active$ to record whether there is an active computation on an object. For new objects, $active$ is initially false. The **fork** o statement asserts that the current thread has write permission for $o.active$ and that o is not active. It also asserts the precondition of o's Run method, denoted by $RunPre(o)$, and transfers the required permissions to the new thread using the Exhale operation. The new thread will then execute o's Run method.

The **join** o statement waits for the computation of the thread that has been forked on object o to complete, and then marks o as no longer being active. The current thread may assume the postcondition of o's Run method, denoted by $RunPost(o)$, and obtains the permissions of the joined thread.

$$\begin{array}{ll}
\textbf{fork } o; \quad\equiv & \textbf{join } o; \quad\equiv \\
\quad \textbf{assert } CanWrite(o.active); & \quad \textbf{assert } CanWrite(o.active); \\
\quad \textbf{assert } \neg Heap[o, active]; & \quad \textbf{assert } Heap[o, active]; \\
\quad \mathsf{Exhale}[\![RunPre(o)]\!] & \quad Heap[o, active] := \textit{false}; \\
\quad Heap[o, active] := \textit{true}; & \quad \mathsf{Inhale}[\![RunPost(o)]\!]
\end{array}$$

Note that requiring write permission for $o.active$ in both **fork** o and **join** o ensures mutual exclusion. In particular, a thread can be joined only once, which prevents a duplication of the permissions returned from that thread.

When the Run method is initiated by a **fork**, then its specification is interpreted from two different threads: the precondition is exhaled by the forking thread and inhaled by the forked thread; the postcondition is exhaled by the terminating thread and inhaled by the joining thread. Therefore, it is necessary for soundness that these interpretations are consistent. We achieve that by restricting the use of thread-local fields. The specification of Run must not mention the $held$ field of any object. Moreover, since **maxlock** is encoded in terms of $held$, it may be used only in the form **maxlock** $\sqsubseteq E$ in positive contexts of the precondition.

Method Calls and Loops. The semantics of method calls exhales the precondition and then inhales the postcondition. In this way, it is like the succession of a fork and a join, except for the *active* machinery, and without the restrictions on the specification of the *Run* method. Indeed, fork and join are nothing but an asynchronous call to a method called *Run*.

The **while** statement exhales the loop invariant and then havocs the variables assigned to in the loop body. Then, it either inhales the loop invariant, assumes the negation of the loop guard, and continues after the loop, or it starts from an empty mask $\mathcal{P}$, inhales the loop invariant, assumes the loop guard, executes the loop body, and exhales the loop invariant. For brevity, we omit the formalization.

5 Related Work

Implicit dynamic frames were first used by Smans *et al.* [18] as a way to use Kassios's dynamic frames [15] but with access predicates instead of explicit modifies clauses. The permissions required by a method precondition implicitly define an access set, which is an upper bound on the fields modified by the method. We extend this work by supporting fractional permissions, which call for the exhale and inhale operations instead of just computing access sets. The havoc in the inhale operation corresponds to the havoc of the heap in the encoding of a modifies clause.

Fractional permissions were proposed by Boyland [4] and used by Zhao [21] for the analysis of concurrent Java programs. Zhao developed a type system to track read and write permissions for fields and to enforce a (fixed) locking order. The type system enforces the absence of data races and deadlocks, but does not support the verification of a program w.r.t. to a programmer-supplied contract.

Methodologies similar to ours have been defined in separation logic by Bornat *et al.* [2], by Gotsman *et al.* [8], and by Hobor *et al.* [11]. These extend Concurrent Separation Logic [17] to allow an unbounded number of locks and threads and to allow fractional permissions and counting permissions, which are similar to our infinitesimal permissions. A difference is that we translate our methodology into first-order verification conditions instead of needing a separate logic. A minor difference with separation logic is that we can handle **old** expressions, which provide a natural way to write postconditions. Unlike these pieces of work, we also verify that programs do not have deadlocks.

Checkers for separation logic include Smallfoot [1], jStar [7], and VeriFast [12], which are all based on some symbolic execution with interspersed calls to a theorem prover. By translating each method to just one formula, we can let the theorem prover perform case splits that a symbolic execution engine would have to resolve at each program point, which is not always possible. On the other hand, we currently have no support for abstract predicates and currently do not check that permissions are not lost.

Boyapati *et al.* [3] present an ownership type system that prevents data races and deadlocks. This system supports thread-local objects and coarse-grained locking of shared objects, where the lock of an object o also protects all objects owned by o. The type system permits concurrent reading only for immutable objects, whereas the fractional permissions in our system support fine-grained locking and concurrent reading. Similar to our work, Boyapati *et al.*'s system prevents deadlocks by enforcing that locks are acquired in a given locking order, and this order can be changed dynamically.

Jacobs *et al.* [13] extend Spec#'s verification methodology to concurrent programs. Like Boyapati, they use ownership to impose a coarse-grained locking strategy, whereas our methodology supports fine-grained locking of arbitrary structures. We adopted their technique of specifying the locking order as part of the **share** statement and extended this capability by allowing locks to be re-ordered.

6   Conclusions

We presented a verification methodology for concurrent, object-based programs, which enforces the absence of data races and deadlocks and allows one to verify code against contracts. Our methodology uses fractional permissions, which allow us to support fine-grained locking and multi-object monitor invariants, sharing and un-sharing of objects, and concurrent reading. Our methodology encodes the locking order via fields in the heap, which enables dynamic changes. These features make our methodology sufficiently expressive to verify advanced concurrency patterns.

We have implemented our methodology in a translator from our experimental source language Chalice to the intermediate verification language Boogie [0] and have used it to verify several challenging examples including hand-over-hand locking for linked lists and a lock re-ordering algorithm. We have designed our methodology to work well with off-the-shelf SMT solvers and, indeed, all of our examples could be verified fully automatically. Our implementation also supports reader-writer locks, which we omitted here for lack of space.

The presented methodology is an expressive foundation for more comprehensive verification techniques. As future work, we plan to prove a formal soundness result including the following properties: (0) Justification of assumptions: the conditions assumed as part of the Inhale operation are guaranteed to hold. (1) Non-interference of threads, in particular, stability of read expressions: no thread can be writing an expression that is being read by another thread. (2) Absence of deadlocks in the presence of our changing locking order. Other plans for future work are to extend our methodology by two-state invariants to permit rely-guarantee reasoning and by abstraction via user-defined functions or predicates. We also want to develop an automatic inference of access predicates and extend Chalice to a full object-oriented language by adding subtyping.

Acknowledgments. We thank the referees for their useful comments. Müller's work was funded in part by the Information Society Technologies program of the European Commission, Future and Emerging Technologies under the IST-2005-015905 MOBIUS project.

References

0. Barnett, M., Chang, B.-Y.E., DeLine, R., Jacobs, B., Leino, K.R.M.: Boogie: A modular reusable verifier for object-oriented programs. In: de Boer, F.S., Bonsangue, M.M., Graf, S., de Roever, W.-P. (eds.) FMCO 2005. LNCS, vol. 4111, pp. 364–387. Springer, Heidelberg (2006)

1. Berdine, J., Calcagno, C., O'Hearn, P.W.: Smallfoot: Modular automatic assertion checking with separation logic. In: de Boer, F.S., Bonsangue, M.M., Graf, S., de Roever, W.-P. (eds.) FMCO 2005. LNCS, vol. 4111, pp. 115–137. Springer, Heidelberg (2006)
2. Bornat, R., Calcagno, C., O'Hearn, P., Parkinson, M.: Permission accounting in separation logic. In: POPL 2005, pp. 259–270. ACM, New York (2005)
3. Boyapati, C., Lee, R., Rinard, M.C.: Ownership types for safe programming: Preventing data races and deadlocks. In: OOPSLA 2002, pp. 211–230. ACM, New York (2002)
4. Boyland, J.: Checking interference with fractional permissions. In: Cousot, R. (ed.) SAS 2003. LNCS, vol. 2694, pp. 55–72. Springer, Heidelberg (2003)
5. Brinch Hansen, P.: Operating systems principles. Prentice-Hall, Englewood Cliffs (1973)
6. de Moura, L., Bjørner, N.: Z3: An efficient SMT solver. In: Ramakrishnan, C.R., Rehof, J. (eds.) TACAS 2008. LNCS, vol. 4963, pp. 337–340. Springer, Heidelberg (2008)
7. Distefano, D., Parkinson, M.J.: jStar: Towards practical verification of Java. In: OOPSLA 2008, pp. 213–226. ACM, New York (2008)
8. Gotsman, A., Berdine, J., Cook, B., Rinetzky, N., Sagiv, M.: Local reasoning for storable locks and threads. In: Shao, Z. (ed.) APLAS 2007. LNCS, vol. 4807, pp. 19–37. Springer, Heidelberg (2007)
9. Herlihy, M., Shavit, N.: The Art of Multiprocessor Programming. Morgan Kaufmann, San Francisco (2008)
10. Hoare, C.A.R.: Monitors: an operating system structuring concept. Commun. ACM 17(10), 549–557 (1974)
11. Hobor, A., Appel, A.W., Nardelli, F.Z.: Oracle semantics for concurrent separation logic. In: Drossopoulou, S. (ed.) ESOP 2008. LNCS, vol. 4960, pp. 353–367. Springer, Heidelberg (2008)
12. Jacobs, B., Piessens, F.: The VeriFast program verifier. Technical Report CW520, Katholieke Universiteit Leuven (August 2008)
13. Jacobs, B., Smans, J., Piessens, F., Schulte, W.: A statically verifiable programming model for concurrent object-oriented programs. In: Liu, Z., He, J. (eds.) ICFEM 2006. LNCS, vol. 4260, pp. 420–439. Springer, Heidelberg (2006)
14. Jones, C.B.: Specification and design of (parallel) programs. In: IFIP Congress, pp. 321–332. North-Holland, Amsterdam (1983)
15. Kassios, I.T.: Dynamic frames: Support for framing, dependencies and sharing without restrictions. In: Misra, J., Nipkow, T., Sekerinski, E. (eds.) FM 2006. LNCS, vol. 4085, pp. 268–283. Springer, Heidelberg (2006)
16. Lea, D.: Concurrent Programming in Java: Design Principles and Patterns. Addison-Wesley, Reading (1999)
17. O'Hearn, P.W.: Resources, concurrency, and local reasoning. TCS 375(1–3), 271–307 (2007)
18. Smans, J., Jacobs, B., Piessens, F.: Implicit dynamic frames. FTfJP 2008, Technical Report ICIS-R08013, Radboud University, pp. 1–12 (2008)
19. Walker, D., Crary, K., Morrisett, G.: Typed memory management via static capabilities. ACM TOPLAS 22(4), 701–771 (2000)
20. Xu, Q., de Roever, W.-P., He, J.: The rely-guarantee method for verifying shared variable concurrent programs. Formal Aspects of Computing 9(2), 149–174 (1997)
21. Zhao, Y.: Concurrency Analysis based on Fractional Permission System. PhD thesis, The University of Wisconsin–Milwaukee (2007)

SingleTrack: A Dynamic Determinism Checker for Multithreaded Programs

Caitlin Sadowski[1], Stephen N. Freund[2], and Cormac Flanagan[1]

[1] University of California at Santa Cruz, Santa Cruz, CA
[2] Williams College, Williamstown, MA

Abstract. Multithreaded programs are prone to errors caused by unintended interference between concurrent threads. This paper focuses on verifying that *deterministically-parallel* code is free of such thread interference errors. Deterministically-parallel code may create and use new threads, via fork and join, and coordinate their behavior with synchronization primitives, such as barriers and semaphores. Such code does not satisfy the traditional non-interference property of atomicity (or serializability), however, and so existing atomicity tools are inadequate for checking deterministically-parallel code. We introduce a new non-interference specification for deterministically-parallel code, and we present a dynamic analysis to enforce it. We also describe SINGLETRACK, a prototype implementation of this analysis. SINGLETRACK's performance is competitive with prior atomicity checkers, but it produces many fewer spurious warnings because it enforces a more general non-interference property that is applicable to more software.

1 Introduction

Multiple threads of control are widely used in software development for many reasons, including their ability to utilize modern multi-core processors. Reasoning about the correctness of multithreaded code is notoriously difficult, however, due to the potential for non-deterministic interference between threads. Thus, methods for specifying and controlling thread interference are crucial for the cost-effective development of reliable multithreaded software. Previous studies have explored analyses for controlling interference by verifying, for example, that a program is free of data races or that methods are atomic (in that they always behave as if they execute serially). Some programs, however, are safe despite the presence of non-atomic methods, and previous studies revealed numerous examples of such methods. Motivated by this experience, this paper explores a more general non-interference property, namely *deterministic parallelism*.

Deterministic Parallelism. A deterministically-parallel computation may use multiple threads, but these threads either do not communicate (as in divide-and-conquer parallelism) or they communicate in a deterministic manner (e.g., via barriers). In either case, the relative scheduling of threads in subcomputations does not affect the program's overall behavior.

G. Castagna (Ed.): ESOP 2009, LNCS 5502, pp. 394–409, 2009.

```
deterministic void quicksort(int[] a) {
  synchronized (a) {
    quicksort_helper(a, 0, a.length-1);
  }
}

void quicksort_helper(int[] a, int lo, int hi) {
  if (hi - lo > 1) {
    int pivot = partition(a, lo, hi);
    Thread t1 = fork { quicksort_helper(a, lo, pivot-1); }
    Thread t2 = fork { quicksort_helper(a, pivot+1, hi); }
    t1.join();
    t2.join();
  }
}
```

Fig. 1. Deterministically Parallel Sort Implementation

To illustrate this concurrency pattern, consider the multithreaded `quicksort` implementation shown in Figure 1. That method synchronizes on the lock for array `a`, and then calls a helper method to sort the array by partitioning it and forking two threads to recursively sort each half. The `quicksort` method is annotated with the non-interference specification "`deterministic`." Each invocation of `quicksort` produces a computation involving multiplie threads: the initial thread and all threads forked by the `quicksort_helper` method. We refer to the execution of a `deterministic` method and its forked threads as a *transaction*.

In general, a program execution may involve multiple, possibly concurrent, transactions, and each transaction may be internally multithreaded (if, as in the `quicksort` function, its code forks new threads). The goal of this paper is to verify that the entire program execution satisfies the following two important non-interference properties. These two properties prevent interference problems between threads in one transaction, and in different transactions, respectively.

1. **Conflict Freedom.** Threads insinde each transaction must be *conflict-free*. That is, if two operations from the same transaction are enabled at the same time, then those operations must not conflict. Thus, all *intra-transaction* race conditions are forbidden, including those on regular variables, on `volatile` variables, and on locks. Deterministic synchronization, such as fork-join patterns and barrier synchronization, is allowed, as is synchronization *between* transactions, as in the quicksort example.
2. **External Serializability.** Threads inside each transaction must not interfere with threads outside that transaction. Note that this notion is different than atomicity, which would require the `quicksort` method to behave as if it executes serially, without interleaved operations from other threads. Since `quicksort_helper` must wait for the forked threads to terminate, `quicksort` cannot execute serially and is not atomic.

Nevertheless, `quicksort` does enjoy a strong atomicity-like property, but only when considering the operations of all threads in the entire `quicksort` transaction, and not just the operations of the thread calling `quicksort`. More specifically, a trace is *externally serial* if each (possibly multithreaded) transaction executes contiguously, without interleaved operations from outside that transaction. A trace is *externally serializable* if it is equivalent to an externally serial trace.

For the interesting special case when the `main` method of an application is annotated as `deterministic`, external serializability becomes a trivial property (since the execution contains only one transaction), but conflict freedom provides a strong determinism guarantee–that the program will behave the same regardless of how its threads are scheduled.[1] This special case of entirely deterministic applications was also addressed by the Cilk Nondeterminator [7], whereas this paper addresses the problem in a more general setting.

Another interesting case is when a `deterministic` method does not fork additional threads, and so conflict freedom becomes trivial (since the transaction contains only a single thread) and external serializability reduces to the traditional notion of serializability or atomicity. Thus, `deterministic` can be viewed as a generalization of `atomic` that better supports deterministically-parallel computations such as quicksort.

In the more general situation, a program execution may consist of multiple (possibly concurrent) transactions, each of which is internally multithreaded, and the above two correctness properties control thread interference both within and between transactions.

Single Track. This paper presents a dynamic analysis for verifying conflict freedom and external serializability. To verify conflict freedom, the analysis employs clock vectors [14] as a compact representation of the happens-before relation, and it uses additional mechanisms to track the current transaction for each thread and to distinguish intra-transaction conflicts (which are forbidden) from inter-transaction conflicts (which are allowed). To verify external serializability, the analysis dynamically constructs a *transactional happens-before* graph [10]. This graph encodes which transactions have operations that happen before operations of other transactions, and it contains a cycle if and only if the observed trace violates external serializability.

Figure 2 contains two code fragments that illustrate common patterns for deterministic parallelism found in programs. In the left column, the `main` method starts three concurrent invocations of the `worker` method, where each `worker` invocation repeatedly reads shared data, blocks on a barrier, and then updates disjoint portions of that shared data. The barrier synchronization ensures the absence of conflicts on the reads and writes of the shared data. Although `main` is not `atomic`, our analysis verifies that it is `deterministic`. The right column of Figure 2 shows an idealized implementation of thread pools, in which the assignment of tasks from the work list to worker threads is scheduler-dependent

---

[1] This property assumes that thread scheduling is the only source of non-determinism.

```
Barrier barrier = new Barrier(3);          class ThreadPool {
int a[] = new int[3];                        BlockingQueue<Runnable> workList
                                               = new BlockingQueue<Runnable>();
deterministic void main() {
  fork { worker(0); }                        ThreadPool(int numWorkers) {
  fork { worker(1); }                          for (int i = 0; i < numWorkers; i++) {
  worker(2);                                     fork {
}                                                  while (true) {
                                                     workList.dequeue().run();
void worker(int id) {                              }
  for (int i = 0; i < 10; i++) {               }
    int tmp = f(a[0],a[1],a[2]);            }
    barrier.await();                       }
    a[id] = tmp;
    barrier.await();                       void execute(Runnable task) {
  }                                          workList.enqueue(task);
}                                          }
                                         }
```
        (a) Barrier synchronization   (b) Thread pools

Fig. 2. Common idioms for Deterministic Parallelism

and so non-deterministic. If a program uses a thread pool to execute tasks with deterministic run methods, our analysis will still verify that these tasks are deterministic, despite the non-determinism at the application level.

We have developed a prototype implementation, called SINGLETRACK, of this dynamic analysis. Experimental results show that SINGLETRACK provides a significant improvement over prior atomicity checkers, largely because deterministic is a more general non-interference specification than atomic and so is applicable to more methods. In effect, this permits us to check more complex code with fewer false alarms than existing tools.

For example, the sor benchmark [1] includes six methods that are not atomic because they involve barrier synchronization along the lines shown in Figure 2(a). Atomicity checkers provide no insight regarding thread interference problems in these methods and, in fact, mask a subtle synchronization defect detected by SINGLETRACK. (The barrier implementation incorrectly relied on writes to a long variable being atomic.) After fixing that bug, SINGLETRACK verified the entire sor benchmark as deterministic, whereas VELODROME, a dynamic atomicity checker [10], still reported spurious atomicity violations on the six methods. In addition, SINGLETRACK verified as deterministic many other problematic non-atomic methods in our benchmarks. Despite its increased generality, SINGLETRACK's performance is competitive with existing atomicity checkers.

Contributions. In summary, this paper:

- identifies a limitation of atomicity for reasoning about the common idiom of deterministic parallelism;
- proposes deterministic as a concise specification for this concurrency idiom that combines conflict freedom and external serializability;
- develops a dynamic analysis for verifying this non-interference specification;

- shows that the analysis reports an error whenever the observed trace violates this specification;
- presents an implementation for multithreaded Java programs; and
- validates the effectiveness and performance on a collection of benchmarks.

2   Semantics of Multithreaded Programs

To provide a sound basis for our dynamic analysis, we begin by formalizing the semantics of multithreaded programs, as summarized in Figure 3. A program consists of a number of concurrently executing threads that manipulate variables $x \in Var$ and locks $m \in Lock$. Each thread has a thread identifier $t \in Tid$. A program *state* Σ maps program variables to values. The state also records the holder (if any) of each lock m: if m held by thread t, then $\Sigma(m) = t$, and otherwise $\Sigma(m) = \bot$. The state also maps each thread identifier t to a local store $\Sigma(t) = \pi$ for that thread, which contains thread-local data such as the program counter and call stack. The distinguished local stores NotStarted and Finished indicate threads that have not started running yet and that have finished running, respectively. Execution starts in an initial state Σ_0, where $\Sigma_0(t) =$ NotStarted for all threads t except the initial thread.

Operations. Each thread proceeds by performing a sequence of operations on the global store. Thread t can perform all operations a from the following list:

- $rd(t, x, v)$ and $wr(t, x, v)$, which read and write a value v from variable x;
- $acq(t, m)$ and $rel(t, m)$, which acquire and release a lock m;
- $begin(t)$ and $end(t)$, which demarcate each **deterministic** block;
- $fork(t, u, \pi)$, which forks a new thread u with initial local store π;
- $stop(t)$, which stops thread t; and
- $join(t, u)$, which blocks until thread t terminates via $stop(t)$.

The relation $T(t, \pi, a, \pi')$ holds if the thread t can take a step from a local store π to a new local store π' by performing the operation $a \in Operation$ on the global store. We assume that T is not defined if either π or π' is the distinguished local stores NotStarted or Finished.

The transition relation $\Sigma \rightarrow^a \Sigma'$ performs a single step of execution. It chooses an operation a by thread t that is applicable in the local state $\Sigma(t)$, performs that operation to yield a new local store π', and returns a new (appropriately updated) state. An operation a is *enabled* in Σ if $\exists \Sigma'$ such that $\Sigma \rightarrow^a \Sigma'$. A state Σ is *final* if the local store for every thread in that state is either NotStarted or Finished. We assume that each operation is deterministic: if $tid(a) = tid(b)$ and $\Sigma \rightarrow^a \Sigma'$ and $\Sigma \rightarrow^b \Sigma''$ then $a = b$ and $\Sigma' = \Sigma''$.

A *trace* α captures an execution of a multithreaded program by listing the sequence of operations performed by the various threads. The behavior of a trace $\alpha = a_1.a_2. \cdots .a_n$ is defined by the relation $\Sigma_0 \rightarrow^\alpha \Sigma_n$, which holds if there exist intermediate states $\Sigma_1, \ldots, \Sigma_{n-1}$ such that $\Sigma_0 \rightarrow^{a_1} \Sigma_1 \rightarrow^{a_2} \cdots \rightarrow^{a_n} \Sigma_n$. We assume that each valid trace is cycle free.

Domains:

$$\Sigma \in \quad State \quad = \quad (Var \rightarrow Value)$$
$$\cup \; (Lock \rightarrow Tid_\perp)$$
$$\cup \; (Tid \rightarrow LocalStore)$$

$$a \in Operation ::= rd(t,x,v) \mid wr(t,x,v)$$
$$\mid acq(t,m) \mid rel(t,m)$$
$$\mid begin(t) \mid end(t)$$
$$\mid fork(t,u,\pi) \mid join(t,u) \mid stop(t)$$

$$u,t \in Tid$$
$$x \in Var$$
$$v \in Value$$
$$m \in Lock$$
$$\pi \in LocalStore$$

Transition relation: $\Sigma \rightarrow^a \Sigma'$

[STEP READ]
$$\frac{a = rd(t,x,v) \quad T(t, \Sigma(t), a, \pi') \quad \Sigma(x) = v}{\Sigma \rightarrow^a \Sigma[t := \pi']}$$

[STEP WRITE]
$$\frac{a = wr(t,x,v) \quad T(t, \Sigma(t), a, \pi')}{\Sigma \rightarrow^a \Sigma[t := \pi', x := v]}$$

[STEP ACQUIRE]
$$\frac{a = acq(t,m) \quad T(t, \Sigma(t), a, \pi') \quad \Sigma(m) = \perp}{\Sigma \rightarrow^a \Sigma[t := \pi', m := t]}$$

[STEP RELEASE]
$$\frac{a = rel(t,m) \quad T(t, \Sigma(t), a, \pi') \quad \Sigma(m) = t}{\Sigma \rightarrow^a \Sigma[t := \pi', m := \perp]}$$

[STEP BEGIN]
$$\frac{a = begin(t) \quad T(t, \Sigma(t), a, \pi')}{\Sigma \rightarrow^a \Sigma[t := \pi']}$$

[STEP END]
$$\frac{a = end(t) \quad T(t, \Sigma(t), a, \pi')}{\Sigma \rightarrow^a \Sigma[t := \pi']}$$

[STEP FORK]
$$\frac{a = fork(t,u,\pi'') \quad T(t, \Sigma(t), a, \pi')}{\Sigma(u) = \texttt{NotStarted} \quad \pi' \neq \texttt{NotStarted}}{\Sigma \rightarrow^a \Sigma[t := \pi', u := \pi'']}$$

[STEP JOIN]
$$\frac{a = join(t,u)}{T(t, \Sigma(t), a, \pi') \quad \Sigma(u) = \texttt{Finished}}{\Sigma \rightarrow^a \Sigma[t := \pi']}$$

[STEP STOP]
$$\frac{a = stop(t) \quad T(t, \Sigma(t), a, \pi')}{\Sigma \rightarrow^a \Sigma[t := \texttt{Finished}]}$$

Fig. 3. Semantics of Multithreaded Programs

Conflicts. Two operations in a trace *conflict* if they satisfy one of the following:

- **Communication conflict**: they read or write the same variable, and at least one of the accesses is a write.
- **Lock conflict:** they acquire or release the same lock.
- **Fork-join conflict:** one operation is $fork(t,u,\pi)$ or $join(t,u)$ and the other operation is by thread u.
- **Program order conflict**: they are performed by the same thread.

The *happens-before relation* $<_\alpha$ for a trace α is the smallest transitively-closed relation on operations in α such that if operation a occurs before b in α and a conflicts with b, then a *happens-before* b.[2]

Two traces are *equivalent* if one can be obtained from the other by repeatedly swapping adjacent non-conflicting operations. Equivalent traces yield the same happens-before relation and exhibit equivalent behavior.

---

[2] In theory, a particular operation a could occur multiple times in a trace. We avoid this complication by assuming that each operation includes a unique identifier, but, to avoid clutter, we do not include this unique identifier in the concrete syntax of operations.

Transactions. A *transaction* in a trace α is the sequence of operations executed by a thread t starting with a $begin(t)$ operation and containing all t operations up to and including a matching $end(t)$ operation. For each operation $fork(t, u, \pi)$ in a transaction, that transaction also includes all operations of the forked thread u. Any operation that does not occur within another transaction is considered to execute in its own (unary) transaction. To simplify some aspects of the formal presentation, we assume $begin(t)$ and $end(t)$ operations are appropriately matched and are not nested (although our implementation does support nested deterministic specifications). We also assume that all locks acquired within a transaction are released within that transaction.

3   Dynamically Verifying Internal Conflict Freedom

We next address how to dynamically verify our notion of conflict freedom, *i.e.*, that each operation in the observed trace does not conflict with any other operation in the same transaction. Thus, for example, a lock acquire should not conflict with any other acquire in the same transaction. Similarly, any read operation in a transaction should not conflict with any write in the same transaction. Note that conflicts between an acquire inside a transaction and an acquire *outside* the transaction are permitted; they may violate external serializability but not conflict freedom.

Our analysis uses clock vectors [14] as a compact representation for the happens-before relation and to identify which operations in a transaction are concurrent. A clock vector $CV : Tid \rightarrow Nat$ maps thread identifiers to clocks. Roughly speaking, if cv is the clock vector for an operation a in a trace, then $cv(t)$ identifies which operations of thread t happen-before that operation a (*i.e.*, those t-operations for which t's clock is less than or equal to $cv(t)$).

Clock vectors are partially-ordered ($\sqsubseteq$) in a point-wise manner, with an associated join operation ($\sqcup$) and minimal element (c_0). In addition, the helper function inc_t increments the t-component of a clock vector:

$$
\begin{aligned}
cv_1 \sqsubseteq cv_2 \quad &\text{iff} \quad \forall t.\ cv_1(t) \leq cv_2(t) \\
cv_1 \sqcup cv_2 \quad &= \quad \lambda t.\ max(cv_1(t), cv_2(t)) \\
c_0 \quad &= \quad \lambda t.\ 0 \\
inc_t(cv) \quad &= \quad \lambda u.\ \texttt{if } u = t \texttt{ then } cv(u) + 1 \texttt{ else } cv(u)
\end{aligned}
$$

Our conflict freedom analysis allocates a unique *transaction identifier* $w \in Xid$ for each transaction in the observed trace and records which threads belong to that transaction. The analysis is an online algorithm based on an analysis state $\sigma = (\mathbb{X}, \mathbb{C}, \mathbb{U}, \mathbb{R}, \mathbb{W})$ where:

- $\mathbb{X} : Tid \rightarrow Xid_\perp$ records the current transaction (if any) for each thread;
- $\mathbb{C} : Tid \rightarrow CV$ records the clock vector of the current operation by each thread;
- $\mathbb{U} : Lock \times Xid \rightarrow CV$ records the clock vector of the last unlock of each lock in each transaction;

[CF BEGIN]
$$\frac{\begin{array}{rcl} X(t) &=& \bot \\ X' &=& X[t := w], \ w \text{ is fresh} \\ C' &=& C[t := inc_t(c_0)] \end{array}}{(X, C, U, R, W) \Rightarrow^{begin(t)} (X', C', U, R, W)}$$

[CF END]
$$\frac{\begin{array}{rcl} X(t) &\neq& \bot \\ X' &=& X[t := \bot] \end{array}}{(X, C, U, R, W) \Rightarrow^{end(t)} (X', C, U, R, W)}$$

[CF ACQUIRE]
$$\frac{\begin{array}{rcl} X(t) &=& w \neq \bot \\ U(m, w) &\sqsubseteq& C(t) \end{array}}{(X, C, U, R, W) \Rightarrow^{acq(t,m)} (X, C, U, R, W)}$$

[CF RELEASE]
$$\frac{\begin{array}{rcl} X(t) &=& w \neq \bot \\ U' &=& U[(m, w) := C(t)] \end{array}}{(X, C, U, R, W) \Rightarrow^{rel(t,m)} (X, C, U', R, W)}$$

[CF READ]
$$\frac{\begin{array}{rcl} X(t) &=& w \neq \bot \\ W(x, w) &\sqsubseteq& C(t) \\ R' &=& R[(x, w) := R(x, w) \sqcup C(t)] \end{array}}{(X, C, U, R, W) \Rightarrow^{rd(t,x,v)} (X, C, U, R', W)}$$

[CF WRITE]
$$\frac{\begin{array}{rcl} X(t) &=& w \neq \bot \\ W(x, w) \sqsubseteq C(t) & & R(x, w) \sqsubseteq C(t) \\ W' &=& W[(x, w) := C(t)] \end{array}}{(X, C, U, R, W) \Rightarrow^{wr(t,x,v)} (X, C, U, R, W')}$$

[CF FORK]
$$\frac{\begin{array}{rcl} X' &=& X[u := X(t)] \\ C' &=& C[t := inc_t(C(t)), u := inc_u(C(t))] \end{array}}{(X, C, U, R, W) \Rightarrow^{fork(t,u,\pi)} (X', C', U, R, W)}$$

[CF JOIN]
$$\frac{C' = C[t := C(t) \sqcup C(u)]}{(X, C, U, R, W) \Rightarrow^{join(t,u)} (X, C', U, R, W)}$$

[CF STOP]
$$\frac{}{(X, C, U, R, W) \Rightarrow^{stop(t)} (X, C, U, R, W)}$$

[CF OUTSIDE]
$$\frac{\begin{array}{c} X(t) = \bot \\ a \in \{acq(t, m), rel(t, m), rd(t, x, v), wr(t, x, v)\} \end{array}}{(X, C, U, R, W) \Rightarrow^{a} (X, C, U, R, W)}$$

Fig. 4. Dynamically Verifying $\underline{C}$onflict $\underline{F}$reedom: $\sigma \Rightarrow^a \sigma'$

- $R : Var \times Xid \to CV$ records the join of all clock vectors for all reads to each variable by each transaction; and
- $W : Var \times Xid \to CV$ records the clock vector of the last write to each variable in each transaction.

In the initial analysis state, no thread is in a transaction and all clock vectors are initialized to c_0, except each $C(t)$ starts at $inc_t(c_0)$ to reflect that the first steps by different threads are not ordered.

$$\sigma_0 \ = \ (\lambda t. \bot, \ \lambda t. inc_t(c_0), \ \lambda(m, w). c_0, \ \lambda(x, w). c_0, \ \lambda(x, w). c_0)$$

The relation $\sigma \Rightarrow^a \sigma'$ is defined in Figure 4. The first rule [CF BEGIN] for $begin(t)$ records that thread t is in a fresh transaction, and resets the clock vector for t. The complementary rule for $end(t)$ records that t is no longer in a transaction. The rule [CF ACQUIRE] checks that each lock acquire happens after the last acquire of that lock in the same transaction. If this check fails, then no rule is applicable and the analysis reports a violation of conflict freedom. Rules [CF READ] and [CF WRITE] check in a similar manner that reads and writes do not conflict with other operations in the same transaction. We update clock vectors for fork and join operations that perform real (non-redundant) synchronization. The rule [CF FORK] for $fork(t, u, \pi)$ performs one "clock tick" for threads t and u, and [CF JOIN] records that a join operation happens-after the last operation (*i.e.*, the stop operation) of the joined thread. Finally, operations outside a transaction are irrelevant and are ignored via [CF OUTSIDE].

We extend the relation $\sigma \Rightarrow^a \sigma'$ from operations to traces in the expected manner: the relation $\sigma_0 \Rightarrow^\alpha \sigma_n$ holds for a trace $\alpha = a_1. \cdots .a_n$ if there exist intermediate analysis states $\sigma_1, \ldots, \sigma_{n-1}$ such that $\sigma_0 \Rightarrow^{a_1} \sigma_1 \Rightarrow^{a_2} \cdots \Rightarrow^{a_n} \sigma_n$.

Correctness. The following lemma summarizes the non-interference guarantee ensured by this analysis. If the entire program trace lies within a single transaction, then conflict freedom guarantees determinism. That is, we can generalize from a single observed trace of the target program to reason about behavior and correctness of all possible traces for that program (assuming of course no sources of non-determinism other than thread scheduling).

Lemma 1 (Single Transaction Determinism). *Suppose $\Sigma_0 \rightarrow^\alpha \Sigma$ where Σ is final and $\sigma_0 \Rightarrow^\alpha \sigma$ and α contains a single transaction. Then for any other trace $\Sigma_0 \rightarrow^\beta \Sigma'$ where Σ' is final, we have that $\Sigma = \Sigma'$.*

4   Dynamically Verifying External Serializability

We next describe our dynamic analysis for the second non-interference property of external serializability. Our analysis allocates a *Node* for each transaction in the observed trace. Then, for each operation in the trace that conflicts with a preceding operation from a different transaction, our analysis adds a directed edge between the nodes for these two transactions. Thus, the analysis computes the *transactional happens-before relation*, where transaction A *happens-before* transaction B in α (written $A <_\alpha B$) if there exists some operations a of A and b of B such that $a <_\alpha b$. Then α is serializable if and only if the transactional happens-before order $<_\alpha$ is acyclic. This analysis generalizes the approach used to identify atomicity violations in the VELODROME atomicity checker [10].

Our external-serializability analysis is an online algorithm that maintains an analysis state $\phi = (\mathcal{C}, \mathcal{L}, \mathcal{U}, \mathcal{R}, \mathcal{W}, \mathcal{H})$ where:

- $\mathcal{C} : Tid \rightarrow \{\text{IN}, \text{OUT}\}$ identifies whether a thread is currently in a transaction;
- $\mathcal{L} : Tid \rightarrow Node_\perp$ identifies the transaction that executed the last operation (if any) of each thread;
- $\mathcal{U} : Lock \rightarrow Node_\perp$ identifies the last transaction (if any) to unlock each lock;
- $\mathcal{R} : Var \times Tid \rightarrow Node_\perp$ identifies the last transaction of each thread to read from each variable;
- $\mathcal{W} : Var \rightarrow Node_\perp$ identifies the last transaction (if any) to write to each variable; and
- $\mathcal{H} \subseteq Node \times Node$ is the happens-before relation on transactions. (More precisely, the transitive closure $\mathcal{H}^*$ of $\mathcal{H}$ is the happens-before relation, since, for efficiency, $\mathcal{H}$ is not transitively closed.)

In the initial analysis state ϕ_0, these components are all empty:

$$\phi_0 = (\lambda t.\text{OUT}, \quad \lambda t.\perp, \quad \lambda m.\perp, \quad \lambda(x,t).\perp, \quad \lambda x.\perp, \quad \emptyset)$$

The relation $\phi \Rightarrow^a \phi'$ shown in Figure 5 updates the analysis state for each operation a of the target program. The first rule [XS BEGIN] for *begin*(t) uses

In all rules, $\phi = (\mathcal{C}, \mathcal{L}, \mathcal{U}, \mathcal{R}, \mathcal{W}, \mathcal{H})$.

[XS BEGIN]
$$\frac{\begin{array}{rcl}\mathcal{C}(t) &=& \text{OUT} \\ \mathcal{C}' &=& \mathcal{C}[t := \text{IN}] \\ \mathcal{L}' &=& \mathcal{L}[t := n],\ n \text{ is fresh} \\ \mathcal{H}' &=& \mathcal{H} \uplus \{(\mathcal{L}(t), n)\}\end{array}}{\phi \Rightarrow^{begin(t)} (\mathcal{C}', \mathcal{L}', \mathcal{U}, \mathcal{R}, \mathcal{W}, \mathcal{H}')}$$

[XS END]
$$\frac{\begin{array}{rcl}\mathcal{C}(t) &=& \text{IN} \\ \mathcal{C}' &=& \mathcal{C}[t := \text{OUT}]\end{array}}{\phi \Rightarrow^{end(t)} (\mathcal{C}', \mathcal{L}, \mathcal{U}, \mathcal{R}, \mathcal{W}, \mathcal{H})}$$

[XS ACQUIRE]
$$\frac{\mathcal{C}(t) = \text{IN} \qquad \mathcal{H}' = \mathcal{H} \uplus \{(\mathcal{U}(m), \mathcal{L}(t))\}}{\phi \Rightarrow^{acq(t,m)} (\mathcal{C}, \mathcal{L}, \mathcal{U}, \mathcal{R}, \mathcal{W}, \mathcal{H}')}$$

[XS RELEASE]
$$\frac{\mathcal{C}(t) = \text{IN} \qquad \mathcal{U}' = \mathcal{U}[m := \mathcal{L}(t)]}{\phi \Rightarrow^{rel(t,m)} (\mathcal{C}, \mathcal{L}, \mathcal{U}', \mathcal{R}, \mathcal{W}, \mathcal{H})}$$

[XS READ]
$$\frac{\begin{array}{rcl}\mathcal{C}(t) &=& \text{IN} \\ \mathcal{H}' &=& \mathcal{H} \uplus \{(\mathcal{W}(x), \mathcal{L}(t))\} \\ \mathcal{R}' &=& \mathcal{R}[(x,t) := \mathcal{L}(t)]\end{array}}{\phi \Rightarrow^{rd(t,x,v)} (\mathcal{C}, \mathcal{L}, \mathcal{U}, \mathcal{R}', \mathcal{W}, \mathcal{H}')}$$

[XS WRITE]
$$\frac{\begin{array}{rcl}\mathcal{C}(t) &=& \text{IN} \\ \mathcal{W}' &=& \mathcal{W}[x := \mathcal{L}(t)] \\ \mathcal{H}' &=& \mathcal{H} \uplus \{(\mathcal{W}(x), \mathcal{L}(t)), (\mathcal{R}(x,u), \mathcal{L}(t)) \mid u \in Tid\}\end{array}}{\phi \Rightarrow^{wr(t,x,v)} (\mathcal{C}, \mathcal{L}, \mathcal{U}, \mathcal{R}, \mathcal{W}', \mathcal{H}')}$$

[XS FORK IN]
$$\frac{\mathcal{C}(t) = \text{IN}}{\mathcal{L}' = \mathcal{L}[u := \mathcal{L}(t)] \qquad \mathcal{C}' = \mathcal{C}[u := \text{IN}]}{\phi \Rightarrow^{fork(t,u,\pi)} (\mathcal{C}', \mathcal{L}', \mathcal{U}, \mathcal{R}, \mathcal{W}, \mathcal{H})}$$

[XS FORK OUT]
$$\frac{\begin{array}{l}\mathcal{C}(t) = \text{OUT} \quad n \text{ is fresh} \quad \mathcal{L}' = \mathcal{L}[t := n, u := n] \\ \mathcal{C}' = \mathcal{C}[u := \text{OUT}] \qquad \mathcal{H}' = \mathcal{H} \uplus \{(\mathcal{L}(t), n)\}\end{array}}{\phi \Rightarrow^{fork(t,u,\pi)} (\mathcal{C}', \mathcal{L}', \mathcal{U}, \mathcal{R}, \mathcal{W}, \mathcal{H}')}$$

[XS JOIN]
$$\frac{\mathcal{C}(t) = \text{IN} \qquad \mathcal{H}' = \mathcal{H} \uplus \{(\mathcal{L}(u), \mathcal{L}(t))\}}{\phi \Rightarrow^{join(t,u)} (\mathcal{C}, \mathcal{L}, \mathcal{U}, \mathcal{R}, \mathcal{W}, \mathcal{H}')}$$

[XS STOP]
$$\frac{\mathcal{C}(t) = \text{IN}}{\phi \Rightarrow^{stop(t)} (\mathcal{C}, \mathcal{L}, \mathcal{U}, \mathcal{R}, \mathcal{W}, \mathcal{H})}$$

[XS OUTSIDE]
$$\frac{\begin{array}{c}\mathcal{C}(t) = \text{OUT} \\ a \in \{acq(t,m), rel(t,m), rd(t,x,v), wr(t,x,v), join(t,u), stop(t)\} \\ \phi \Rightarrow^{begin(t)} \phi_1 \qquad \phi_1 \Rightarrow^a \sigma_2 \qquad \phi_2 \Rightarrow^{end(t)} \phi'\end{array}}{\phi \Rightarrow^a \phi'}$$

Fig. 5. Dynamically Verifying External-Serializability: $\phi \Rightarrow^a \phi'$

the operation $\mathcal{H} \uplus E$ to extend the happens-before graph with additional edges $E \subseteq Node_\perp \times Node_\perp$, filtering out self-edges and edges that start or end on $\perp$:

$$\mathcal{H} \uplus E \stackrel{\text{def}}{=} \mathcal{H} \cup \{(n_1, n_2) \in E \mid n_1 \neq n_2,\ n_1 \neq \perp,\ n_2 \neq \perp\}$$

Thus, in [XS BEGIN], if $\mathcal{L}(t) = \perp$, then the happens-before graph is unchanged. Otherwise it is extended with an edge from the last transaction of thread t to the current transaction of t. The rule [XS ACQUIRE] for $acq(t, m)$ updates the happens-before graph with an edge from the last release $\mathcal{U}(m)$ of that lock. Conversely, [XS RELEASE] for $rel(t, m)$ updates $\mathcal{U}(m)$ with the current transaction.

The rule [XS WRITE] for $wr(t, x, v)$ records that this write happens-after all previous accesses to x, and updates $\mathcal{W}(x)$ to denote the current transaction. The rule [XS READ] for $rd(t, x, v)$ records that this read happens-after the last write to x, and records that the last read to this variable by this thread is the current transaction. For a fork operation within a transaction, the rule [XS FORK IN] records that the forked thread also executes within that transaction. For forks outside a transaction, [XS FORK OUT] creates a fresh unary transaction n for the fork operation. For other operations outside a transaction, [XS OUTSIDE] enters a new transaction, performs that operation, and then exits that (unary) transaction. We extend the relation $\phi \Rightarrow^a \phi'$ from operations to traces.

Correctness. The set *Error* denotes analysis states that contain a non-trivial cycle in the happens-before relation:

$$Error \overset{\text{def}}{=} \{(\mathcal{C}, \mathcal{L}, \mathcal{U}, \mathcal{R}, \mathcal{W}, \mathcal{H}) \mid \mathcal{H}^* \text{ contains a non-trivial cycle}\}$$

Our dynamic analysis is sound and in that it identifies exactly those traces that are not externally serializable.

Lemma 2 (External Serializability). *Suppose $\Sigma_0 \to^\alpha \Sigma$ and $\phi_0 \Rightarrow^\alpha \phi$. Then α is externally serializable if and only if $\phi \notin Error$.*

The preceding lemmas characterize the correctness guarantee provided by each of the conflict-freedom and external-serializability analyses. We now describe how the combination of these two analyses provides a determinism guarantee for programs with multiple transactions (each of which may be internally multithreaded).

The *begin-order* of a serial trace is simply the projection of *begin* operations in that trace, which identifies the order in which the transactions execute while ignoring internal scheduling within each transaction.

$$begin\text{-}order(\alpha) = \text{projection of } begin \text{ operations in } \alpha, \text{ where } \alpha \text{ is serial}$$

We say that two serializable traces α and β have the *same commit order* if α and β have equivalent serial traces α' and β' respectively, such that

$$begin\text{-}order(\alpha') = begin\text{-}order(\beta')$$

Suppose that α is a program trace that satisfies our analyses. Clearly, a different schedule β of the various transactions could change the program's behavior and, for example, cause it to execute code not covered by our analyses. However, if β is a serializable trace that has the same commit order as α, then β is guaranteed to terminate in the same final state as α, and thus yield the same observable behavior (where we assume all observations are made by inspecting this final state).

Theorem 1 (Determinism). *Suppose $\Sigma_0 \to^\alpha \Sigma$ and $\sigma_0 \Rightarrow^\alpha \sigma$ and $\phi_0 \Rightarrow^\alpha \phi$ where Σ is a final state and $\phi \notin Error$. Then any serializable trace that has the same commit order as α will terminate in the same final state.*

5   Implementation and Evaluation

We have developed a prototype implementation, called SINGLETRACK, of our dynamic analysis for deterministic parallelism. The analysis takes as input a

Java bytecode program and a specification of which methods should be deterministic. It then monitors program execution and reports a warning whenever a determinism specification is violated. For a conflict freedom error, SINGLE-TRACK identifies the two operations within a transaction that conflict. For an external serializability error, SINGLETRACK identifies the corresponding cycle in the transactional happens-before graph.

SINGLETRACK is implemented as a component in ROADRUNNER, a framework we have designed for developing dynamic analyses for multithreaded software. ROADRUNNER is written entirely in Java and runs on any standard JVM. ROADRUNNER inserts instrumentation code into the target bytecode program at load time. This code generates a stream of events for lock acquires and releases, field and array accesses, method entries and exits, etc. Back-end tool components, such as SINGLETRACK, process this event stream as it is generated. Re-entrant lock acquires and releases (which are redundant) are filtered out by ROADRUNNER to simplify these analyses.

Our SINGLETRACK implementation extends the analysis described so far in a number of respects, including by supporting additional synchronization primitives such as barriers and semaphores. It also supports nested deterministic blocks. When a determinism error is identified, the tool reports a warning for each deterministic block being violated, and so a single bug may lead to multiple determinism warnings. It also includes a fast happens-before analysis to verify that all array elements and non-volatile fields are accessed in a race-free manner. Hence, only synchronization operations and accesses to volatile fields must be analyzed for conflict freedom and external serializability, which significantly improves SINGLETRACK's performance.

We have applied SINGLETRACK to eight JavaGrande [1] benchmarks (crypt, lufact, series, sor, sparse, moldyn, montecarlo, and raytracer), hedc (a query engine that downloads astronomical data from the web [23]), and four additional programs written by us: quicksort, which recursively quicksorts an array, spawning new threads for the recursive calls; matrixmultiply, which implements a multithreaded, divide-and-conquer matrix multiplication; queue-mm, which uses a thread pool and work queue to perform a number of matrix multiplies simultaneously; and queue-jg, which uses a thread pool and work queue to execute the first five JavaGrande benchmarks. All JavaGrande benchmarks were configured to use the small data size and four threads, hedc was configured to use four worker threads, and the thread pool programs were configured to use pools with two worker threads.

We performed all experiments on an Apple Mac Pro with dual quad-core 3GHz Pentium Xeon processors and 4GB of memory, using OS X 10.5 and Sun's Java HotSpot Client VM, version 1.5.7. All classes loaded by the benchmark programs were instrumented, except those from the standard Java libraries.

Table 1 presents the size, number of threads, and uninstrumented base running time of each program, as well as the slowdown (as a ratio to the base time) of each program when checked by three dynamic analyses: EMPTYTOOL (which does no work and simply measures the instrumentation overhead), SINGLETRACK, and

Table 1. Benchmark Programs

Program	Size (lines)	Num. Threads	Base Time (sec)	Slowdown Empty Tool	Slowdown Single-Track	Slowdown Velo-drome	Velodrome Atomicity Warnings	SingleTrack Deterministic Warnings
crypt	1,241	7	0.3	3.6	18.5	18.9	4	0
lufact	1,627	4	0.2	6.9	15.3	15.2	5	0
series	967	4	2.0	1.3	1.2	1.4	4	0
sor	876	4	0.2	3.8	7.7	7.5	6	6
sparse	868	4	0.3	7.7	24.6	24.4	4	0
moldyn	1,402	4	0.7	5.1	18.6	16.2	6	0
montecarlo	2,669	4	1.6	2.2	6.7	6.9	5	0
raytracer	1,970	4	0.9	13.3	19.5	19.9	5	1
matrixmult	301	7	0.04	4.1	5.8	6.0	5	0
quicksort	292	29	0.05	4.2	5.9	5.8	5	0
hedc	6,400	6	25.9	1.0	1.0	1.0	0	0
queue-jg	3,906	9	4.1	2.1	9.6	10.0	28	0
queue-mm	449	11	1.0	1.3	1.3	1.3	7	0

the VELODROME atomicity checker [10]. Both SINGLETRACK and VELODROME used the same fast happens-before race detector mentioned above to avoid the overhead of analyzing race-free data accesses. The average slowdowns for these three tools are 4.3, 10.4, and 10.3, respectively, indicating that SINGLETRACK does not introduce much additional overhead over VELODROME, despite checking a more complex non-interference property.

The first ten programs in the table use various fork-join, barrier, and divide-and-conquer idioms, and were designed to be deterministic. For these benchmarks, all methods were specified as deterministic for SINGLETRACK and atomic for VELODROME. Experiments using VELODROME produced 49 reports of non-atomic methods. Further inspection revealed that these methods were never intended to be atomic, however, since they involve multithreaded subcomputations. Thus, VELODROME is essentially enforcing the wrong non-interference specification. Consequently, VELODROME provides no useful information about the correctness of these methods. In contrast, SINGLETRACK eliminates all warnings except those caused by two programming errors: raytracer has a known race condition on a checksum field that causes nondeterminism, and sor contains a barrier implementation that assumes operations on long values are atomic. Fixing these two errors enables SINGLETRACK to verify that all ten programs are deterministic.

The last three programs submit jobs to a work queue. As illustrated in Figure 2(b), concurrent worker threads introduce non-determinism. VELODROME could verify only that the hedc tasks were atomic, but reported atomicity violations for the tasks in queue-jg and queue-mm. In contrast, SINGLETRACK successfully verified that the tasks in all three of these benchmarks were deterministic.

To summarize, SINGLETRACK can verify important non-interference properties for programs that are not supported by current checkers. This greatly reduces the burden on the programmer by eliminating spurious warnings that would otherwise have to be examined manually. In the programs studied, only 10% of the warnings reported by VELODROME reflect real interference errors, whereas all of the SINGLETRACK warnings reflected real synchronization errors.

6   Related Work

Netzer and Miller [16] provide a good overview of various kinds of thread inference errors in multithreaded programs. Much previous work has addressed dynamically detecting race conditions, including via race detectors based on the happens-before relation [4,20,5] as well as via extensions of Eraser's lockset algorithm [19], for example, to object-oriented languages [23] and for improved precision or performance [3,17]. Dynamic race detectors have also been developed for other settings, including for nested fork-join parallelism [15].

A variety of tools have been developed to detect atomicity violations, both statically and dynamically. The Atomizer [8] uses Lipton's theory of reduction [13] to check serializability. Wang and Stoller developed more precise *commit-node* algorithms that address both conflict-atomicity (referred to as atomicity in this paper) and view-atomicity [24].

The Cilk project investigated verifying determinism of entire multithreaded applications, first addressing a more restricted fork-join concurrency structure [7] and later extending that approach to more general locking idioms [2]. While successful for deterministic Cilk applications, this approach does not support applications (like hedc, queue-jg, and queue-mm) that are non-deterministic but contain deterministic subcomputations.

Lightweight transactions (see *e.g.* [21,11,12,22]) offer an interesting alternative to explicit concurrency control, and we believe that a combination or synthesis of these two approaches may yield an attractive programming model. In particular, language runtimes could implement determinism via techniques similar to those used to implement transactions, combined with a deterministic scheduler for threads inside transactions.

Static analyses for verifying atomicity include type systems [9,18] as well as techniques that look for cycles in the happens-before graph [6]. Compared to dynamic techniques, static systems provide stronger soundness guarantees but typically involve trade-offs between precision and scalability. An interesting topic for future work is the development of static analyses that provide better support for deterministically-parallel software.

7   Conclusions

Tools for identifying concurrency errors continue to grow in importance. To be effective, they must be able to verify properties of complex software without burdening the programmer with spurious warning messages. This work attempts to achieve this goal by (1) introducing deterministic, a new non-interference specification that generalizes atomic, and which provides better support for deterministically-parallel software, and (2) by developing a new sound dynamic analysis to identify deterministic specification violations. Experimental results demonstrate the our analysis provides a significant improvement over prior checkers, particularly in terms of its ability to detect bugs and verify non-interference properties for deterministically-parallel software. One avenue for future work is to explore how to best design systems around this property.

This work was supported in part by NSF Grants 0341179, 0341387, 0644130, and 0707885.

References

1. Java Grande benchmark suite (2008), http://www.javagrande.org
2. Cheng, G.-I., Feng, M., Leiserson, C.E., Randall, K.H., Stark, A.F.: Detecting data races in Cilk programs that use locks. In: SPAA, pp. 298–309 (1998)
3. Choi, J.-D., Lee, K., Loginov, A., O'Callahan, R., Sarkar, V., Sridhara, M.: Efficient and precise datarace detection for multithreaded object-oriented programs. In: PLDI, pp. 258–269 (2002)
4. Christiaens, M., Bosschere, K.D.: TRaDe: Data Race Detection for Java. In: Alexandrov, V.N., Dongarra, J., Juliano, B.A., Renner, R.S., Tan, C.J.K. (eds.) ICCS-ComputSci 2001. LNCS, vol. 2074, pp. 761–770. Springer, Heidelberg (2001)
5. Elmas, T., Qadeer, S., Tasiran, S.: Goldilocks: a race and transaction-aware Java runtime. In: PLDI, pp. 245–255 (2007)
6. Farzan, A., Madhusudan, P.: Causal atomicity. In: Ball, T., Jones, R.B. (eds.) CAV 2006. LNCS, vol. 4144, pp. 315–328. Springer, Heidelberg (2006)
7. Feng, M., Leiserson, C.E.: Efficient detection of determinacy races in Cilk programs. In: SPAA, pp. 1–11 (1997)
8. Flanagan, C., Freund, S.N.: Atomizer: A dynamic atomicity checker for multithreaded programs. In: POPL, pp. 256–267 (2004)
9. Flanagan, C., Freund, S.N., Lifshin, M., Qadeer, S.: Types for atomicity: Static checking and inference for Java. TOPLAS 30(4), 1–53 (2008)
10. Flanagan, C., Freund, S.N., Yi, J.: Velodrome: A sound and complete dynamic atomicity checker for multithreaded programs. In: PLDI (2008)
11. Harris, T., Fraser, K.: Language support for lightweight transactions. In: OOPSLA, pp. 388–402 (2003)
12. Harris, T., Marlow, S., Peyton-Jones, S., Herlihy, M.: Composable memory transactions. In: PPOPP, pp. 48–60 (2005)
13. Lipton, R.J.: Reduction: A method of proving properties of parallel programs. Communications of the ACM 18(12), 717–721 (1975)
14. Mattern, F.: Virtual time and global states of distributed systems. In: International Workshop on Parallel and Distributed Algorithms (1988)
15. Mellor-Crummey, J.: On-the-fly detection of data races for programs with nested fork-join parallelism. In: Supercomputing, pp. 24–33 (1991)
16. Netzer, R.H.B., Miller, B.P.: What are race conditions? some issues and formalizations. LOPLAS 1, 74–88 (1992)
17. Pozniansky, E., Schuster, A.: Efficient on-the-fly data race detection in multithreaded C++ programs. In: PPOPP, pp. 179–190 (2003)

18. Sasturkar, A., Agarwal, R., Wang, L., Stoller, S.D.: Automated type-based analysis of data races and atomicity. In: PPOPP, pp. 83–94 (2005)
19. Savage, S., Burrows, M., Nelson, G., Sobalvarro, P., Anderson, T.E.: Eraser: A dynamic data race detector for multi-threaded programs. TOCS 15(4), 391–411 (1997)
20. Schonberg, E.: On-the-fly detection of access anomalies. In: PLDI, pp. 285–297 (1989)
21. Shavit, N., Touitou, D.: Software transactional memory. In: PODC, pp. 204–213 (1995)
22. Vitek, J., Jagannathan, S., Welc, A., Hosking, A.L.: A semantic framework for designer transactions. In: Schmidt, D. (ed.) ESOP 2004. LNCS, vol. 2986, pp. 249–263. Springer, Heidelberg (2004)
23. von Praun, C., Gross, T.: Object race detection. In: OOPSLA, pp. 70–82 (2001)
24. Wang, L., Stoller, S.D.: Accurate and efficient runtime detection of atomicity errors in concurrent programs. In: PPOPP, pp. 137–146 (2006)

Author Index